AF802577

Angiography and its latest aspects
Angiographie und ihre neusten Erkenntnisse

Angiography and its latest aspects
Angiographie und ihre neusten Erkenntnisse

Internationale Arbeits- und Fortbildungstagung
Salzburg, 27. – 29.4.1972

Herausgegeben von Kurt Egon Loose

Mit 300 Abbildungen und 55 Tabellen

Walter de Gruyter · Berlin · New York 1975

Tagung der
Internationalen Vereinigung
für Angiographie

Herausgeber
Prof. Dr. K. E. Loose

Chefarzt der Chirurgischen und
Angiologischen Abteilung
der Städt. Krankenanstalten Itzehoe/Holst.

Unter Mitarbeit von
Dr. med. D. A. Loose
Wiss. Ass. an der
Chirurgischen Klinik u. Poliklinik
der Universität Düsseldorf
4 Düsseldorf
Moorenstraße 5

Die Wiedergabe von Gebrauchsnamen, Handelsnamen, Warenbezeichnungen und dgl. in dieser Monographie berechtigt nicht zu der Annahme, daß solche Namen ohne weiteres von jedermann benützt werden dürften. Vielmehr handelt es sich häufig um gesetzlich geschützte Warenzeichen, auch wenn sie nicht eigens als solche gekennzeichnet sind.

ISBN 3 11 004395 5

© Copyright 1974 by Walter de Gruyter & Co., vormals G. J. Göschen'sche Verlagshandlung, J. Guttentag, Verlagsbuchhandlung Georg Reimer, Karl J. Trübner, Veit & Comp., Berlin 30.

Alle Rechte, insbesondere das Recht der Vervielfältigung und Verbreitung sowie der Übersetzung, vorbehalten. Kein Teil des Werkes darf in irgendeiner Form (durch Photokopie, Mikrofilm oder ein anderes Verfahren) ohne schriftliche Genehmigung des Verlages reproduziert oder unter Verwendung elektronischer Systeme verarbeitet, vervielfältigt oder verbreitet werden. Printed in Germany.

Satz: IBM-Composer, Walter de Gruyter & Co., Berlin.
Druck: Karl Gerike, Berlin.
Bindearbeiten: Lüderitz & Bauer, Berlin.

Library of Congress Catalog Card
Number: 73-82435

Präsidialkreis der Tagung:

A. Breit	Passau	Wm. Penn	Nimwegen
J. Ecoiffier	Paris	O. Olsson	Lund
H. H. Ellegast	Salzburg	H. Pokieser	Wien
W. Frommhold	Tübingen	N. Schad	St. Louis/USA
W. A. Fuchs	Bern	F. E. Stieve	Berlin/München
E. Kotscher	Wien	J. Wellauer	Zürich
K. E. Loose	Itzehoe/Holst.	O. Wichtl	Wien

Vorwort

Zum 4. Male fand sich ein Kollegen- und Freundeskreis aus Klinikern, Radiologen und Technikern zusammen, um die *neuesten Erkenntnisse der Angiographie* aus röntgenologischer sowie klinischer Sicht aufzuzeigen. Gerade diese haben in den vergangenen Jahren eine noch kaum übersehbare Bedeutung für alle Fachgebiete der Medizin erlangt. So vermochte die moderne Angiographie als grundlegende Diagnostikmethode unter anderem die Kenntnisse über Morphologie und Funktion der Kreislauforgane in beachtlichem Maße zu verbessern. Hierdurch wurden maßgebende Fortschritte sowohl in der Diagnostik als auch in der Behandlung der Herz- und Gefäßleiden ermöglicht. Wir alle sind von dieser Entwicklung beeindruckt, und deshalb nimmt es nicht wunder, daß sich in Salzburg ein weiter Kreis gleichinteressierter Kollegen aus dem In- und Ausland zusammenfand, den die Anwesenheit verehrter Gäste und Freunde auszeichnete. So konnte ich der Freude Ausdruck geben, eine große Zahl von Kongreßteilnehmern aus 16 Ländern begrüßen zu dürfen, als Zeichen einer engen wissenschaftlichen und menschlichen Verbundenheit, wie sich diese bei den 3 vorangegangenen Kongressen bereits manifestierte. Im besonderen wurde den Herren aus USA und dem großen Kollegenkreis aus den Niederlanden ein Willkommensgruß entgegengebracht. Für ihr aller Kommen und ihre Kongreßteilnahme, die vielfach mit Mühen und vorherigem intensiven Arbeitseinsatz verbunden war, gebührt ihnen der allerherzlichste Dank.

Die Organisation und Durchführung eines solchen Kongresses war nicht möglich ohne die verständnisvolle Hilfe und die Programmführung durch Herrn Professor Stieve und Herrn Professor Ellegast, die als Mitgestalter des 4. Angiographie-Kongresses unseres herzlichsten Dankes gewiß sein dürfen.

Es war mir persönlich eine große Freude, mit beiden Herren und in Zusammenarbeit mit Herrn Professor Breit unseren Salzburger Kongreß ausrichten zu können.
Im weiteren ist eine so große Tagung undenkbar ohne die Hilfe, die wir auch dieses Mal von seiten der Industrie mit anerkennenswerter Bereitschaft und besonderem Verständnis namhafter Firmen entgegennehmen konnten. Hierfür darf ich unser aller Dank zum Ausdruck bringen.

Durch die wertvolle Kooperation mit den maßgebenden Stellen in Salzburg ist der Kongreß gewachsen. Sein Ziel ist: eine Übersicht über den fortschrittlichen Stand der als Hauptthemen genannten derzeitigen aktuellen Probleme durch namhafte und erfahrene Fachleute zu geben, um damit die neuesten Erkenntnisse der Angiographie zu vermitteln.
Sie alle mögen prüfen, was gelungen ist oder was erreicht wurde und was noch nicht befriedigend gelöst werden konnte.
Der Dank gilt den Herren Referenten, Vortragenden und Diskussionsteilnehmern sowie den Mitarbeiterinnen und Mitarbeitern für die Mitwirkung an der gemeinsamen großen Aufgabe: unserer Tagung Rahmen und Inhalt zu geben, so daß alle Erwartungen in wissenschaftlicher sowie menschlicher Beziehung erfüllt wurden.

Mögen Sie alle die Stadt Salzburg erleben

„Als Bauwerk zwischen dem Städtischen
und dem Ländlichen,
dem Uralten und dem Neuzeitlichen,
dem Barock-fürstlichen
und dem lieblich – ewig Bäuerlichen!",

in dem immer wieder *Mozart* der Ausdruck von alledem ist.
Wir möchten *Hofmannsthal* voll und ganz beipflichten, wenn er über Salzburg begeistert äußert:
„Das mittlere Europa hat keinen schöneren Raum".

Itzehoe, im September 1974
Prof. Dr. K. E. Loose

Inhaltsverzeichnis

* Literatur kann bei den Verfassern angefordert werden

I. DIE ANGIOGRAPHIE MIT DER KATHETERMETHODE UND DEREN GEFAHREN

Controllable Catheter Systems

M. H. Wholey

Presently, there are five basic systems for controlling or manipulating an angiographic catheter within the cardiovascular compartment.
Firstly we can rely on the torque of natural solid wall extruded plastic tubing. The composition can be polyvinyl chloride, polyethylene, polytetrafluoroetylene or polyurethane. Opacifying agents and color additives are incorporated into the wall composition during the extrusion. These opacifying agents can be combinations of tin, barium, bismuth, lead or their salts and in general have no major alterations in the physical properties of the basic plastic. Obviously no one catheter is best for all procedures. As a matter of fact when asked why he chooses a particular catheter the radiologist frequently responds "it feels right". To convert "it feels right" into engineering terms one has to consider certain characteristics: A) Composition hardness; B) Material friction; C) Body tissue compatibility; D) Bursting pressure etc. Next one has to consider the catheter curve, wall thickness, length, and each angiographers technique preferences. Obviously then it is difficult to recommend a single all purpose catheter that is adequate for renal, adrenal, carotid, coronary or pulmonary arteriography. One whose flow rates could adjust from 6 cc. per second in the renal to 25 cc. per second in the aortic arch. One whose dimensions are not greater than safety precludes for selective catheterization of smaller vessels. One whose surfaces are biologically inert. Thrombogenesis on internal and external catheter surfaces has been well established by means of scanning electron microscopy. Catheters of polyurethane and polyethylene were studied before and after intra arterial placement. The polyurethane displayed a variety of defects including irregular bands, troughs, and lacunae, measuring 1–2 mu. in size. The polyethylene showed some degree of linear grooving but generally appeared more homogenous and smooth than polyurethane at magnification up to 3,000 times. Studies have shown that surface irregularities may be important factors in the initiation of thrombogenesis, and embolization of thrombus fragments. Surface roughness decreases the degree of blood compatibility and fibrin deposition, platelet aggregation and red thrombus formation occurs on both the external and internal surface of the catheters.

Although these limitations exist, solid wall tubing remains the simplist and certainly the most widely used method for selective catheter control. With few exceptions essentially every vessel in the body can be selectively catheterized and within a matter of minutes.
The second system for catheter control employed a linear or preformed metallic wire. As early as 1949 the limitations of the straight catheter for selective vessel examination was apparent. *Radner* utilized a preformed wire to deflect a straight ureteric catheter for entrance to the vertebral artery. *Gollman* and *Nordenström* employed similar mechanisms. *Viamonte and Stevens* slightly

varying this approach used a straight guide to alter a permanently curved tip. All of these methods have major limitations in that the metallic wire used to alter the curve is of such high flexural rigidity that its use in tortuous vessels is hazardous. Perforation, embolization and damage to the internal surface of the catheter can occur. Contrast injection with the guide in place by these original methods was not feasible and the actual improvement in torque control was only marginal. These early methods have been largely abandoned by todays standards.

A basic improvement in this approach, however, was introduced by *Cope*. The most recent *Cope* system utilizes a preformed (Fig 1) polyethylene single end open catheter with an I. D. of .062 inches and an O. D. of .082 inches diameter.

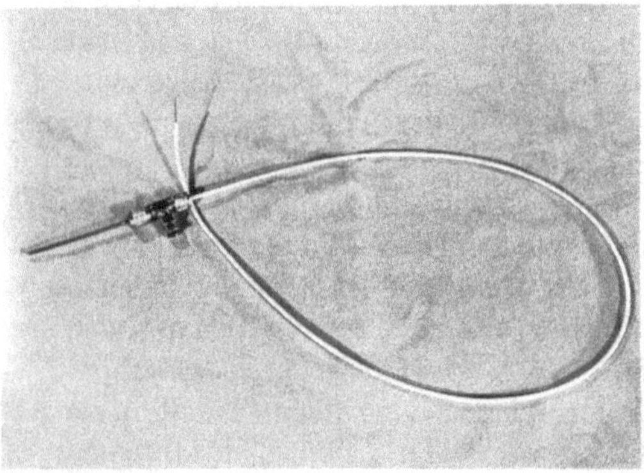

Fig. 1: Cope – catheter guide system with "anti flipper" guide in position.

Supposedly these dimensions allow a flow rate of 20 cc. per second with the guide wire in position during injection. For non-selective examinations the straight "anti flipper" 23 gauge wire is inserted and projects 1–2 cm. beyond the tip of the catheter. This in effect straightens the catheter and positions it in a mid aortic location while the guide tip rests on the aortic wall. Intimal extravasation is minimized. In theory this is related to the fact that the jet nucleus or linear velocity at high flow rate is greatest with single end hole catheters. Fortunately this linear velocity or motion energy I. E. Kinetic energy of the injection stream dissipates exponentially so that 1 cm. distant from the tip of the catheter the force is essentially 10 % of its original. Our studies with system demonstrates excessive reaction forces and recoil activity during high flow injections. The single end opening with additional cross sectional narrowing by the anti flipper wire created an unstable injection profile as studied by cine analysis. After removal of the anti flipper wire the preformed torque control wire is positioned for selective examinations. The tip of the torque control is 27 gauge size and similarly injection with a guide in place can be performed. Although the system has been used extensively and quite successfully by *Cope* certain limitations occurred during our evaluation. First the rigidity of the torque control guide can perforate the thin (Fig. 2a & b) walled polyethylene catheter. This is especially

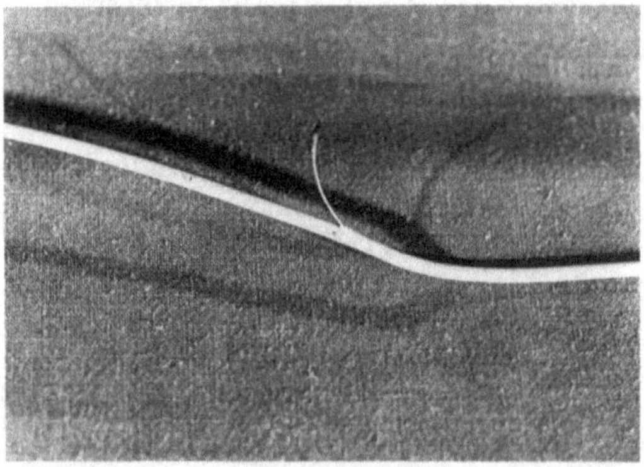

Fig. 2a: Perforation of thin walled polyethylene tubing by linear preformed torque control guide.

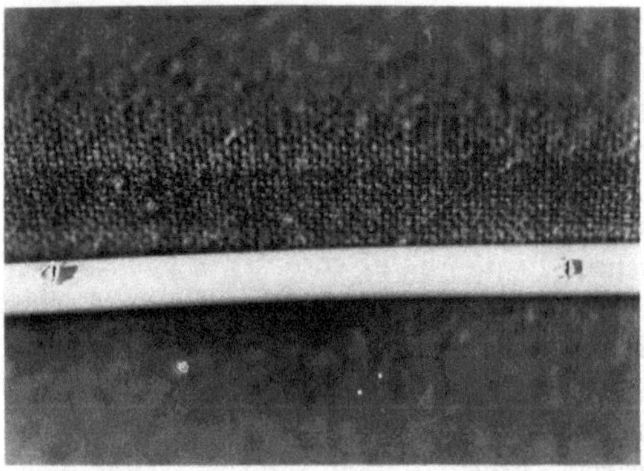

Fig. 2b: Magnification view of catheter perforations with Cope torque control guide.

true in obese patients in whom increased distance from the skin puncture site to the femoral artery exists, or in whom a tortuous iliac vessel is being negotiated. Secondly the torque control guide because of this rigidity scrapes the catheter wall for its entire length during injection and fragments from the wall can be embolized. (Fig. 3) This

Fig. 3: Plastic embolic fragments from catheter wall over the torque guide.

plastic fragmentation not only acts as an embolic source but now with iatrogenic internal catheter surface irregularities the complex biophysical properties of catheter damage and accelerated thrombogenesis as outlined above are initiated. Consequently although torque control is improved with this system its restrictions in our experiences were significant.

A third approach to catheter control included a large group of catheter deflectors that employ either a flexible spring guide or solid tubing but both incorporating a central traction core wire. When force is applied to the central core wire the distal tip flexing member bends in the direction of the free core wire. In 1965 we built such a system utilizing stainless steel tubing of .025 inches (6 mm.) O. D. diameter. The core wire (.007 inches) moves freely within the tubing and extends 2 cm. beyond the distal tubing body and is firmly soldered to a second piece of stainless tubing laid back along the core wire. The lower end of the guide is fitted with a small sleeve which is also soldered to the catheter body and the entire assembly is positioned in a control handle. In the event a guide wire is damaged it may be released from an actuating assembly and a new one is simply inserted. Its advantages were its simplicity, size and flexural strength. (Fig. 4 a) Because of

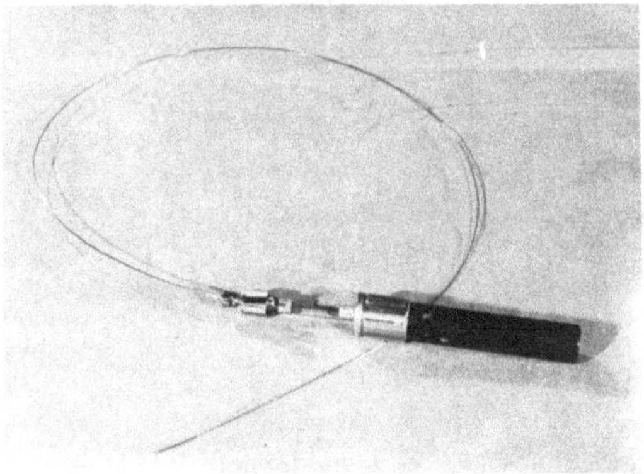

Fig. 4 a: *Wholey* controllable guide.

the .6 mm. O. D. it could be inserted into essentially any catheter system. Its disadvantages, however, exceeded its merits. Firstly, we rarely had occasion for its use. Secondly, it was essentially a linear body, possessing all the disadvantages enumerated above for linear wires; i. e. catheter and/or vessel perforation, internal catheter surface erosion, and tear by the force wire, thrombogenesis and finally wire fracture. We essentially discontinued its use other than for occasional rebirth of an experimental idea i. e. control of a bronchographic catheter; directional control of our percutaneous balloon catheter. The *Muller* – U.S.C.I., *Cook,* and *Bing-Gadd* controllable guides utilize a similar principle. Both the *Muller* and the *Cook* (Fig. 4 b & c) utilize a flexible .038"

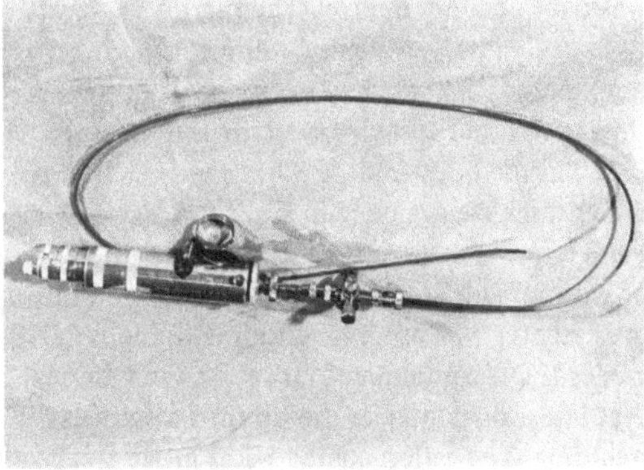

Fig. 4 b: *Müller* – U.S.C.I. controllable guide.

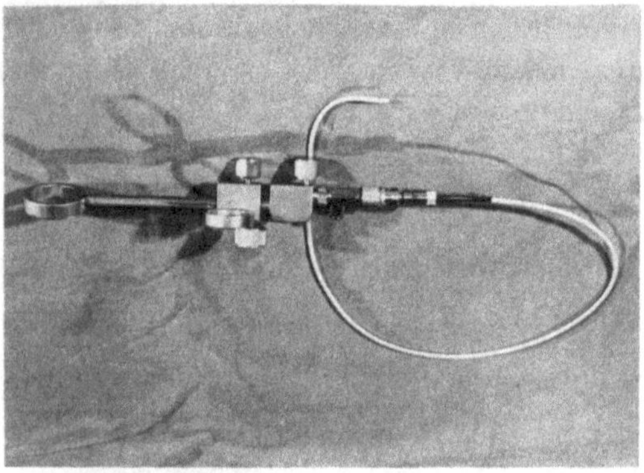

Fig. 4c: *Cook* controllable guide.

guide that when retracted deflects the catheter tip in a single plane. It would appear that the flexible guide has definite advantages over our original solid tubing. A singular advantage is that when a catheter is bent and the guide is in position the catheter may be then passed further over the guide into a subselective vessel. This is not possible when the core wire is exposed as occurs in ours or in the *Almen* system. This creates a very high friction coefficient between the guide and the catheter during flexion. The *Almen* system does allow flexion in two directions in the same plane. Most of these systems also allow alteration in either the length of the catheter to be deflected or the angle of deflection. For selective vessel examinations, injection can be performed in the lower flow rate ranges with the guide in position. Higher flows are not intended with these systems.

The fourth group of controllable catheter systems was developed by *Bentov*. The method consists of extruded polyethylene tubing containing 5 longitudinal lumens. The main central lumen is similar to other catheter systems and measures .042" in the body and .038" at the tip. External dimensions are available in Fr. 7 & 8 sizes. The Fr. 8 is available in a single end open catheter with or without side slit openings. Incorporated into the catheter wall are 4 longitudinal lumens (.010 inches I. D.) containing four teflon wire guides that insert distally near the tip into a stainless steel ring. The teflon coated wires move freely and control the flexibility of the very soft distal tip. A control handle using thumb type operation allows tip control in any plane through 360 degrees rotation. Manual rotation of the assembly body and catheter are not only unnecessary for tip control but can be injurious. The catheter body configuration is slightly square and rotation at the puncture site with such a large catheter may induce puncture site bleeding and hematoma formation. Obvious advantages in this type of catheter control exists. First, the tip is hermetically bonded polypropylene to the body of the catheter. It is extremely soft and avoids any trauma to the intima. The softness also allows for easy flexibility. Secondly, the lumen can be left open during manipulation; injection rates are not impaired by reducing the cross sectional dimensions with a guide and theoretically thrombogenic tendencies should be less. A particular curve can be locked into the system during injection. Thirdly, although all of the systems lose certain flexural capabilities when the catheter has passed multiple tortuous curves since the stress force for deflection is increased, and the resistance coefficient between wires and catheters is significant, the Meditech system did maintain moderate tip control under those circumstances.

The fifth and final group of controllable catheter systems involves a reversion to the original solid tubing. Incorporated, however, into the extruded plastic can be a woven dacron, or more recently a braided woven stainless steel. We presently are evaluating a bonded metal-plastic combination catheter that in tests has very substantial torque control. Incorporation of flexible metals into the wall composition does not interfere with catheter dimensions and consequently flow rates are not altered. Ordinarily the tip is free of the braided metal and consequently remains relatively soft. The value of these catheters with reference to torque control has been documented by their extensive application to coronary arteriography. Additional applications include catheterization of the brachiocephalic vessels, and the abdominal viscera. These catheters are available as either polyurethane or polyethylene. In order to obtain these torque control advantages an additional flexural rigidity in the catheter body, atherosclerotic plaques may be dislodged. Certainly this is true for all catheters and consequently rotatory motions, especially in those catheters passing over the aortic arch should be gentle.

Finally, I would like to mention as early as 1951 *Tillander* was interested in the deflection of the catheter tip by means of an electromagnet. Hilal currently is using magnetic force for catheter direction in an interventional approach in certain neuroradiologic procedures. Magnetic steering of catheters presents certain technical problems relative to the catheter, examination table, construction and size of the magnet, and use with conventional image intensifiers. The magnetic field may deflect the electrons within the vacuum tube.

Summary

There has been a continuing effort in the past 20 years to improve the selectivity of vascular examinations by means of catheter control either remotely or directly at the catheter level. Five system categories have been evaluated both clinically and experimentally in a fluid model by means of cine analysis. There is no single system for all applications. It would appear, however, that the simplist and most expedient approach to most examinations remains with the conventional polyethylene opaque solid wall tubing. Modifications in the wall utilizing braided steel wire constitutes a significant contribution as documented by their wide spread acceptance and simplicity in operation. The braided steel mesh has resulted in striking improvement in torque control. Its principle application has been in the area of coronary arteriography. The trend for controllable catheters is in this direction of metal bonding as a part of the wall composition.

There remains a large group of controllable guides operating as outlined by means of traction forces on the central core wire. As the guide bends similar flexion of the catheter occurs. The original intent was for guides of this nature to be used routinely. In practice however there is an almost inverse arithmetic proportion between the experience of the angiographer and the occasions during conventional angiography when a controllable guide is needed. The routine use of controllable guides for universal angiography is both time consuming and impractial. Most examinations are presently being done in a matter of minutes and utilization of ancillary guiding instruments separate from the catheter proper only prolong the examination time. Unfortunately in our experience a significant number of complications occurred during routine use of the guiding mechanisms. When the linear torque control guides are being inserted perforation of the catheter may occur with the very obese patients. The linear guides should never be used to advance the catheter since intimal lacerations through an atherosclerotic plaque may occur. Excessive rotation of the catheter when either the linear or tip deflecting guides are in position should be avoided. The additional rigidity may dislodge intimal plaques or result in widening at the original puncture site with puncture site bleeding. This is especially true with the Meditech guides which should not be rotated since tip precision control does not depend on torque but on the flexing action related to the 4 member wires incorporated into the catheter wall. Since the catheter is squared at its edges, rotation of the catheter and assembly will produce puncture site bleeding. None of the catheters evaluated with the guiding instruments have a stable injection profile at high flow rates and consequently, during aortography excessive reaction forces occur.

Where then are accessory guiding mechanisms of any value? Certainly not for the routine selective exam or during coronary artery examinations. It would appear that their principle value is in modifying a primary or secondary curve in a catheter of multiple curves. Multiple curves meaning two or more configurations in a primary entrance catheter. For example, if one can alter the primary curve to enter the left renal vein then the secondary curve passes freely to the left adrenal vein; or if one is in the left pulmonary artery and passage to the right is necessary, or if one desires the external carotid artery and/or the internal carotid artery. There is also an application in extending the catheter configuration to passage into a subselective branch. For example catheterization of the gastroduodenal artery from the hepatic or left gastric artery.

It would seem feasible that most radiology departments incorporating vascular examinations should have within the department one of the above described controllable guide machanisms. The occasions for utilization may be extremely infrequent but there will be occasions and in those instances when properly used the systems will prove a valuable contribution.

Plastic Materials for Catheters

T. Olin

Catheters are usually manufactured by some plastic materials.

Plastics can be classified in three main groups:

Duroplastics (thermosetting)
Thermoplastics
and Elastomers.

Thermosetting plastic is a term applied to that type of material which undergoes irreversible chemical change when heated to form an insoluble, infusible mass which will not soften on later heating. Overheating causes chemical decomposition. A *thermoplastic* is a material which can be softened by heating to a pliable mass, then shaped to a desired form, which is retained on cooling to the solid state. This process of softening can be repeated a number of times without damage to the material, provided that the heat applied is not such as to cause chemical decomposition. *Elastomers* (rubber and the like) are high polymeric materials which exhibit elasticity when subjected to stress. Of these three groups the thermoplastics are the most important catheter material but to some extent also elastomers are used, e. g. for flow guided catheters.

Plastic materials for catheters must be somewhat flexible and elastic, neither too soft, nor to rigid. If it is too soft they can not be guided into the desired part of the vascular system to be studied and if too rigid, they are liable to damage the vascular wall.

Among the *thermoplastics* the *polyolefins* are widely used. Polyolefins is a blanket name for polymerized, unsaturated, aliphatic hydrocarbons. The best known product belonging to this group is *polyethylene,* often abbreviated to polythene. The polyethylene first synthetized was of so called *low density* type with a specific gravity of 0.91–0.925. Owing to the process by which it is manufactured it is also called high pressure polyethylene. Later also denser types of polyethylene have been developed, *middle density* and *high density* polyethylene. The last mentioned product is sold under different names such as low pressure polyethylene, *Ziegler* or *Phillip's* polyethylene. Owing to the arrangement of the molecular chains with a minimum of branched chains, high density polyethylene is sometimes called linear polyethylene. The properties of high density polyethylene as compared to low density polyethylene may be summarized as follows: High density polyethylene is denser, stronger, more rigid and has a higher softening temperature than the ordinary low density polyethylene.

A polyolefin which is getting more and more popular is polypropylene, or often abbreviated polypropene. It is not a homogenous substance but is made out of several types, all of which are very light. Its specific gravity is 0.91. Owing to the arrangement of the methyl groups a distinction is made between atactic and isotactic polypropene. The former is soft and somewhat sticky and not suitable for the manufacture of tubing, while the isotactic type is. Polypropene differs from low density polyethylene by the fact that it tolerates higher temperatures, is stronger but more rigid though relatively elastic.

Among *halogenated thermoplastics* the most important substances are *teflon* and different types of *polyvinyl* plastics. *Polytetrafluoroethylene* or PTFE or *teflon,* other manufacturing names are Fluon and Fluorothene, is an expensive plastic material but owing to its good properties, it is fairly widely used. This material tolerates high temperatures and is resistant to most chemicals and has a very low friction coefficient against metal. *Polychlorotrifluoroethylene,* (Kel-F, Hostaflon etc) is closely related to polytetrafluoroethylene and really it was a predecessor to this substance. It is, however, relatively rigid, and has not been used for catheters. *Polyvinyl plastics.* The most common polyvinyl plastic material is probably polyvinyl chloride (PVC). It is a hard rigid material and not suitable for the manufacture of catheters. It can, however, be softened by addition of special plasticizers. Two principally different types of plasticizers are available, namely inner and outer plasticizers. *Inner plasticizers* are added to the monomer before polymerization and incorporated in the molecular chain, so called co-polymerization, which decreases the tendency of crystallization. Such inner plasticizers are e. g. vinyl-acetate, vinylidene chloride, acryonitril and vinyl stearate. PVC can be modified to the desired degree by varying the amount of plasticizers. On addition of 15 % vinyl acetate a produkt will be obtained which is widely used and often known as rigid polyvinyl chloride.It has better mechanical properties than pure polyvinyl chloride. *Outer plasticizers* are added to the resin during the manufacturing process and by solubility effects converts the pure resin into an ordinary plastic.The solvent acts by separating portions of the long molecular chains of the resin, thus reducing the intermolecular attraction between these chains. By varying the amount of outer plasticizers material can be obtained with a number of different properties and even made rubber like. Such flexible or soft PVC is often made not from pure polyvinylchloride but from co-polymers between PVC and vinyl acetate. Thus, two main types of *polyvinyl chloride* are available, *one hard and rigid, the other soft and rubber like.* An intermediate type of PVC, so called *semirigid* polyvinyl chloride with properties resembling those of polyethylene but often stronger, appears to have attracted less medical attention. Many of the outer plasticizers which are added to PVC to give the latter a suitable mechanical property, often irritates the tissue. Reports on medical trials with polyvinyl plastics hold only for the actual material studied because of the wide variety of additives used by different manufacturers.

Polyvinylidene chloride which is closely related to polyvinyl chloride is often known as Saran, the name given by the first manufacturer. The pure product is hard and rigid but can be modified by inner plasticizers with PVC or acryonitrile, for example, but even it is rather rigid. It has not been used for manufacturing of catheters.

Polyamide is often known as nylon, the name given by the first manufacturer, *du Pont Co.* Various types of nylon are available, e. g. nylon 6, nylon 6–6, nylon 6–10 and nylon 11, where the numbers indicate the numbers and arrangement of C-atoms in the monomer. The polyamides are characterized by their relatively high strength and high softening temperature and by the fact that at a certain critical temperature they change from solid to fluid state without any intermediate softening state. Other thermoplastics usually have a melting range rather than a melting point. Nylon 6 and nylon 11 have been used for medical catheters.

Mixed materials are getting more and more common.

These plastics are often called taylored resins and contain for example middle density polyethylene mixed with polyisobuthylene which makes it softer and more pliable. Another example of taylored resins is chlorinated polyethylene. The mechanical properties of for example polyethylene will change considerably if it is exposed to strong ionized radiation, due to the fact that chemical bonds are formed between adjacent molecular chains. The important *technical properties* of polymers used for medical purpose are density, radiopacity, tensil strength, flexural strength, modulus of elasticity, maximum service temperature, heat distortion temperature and water absorbtion. Tensil strength will give a measure about how high injection pressure a catheter may stand. Flexural strength indicates if a catheter easily will break or not. The modulus of elasticity is a measure of how stiff a catheter will be.

Tab. 1: Technical properties of polymers used for medical purposes.

Abreviations:

L.D.P.E.	low density polythene
M.D.P.E.	middle " "
H.D.P.E.	high " "
P.T.F.E.	polytetrafluoroethylene
P.C.T.F.E.	polychlorotrifluoroethylene
P.V.C.	polyvinyl chloride
P.V.L.C.	polyvinylidene chloride
E	modulus of clasticity (bending)

The values are obtained from Plastvärlden (1962).

The higher this value is, the stiffer the catheter is. Maximum service temperature and heat distortion temperature indicate e. g. if a catheter can be heat-sterilized. Water absorbtion indicates eventual resorbtion of water soluble drugs on the surface of the catheter, e. g. Heparin. A survey of the technical properties of some plastics of medical importance are given in Table 1.

When a radiologist tries to evaluate the suitability of a new catheter he usually just takes it in his hand, bends it and touches it and so tries to judge. In a more scientific way this can be done according to the principles applied when the strength of materials are studied technologically. A piece of a catheter is fixed at one end and loaded with a concentrated force at the other end, a. s. c. cantilever beam (Fig. 1). At the same time the deflection of the end of the beam is registered. This deflection (Δ) of the catheters as the beam is loaded on bending follows the law:

$$\Delta = \frac{1}{3} \cdot \frac{F}{E} \cdot \frac{l^3}{I}$$

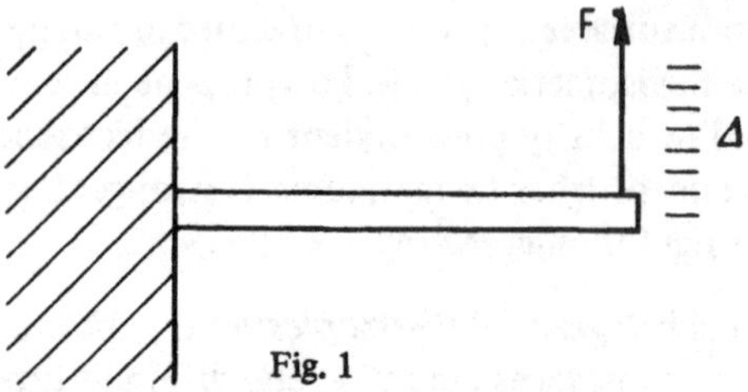

Fig. 1

where F is a concentrated force acting on the beam, E the modulus of elasticity, l the length of the beam, I the monent of inertia of the transverse section of the beam.

If the transverse section is annular as it usually is in a catheter

$$I = \frac{\pi}{64} \cdot (D^4 - d^4)$$

where D is the outer diameter and d the inner diameter. The force necessary to cause a deflection of the end of the beam will then be

$$F = \frac{3\pi}{64} \cdot \frac{\Delta(D^4 - d^4) \cdot E}{l^3}$$

The determinations of course have to be made in a thermostatically controlled water bath at 37° C in order to mimic conditions in the human body.

Tab. 2: Modulus of elasticity at 37°/C for some catheter materials

Polyethylene, non opaque	$0.9 \cdot 10^3$	kp/cm²
Polyethylene, opaque ÖL Kifa	1.3	"
Polypropene	6.2	"
Polyamide, nylon 11	2.6	"
Teflon, non opaque	4.2	"
Teflon, opaque	4.9	"
PCTFE	8.0	"

Modulus of elasticity measured for some different catheters. Table 2. Low density polyethylene of the ordinary type, nonopaque, has a modulus of elasticity of $0.9 \cdot 10^3$. If it is made radiopaque, Kifa ÖL, the modulus of elasticity will increase to $1.3 \cdot 10^3$. Some types of radiopaque polyethylene are even stiffer. Polypropene is very stiff with a modulus of $6.2 \cdot 10^3$. Vinyl plastics are so soft and pliable that usually the modulus of elasticity can not be measured.

Nylon 11 has a modulus of elasticity of $2.6 \cdot 10^3$ and non-opaque teflon $4.2 \cdot 10^3$. If made radiopaque it will be stiffer with a modulus of $4.9 \cdot 10^3$. Kel-F is very stiff and has a modulus of elasticity of $8.0 \cdot 10^3$.

The plastic which is most commonly used as catheter material at present is low density polytene often made radiopaque by lead or some other heavy metal. These catheters can easily be preshaped in hot water or over a hot air gun and the tip can be drawn out so that it will fit snuggly around the guide wire. Although widely used some drawbacks now and then are revealed for these low density radiopaque polyethylene tubes. At high injection pressure they might rupture sometimes and if so, stronger materials, e. g. woven dacron or stronger plastics as teflon or nylon have to be used instead. The low modulus of elasticity of polyethylene even when it is radiopaque is usually a benefit since the risk for mechanical damage of the vessel walls is kept reasonably low. Catheters made of teflon and nylon, especially if they have a large bore and a thick wall increase the risk for damage and should be handled with much care. Another problem with the polyethylene is that it is next to impossible to glue anything on and therefore balloon catheters often are made of polyvinyl. The so called memory of polyvinyl is bad. this means that a curve of a catheter which is shaped outside the body and stretched out during the introduction, will only reappear to a minor extent inside the body. This memory can be made better by reinforcement of the catheter with for example a metal wire incorporated into the plastic.

Some catheters made for a specific purpose are not made of a pure plastic but represent a woven material related to vascular prostheses. Cardiac catheters of different types are thus often made by woven terylene which is a manufacturer's name for a polyester or terephthalic acid and ethylene glycol. Other names are: Dacron, Mylar and Hostaphan. The technique with the woven material in the catheter wall will reinforce the catheter considerably. This can also be increased by a mesh of stainless steel in the wall. The advantage with catheters of this type is that they can stand a high pressure and that the rotation control of the catheter is good at the same time as the stiffness is not very high. The drawback with these catheters is that they cannot be cut off and modeled to the same extent as ordinary pure plastic catheters.

The surface of catheters varies with the plastic. It can easily be studied in a microscope. The surface of non-opaque and opaque polyethylene catheters are quite ragged which most certainly will stimulate clotting onto it (Fig. 2). Other plastics have a smoother surface, e. g. nylon and teflon. These problems will, however, be discussed in another paper from this meeting.

Fig. 2: Photography of two catheters. Above a non-opaque polyethylene tube (PE 160) and below a radiopaque polyethylene catheter (Kifa, Ö,L. 1). Note the ragged surface.

To sum up. Catheters can be made by many different materials. Pure plastics, mixed plastics, different types of reinforcements can be used and so the properties can be modified to fit the need for a certain examination. Sometimes it is difficult for the radiologist to know what catheter material he really is using. To make a rapid diagnosis of what catheter you use, a burning match and your nose may be enough for the diagnosis. If it is polyethylene material you will get a Christmas feeling due to the candle light smell. Polyvinyl will irritate your nose due to chlorine and chlorinated products. Polyamides, the nylons, smell like burning feathers. Teflon, finally, if heated to extremely high temperatures, will cause so called polymer-fume fever which resembles brassfounders ague (Fig. 3).

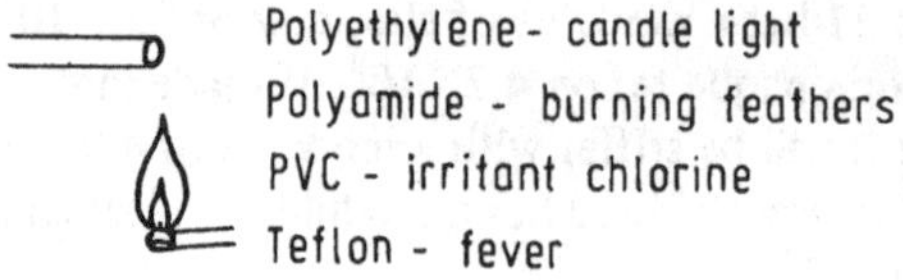

Fig. 3

The rapid development of catheter angiography is very closely related to, and dependent on, the rapid development of the plastic industry. Without the fruitful collaboration which has taken place we would have been back at the stage before the second world war.
The development of plastic materials is going on all the time and so will catheter angiography too.

Angiography by Cathetermethods. Risks and Complications

B. Jacobsson

Thromboembolism is the most common serious complication of vascular catheterisation. It has been clearly shown that the thromboemboli are caused by the formation of thrombi on the surface of the catheter. The thrombotic masses are wiped off in connection with the withdrawal of the catheter and may in this way cause thrombi at the sight of puncture and/or emboli distally thereto. Thrombi may also form in the tip of the catheter and be injected into the bloodstream. The frequency of thromboemboli after arterial catheterisation diagnosed on clinical grounds alone varies widely. This variation can be explained, at least to a certain extent, by the differences in the extent of the search for the complication. Unless the patient is thoroughly examined, even severe thrombosis is apt to be missed. Let me give you an example: An arteriography of a seven year old boy in whom the femoral artery had been catheterised four years earlier schowed occlusion of the artery. No signs of arterial occlusion had been noticed after the original catheterisation. When the boy was seen again four years later for check-up of his congenital heart disease the right leg was found to be shorter and thinner than left, and questioning revealed intermittent claudication.

33 children who had been subjected to catheterisation of the femoral artery at the age of 1–13 years were therefore reviewed between 2 and 10 years later. The review regularly included palpation of the pulses, measurement of the size of the limb and questioning for symptoms of ischemia. In selected cases angiography and plethysmography were also performed. At the time of catheterisation no thrombotic complications were suspected. More than one third of the children had weak arterial pulsations and signs of atrophy. In 4 of the 5 children in whom arteriography was performed the femoral and/or the iliac artery was occluded in the groin. In the fifth the femoral artery was partially obstructed. In the 8 children studied with plethysmography the maximal flow through the catheterised leg was found to be decreased by 5 to 50 % as compared with that through the contralateral leg. The difference in flow was statistically significant ($p < 0.05$).
We thus see that even serious complications may sometimes produce only negligible symptoms. This means that catheterisation should always be followed by careful examination for complications. An objective method like oscillography is recommended. Many authors warn against regarding loss or weakness of pulsations after catheterisation

as a sign of spasm. Judging from our experience, if the pulsations are weak for more than 3 hours after withdrawal of the catheter, spasm can be excluded. Some examinors set the limit at 4 or 8 hours. What should be done if the pulsations remain weak? In the absence of special contraindications reangiography to locate the occlusion is recommended. If the obstruction is substantial, the patient should be operated upon as quickly as possible. A delay of more than 12 hours may have serious consequences. The use of spasmolytics to releive a suspected vascular spasm is questionable and may have a negative effect if it delays surgery. If surgery for some reason is contraindicated, fibrinolytic therapy should be considered. In an article in Lancet 1972 *Machleder* and coworkers report a long term follow-up after catheterisation of the brachial artery. They found the radial pulse to be weak or absent in 24 % of the patients and conclude that no patient who has either no radial pulse, or a weak pulse and symptoms of ischemia after catheterisation should be allowed to leave the hospital without arterial exploration.

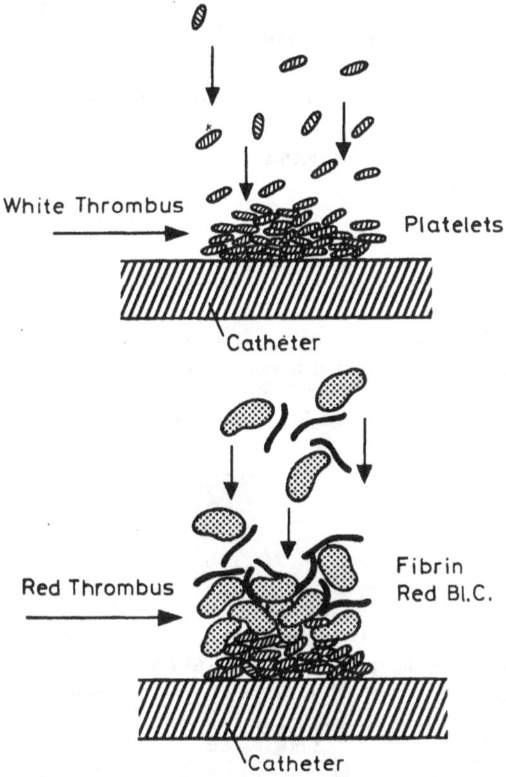

Fig. 1: Schematic illustration of thrombus formation on vascular catheters.

Recent angiographic research has shown the frequency of thrombi on catheters to be much higher than that expected from the frequency of reported clinical complications and vary between 50–100 %. One might thus even suspect that every vascular catheterisation leads to thromboemboli of varying degree. The formation of thrombi on an artificial material placed in the circulation differs from other etiological factors of thromboembolism in that it is created by modern medicine itself and may be classed under the heading of pathology of progress. This makes it all the more necessary to search for means of preventing such complications. What are the possibilities of doing this? Fig. 1 shows how a thrombus forms. It begins by platelet adhesion, followed by platelet aggregation. This results in the formation of a white thrombus.

Then, secondly, comes coagulation with conversion of fibrinogen to fibrin and incorporation of blood corpuscles. In addition the foreign surface is covered by a film of protein of unknown nature. There are two essentially different ways to reduce such thrombus formation. Either to influence one or more of the factors taking part in thrombus formation by pretreatment of the patient. Or to use catheters with the least possible thrombogenicity in other words a catheter made of material with as small a tendency as possible to initiate thrombus formation. By pretreatment of the patient one may either influence the first step in thrombus formation i. e. the platelet reaction e. g. by dextran or the second step i. e. coagulation by heparin. So far there are no reports on the thrombogenicity of different catheter material. But such an investigation has been performed in cooperation with Dr. *David Schlossmann.*

As the thrombogenicity of a material might be adequately defined as its tendency to initiate thrombus formation platelet adhesion seems to be a well founded measure for thrombogenicity.

Table 1 gives the adhesion of platelets to different catheter materials *in vitro.*

Tab. 1: Adhesion (%) of labelled and unlabelled platelets to different vascular catheter materials
n = number of experiments

	^{51}Cr dog platelets	Dog platelets	Human platelets
Radiopaque polyethylene	32	35	47
Polyethylene	23	27	42
Teflon	13	18	38
n	9	9	12

Tab. 2: Adhesion (%) of platelets to vascular catheter materials in vitro. Mean values of five experiments

	^{51}Cr dog platelets	Dog platelets	Human platelets
Polyethylene	23	32	34
Heparinised polyethylene	0	13	1

The same three materials were also tested simultaneously in vivo. The testing was performed in dogs after labelling of the platelets with ^{51}Cr. The test devices used were made out of three pieces of catheters connected with wooden pins and provided with the same number of side-holes. The device was inserted into the aorta by transfemoral catheterisation. The side-holes permitted the flow of blood through the pieces and thereby the formation of thrombi on their inner surface. On withdrawal of the devices thrombi adhering to the pieces of materials were thus readily available to analysis. The results of the *in vivo* tests were principally the same as the *in vitro* ones.

Theoretically one might imagine 3 possibilities of reducing the thrombogenicity of a given catheter. One may thus change the surface charge, one may give the catheter a suitable protein coating or one may bind heparin to the catheter. We have tried all three possibilities and have so far found binding of heparin to be the most promising procedure. Table 2 shows the effect of heparinisation according to the method of *Eriksson* and coworkers (1967) when tested in vitro and in vivo.
As the test results with heparin-binding to the catheter have been promising a clinical trial has started.

Thrombogenicity of vascular catheter materials in vivo. Mean values of six experiments in each of two (=A and B) dogs. Values for non-heparinised catheter in corresponding positions in control and test devices were said to be 100.

	Control			Test		
	Polyethylene	Polyethylene	Polyethylene	Polyethylene	Heparinised and sterilised polyethylene	Heparinised polyethylene
A	100	108	99	100	31	35
B	100	113	104	100	40	40

Gefahren und Komplikationen

J. Kaude

Bei jeder Angiographie ist ein Patient allein schon durch die Lokalanästhesie und die anschließende Arterienpunktion einem Risiko und somit Komplikationen ausgesetzt. Die Gefahr für das Auftreten von Komplikationen bleibt noch bis zu einigen Tagen nach der Untersuchung bestehen. Der Angiographiker muß alle nur möglichen Komplikationen gut kennen, um sie einerseits vermeiden zu können, und um andererseits eventuell dem behandelnden Kliniker mit Rat zur Seite zu stehen oder falls notwendig bestimmte Komplikationen selber unmittelbar behandeln zu können. Ich darf in diesem Zusammenhang nur diejenigen Komplikationen erwähnen, die durch die Kathetertechnik, die Gefäßpunktion und die Kontrastmittelinjektion durch den Katheter zustande kommen können, und von solchen Komplikationen, die durch chemisch-pharmakologische Eigenschaften des Kontrastmittels bedingt sind, absehen.

In der Tab. 1 sind die Komplikationen aufgezählt, die bei der perkutanen *Seldinger*-Technik auftreten können.

Tab. 1: Komplikationen bei Angiographie mit Katheter

1. Vasovagaler Reflex
2. Hämatom an der Punktionsstelle
3. Embolus (Blutkoagel, atheromatöses Material, Luft)
4. Thrombose an der Punktionsstelle
5. Gefäßperforation (durch Führungsdraht)
6. Subintimale, extravasale Kontrastmittelinjektion, Dissektion
7. Gefäß-Spasmus
8. Gefäßverschluß durch den Katheter (Ischämie, Infarkt)
9. Abbrechen des Führungsdrahtes oder Katheters
10. Unstillbare Blutung aus dem Stichkanal. Aneurysma. A-V-Fistel
11. Infektion

Da Vorbeugen besser ist als Heilen, darf ich den Schwerpunkt meiner Ausführungen auf die Vermeidung der ausgezählten Komplikationen legen:

1. Durch vorherige Gabe von 0,75–1,0 mg Atropin kann man das Auftreten eines vagovasalen Reflexes mit Blutdruckabfall und Bradykardie vermeiden. Die Behandlung eines vagovasalen Reflexes erfordert höhere intravenöse Atropingaben und häufig muß die Untersuchung abgebrochen werden.

Zur Vermeidung eines möglichen ekzessiven Blutdruckanstieges beim Vorliegen eines Phäochromozytoms ist eine zusätzliche vorherige Gabe von alfa-Rezeptorenblockern unbedingt erforderlich.

2. An der Punktionsstelle kommt es immer zu einem mehr oder weniger ausgeprägten Hämatom. Bei langer Untersuchungsdauer, bei technisch schwierigen selektiven Untersuchungen oder bei mangelhafter Kompression nach Katheterentfernung kann es zu einer massiven Hämatombildung im Bereich der Punktionsstelle kommen. Darum ist es wichtig, die Verletzung der Gefäßwand und somit die Ursache der Hämatombildung so klein wie möglich zu halten. Die meisten arteriellen Untersuchungen, ausgenommen der Bereich des Herzens und der thorakalen Aorta, können mit einem Katheter von ID 1,45 und AD 2,2 mm, oder sogar mit ID 0,86 und AD 1,37 mm durchgeführt werden.

Kommt es schon unmittelbar nach Arterienpunktion zur Hämatombildung, so ist eine dauernde Kompression der Arterie oberhalb der Punktionsstelle während des gesamten Untersuchungsganges notwendig. Nach meiner Erfahrung läßt sich eine Hämatombildung durch die Punktion nur der vorderen Arterienwand nicht verhindern. Im Gegenteil, es scheint vielmehr so zu sein, daß ein durch die gleichzeitige Punktion der hinteren Arterienwand entstandenes kleines Hämatom eine gewisse Kompression auf das Gefäß ausübt und dadurch die Zunahme der Hämatombildung unterbindet. Durch lokale Injektion von 30–40 IE Hyaluronidase läßt sich die Resorption größerer Hämatome beschleunigen. Es ist unbedingt ratsam, die Arteria femoralis immer distal des Leistenbandes zu punktieren, weil somit eine Kompression oberhalb der Punktionsstelle möglich ist und eine retroperitoneale Blutung verhindert werden kann.

3. Durch Einschwemmen von Koageln in den Blutkreislauf, die sich während der Angiographie innerhalb des Katheterlumens an der Katheterspitze oder in Seitenlöchern des Katheters gebildet haben, kann es zu Embolien mit sekundärer Infarktbildung kommen. Auf den Zusammenhang zwischen Koagelbildung und Kathetermaterial, Katheterlänge bzw. die Dauer der Untersuchung hat *Jacobsson* hingewiesen. Besonders groß ist die Emboliegefahr nach längeren Manipulationen mit dem Führungsdraht im Katheterlumen. Durch Spülung mit Heparin-Kochsalzlösung (5000 IE/ 500 ml physiologische Kochsalzlösung) läßt sich eine intraluminale Koagelbildung weitgehend verhindern. Diese Injektion sollte mit kräftigem Druck durch den Katheter erfolgen, damit alle Katheterlöcher gut durchspült werden. Meist wird eine Koagelbildung in einem Seitenloch nicht bemerkt, da der Katheter durch das Spitzenloch durchgängig ist. Es sollte niemals eine Spülung oder eine Injektion ohne vorherige Aspiration durchgeführt werden.
Bei der Angiographie arteriosklerotischer Gefäße sind Embolien durch abgelöstes atheromatöses Material beschrieben worden, wobei es zu fatalen Folgen gekommen war. Auch diese Komplikation läßt sich durch Verwendung von englumigen Punktionskanülen und von Kathetern mit kleinem Durchmesser weitgehend vermeiden.
Ein Katheteraustausch soll immer distal der Abgänge der Nierenarterien durchgeführt werden, da es sonst zu Gehirn-, Darm- oder Nierenembolien kommen kann.

4. Eine Thrombose an der Punktionsstelle kann dadurch entstehen, daß an der Katheteraußenwand haftende Koagel beim Entfernen des Katheters das Gefäßlumen verschließen (Abb. 1). Zum anderen kann eine Thrombose dadurch entstehen, daß arteriosklerotische Gefäße lange und stark komprimiert worden sind. Es hat sich bei uns bewährt, während der Entfernung des Katheters zu aspirieren, weil dabei eventuell an der Spitze oder in einem Seitenloch haftende Koagel mit entfernt werden können. Es ist ratsam, nach Entfernung des Katheters zu kontrollieren, ob es frei aus dem Punktionskanal blutet. Bei arteriosklerotischen Gefäßen sollte nur 2–3 Minuten lang ein leichter Druck mit flachem Finger ausgeübt werden. Ein Kompressionsverband empfiehlt sich nicht, sondern vielmehr sollte die Punktionsstelle über mehrere Stunden frei beobachtet werden.

Abb. 1: Blutkoagel an der Außenseite eines grauen Kifa-Katheters bei Nierenphlebographie. Klinisch keine Komplikationen nach der Untersuchung.

5. Zu Gefäßperforationen kommt es zumeist durch Manipulationen mit dem Führungsdraht in arteriosklerotischen Gefäßen, besonders dann wenn die Beckenarterien geschlängelt sind. Solche Perforationen brauchen keine gravierenden Folgen zu haben. Vermeiden lassen sie sich lediglich durch vorsichtige Manipulationen beim Katheterisieren, wobei niemals mit einem Führungsdraht forciert vorgegangen werden sollte, sondern lieber

ein Führungsdraht oder Katheter mit gebogener, weicher Spitze als Führungsteil des Systems verwandt werden sollte.

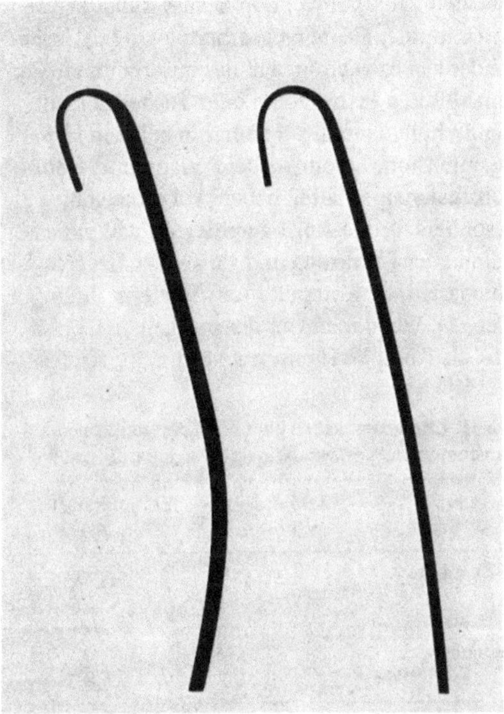

Abb. 2: Katheter mit ausgezogener, umgebogener Spitze für Aortographie und Kardioangiographie (*Boijsen, Olin*).

6. Ebenso läßt sich eine subintimale Kontrastmittelinjektion in die Aorta oder eine subendokardielle Injektion im Herzen durch Verwendung eines Katheters mit gebogener, weicher Spitze vermeiden (Abb. 2). Bei selektiven Untersuchungen kann es zur subintimalen Injektion bei Verwendung ungeeigneter Katheterspitzen kommen durch Lageveränderungen des Patienten. Allein schon durch ein tiefes Ein- oder Ausatmen nach der Testinjektion kann die Katheterspitze gegen die Gefäßwand gedrückt werden. Dabei bleibt die Strömung durch ein Seitenloch erhalten, so daß der Verschluß der Katheterspitze gar nicht bemerkt werden kann. Wird dann nachfolgend das Kontrastmittel mit starkem Druck injiziert, so kann es zu einer schweren Verletzung der Gefäßwand kommen (Abb. 2).

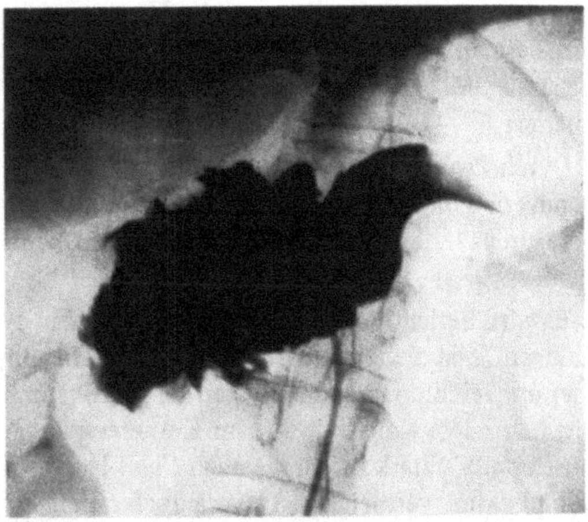

Abb. 3: Perforation der A.lienalis mit massivem Kontrastmittelextravasat bei Anwendung eines ungeeigneten Katheters (selektive Katheterisierung der A. lienalis mit einem sog. „Kobrakatheter", versehen mit einem Seitenloch). Freie Strömung bei Probeinjektion und Aspiration vor der Kontrastmittelinjektion war durch das Seitenloch vorhanden. Die Katheterspitze muß jedoch direkt gegen die Arterienwand gerichtet sein. Der Patient empfand starke Schmerzen bei der Injektion und reagierte mit kurzfristigem Blutdruckabfall. Das Kontrastmittel war später frei in der Bauchhöhle verteilt, die A. lienalis hatte bei Kontrollinjektion in die A. coeliaca schon 10-15 Minuten später ein normales Aussehen. Keine Spätfolgen.

Bei selektiven Nierenangiographien verwenden wir immer Katheter ohne Seitenlöcher. Zur Darstellung kleiner Arterien und zur Nebennierenphlebographie empfiehlt sich nach vorsichtiger Testinjektion immer die manuelle Injektion.

7. Besonders bei Kleinkindern kommt es häufiger zu einem Gefäßspasmus als Folge der Punktion bzw. der Katheterisierung, der jedoch nach Entfernen des Katheters sich wieder löst. Beim Erwachsenen läßt sich ein solcher Spasmus durch intraarterielle Gabe von 25 mg Priscol gut lösen (*Hawkins*). Bei selektiver Nierenangiographie entsteht ein solcher Spasmus zumeist auf dem Boden eines zu langen Spitzenteils, der dann zu weit in die Arteria renalis vorgeschoben wird. Andererseits kann es bei Katheterisierung zu kleiner Nierenarterien ebenfalls zum Gefäßspasmus kommen. Wird das Nierenarterienlumen völlig vom Kathe-

ter verschlossen, so ist die arterielle Versorgung der Niere erheblich gestört und es kommt zur Ischämie, die die Niere jedoch für kürzere Zeit toleriert.

8. Durch Embolie einerseits oder durch Gefäßwandverletzung mit anschließender totaler Lumenverlegung kann es zum ischämischen Infarkt kommen.

9. Es wird berichtet, daß bei 1 Million Untersuchungen 7mal die Führungsdrahtspitze im Herzen oder im Gefäßlumen abgebrochen sein soll. Durch eine besondere Konstruktion der Katheterspitze mit einem Verstärkungsdraht nach *Cook* ist diese Komplikation vermeidbar. Es ist jedoch möglich, die abgebrochene Spitze mit einer Schlinge, die durch einen gröberen Katheter vorgeschoben wird, zu entfernen *(Henley)*. Nach *Cook* ist das Abbrechen des Führungsdrahtes dadurch bedingt, daß es durch häufiges Sterilisieren in Kochsalzlösung oder durch Behandlung des Führungsdrahtes mit warmer Kochsalzlösung zu Korrosionen kommt.

10. Selten kommt es vor, daß nach Entfernen des Katheters sich die Gefäßwand um die Punktionsöffnung herum nicht kontrahiert und der Stichkanal offen bleibt, so daß es zu einer massiven Blutung kommt. In einem solchen Falle ist eine Gefäßnaht notwendig. Junge, lebhafte Patienten müssen besonders überwacht werden, daß sie einige Tage nach der Untersuchung sich ruhig verhalten. Wir haben einmal bei einem jungen Mann, zwei Tage nach Angiographie, die Bildung eines falschen Aneurysmas beobachtet: Er hatte einen schweren Wagen geschoben und war außerdem nach der Angiographie heparinisiert worden. Selten kann es auch einmal zu einer A-V-Fistel kommen, die durch versehentliche gleichzeitige Arterien- und Venenpunktion zustande gekommen ist. In einem solchen Falle muß die Fistel operativ beseitigt werden.

11. Infektionen oder Sepsis haben wir nach Angiographie nicht beobachtet. Leichte, vorübergehende Temperaturerhöhungen können jedoch vorkommen. Ebenso kann es zur Abszedierung eines Hämatoms im Punktionsbereich kommen. Somit muß unbedingt unter sterilen Kautelen gearbeitet werden, insbesondere ist es wichtig, daß das mitarbeitende Personal blutige Instrumente oder Tücher nur mit Handschuhen anfaßt um einer möglichen Hepatitisinfektion, besonders bei Patienten, die Bluttransfusionen erhalten haben, vorzubeugen.

Besonders für die Angiographie gilt, daß mit zunehmender Erfahrung und steigender Untersuchungszahl die Komplikationsfrequenz abnimmt (Tab. 2). Wenn man von der mangelnden Erfahrung als Komplikationsursache absieht, so sind die häufigsten Gründe für das Auftreten von Komplikationen die Anwendung von zu großen Punktionskanülen, zu groben Kathetern, ungeeignetem Kathetermaterial, grobes Manipulieren mit dem Katheter und ungeeignete Katheterspitzen, besonders bei selektiven Untersuchungen. Darum ist es wichtig, daß der Untersucher die Kathetertechnik erlernt ohne Zuhilfenahme eines Lenkinstrumentes, das niemals das „Fingerspitzengefühl" ersetzen kann.

Tab. 2: Literaturangaben über die Komplikationen bei transfemoraler Aortographie und Angiokardiographie

Verfasser	Zahl d. Untersuchungen	Komplikationen (%)
Lang, 1963*	11 402	0.77 (0.06 Mortalität)
Seidenberg u. Hurwitt 1966	1 500	1.8
Halpern, 1964	1 000	2.4
Diemel u. Schmitz-Dräger, 1968	241	3.7

* Sammelstatistik

Experimentelle und histologische Untersuchungen über das Einbringen von Kathetern in Gefäße

K. H. van de Weyer

Welche Folgen haben Kathetermanipulationen an der Gefäßinnenwandung? Mit dieser Fragestellung und unter der Annahme, daß der Verletzungsmechanismus bei Mensch und Tier gleichartig ist, haben wir Untersuchungen an 51 Hunden durchgeführt. Bei allen Tieren wurden Pankreasangiographien mit Kontrastmittelinjektionen in die A. coeliaca und die A. mesenterica superior durchgeführt.

Makroskopisch festgestellte Gefäßläsionen nach Pankreasangiographie (Abb. 1a)

Versuchsgruppe 1

(Vorschieben mit gekrümmter Katheterspitze, rote ÖDMAN-LEDIN-Katheter)

Nr. des Versuchstieres	Aorta abdominalis	A. coeliaca	A. mes. cran.	Aa. renales
1	–	–	–	–
2	++ P	–	–	+
4	–	–	–	–
5	+ P	–	–	++
7	++ P	–	–	–
9	–	–	–	–
10	+++ P	–	–	–
11	–	–	–	–
12	+++ P	P*	–	–
13	+++	–	–	–
14	+ P	–	–	+
16	+++ P	–	–	–
17	++ P	+	–	–

Zeichenerklärung:

- – keine Veränderung
- \+ geringgradige Läsion
- ++ mittelgradige Läsion
- +++ schwere Läsion
- P Parietalthrombose

* Bemerkung:

Die Thrombose der Arteria coeliaca bei Versuchstier 12 wurde arteficiell durch Ausspritzen eines Thrombus aus dem in der Arteria coeliaca liegenden Katheters verursacht.

Makroskopisch festgestellte Gefäßläsionen nach Pankreasangiographie (Abb. 1b)

Versuchsgruppe 2

(Vorschieben mit gestreckter Katheterspitze, rote ÖDMAN-LEDIN-Katheter)

Nr. des Versuchstieres	Aorta abdominalis	A. coeliaca	A. mes. cran.	Aa. renales
18	+ P	–	–	–
19	–	–	–	–
20	–	–	–	–
22	–	–	–	–
23	+ P	–	–	–
24	–	–	–	–
25	–	–	–	–
26	–	–	–	–

Fortsetzung von Abb. 1 b:

Nr. des Versuchstieres	Aorta abdominalis	A. coeliaca	A. mes. cran.	Aa. renales
27	++ P	–	–	–
28	–	–	–	–
29	–	–	–	–
30	–	–	–	–
31	–	–	–	–
32	++ P	–	–	–
33	–	–	–	–
34	++ P	–	–	–
35	–	–	–	–
37	–	–	–	–
38	–	–	–	–
39	–	–	–	–
40	+ P	–	–	–
41	–	–	–	–
42	–	–	–	–
43	–	–	–	–
44	–	–	–	–
45	+ P	–	–	–
46	+++	–	–	–
47	–	–	–	–
48	+++ P	–	–	–
49	–	–	–	–
50	–	–	–	–
51	–	–	–	–
53	++	–	–	–
54	–	–	–	–
55	–	–	–	–
56	–	–	–	–
57	–	–	–	–
58	–	–	–	–

Zeichenerklärung:

– keine Veränderung
+ geringgradige Läsion
++ mittelgradige Läsion
+++ schwere Läsion
P Parietalthrombose

Es wurden zwei Versuchsgruppen gebildet. Bei der ersten Gruppe wurden die Katheter über große Gefäßstrecken in gekrümmtem Zustand im Gefäßlumen vorgeschoben und zunächst, um eine bessere Spitzenkrümmung zu erreichen, in eine Nierenarterie eingeführt. Unter weiterem Vorschieben sprangen die Katheter gekrümmt zurück in die Aorta. Durch Rotation der Katheterspitze erfolgte dann die Sondierung der Oberbaucharterien. Bei der zweiten Gruppe wurde die Spitzenkrümmung der Katheter durch Einführung eines starren Führungsdrahtes ausgeglichen. Die Katheterspitzen wurden in gestrecktem Zustand bis an die Abgänge der Oberbaucharterien herangebracht. Nach Zurückziehen des Drahtes nahmen die Katheter ihre vorgegebene Spitzenkrümmung zur selektiven Sondierung ein.

Die Abb. 1 a gibt die makroskopisch festgestellten Gefäßlaesionen bei der Gruppe 1 wieder. Bei 9 von 13 Hunden fanden sich Defekte der Intima, die bei zwei Tieren geringgradig (bis zu Streichholzkopfgröße), in zwei Fällen mittelgradig (bis zu 0,5 cm Länge) und bei vier Versuchstieren schwer (0,5–3 cm Länge) waren. Bei drei Versuchstieren fanden sich Verletzungen an Nierenarterien.

Die Abb. 1 b gibt die Befunde der Versuchsgruppe 2 wieder. Bei 38 mit dieser Methode untersuchten

Hunden fanden sich nur 10 Gefäßlaesionen, die auf die Katheterisation zurückzuführen waren. Bei vier Hunden fanden sich geringgradige Verletzungen, 4 x mittelgradige und 2 x schwere Gefäßwanddefekte.

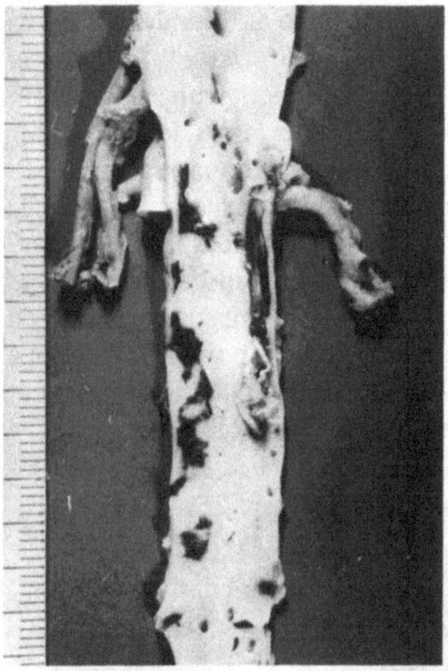

Abb. 2a

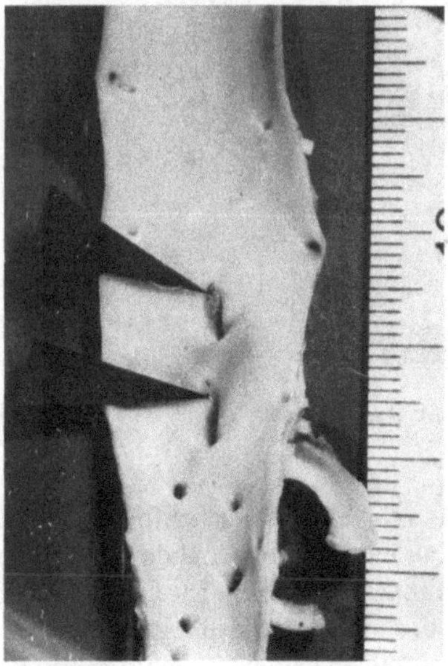

Abb. 2b

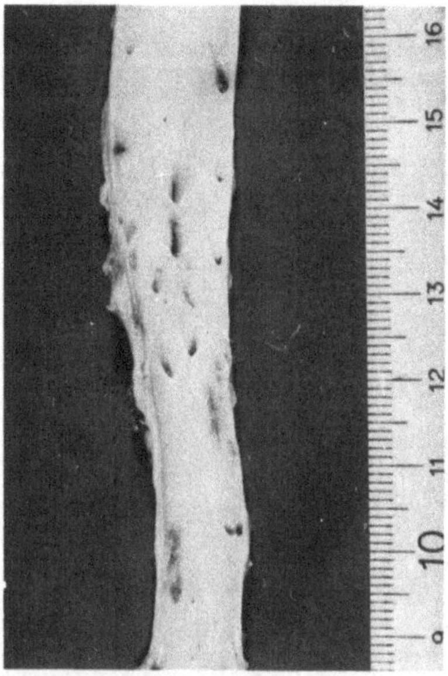

Abb. 2c

Abb. 2a–c: Umschriebene Angiomatose des Oberschenkels.

Die Abb. 2a zeigt eine Hundeaorta, bei der die Katheter über größere Gefäßstrecken in gekrümmtem Zustand hochgeschoben und rotiert wurden. Man sieht zahlreiche schwergradige Intimaabschürfungen, die von Parietalthromben bedeckt sind. Das Tier wurde 2 Std. nach der Angiographie abgetötet.

Abb. 2b: Frische Abschürfungen waren stets von Parietalthromben bedeckt.
Bei den mehrere Tage nach der Angiografie abgetöteten Tieren fanden sich an der Intima graugelbe polsterartige Verdickungen an den Stellen der stattgehabten Wandlaesionen.
Abb. 2c: Hundeaorta 5 Tage nach Angiografie.
Nach unseren histologischen Untersuchungen werden sicher in den allermeisten Fällen die Gefäßverletzungen ohne Folgen abheilen.

Die Abb. 3a zeigt das histologische Bild eines frischen Endotheldefektes mit Einriß der lumennächsten elastischen Lamelle sowie mit frischer Parietalthrombose (Abtöten des Tieres 4 Std. nach der Angiographie. Van Gieson-Färbung).
Die Abb. 3b zeigt die Aorta abdominalis eines Versuchstieres mit zellreichem Intimapolster, ei-

nem schon weitgehend organisierten Parietalthrombus nach Katheterangiographie entsprechend (Abtöten des Hundes 48 Std. nach der Angiographie).

Die Abb. 3c zeigt die Aorta abdominalis mit einem flachen, weitgehend organisierten Parietalthrombus (Abtöten des Hundes 4 Tage nach der Angiographie).

Auch tiefere Gefäßverletzungen heilen meist folgenlos ab. Selbst bis in die tieferen Wandregionen hineinreichende Verletzungen zeigten bei unseren histologischen Untersuchungen nach einigen Tagen gute Abheilungstendenz.

Die Parietalthromben, insbesondere die wärzchenförmigen Parietalthromben, tragen jedoch die Gefahr der Ablösung in sich. Dann kann es zu peripheren Embolien und im Bereiche der Endarterien zu Infarkten kommen.

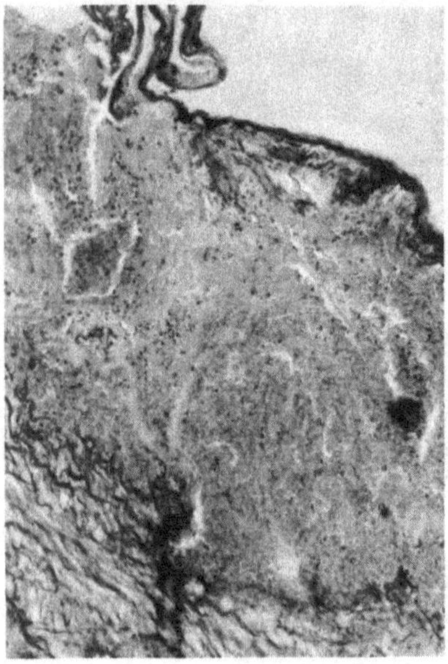

Abb. 3a

b. 3b

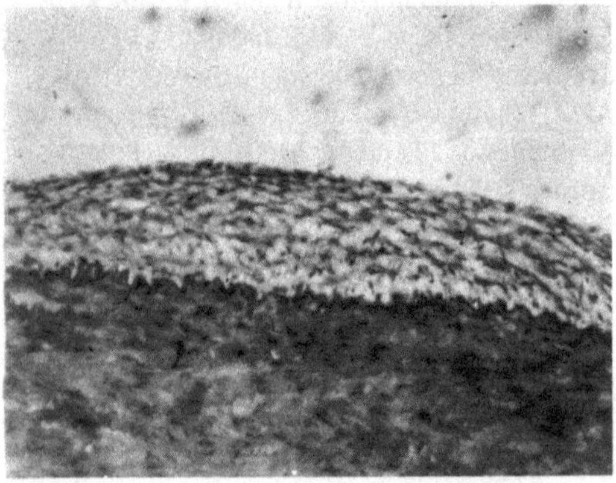

b. 3c

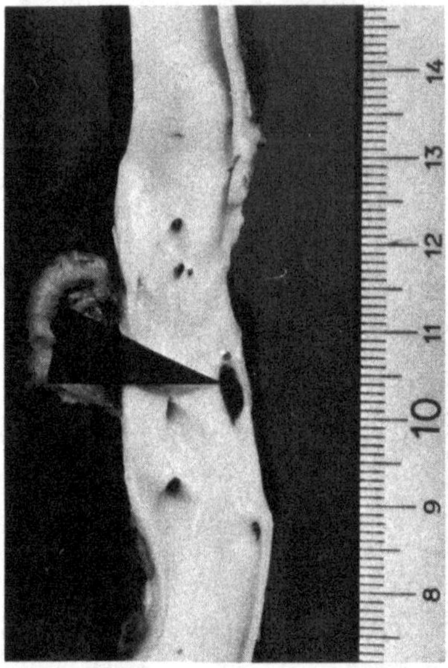

Abb. 4a

Abb. 4a zeigt einen wärzchenförmigen Parietalthrombus im Bereiche der abdominellen Aorta eines Hundes (Abtöten 3 Tage nach Angiographie). Die Abb. 4b zeigt das histologische Bild. Man sieht den zellreichen, wärzchenförmigen Parietalthrombus.

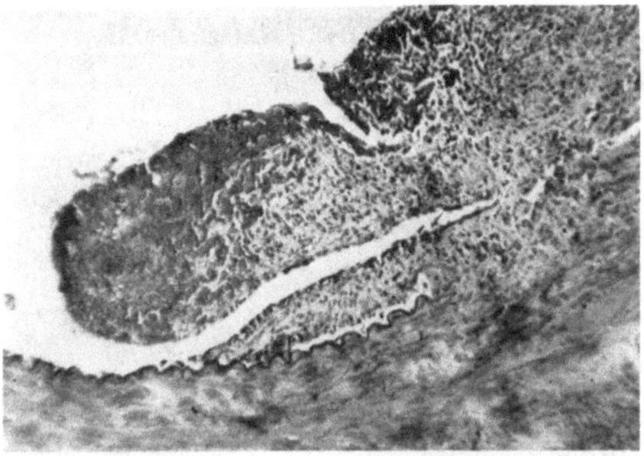

Abb. 4b

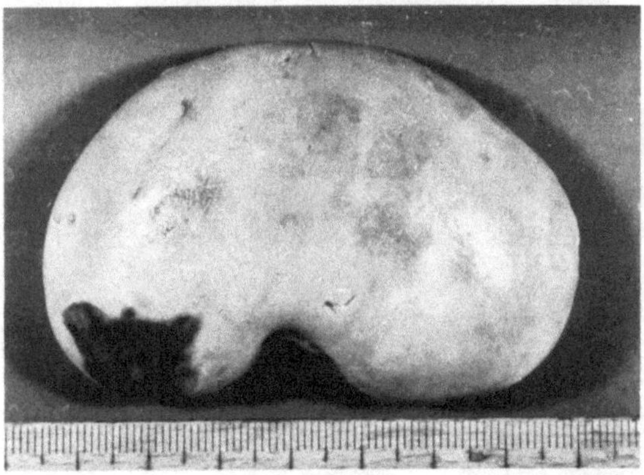

Abb. 4c

Die Abb. 4c zeigt einen Niereninfarkt am unteren Pol der rechten Niere.

Unseren tierexperimentellen Befunden kann entgegengehalten werden, daß die Gefäßintima des Hundes vulnerabler sei als die des Menschen. Zudem ist die Aorta des Hundes wesentlich enger, so daß gebogene Katheter leichter und häufiger zu Verletzungen der Gefäßwand führen. Der Mechanismus der Intimaverletzungen ist jedoch bei Hund und Mensch der gleiche. Ein Unterschied zwischen unseren Tierexperimenten und der Katheterangiographie beim Menschen bedeutet die Tatsache, daß es sich immer um gefäßgesunde Hunde handelte. Unsere Patienten, die zur Angiographie kommen, weisen dagegen häufig arteriosklerotische Veränderungen auf.

Zusammenfassend ist festzustellen, daß offensichtlich das Vorschieben von Kathetern in gekrümmtem Zustand größere Gefahren für die Intima mit sich bringt als das Vorschieben von Kathetern in gestrecktem Zustand. Intimalaesionen werden immer von Parietalthromben bedeckt. Offenbar heilen diese und auch tiefere Gefäßverletzungen meist folgenlos aus. Die sich auf den Endothellaesionen ausbildenden Parietalthromben, insbesondere die wärzchenförmigen Parietalthromben, tragen die Gefahr der Ablösung in sich. Es kann dann zu peripheren Embolien und Infarkten kommen.

Grenzen der Katheterverfahren bei der Darstellung von Angiomatosen und Gefäßmißbildungen

R. Schuster

Neurosegmentäre und ossäre Angiomatosen sind ausschließlich arteriell nur begrenzt darstellbar. Das arteriell verabfolgte Kontrastmittel gelangt nur teilweise in venöse Gefäßmißbildungen und wird hier ungleichmäßig verteilt und verdünnt, so daß eine ausreichende Beurteilung nicht gegeben ist. Das gilt besonders für ossäre Angiomatosen mit osteolytischer Komponente (*Gorham–Stout*). Diese Angiomatosen können am ehesten durch arterielle und venöse Kontrastmittelverabfolgung in ihrer Gesamtausdehnung erfaßt werden. Dabei lassen sich über den arteriellen Weg am ehesten mit Hilfe eines Katheterverfahrens auch parossale Weichteilveränderungen darstellen, während die ossären Gefäßfehlbildungen transossal für die Kontrastmittelverabfolgung am besten zugänglich sind (Abb. 1a–c). Die transossale Kontrastmittelgabe erfolgt dabei möglichst über verschie-

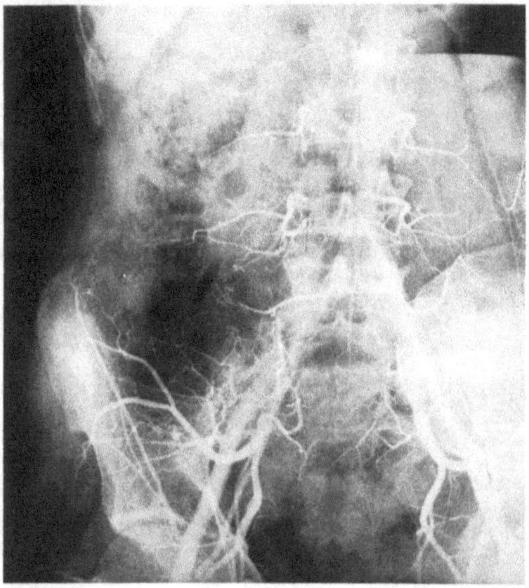

Abb. 1 b

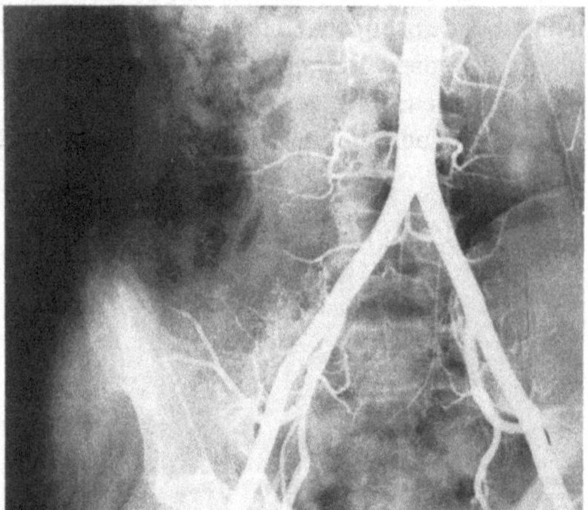

Abb. 1 a

Abb. 1 a bis c: Ossäre Angiomatose der Beckenschaufel (*Gorham–Stout*).

a. Früharterielle Phase.

b. Spätarterielle Phase.

c. Transossales Phlebogramm.

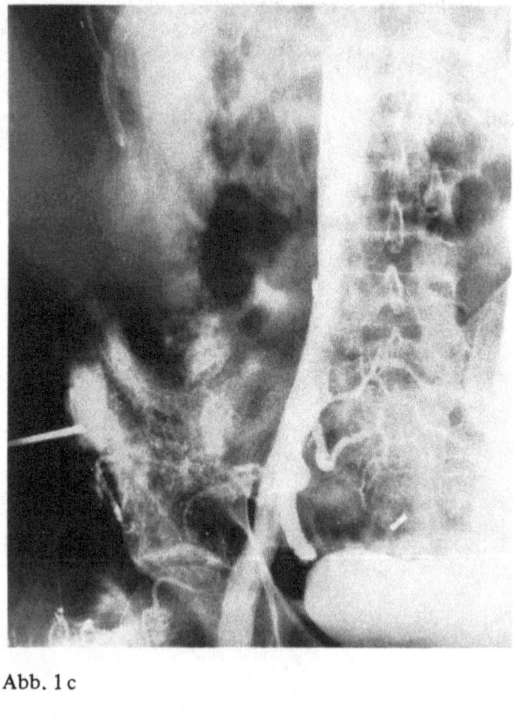

Abb. 1 c

dene Injektionsstellen außerhalb des angiomatösen Bereiches, um unterschiedliche Kontrastmittelanreicherungen in umschriebenen Angiomanteilen zu vermeiden.

Neurosegmentäre Angiomatosen der Extremitäten mit Riesenwuchs (*Klippel–Trenaunay*) oder mit ausschließlichen Weichteilveränderungen (*Gormley, Dockerty, Johnson*) sind vorwiegend durch die venöse Kontrastmittelverabfolgung darstellbar, und zwar am ehesten durch die periphere Extremitäten-Phlebographie. Die direkte Kontrastmittelinjektion in das Angiomgewebe ermöglicht keine ausreichende Information über Art und Umfang der Gefäßmißbildungen. Eine ausschließliche arterielle Darstellung ist bei den genannten Angiomatosen im Bereich der venösen Angiomanteile unergiebig.

Umschriebene Angiomatosen sollten in jedem Falle arteriell und venös, und zwar in Abhängigkeit von der Lokalisation mit einem Katheterverfahren dargestellt werden, da eine differentialdiagnostische Abgrenzung gegenüber vaskularisierten malignen Geschwülsten sonst nicht möglich ist.

An den Extremitäten ist die venöse Darstellung auch zur Unterscheidung zwischen angiomatösen Venenveränderungen und primären Venenerkrankungen angezeigt (Abb. 2a–c) (Tab. 1).

Insgesamt wurden 27 Angiomatosen aus einem

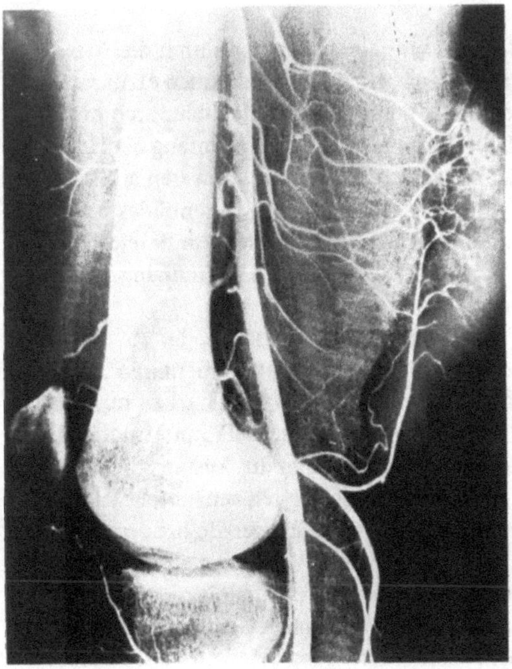

Abb. 2a

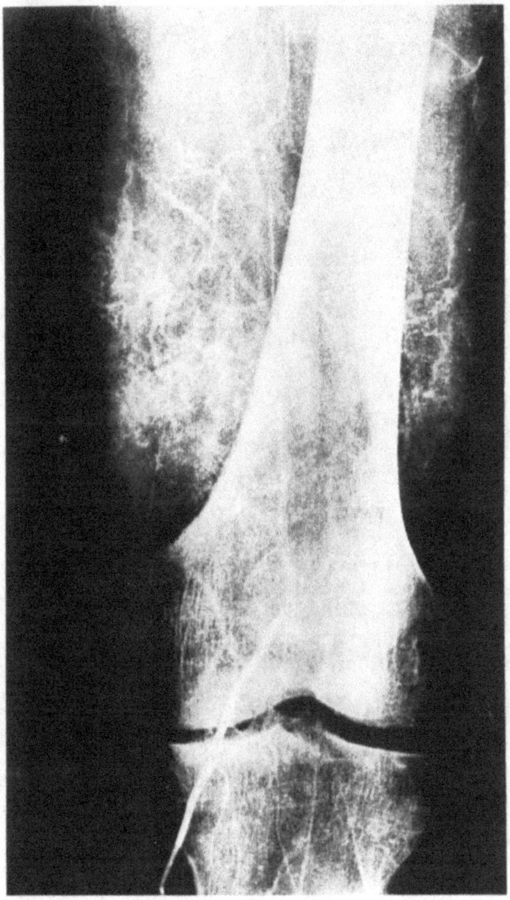

Abb. 2b

Abb. 2a–c: Umschriebene Angiomatose des Oberschenkels.
a u. b. Arteriogramm.
c. Peripheres Phlebogramm.

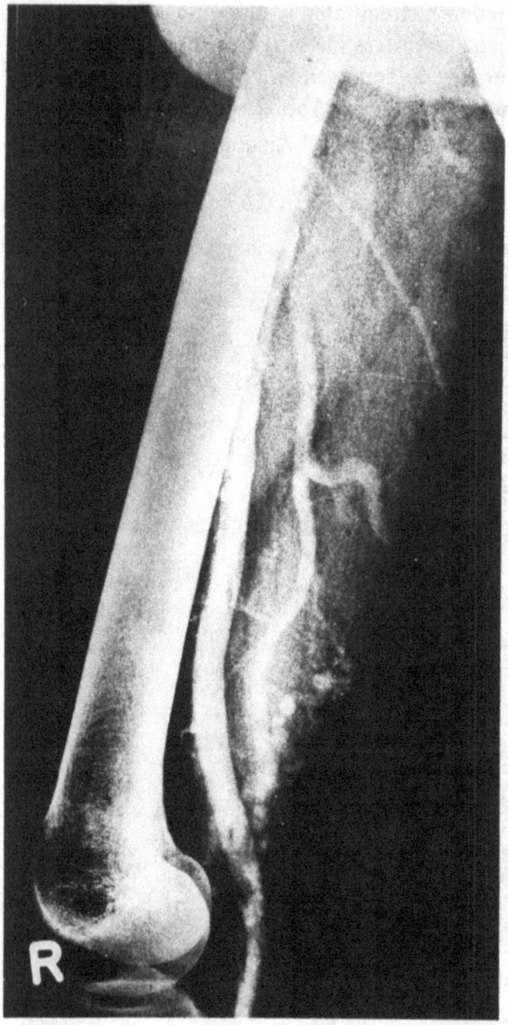

Abb. 2c

Tab. 1:

Darstellung von ANGIOMATOSEN

Kontrastmittel-verabfolgung		Art der Angio-matose	
arteriell	Katheter	Neurosegmentäre Angiomatosen, umschrieben	Ossäre Angiomatosen (*Gorham–Stout*)
venös	Katheter	„	–
venös	direkt	„	–
venös	transossal	–	Ossäre Angiomatosen (*Gorham–Stout*)
venös	peripher	Neurosegmentäre Angiomatosen einer Extremität mit und ohne Riesenwuchs (*Klippel–Trenaunay, Gormley, Dockerty*)	

Krankengut von 5000 angiographischen Untersuchungen hinsichtlich ihrer Darstellungsmöglichkeiten überprüft. Von 4 ossären Angiomatosen (*Gorham–Stout*) konnten 3 transossal in vollem Umfang und davon auch ein Fall z. T. arteriell dargestellt werden. Bei einem weiteren histologisch gesicherten Fall war eine angiographische Beurteilung nicht möglich. Von 15 Weichteilangiomatosen ohne Riesenwuchs der betroffenen Skeletteile wurden phlebographisch 11 abgeklärt. Bei 4 dieser Fälle ließen sich durch die Arteriographie zusätzliche Informationen erzielen. 4 weitere Fälle konnten ausschließlich durch die arterielle Darstellung in vollem Umfang beurteilt werden. 8 weitere Angiomatosen waren an Hand der Symptomatik des venösen Gefäßbildes bei nicht eindeutigem klinischen Bild dem Bereich der *Klippel–Trenaunay*'schen Erkrankung zu zuordnen.

Zusammenfassend ist zu sagen, daß sowohl bei ossären als auch bei neurodegmentären Angiomatosen die vollständige Darstellbarkeit nur durch die arterielle und venöse Gefäßuntersuchung zu erzielen ist. Auch wenn die Aussagemöglichkeit der Arteriographie bei den genannten Angiomatosen begrenzt ist, sollte gerade bei den ossären und umschriebenen Weichteilangiomatosen im Hinblick auf die Differentialdiagnose gegenüber vaskularisierten malignen Geschwülsten die arterielle Gefäßdarstellung in jedem Falle erstrebt werden.

Zerebrale Katheterangiographie

B. Kunkel

In der neuroradiologischen Abteilung der Universitäts-Nervenklinik München machten bis 1970 die Katheteruntersuchungen maximal 10% der zerebralen Angiographien aus. Seit der Anwendung dünner Polyäthylenkatheter (unter gleichzeitiger Erweiterung der Indikationsstellung) stiegen die Katheteruntersuchungen auf 17% aller Angiographien an. Derzeit wird schon jede 4. Angiographie mittels transfemoralen Katheters ausgeführt. (1972 bereits 34 %) Wurde in früheren Jahren lediglich die Arteria vertebralis katheterisiert, so werden heute zu gleichen Teilen die Carotis interna, Carotis externa und die A. vertebralis untersucht. Es wird dabei nicht nur ein Einzelgefäß dargestellt, sondern es werden mehrere Gefäßbereiche nacheinander abgebildet. Die Indikationen zur Katheterdiagnostik sind:

1. Verdacht auf Gefäßprozesse im Halsteilabschnitt oder am Abgang der großen Hirngefäße aus Aorta und Subclavia.

2. Einseitige Gefäßveränderungen, die die Beurteilung der übrigen Hirngefäße miterfordern.

3. Mehrgefäßdarstellung zur zerebralen Aneurysma-Suche.

4. Dokumentation der Gefäßverhältnisse nach operativen Eingriffen am Hals, besonders nach Unterbindungen der A. carotis externa, da hier die Direktpunktion der A. carotis nicht unbedenklich ist.

5. Verdacht auf Prozesse der hinteren Schädelgrube, die eine gleichzeitige Übersicht über den Carotiskreislauf erforderlich machen.

6. Verdacht auf Durchblutungsstillstand in der Carotis- und in der Vertebralisstrombahn (Hirntod).

7. Gleichzeitige zerebrale und periphere Angiographie, z. B. der Nieren- oder der Herzkranzarterien.

Bei der zerebralen Angiographie sind wie bei der peripheren Angiographie bestimmte Bedingungen an das Kathetersystem zu stellen. Die Kanülen sollen möglichst dünn sein, damit die Gefäßwand nur gering verletzt wird. Die Katheter selbst müssen dünn genug sein, um auch während der gesamten Untersuchung in einem Einzelgefäß belassen werden zu können. Ferner müssen die Katheter ohne Führungsdraht und Kontrastmittel ausreichend röntgendicht sein, damit ihre Lage unter der Durchleuchtung gut zu erkennen ist.

In unserer Klinik haben sich am besten bewährt: BD-Polyäthylen-Einmalkatheter. Sie erfordern jedoch die sterile Anfertigung eines Kelches für das Ansatzstück und das Ausziehen einer Spitze zu Beginn der Untersuchung. Der Formocath-blue-Katheter, in der jeweils gewünschten Länge, kann mit Kelch und Spitze unsteril schon lange vor der Untersuchung versehen werden, ist aber dann möglichst zu gassterilisieren. Die günstigsten Kathetermaße für die Untersuchung von Erwachsenen sind u. E.: Äußerer Durchmesser 1,6 mm, innerer Durchmesser 1,14 mm. Weitere Kathetermaße (Kleinkinder und Säuglinge) siehe Tabelle 1.
Die teflonbeschichteten *Cook*-Führungsdrähte, mit gerader oder gebogener Spitze, mit oder ohne Seele, haben einen Durchmesser von 0,9 mm. Die Drähte sollen so lang sein, daß sie bis in die untere Aorta vorgeführt werden können, ohne sie nach Einführen des Katheters zurückziehen zu müssen. Die von uns benutzten Kanülen 18G ohne Mandrain haben einen äußeren Durchmesser von 1,25 mm und einen inneren von 0,98 mm.* Die dünnere Kanüle vermeidet gerade bei älteren Patienten gröbere Gefäßwandverletzungen oder das evtl. Loslösen atherosklerotischer Plaques. Nach Entfernen des Katheters ist dann auch die Gefahr einer Nachblutung geringer.

Tab. 1: Maße der Kanülen, Führungsdrähte und Katheter

	Erwachsene		*Kleinkinder*		*Säuglinge*	
	äußerer ϕ	innerer ϕ	äußerer ϕ	innerer ϕ	äußerer ϕ	innerer ϕ
Kanüle	*18G* 1,20 mm 0,047"(inch.)	0,98 mm	*19G* 1,1 mm 0,0425"	0,8 mm	*21G* 0,9 mm 0,035"	
Führungsdraht	0,812 mm 0,032" (inch.)		0,635 mm 0,025"		0,533 mm 0,021"	
B-D Polyäthylen weiß*	1,65 mm 0,065" (inch.)	1,14 mm 0,045"	1,36 mm 0,054"	0,94 mm 0,037"	–	
Formocath-blue*	1,57 mm 0,062" (inch.)	1,14 mm 0,045"	1,22 mm 0,048"	0,94 mm 0,037"	0,965 mm 0,038"	0,635 mm 0,025"

* = B-D Katheter: Becton und Dickinson, Rutherford N. Y.

Der Katheter wird in typischer Weise über die A. femoralis bis zum Aortenbogen vorgeführt. Unter Durchleuchtungskontrolle werden die Gefäßangänge, der Truncus brachiocephalicus wie die li. A. carotis communis und die li. A. subclavia betrachtet. Sieht man keine stärkeren Einengungen an den Gefäßabgängen, so wird der Katheter in das gewünschte Gefäß vorgeschoben und die Angiographie mit Einzelaufnahmen, schneller Bildserie, Vergrößerungsaufnahmen oder Kinofilm abgeschlossen. Führt man den Katheter in einem Einzelgefäß sehr weit nach cranial (bis 2 oder 3 cm) unterhalb der Schädelbasis vor, wird eine übersichtliche und kontrastreiche Darstellung der jeweiligen intrazerebralen Gefäße schon mit kleinen Kontrastmittelmengen (bis zu 3 ml) erreicht.

Dünne Polyäthylenkatheter erlauben eine längere, d. h. reizlose Verweildauer im Einzelgefäß. Das Aufsuchen der Einzelgefäße wird erleichtert durch Wechselspiel zwischen Führungsdraht und Katheter, der für die rechte

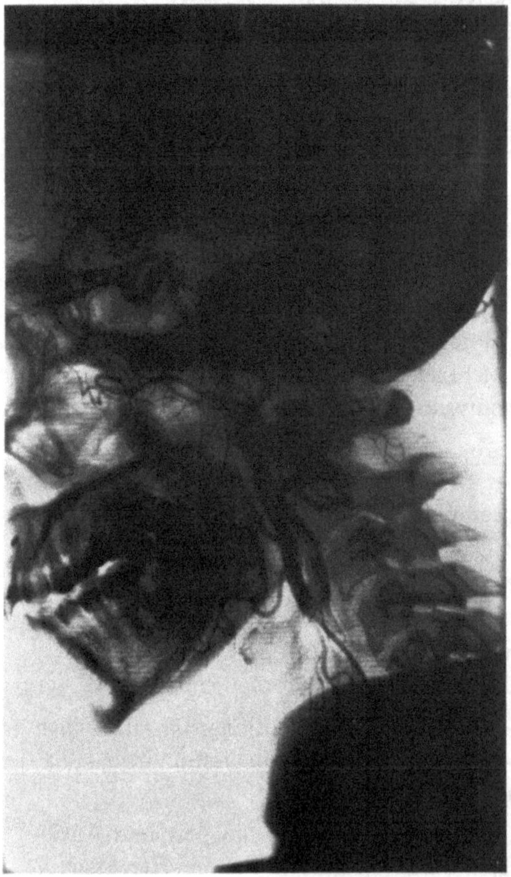

→

Abb. 1: Lage der Katheterspitze: A. carotis communis. Darstellung der Carotis interna und externa mit ihren Ästen.

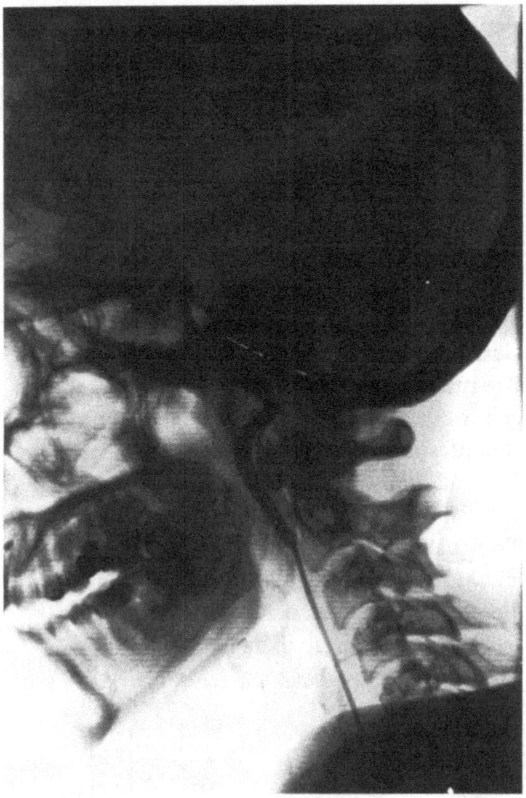

Abb. 2: Isolierte Darstellung der Carotis interna und ihrer intrazerebralen Aufzweigungen.

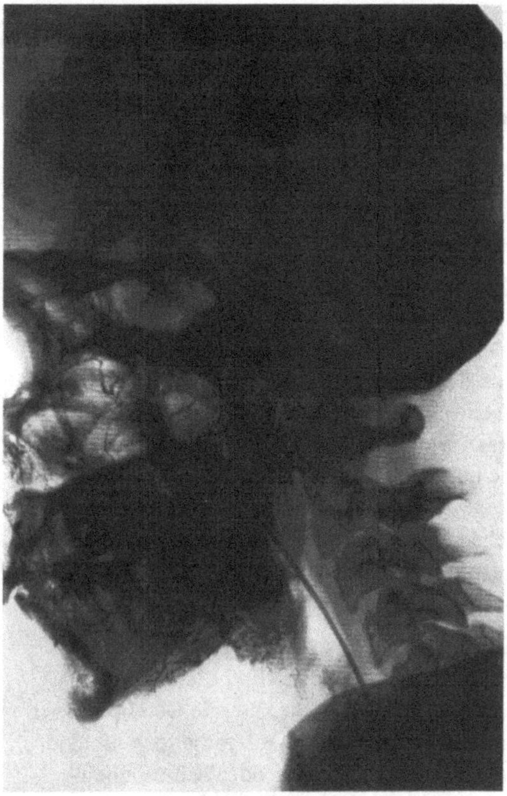

Abb. 3: Lage der Katheterspitze: A. lingualis. Darstellung der A. lingualis-Äste (A. submentalis, A. labialis mandibularis et maxillaris.) und des Gefäßnetzes der Submandibulardrüse.

Carotis und bei jüngeren Patienten mit einer abgebogenen Spitze von etwa 120 Grad zu versehen ist. Für die Untersuchung älterer Patienten und für die linke A. carotis ist eine abgebogene Spitze von 60–90 Grad erforderlich. Durchleuchtungskontrollen lassen unter jeder Kontrastmittelinjektion und danach den einwandfreien Abfluß erkennen. Gerade ältere, unruhige und sehr empfindliche Patienten tolerieren den transfemoralen Katheter eher als die Gefäßdirektpunktion* am Hals.

Die routinemäßige Anwendung dieses Kathetersystems ermöglichte in den letzten 1 1/2 Jahren die ambulante Vornahme von mehr als 40% der Katheteruntersuchungen. Unter 535 mittels Katheter angiographierten Patienten der letzten 4 Jahre waren 60 über 60 Jahre alt (11%). Seit Anwendung der dünnen Polyäthylenkatheter wurden keine Komplikationen mit bleibenden neurologischen Ausfällen beobachtet.

* für die Direktpunktion der Carotis: Kanüle 20G – äußerer ϕ – 1,0 mm.

Superselektive Pankreasangiographie – anatomische und technische Probleme*

H. Pokieser

Superselektive Injektionen in Organarterien des Pankreas oder in deren Muttergefäße sind komplementäre Verfahren zur Zoeliako- und Mesenterikographie. Sie erbringen die weitreichendste Füllung der Parenchymgefäße und sind damit zur Zeit die sicherste Methode zum Nachweis umschriebener pathologischer Prozesse. Grenzen werden dem Verfahren durch die normale und pathologische Anatomie der Eingeweidegefäße gezogen. Die dafür maßgeblichen Faktoren sollen auf der Basis einer Auswertung von 500 selektiven und 120 superselektiven Visceralarteriographien erörtert werden.

Auf der Wegstrecke zwischen inguinaler oder axillärer Punktionsstelle und dem Truncus coeliacus können obliterierende Gefäßprozesse den Zugang hemmen, häufiger jedoch blockiert ein Kinking der Becken- oder Schlüsselbeinarterie den bereits im Truncus coeliacus liegenden Katheter. In dieser Situation hilft auch ein Deflektorsystem nicht weiter.

Die Verlaufsrichtung des Truncus coeliacus beeinflußt das weitere Vorschieben des Katheters unterschiedlich, je nach dem ob dieser von axillär oder inguinal eingeführt wurde. Mit Bevorzugung pyknisch-adipöser Patienten beobachten wir bei etwa einem Drittel der Fälle, ähnlich wie *Lunderquist* (1967) cranialen Truncusverlauf, ein Typ der leichter von inguinal überwunden wird. In der Mehrzahl zieht der Truncus jedoch nach caudal rechts, ein Verlauf der die Katheterisierung von cranial, besonders im Hinblick auf das Zielgebiet der Arteria gastroduodenalis begünstigt. Mit Hilfe eines Deflektorsystems kann die Truncusstrecke jedoch in der Regel auch von inguinal passiert werden.

Pathologische Zustände die eine Katheterpassage durch den Truncus beeinträchtigen sind Verschlußprozesse auf degenerativer oder tumoröser Basis und Kompressionen von außen. Im Gesamtkollektiv hatten 10% der Fälle derartige primäre oder sekundäre Gefäßveränderungen, wobei extreme Depressionen des Truncusverlaufes nach caudal mit einem Winkel von 20 Grad und weniger zur Aorta etwa die Hälfte, also 5% insgesamt darstellen. Unsere Fälle mit Truncuskompression durch das Ligamentum arcuatum des Zwerchfells sind durchwegs in dieser Gruppe. Auch ohne höhergradige Gefäßstenose mißlingen in dieser Situation

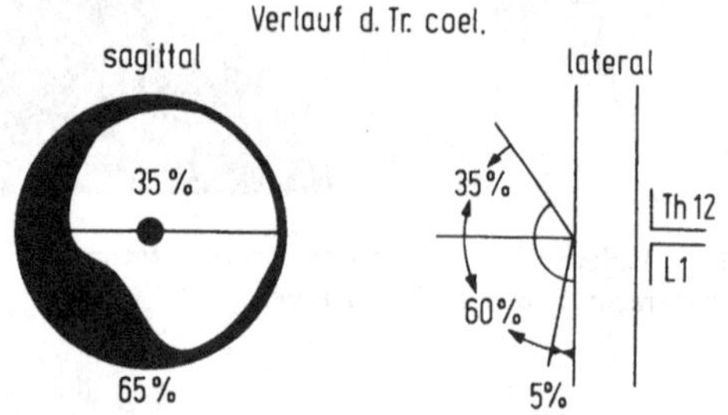

Abb. 1

Katheterpassagen von axillär und inguinal (Abb. 1).

Pankreasgefäße vom Truncus coeliacus bzw. von seinen Hauptästen abgehend, versorgen vier Fünftel des Organes, ausgenommen bleibt lediglich ein kleiner Teil des dorso-caudalen Caputbereiches der durch die Arteria pancreaticoduodenalis inferior anatomisch dem Mesenterikagebiet angeschlossen ist. Angiographisch kann dieses Areal jedoch über konstant vorhandene Verbindungen zu zoeliakalen Kopf- und Körperästen retrograd dargestellt werden, so daß auf eine Sondierung der unteren Pankreasarterie

* Mit Unterstützung der Ludw. Boltzmanngesellschaft zur Förderung der wissenschaftlichen Forschung in Österreich.

meist verzeichtet werden kann. Die hohe Frequenz von Abgangsvarianten dieses Gefäßes macht überdies ein derartiges Beginnen problematisch.
Bevorzugte Zielpunkte superselektiver Sondierungen sind die A. lienalis als Stammgefäß von Körper- und Schwanzarterien, die Arteria gastroduodenalis als Ursprungsort der Kopfarkaden und fakultativ die Arteria pancreatica dorsalis. Wenig Mühe bereitet die Sondierung der Milzarterie. Als stärkster Truncusast ist sie auch bei rechtsläufigem Truncus gut zu erreichen. Die Katheterspitze soll jedoch im Anfangsabschnitt bleiben, um die zu etwa 40% von ihr abgehende A. pancreatica dorsalis mitzuerfassen. Isolierter Abgang aus der Aorta, meist als Truncus lienogastricus, ist in 3 bis 5% der Fälle zu erwarten und erleichtert die Untersuchung. Ursprung der Milzarterie aus der A. mesenterica superior ist überaus selten. (0,3 bis 1,5% nach *Michels* (1955) und *Lunderquist* (1967)).
Größere Schwierigkeiten kann die Sondierung der A. gastroduodenalis bereiten. Der linksläufige Truncus coeliacus oder spitzwinkeliger Abgang aus der A. hepatica sind Hauptursachen dafür. Ursprungsvarianten sind der Abgang aus einer aberranten Leberarterie, Frequenz 3,5% oder direkt aus der A. mesenterica superior (1%) (Abb. 2).

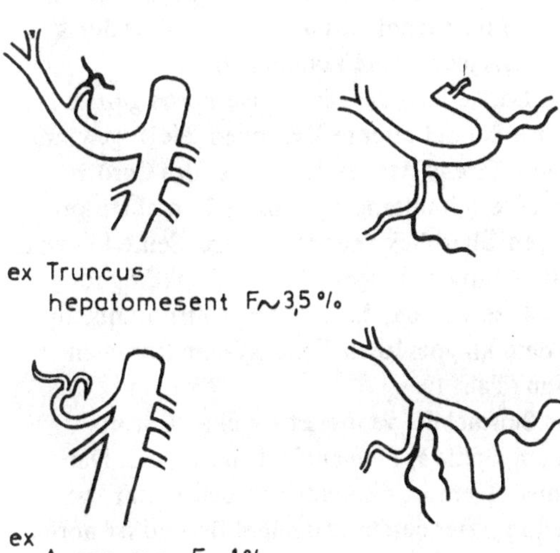

Abb. 2

Gelingt die Sondierung der A. gastroduodenalis, soll auch hier der Katheter nur ein kurzes Stück eingeführt werden, da häufig Spasmen auftreten und überdies die hintere Kopfarkade knapp nach dem Abgang aus der Leberarterie entspringen kann. Die Mitfüllung dieses Astes ist besonders wichtig, da einerseits von hier aus häufig Longitudinalarterien in den Pankreaskörper abgehen und andererseits die enge Lagebeziehung der hinteren Arkade zum intrapankreatischen Choledochus von diagnostischer Relevanz sein kann (Abb. 3).

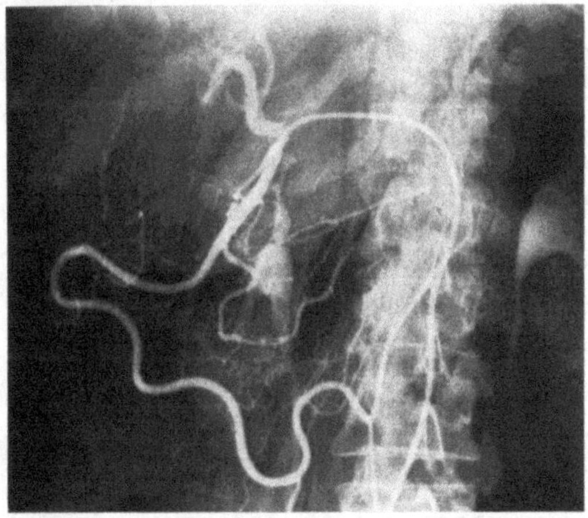
Abb. 3

Als fakultativ zugängliche Organarterie verbleibt die A. pancreatica dorsalis. Das Gefäß schwankt im Kaliber zwischen 1 und 4 mm, während als Ursprungsort neben dem Truncus coeliacus auch alle seine Äste und die A. mesenterica superior in Frage kommen (Abb. 4). Der

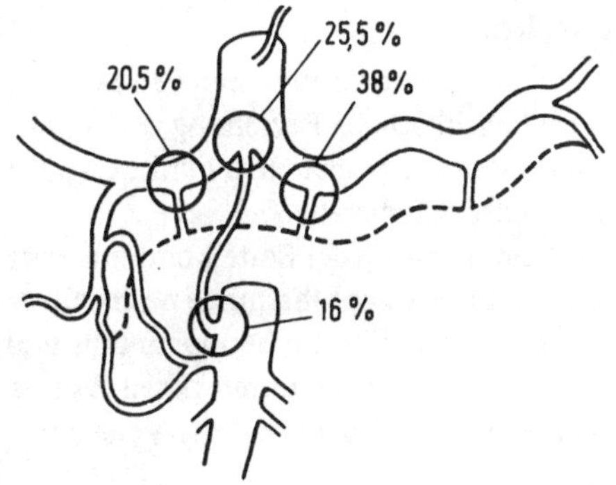

Abb. 4

Versuch einer superselektiven Sondierung lohnt sich nur, wenn auf den vorangehenden Zoeliaka- und Mesenterikaserien eine kaliberstarke Pankreaskörperarterie mit Abgang aus dem Truncus coeliacus oder knapp danach aus der Leber- bzw. Milzarterie zu identifizieren ist. Der große Darstellungsumfang einer Kontrastinjektion in die A. pancreatica dorsalis entschädigt für die Mühe des Aufsuchens. Optimale Füllung der Longitudinalgefäße, der A. pancreatica transversa mit Verbindungen zu den Kopfarkaden, zur A. pancreatica magna im Schwanz und Füllung feiner Äste zum Processus uncinatus sind die Regel (Abb. 5).

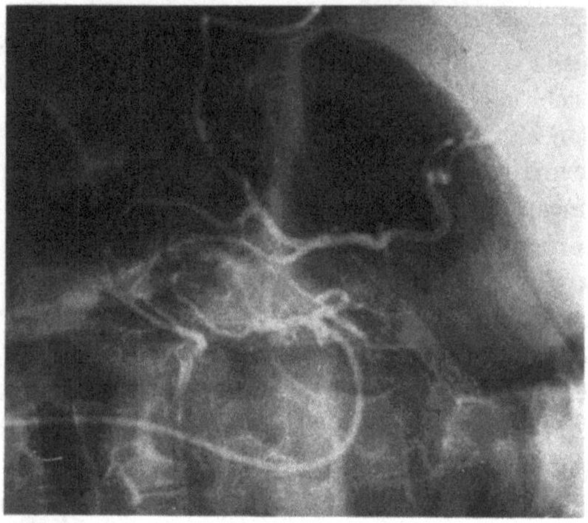

Abb. 5

Die Kürze der Zeit gestattet keine Erörterung methodischer Fragen. Unsere Hoffnungen und Bestrebungen, die Diagnostik von Pankreastumoren in einer therapeutisch noch nutzbaren Phase vorzunehmen, stützen sich wesentlich auf die Weiterentwicklung von Kathetermaterial und Lenksystemen zur superselektiven Organarteriographie. Für die sichere und sinnvolle Anwendung dieser hochwertigen angiographischen Methoden erscheint uns die Berücksichtigung der variablen Topik von Gefäßstämmen und der zahlreichen Abgangsvarianten von Organarterien bedeutungsvoll und einer Analyse wert.

Die selektive Phlebographie des Sinus cavernosus

R. Oberson und R. Otto

Der diagnostische Wert einer positiven Darstellung des paarig angelegten Sinus cavernosus ist unumstritten. Sie ist insbesondere indiziert zur Beurteilung von intra- und parasellären expansiven Prozessen oder etwaigen Thrombosen dieser Region.

Lage der Sinus cavernosi zwischen den Schädelgruben und nachbarliche Beziehung zu Hypophyse und Orbitae betonen ihre Funktion als zentrale venöse Schaltstelle.

Der Sinus cavernosus jeder Seite kommuniziert nach vorn mit der V. ophthalmica, nach seitwärts oben mit dem Sinus sphenoparietalis und der V. cerebri media; nach unten gehen Zweige an den Plexus pterygoideus und die Vene des Foramen ovale ab.

Nach hinten schließen sich die Sinus petrosi superiores und inferiores an, die wiederum mit dem Sinus sigmoideus bzw. den Bulbus der V. jugularis jeder Seite kommunizieren.

Zur Darstellung des Sinus cavernosus gibt es indirekte und direkte Methoden. Meist gewinnt man während der venösen Phase des Carotis- oder Vertebralisangiogramms schon einen gewissen Überblick über seine Lage. Seine fehlende Darstellung ist hingegen nicht als pathognomisch zu werten, da es zu einer Stromumkehr in dem klappenlosen Venensystem kommen kann (Tab. 1).

Als Beispiel die venöse Phase einer Carotisangiographie bei einem 5-jährigen Kind. Der Sinus cavernosus kommt angedeutet zur Darstellung. Der cerebrovasculäre Befund ist normal. Die direkte Darstellung des Sinus caver-

Tab. 1: Phlebographie des Sinus cavernosus

Nicht selektiv:	Carotisangiographie (venöse Phase) Vertebralisangiographie (venöse Phase)	
Semiselektiv:	V. ophthalmica via	– V. angularis – V. frontalis
	Sinus petrosus inferior via V.jugularis interna	
Selektiv:	Sinus cavernosus via Sinus petrosus inferior	

nosus gelingt durch Punktion der V. angularis unter gleichzeitiger Mitfüllung der Vena ophthalmica superior. Technisch ist diese Methode aber schwieriger, da die V. angularis freigelegt werden muß.
Eine patentere Lösung ist die Punktion der V. frontalis, die in 9 von 10 Fällen gelingt. Durch Füllung beider Vv. ophthalmicae superiores ist der Sinus cavernosus normalerweise gut darstellbar, wie bei diesem 2-jährigen Kind mit Normalbefund.
Gelegentlich reicht diese Methode aber nicht aus, um den Sinus cavernosus sichtbar zu machen. Das kann bei einem ausgesprochen großen intrasellären Prozeß der Fall sein oder bei Vorliegen einer Thrombose, ferner bei einer orbitalen Hypertonie oder einer arteriovenösen Fistel mit entsprechender venöser Hypertonie.
Die Darstellung des Sinus cavernosus über die V. jugularis interna ist der sicherste diagnostische Weg. Die bloße Punktion auf Höhe des Schildknorpels genügt jedoch nicht. Besser ist es, einen Katheter mindestens bis auf Höhe des Bulbus der V. jugularis zu führen und dann das Kontrastmittel zu injizieren. Die Einführung des Katheters kann dabei auch von einer Armvene oder sogar von der V. femoralis erfolgen.
Oft gelingt es sogar, wie wir es empfehlen, den Katheter bis in den Sinus petrosus inferior vorzuschieben, sofern keine Gefäßanomalie vorliegt. Diese kann eine sehr unterschiedliche Form haben, und nur in 50% der Fälle ist der Sinus petrosus inferior so ausgebildet, daß er sich leicht sondieren läßt.
Diese 53-jährigen Frau hatte die für einen Hypophysentumor typische Gesichtsfeldeinschränkung. Im Carotisangiogramm war bereits eine Abweichung des rechten Carotissiphons nach lateral erkennbar. Der Sinus cavernosus ist erheblich nach lateral verlagert und deformiert. (Abb. 1 und Abb. 2).

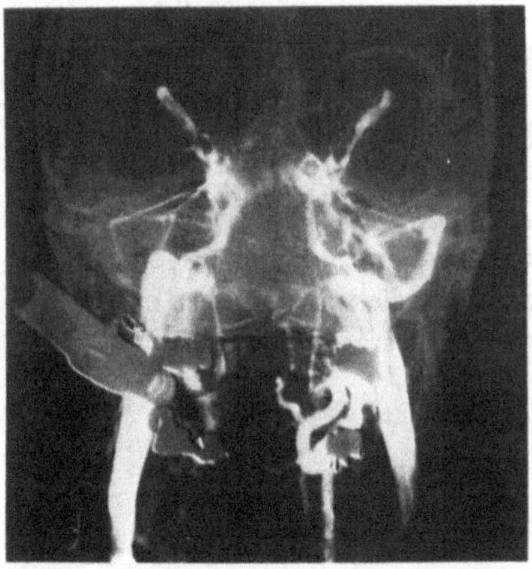

Abb. 1: Darstellung des Sinus cavernosus beiderseits bei einer 53-jährigen Patientin mit einem Hypophysentumor. Halbaxiale Aufnahme.

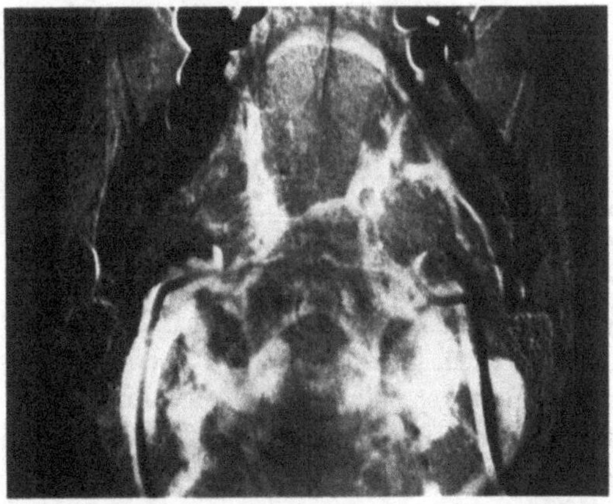

Abb. 2: Gleiche Patientin wie Abb. 1. Axiale Aufnahme. Sonden beiderseits im Sinus petrosus inferior liegend.

Daß der Sinus petrosus inferior sogar beim Säugling sondiert werden kann, zeigen diese Aufnahmen von einem nicht einmal 3 Monate alten Kind. Die schwache Darstellung des Sinus cavernosus auf die Hypertonie im Venensystem zurückführen, der ein großes artero-venöses Aneurysma der A. ophthalmica zugrunde lag. In diesem Fall konnte mit der Carotisangiographie der Sinus cavernosus besser dargestellt werden.
Wenn der Sinus petrosus inferior groß genug ist, kann der Sinus cavernosus sogar direkt sondiert werden. Auf dieser Aufnahme stößt die Katheterspitze gegen das Dach des Sinus cavernosus. Bei dem 45-jährigen Kranken mit Exophtalmie fand sich eine Thrombose der V. ophthalmica superior. Weder die Punktion der V. frontalis noch die direkte Sondierung des Sinus cavernosus erlaubten die Darstellung des Gefäßes (Abb. 3).

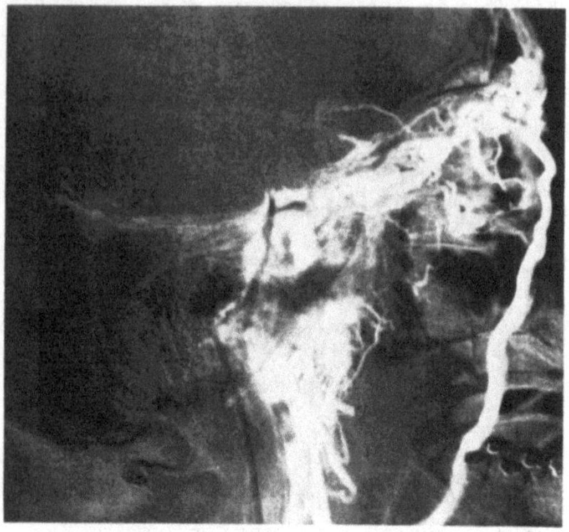

Abb. 3: Darstellung des Sinus cavernosus durch direkte Sondierung. Seitliche Aufnahme. Die Katheterspitze stößt gegen das Dach des Sinus cavernosus. Thrombose der V. ophtalmica superior.

Arteriopathies as demonstrated by Arteriography and respective Surgical Indications

(Experience with 5 000 consecutive Arteriographies)

G. E. Poulias, S. Benetatos, E. Prombonas, B. Skoutas, L. Polemis and S. Syribeis

Phenomenal growth in reconstructive vascular surgery during the last decade, has been directly proportional to the refinements in arteriographic investigation together with overall sophisticated diagnostic management. Indeed intelligent participation of modern arteriography and its generalized acceptance upon clinical basis, enabled contemporary clinicians to form a better knowledge of vascular pathology and on the other hand outline precisely the surgical tactic to be applied. To day's surgical philosophy in regard to vascular morphology as presented by arteriography, is practically based upon respective dynamic findings which constitute the major factor determining surgical indication and selective reconstructive undertaking. It is the purpose of this particular communication to present our compact experience with 5000 consecutive arteriographies, together with dynamic evidence of vascular pathology and respective surgical indications. Total material represents clinical product from the same group, within the same service and identical technical approach in routine use. There was no death and/or significant morbidity in the entire series of arteriographies Tab. 1. Technicwise mainly direct percutaneous needle arteriography was the method of choice in the majority of cases minus thoracic aorta, where catheterization

Tab. 1: Arteriopathies
Arteriographic investigation and surgical indications

Total No of arteriographies. . . . 5000	Period	January 1965
Surgical Indications 1800		March 1972

Overall surgical philosophy

I.	Clinical evaluation and orientation
II.	Localization of involved area
III.	Complete arteriographic controle
IV.	Investigation of associated pathology
V.	Anticipated age limit
VI.	Selective surgical indication
VII.	Surgical reconstitution
VIII.	Post – operative assessment
IX.	Long term follow up
X.	Follow up clinic organization

Tab. 1: Classification of factors influencing and finally determining reconstructive surgery in all cases of arterial pathology as detected by selective arteriography. Mainly emphasis is given to the overall clinical essessment in association with the type, location and characyeristics of disease detected. Associated pathology as well has been a matter of direct clinical attention influencing most of the time not only indication per say but priority of reconstructive operations planned as well. Post operative controle in our service has been organized in terms "of follow up clinic" and an effort is made for all these patients to be followed as close as possible. In this regard referring physicians are the main source of informations, relatives and the patient himself, while admission for subjective estimation of cardiovascular status is always attempted and in most cases succeded.

was performed. It is our strong belief that direct arteriocentesis represents a highly justified diagnostic procedure eliminating the drawbacks, enabling simplicity and providing quality of films coupled with safety in performance. Accordingly all cases in this report represent angiopathology as depicted by direct percutaneous needle arteriography, except 148 cases of thoracic aorta an area investigated by means of catheter introduction at the level of ascending portion and forceful injection via pressor injector (Tab. 2). As far as technical approach is concerned, two new personal methods of arteriography are introduced e. g. retrograde carotid arteriography and simplified femoral aortography. Both methods consist of manual injection of contrast medium in retrograde fashion into the common carotid or even inomminate artery and at the level of common femoral. With the former perfect visualization of inomminate, subclavian, vertebral and carotid bifurcation can be obtained, while the latter enables excellent outlining of the bifurcation area with all intrapelvic arterial distributions. Total amount of dye is usually 40cc for this type of aortography while all mechanical devices are eliminated by hand injection. Thus translumbar aortography remains a selective procedure in our hands for cases of advanced involvement or even complete occlusion of abdominal aortic trunk. Statistical data concerning all technical details, medium used, age distribution and frequency together with regional approach and selective punctures, are detaily appeared at the text in terms of graphic illustrations (Tab. 3–4). For all practical reasons and on the basis of angiopathology detected, total clinical material has been classified according to the following schema: Brachiocephalic pathology, Thoracoabdominal pathology, abdominal pathology,

Tab. 2: Arteriopathies with respective surgical indications direct percutaneous needle arteriography

Total No of cases	5000	Period	January 1965
Minus	148		March 1972
Total No of Indications	1800		

Classification according to arterial involvement and selective puncture

I. Brachiocephalic	a. Subclavian	155
	b. Upper brachial	32
	c. Lower brachial	68
	d. Common carotid	425
II. Aorto – iliac	a. Abdominal aorta	750
	b. External iliac	322
	c. Common femoral	300
III. Femoro – popliteal	a. Common femoral	1600
IV. Combined	a. Abdominal aorta	485
	b. Common femoral	715

Tab. 2: General evidence of the total number of arteriographies performed in association with diseased area as classified according to involvement seen. Note that 148 arteriographies have been excluded from the total number of 5000, for they represent cases where catheter introduction and mechanical injection under pressure was necessary. This mainly reflects cases of thoracic aorta disease, for in all others direct percutaneous puncture in strategic places was the method routinely instituted. Subclavian punctures were primarily performed for vertebral artery disease but axillo-brachial region was investigated by that route of injection as well. Upper brachial puncture was used for outlining of the right brachiocephalic system, while the lower one was saved for lesions reaching the level of innominate junction. Abdominal aorta was punctured at the level or about the renal arteries and external iliac with common femoral were used for controle of respective sides or retrograde femoral aortography, a technic described in the text.

Aorto-Iliac pathology, Femoro-popliteal pathology and combined one (Fig. 1).

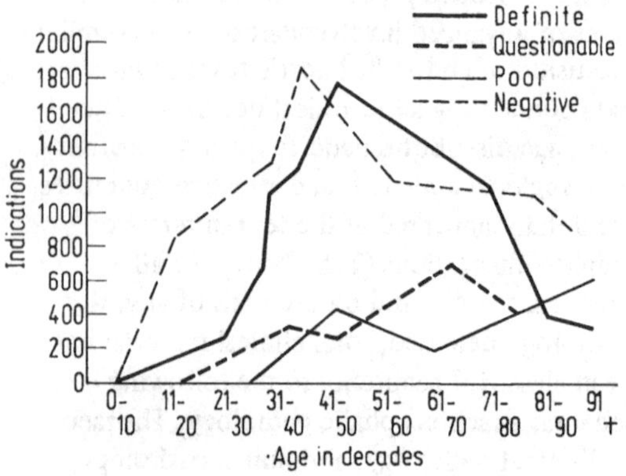

Fig. 1: Graphic illustration indicating surgical tactic followed with respective scaling, in the total number of 5000 arteriographic procedures performed and respective indications. It is noteworth that definite indication follow actually a parallel course with questionable while the level of poor and negative indications fall considerably in comparison. It has been also interesting to observe that increased rate of indications cover the limits between the third and fifth decade of age, with poor and negative ones noted in sixth and seventh decade. This is of course a matter of surgical aggressiveness in dealing with younger individuals more susceptible in major surgical efforts justified and well accepted approach. There is also evidence of two distinct differences noted in the curves of poor and questionable indications, with sharp elevations oposed in the fourth and then again in the seventh decade.

Tab. 3: Arteriopathies
Surgical indications

Factors considered in surgery			
Total No of arteriographies. . . .	5000	Period	January 1965
Total No of indications	1800		March 1972

I.	Segmental disease
II.	Proximal free lumen
III.	Free periphery with low resistance
IV.	Diabetes mellitus
V.	Age
VI.	Combined pathology
VII.	Diffuse involvement
VIII.	Progressive disease
IX.	Associated pathology
X.	Coronary artery disease

Tab. 3: Outlining of factors taken into consideration prior to any decision for major surgical undertaking. Segmental disease with free central flow and decreased peripheral resistance were primary indications although aggressiveness in this regard can very well be justified in an attempt for salvage of threatened limb. Coincidence of diabetes was not very high in our cases and with obstructive lesions located proximally e. g. cephalad to Poupart's ligament, no difference was noted comparatively. However as far as post operative course is concerned it must be added that the rate of complications from cardiovascular system, was higher in diabetic individuals. Graft occlusion, renal insufficiency, cerebrovascular insufficiency and myocardial infarctions were predominant in that list of patients.

Arteriographies performed in brachiocephalic system, were based primarily upon clinical manifestations suggestive of cerebrovascular insufficiency with main attention focused upon carotid arteries and vertebrals. In addition however subclavian trunks were constantly within the diagnostic scope while upper extremities vascular disorders represented another indication for such a diagnostic undertaking. Respective surgical indications were outlined in association with clinically detected cerebral insufficiency, the major indication being cases of intermittent ischemic attacks. A definitely selective surgical attitude was followed in cases of progressive ischemia and even more in complete one. Special attention was also given to subclavian steal syndrome and all its caracteristic hemodynamic changes. In general degree of occlusive process, type of organic lesion, free peripheral lumen and general clinical status were primarily considered as major factors determining final surgical indication. Unusual pathology was also encountered such as fibrous dysplasia and congenital anomalies and discussed accordingly (Fig. 2 and Fig. 3).

Thoraco-abdominal pathology was detected mainly by means of retrograde catheterization and mechanical injection in most of the cases. In this particular area pathology disclosed was of the type of congenital malformations and aneurysmal disease. Surgical indications were based upon resectability and reconstitution of aortic continuty by prosthesis interposition. In this regard, coarctation of the classical type and proximal location as well was predominant in the pathology depicted, together with increased rate of surgery.

Abdominal pathology was primarily investigated in terms of lesions involving superior mesenteric and renal arterial trunks. Hypertension, mainly diastolic, and abdominal angina

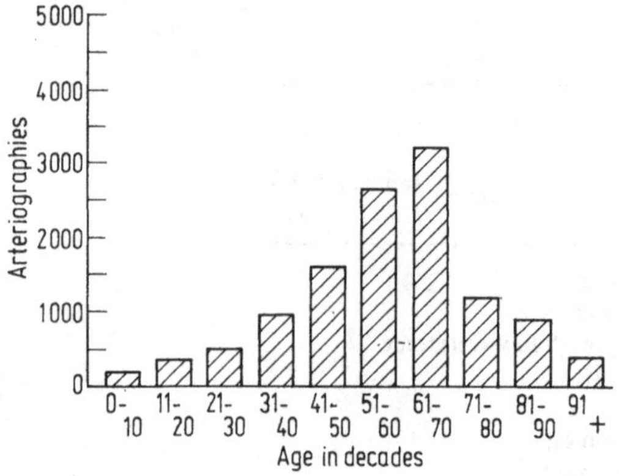

Fig. 2: Statistical data indicative of the incidence of arteriographic controle, reflecting total number of cases plotted with age. There is a distinct elevation of respective level between the 5th and 7th decade of age, suggestive of increased incidence of disease picked up by arteriography. Indeed high rate of diagnostic procedures in this group of patients is definitely related to the fact that they themselves seak medical advise and specialized treatment. In the contrary individuals falling in the 8th and 9th decade, are mainly resitant resulting in a plasmatic fall of disease incidence which actually does not exist. Thus this particular group in a limited number will accept hospital evaluation and further surgical reconstruction of their functional defficiet. Interesting also is indication for arteriography in the first three decades of age. Pathology revealed in this particular group was dominated by congenital lesions e. g. A–V fistulas, absence of major trunks, and anomalous taking off in main arterial origins. In addition however non specific arteriopathies were revealed of the Buerger's type, dysplasia and atheromatous processes in individuals even at the age of 25 and 35.

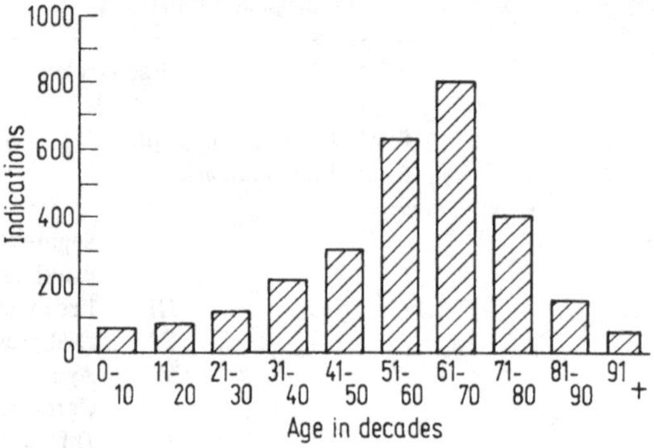

Fig. 3: Graphic illustration depicting different degree of indications for arteriography, in the entire series of 5000 injections performed. Increased rate of diagnostic procedures is present in the 5th, 6th and 7th decade of age which actually seem to be parallel to surgical indications as shown in respective graphs. It has to be pointed again that decreased index of arteriographies after the 7th decade does not necessarily reflect low incidence of vascular involvement, whatever the pathology, but simply shows the fact of limited number of these individuals who reach the hospital while others simply do not accept suggestion for specialized evaluation. However it has to be emphasized that according to our philosophy, no indication for arteriography is placed unless there is a foreseen possibility for surgical undertaking. Otherwise we really believe that arteriographic investigation, regardless of simplicity, is by no means justified.

constituted the major indication in this particular group of patients, while reconstructive undertaking was based upon technically approachable lesion shown by arteriography.

The highly vulnerable area of aorto-iliac bifurcation was particularly investigated, with surgical indications following the patterns of arterial morphology. In this particular type of arterial disease, translumbar aortography and simplified femoral one were the method of choice in applying arteriographic principle and attempting localization of the disease and operability of the respective functional disorder. Particularly retrograde femoral injection, as has been already mentioned, proved to be extremely useful in detecting proximal lesion and recognizing peripheral status. Data collected confirmed the presence of different pathological patterns at levels usually not encompassed and of a morphology actually unsuspected. Our clinical data covering in the majority atherosclerotic involvement, has been classified on the basis of arteriographic evidence, in three major

Tab. 4: Arteriopathies
Respective surgical indications

Direct percutaneous needle arteriography

Total No of arteriographies. . . .	5000	Period	January 1965
Minus	148		March 1972

Classification according to arteriocenteses, type of injection and contrast medium used

Arteriocentesis	*Type of injection*		*Contrast medium used*	
I. Brachiocephalic	a. Antegrade . . .	430	Hypaque	50%
	b. Retrograde . . .	250	Hypaque	50%
II. Aorto – iliac	a. Antegrade . . .	850	Hypaque	75%
	b. Retrograde . . .	522	Hypaque	50%
III. Femoro – popliteal	a. Antegrade . . .	1700	Hypaque	50%
IV. Combined	a. Antegrade . . .	785	Hypaque	75%
	b. Retrograde . . .	315	Hypaque	50%

Tab. 4: Table indicating the technic which was generally followed in all direct percutaneous arteriocenteses together with contrast medium used and type of injection made. Classification of involved areas follow the same pattern but is noteworth the method of retrograde injection which was followed in carotid and common femoral artery as well. The first type of injection represents our technic of visualization of the right brachiocephalic system with only one manual introduction of dye. The second one shows the number of simplified aortographies performed obviating translumbar puncture and all other mechanical devices including catheters. With the No 17 atraumatic type needle well into the common femoral, the entire bifurcation area with all intrapelvic distribution was observed in a higher quality that the one noted in translumbar aortographies. This is obviuously due to the high concentration of dye injected in retrograde fashion as compared with the antegrade one in routine aortic punctures with the inevitable dilution. The particular mechanism is discussed in the text. Both technics have been highly gratifying and upon selective basis constitute a routine in our hands.

patterns e. g. patterns of segment occlusion enable to surgery, patterns of diffuse involvement, beyond limits of surgical relief, and patterns of total occlusion with or without peripheral flow. A rather unusual pathology demonstrated in that area were the stages of aortic trunk "amputation" and the high juxta renal occlusion simmulating "butterfly" as described by us in terms of "butterfly appearence", a distinct morphological entity amenable to surgical reconstitution. In addition abdominal coarctation and atypical rather iliofemoral distribution of organic involvement were disclosed as well.

Femoro-popliteal pathology was dominated by superficial femoral organic involvement, although some unusual patterns were encountered along the course of common femoral and profunda.

In evaluating femoropopliteal area, aortic bifurcation was routinely investigated and in this regard is like to stress the obvious by giving praise to such a tactic taking into consideration the high frequency of overlooked disease cephalad to Poupart's ligament (Tab. 5, Tab. 6).

From the technical standpoint all arteriocenteses were performed with atraumatic thin wall needles e. g. No 18 for carotids (*Gournand–Grillo*), No 17 for subclavians and brachials, No 17 for abdominal aortic puncture and No 17 (*Grillo type*) for all femoral punc-

Tab. 5: Arteriopathies
Direct percutaneous needle arteriography

Total No of cases	5000	Period	January 1965
Minus	148		March 1972

Results in general

Type of injection	*Excellent*	*Good*	*Repeated*	*Death*
Brachiocephalic	640	28	12	0
Aorto – iliac	1302	30	70	0
Femoro – popliteal	1418	115	67	0
Combined	1000	60	60	0

Tab. 5: Table indicative or results in our total number of arteriographies. Scaling of pictures obtained is based upon categories seen in terms of excellent, good and rather poor results necessitating repetition of diagnostic procedure. There was no death or major complication while the minors encountered were other extravasation type and spontaneously resolved local hematomas. No operation was undertaken to solve complication occured in the course of arteriographic controle as presented in this communication.

Tab. 6: Arteriopathies
Arteriographic investigation and surgical indications

Total No of arteriographies	5000	Period	January 1965
Surgical indications	1800		March 1972

Operations performed

I.	Brachiocephalic system	75
II.	Thoracic aorta	42
III.	Abdominal aorta & branches	85
IV.	Aorto – iliac system	225
V.	Ilio – femoro – popliteal	140
VI.	Femoro – popliteal	202
	Total	769

Tab. 6: Total number of operations performed on the basis of indications based primarily upon arteriographic estimation and disease outlining. Operative approach includes different types of arteriopathy from congenital malformation to arteriosclerosis obliterans. The latter has been dominant in the entire series of cases presented. Thoracic aorta was the area where most of congenital anomalies were picked up with the periphery been involved mainly by obstructive type of disease. As far the technic applied, endarterectomy with arterioplasty, together with institution of synthetic prosthetic material were the two methods of choice upon selective basis. However index of prosthetic material in terms of direct reconstitution of continuity or bypass of the lesion, was the preferable method plotted with endarterectomy which in cases of extensive involvement is deffinitely limited. However synthetic material was not used below the Poupart's ligament and venous grafts from the saphenous vein were applied instead. Indeed it is our strong belief that arterial prostheses, no matter what the material is, have no place in femoro-popliteal pathology, for the length required for by pass is in deffinite disproportion with the resistance developed in the provided flow, resulting in early occlusion. Our personal experience goes parallel to the others in this regard unless vein for one reason or the other is not available and the legs integrity is at the stake. Endarterectomy with arterioplasty was the method of choice in all cases practically of cerebrovascular reconstruction. Bypass principle however was applied in cases of aortic arch involvement including some cases of subclavian steal syndrome. Patch angioplasty was also thought as method of choice in cases of superficial involvement too and if the occlusive process was less than 15 cm in length for otherwise bypass was considered necessary.

tures including retrograde injection for aortography. In practically all instances contrast medium was introduced manually, via a 10″ plastic connector and a two ways stop cock. The only occasion in which pressor injector was applied, was femoral aortography in hypertensive individuals with pressure applied ranging from 4 to 6 kg/cm²/ Contrast medium used was Hypaque 75% for aorta and its branches while in all other cases 50% solution proved to be the concentration of choice. Particularly the low viscocity of 50% solution was extremely helpful in cases of femoral aortography facilitating forceful manual injection and counteracting the descending flow. Even more than that a better contrast of films were obtained as compared with antegrade translumbar injection, because of the concentration that takes place during retrograde introduction of 50% solution. Indeed that is the case for the first wave of dye on its "way down" meets the second one on its "way up" a mechanism resulting in high contrast indeed. Selective injections with individual technical approach are clearly indicated in respective figures and graphic illustrations in the text. Average amount of dye used was 20cc for brachiocephalic group in each side, 30–50cc for the abdominal aorta and its branches and 2cc/kg/Body weight for the thoracic aorta, femorals and combined pathology. There was no death in the entire series of arteriographies and no significant morbidity was encountered. Complications seen were of minor significance as can be confirmed by data provided.

Summary

A compact experience with 5000 cases subjected to arteriographic investigation is presented, with all respective surgical indications bases primarily upon arteriographic morphology and patterns of organic disease detected. In view of to day's experience and respective conceptual changes in dealing with vascular pathology, clinical orientation of any type can by no means conceived in the absence of full objective evidence of underlying pathology as presented by complete arteriographic controle as this is considered to day. Simplicity together with safety in performance are features who need no further emphasis and the technic of direct percutaneous needle arteriography is highly praised. It was this approach which was practically used in all cases minus thoracic aorta. Two new personal methods of arteriographic controle are presented such as retrograde carotid arteriography and simplified femoral needle aortography. No death or major complication was encountered in the entire series presented.

Komplikationen bei Katheterangiographien –

Kritischer Bericht über 2 900 Angiographien mit der Seldinger-Technik

H. F. Schirmer, S. Bayindir, N. Heger und R. Steckenmesser

In der Röntgenabteilung der Chirurgischen Universitätsklinik Gießen wurden in den letzten 8 Jahren 2900 Katheterangiographien nach Seldinger-Technik durchgeführt (Tab. 1). Die Tabelle zeigt in der 1. und 2. Kolonne die Verteilung der einzelnen Angiographien auf die Gesamtzahl. Selektive Renovasographien, Coeliacographien und Darstellung der A. mesenterica superior nehmen in unserem Untersuchungsgut den größten Raum ein.

In den beiden letzten Spalten der Tabelle haben wir die Verteilung schwerer Komplikationen auf die einzelnen Untersuchungsarten in absoluten und Prozentzahlen angegeben. Die Zwi-

Tab. 1: Katheterangiographien mittels Seldinger-Technik vom 1. 1. 64 – 10. 4. 72 2900

	Zahl	Komplikationen	%
Coeliacographien 304mal mit Mesenterica	724	5	0,7
Renovasographien	636	5	0,8
Becken + Femoralis	643	6	0,9
Aortographie	480	3	0,6
Femoralis	197	1	0,5
Brachialis	97	2	2
Blasenangiographie	78	–	–
Coronarangiographie	23	2	10
Sel. lumbal + intercostal	20	–	–
Sel. Nebenniere	2	–	–
	2900	24	0,8

Tab. 2: Art und Zahl der Komplikationen bei 2900 Katheter-Angiographien

Komplikationen	Zahl	operative Behandlung	konservative Behandlung
Blutung bzw. ausgedehntes Hämatom am Punktionsort	10	5	5
Arteriele Thrombose in Höhe der Punktionsstelle	7	5	2
Arterielle Embolie	2	1	1
Falsches Aneurysma (Aneurysma spurium)	2	2	–
Ausgedehntes Bauchwandhämatom (Abweichen des Guides in die arteria epigastrica inferior mit Gefäßruptur	1	–	1
Kontrastmittelzwischenfall	1	–	1
zentraler Zwischenfall	1	–	1
	24	13	11

schenfälle verteilen sich gleichmäßig auf alle Angiographiearten. Insgesamt kamen bei 2900 Angiographien 24 schwerere Komplikationen vor, d. h. in 0,8% der Fälle (Tab. 2).

Die nächste Tabelle zeigt eine Aufstellung der von uns beobachteten, als schwer anzusehenden Komplikationen: 10 Hämatome und Blutungen, 7 Thrombosen, 2 Embolien, 1 ausgedehntes Bauchwandhämatom infolge Abweichens des Führungsdrahtes in die A. epigastrica inferior, 2 Aneurysmata spuria der A. femoralis, 1 Zwischenfall am Zentralnervensystem und 1 Kontrastmittelunverträglichkeit. Weitere Unverträglichkeitsreaktionen kamen, abgesehen von gelegentlicher Übelkeit, nicht vor. Wir verwenden Jothalamate in Form von 60- und 70%igem Conray[1]. Insgesamt mußte 13mal chirurgisch eingegriffen werden.
Wegen seiner Besonderheiten nehmen wir den folgenden Fall heraus:

Es handelt sich um eine 51-jährige Patientin, die in einer auswärtigen Klinik zur Klärung einer Hypertonie angiographiert wurde. Trotz des großen Hämatoms wurde 14 Tage lang eine konservative Therapie versucht und erst dann ein Gefäßchirurg unserer Klinik konsiliarisch hinzugezogen, dem sich dieses Bild bot: Unterhalb des rechten Leistenbandes überkindskopfgroße Schwellung, eine verfärbte Haut mit Spannungsblasen sowie eine zweimarkstückgroße Nekrose mit Blutung. Das infizierte Hämatom konnte ausgeräumt werden.
Wir stehen auf dem Standpunkt, daß beim Auftreten von schweren Komplikationen, z. B. größeren Hämatomen und Arterienverlegungen mit chirurgischen Maßnahmen nicht gezögert werden sollte, um spätere irreparable Schäden zu vermeiden.

Typische Komplikationen nach Katheterangiographien aus chirurgischer Sicht

G. Baumann

Von Januar 1966 bis 31. März 1972 haben wir in der Chirurgischen Universitätsklinik in München 53 Patienten nach einer Katheterangiographie operiert. In 36 Fällen handelte es sich um Thrombosen der Arteria femoralis und iliaca, 9 mal fanden sich Thrombosen der Arteria brachialis. Bei 4 Kranken bestanden pulsierende Hämatome, 3 mal war ein Teil des *Seldinger*-Führungsdrahtes abgebrochen, und einmal kam es zu einer Wanddissektion im Bereich der Arteria iliaca communis. Diese Zahl der Zwischenfälle bezieht sich auf einige tausend Angiogramme, die in 7 verschiedenen Instituten mit jeweils mehreren Kollegen durchgeführt wurden. Insgesamt liegt die Komplikationsrate also niedrig und dürfte der Sammelstatistik von *Zeitler* entsprechen. Einige charakteristische Fälle zur Demonstration:

1. 12-jähriger Junge mit Aortenisthmusstenose. Thrombose der linken Arteria cubitalis, gut kollateralisiert, jedoch *Ratschow*'sche Probe positiv. In Lokalanaesthesie Ausräumung der Thrombose, Verschluß der Arteriotomie durch einen Venenstreifen aus einer oberflächlichen Vene in der Ellenbeuge.

2. 51-jährige Stenotypistin 1/2 Jahr nach Koronarographie. Verschluß der gesamten

[1] Fa. Byk-Gulden, Konstanz.

rechten Arteria brachialis. Axillo-cubitaler autologer Venen-Bypass aus der rechten Vena saphena magna. 4 Stunden Operation.

3. 53-jährige Patientin. Renovasographie von der linken Arteria femoralis aus nach *Seldinger*-Technik. Dissektion der Wand in der Arteria iliaca externa und communis bis in die Aorta hinein. Wiederherstellung nach einigen Wochen nur mit einem aortofemoralen Dacron-Bypass mit 6 mm Durchmesser möglich.

4. 49-jährige Patientin. 5 Tage nach Katheter-angiogramm von der rechten Leiste aus. Riesiges pulsierendes Hämatom, Hb-Abfall auf 7 g%. Die Leistenbeuge war mit einem Sandsack unkontrolliert komprimiert worden. In Lokalanaesthesie Verschluß der Punktionsstelle mit 6 × 0 Naht, Ausräumung des riesigen Hämatoms, Einlegen einer Redondrainage.

5. 66-jähriger Patient in sehr schlechtem Allgemeinzustand. Perforation der linken Arteria iliaca externa mit einem *Seldinger*-Führungsdraht, der dort abbrach. In Lokalanaesthesie Extraktion des Fremdkörpers von einem Inguinalschnitt aus. Übernähung der Perforationsstelle.

6. 59-jähriger Patient. Aortenbogen-Darstellung nach *Seldinger*-Technik. Abbruch eines 32 mm langen Stückes des Führungsdrahtes in der linken Arteria vertebralis. Supraclaviculäre Freilegung des Vertebralis-Abgangs. Extraktion des Fremdkörpers nach distal aus der Arteria subclavia.

Die geschilderten Fälle zeigen, daß bei aller Vorsicht immer wieder einmal Komplikationen auftreten können, die zu chirurgischem Vorgehen zwingen. Aus unserer Sicht möchten wir dafür folgende Empfehlungen geben:

1. Vor jeder Katheter-Untersuchung sollte ein genauer Pulsstatus der betreffenden Extremität erhoben und dieser nachher überprüft werden. Wenn bei sichtlich nicht bedrohter Extremität am nächsten Tag noch immer ein Puls nicht zu tasten ist, muß angiographiert werden und möglichst bald das Hindernis beseitigt werden. Zu diesem Zeitpunkt bereitet dies noch keine Schwierigkeiten, nach Wochen hingegen, wenn die ungenügende Belastbarkeit auffällt, wird die Rekonstruktion oft nur mit einem größeren Eingriff möglich sein.

2. Bei Ischämiezeichen nach der Angiographie sollte man nicht länger als 2 Stunden unter spasmolytischer Behandlung verstreichen lassen.

3. Führungsdrähte sollten nicht zu lange benutzt und nicht mit Gewalt eingeführt werden.

4. Unkontrollierte mechanische Kompression mit Sandsäcken oder Druckverbänden sollte vermieden werden. Wenn man sich die nötige Zeit zur dosierten manuellen Kompression nimmt, wird sowohl die Zahl der Thrombosen wie auch die der pulsierenden Hämatome geringer werden.

5. Im Bewußtsein, daß ein kleiner Prozentsatz an Komplikationen unvermeidbar ist, sollte man sich nicht scheuen, frühzeitig einen Gefäßchirurgen zuzuziehen. Bei guter interdisziplinärer Zusammenarbeit können Dauerfolgen für den Patienten leicht vermieden werden.

Komplikationen bei Katheterangiographien, Ursachen und deren Behandlung

F. Olbert, H. Denck und L. Wicke

Komplikationen bei Katheterangiographien haben verschiedene Ursachen: sie können allgemein durch das Kontrastmittel selbst, im Rahmen von Narkosezwischenfällen, sie können durch die Punktion, und sie können auch durch den Katheter verursacht werden.
Wir haben an unserer Abteilung in den letzten Jahren 981 Katheterangiographien durchgeführt (Tab. 1, 2).

Die in der Tabelle angeführte Amaurose geschah nach einer Aortenbogenangiographie, wobei es vermutlich durch ein Kontrastmittelüberangebot im Bereiche der Fissura calcarina zu einer passageren Erblindung kam.
Wir haben beobachtet, daß die Thrombosen ausnahmslos nach Zwei- und Mehrfachgebrauch eines Katheters zustande kamen. Dies wird verständlich, wenn wir uns die Katheteroberfläche bzw. Innenfläche eines solchen gebrauchten Katheters im Elektronenmikroskop näher betrachten. Ein ungebrauchter Katheter hat eine glatte, bzw. leicht gekörnte Oberfläche ohne Schliffurchen, während ein gebrauchter Katheter eine große, mit Vertiefungen charakterisierte Oberfläche aufweist, die sowohl an der Innenfläche, als auch an der Außenfläche einerseits durch den Führungsdraht, andererseits durch das Vorschieben, offensichtlich im Bereich der Punktionsstelle Ziehspuren aufweist (Abb. 1a). Auch durch Formalin kommt es zur beträchtlichen Schädigung der Innen- und Außenfläche eines solchen Katheters, die es verständlich macht, daß es zu einer erhöhten Thrombozytensedimentation kommt (Abb. 1b). Als zweite Ursache bei solchen Thrombosen glauben wir einer beschädigten Katheterspitze ebenso wie einem unsauber ausgestanzten Seitenloch eine erhebliche Schuld für eine entstandene Thrombose zuschie-

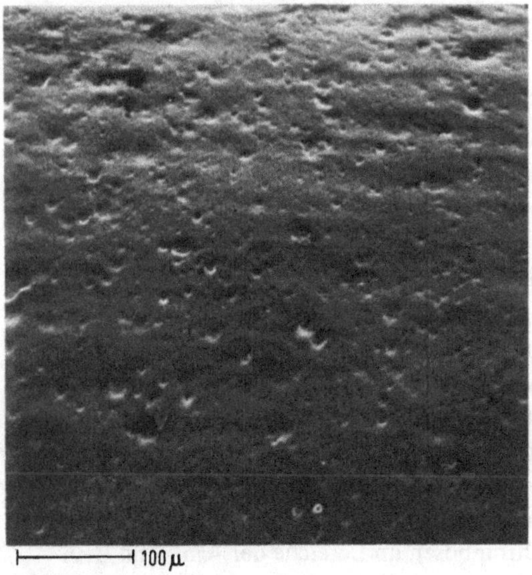

Abb. 1a

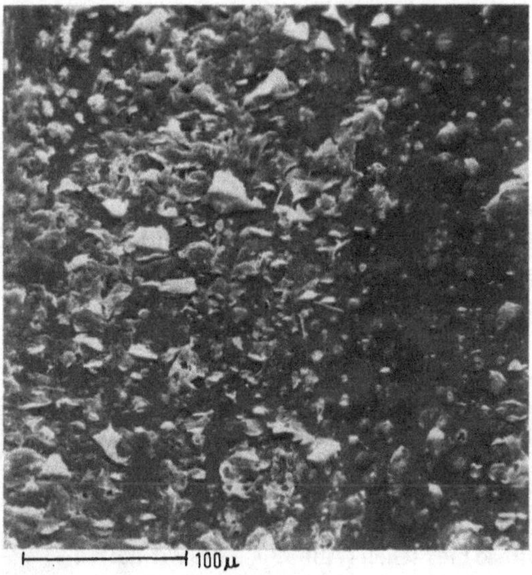

Abb. 1b

Tab. 1:

Aortenbogen	372
Nierenangiographie	330
Coeliacographie	177
Angiographie der weiblichen Brust	35
Bronchialisangiographie	35
Armangiographie	32
Summe	981

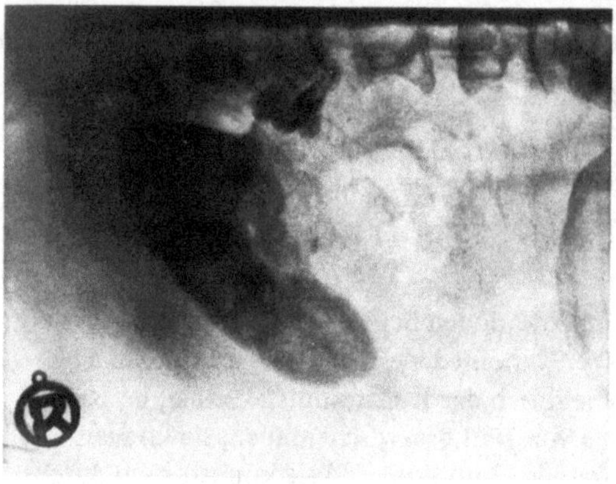

Abb. 2

Tab. 2: Komplikationen bei 981 Katheterangiographien

Art	Anzahl	%
Todesfälle	0	0,0
Intramurale Injektion (Niere, Aortenbogen)	2	0,2
Gefäßperforation durch den Führungsdraht (im Beckenbereich)	4	0,4
Thrombosen (5 Arm, 3 Bein)	8	0,8
Amaurose nach Aortenbogenangiographie	1	0,1
1 Übernähung im Leistenbereich	1	0,1
Summe	16	1,6

ben zu können. Die Spitze eines Katheters soll eine ideale Krümmung aufweisen. Diese Krümmung soll nicht abrupt erfolgen.
Wir haben einmal bei einer Untersuchung mit einer solchen in Stufen verlaufender Katheterkrümmung eine intramurale Injektion im Rahmen einer Nierenarterienuntersuchung gesetzt, die wir anläßlich eines Tumorverdachtes im Bereiche der rechten Niere durchführten (Abb. 2).

Auch bei Aortenbogenangiographien, insbesondere beim alten Menschen ist es möglich, eine intramurale Kontrastmittelinjektion zu setzen, wie wir sie hier sehen (Abb. 3a, 3b). Wir halten es daher für notwendig, Aortenbogenangiographien, insbesondere bei älteren Personen, nach der Methode von *Olin* durchzuführen, die nicht nur das Rückschnellen des Katheters während der Injektion verhindert, sondern damit auch verhindert, daß sich die Katheterspitze an einem Plaque verhängt und so eine intramurale Injektion begünstigt.

Die Behandlung der intramuralen Injektion im Bereiche des Aortenbogens war nicht notwendig. Der Schaden durch die intramurale Kontrastmittelinjektion im Bereiche der Nierenarterie mußte durch eine Veneninterposition behoben werden.
Thrombosen im Bereiche der Arm- und Beinarterien nach Katheterangiographien, die wir

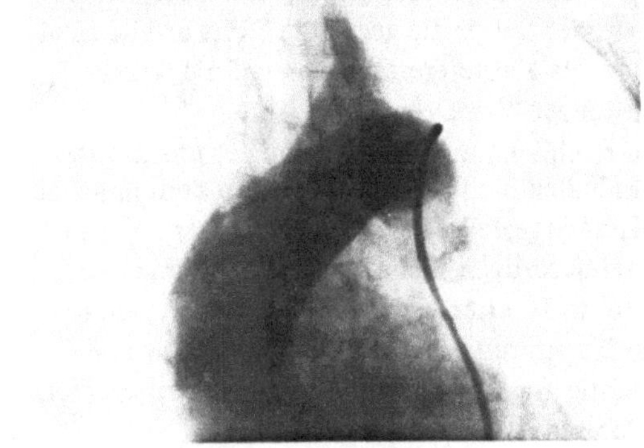

Abb. 3a

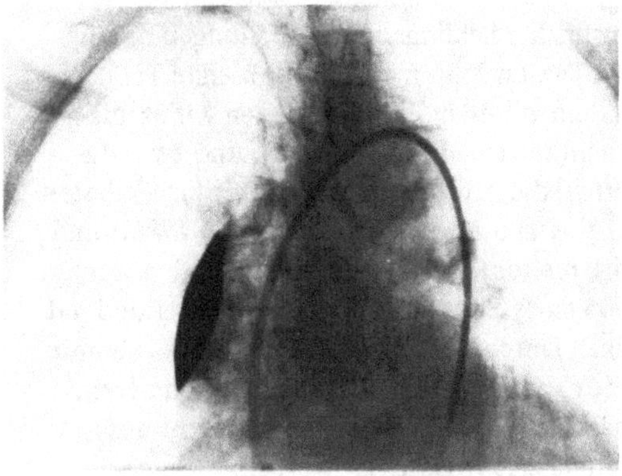

Abb. 3b

selbst an unserer Abteilung 8 mal und von auswärts 9 mal zur Behandlung bekamen, wurden chirurgisch behandelt. Wir haben bei diesen Komplikationen 3 Verschlußtypen beobachtet:

1. Die Thrombose im unmittelbaren Bereich der Punktionsstelle.

2. Die Embolie im distalen Abschnitt der Arteria femoralis, bzw. im Bereiche der Arterie poplitea.

3. Der embolische Verschluß einer Beckenarterie, offensichtlich durch Thrombose am Katheter, weil während der Operation ein Gefäßschaden nicht nachzuweisen war.

Wir sind auf Grund unserer Erfahrung der Meinung, daß Katheterangiographien nur mit Einmalkathetern durchgeführt werden sollten, daß die Thromboseneigung im Katheter einerseits durch häufige Heparinspülung des Katheters und andererseits durch eine möglichst kurze Untersuchungsdauer verringert wird. Jede Katheteruntersuchung sollte erst nach einem genauen vorhergehenden Gefäßstatus erfolgen, um das Loslösen von Plaques zu verhindern. Bei Ischämie sollte eine sofortige Kontrollangiographie durchgeführt werden, um schwerere Schäden zu vermeiden.

Verhütung von Katheterisierungskomplikationen durch Führungsdraht mit J-Spitze und beweglichem Kern

R. Köhler

In meiner Abteilung besteht über die Hälfte aller Angiographiepatienten aus Arteriosklerosefällen entweder mit Symptomen von den unteren Extremitäten oder mit solchen vom Cerebrum. Beide Fälle erfordern eine optimale Untersuchung mit Seldinger-Technik, mit Darstellung der Beckenarterien und den unteren bzw. oberen Aorta. Dies kann auf Schwierigkeiten stoßen, und es können Gefährdungen aufkommen für den Patienten, wenn die Gefäße arteriosklerotisch gewunden und/oder vielleicht mit intimalen Unebenheiten erfüllt sind.

Die Anzahl vollständiger Mißerfolge bei unseren inguinalen Seldinger-Untersuchungen hat in den letzten Jahren eine zunehmende Tendenz erkennen lassen. Plötzlich haben wir es wie mit einem rettenden Engel zu tun, und zwar dadurch, daß ich einen Spezialleiter für Katheter-Angiographie anschaffte, der von *Judkins* und Mitarbeitern 1967 beschrieben worden war. Sein eines Ende ist j-förmig gekrümmt und hat einen Durchmesser von 3 mm. Das gekrümmte Ende kann unter Zuhilfenahme des inneren, mandrinbetonten, recht steifen Kerns des Leiters gerade gerichtet werden.

Vor dem Einführen durch die *Seldinger*-Nadel wird die Spitze dadurch ausgestreckt, daß der Kern bis zur Spitze des Leiters herausgeführt wird. Nachdem der Leiter die Nadel passiert hat, wird der Mandrin 2–3 cm herausgezogen, und der Leiter nimmt wieder seine J-Form an. Unter Durchleuchtungskontrolle gelingt es danach meistens den Leiter durch die Iliakalarterie und untere Aorta hinauszuführen. Nachdem der Leiter die geeignete Höhe erreicht hat, geht die Kathetereinführung auf die übliche Seldinger-Weise vor sich.
In reichlich zwei Jahren gelang es uns in rund 80 Fällen nicht, die Katheter mit dem üblichen Kifa-hergestellten Leiter einzuführen. Nur in drei derartigen Fällen konnte der danach erprobte J-Leiter nicht eingebracht werden, und in 2 weiteren Fällen konnten Katheter und richtig angebrachter Führungsdraht zusammen nicht aufwärts vordringen.

Die folgenden Abbildungen zeigen Beispiele für geglückte Katheterpassagen trotz schwerer iliakaler Arteriosklerose. Die größte Schwierigkeit bei der Einführung wird verursacht durch schwere distale iliakale Schlängelung in Kombination mit großen Plaques. Die einwärts vorrückende, auf den Leiter übertragene Kraft wird dabei durch einen quergestellten Gefäßverlauf absorbiert,

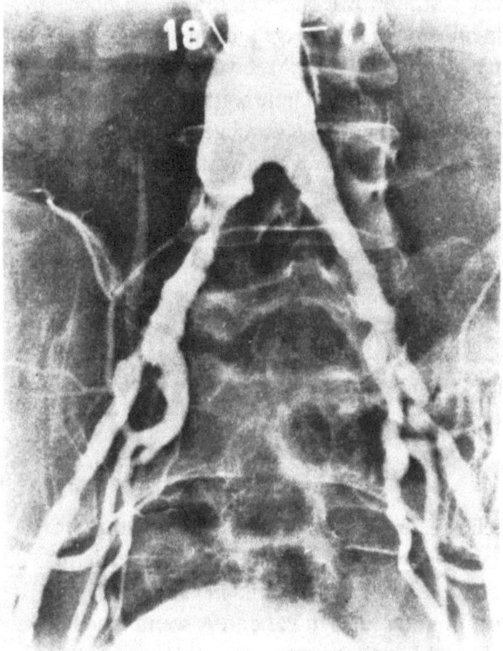

Abb. 1a

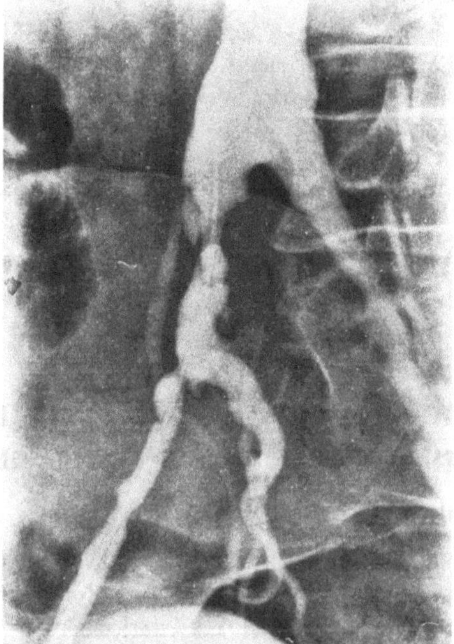

Abb. 1b

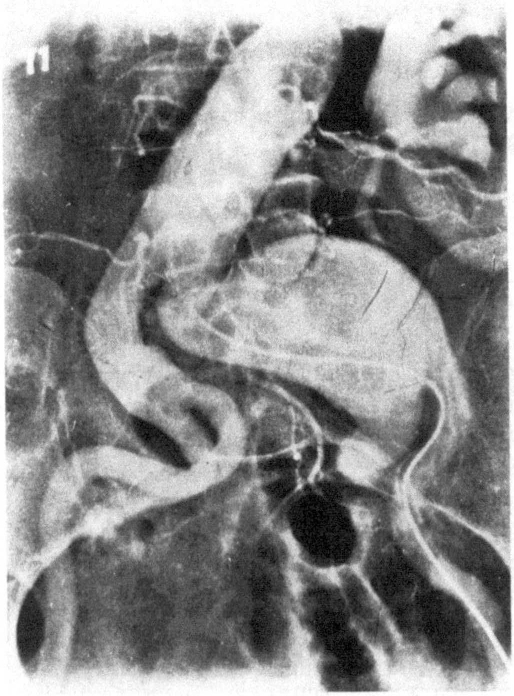

Abb. 2

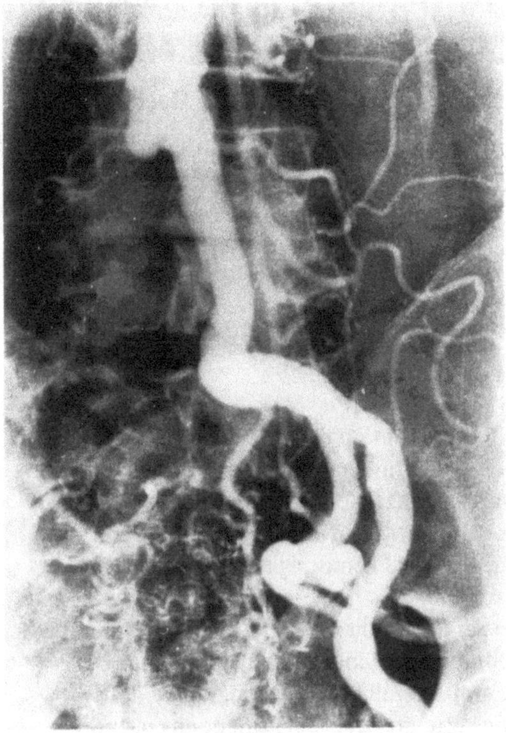

Abb. 3

und entweder der Leiter oder Leiter und Katheter vermögen nicht weiter einwärts vorzudringen.
Der Führungsdraht mit J-Spitze wird nun in meiner Abteilung bei Verdacht auf Bauchaorten-Aneurysma systematisch angewandt und stets dann ergriffen, wenn ein gewöhnlicher gerader Leiter mit weicher Spitze in den Iliakalarterien aufwärts stecken bleibt.
Aus Sparsamkeitsgründen machen wir zunächst einen Versuch mit geradem Leiter, denn der J-Leiter ist recht kostspielig und nur für einmaligen Gebrauch vorgesehen. Das Auswechseln des Leiters verzögert die Untersuchung nicht nennenswert.

Les Indications de l'Arteriographie abdominale selective d'Urgence dans les Hematemeses graves

F. Weill, J. P. Ricatte et J. C. Becker

L'angiographie dans les hématémèses abondantes a été proposée dés 1963; nous avons réuni 32 observations où cet examen a été pratiqué en urgence et avant toute opacification barytée.

Les images anormales

– La constitution d'une tache opaque, apparaissant à la fin du temps artériolaire et persistant pendant un certain temps après la disparition des images de pariétographie, traduit directement l'hémorragie et s'explique par le passage dans la lumière digestive de sang opacifié par le produit de contraste. Ceci suppose un débit hémorragique ponctuel minimum de 0,5 ml par minute: l'artériographie doit donc être pratiquée réellement en cours d'hemorragie pendant que se poursuit la thérapeutique réanimatrice.

– Des déformations artérielles peuvent aussi traduire le siège d'une lésion: artérioles de diamètre anormalement grand se dirigeant vers un cratère ulcéreux; déformation d'un petit élément vasculaire au voisinage d'une lésion.

– Le renforcement du dessin artériolo-capillaire est un simple signe d'appel lors de la confrontation d'un examen angiographique à priori négatif avec les clichés du transit qui a suivi.

– Les signes d'hypertension portale enfin sont trop connus depuis les travaux de *Léger* pour que nous les rappelions.

Le tableau 1 résume les résultats de nos 32 examens:

Tab. 1:

Nombre total d'examens vasculaires	Nombre d'examens négatifs	Taches opaques	Déformations artérielles	Renforcement artériolo-capillaire	HTP
32	8	7	3	8	8

Apports de l'angiographie dans le diagnostic du siège de l'hémorragie et de l'étiologie

Parmi les 32 malades examinés par angiographie, 29 l'ont été par transit immédiatement après. Cet examen a été le seul à aboutir à un résultat positif chez 5 d'entre eux.

Chez 14 malades (43%), le diagnostic a été fait grâce à la conjonction des signes parfois isoléménť non déterminants de l'angiographie et du transit.

Enfin chez 8 malades seule l'angiographie a permis un diagnostic (25% des cas) (Tab. 2).

L'hypertension portale a été radiologiquement confirmée chez 11 des 17 cirrhotiques seulement: chez 8 malades, ont été retrouvés les signes angiographiques classiques: veines anormales dans la région du hile de la rate, reflux, etc... Trois fois seulement le diagnostic a été le fait du transit par la mise en évidence de varices oesophagiennes perdent leur relief. Parmi les période d'hématémèse abondante les varices oesophagiennes perdent leur relief' Parmi les 6 malades chez qui l'image de retour porte n'était pas de densité suffisante pour démontrer une anomalie hémodynamique ou était apparemment normale, l'un présentait pourtant à l'intervention des varices oesophagiennes et tubérositaires considérables.

4 patients présentaient des lésions ulcéreuses associées à une hypertension portale. Elles ont toutes été mises en évidence par le transit. L'angiographie a permis le diagnostic simultané de l'hypertension portale et de l'ulcère dans 2 cas. Elle a montré dans I cas l'ulcère seule-

Tab. 2:

Nombre d'examens	Pas de diagnostic	Examen responsable du diagnostic		
		transit	artériographie	artériographie + transit
32	5	5	8	14
	15,6%	15,6%	25%	43%

ment et dans I autre cas l'hypertension portale seulement, qui aurait échappé au transit seul.

Il faut à notre avis retenir de ces chiffres, dans ce domaine de l'exploration radiologique des hématémèses graves:
– l'apport considérable de l'angiographie, malgré des échecs dans le diagnostic de l'hypertension portale.
– l'apport déterminant de l'angiographie dans le diagnostic lésionnel en général, puisque dans 25% des cas elle a représenté la seule voie du diagnostic du siège de l'hémorragie.

Indications

1. *Chez le sujet jeune* (moins de 30 ans): La réanimation médicale est habituellement très ëfficace: un retard de 24 ou 36 heures dans la thérapeutique chirurgicale n'aura en régale générale pas de conséquence dramatique. Par ailleurs, le risque local de thrombose artérielle est le plus élevé.
Nous pensons donc, surtout s'il existe des éléments en faveur d'une lésion ulcéreuse, qu'il est préférable de recourir d'abord aux explorations conventionnelles, précédées si cela est possible d'une fibroscopie d'urgence.
2. *Chez le sujet agé* (plus de 60 ans): La réanimation est plus délicate, l'artériographie moins dangereuse et la décision opératoire plus importante, étant donné les risques chez ces malades des interventions tardives ou itératives.

Dans ce cas, l'angiographie première mérite d'être systématique chaque fois que la fibroscopie n'a pas permis une exploration satisfaisante.

3. *Entre 30 et 60 ans*: La discussion est plus difficile et les indications devront être pesées cas par cas.
Il semble logique de pratiquer l'artériographie avant l'exploration par transit:
– dans les cas d'hémorragie abondante où la tension artérielle ne remonte pas malgré les transfusions sanguines (on est alors à peu près sûr d'être «en période hémorragique»).
– dans tous les cas où le transit est impossible par suite de l'état général ou neurologique du malade.
– quand l'hémorragie est une récidive, les épisodes antérieurs étant demeurés inexpliqués par la fibroscopie ou / et par les explorations barytées habituelles.
– en cas d'impossibilité ou d'échec de l'endoscopie, lorsque le diagnostic d'une affection susceptible de provoquer des hémorragies digestives est connu, et que le seul problème consiste à localiser le saignement, par example, dans l'association ulcère-HTP.

Der klinische, röntgenologische und enzymchemische Nachweis von Komplikationen anläßlich der Nierenangiographie

H. Wieners und H. C. Siemensen

Die Objektivierung ischämischer Nierenschäden nach Kontrastmittelanwendung, insbesondere nach Angiographien ist unverändert problematisch. Meistens sind ischämische Komplikationen im Bereiche der Nieren jedoch mit einem entsprechenden klinischen Befund (Abb. 1) korreliert. Dabei kann das akute

Abb. 1: Klinische Befunde bei komplizierter Renovasographie.

a. Lokale Mißempfindung, Flankenschmerz, Peritoneäler Reizzustand.
b. Tachykardie, Atemnot, Erbrechen.
c. Kreislaufhypotonie, Kollaps, Cyanose, Blässe.
d. Mikro- und (Makrohämaturie), Proteinurie.
e. Subfebrile Temperaturen, Leukocytose, BSG-Anstieg.

klinische Bild bei spastisch, thrombotisch und thromboembolisch bedingter Nierenischämie weitgehend ähnlich sein.
Im Angiogramm findet sich ein mehr oder weniger ausgedehnter, perfusionsgestörter Nierenanteil, der anatomisch der segmentalen Gliederung des Nierengefäßsystems entspricht. Eine zutreffende Aussage über eine bestehende Dauerischämie der Nieren ist während der Angiographie nicht immer zu machen. Das trifft besonders für die Fälle zu, die nicht während der Angiographie, sondern erst im Anschluß an die Untersuchung eine ischämische Nierenkomplikation entwickeln. Die definitive Diagnose, ob eine spastisch bedingte passagere Ischämie oder eine thromboembolisch bedingte Dauerischämie vorliegt, kann mit radiologischen Mitteln nur durch angiographische, urographische und nierenszintigraphische Nachuntersuchungen möglich sein.

Die Bestimmung von Enzymaktivitäten im Serum zur Diagnostik von Nierenschäden hat aufgrund bisheriger Erfahrungen noch keinen wesentlichen Beitrag zu leisten vermocht. Nach Niereninfarkten sind Anstiege unspezifischer Enzyme (Abb. 2), wie die Glutamat-Oxalacetat-Transaminase (GOT), Glutamat-Pyruvat-Transaminase (GPT), Alkalische Phosphatase (AP) und Lactat-Dehydrogenase (LDH) im Serum gesichert. Das Verhalten nierenspezifischer Enzyme wie Renin und Erythropoetin ist bisher noch nicht umfassend geprüft worden.

Abb. 2: Untersuchung der Serum- und Plasmaenzyme bei unkomplizierter Renovasographie und nach Niereninfarkt.

Unspezifische Serumenzyme:

Lactat-Dehydrogenase (LDH)
Glutamat-Oxalacetat-Transaminase (GOT)
Glutamat-Pyruvat-Transaminase (GPT)
Alkalische Phosphatase (AP)

Nierenspezifische Enzyme:

Reninaktivität im Plasma (PRA)
(Erythropoetin (EP) (nicht untersucht)).

Material und Methode

In Form einer prospektiven Untersuchung haben wir 1970 und 1971 aus einer Serie von 187 Nierenangiographien, die als Aorto-Renographie mit anschließend selektiver Katheterisierung mindestens einer Nierenarterie durchgeführt wurden, systematisch bei 11 Patienten vor der Renovasographie und 1 1/2 Stunden bis zu 14 Tagen nach der Renovasographie die Reniaktivitäten im Plasma (PRA)* und die unspezifischen Serumaktivitäten GOT, GPT, AP und LDH bestimmt.

Das Durchschnittsalter der Patienten betrug 35 Jahre (23–56), wir untersuchten 3 Frauen und 8 Männer.
Bei 3 Patienten (1 weibl., 2 männl.) konnte nach Katheterwechsel angiographisch ein Infarkt von mindestens 4 Segmenten beobachtet werden. Die Infarkte sind durch den klinischen Befund und durch spätere Kontroll-Urographien und Nierenszintigraphien bestätigt worden. 8 weitere untersuchte Fälle boten einen unkomplizierten Verlauf der kombinierten Renovasographie.

Ergebnisse

Nach unkomplizierter Renovasographie kam es bei 8 Patienten zu keiner Aktivitätssteigerung von AP, GOT, GPT und LDH im Serum, es fanden sich lediglich Schwankungen im Normbereich. 3 Patienten mit Niereninfarkt wiesen passagere Anstiege der AP, GOT und LDH von 24 Stunden bis zu 2 Tagen nach der Untersuchung auf, während die GPT unbeeinflußt blieb.
Die PRA lag auch bei Patienten mit unkomplizierter Renovasographie 1 1/2 Stunden nach

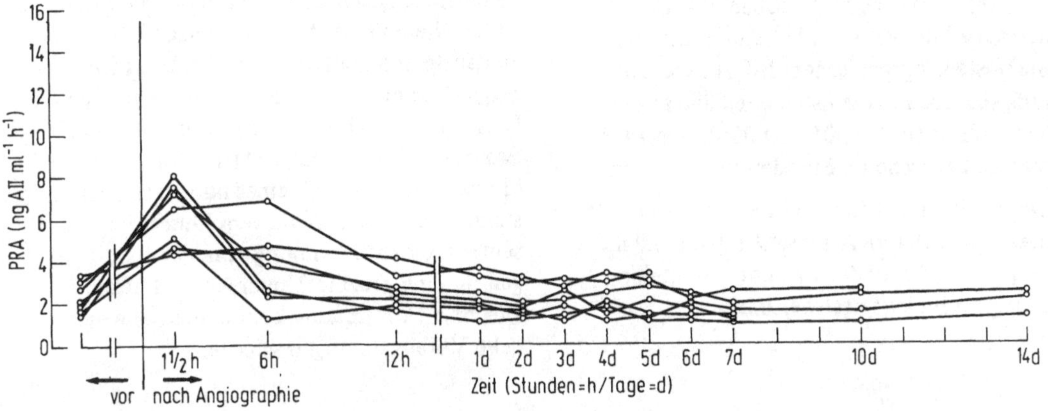

Abb. 3: Verlaufskontrolle der Plasma-Renin-Aktivität (PRA) vor und nach unkomplizierter Renovasographie bei 8 Patienten.

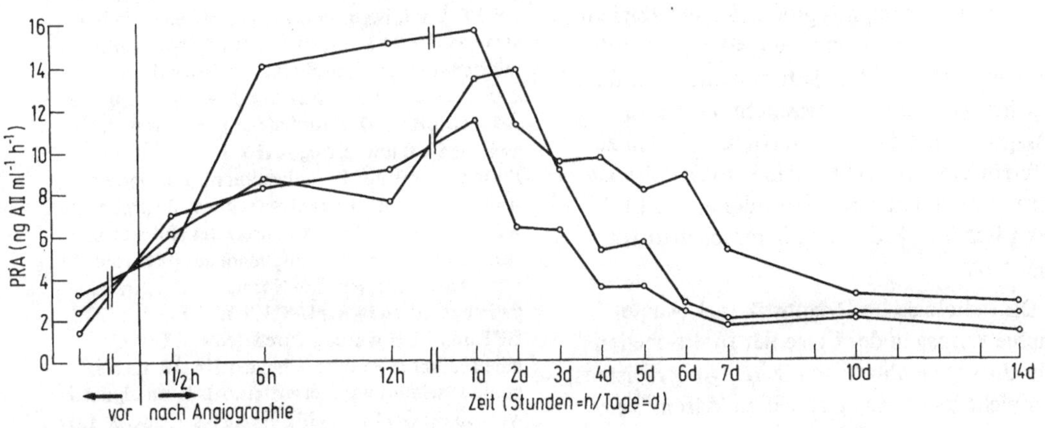

Abb. 4: Verlaufskontrolle der Plasma-Renin-Aktivität (PRA) vor und nach Renovasographie bei 3 Patienten mit nachgewiesenem Niereninfarkt.

der Gefäßdarstellung signifikant über den Ausgangswerten ($p < 0{,}001$) (Abb. 3). Diese PRA-Erhöhung hielt sich auch nach 6 Stunden noch über Normalwerten. Signifikante Differenzen ließen sich aber wegen bestehender Schwankungen nach 6 Stunden nicht mehr nachweisen. 12 Stunden nach der Angiographie waren die PRA-Werte normalisiert.

Kam es zur Ausbildung eines Niereninfarktes wurden starke und langanhaltende PRA-Steigerungen bis zu 3 Tagen (Abb. 4), in einem Fall bis zu 7 Tagen beobachtet. Gegenüber Werten vor der Renovasographie wurde eine signifikante Erhöhung auf dem Niveau ($p < 0{,}001 - p < 0{,}005$) beobachtet. Der Unterschied der PRA bei Patienten mit und ohne postangiographischem Infarkt war eindeutig signifikant zugunsten der Fälle mit Niereninfarkt ($p < 0{,}001 - 0{,}005$), und zwar in der Zeit zwischen 6 Stunden und 6 Tagen.

Dagegen sind statistisch eindeutig zu sichernde Unterschiede der PRA zwischen den beiden Gruppen 1 1/2 Stunden nach der Gefäßdarstellung noch nicht nachweisbar.

Diskussion

1. Klinische Befunde nach komplizierter Renovasographie können mit großer Regelmäßigkeit einen Nierenschaden anzeigen, sie sind jedoch nicht ausreichend spezifisch, um zwischen funktionellem und morphologischem, zwischen passagerem und dauerndem Nierenschaden zu differenzieren. Sie geben keine zuverlässige Erklärung, ob ein ischämischer oder ein nicht durch Ischämie bedingter Nierenschaden vorliegt.

2. Die radiologische Diagnostik incl. Angiographie vermag in der Frage der funktionellen oder thromboembolischen Schädigung meistens, aber nicht immer ausreichend zu klären. Sie zeigt aber das Ausmaß der aktuellen Nierenperfusionsstörung an.

3. Unspezifische Serumenzyme wie GOT, LDH und AP zeigen keine Änderung in ihrer Aktivität bei unkomplizierter Renovasographie; beim postangiographischen Niereninfarkt frühestens nach 24 Stunden. Für die Frühdiagnose eines Niereninfarktes, die die Voraussetzung für eine kausale Therapie ist, sind diese Enzymveränderungen zu träge und auch zu unspezifisch.

4. Die Auswirkungen der postangiographischen, ischämischen Nierenläsion, gleichgültig ob funktionell oder thromboembolisch bedingt, werden offensichtlich am geeignetsten mit Hilfe nierenspezifischer Enzyme erfaßt. Die PRA ist bei Niereninfarkten bereits nach 6 Stunden eindeutig und anhaltend erhöht. Die PRA reagiert damit rascher und intensiver auf einen Nierenparenchymuntergang als unspezifische Enzyme, wie z. B. AP, GOT u. LDH. Die klinische Problematik eines nun einmal entstandenen renalen Gefäßverschlusses liegt in seiner raschen Erkennung, um Voraussetzungen für eine gezielte Therapie zu schaffen. Die PRA-Bestimmung könnte hierbei wesentliche Voraussetzungen schaffen.

* Die PRA wurde mit dem von *Boucher* et al. angegebenen Verfahren nach Inkubation über 12 Stunden bei 39° C mit hetorologem Schafsubstrat im bioassay an der 24 Stunden vorher bilateral nephrektomierten und mit Pentolinium vorbehandelten Ratte durch Gabe äquipressorischer Dosen von Angiotensin II ermittelt. Die Normalwerte im Plasma lagen zwischen 1,0 und 2,2 ng A II $\times$ 1,0 ml^{-1} $\times$ 1 h^{-1}. Die Blutentnahme zur Reninbestimmung erfolgte nur nach 4 Stunden vorher eingehaltener Bettruhe. Die AP wurde mit Hilfe eines Farbtestes (Freisetzung von Phosphat und p-Nitrophenol aus p-Nitrophenylphosphat) gemessen. Die Normalwerte schwankten zwischen 20 und 48 mU $\times$ 1,0 ml^{-1} Serum. GOT, GPT und LDH wurden durch den UV-Test über eine Indikator-Reaktion, bei der NADH als Meßgröße bestimmt wird, ermittelt. Als Normalgrenze wurden für GOT und GPT Werte bis 20 mU $\times$ 1,0 ml^{-1} Serum festgesetzt. Als Normalbereich gelten bei der LDH Werte bis 195 mU $\times$ 1,0 ml^{-1} Serum.

Arterienkomplikationen bei Linksherzsondierung mit der Sones-Technik

G. Kober, H.-J. Becker, E. Krause und M. Kaltenbach

Zur Linksherzsondierung wird von den meisten Untersuchern der perkutane transfemorale Zugang nach Seldinger oder Hettler bevorzugt. Erst in den letzten Jahren hat nach Einführung der selektiven Koronarangiographie durch Sones der transbrachiale Zugang eine immer größere Anwendung gefunden.
Von vielen Untersuchern wird diese Methode jedoch abgelehnt, da sie eine Freilegung, Eröffnung und anschließende Versorgung der Arteria brachialis durch Naht notwendig macht und Komplikationen von seiten des Gefäßes, vor allem Gefäßverschlüsse mit Pulsverlust und ischämischen Beschwerden gefürchtet werden.
In der Tabelle sind die in unserem Katheterlabor beobachteten Gefäßkomplikationen getrennt nach den benutzten Nahttechniken aufgeführt. Die Einzelknopfnaht wurde in den ersten 182 Untersuchungen angewendet und aufgegeben, da sie bei größeren methodischen Schwierigkeiten gegenüber den übrigen Techniken keine Vorteile besitzt. Heute wird bei kräftigem Gefäß vor der Arteriotomie eine Tabaksbeutelnaht angelegt, die nach Beendigung der Untersuchung zugezogen wird, wodurch in der Regel eine sofortige Blutstillung erzielt werden kann. Schlanke Gefäße werden im Anschluß an die Untersuchung durch eine fortlaufende Naht versorgt.
Initiale Verluste des Radialispulses wurden insgesamt in 4,3% der Fälle beobachtet. Bei fehlendem Puls empfiehlt sich die sofortige Revision der Arterie mit Hilfe des Thrombektomie-Katheters nach *Fogarty*, wobei der Katheter nach cranial bis zur Axilla und nach distal bis zum Handgelenk vorgeschoben werden muß. Die Versorgung brüchiger Gefäße ist bisweilen mit Schwierigkeiten verbunden. Ein Ausreißen der Nähte kann hier die plastische Deckung des Defektes mit einem Venenpatch oder die Interposition eines Venenstückes erforderlich machen. Die anfangs verwendete Fibrinolyse wird von uns nicht mehr eingesetzt, da sie leicht größere Haematome verursacht.

Bei sorgfältiger Nahttechnik und sofortiger Revision bei Pulsverlust lassen sich bleibende Pulsverluste fast immer vermeiden, wie unsere Statistik mit nur zwei entsprechenden Fällen beweist. Bei dem einen Patienten handelte es sich um eine unserer ersten Untersuchungen. Hier wurde die Thrombektomie erst 14 Tage nach der Untersuchung ohne Erfolg versucht. Bei dem zweiten Patienten kam es zu einem erneuten Pulsverlust allerdings ohne Beschwerden, nachdem ein Venenpatch gute Durchblutungsverhältnisse geschaffen hatte.

Insgesamt sind Arterienkomplikationen beim transbrachialen Vorgehen bei genügender Erfahrung selten und kaum häufiger als bei der transfemoralen Technik. Gefäßverschlüsse der unteren Extremität wirken sich darüber hinaus in der Regel ernster für den betroffenen Patienten aus. Der größere Aufwand der transbrachialen Methode durch Freilegen und Nahtversorgung des Gefäßes wird dadurch aufgewogen, daß unter Sicht des Auges eine sorgfältige Blutstillung vorgenommen werden kann, wodurch Haematome nur selten beobachtet werden und Patienten auch unter vollwirksamer Antikoagulantienbehandlung untersucht werden können. Das beschriebene Vorgehen hat sich inzwischen bei über 1000 Patienten bewährt. Ein weiterer bleibender Pulsverlust ist nicht mehr aufgetreten (Stand Oktober 1973).

Einzelknopf-Naht 182	Tabaksbeutel-Naht 131	Fortlaufende Naht 203	
13 (7,1%)	4 (3,1%)	5 (2,5%)	Pulsverlust initial 22 (4,3%)
			Normalisierung
1	–	–	a. spontan
6	3	3	b. Thrombektomie (Fogarty)
1	1	2	c. Thrombektomie + Venenpatch
4	–	–	d. Fibrinolyse
			Bleibender Pulsverlust 2 (0,4%)
1	–	–	a. mit Arbeitsischaemie
–	–	1	b. ohne Arbeitsischaemie
5	2	4	Deutliche Pulsabschwächung ohne Beschwerden 11 (2,1%)

Abb. 1: Nahttechniken und Komplikationen (Stand 15. 4. 1972) nach Arteriotomie der A. brachialis bei 516 Patienten.

II. FREIE VORTRÄGE

Die Angiographie in der Unfallchirurgie

H. Hackstock und E. Spritzendorfer

Die Problematik der Angiographie in der gesamten Traumatologie einigermaßen zu beschreiben ist in der Kürze der 5-minütigen Vortragszeit nicht möglich. Wir wollen daher nur einige spezielle Probleme der Extremitätenangiographie herausnehmen und diese mit einzelnen Beispielen beleuchten.

Offene Verletzungen

Tiefgreifende Wunden an den Extremitäten bzw. offene Frakturen stellen immer eine sofortige Operationsindikation dar. In diesen Fällen ist die angiographische Darstellung der Gefäße meist überflüssig, da während der Operation die Freilegung des Gefäßes und die direkte Überprüfung seiner Durchgängigkeit von größerer diagnostischer Bedeutung ist als die Angiographie. Beim echten Gefäßspasmus kommt aber der Angiographie eine überragende dokumentarische Bedeutung zu. Sie soll dann aber intraoperativ ausgeführt werden, so daß kein Zeitverlust entsteht.

Geschlossene, stumpfe Traumen

Die klinische Symptomatik der Durchblutungsstörung bei stumpfen Traumen hängt ab vom Zeitraum zwischen Verletzung und Untersuchung. Der primär meist geringfügige Intimaeinriß macht oft eine nur geringe Symptomatik, die oft zu Fehldiagnosen führt. Die in weiterer Folge auftretende Einrollung der Intima mit Thrombosierung macht die klinische Diagnose eindeutiger. Pulskontrollen allein können hier niemals den Wert der Angiographie nur einigermaßen wettmachen.

In diesen Fällen zeigt aber die angiographische Darstellung der Gefäße schon im frühesten Stadium das wahre Verletzungsausmaß, und es wird wertvolle Zeit gewonnen.

Verlaufskontrolle

Jedes chirurgische Vorgehen bedarf zur kritischen Bewertung einer exakten Verlaufskontrolle. Jede Gefäßnaht muß – sei sie nun durch direkte Naht vereinigt, oder mit verschiedenen Gefäßnähapparaten (z. B. *Nakayama*-Gerät) durchgeführt – der genauen Kontrolle. Gerade in den Fällen mit blander klinischer Symptomatik ist die Kontrolle unerläßlich, da sie oft Jahre später unerwartete Veränderung aufzudecken vermag.
Implantationen von Gefäßprothesen, Homoio- oder Autotransplantaten müssen auf Jahre hinaus angiographisch kontrolliert werden. So zeigten z. B. anfangs die kältekonservierten Arterientransplantate eine gute Funktion. Bei der Kontrolle waren aber die meisten verschlossen. Inzwischen wissen wir, daß Arterientransplantate zur Überbrückung von Gefäßdefekten ungeeignet sind und die Implantation von autologen Venenstücken das Verfahren der Wahl darstellt. Dies war aber nur dank der Angiographie möglich.
Drei Beispiele mögen das Gesagte erläutern:

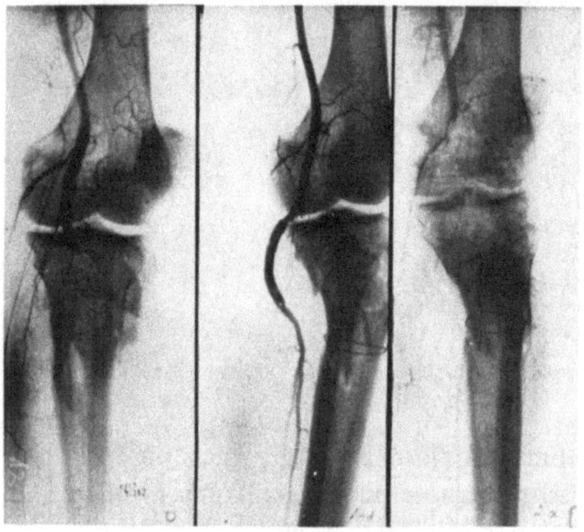

Abb. 1: Ein 53jähriger Mann zog sich als Motorradfahrer bei einem Zusammenstoß mit einem PKW eine offene Unterschenkelfraktur zu. Bei der Aufnahme im Krankenhaus war das Bein nur angedeutet kühler als das unverletzte, die Fußpulse waren schwach tastbar. Die Femoralisangiographie zeigte einen Kontrastmittelstop in Höhe des Kniegelenkspaltes! Die reichlich vorhandenen Kollateralen erklärten die geringe klinische Symptomatik und gaben gleichzeitig eine gute Prognose für die Wiederherstellung. Es wurde ein kältekonserviertes Arterienstück eingesetzt, welches nach 13 Tagen noch gut durchgängig, nach 1/2 Jahr aber bereits verschlossen war. Unser Patient konnte sich aber wegen der geringen Beschwerden nicht zu einem neuerlichen Eingriff entschließen. – Fall aus dem Jahre 1956. –

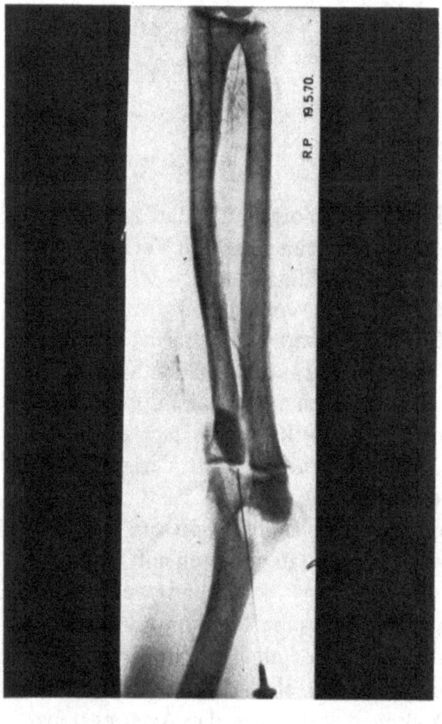

Abb. 2: Ein 29jähriger Mann erlitt einen Messerstich am linken Vorderarm. Es handelte sich um eine perforierende Verletzung mit einer 2 cm langen Wunde radial-beugeseitig und einer 2 cm langen Wunde ulnar-streckseitig knapp unterhalb des Ellenbogengelenkes. Keine besondere Blutung, keine Nervenläsion, gut tastbare Pulse der A. radialis und A. ulnaris. Es wurde daher bei der primären Versorgung eine Wundexzision mit Austastung des Stichkanals und Drainage durchgeführt. Nach 2 Tagen stellte sich eine pulsierende Schwellung an der Verletzungsstelle ein, weshalb nun eine ausgedehnte Wundrevision durchgeführt wurde. Nach Freilegung der A. cubitalis wurde zunächst eine Angiographie durchgeführt. Diese zeigte eine gute Füllung der A. radialis und der A. interossea, ein Extravasat knapp distal der Aufteilungsstelle der A. cubitalis und eine Füllung der V. basilica und der V. cephalica. Bei der weiteren Revision der Wunde stellte sich heraus, daß die Aufteilungsstelle der A. cubitalis auf 3 mm eröffnet worden war und daß eine Verbindungsvene ebenfalls auf der selben Strecke verletzt war. So erklärte sich einerseits die arterio-venöse Fistel bei andererseits guter Füllung der A. radialis. – Fall aus dem Jahre 1970. –

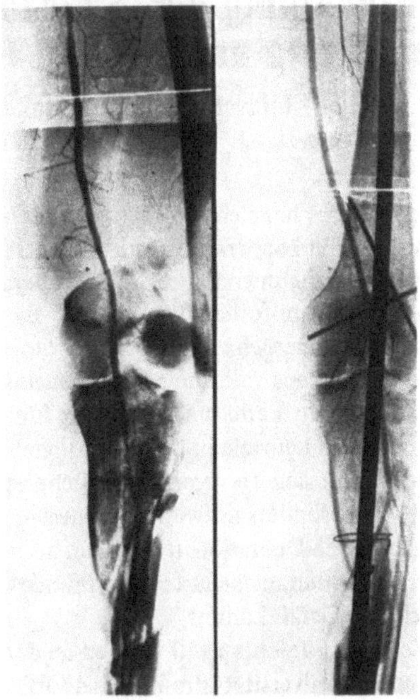

Abb. 3: Ein 17jähriges Mädchen war als Beifahrerin eines Mopeds bei einem PKW-Zusammenstoß verletzt worden. Es handelte sich um einen schwersten offenen dia- und supracondylären Oberschenkelbruch, einen offenen Schienbeinkopfbruch und einen offenen Trümmerbruch des Unterschenkels. Bei der Einlieferung war das Bein kalt und blaß, das Hautgefühl fehlte. Die Femoralisangiographie zeigte eine gute Kontrastdarstellung bis knapp unterhalb des Kniegelenkspaltes und von da nach peripher eine fragliche fadenförmige Kontrastmittelstraße. Bei der Revision zeigte sich die A. poplitea unverletzt, aber spastisch. Noch während der Operation löste sich der Spasmus, so daß das Kontrollangiogramm nach Beendigung der Operation – wie auf dem Bild gut sichtbar – einen freien Durchfluß des Kontrastmittels darstellt. – Fall aus dem Jahre 1971. –

Zusammenfassend stellen wir fest:

Die Traumatologie der Gefäße ist eine Chirurgie der Dringlichkeit. Alle diagnostischen und therapeutischen Maßnahmen haben sich daher dem Ziel der schnellstmöglichen Wiederherstellung der Gefäßstrombahn unterzuordnen.

Angiographische Darstellungen erübrigen sich meist bei schweren offenen Verletzungen, die ohnedies eine Gefäßrevision einschließen. Im Falle des echten Gefäßspasmus ist aber die Angiographie auch in diesen Fällen wertvoll.

Von größter diagnostischer Bedeutung ist die Angiographie bei stumpfen Extremitätentraumen mit diskreten Durchblutungsstörungen. Das erste Stadium der Gefäßverletzung – der Intimaeinriß – ist klinisch praktisch nicht diagnostizierbar. Jedoch bei Progredienz der Symptomatik steht die Indikation zur Angiographie außer Zweifel, da nur sie allein das wahre Ausmaß und die Lokalisation der Gefäßverletzung darstellt.

Die Bedeutung der Arteriographie für die Langzeitbeobachtung nach AV-Fistel-Operationen

D. A. Loose, F. Kleinschmidt und J. Balau

Die Angiographie hat sich im Rahmen der Gefäßchirurgie als praeoperative, zum Teil intraoperative und zunehmend auch als postoperative Kontrolle einen festen Platz erobert. Es lassen sich dadurch nicht nur das morphologische Ergebnis der Rekonstruktion, sondern auch die hämodynamischen Verhältnisse und das funktionelle Resultat beurteilen. Nach AV-Fistel-Operationen hat sich die arteriographische Spätkontrolle als besonders notwendig erwiesen, da es nach diesen Operationen in einem hohen Prozentsatz zu therapiebedürftigen Befunden am operierten Gefäß kommt.
In der Zeit von 1959 bis 1970 wurden an der Chirurgischen Universitätsklinik Düsseldorf 32 AV-Fisteln beobachtet, von denen 23 traumatischer, 2 iatrogener und 5 angeborener Ätiologie waren. Bei 2 AV-Fisteln war die Genese ungeklärt (s. Tab. 1a). 18mal waren die

Tab. 1a: Ätiologie der AV-Fisteln

traumatisch	23 x
iatrogen	2 x
angeboren	5 x
ungeklärt	2 x
Total	32

AV-Fisteln an den unteren Extremitäten, 7mal im Bereich der Hals- und Kopfgefäße, 4mal im Bereich der oberen Extremitäten und 3mal an inneren Organen lokalisiert (s. Tab. 1b). Es handelt sich insgesamt um AV-Fisteln, die wenigstens ein halbes Jahr und längstens 26 Jahre bestanden haben. Von ihnen wurden 30 operiert, wobei 21mal die Separationsmethode, 1mal der transvenöse Fistelverschluß und 8mal die Kontinuitätsresektion und Wiederherstellung der Strombahn durchgeführt wurde (s. Tab. 1c).

Tab. 1b: Lokalisationen der AV-Fisteln

untere Extremität	18 x
Hals- und Kopfgefäße	7 x
obere Extremität	4 x
innere Organe	3 x
Total	32

Tab. 1c: Op-Methoden zum Verschluß von lange bestehenden AV-Fisteln

Separationsmethode	21 x
Kontinuitätsresektion und Wiederherstellung der Strombahn	8 x
transvenöser Fistelverschluß	1 x
Total	30

Die postoperativ wenigstens nach einem Jahr und längstens nach 9 Jahren durchgeführten arteriographischen Kontrollen ergaben in einigen Fällen therapiebedürftige Gefäßbefunde, von denen drei Beispiele demonstriert werden:
Eine typische Komplikation nach einer AV-Fistel-Operation ist zum Beispiel eine arterielle Thrombose der ektatischen Fistelarterie. Diese kommt häufig zustande, weil nach Unterbrechung des Kurzschlußkreislaufes die Strömungsgeschwindigkeit abnimmt. Einen typischen Verlauf konnten wir bei einem Patienten beobachten, bei dem im praeoperativen Angiogramm (s. Abb. 1a) eine AV-Fistel zwischen distaler Arteria und Vena femoralis bestand. Im postoperativen Kontroll-Arteriogramm nach Durchtrennung der Fistel (s. Abb. 1b) findet sich eine gute Darstellung des distal der ehemaligen Fistel gelegenen arteriellen Stromgebietes. In einer weiteren postoperativen

Kontroll-Angiographie nach 9 Jahren (s. Abb. 1c) zeigt sich eine wandständige Thrombose der ektatischen Arteria femoralis superfizialis. Bei der dann notwendigen Operation wurde die ektatische, mittlerweile völlig thrombosierte Arterie reseziert (s. Abb. 1d und 1e) und ein Vena saphena Transplantat interponiert.
Ein anderer hin und wieder zu beobachtender Befund bei der arteriographischen Spätkontrolle nach AV-Fistel-Operationen ist eine Rest- oder Rezidivfistel. In unserem Falle wurde 1953 eine AV-Fistel der Arteria und Vena femoralis in Höhe des Adduktorenkanals durchtrennt. Erst bei der angiographischen Spätkontrolle nach 2 Jahren (s. Abb. 2a) fand sich eine erneute kleine Fistel zwischen Arteria femoralis superior und einem Ast der

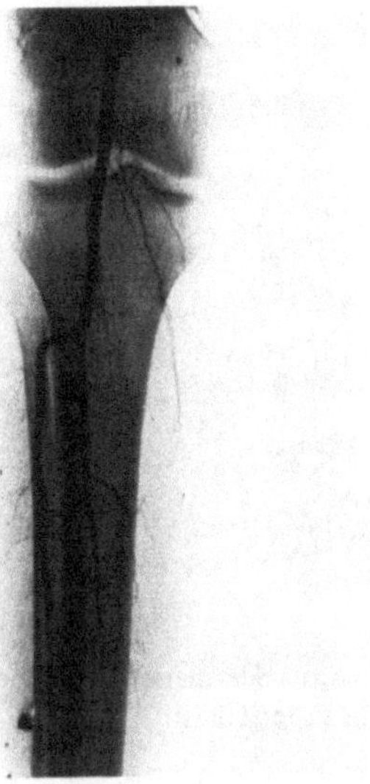

Abb. 1b: Postoperatives Kontroll-Angiogramm nach Fisteldurchtrennung: Gute Darstellung des arteriellen Stromgebietes distal der ehemaligen Fistel.

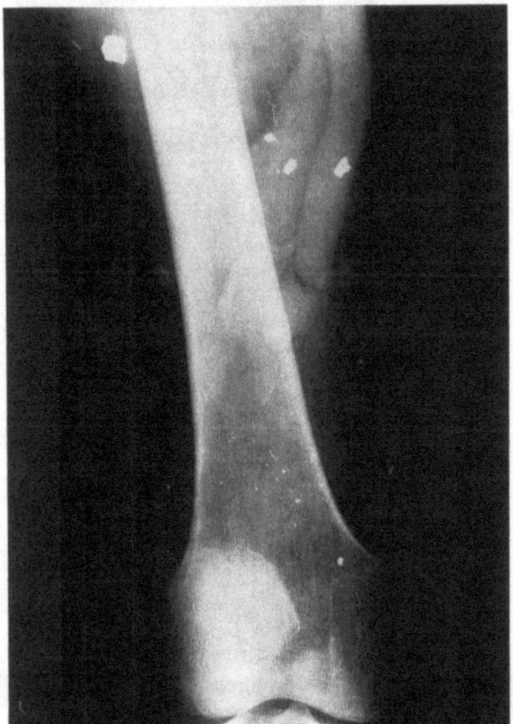

Abb. 1a: AV-Fistel zwischen distaler Arteria und Vena femoralis durch Granatsplitterverletzung. Fehlende Darstellung der Arteria poplitea.

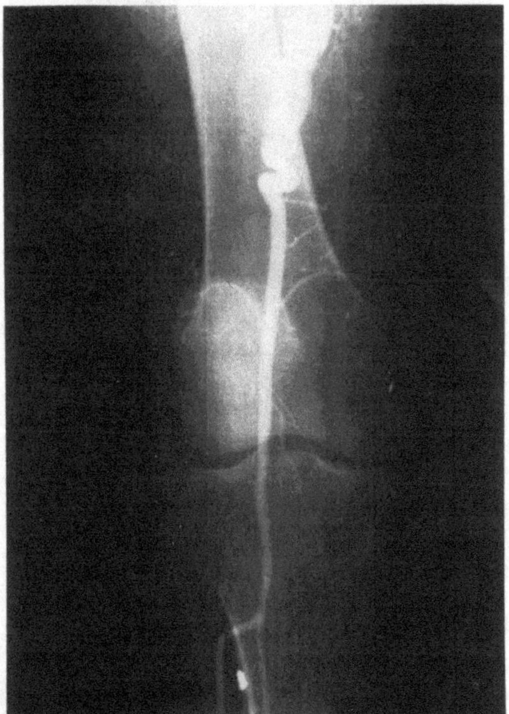

Abb. 1c: Postoperatives Kontroll-Angiogramm nach 9 Jahren: Wandständige Thrombose der ektatischen Arteria femoralis superfizialis und dadurch mäßige Kontrastdarstellung der Arteria poplitea.

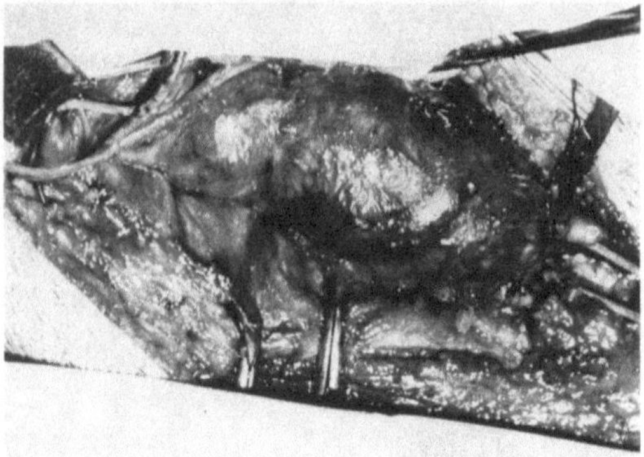

Abb. 1d: Operationssitus der aneurysmatischen distalen Arteria femoralis superfizialis.

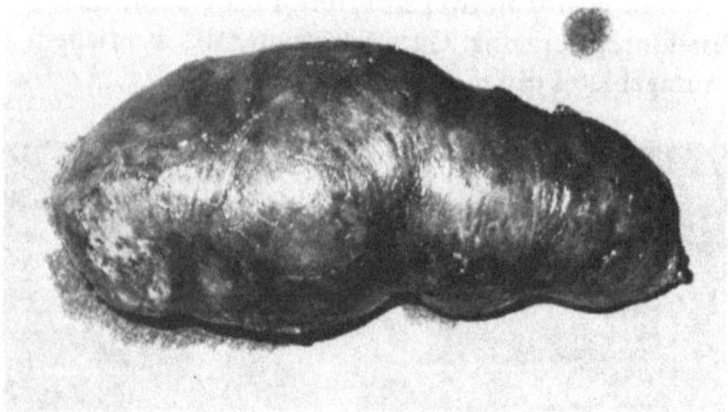

Abb. 1e: Op-Präparat: Aneurysmatisches Arteriensegment der distalen Arteria femoralis superfizialis.

Vena saphena magna bzw. der Vena femoralis (s. Abb. 2b) sowie ein postfistulärer Verschluß der Arterie (s. Abb. 2a). Intraoperativ zeigte sich eine Thrombose des distalen Arterienabschnittes, und es wurde eine Kontinuitätsresektion und Interposition eines Vena saphena Transplantates durchgeführt.

Auch in der Gefäßchirurgie erlebt man immer wieder, daß sich Patienten einer notwendigen weiteren Gefäßoperation entziehen. So in einem Falle (s. Abb. 3a), in welchem bei der ersten Gefäßoperation eine AV-Fistel der Arteria femoralis profunda und der Vena femoralis beseitigt wurde. Als weitere Gefäßoperation war die Beseitigung des Kingking-Syndroms (s. Abb. 3b) der rechten Arteria iliaca communis angezeigt, das sich im prae-

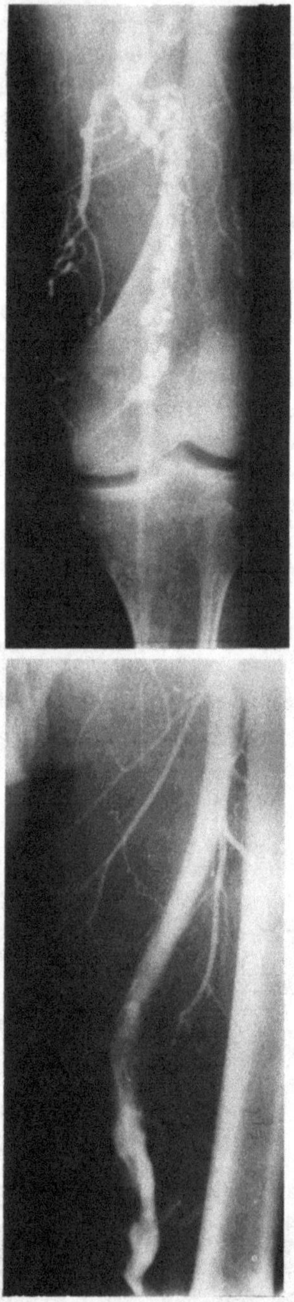

Abb. 2a: Postoperatives Kontroll-Angiogramm. Durchtrennung einer AV-Fistel zwischen Arteria und Vena femoralis in Höhe des Adduktorenkanals. Jetzt stellt sich eine kleine Fistel zwischen Arteria femoralis superior und b: einem Ast der Vena saphena magna bzw. der Vena femoralis dar. Außerdem besteht ein postfistulärer Verschluß der Arteria femoralis superfizialis.

operativen Angiogramm dargestellt hatte. Dieser Operation entzog sich der Patient, da er damals keine Beschwerden hatte. Inzwischen ist der arterielle Zustrom funktionell so stark behindert, daß die damals schon notwendige weitere Gefäßoperation jetzt unzugänglich wird; in der nach 5 Jahren durchgeführten postoperativen Kontroll-Angiographie (s. Abb. 3c und d) zeigt sich ein stark verzögerter Kontrastmittelabfluß im Bereich der rechtsseitigen Arteria iliaca communis und Arteria iliaca externa.

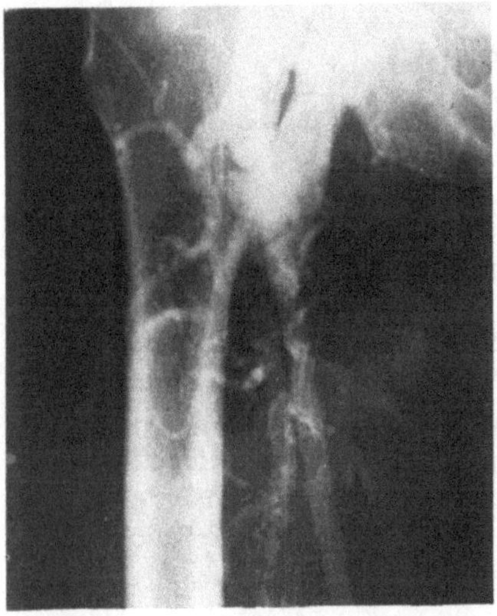

Abb. 3a

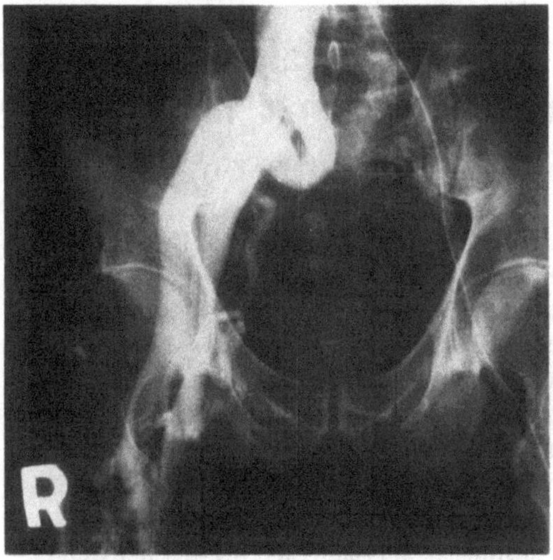

Abb. 3b

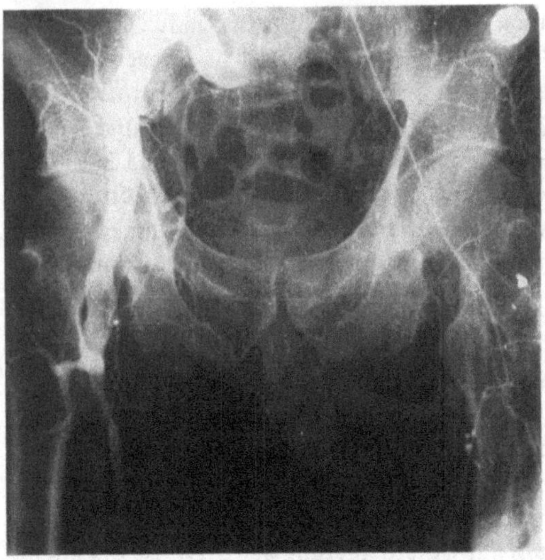

Abb. 3c

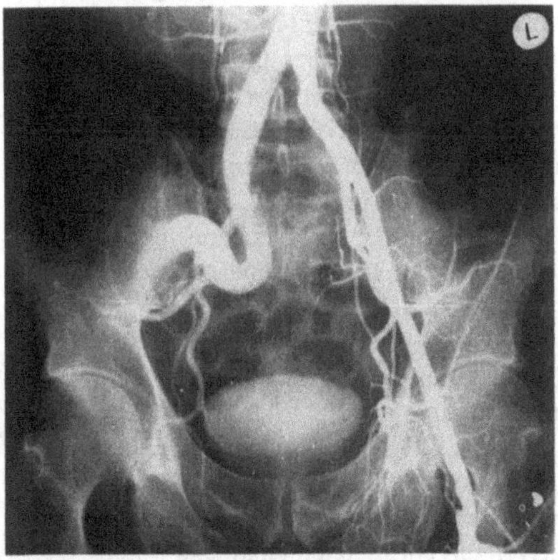

Abb. 3d

Abb. 3a: Praepoerative Angiogramm: AV-Fistel zwischen Arteria femoralis profunda und Vena femoralis. b: Gleichzeitig besteht ein Kingking-Syndrom der rechten Arteria iliaca communis. Nach der durchgeführten AV-Fisteloperation lehnt der Patient die operative Beseitigung des Kingking-Syndroms ab. c: und d: Postoperative angiographische Spätkontrolle: Starke Verzögerung des arteriellen Zustromes in die rechte untere Extremität bei einem ausgeprägten Kingking-Syndrom der Arteria iliaca communis.

Zur Vermeidung von therapiebedürftigen Spätbefunden am operierten Gefäß nach AV-Fistel-Operationen sind nach unseren Erfahrungen zum einen die frühestmögliche Operation und zum anderen regelmäßige postoperative Kontroll-Arteriographien notwendig.

Zur Differentialdiagnose funktioneller und morphologischer Veränderungen am Gefäßbild der Hand

H. H. Wagner, K. Alexander, U. Jobst und A. Wittenborg

In zahlreichen arteriographischen Untersuchungen kommt die Unsicherheit in der Abgrenzung funktioneller und organischer Komponenten bei der Beurteilung der peripheren, insbesondere akralen Durchblutungsstörungen der oberen Extremität zum Ausdruck. Eine Differenzierung ist aber sowohl für die Beurteilung der Pathogenese des Leidens als auch für die Therapie von großer Bedeutung.

Bemühungen, die Häufigkeit organischer Gefäßveränderungen bei der PCP zu bestimmen, veranlaßten uns, bei unserem Patientengut mit Durchblutungsstörungen im Handbereich zur Abgrenzung funktioneller und morphologischer Gefäßveränderungen die Pharmakoradiographie durchzuführen. Entscheidend und Ausgangsbasis für den Einsatz des Pharmakons war die Erstangiographie: in allen Fällen, wo vermutet werden konnte, daß eine funktionelle Engstellung der peripheren arteriellen Strombahn den Einstrom des Kontrastmittels beeinflußte, wurde eine intraarterielle pharmakologische Vasodilatation versucht.

In keinem unserer Fälle sahen wir nach der Arterienpunktion oder der intraarteriellen Applikation des Kontrastmittels „Conray 60" sowie des Vasodilatans Zwischenfälle.

Die von uns eingesetzten Pharmaka waren Ronicol compositum® und Vasculat®. Während Ronicol in keinem Fall zu einer Veränderung des angiographischen Bildes führte (25 Probanden), hatte Vasculat® bei jedem 5. Fall einen deutlichen Effekt auf die arterielle und venöse Strombahn und die Zirkulationszeit. Abb. 1a und 1b zeigen das Handarteriogramm einer 69jährigen Patientin mit PCP vor und nach intraarterieller Gabe von Vasculat®. Man erkennt deutlich, daß der Verzicht auf die Pharmakoradiographie zur Diagnose einer generalisierten akralen Verschlußkrankheit geführt hätte, während es sich in Wirklichkeit ganz überwiegend um eine funktionelle Durchblutungsstörung handelt.

Neuerdings untersuchen wir in einer vergleichenden Studie die Effektivität einer Stellatumblockade und pharmakologisch induzierter Vasodilatation. Abb. 2a und 2b belegen im Gegensatz zur neuesten Mitteilung *Horvaths* u. Mitarb. die Möglichkeit, funktionelle und morphologische Komponenten (2. und 3. Finger) einer peripheren Durchblutungsstörung zu differenzieren. Diese Untersuchung konnte mit der Thermographie methodisch ergänzt und bestätigt werden.

Wir sind heute der Meinung, daß eine einmalige Angiographieserie keine differenzierte Aussage über das Vorliegen organischer oder funktioneller Gefäßveränderungen zuläßt, soweit eine periphere Engstellung der arteriellen Strombahn nachweisbar ist. In diesen Fällen muß zur Untermauerung der Diagnose organische Arteriopathie eine Zweitangiographie nach intraarterieller Applikation von nachweislich wirksamen Vasodilatantien wie Vasculat® oder Stellatumblockade gefordert werden, zumal sich aus dem Untersuchungsergebnis therapeutische Konsequenzen ergeben können.

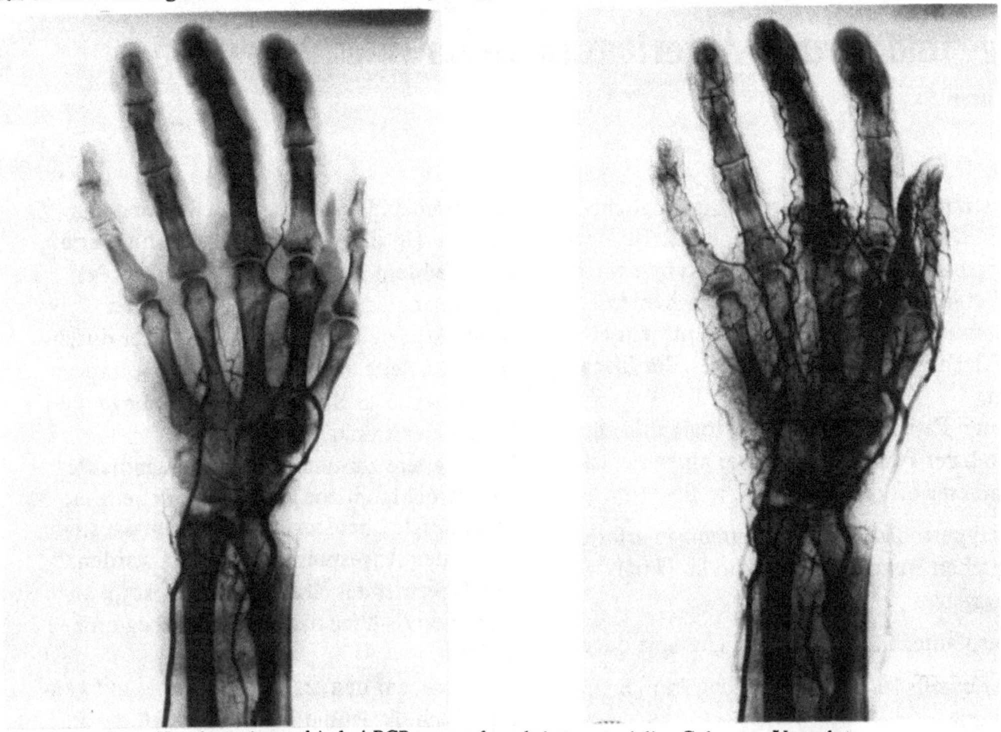

Abb. 1a und 1b: Handarteriographie bei PCP vor und nach intraarterieller Gabe von Vasculat

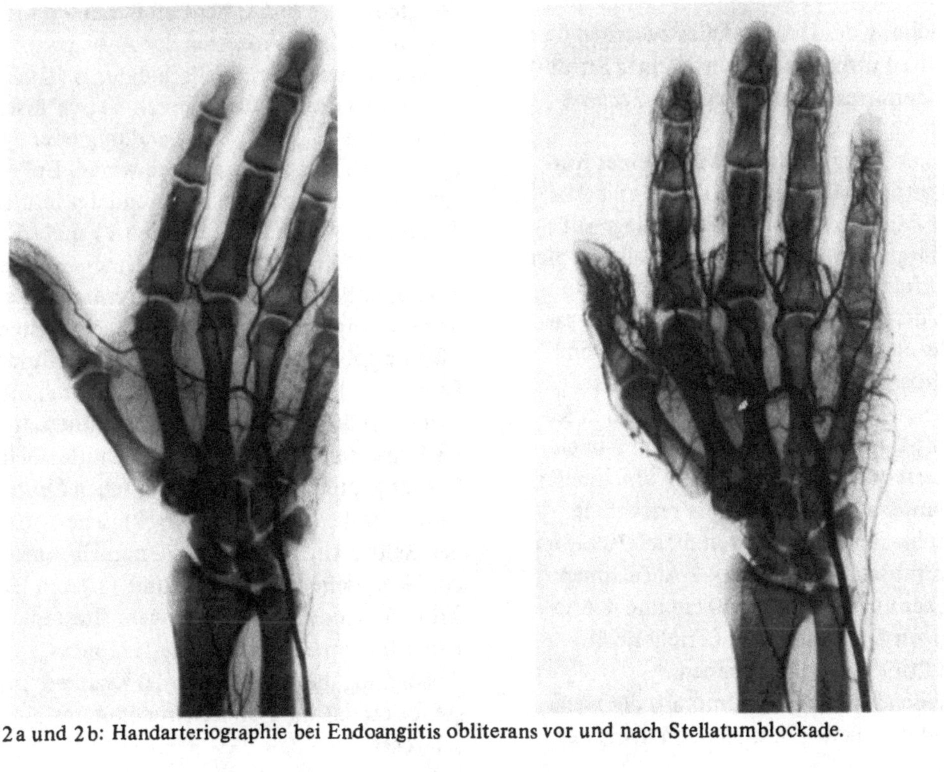

Abb. 2a und 2b: Handarteriographie bei Endoangiitis obliterans vor und nach Stellatumblockade.

Saug- und Druck-Arteriographie im Beckenbereich

H. Richter

Die im letzten Jahre an unserer Angiologischen Klinik in Darmstadt-Eberstadt entwickelte Methode ergab sich aus den Notwendigkeiten einer möglichst schonenden röntgenologischen Arteriendarstellung bei Gefäßkranken mit einseitigen Verschlußprozessen im Bereich der Iliacalarterien.

Bei älteren Patienten ist eine Aortographie nach translumbaler Punktion oder über einen Femoralis-Katheter oft nicht möglich: z. B.

1. Bei Hypertonikern mit hochgradigen arteriosklerotischen Wandveränderungen im Untersuchungsgebiet
2. bei geplanter fibrinolytischer Therapie oder
3. unter bereits laufender Antikoagulantienbehandlung
4. bei Tumor- oder Aneurysma-Verdacht.

Zur Erhöhung des Druckgefälles zwischen den Abschnitten proximal und distal eines Strombahnhindernisses hat sich folgende *Technik* bewährt:

Die Vorbereitung geschieht wie zu einer Katheter-Aortographie. Nach Intubationsnarkose liegt der Patient relaxiert in Rückenlage auf dem Röntgentisch. Mittels Ultraschall-Doppler-Sonde erfolgt die Lokalisation der Punktionsstelle in der Leistenbeuge distal der Obliteration oder Stenose im Becken. Eventuell sind Beckenhochlagerung und medikamentöse Blutdruckanhebung nötig. Wir verwenden Kanülen mit Doppelmandrin und einem Außendurchmesser von 1,2 mm. Als 1. Aufnahmeserie erfolgt unter Atemstillstand die retrograde Ilicographie mit Injektion von 50 ml 70%igem Kontrastmittel. Es werden 1–2 Aufnahmen des Beckens in Format 40/40 cm und 4 Aufnahmen zur Darstellung der Peripherie in Format 20/96 cm vorgenommen.

Anschließend wird die A. femoralis der weniger befallenen Seite punktiert und distal der Punktionsstelle eine arterielle Stauung von 300 mm Hg angelegt. Die 2. Aufnahmeserie von 4 Bildern in Format 40/40 cm erfolgt nach retrograder Injektion der gleichen Kontrastmittelmenge von der weniger durchströmten Seite aus. Gleichzeitige Aspiration von 50–100 ml Blut über die noch liegende Kanüle der kranken Seite.

Eine weitere Erhöhung des Druckgradienten vom Bauchraum zur peripheren Extremität kann durch Überdruck im Beatmungssystem durch den Anaesthesisten erreicht werden. Der Übertritt des Kontrastmittels ist im allgemeinen 6–8 sec nach Injektionsbeginn beendet.

Für diese, auf den ersten Blick etwas aufwendige Technik, ist die *Indikationsstellung* auch in unserem Krankengut noch nicht sehr groß. Wir stellten sie bisher bei Gefäßkranken mit asymmetrischen Prozessen der A. iliaca communis und/oder A. iliaca externa (auch in Kombination mit peripheren Verschlüssen), die für eine baldige Lysebehandlung oder operative Therapie vorgesehen waren. Bei rund 700 Angiographien während der letzten 13 Monate wurde das Verfahren 11 mal (d. h. in einer Häufigkeit von 1,5%) ohne besondere Komplikationen angewandt. Im Vergleich zu anderen angiographischen Untersuchungstechniken ergaben sich bemerkenswerte Befunde. Es wurden lediglich männliche Patienten im Alter von 50–72 Jahren. (Durchschnittsalter 58 Jahre) mit der neuen Methode untersucht. Soweit geprüft, lagen die systolischen Druckwerte auf der vom Iliaca-Verschluß betroffenen Seite zwischen 50 und 70 mm Hg, auf der Gegenseite zwischen 90 und 110 mm Hg. Klinisch handelte es sich bei dem ältesten Patienten um ein thrombosiertes Iliaca-Aneurysma, bei den übrigen 10 Kranken um stenosierende oder obliterierende Arteriosklerosen.

Aus den Bildern der Routine-Serie und den nach der Saug-Druck-Methode gewonnenen Aufnahmen läßt sich ein befriedigendes Panorama der Arterienverhältnisse im Becken zusammensetzen. Auch den Gefäßchirurgen dürften solche Bilder zur Entscheidung für ihr operatives Vorgehen genügen.

Zusammenfassung

Bei Arteriosclerosis stenosans oder obliterans mit asymmetrischem Befall der Iliacal-Gefäße lassen sich pathologische Gefäßprozesse und Kollateralen im Becken durch eine neue, risikoarme Angiographie-Methode exakt beurteilen, auch wenn eine Aortographie oder Katheter-Untersuchungen nicht durchgeführt werden können. Die Injektion des Kontrastmittels erfolgt von der gesunden A. femoralis aus unter distaler Abstauung, retrograd über die Aortengabel zur Gegenseite; dort wird gleichzeitig distal des Verschlusses ein Unterdruck durch Absaugen von Blut über eine zweite Femoralis-Kanüle erzielt. Während der Absaug- und Injektionsperiode lassen sich 4 Serien-Aufnahmen des Beckens vornehmen. Es wird über 11 eigene Fälle berichtet.

Transhepatische Cholangiographie und viszerale Angiographie bei Ikterus

J. Göthlin, M. Mansoor und K. Tranberg

Bei Patienten mit Okklusions-Ikterus kann die Lokalisation des Hindernisses durch die perkutane transhepatische Cholangiographie (PTC) gestellt werden. Mit Hilfe dieser Untersuchungs-Methode ist es selten möglich, Art, Ursprung und Ausbreitung des pathologischen Prozesses zu bestimmen. Besonders wertvoll ist diese Methode für den Chirurgen zur Abklärung einer operativen Situation im Sinne eines Pro oder Contra. Die selektive viszerale Angiographie

		PTC			Angiographie		
Endgültige Diagnose	Anzahl Fälle	+	-	F	+	-	F
Freie Gallenwege	2			1		2	
Choledocholithiasis	4	2		2		4	
Operative Läsionen	4	4				3	1
Inflammatorische Stenosen	4	3		1	4		
Tumoren im Bereich der extrahepatischen Gallenwege	33	30		3	29	3	1
Lebertumoren	3	1		2	3		
Total	50	40		9	36	12	2

bietet in dieser Hinsicht eine ebenfalls gute Ergänzung zur perkutanen transhepatischen Cholangiographie.
Bei 50 Patienten mit Verdacht auf Okklusions-Ikterus wurde zuerst eine selektive viszerale Angiographie ausgeführt und am Operationstag eine perkutane transhepatische Cholangiographie durchgeführt. Die Resultate zeigen folgende Tabelle, wo + eine richtige Diagnose, - eine falsche Daignose und F ein Mißlingen der Untersuchung bedeuten.
Bei intraoperativen Verletzungen der Gallenwege war die Diagnose mit der Cholangiographie in allen Fällen richtig. Mit der viszeralen Angiographie konnten Gefäßverletzungen bei 3 von diesen Patienten diagnostiziert werden.

In der nächsten Gruppe mit inflammatorischen Veränderungen war die Diagnose mit der viszeralen Angiographie bei 4 Patienten richtig. Die Gruppe, die am interessantesten ist, ist die Tumorgruppe. Bei 30 von 33 Patienten wurde die Diagnose mit Hilfe der Cholangiographie gestellt – jedoch wußte man wenig von dem Ursprung und der Ausdehnung des Tumors. Diese Auskünfte wurden durch die viszerale Angiographie gegeben. Zusammen gaben die Untersuchungen eine korrekte Diagnose bei sämtlichen 33 Patienten.
Lebermetastasen wurden am besten mit der viszeralen Angiographie nachgewiesen.
Wir empfehlen die perkutane transhepatische Cholangiographie und die selektive viszerale Angiographie bei Patienten mit Okklusions-Ikterus, falls operative Eingriffe vorgesehen sind.

Angiographische Untersuchungen bei Aortenaneurysmen

V. Kammerer, H. K. Deininger, V. Piepgras und M. Podzich

Die Klärung eines aneurysmaverdächtigen Befundes an der Aorta erfordert, besonders wenn therapeutische Konsequenzen zu ziehen sind, eine angiographische Untersuchung, da nur durch direkte Darstellung die anatomischen und funktionellen Verhältnisse ausreichend exakt beurteilt werden können. Die technisch unkompliziertere indirekte Darstellung mit läsionsferner Punktion und ante- oder retrograder Kontrastmittelinjektion ohne Katheterismus ist bei Aneurysmen der Aorta selten erfolgreich, da eine zur Beurteilung ausreichende Kontrastdicht meist nicht erzielt wird. Dies gilt auch für die Aortendarstellung nach intravenöser Injektion des Kontrastmittels.
Die besseren Ergebnisse bringt die Katheterangiographie. Das Risiko der Untersuchung ist in der Gefahr begründet, die instabile Gefäßwand im Aneurysmabereich durch brüske Manipulationen zu beschädigen, eine möglicherweise vorhandene Dissektion zu erweitern oder eine via falsa herzustellen. Zudem muß vermieden werden, Teile von wandständigen Thromben abzulösen und so eine arterielle Embolie zu provozieren. Hingegen stellt der Druckanstieg bei der Injektion des Kontrastmittels im allgemeinen keinen Risikofaktor dar. Zugangsweg und Untersuchungsgang sind vom jeweils zu erwartenden Befund abhängig. Häufig ist die Punktion mehrerer Gefäße mit mehrfacher Katheterisierung erforderlich. In unserem Stuttgarter Arbeitskreis haben wir in den letzten Jahren 15 Patienten mit Aneurysmen der Aorta untersucht. Etwa die Hälfte war mit dem klinischen Bild eines akuten abdominellen oder thorakalen Schmerzsyndroms (häufig unter der Diagnose Herzinfarkt) eingewiesen worden. Das Alter der Patientin – es handelt sich um 13 Männer und 2 Frauen – war zwischen 18 und 69 Jahren. Bei 7 der

15 Patienten mußte von mehreren peripheren Arterien aus punktiert bzw. katheterisiert werden. Komplikationen in Verbindung mit der Angiographie wurden hierbei nicht beobachtet. Die *Lokalisation,* sowohl der sackförmigen als auch der fusiformen Aneurysmen mit und ohne Dissektion geht aus Abbildung 1 hervor. Bei Überschreitung der willkürlich gewählten Segmentgrenzen wurden die Aneurysmen dem überwiegend getroffenen Segment zugezählt, um eine Doppelzählung zu vermeiden. In der gleichen Abbildung ist die Untersuchungstechnik skizziert, wobei infolge der erforderlichen Punktionen mehrerer Gefäße beim selben Patienten eine höhere Summe als 15 erscheint.

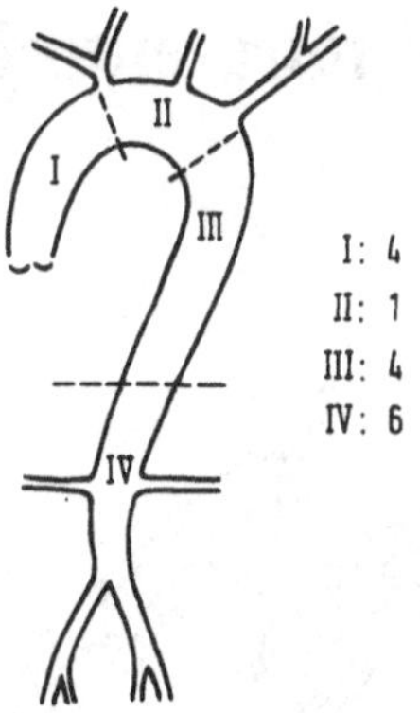

Abb. 1: Schematische Übersicht der Lokalisation von 15 Aortenaneurysmen (obere Bildhälfte) und der Untersuchungstechnik (untere Bildhälfte).

Bei 3 Patienten mit Aneurysmen der thorakalen Aorta muß eine traumatische Ursache angenommen werden, wobei das Trauma immer mehrere Jahre zurücklag. Bei einem Patienten bestand eine Lues-Anamnese.
Unter diesen 15 Patienten stellen 2 Fälle interessante und mitteilungswerte Einzelbeobachtungen dar:

1. Ein 30jähriger Mann, der längere Zeit wegen therapieresistenter Rechtsherzinsuffizienz behandelt worden war. Auf der Thoraxübersichtsaufnahme fand sich eine leichte Verminderung der Gefäßzeichnung rechts. Die Pulmonalisangiographie (Abb. 2) ergab den Befund einer peripheren Stenose am Anfangsteil der rechten Pulmonalarterie, deren Ursache erst intraoperativ als Aneurysma der Aortenwurzel mit großem intramuralem Hämatom erkannt wurde. Anamnestisch Motorradunfall vor Jahren.

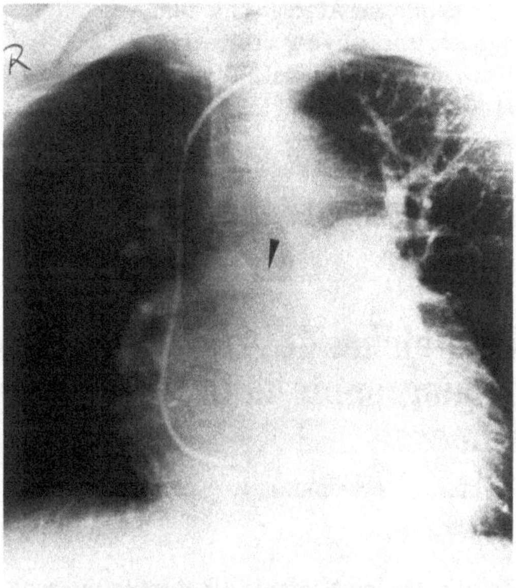

Abb. 2: Traumatisches intramurales Hämatom der Aortenwand als Ursache einer peripheren Pumonalstenose rechts (Pfeil).

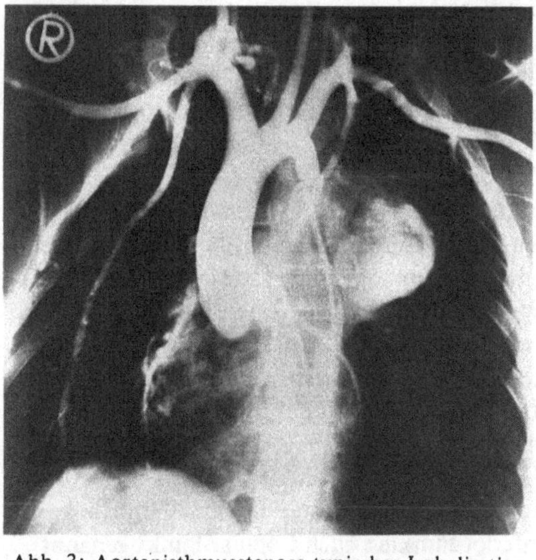

Abb. 3: Aortenisthmusstenose typischer Lokalisation mit poststenotischem sackförmigem Aneurysma der deszendierenden Aorta.

Der zweite Fall ist der einer 18jährigen Patientin, bei der im Rahmen der Schirmbildreihenuntersuchung ein tumorverdächtiger Befund am linken Hilus aufgefallen war, der auf einer Thoraxaufnahme 2 Jahre zuvor nicht bestanden hatte. Von einer Thoraxspezialklinik wurde die Patientin zur Angiographie zum Ausschluß eines Aortenaneurysma überwiesen. Bei der retrograden transfemoralen Katheterisierung gelangte man in ein sackförmiges Aneurysma im oberen Deszendensbereich. Nach transaxillärer Aortenbogendarstellung (Abb. 3) erkennt man eine Aortenisthmusstenose typischer Lokalisation und unmittelbar distal gelegen das sackförmige Aneurysma. Diese Kombination einer Isthmusstenose mit einem Aneurysma stellt einen nicht häufigen Befund dar. Als Ursache des Aneurysma werden sowohl die lokale Schädigung der Aortenwand durch den vom düsenförmigen Stenosenquerschnitt geformten Blutstrom als auch lokale, bakterielle Entzündungen, die zu einer umschriebenen Schwäche mit Einriß der Wand und Ausbildung des Aneurysma führen, diskutiert.

Vergleichende Analyse der Ergebnisse der Vertebralis-Angiographie und der Pneumographie bei infratentoriellen Tumoren

F. Thun, G. Friedmann, K. Schmücker und R. Tismer

50 Patienten mit Verdacht auf einen infratentoriell raumfordernden Prozeß wurden angiographisch und pneumographisch untersucht. Die Gefäßdarstellung erfolgte in 42 Fällen als selektive Vertebralisangiographie mit der Kathetermethode nach *Seldinger*, 7 mal als Brachialis-Gegenstromangiographie und einmal als direkte Vertebralisangiographie. Die Pneumographien führten wir gesteuert im Mimer III 33mal als Encephalo-Cisternographie und 17mal als Ventrikulographie durch. Retrospektiv analysierten wir die Vertebralisangiogramme vergleichend mit den Pneumogrammen sowie den intraoperativen und histologischen Befunden. Bei der Auswertung der Vertebralisangiographien ergänzten wir die genaue Analyse des Ursprungs und Verlaufs der infratentoriell angiographisch erkennbaren Gefäße – wenn möglich – durch die Bestimmung des Colliculo-Central-Punktes, des Chorioidalis-Punktes und des Vermis-Inferior-Punktes, auch Copular-Punkt genannt (Abb. 1).

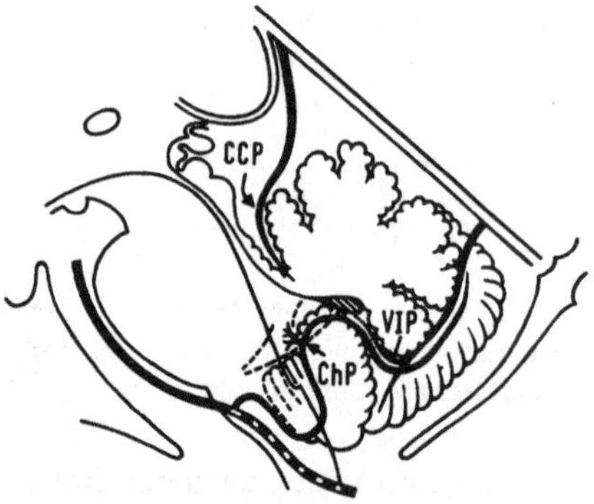

Abb. 1: Meßpunkte im Vertebralisangiogramm.
Colliculo-Central-Punkt (CCP)
Chorioidalis-Punkt (ChP)
Vermis-Inferior Punkt (VIP)

Bei 16 der hier analysierten 50 Patienten bestätigte sich im weiteren Verlauf der anamnestisch und klinisch begründete Verdacht auf einen raumfordernden Prozeß der hinteren Schädelgrube nicht. Alle wiesen ein normales Vertebralisangiogramm und Pneumogramm auf. Bei 34 der 50 Patienten lag ein infratentorieller Tumor vor (Tab. 1), der in 28 Fällen auch operativ und pathologisch-anatomisch gesichert werden konnte. Die Histologie dieser Tumoren ist in dieser Tabelle angegeben. 5 mal bestand Inoperabilität; ein Patient wurde noch nicht operiert.

Tab. 1: Verteilung der 34 infratentoriellen Tumoren

Medulloblastom	2
Spongioblastom	3
Ependymom	6
Gliom	4
Kleinhirnbrückenwinkelneurinom	7
Tentoriummeningeom	1
Kleinhirnbrückenwinkelmeningeom	2
Angioblastom	2
Epidermoid	1
Gangliocytom	1
Clivuschondrom	2
Metastase	3
	34

Angiographisch wurden diese Tumoren 31mal richtig lokalisiert (Tab. 2). In 3 Fällen ergab sich aufgrund der Vertebralisangiographie lediglich der Verdacht auf einen raumfordernden infratentoriellen Prozeß; dabei handelte es sich in einem Fall um ein kleines Akustikusneurinom und je einmal um einen nicht sehr ausgedehnten Tumor in der linken Kleinhirnhemisphäre bzw. im Wurm. Somit wurde bei keinem der Patienten mit gesichertem infratentoriellem Tumor das Vertebralisangiogramm als normal gedeutet. Eine so hohe Trefferquote ist jedoch nur dann zu erreichen, wenn

Tab. 2: Ergebnis der Vertebralisangiographie (VAG) und der Pneumographie (PEG/VP) bei 34 Patienten mit infratentoriellem Tumor

	VAG	PEG/VP
Richtige Tumorlokalisation	31	31
Suspekter Befund	3	1
Diagnostisch unzureichende Füllung infratentoriell	–	2
	34	34
Davon artdiagnostisch richtig zugeordnet	5	1

auch die Morphologie der kleinen Gefäße sorgfältig beachtet wird. Die Kriterien, auf die sich die angiographische Lokalisation der lateral bzw. median gelegenen infratentoriellen Tumoren stützt, zeigt Tab. 3. Neben der Lokalisation des Tumors war 5mal seine Artdiagnose möglich: 1mal handelte es sich um ein Tentoriummeningeom, in 2 Fällen um Metastasen eines Carcinoms und 2mal um ein Angioblastom. Ein Beispiel sei demonstriert (Abb. 2a).

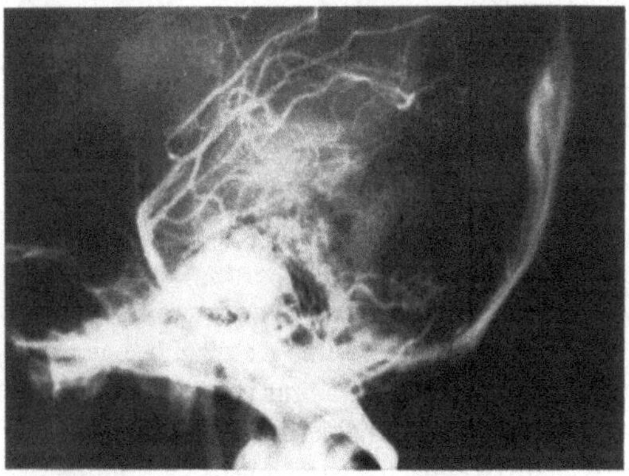

Abb. 2a

Im Seitenbild ist der Chorioidalispunkt deutlich nach ventral und weniger stark auch nach caudal verlagert. Retrotonsillär hebt sich eine 9 mm große Anfärbung mit zentraler Aufhellung ab. Die Hemisphärenäste des Ramus tonsillo-hemisphaericus verlaufen gestreckt und umgreifen einen größeren gefäßarmen Bezirk. Die A. vermiana superior und die Hemisphärenäste der A. cerebelli superior sind kuppelförmig angehoben, die Aa. cerebelli superiores verlaufen gestreckt und horizontal. Im Sagittalbild (Abb. 2b) sind die hochgradige Verdrängung der linken A. cerebelli inferior posterior bis nach paramedian rechts und die gestreckten Hemisphärenäste links auffällig. Eine mäßige Dislokation der linken A. cerebelli superior zeigt die Verlagerung des Hirnstammes zur Gegenseite. Neben dem kleinen Angioblastom liegt also eine große Cyste in der linken Kleinhirnhemisphäre vor.
Auch pneumographisch (Tab. 2) konnte der infratentorielle Tumor bei 31 der 34 Patienten

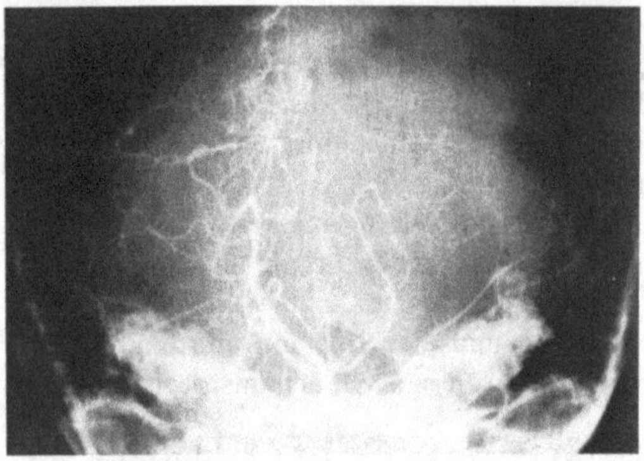

Abb. 2b

richtig lokalisiert werden. In einem Fall lag nur der Verdacht auf einen pathologischen Prozeß vor, 2mal konnte trotz optimaler Füllungstechnik encephalographisch keine diagnostisch ausreichende Kontrastierung der inneren und äußeren Liquorräume der hinteren Schädelgrube erreicht werden. Eine Artdiagnose gelang aufgrund des Pneumogramms in einem Fall, bei dem ventrikulographisch ein Epidermoid im 4. Ventrikel nachgewiesen werden konnte.

Als Schlußfolgerung ergibt sich: die Vertebralisangiographie und die Pneumographie besitzen für den Nachweis und die Lokalisation infratentorieller Tumoren eine gute Treffsicherheit, die bei unserem Krankengut für beide Verfahren jeweils 91% betrug. Bei der Erfassung kleiner Tumoren im Kleinhirnbrückenwinkel ist jedoch die Cisterno-Pneumographie überlegen. Andererseits wird der frühzeitige pneumographische Tumornachweis um so schwieriger, je weiter die Geschwulst von den inneren Liquorräumen oder größeren Cisternen entfernt ist. In diesen Fällen ist die Vertebralisangiographie leistungsfähiger. Artdiagnostisch war die Angiographie überlegen. Untersuchungsrisiko und Belastung des Patienten sind bei der Vertebralisangiographie geringer als bei der Ventrikulographie, halten sich jedoch im Vergleich zur Encephalographie die Waage. Die subjektiven Beschwerden sind bei der Cisternographie sicherlich intensiver als bei der Vertebralisangiographie.

Tab. 3: Wichtigste angiographische Veränderungen bei raumfordernden Prozessen infratentoriell

Lateral lokalisiert

Kleinhirnbrückenwinkel

A. cerebelli inf. ant. angehoben
A. cerebelli sup.: 1. und 2. Segment angehoben, 2. Segment zudem nach medial verlagert; A. marginalis angehoben und gestreckt
A. cerebri post.: Segment P_2 mäßig angehoben und nach medial disloziert
V. petr. sup.: angehoben oder/und lateral verlagert; fehlt homolateral bei Darstellung der gegenseitigen V. petr. sup.

Kleinhirnhemisphäre

A. cerebelli sup.: Hemisphärenäste angehoben und gestreckt; A. verm. sup. (und V. verm. sup.) zur Gegenseite verdrängt
CCP → ventral

Kleinhirntonsille

A. cerebelli inf. post.: posterobulbäres oder/und supratonsilläres Segment nach medial verlagert.
ChP angehoben. VIP → dorsal. Sag. Tonsillendurchmesser vergrößert

Median lokalisiert

Oberer Hirnstamm

A. cerebelli sup. und A. cerebri post.: peripedunculär vorwiegend nach lateral verdrängt und gespannt; ebenso die V. mesenceph. posterior. V. pontomesenc. ant.: clivusnah. CCP → dorsal

Unterer Hirnstamm

V. pontomesenc. ant. clivusnah
ChP und VIP → dorsal

IV. Ventrikel

A. cerebelli inf. post.: supratonsilläres Segment nach lateral disloziert
V. pontomesenc. ant. clivusnah
ChP nicht (oder gering ventral) verlagert.
VIP → dorsal. Sag. Tonsillendurchmesser vergrößert.
CCP angehoben

Unterwurm

A. cerebelli inf. post.: A. verm. inf. (wie auch V. verm. inf.) nach lateral verdrängt
ChP → ventral. VIP → ventral

Percutaneous transcatheter embolization of vascular Tumors

R. E. M. Hekster, W. Luyendijk and B. Matricali

Summary

Feeding vessels of vascular tumors have been demonstrated by means of superselective catheterangiography, after which these vessels have been occluded by superselective embolization by means of injection of muscle particles through the same catheters used for the diagnostic studies. Only tumors not readily accessible to (neuro) surgery have been treated in this manner up to now. However good objective short-term results have been achieved. The technique of transcatheter embolization is described and illustrated.

The collapse of angiomatous blood spaces in vascular malformations and highly vascular tumors after termination of the blood supply to these lesions, a collapse inducing thrombosis of these blood spaces has inspired us to try and obstruct feeding vessels of very vascular tumors in order to investigate the quality of this procedure as a possible alternative to sometimes hazardous surgical treatment.

Materials and Methods

The patient's own (tensor fascia latae) muscle has been selected as a very suitable embolizing material. Since 1931, when muscle was used as artificial embolus material in the treatment of carotid-cavernous fistulae it has been used in a great variety of neurosurgical proce-

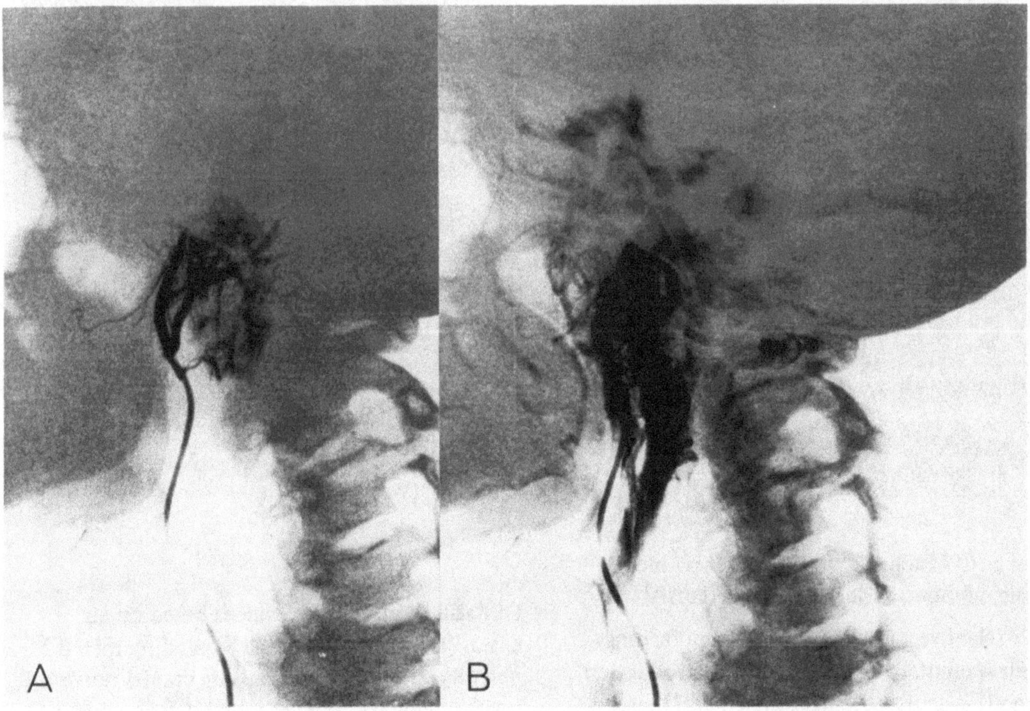

Abb. 1

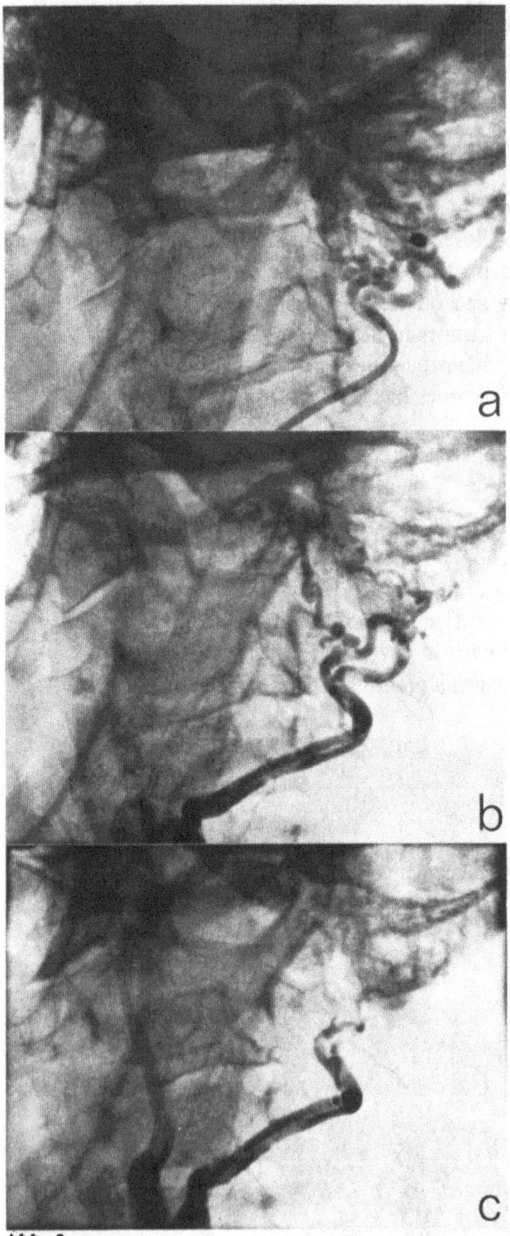

Abb. 2

dures both inside and around cerebral blood vessels, without noticeable side-effects.

After selective catheterization of the feeding vessels (percutaneous "seldinger" introduction method) is achieved, muscle particles, measuring approximately 2 X 2 X 4 mm. each are introduced into a stopcock, which then is attached to the catheter. The particles are injected manually into the artery by means of a following injection of diluted contrast medium. Contrast medium is also injected after the passage through the catheter of each piece of muscle both to check catheter position and changes in local flow.

As a rule thin radiopaque catheters (rothene 1,7 mm) are used, occasionally it may be necessary to use a catheter with better torque-control (RPX 062).

All catheterizations are performed under local anesthesia at the puncture site only. Control serial angiography six weeks after embolization is performed.

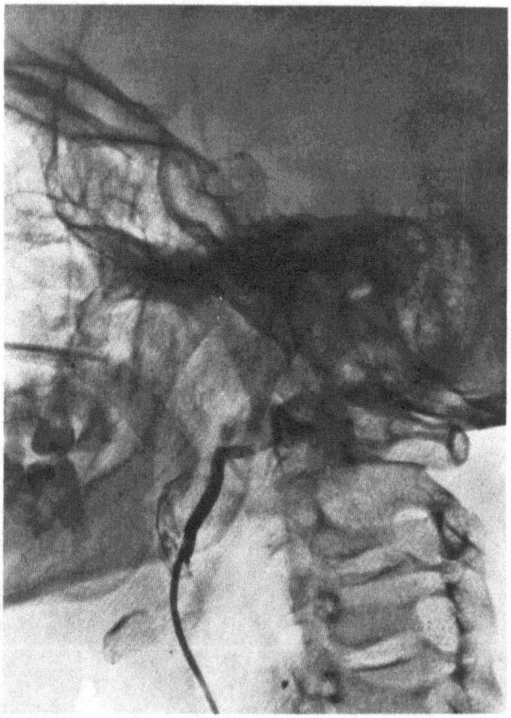

Abb. 3

Our still limited experience is based on six cases. (five chemodectoma expanding into the petrous temporal bone causing cranial nerve involvement and one vertebral haemangioma causing spinal cord compression).

Discussion

Progress in radiodiagnostic procedures (a. o. superselective catheter angiography) has extended the transcatheter occlusion therapy to vessels difficult to reach surgically. Although by occlusion of its feeding vessels the angiomatous lesion will be placed "hors de combat" by induced thrombosis, the permanency of this method of treatment remains questionable as the lesion is not removed and revascularisation will eventually occur. However, the procedure can be repeated without additional risk, while the use of a less dangerous probable alternative to (neuro) surgery or radiotherapy in cases where these methods of treatment can be very hazardous or almost hopeless is felt to be completely justified.

Especially in tumors of the glomus jugulare (chemodectoma), where optimal treatment, i. e. complete surgical excision is very often impossible because of the size and extent of the tumor, repeated embolization seems to be an acceptable method of treatment.

We have treated several patients in whom no other acceptable treatment could be considered due to enormous risks of operation, radiotherapy or even ligation of main vessels (this last method not being effective as a long-term treatment anyway) by means of transcatheter embolization. Short-term results varying from six to twelve months, have been satisfactory.

Phlebography with Compression

P. Vuorinen

The amount of venous blood is the same as the amount of arterial blood. The circulatory conditions in the veins are quite different from those in the arteries. The venous flow has a low pressure, the veins are wide and the flow is passive without any central pump and there are ample collateral nets.

If there is a pathologic condition like pathologic back flow or pathologic dilatations or occlusions and defects in the veins, venous flow tends to avoid that area.

In order to demonstrate pathologic conditions we must force the venous flow which is visualized through the contrast medium flow to the pathologic area. Different factors may be used to influence the venous flow and to direct the way of the contrast medium. We can use the gravity force, muscular pump of the veins or we may choose an optimal site of injection and use a high injection pressure in order to force the contrast medium in the desired direction.

Compression of different parts of the veins may be used in order to be able to demonstrate different pathologic conditions.

In Oulu we have used this compression technique at phlebography in examination of the uterine veins and the intra-osseal venous circulation.

In uterine phlebography the contrast medium is injected into the uterine muscle in the fundus uteri and it flows very rapidly into uterine and ovarian veins. Because all parts of the uterine venous plexuses or draining veins are not demonstrated in every case, a compression bag (similar to the IVP compression) has been used to direct the venous flow. With the compression bag ovarian veins or vena cava can be compressed. Fig. 1 shows the effect of compression. With compression of the left

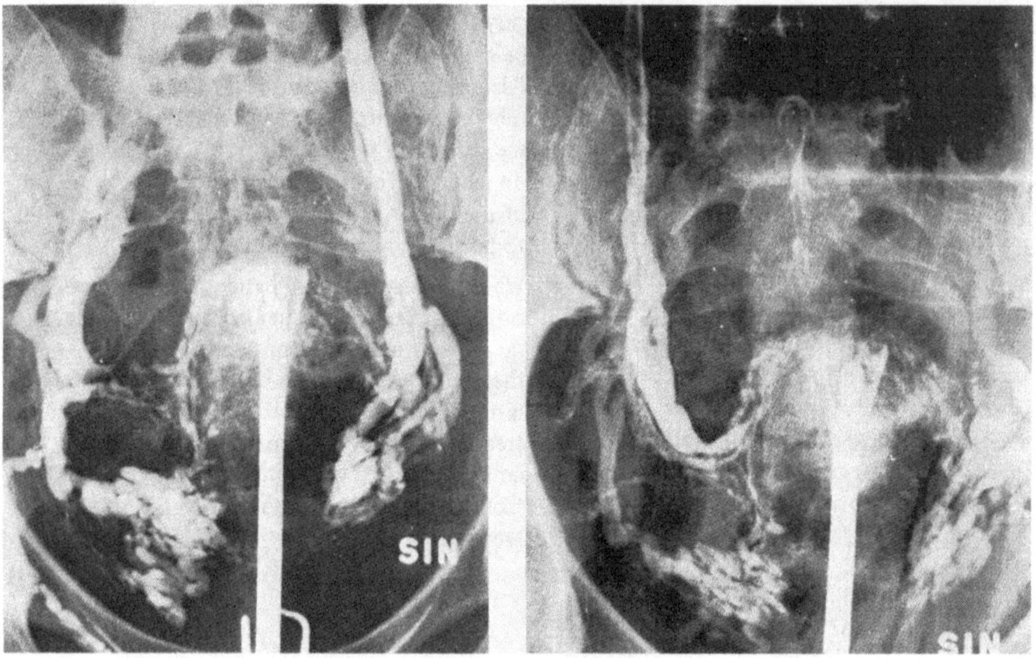

Fig. 1: Without compression (left) there is no filling of the right ovarian vein. With compression of the left ovarian vein and the vena cava, a thrombus in the right ovarian vein is visualised.

ovarian vein and the vena cava the contrast medium is forced to fill the right ovarian vein where a thrombotic process is demonstrated.

We have used this method for detecting varicose veins, uterine tumours and for investigating unclear cases of pelvic pain.
Another use of compression phlebography is compression osteomedullography of the tibia. The contrast medium is injected by hand inside the tibia. When a compression bag with compression pressue of 450 mm of Hg is applied around the fracture area in the tibia, a diagnosis of vascular connections between the fragments can be made. A dealyed union or non-union of the fracture can be predicted at early phase and the treatment adjusted accordingly. The

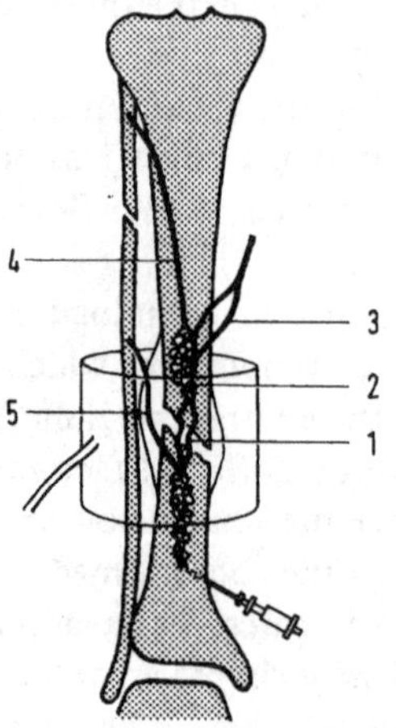

Fig. 2: A schematic presentation of the criteria for the assessment of intra-osseous venous connections through the fracture. The presence of one or more of the following signs was considered as sign of venous flow through the fracture: contrast filling of (1) intra-osseous veins crossing the fracture, (2) the sinusoid net of the proximal fragment, (3) periosteal veins of the proximal fragment, (4) the ascending branch of the main efferent vein, (5) veins passing along the periosteal callus from one fragment to another.

signs of flow through the fracture area are demonstrated in Fig. 2. Without compression the extra-osseal veins are easily filled but when the compression is applied the intra-osseal flow can be easily demonstrated (Fig. 3). In the fracture with non-union there is no flow through the fracture area. This examination seems to have very good clinical correlation.
The use of the compression technique has shown its value in these two types of phlebographic examinations and the same technique may most probably be used even on a large scale in phlebography.

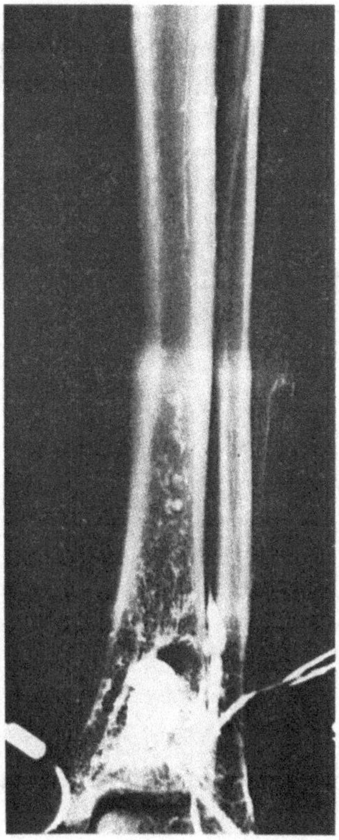

→

Fig. 3: Intra-osseal contrast injection with compression around the soft tissues of the leg demonstrates the intra-osseal venous flow in a normal tibia.

Erfahrungen mit der Nebennierenphlebographie

M. Georgi, H.-H. Wendenburg und P. Weber

Die konventionelle Röntgendiagnostik unter Einschluß des Retropneumoperitoneums ist zum Nachweis pathologischer Nebennierenprozesse unbefriedigend. Die Aortographie leistet nur dann einen wesentlichen Beitrag, wenn Nebennierentumoren – wie das Phächromocytom – gut vascularisiert sind. Die selektive Nebennierenarteriographie ist wegen der komplexen Gefäßversorgung der Nebennieren nur schwierig durchzuführen.
Daher wird vor allem im angelsächsischen und skandinavischen Schrifttum seit Mitte der 60er Jahre die Nebennierenphlebographie propagiert. Als Indikation für diese Untersuchungsmethode werden angesehen: das Conn-Syndrom, M. *Cushing*, das Phäochromocytom, Abklärung retroperitonealer Tumoren sowie der Nachweis von Nebennierenmetastasen.
Wir haben die Nebennierenphlebographie bisher bei 22 Patienten durchgeführt. Die anfänglich schwierig erscheinende Technik konnte für die *linke* Nebenniere stabilisiert werden. Nach Punktion der V. femoralis in Seldinger-Technik wird zunächst ein vorn gebogener roter *Oedman*-Katheter in die linke Nierenvene eingelegt. Danach wird in Anlehnung an *Cerny* und Mitar-

beiter ein sehr flexibler Führungsdraht bis zum Nierenhilus vorgeschoben (Abb. 1). Der erste Katheter kann dann leicht gegen einen zweiten ausgewechselt werden, dessen Form die Sondierung der linken Nebennierenvene erlaubt.

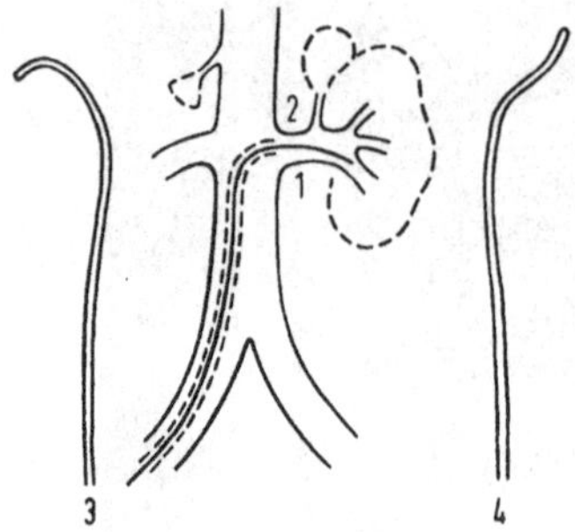

Abb. 1: Schema der Anatomie der Nebennierenvenen, sowie Skizze der zur Sondierung geeigneten Katheterformen. Erläuterung der Technik der linksseitigen Nebennierenvenensondierung.

Von sieben Fehlversuchen entfielen vier auf die ersten sechs Untersuchungen, bei denen diese Technik noch nicht angewendet wurde. Einmal verhinderte eine Kompression der V. cava inferior die Sondierung der Nierenvene.
Ein normales Nebennierenphlebogramm zeigt Abb. 2. Die Nebenniere ist normal groß, ihr venöses Gefäßbild harmonisch. Bei einem präoperativ diagnostiziertem Phäochromocytom (Abb. 3) verursacht der ca. 2 cm große Tumor eine Kompression der Nebennierenvenen. Gestaute Venen an seiner oberen und lateralen Begrenzung ergeben ein sehr genaues Abbild seiner Form und Größe.
Bei einer Patientin mit einen *Conn*-Syndrom sieht man eine Rarefizierung der Venenstruktur an der lateralen Begrenzung der Nebenniere. Die histologische Untersuchung des Operationspräparats ergab als seltenere Form dieses Krankheitsbildes eine mikro- und multinoduläre Hyperplasie nicht nur der äußeren Nebennierenrindenschicht.
Bei einer Patientin mit *M. Cushing* war die linke Nebenniere lediglich vergrößert. Eine unter der Injektion erfolgte Ruptur der Nebennierenvene verursachte einen temporären Schmerzzustand und blieb klinisch ohne Folgen.
Bei einer Patientin mit metastasierendem Mamma-Carcinom ergab das Phlebogramm eine erhebliche Vergrößerung der linken Neben-

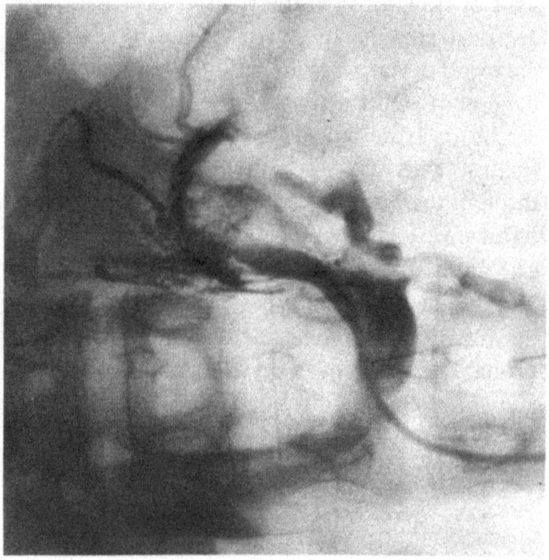

Abb. 2: Phlebogramm bei Phäochromocytom der linken Nebenniere.

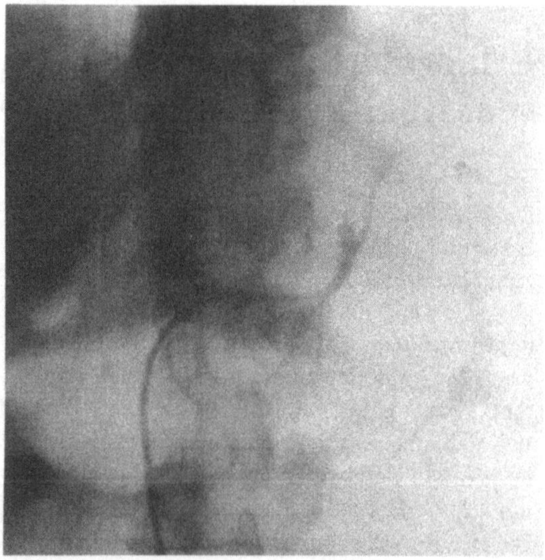

Abb. 3: Verdacht auf Nebennierenmetastase links bei Mamma-Carconom (keine Autopsie!).

niere. Die Hauptvene ist gestaut und bricht ab, andere Venen verlaufen gespannt über das vergrößerte Organ (Abb. 3). Der Befund wurde als Nebennierenmetastase gedeutet.
Unsere Versuche, auch die *rechte* Nebenniere mit gleicher Zuverlässigkeit darzustellen, sind bisher fehlgeschlagen. Ihre Vene ist außerordentlich dünn und läßt sich nur schwer sondieren. Oft werden Lebervenen gefüllt.
Ein Vorteil der Nebennierenphlebographie ist die Möglichkeit, aus der Nebennierenvene gezielt Blut für Hormonbestimmungen zu entnehmen. Ernste Komplikationen wurden bei der angewendeten Technik nicht beobachtet.

Zusammenfassung

Die Nebennierenphlebographie wurde bei 22 Patienten vorgenommen. Sie gelang vorwiegend linksseitig. Die dabei angewendete Technik wird beschrieben. Indikationen und Ergebnisse bei einigen Nebennierenerkrankungen werden besprochen.

Abflußwege und ihre Bedeutung beim Achselvenenverschluß

H. Sieberns

Das mediastinale Phlebogramm hat in der Literatur relativ selten Erwähnung gefunden (*Brandt, Drewes, Loehr, Süsse, Tiwisina* u. a.). Die Ursache hierfür liegt in der geringen Symptomatik (*Gullmo, Schäfer* u. *Thies* u. a.) und den leider oft wenig ergiebigen Röntgenbildern, die vielfach auch mit einer zu geringen Kontrastmittelmenge durchgeführt werden, so daß mancher Verschluß sich nicht dokumentiert (*Reinhardt*).
Die Indikation zur Phlebographie wird von der Klinik aus bei folgenden Symptomen gestellt:

Pralle bis derbe Schwellung des Armes, Schweregefühl mit Kribbeln beim Hängenlassen des Armes, das beim Heben verschwindet,
gleichmäßiges fleckiges Hautkolorit,
Ausbildung von erweiterten Hautvenen am Oberarm, Schulter, Brust gegebenenfalls Einflußstauung.

Alle klinischen Erscheinungen können getrennt voneinander auftreten und sehr diskret bleiben, so daß die Diagnosestellung erschwert ist (*Drewes, Sieberns, Tagariello*). Bei klinischem Verdacht sollte in jedem Fall eine sorgfältige Palpation der Achselhöhle, der Supraclaviculargrube und der lateralen Thoraxwand durchgeführt werden. Verhärtungen von Venen in diesen Regionen oder atypische Tastbefunde der Achselgruben oder auch zart durchschimmernde erweiterte Venen der lateralen Thoraxwand können gelegentlich der einzige Hinweis auf einen Verschluß der Vena subclavia sein.
In Einzelfällen ist ein Schwindelgefühl mit vermehrtem Blutandrang beim Bücken das einzige klinische Symptom bei sonst fehlender orthostatischer Dysregulation.
Aufmerksamkeit sollte vermehrt den Patienten gewidmet werden, bei denen wegen einer Notwendigkeit einer parenteralen Zufuhr ein Cavakatheter von der Ellenbeuge aus gelegt werden mußte (*Dietz* u. *van de Weyer*), nach Angiocardiographien und transvenösen Schrittmacherimplantationen (*Balau* u. Mitarb.) oder nach Dialysen.
Das unterschiedliche klinische Bild ist weniger geprägt von dem akuten Auftreten einer Okklusion als von der Lage des Verschlusses und seiner Ausdehnung. Lateral gelegene und

kurzstreckige Abflußhindernisse bedingen in der überwiegenden Zahl der Fälle einen kurzen Umgehungskreislauf, der entweder über die Venen der Supraclaviculargrube, die Halsmuskelvenen oder über Venen der vorderen Thoraxwand (Abb. 1) geht und nur gelegent-

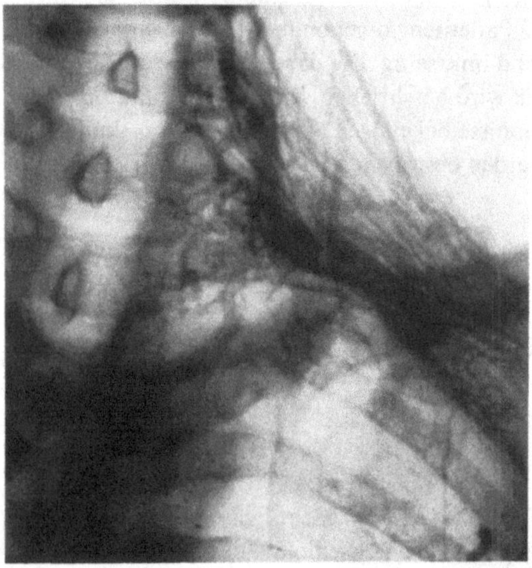

Abb. 1

lich über die Vena thoracalis lateralis. Letzterer Weg öffnet sich dann, wenn ein ausgedehnter Verschluß besteht und der Abfluß über die o. g. Wege nicht mehr ausreicht. Sie sind dann oft trotz klinischen Nachweises von erweiterten Hautvenen nicht mehr darstellbar (*Reinhardt*), auch dann nicht, wenn durch Kompression der erweiterten Vena thoracalis lateralis dieser Weg versperrt ist, wie eigene Untersuchung gezeigt haben. Die Kompression erfolgt dabei mittels einer elastischen Binde. Sie bewirkte bei 6 Patienten, bei denen dieser Versuch durchgeführt wurde, einen unangenehmen Blutandrang im Kopfe, der sich nach Lösung der Kompression sofort wieder gab.

Die Vena thoracalis lateralis stellt sich regelmäßig als kleinfingerdickes Gefäß (Abb. 2) dar und ist bei Einbeziehung der gesamten Vena subclavia und der V. anonyma in den thrombotischen Prozeß nahezu das einzige Gefäß für den Abtransport des Venenblutes des Armes.

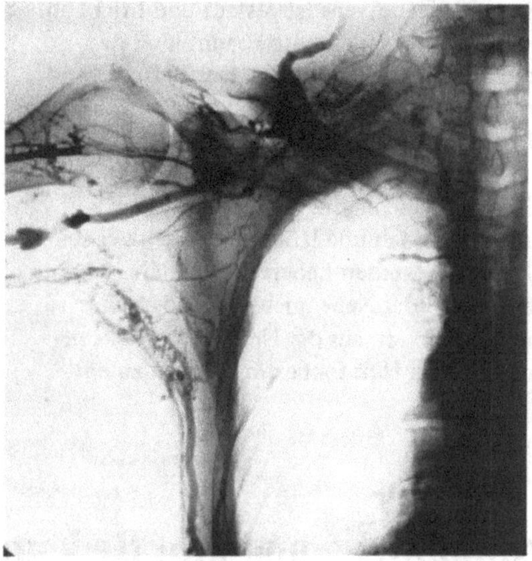

Abb. 2

Nur ein kleiner Teil des Kontrastmittels wird über Venen der Supraclaviculargrube zu den Venen der Wirbelsäule abgeleitet. Die Unterbrechung der Vena thoracalis lateralis würde bei solch ausgedehnter Thrombose zu schweren Ausfallserscheinungen führen müssen.

Der weitere Abtransport des venösen Blutes erfolgt in diesen Fällen über die Intercostalvenen. Hierbei werden normalerweise in unterschiedlichem Ausmaße die Venen der 3. – 10. Rippe einbezogen. Oft jedoch sind nur 2 Venen gefüllt, wobei wiederum die ventralen Gefäße nicht unbedingt den dorsalen entsprechen müssen. Rechtsseitig wird in einer großen Zahl der Fälle ein Abfluß zur Vena intercostalis suprema sichtbar. Eine gleichzeitige Füllung aller Intercostalvenen einer oder beider Seiten ist in der Literatur bisher nicht verzeichnet.

Die Öffnung des Weges über die Vena thoracalis lateralis zur Vena thoraco-epigastrica erfolgt nur selten. Er öffnet sich dann, wenn der thrombotische Prozeß die obere Hohlvene mit erfaßt hat und der Transport des venösen Blutes zum Herzen auf diesem Wege blockiert ist.

Damit ist auch der Einstrom des venösen

Blutes in die obere Hohlvene ausgeschlossen, es muß ebenso wie das der Arme über die V. thoracalis lat. weitertransportiert werden.

Wohl öffnen sich Intercostalvenen, doch ermöglichen sie in diesen Fällen keinen Transport von der V. acygos bzw. hemiacygos zum re. Herzen. Das gleiche gilt für die V. mammaria interna. Aus diesem Grunde muß die Ableitung des gesamten Blutes zur V. cava inf. erfolgen. Damit wird eine Öffnung des Weges zur V. thoraco-epigastrica oder über ein Venenkonvolut notwendig, das wiederum eine Verbindung zur V. phrenica besitzt. In jedem Fall wird die V. phrenica mit einbezogen.
Gelegentlich zeigt sich die Möglichkeit einer starken Erweiterung der V. pericardii, die über die V. hemiacygos accessoria aufgefüllt wird. Sie findet in Höhe des Zwerchfelles wieder Anschluß an das übrige Kollateralsystem. Im weiteren Verlauf kontrastieren sich im Serienablauf zunehmend die unteren Anteile der V. acygos bzw. hemiacygos, die dann das Blut über die Vv. Lumbales und die V. ovarica (spermatica) in die V. iliaca interna weitergeben. Auf diese Weise wird das gesamte venöse Blut des Kopfes und der oberen Extremitäten in die V. cava inf. abgeleitet. Das stellt für den Kreislauf eine enorme Belastung dar, die sich jedoch klinisch bei jungen Leuten kaum manifestiert. Ein vermehrter Blutandrang im Kopfe beim Bücken kann das einzige Symptom sein.
Die Ausbildung der Kollateralbahnen richtet sich nach dem Ausmaß der Thrombosierung. Je nach der Ausdehnung kommt es zu einem direkten Abfluß über die Schulterregion, bei ausgedehnteren Verschlüssen reichen diese Wege nicht mehr aus, und es kommt zur Öffnung der V. thoracalis lat. Ist gleichzeitig der Abstrom zur oberen Hohlvene blockiert, so werden erst dann weitere Kollateralbahnen mit zum Abtransport herangezogen.

Angioszintigraphie der oberen Extremität bei verschiedenen Stadien der PCP

E. Ogris und F. Olbert

Einleitung

Von mehreren Autoren wurde daraufhingewiesen, daß den periarticulären Gefäßwandveränderungen in der Pathomorphologie der rheumatoiden Arthritis eine entscheidende Rolle zukommt, und daß auf Grund der nachgewiesenen Gefäßveränderungen auch mit erheblichen Zirkulationsstörungen zu rechnen ist. Wir haben versucht, diese in den verschiedenen Stadien der PCP auftretenden Zirkulationsveränderungen mittels der Angiographie sowie mit Hilfe nuklearmedizinischer Methoden zu erfassen.

Methodik

Die angiographische Kontrastdarstellung der Hand- und Fingerarterien erfolgt in der üblichen Weise durch Direktpunktion der A. brachialis.
Die nuklearmedizinische Untersuchung wurde mit einer Szintillationskamera in Verbindung mit einem 4096-Vielkanalkernspeicher ausgeführt. Als radioaktive Tracer wurden ^{131}J-MAA intraarteriell und ^{99m}Tc intravenös verwendet. Die jeweils im Bereich der MCP (Metacarpophalangeal-) und PIP (proximalen Interphalangealgelenke) registrierten Inte-

gralaktivitäten wurden als sogenannte AOIs (areas of interest) mit Hilfe des 4096-Kanalkernspeichers bestimmt und in Prozent der vom Detektor gesehenen Gesamtaktivität ausgedrückt. Die im Bereich der einzelnen Gelenke nach ^{99m}Tc bzw. ^{131}J-MAA gemessenen Aktivitäten wurden einander vergleichend gegenübergestellt und als Aktivitätsprofil dargestellt.
18 Patienten mit verschiedenen Stadien der PCP wurden auf die beschriebene Weise kombiniert untersucht.

Ergebnisse

Angiographisch konnten im wesentlichen zwei Typen von Gefäßveränderungen festgestellt werden:

1. occlusive Veränderungen aller Schweregrade, die eine oder mehrere Fingerarterien betrafen. Sie reichten gradmäßig von partieller Engstellung einzelner Gefäßabschnitte über umschriebene Lumeneinengungen bis zum totalen Verschluß einer Digitalarterie. Letzterer war häufig kombiniert mit feinen, querverlaufenden, von der gesunden zur kranken Seite ziehenden Kollateralen. An sämtlichen Fingern wurden occlusive Veränderungen mit derselben Häufigkeit angetroffen.

2. Hypervascularisierte Bezirke
Sie waren anzutreffen in Arealen mit gesteigerter Synovialproliferation, im Bereich entzündlich veränderter Gelenke oder Sehnenscheiden sowie weiterhin im Bereich lokaler Knorpelcorosionen.

Um quantitative Aussagen über den Grad der arteriellen Blutversorgung der Synovia treffen zu können, wurden Angioszintigramme nach intraarterieller Injektion von ^{131}J-MAA angefertigt. Die Injektion erfolte in die A. brachialis im Anschluß an die Angiographie. Intraarteriell injiziertes MAA folgt in seiner Verteilung dem relativen Blutfluß zu einer bestimmten anatomischen Region. Die Aktivitätsverteilung im Versorgungsgebiet einer Arterie repräsentiert daher die relative arterielle Blutverteilung, also den Grad der Perfusion. Teilbereiche im Versorgungsgebiet einer Arterie, die relativ gesehen besser durchblutet sind als etwa umgebende Areale zeigen daher auch eine bessere szintigraphisch nachweisbare Aktivitätsanreicherung, selbst wenn diese Arterie absolut gesehen eine verminderte Durchblutung aufweist.

Bei unseren Untersuchungen fanden wir eine Herabsetzung bzw. ein Fehlen der Aktivitätsanreicherung im Versorgungsbereich von Arterien, die occlusive Veränderungen verschiedener Schweregrade aufwiesen. Andererseits war eine deutliche Aktivitätsanreicherung im Bereich hypervascularisierter Bezirke anzutreffen. Gegenüber dem normalen Angioszintigramm der Hand, wo eine Aktivitätsanreicherung hauptsächlich in den gefäßreichen Muskelpartien des Thenar und Hypothenar stattfindet, und die Gelenke zufolge ihrer relativen Gefäßarmut eine geringe Anreicherung radioaktiver Partikel aufweisen, läßt das, bei verschiedenen Stadien der PCP gesehene Aktivitätsmuster den Schluß zu, daß durch die vermehrte Perfusion hypervascularisierter Gewebsbezirke eine relative Minderdurchblutung und somit zirkulatorische Schädigung angrenzender, nicht unmittelbar betroffener Gewebsbezirke stattfindet. Eine weitere Verschlechterung der Zirkulation ist durch vermehrt auftretende arteriovenöse Shunts anzunehmen, die wir eindeutig szintigraphisch durch eine Partikelanreicherung in der Lunge nachweisen konnten, wo sie angiographisch nur zu vermuten waren. Das Fehlen einer Aktivitätsanreicherung in einem bestimmten Areal im Angioszintigramm läßt nicht notwendigerweise den Schluß zu, daß im betreffenden Gebiet eine Minderperfusion durch Gefäßverschlüsse vorliegt. Es kann dies vielmehr auch der Ausdruck von präkapillären arteriovenösen Kurzschlüssen sein, durch die das betreffende Areal zirkulatorisch umgangen wird. Der Angiographie kommt die Aufgabe zu, den Nachweis zu erbringen, ob im minderperfundierten Gebiet Gefäße nachzuweisen sind oder nicht. Sind die Befunde beider Methoden identisch im Sinne eines Fehlens von Gefäßen im Angiogramm bzw. einer Aktivitätsanreicherung von markiertem MAA im Angioszintigramm, so liegt tatsächlich eine Minderperfusion des betreffenden Gebietes vor. Können bei Fehlen einer Aktivitätsanreicherung im Angioszintigramm mit Hilfe der Angiographie aber Gefäße dargestellt werden, so liegen präkapilläre arteriovenöse Anastomosen oder pathologische Gefäße vor. Während der Nachweis solcher arterio-venöser Shunts angiographisch nicht immer leicht gelingt, ist dieser mittels der Angioszintigraphie, wo im Falle von Kurzschlüssen distal der Injektionsstelle eine gut nachweisbare Aktivitätsanreicherung im Bereich der Lungen durch Fixation markierter Partikel stattfindet, sehr leicht möglich. Die Aussagen beider Methoden ergänzen einander daher auf ideale Weise.

Um auch Aussagen über den Grad der bestehenden Synovitis machen zu können, wurde auf dieselbe Weise die Aufnahme von ^{99m}Tc in den betreffenden Gelenken gemessen. Wie bekannt, reichert sich ^{99m}Tc im entzündeten Synovialgewebe etwa 20–30% stärker als in der Umgebung an. Als Ursache dafür wird heute die in diesem Gebiet gesteigerte Gefäßpermeabilität angesehen. Die ^{99m}Tc Aufnahme entspricht somit in Lokalisation und Intensität dem Grad der bestehenden Synovitis. Setzt man die Aufnahme der beiden Isotope im Bereich der untersuchten Gelenke zueinander in Beziehung, die einerseits den Perfusionsgrad andererseits den Grad der bestehenden Synovitis repräsentieren, so sind unserer Ansicht nach prognostische Aussagen möglich. Es konnte nämlich festgestellt werden, daß beide Komponenten an ein und demselben Gelenk nicht immer parallel gehen.

Diskussion

In den Frühstadien der PCP geht im Allgemeinen die im Bereich der einzelnen Gelenke szintigraphisch nachweisbare Aktivitätsanreicherung von ^{99m}Tc und ^{131}J-MAA parallel, wie aus den dargestellten Aktivitätsprofilen gut ablesbar ist. Es herrschen eindeutig die Zeichen der Exsudation vor, was in der gesteigerten, auf eine Permeabilitätsstörung zurückgehende Anreicherung von ^{99m}Tc zum Ausdruck kommt (Abb. 1a, b, c, d).

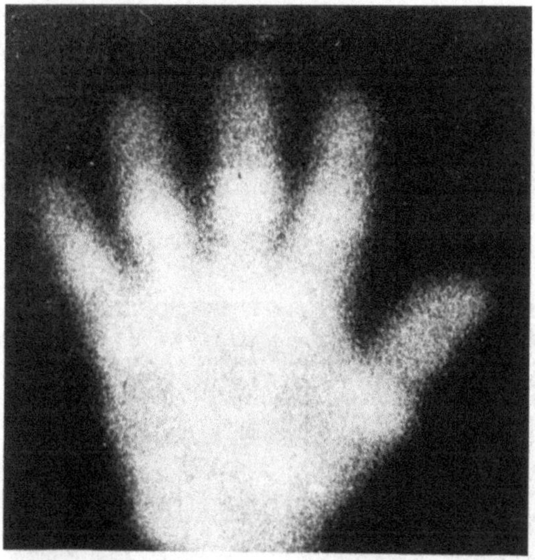

Abb. 1a: ^{99m}Tc Szintigramm der rechten Hand (von volar) eines 52jährigen Patienten mit den klinischen Zeichen eines akuten entzündlichen Schubes im Bereich der Fingergelenke beider Hände bei bisher neunmonatiger Krankheitsdauer. Die gleichmäßig gesteigerte Aktivitätsanreicherung im Bereich der MCP und PIP läßt auf eine gradmäßig alle dargestellten Gelenke ziemlich gleichmäßig betreffende Synovitis schließen.

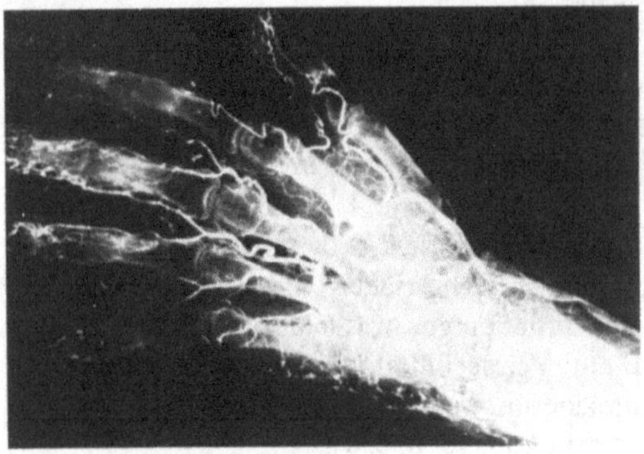

Abb. 1b: Angiogramm derselben Hand mit partieller Engstellung der Fingerarterien des 4. und 5. Strahles ulnar und des 2. und 3. Strahles radial in deren distalem Verlauf. Andererseits ausgeprägte Hypervascularisation im Bereich des Daumengrundgelenkes. Am deutlichsten im Bereich des 2. PIP und 5. MCP, angedeutet beim 3. und 4. PIP frühzeitiger venöser Rückfluß, durch arteriovenöse Shunts bedingt.

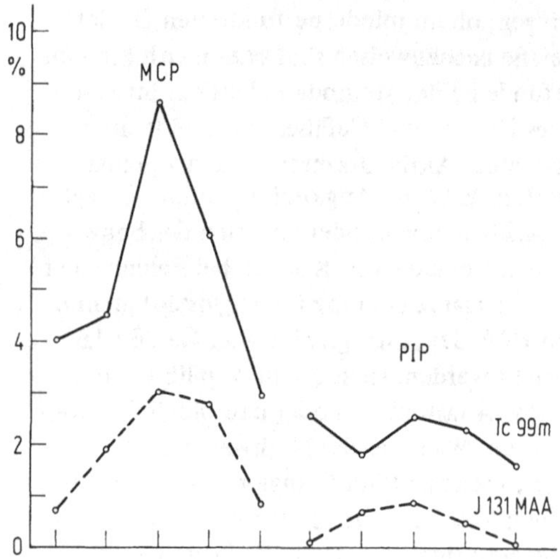

Abb. 1d: Aktivitätsprofile der MCP und PIP. Abszisse: relative Aktivitätsanreicherung im Bereich der dargestellten Gelenke in Prozent. Ordinate: die einzelnen Punkte repräsentieren von links nach rechts jeweils den 1. – 5. Strahl. Während die Aktivitätsprofile von ^{99m}Tc und ^{131}J-MAA im Bereich der PIP – mit Ausnahme der 1. PIP – ein gleichsinniges Verhalten zeigen, ist im Bereich des 2. und 3. MCP eine gesteigerte Aktivitätsanreicherung von MAA als Ausdruck einer, durch die angiographisch nachgewiesene Hypervascularisation bedingten gesteigerten Perfusion im Bereich dieser Gelenke festzustellen.

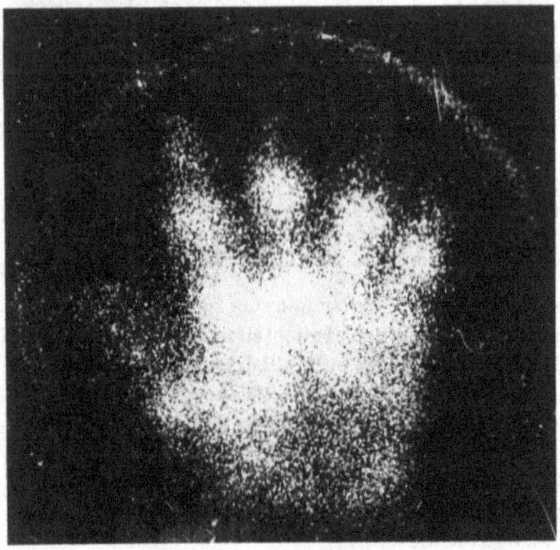

Abb. 1c: Angioszintigramm derselben Hand nach ^{131}J-MAA intraarteriell. Deutliche Aktivitätsanreicherung im Bereich aller PIP und MCP. Am stärksten im Bereich des 2. und 3. MCP. Weniger ausgeprägt im Bereich des 4. und 5. MCP.

Kommt es jedoch zur Ausbildung eines Granulationsgewebes mit Gefäßneubildungen, so findet die angiographisch nachweisbare Hypervascularisation und die damit verbundene Perfusionsstörung ihren Ausdruck in der verstärkten Aktivitätsanreicherung von ^{131}J-MAA im Angioszintigramm.
Bei unseren Untersuchungen war auffallend, daß die Gefäßneubildungen im Bereich einzelner Gelenke bei einigen Patienten sehr frühzeitig (etwa 2–3 Monate nach Beginn der Erkrankung) bereits nachweisbar waren und dabei einzelne Gelenke isoliert betrafen (Abb. 2a, b, c, d). Diese Gelenke zeigten im weiteren

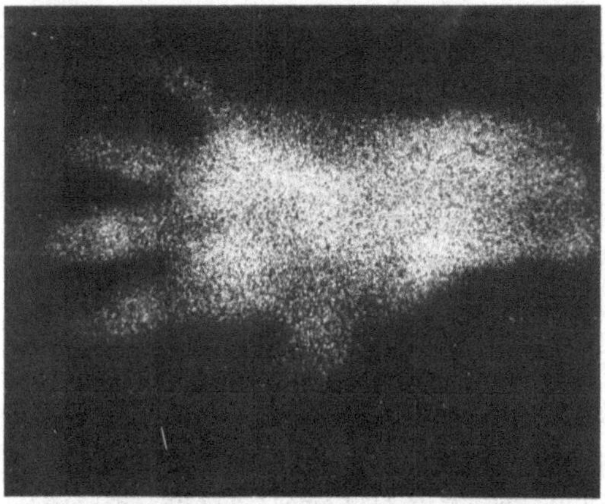

Abb. 2a: ^{99m}Tc Szintigramm der linken Hand (von volar) eines 57jährigen Patienten mit frischer PCP von etwa drei Monaten Dauer. Auffallend die gleichmäßige Aktivitätsanreicherung im Bereich aller PIP und MCP.

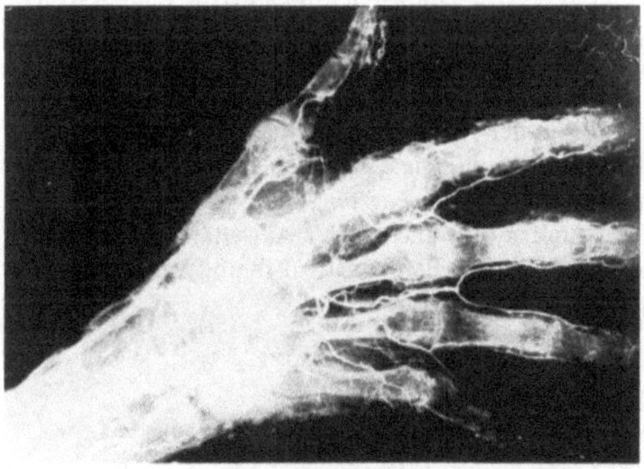

Abb. 2b: Relativ gute Gefäßversorgung im Bereich der Finger mit Ausnahme des 1. und 2. Strahles radial, die eine Engstellung der Gefäße aufweisen. Hier jedoch, sowie im Bereich des 5. Fingers quer verlaufende Kollateralgefäße. Hypervascularisationen im Bereich des 3. und 4. PIP, sowie des 2., 3. und 4. MCP erkennbar.

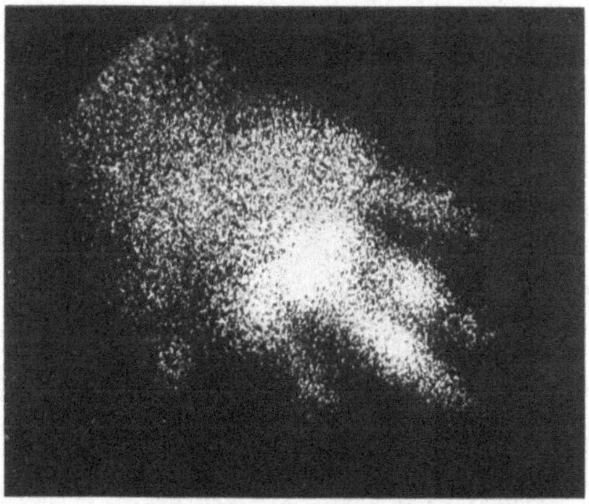

Abb. 2c: Angioszintigramm mit auffallender Aktivitätsanreicherung im Bereich des 3. und 4. PIP, sowie des 2., 3. und 4. MCP.

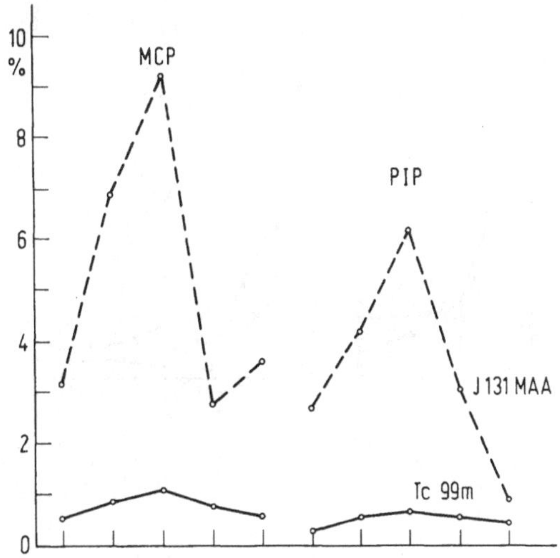

Abb. 2d: Aktivitätsprofile mit auffallender Diskrepanz durch isoliert gesteigerte Aktivitätsanreicherung von ^{131}J-MAA über den 3. und 4. PIP, sowie über den 2., 3. und 4. MCP als Ausdruck einer, bei der vorliegenden Krankheitsdauer frühzeitigen Vascularisation im Bereich einzelner Gelenke.

klinischen Verlauf der Erkrankung eine besonders rasch fortschreitende Destruktion. Exsudations- und Vaskularisationsgrad zeigten also an diesen Gelenken nicht immer ein paralleles Verhalten. Als therapeutische Konsequenz wurde daher von uns in diesen Fällen die Frühsynovektomie angesehen.
Im chronischen Stadium der Krankheit, wo die Zahl der Gefäßneubildungen abnimmt, die Destruktion der Gelenke jedoch durch bindegewebige Umwandlung fortschreitet, zeigt andererseits die Anreicherung von ^{99m}Tc bei Fehlen einer solchen von ^{131}J-MAA an, daß sich in dem betreffenden Gelenk noch frische, entzündliche Prozesse abspielen (Abb. 3).

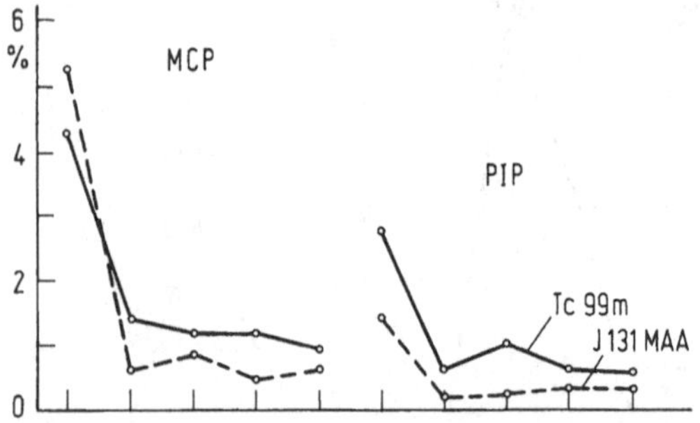

Zusammenfassung

1. In der Mehrzahl der Fälle gehen im Frühstadium der PCP der Grad der Synovitis und der Vascularisation parallel.

2. Zeigen einzelne Gelenke bereits im Frühstadium ein auffallendes Überwiegen der Vascularisation, so ist dies als prognostisch ungünstiges Zeichen zu werten, da diese Gelenke eine rasch fortschreitende Destruktion zeigen. Die Behandlung sollte in diesen Fällen in einer Frühsynovektomie bestehen.

3. Im chronischen Stadium der Erkrankung kann eine, im Bereich eines Gelenkes nachweisbare ^{99m}Tc Anreicherung anzeigen, daß das Gelenk noch zu einer entzündlichen Reaktion fähig ist und demnach eine Lokaltherapie noch sinnvoll ist.

←

Abb. 3: Aktivitätsprofil der linken Hand eines 53jährigen Patienten mit einer seit 19 Jahren bestehenden PCP mit schweren klinischen und röntgenologischen Veränderungen im Bereich aller Gelenke. Im Bereich der PIP in den Aktivitätsprofilen auffallend, daß im Bereich des 3. PIP als Zeichen einer noch nennenswerten Synovitis eine gesteigerte ^{99m}Tc-Aufnahme festzustellen ist, während eine Aktivitätsanreicherung von ^{131}J-MAA im Bereich aller PIP und MCP mit Ausnahme des 3. MCP fehlt.

Angiographie im Farbröntgenfilm

W. Wenz, A. Porkert, D. Beduhn und F.-J. Roth

1969 zeigt *Kunnen* erstmals einen farbigen Röntgenkinofilm. Er stellt diesen Farbfilm in einem indirekten Verfahren über eine Farbkopiermethode her und projiziert ihn abwechselnd über verschiedene Farbfilter.

Im Folgenden stellen wir ebenfalls ein indirektes Verfahren zur Herstellung eines farbigen Röntgenkinofilmes vor.

Unseren Versuchen legten wir zugrunde: Beim Abfotografieren eines Schwarzweißbildes auf einen Colorfilm unter Vorschalten eines Farbfilters entsteht ein Bild, das ausschließlich der Farbe des Filters entspricht. Ausgenommen davon bleiben die im Bild schwarz erscheinenden Strukturen, z. B. die Arterien eines Angiogrammes. Durch Zweitbelichtung lassen sich diese noch freien Areale beim Abfotografieren unter Vorschalten eines 2. Farbfilters in einer neuen, dem Filter entsprechenden Farbe darstellen. Gleichzeitig erscheinen die doppelt belichteten Bildanteile in der von der jeweiligen Filterkombination abhängigen Mischfarbe, die durch additive Farbmischung entsteht.

1968 bedienen sich *Groh* und *Häendle* dieser Möglichkeit, um farbige Röntgenbilder von Serienangiogrammen herzustellen. Um kontrastreiche überlagerungsfreie Aufnahmen zu erhalten, werden die Angiogramme elektronisch subtrahiert, und dann in Farbe transformiert.

Über erste klinische Erfahrungen mit dieser Methode berichten 1969 *Roth* und *Wenz*.

Da die Bildsubtraktion beim Röntgenkinofilm aufwendig und mühsam ist, verzichteten wir zunächst darauf.
Unsere Methode (Abb. 1) besteht darin, daß zunächst der Negativfilm einer Arteriografie unter Vorschalten eines Farbfilters auf einen Farbfilm aufgenommen wird. Anschließend wird seine Positivkopie synchron und deckungsgleich in Zweitbelichtung unter Vorschalten eines anderen Farbfilters darüber belichtet.
Es entsteht durch additive Farbmischung ein mischfarbenes Bild, das die Farben des 1. und 2. Filters enthält. Ausgenommen von der Farbmischung bleiben lediglich die durch die schwarze Farbe der Positivkopie abgedeckten Arterien.

1. Schwarz-weiß-Phase
   Rö.-Negativfilm → Positivkopie

2. Farbphase (z. B. Angiogramm)
   Rö.-Negativ → Rotfilter
   Rö.-Positiv → Grünfilter
   → Farbfilm (z. B. Gefäße rot, Hintergrund gelb)

Abb. 1: Röntgenkinematographie in Farbe (photographische Methode).

Wie die Demonstration des Farbfilmes zeigt, besitzt der farbige Röntgenkinofilm einen unbestrittenen Wert für alle Gebiete der Lehre.

Unserer Meinung nach wird es mit dem Farbröntgenkinofilm möglich sein, schwierige Gefäßsituationen, wie arterio-venöse Kurzschlüsse, leichter und rascher als im üblichen Film zu differenzieren. Die Abgrenzung von kontrastarm dargestellten Organen sowie die Beurteilung von Tumorausdehnungen wird erleichtert werden.

Erfahrungen mit der Photosubtraktion unter Verwendung maschinell verarbeitungsfähiger Umkehrfilme

K. Rittmeyer und J. Freyschmidt

Gewisse Sektoren angiographischer Diagnostik erfordern die routinemäßige Anwendung des Subtraktionsverfahrens. In diesem Zusammenhang sei besonders auf die Schwierigkeiten bei der Auswertung von Vertebralis- und Spinalarteriographien verwiesen.

Einer routinemäßigen Anwendung des photographischen Subtraktionsverfahrens standen bisher besondere Einwände von Seiten des hohen methodischen und zeitlichen Aufwandes im Wege; für das elektronische Verfahren gelten in erster Linie der hohe finanzielle Aufwand und das Problem der Befunddokumentation.
Seit etwa einem halben Jahr stehen maschinell verarbeitungsfähige Subtraktionsfilme zur Verfügung, die für die photographische Subtraktion geeignet sind.
Unsere Erfahrungen erstrecken sich auf den

Subtraktionsfilm der Firma Kodak und Agfa Gevaert.
Bei Verwendung von 90"-Entwicklungsautomaten steht das fertige Subtraktionsbild im Orginalformat etwa in einem Zeitraum von 5' zur Verfügung.

Methode

Im Kontaktverfahren wird von dem Leerbild eines Serienangiogramms eine Negativkopie, die sog. Maske hergestellt. Die dazu erforderliche Ausrüstung besteht lediglich in einem üblichen, photographischen Belichtungsrahmen. Als Lichtquelle hat sich eine normale 15-W-Lampe bewährt, die etwa in einem Abstand von 1m von dem Kopierrahmen entfernt sein soll. Die Expositionszeit des Umkehrfilmes beträgt bei dieser Anordnung ca. 10–15 Sekunden. Stärkere Lichtquellen erzeugen nach unseren Erfahrungen deutliche Filmschleier, da der sehr empfindliche Film stark auf Streulicht reagiert.

Das zur Subtraktion bestimmte Röntgenbild aus der Serienangiographie wird mit der Maske zur Deckung gebracht. Die Kontaktkopie aus Maske und Angiogramm ergibt das Subtraktionsbild. Die Expositionszeit beträgt jetzt ca. 60".
Um dem Einwand zu begegnen, daß mit einer so einfachen Methode und Ausrüstung keine brauchbaren Resultate zu erzielen sind, seien folgende Beispiele demonstriert (Abb. 1–4).

Abschließend seien folgende Vorzüge der photographischen Subtraktion mit den jetzt zur Verfügung stehenden Filmen hervorgehoben:

Die Bildgüte bei der photographischen Subtraktion auch unter Verwendung maschinell verarbeitungsfähiger Filme ist der des elektronischen Verfahrens überlegen.
Der zeitliche Aufwand ist gering.
Der finanzielle Aufwand ist vergleichsweise minimal.
Die Dokumentation des Befundes bereitet keine Schwierigkeiten, da die Subtraktionskopie im Originalformat zur Verfügung steht.

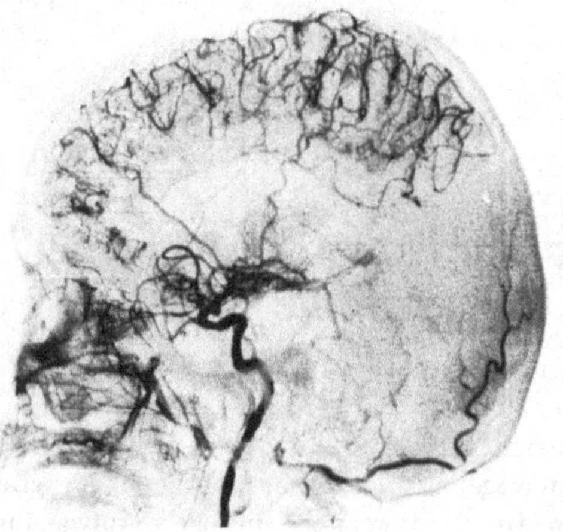

Abb. 1: Die auf photographischem Weg erzielte Subtraktionskopie vermittelt durch Auslöschung überlagernder Strukturen, die teilweise sehr kontrastreich sind, einen guten Einblick in Gefäßverläufe. Namentlich im Bereich der Orbita kommen Gefäßstrukturen zur Darstellung, die anhand des ‚normalen' Angiogramms nicht sicher beurteilt werden können.

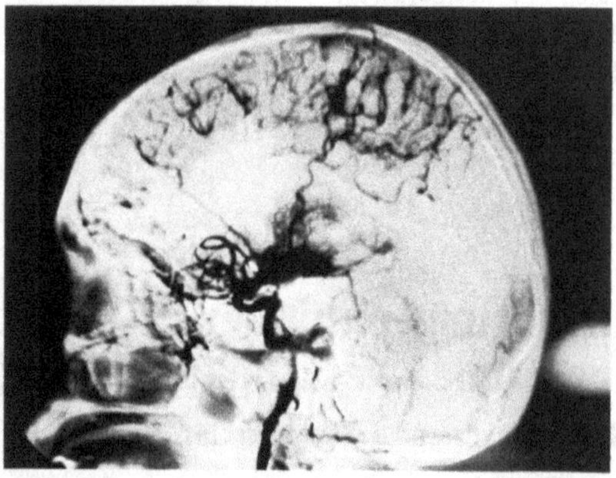

Abb. 2: Zum Vergleich die auf elektronischem Weg erzielte Subtraktionskopie. Feinere Gefäßstrukturen, insbesondere im Bereich der Orbita sind eindeutig schlechter wiedergegeben.

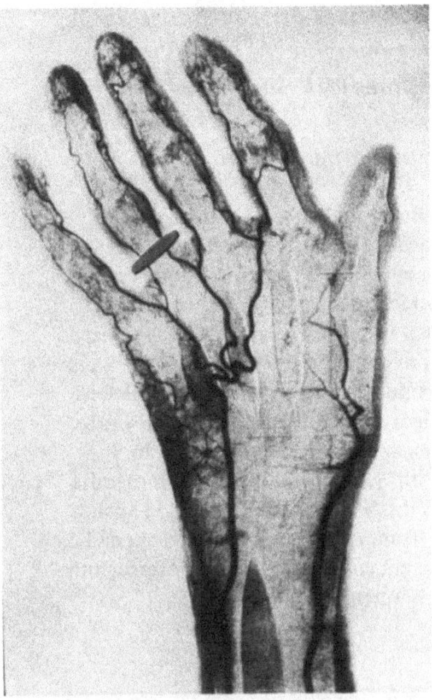

Abb. 3: Photographische Subtraktionskopie aus der arteriellen Phase einer Handarteriographie. Die Wiedergabe zeichnet sich durch eine hohe Detailerkennbarkeit auch im Bereich feinster Gefäßstrukturen aus.

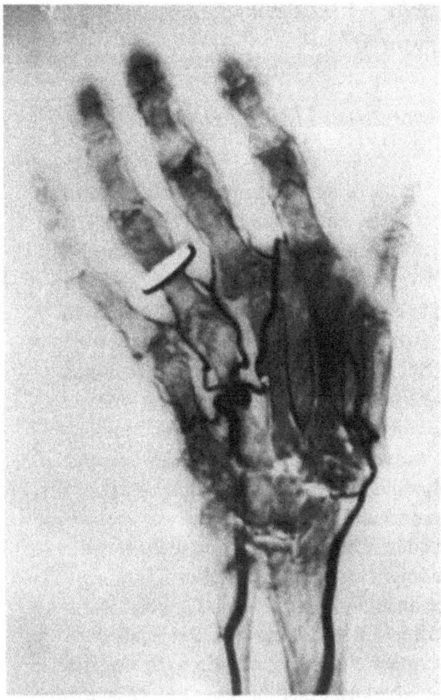

Abb. 4: Zum Vergleich das auf elektronischem Weg erzielte Subtraktionsbild. Die Überlegenheit der photographischen Subtraktionsmethode bei der Darstellung feiner und feinster Gefäßstrukturen kommt hier besonders zum Ausdruck.

Sicher sind noch technische Verbesserungen z. B. bei Lichtverteilung und Filmandruck notwendig, um optimale Ergebnisse zu erzielen; die einfache und schnelle Handhabung der beschriebenen Methode gestattet aber jetzt schon eine Anwendung auf breiter Basis.

Diskussionsbeitrag (E. Löhr) zum Vortrag

Zur Differentialdiagnose funktioneller und morphologischer Veränderungen am Gefäßbild der Hand

Von A. Wagner und Mitarbeitern, vorgetragen durch Dr. Jobst

Wurden die Untersuchungen in Narkose durchgeführt – und welches Kontrastmittel wurde verwendet? Es ist allgemein bekannt, daß auch ohne Pharmaka bei einer 2. distalen Gefäßangiographie eine Weiterstellung der Gefäße beobachtet wird, eine Reaktion, die wahrscheinlich durch lokale Veränderungen des Kontrastmittels selbst bewirkt werden. Es ist noch hinzuzufügen, daß bereits *Hettler*, ich glaube 1961, über die gefäßdilatierende Wirkung von Pharmaka bei seinen Untersuchungen im Rahmen der peripheren Beinarteriographie berichtet hat.

Angiographische Untersuchungen bei Aortenaneurysmen

Von V. Kammerer und Mitarbeitern

Sehr geehrter Herr Kollege *Kammerer*, wie Ihnen bekannt ist, berichteten bereits im Jahre 1968 *I. Steinberg* im Am. Journal of Roentgenology und auch wir in den „Fortschritten auf dem Gebiet der Röntgenstrahlen" über Ergebnisse der angiographischen Darstellungen von thorakalen und abdominalen Aneurysmen. Bei unseren eigenen Untersuchungen haben wir bei keinem Patienten Komplikationen gesehen. Auch hinsichtlich des fraglichen Druckanstieges sind von meinem Kollegen *Göbbeler* und mir diesbezügliche direkte Messungen im Aortenrohr bei thorakalen und abdominalen Aneurysmen vorgenommen worden. Der Druckanstieg während der Kontrastmittelinjektion geht nicht über 5 mm Hg heraus. Viel gefährlicher sind die häufig über Minuten anhaltenden erheblichen Senkungen des Systemdruckes, die wahrscheinlich durch die pathologisch veränderten Gefäßwandungen hervorgerufen werden. Bislang waren in Übereinstimmung mit den Untersuchungen von *Steinberg* die thorakalen Aneurysmen fast ausschließlich luetischer und die abdominalen arteriosklerotischer Genese. Die Notfalluntersuchungen haben hier jedoch eine Änderung des Patientengutes erbracht, so daß wir innerhalb von 6 Monaten 3 Patienten mit einem traumatischen thorakalen Aneurysma angiographisch untersucht haben. In diesem Zusammenhang weise ich auch auf die neuesten Untersuchungen von *Weinz* und Mitarbeitern hin.

Vergleichende Analyse der Ergebnisse der Vertebralis-Angiographie und der Pneumographie bei infratentoriellen Tumoren

Von F. Thun und Mitarbeitern

Ihre hohe Erfolgsquote bei der Aufdeckung von pathologischen Gefäßveränderungen des Vertebralis-Angiogrammes bei infratentoriellen Tumoren ist sehr aufschlußreich und ermutigend zugleich, da bekanntermaßen bisher die angiographische Diagnostik der Tumoren der hinteren Schädelgrube, wenn diese nicht eine durch ihre pathologischen Gefäße typische Konfiguration aufwiesen, sehr schwierig ist. Bislang war nur die Encephalographie in Verbindung auch mit Schichtuntersuchungen hier die Methode der Wahl. Wahrscheinlich werden auch besonders kleine Tumoren des Kleinhirnbrückenwinkels eher durch eine encephalographische Untersuchung erfaßt werden können.

Erfahrungen mit der Photosubtraktion unter Verwendung maschinell verarbeitungsfähiger Umkehrfilme

K. Rittmeier und Mitarbeiter

Ich möchte mir erlauben, Ihnen zu Ihren Erfahrungen mit der photographischen Subtraktion unter Verwendung der 90-Sekunden-Entwicklungsmaschine noch eigene Erfahrungen hinzuzufügen:
Wir haben gleich gute Erfahrungen mit dem Dupont-Kopierfilm gewonnen. Den Filmandruck von Maske und Kopie sowie die bessere gleichmäßige Belichtung kann man durch einen Lumoprint Kopiergerät erreichen, dessen Lichtstärke mit einem Potentiometer gesteuert wird. Eine diesbezügliche Mitteilung befindet sich bereits im Druck.

III. MIKROANGIOGRAPHIE

Technische Lösungen zur Abbildung kleiner Details im Röntgenbild

H. Woelke

Bei der Beurteilung der technischen Bildgüte einer Röntgenaufnahme werden in der Regel das Auflösungsvermögen des gesamten Abbildungssystems sowie der Kontrast als Kriterien herangezogen.
Es ist bekannt, daß diese beiden Komponenten vorhanden sein müssen, um dem menschlichen Auge die Wahrnehmbarkeit kleiner Details zu ermöglichen.
Es soll hier versucht werden aufzuzeigen, welche technischen Erfordernisse an die Aufnahmeapparatur gestellt werden, um die Darstellung kleiner Details bei angiographischen Aufnahmen zu gewährleisten. Mit der Definition des Begriffes – Detail – haben sich zahlreiche Autoren befaßt.
Zusammenfassend läßt sich sagen, daß unter einem Detail eine Einzelheit innerhalb eines interessierenden Objektbereiches verstanden wird. Dieses Detail wird z. B. durch seine Form, Größe, chemische Zusammensetzung im Verhältnis zur Umgebung und seinen Kantenübergang charakterisiert.
Bedingt durch die unterschiedlichen Charakteristika dieser Details bei den verschiedenen Fragestellungen, ist es notwendig, das Aufnahmesystem den jeweiligen Anforderungen anzupassen. Dieses wird besonders deutlich an einem Vergleich einer Aufnahmeapparatur für mikroradiographische Untersuchungen von histologischen Präparaten mit einem angiologischen Arbeitsplatz für Schnellserien-Aufnahmetechnik.
Welche Komponenten der Aufnahmeapparatur sind nun für die Abbildung kleiner Details von Bedeutung?

Strahlenquelle	------	– Brennfleckgröße – Leistung – Aufnahmespannung – (Strahlenqualität)
Objekt	------	– chem. Zusammensetzung – Größe – Dichte – Form – Bewegung
Geometrie	------	– Brennfleck-Film-Abstand – Objekt-Film-Abstand
Empfänger	------	– Empfindlichkeit – Signal-Rausch-Verhältnis – Gradation

Abb. 1: Einflußgrößen bei der Abbildung kleiner Details.

Die Optimierung dieser verschiedenen Größen für angiographische Aufnahmen ist einer systematischen Untersuchung eher zugänglich als für andere diagnostische Aufgaben, da die Form der darzustellenden Objekte, der Gefäße, relativ einfach in Phantomversuchen nachzubilden ist. Ferner sind die Eigenschaften des Kontrastmittels weitgehend bekannt.
Anhand eines Modellversuches soll demonstriert werden, welche wichtigen Erkenntnisse sich daraus für die Praxis ergeben. Ein 20 cm starkes Wasserphantom soll die Bedingungen einer Nierenangiographie hinsichtlich Absorption und Streuung erfüllen. Als Kontrastphantom werden kontrastmittelgefüllte Röhrchen mit unterschiedlichen Durchmessern verwendet. Zusätzlich wer-

den diese Röhrchen mit einer Geschwindigkeit von 10 mm pro sec quer zum Strahlengang bewegt. Die weiteren Aufnahmebedingungen entsprechen einer repräsentativen Anlage für Nierenangiographie, auf deren nähere Beschreibung hier verzichtet werden soll.

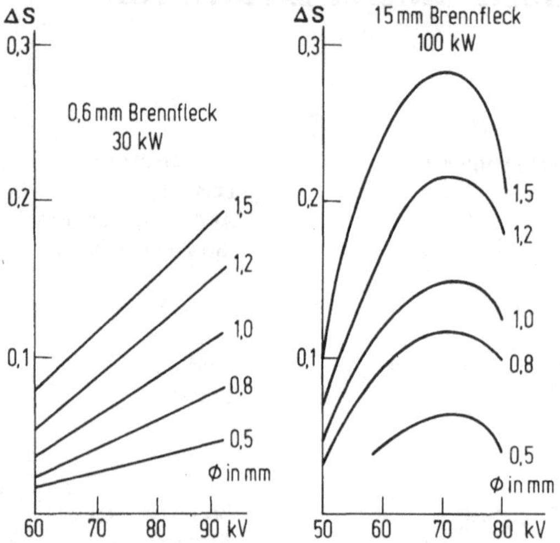

Abb. 2: Gefäßkontraste bei 20 cm Wasserphantom: KM Urografien 60 % Objektgeschwindigkeit 10 mm/s.

In diesem Diagramm sind die Gefäßkontraste in Abhängigkeit von der Aufnahmespannung aufgetragen. Erwartungsgemäß nehmen die Gefäßkontraste mit kleiner werdenden Durchmessern stark ab. In den unteren Spannungsbereichen nehmen die Belichtungszeiten zu, wodurch die Gefäßkontraste infolge der Verwischung durch die Objektbewegung absinken. Mit höheren Aufnahmespannungen und kürzeren Belichtungszeiten steigen die Kontraste an. Bei dem 0,6 mm Brennfleck ist in dem Spannungsbereich bis 90 kV kein Kontrastmaximum zu verzeichnen. Bei dem höher belastbarem 1,5 mm Brennfleck ist festzustellen, daß die Gefäßkontraste insgesamt höher sind als beim kleinen Brennfleck. Bei einer Aufnahmespannung von ungefähr 70 kV besitzen die Kontrastkurven ein Maximum und sinken mit zunehmender Spannung wieder ab. Diese Kontrastabnahme wird durch die hohe Aufnahmespannung verursacht. Die Bewegungsunschärfe ist hier nur noch von geringer Bedeutung, so daß sich diese Kurventeile mit Messungen am ruhenden Phantom decken müßten.

Diese Gefäßkontrastkurven verdeutlichen, daß für diese Untersuchung der große Brennfleck dem kleinen überlegen ist. Der kleine Brennfleck bietet nur dann Vorteile, wenn geringe Gefäßbewegungen zu erwarten sind, da sich die höhere

		(z. B. Nierenangiographie)
Brennfleck	– möglichst klein jedoch mit	– ca. 1,5 mm
Leistung	– hoher Leistung im	– ca. 1500 mA
Aufnahmespannung	– mittlerer Spannungsbereich	– ca. 70 kV
Aufnahmefrequenz	– entsprechend der Blutzirkulationsgeschwindigkeit	– max. 3 B/s
Aufnahmeanzahl	– entsprechend der Zirkulationsdauer	– ca. 10 Aufn.

Abb. 3: Forderungen an eine Röntgenröhre für Angiographie am Beispiel einer Nierenangiographie.

Abbildungsschärfe sonst nur bei relativ hohen Aufnahmespannungen auswirkt, die wegen des verminderten Bildkontrastes nicht empfohlen werden können.

Welche Forderungen lassen sich daraus an eine Röntgenröhre für die Darstellung kleiner bewegter Objekte ableiten?

Diese Forderungen, welche teilweise konträr zueinander stehen, werden durch technologische Grenzen eingeengt. Bei den Hochleistungsröhren stehen wärmetechnische Probleme im Vordergrund. Der Einsatz von Röntgenröhren mit Verbundanoden aus Wolfram-Molybdän ermöglichte eine Erweiterung der Leistungsgrenzen. Einen weiteren Schritt zur Leistungserhöhung von Röntgenröhren stellt die sogenannte Graphitanode dar. Der Anodenteller besteht dabei aus herkömmlichem Schwermetall. In engem Kontakt mit diesem befindet sich darunter ein weiterer Teller aus Graphit. Graphit zeichnet sich im Vergleich zu den konventionellen Materialien durch eine höhere Wärmespeicherfähigkeit, Wärmeleitfähigkeit und Wärmeabstrahlung aus.

Aufgrund dieser Eigenschaften ist eine Graphit-

anodenröhre im Mittel- und Langzeitbereich höher belastbar.
Die Bemühungen um eine Leistungserhöhung des Aufnahmesystems beschränken sich jedoch nicht nur auf die Strahlenerzeugerseite. Empfindlichere Verstärkerfolien und Filme, sowie eine bessere Abstimmung von Streustrahlenrastern leisten einen Beitrag zur Verbesserung der Empfängerseite.
Auch unter günstigsten Aufnahmebedingungen wird es eine durch das Film-Folien-System bedingte Grenze geben, unterhalb derer feine Objektstrukturen nicht mehr abgebildet werden können. Zur Überwindung dieser Grenze ist es erforderlich, die abzubildende Struktur so groß wie möglich auf den Film zu projizieren. Diese Vergrößerung kann durch Verschieben des Objektes gegen den Brennfleck erzielt werden. Bedingt durch die endliche Ausdehnung des Brennflecks treten dabei jedoch auch Halbschatteneffekte auf, die mit steigender Vergrößerung wachsen. Bei geringer Vergrößerung ist das Foliensystem die auflösungsbegrenzende Komponente. Mit steigender Vergrößerung beginnen sich die Rollen zu vertauschen. Jetzt begrenzen die Halbschatteneffekte des Brennflecks die Auflösung. Ein Maximum an Übertragungsfähigkeit wird etwa dann erreicht, wenn die Unschärfen der beiden Komponenten die gleiche Größenordnung besitzen.
Diese Erkenntnisse führten zur Anwendung noch kleinerer Brennflecke. Der 0,3 mm Brennfleck hat sich in der Vergrößerungstechnik bereits lange bewährt.
Von Untersuchungen mit noch kleineren Brennflecken, wie z. B. 0,1 mm und 50 μ wurde in den vergangenen Jahren berichtet.
Diese Brennflecke gestatten zwar eine hohe Auflösung, sind aber in ihrer Anwendbarkeit stark eingeengt. Die äußerst geringen Leistungen bedingen lange Belichtungszeiten bzw. hohe Aufnahmespannungen, so daß merkliche Vergrößerungen in der Angiographie nur an ruhenden oder sehr langsam bewegten Objekten sinnvoll sind.

Die Vergrößerungstechnik wird deshalb in der Herzangiographie ohne Bedeutung sein, wohl aber in der cerebralen und der Extremitäten-Angiographie. In der Nierenangiographie wird diese Technik nur dann einen Gewinn bringen, wenn sich die aufgenommenen Objekte nicht schneller als 2 mm pro sec bewegen.
Die Vergrößerungstechnik wird in der Regel bei schwieriger diagnostischer Deutung eng umschriebener Objektbereiche als ergänzende Untersuchungsmethode der konventionellen Untersuchung angeschlossen. Die gerätetechnische Ausrüstung sollte so ausgelegt sein, daß der Übergang von der einen zur anderen Technik möglichst komplikationslos sowohl für den Patienten als auch für das Personal vonstattengeht.
Dieses soll am Beispiel einer cerebralen Untersuchung demonstriert werden.
In Abb. 4 ist zunächst die Anordnung bei der üblichen 2-Ebenen-Aufnahmetechnik zu sehen. Der Patientenlagerungstisch sowie das Stativ des a. p.-Wechslers sind motorisch höhenverstellbar.

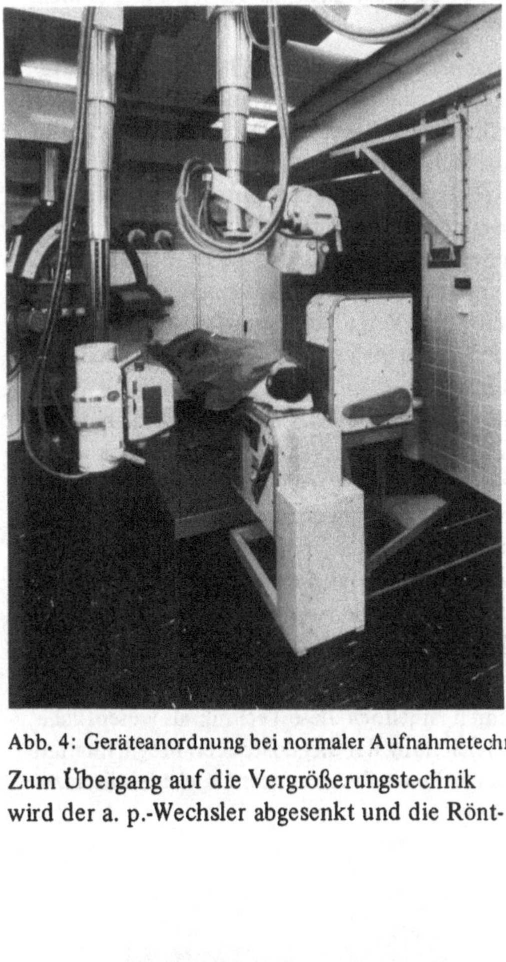

Abb. 4: Geräteanordnung bei normaler Aufnahmetechnik.

Zum Übergang auf die Vergrößerungstechnik wird der a. p.-Wechsler abgesenkt und die Rönt-

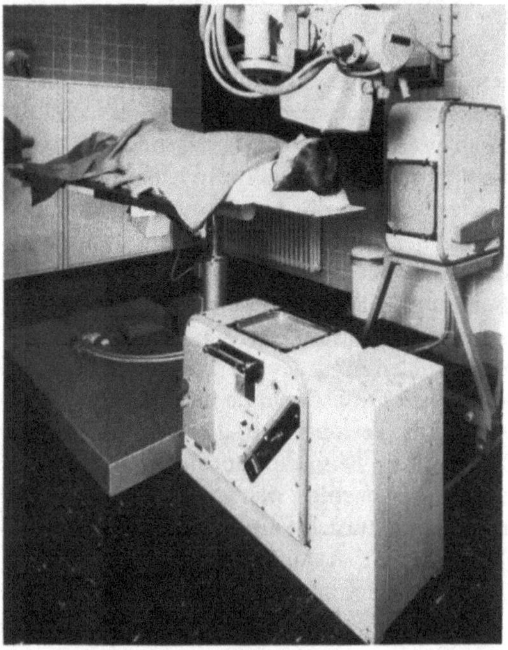

Abb. 5: Geräteanordnung für Vergrößerungsaufnahmetechnik.

genröhre erneut zentriert. Durch Anheben des Patienten kann eine Vergrößerung bis zum Vierfachen gewählt werden. Der große Objekt-Film-Abstand, der bei dieser Technik erforderlich ist, ermöglicht ein Arbeiten ohne Streustrahlenraster. Dadurch werden kürzere Belichtungszeiten bzw. geringere Aufnahmespannungen möglich. Bei Verwendung eines 0,1 mm großen Brennflecks und einem Vergrößerungsmaßstab von 3,5 lassen sich Gefäße bis zu einem Durchmesser von 60 μ abbilden.
Gegenüber der konventionellen Aufnahmetechnik ermöglicht die Vergrößerungstechnik unter gewissen Bedingungen einen beachtlichen Gewinn an Auflösungsvermögen. Die Anwendbarkeit dieser Technik in der Angiographie unterliegt jedoch erheblichen Beschränkungen, die durch die Eigenbewegung des abzubildenden Objektes bedingt sind.

Neben der Aufnahmetechnik mit Hochleistungsröhren ist jedoch diese Technik als wesentliche Bereicherung der diagnostischen Möglichkeiten bei der Beurteilung feinster Objektdetails anzusehen.

Zusammenfassung

Die Darstellung kleiner bewegter Details bei angiographischen Aufnahmen stellt hohe Leistungsanforderungen an das Aufnahmesystem. Einerseits wird ein möglichst kleiner Brennfleck gefordert, andererseits eine hohe Aufnahmeleistung.
Neue technologische Entwicklungen, wie z. B. die Graphitanodenröhre, ermöglichen eine Erweiterung der Leistungsgrenzen.
Zur Darstellung von Objektstrukturen, deren Größe unterhalb der Unschärfe der Verstärkerfolien liegt, wird die Vergrößerungstechnik angewendet.
Bedingt durch die dabei zu verwendenden kleinen und wenig belastbaren Brennflecke, beschränkt sich diese Technik jedoch nur auf die Darstellung ruhender oder wenig bewegter Objekte.
Bei Objekten mit einer Eigenbewegung von mehr als 2 mm/s ist die Vergrößerungstechnik der konventionellen Aufnahmetechnik mit Hochleistungsröhren unterlegen.

Technische Gesichtspunkte bei der Kurzzeitangiographie

K. Franke

Wir haben von Professor *Ecoiffier* in sehr eindrucksvoller Weise gezeigt bekommen, welchen medizinischen Erfolg man erzielen kann, wenn bei der Angiographie sehr kontrastreiche Röntgenaufnahmen erstellt werden. Dazu möchte ich einige Bemerkungen zur Technik und Aufnahmeunschärfe machen.

Bei der Beurteilung jeder Angiographie sind 3 Kriterien gegeben,

der Kontrast,
die kleinste Bewegungsunschärfe und
die hohe Detailerkennbarkeit.

Der hohe Kontrast soll durch eine möglichst niedrige Röhrenspannung, etwa 60–80 kV, erzielt werden. Selbstverständlich muß auch auf eine kleine Bewegungsunschärfe Wert gelegt werden.
Wissen wir doch, daß sich Gefäße in der Niere mit ca. 25 mm/sec bewegen; am Herzrand dagegen können Gefäßbewegungen bis über 100 mm/sec auftreten. Eine kleine Bewegungsunschärfe

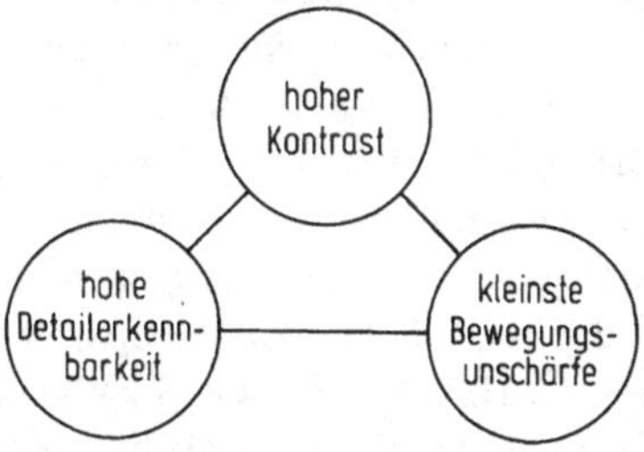

Abb. 1: Kriterien der Angiogramme.

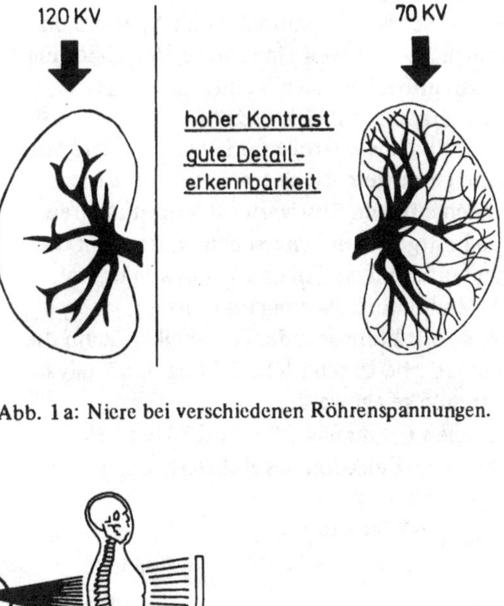

Abb. 1 a: Niere bei verschiedenen Röhrenspannungen.

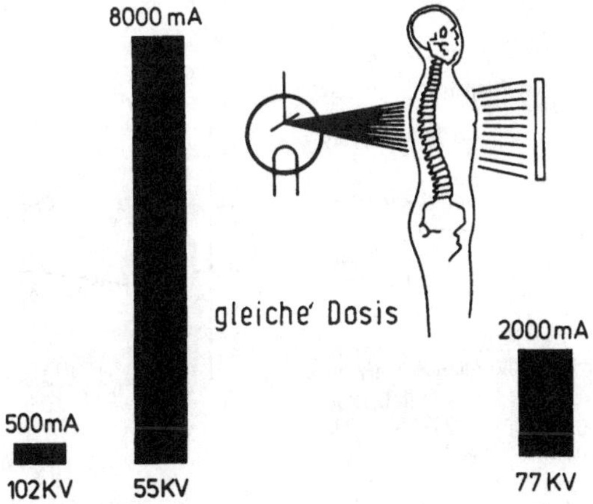

Abb. 1 b: Dosis und Röhrenleistung.

zu erzielen heißt aber, die im Brennfleck umzusetzende Leistung möglichst hoch zu wählen, um zu möglichst kurzer Belichtungszeit zu kommen.
Haben wir etwa gefunden, daß für eine kleine Bewegungsunschärfe 400 mA und 110 kV Röhrenleistung notwendig wären, so bräuchte man, um die gleiche kurze Belichtungszeit zu erzielen, die sagenhafte Zahl von 8 000 mA bei 55 kV. Eine solch starke Spannungsminderung ist also unmöglich. Ein riesenhaft großer Brennfleck wäre die Folge. Setzt man die Spannung dagegen von ca. 102 kV auf etwa 77 kV herab, so vergrößert sich, bei gleicher Belichtungszeit, der Strom von 500 mA auf nunmehr 2000 mA. Aufgrund dieser Stromerhöhung wird der Brennfleck etwa 1,8 × 1,8 mm^2 groß.
Für die Schärfe der Aufnahmen ist also zu untersuchen, inwieweit eine solche Vergrößerung des Brennfleckes einen Verlust an Detailerkennbarkeit mit sich bringt.
Wir wollen diese Größe für Niere und Herz analytisch ermitteln. Nach einer von den Vortragenden auf dem Stuttgarter Röntgenkongreß 1968 mitgeteilten Untersuchung, ist es für die hier vorliegenden Fälle nicht notwendig, mit der Modulationsübertragungsfunktion zu operieren. Mit hinreichender Genauigkeit kann die quadratische Unschärfebeziehung der Analyse zugrunde gelegt werden.
Sie sehen auf diesem Bild für die Niere die Unschärfe als Funktion des Röhrenstromes aufgetragen. Die Bewegungsgeschwindigkeit dieser Gefäße wurde zu 25 mm/sec angenommen.
Die obere Kurve gilt für eine Vergrößerung von v = 1,2, die untere für die eigentlich nur theoretisch mögliche Vergrößerung v = 1,1. Die bei dieser geringen Vergrößerung erzielte Verkleinerung der Unschärfe ist aber nicht sehr bedeutsam. Die geringste Unschärfe liegt bei ca. 3000 mA und 2,3 mm Brennfleckgröße. Etwa die gleiche Detailerkennbarkeit kann man bei ca. 2000 mA durch einen wesentlich kleineren Brennfleck, nämlich 1,8 × 1,8 mm^2 erreichen. Wir sehen an der oberen Kurve, daß das Unschärfeminimum bei etwa 2000 mA Röhrenstrom liegt.
Ganz anders sehen die Verhältnisse bei der Angiocardiographie mit Bewegungsgeschwindigkeiten von gut 100 mm/sec aus.

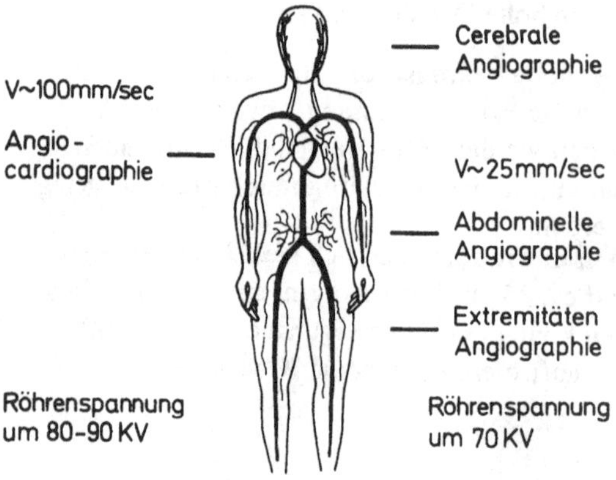

Abb. 2a: Organgeschwindigkeiten und Röhrenspannungen.

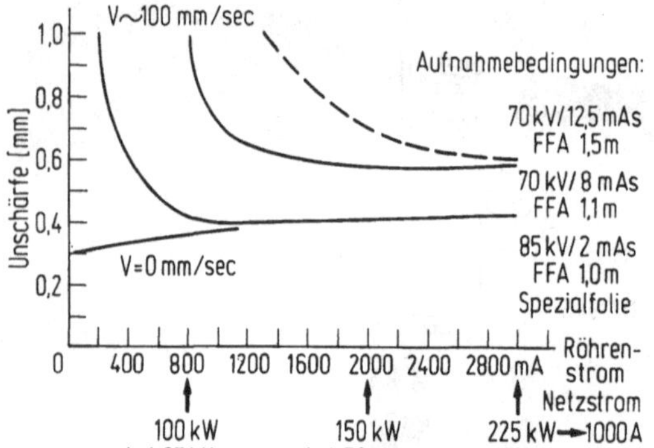

Abb. 2: Unschärfe und Röhrenströme bei Nierenaufnahmen.

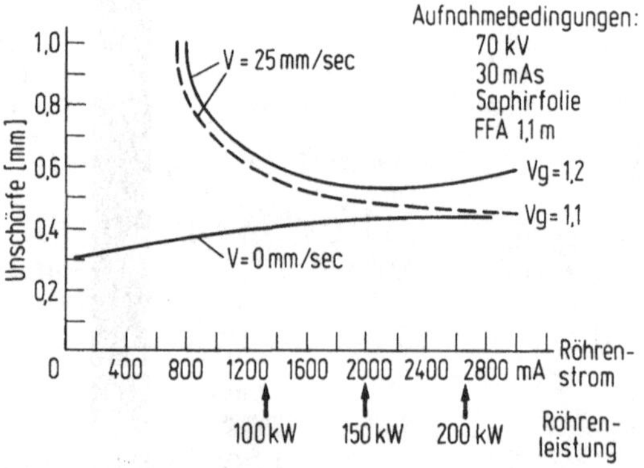

Abb. 2b: Unschärfe und Röhrenströme bei Herzaufnahmen.

Die oberste Kurve, bei ihr wurde ein Fokus-Filmabstand von 1,5 m zugrunde gelegt, zeigt, daß erst bei 3000 mA ein relativ kleiner Unschärfewert erreicht wird. Er liegt trotzdem noch zu hoch. Die Ursache dieser großen Unschärfe liegt in der bei 70 kV trotz der großen Milliamperezahl und des großen Abstandes noch erforderlichen hohen Belichtungszeit; sie beträgt nahezu 100 ms.

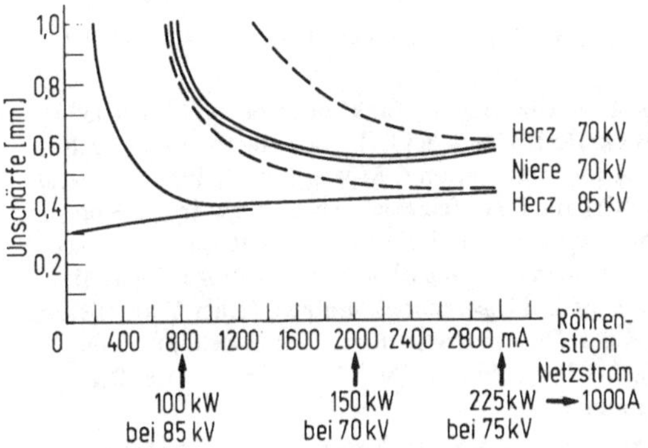

Abb. 2c: Unschärfe Herz, Niere.

Die Kurve links unten zeigt wesentlich bessere Ergebnisse. Die Unschärfe ist hier auf 0,4 mm herabgesunken, weil mit 800 mA ca. 80–90 kV, 1 m Abstand und etwa 20 ms gearbeitet wurde. Der Unschärfewert ist also gut 1/3 kleiner als die bei 3000 mA und 70 kV erreichbare Unschärfegröße.
Was kann man aus dem Gesagten für Folgerungen ziehen?

Sie sehen dies in den beiden letzten Bildern.

1. Bei Angiogrammen im Abdomenbereich, wo wir mit Gefäßgeschwindigkeiten in der Größenordnung von 25 mm/sec rechnen können, bietet die Weichstrahltechnik mit hohen Strömen unbestreitbare Vorteile.
Die Unschärfe verringert sich wesentlich bei Röhrenströmen bis zu 2000 mA. Darüber hinaus ist keine Unschärfeverringerung bemerkbar.

2. Bei Angiogrammen im Herzbereich empfiehlt es sich wegen der hohen Gefäßgeschwindigkeiten auf Spannungen um 80–90 kV zu gehen.

Radiologische Vergrößerungstechnik. Prinzip und Theorie

M. Pfeiler

Bei besonderen Ansprüchen an die Zeichenschärfe eines radiologischen Bildaufzeichnungssystems wird man feststellen, daß auch hochauflösende Film-Folien-Kombinationen noch unschärfebehaftet sind. Bei Abbildung einer dünnen Objektlinie ist nämlich eine endliche Breite ihres Bildes nicht zu unterschreiten, selbst wenn man die Linie im Objekt beliebig schmal macht. Die Bilder zweier benachbarter Linien im Objekt können deswegen zusammenlaufen; die Linien werden nicht mehr aufgelöst.

Nähern wir das Objekt dem hier als ideal punktförmig angenommenen Brennfleck, so wird das Objekt vergrößert abgebildet, d. h. der Abstand der beiden Objektlinien im Bild vergrößert sich. Im Gegensatz zur Normalaufnahme wird jetzt das Linienpaar aufgelöst.

Wir setzen nun anstelle des ideal punktförmigen Brennflecks einen realen Brennfleck endlicher Größe und verfolgen die von ihm ausgehenden und durch die benachbarten Objektschlitze tretenden Strahlen. Trotz Annahme einer ideal scharfzeichnenden Film-Folien-Kombination werden mit zunehmender Vergrößerung die Objektlinien zunehmend breiter abgebildet. Die Bilder der Schlitze können ineinander fließen.
Die endliche Brennfleckgröße steht also der Möglichkeit entgegen, mit Hilfe der Vergrößerungstechnik die Zeichenschärfe des gesam-

ten Aufnahmesystems über die der Film-Folien-Kombination hinaus beliebig zu steigern.

Die Übertragungsfunktion (Abb. 1) ist ein bewährtes Mittel, die resultierende Zeichenschärfe des Aufnahmesystems für verschiedene Brennfleckgrößen und Film-Folien-Kombinationen in Abhängigkeit von der Vergrößerung darzustellen. Man sieht sofort, daß für einen Brennfleck von 1 mm × 1 mm die Vergrößerungstechnik sinnwidrig ist. Der von der Übertragungsfunktion überdeckte Ortsfrequenzbereich oder die „Perioden pro mm" werden mit zunehmender Vergrößerung kleiner. Bei einem Brennfleck 0,3 mm × 0,3 mm erzielen wir bei Vergrößerungen bis etwa zu einem Faktor 2 eine Verbesserung der Zeichenschärfe. Bei höheren Vergrößerungen wird die Auflösung wieder schlechter. Mit einem 0,1 mm × 0,1 mm Brennfleck dagegen läßt sich die Zeichenschärfe weiter steigern.

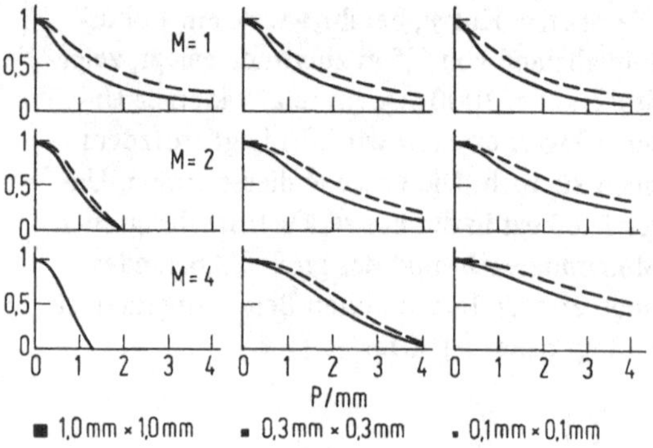

Abb. 1: Übertragungsfunktionen für verschiedene Brennfleckgrößen bei Gebrauch einer Universal-Film-Folien-Kombination („Spezial-Folie", durchgezogene Linie) und einer feinzeichnenden Film-Folien-Kombination („Rubin-Folie", gestrichelte Linie). Betrachtet werden die Fälle ohne Vergrößerung (M = 1, die oberen drei Diagramme), mit zweifacher Vergrößerung (M = 2, Diagramme in der mittleren Zeile) und vierfacher Vergrößerung (M = 4, die unteren drei Diagramme).

Abb. 2: Kontrastmittelgefülltes Schweinenierenpräparat. Das Präparat einschließlich einer 4 cm starken Plexiglasschicht zur Weichteil-Simulation wurde ohne und mit dreifacher Vergrößerung (Brennfleckgröße 0,1 mm × 0,1 mm, Spezial-Folie unter strenger Beibehaltung der Aufnahmeprojektion, also in beiden Fällen mit identischem Fokus-Objekt-Abstand aufgenommen. Die Vergrößerungsaufnahme zeigt z. B. in der Gefäßgabel (Pfeil) viel mehr Gefäße feinen Kalibers und die größeren Gefäße schärfer dargestellt als die normale Aufnahme ohne Vergrößerung. Ebenso aufschlußreich ist ein Vergleich der peripheren Gefäße.

Drei im Vortrag gezeigte cerebralangiographische Bilder nach *H. Hacker*, Johann Wolfgang von Goethe-Universität Frankfurt, können die Leistungsfähigkeit der Vergrößerungstechnik demonstrieren: zuerst die Normalaufnahme mit dem für die Vergrößerung vorgesehenen Feld, dann die photographische Nachvergrößerung dieses Feldes und schließlich die in der Auflösung verbesserte zweifache direkte Vergrößerung. Durch die Praxis bedingte unterschiedliche Projektion von Normalbild und Direktvergrößerung und die Möglichkeit unterschiedlicher Füllungsphasen können einen Vergleich unvollkommen erscheinen lassen. Ein exakter, wenn auch praxisferner Vergleich mit streng beibehaltener Projektion kann mit einer durch ein anatomisches Phantom gewährleisteten unveränderten Struktur durchgeführt werden. Aus dem Normalbild wird der Ausschnitt photographisch nachvergrößert, der auch von der mehr Daten zeigenden Direktvergrößerung erfaßt wird. Unter diesen Aufnahmebedingungen wurde ein Schweinenieren-Präparat angiographiert (Abb. 2): rechts die photographische Nachvergrößerung, links die dreifache direkte Vergrößerung, die mehr Gefäße sichtbar macht.
Es stehen also mit den Nenn-Abmessungen 0,3 mm X 0,3 mm (12 kW), 0,2 mm X 0,2 mm (6 kW) und 0,1 mm X 0,1 mm (3 kW) Fein- und Feinstbrennflecke zur Verfügung, mit denen man Vergrößerungsaufnahmen erzielen kann, die den Normalaufnahmen in der Darstellung feiner Details beachtlich überlegen sind. Ihre Anwendung wird jedoch dadurch stark eingeschränkt, daß mit abnehmender Brennfleckgröße naturgemäß die Strahlenbelastung der Röntgenröhre abnimmt und damit die für eine Aufnahme notwendigen Belichtungszeiten zunehmen. Betrachtungen auf der Basis der Übertragungsfunktion zeigen, daß ein durch die Vergrößerungstechnik erzielter Auflösungsgewinn durch die Bewegungsunschärfe zunichte gemacht wird, wenn die Objektbewegungen schneller als mit 5 mm/s erfolgen und wegen der Objektdicke Belichtungszeiten länger als 50 ms notwendig werden.

Deshalb ist eine Domäne der Vergrößerungstechnik die cerebrale Angiographie, bei der die Blutgefäße sich praktisch nicht bewegen und die Darstellung der Blutgefäße bis zu feinsten Verzweigungen für die Diagnose von Bedeutung ist. Bei den für die Angiographie wichtigen Aufnahmeserien sind bei den Feinstbrennflecken mit den relativ kleinen Strahlungsleistungen mehr Aufnahmen möglich als bei Normalbrennflecken. Der Feinstfokus mit einer Brennfleckgröße von 0,1 mm X 0,1 mm und 3 kW max. Strahlungsleistung erlaubt z. B. bei einer Bildfrequenz von 2 B/s Serien bis zu 50 Aufnahmen, wenn zwischen den Serien eine Pausenzeit von wenigstens 5 min liegt.

Abschließend sei unter Hinweis auf eine Einrichtung bei E. Zeitler, Aggertalklinik Engelskirchen, erwähnt, daß man mit verfügbaren flachen Filmwechslern (links in Abb. 3) Vergrößerungsaufnahmen auch in Sagittalrichtung anfertigen kann, ohne den Patienten mit Hilfe eines speziellen Untersuchungstisches in unbequeme Höhen zu heben.

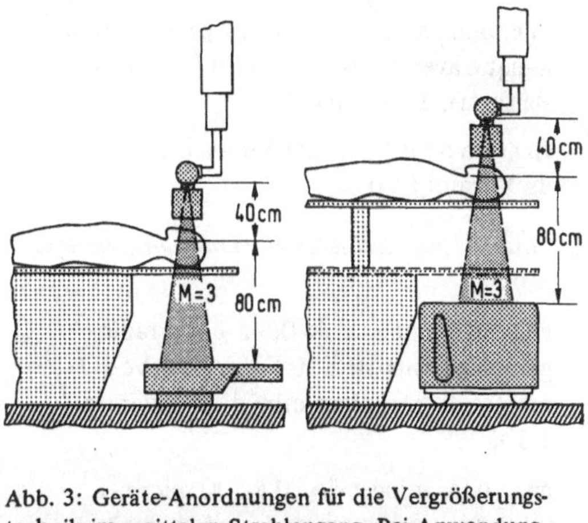

Abb. 3: Geräte-Anordnungen für die Vergrößerungstechnik im sagittalen Strahlengang. Bei Anwendung eines flachen, auf seinem Spezialstativ absenkbaren Filmwechslers (PUCK) braucht der Patientenlagerungstisch für den Übergang von normaler Aufnahmetechnik zur Vergrößerungstechnik (im Bild für dreifache Vergrößerung) nicht angehoben werden.

Confrontations microangiographiques et arteriographiques dans les Tumeurs du Rein

A. Pinet, F. Pinet, V. Tran-Minh et A. Clermont

La microangiographie sur pièces de néphrectomie est une technique de recherche très précise qui objective les plus fines modifications de la vascularisation du rein.
19 tumeurs malignes du rein inventoriées par artériographie pré-opératoire ont été étudiées par microangiographie de la pièce opératoire.

La confrontation de l'artériographie pré-opératoire, de la coupe anatomique et de la microangiographie incite à considérer avec beaucoup de modestie les résultats actuels de l'artériographie et à tout mettre en oeuvre pour les améliorer.

Technique de microangiographie

Elle comporte plusieurs temps:

1. Préparation du rein

- injection lente du rein à une pression physiologique avec du Micropaque (Sulfate de Baryum), dilué à 10%'
- fixation de la pièce pendant 2 à 3 jours dans du Formol à 10%.

2. Coupes longitudinales du rein et microangiographie

- en coupes épaisses de 0,5 à 1 cm, radiographiées sous 10 à 20 KV avec tube à fenêtre de béryllium mini d'un foyer de 1,5 X 1,5.
- en coupes minces de 10 à 500 microns, microradiographiées dans une chambre à vide sous 3 à 7 KV, avec un tube à fenêtre de béryllium de foyer 0,3 X 0,3, à courte distance focale.
  Les films sont à haute résolution.

Resultats

La microangiographie retrouve dans les tumeurs malignes hypervascularisées la désorganisation artérielle, les irrégularités de calibre des vaisseaux, les lacs sanguins néoformés, mais son intérêt est beaucoup plus grand dans les tumeurs hypovascularisées.

3 constatations ont été faites:

1. La tumeur au point de vue anatomique et microangiographique est toujours plus volumineuse que ne le laisse supposer l'artériographie.

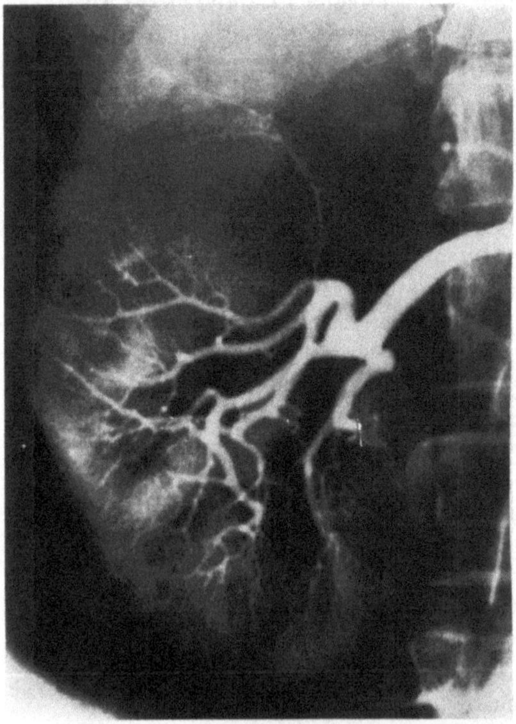

Fig. 1: Femme âgée de 58 ans. Hypertension isolée.
Artériographie: Tumeur maligne hypovascularisée du pôle supérieur du rein droit.

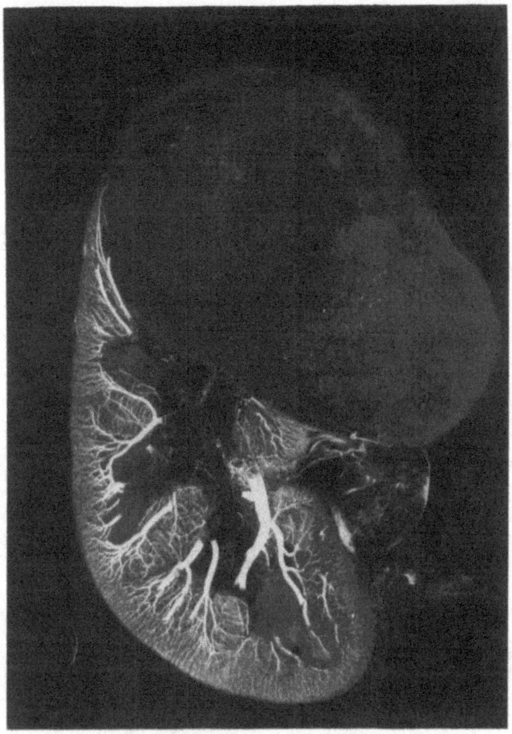

Fig. 2: Même malade que fig. 1.
Microangiographie: Tumeur volumineuse du pôle supérieur avec capillaires néoformés au sein de la masse tumorale nécrosée.

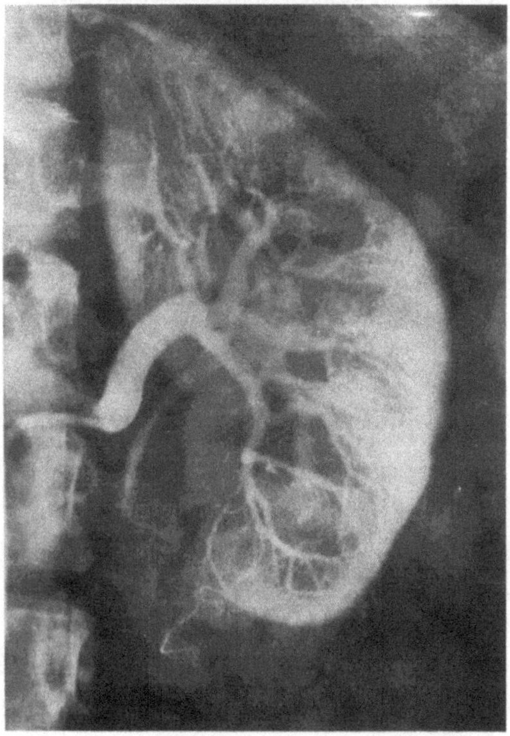

Fig. 3: Femme de 29 ans. Douleurs lombaires vagues. Pôle inférieur du rein gauche suspect à l'U.I.V.
Artériographie: Artères anormales, irrégulières au pôle inférieur gauche.

2. Il y a toujours plus de vascularisation sur les microangiographies que sur l'artériographie.
3. Il n'y a pas de tumeur maligne sans vascularisation anarchique. Même dans les tumeurs nécrosées, apparemment avasculaires il y a toujours présence de vaisseaux néoformés en périphérie qui permettent d'affirmer la malignité et qu'il faut s'appliquer à mettre en évidence en angiographie in vivo.

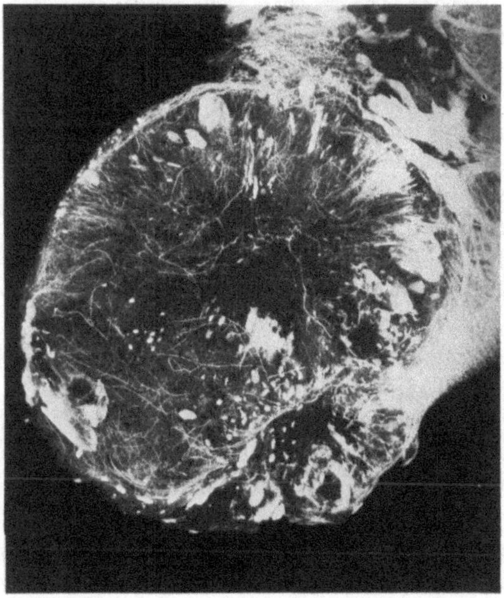

Fig. 4: Même malade que fig. 3.
Microangiographie: coupe de 1 cm.
Noter l'abondante vascularisation intra-tumorale.
Histo: Néphroblastome.

Ces constatations ont *une incidence pratique.*

L'artériographie in vivo telle qu'elle est pratiquée actuellement ne montre qu'une partie de la néovascularisation.
Aussi il faut s'attacher à améliorer la qualité de l'artériographie:

- par l'augmentation de la quantité de produit de contraste en injection sélective.
- par l'usage de produits pharmacodynamiques qui mettent en évidence les artères anormales
- par la recherche d'une meilleure définition radiologique et le recours à l'agrandissement angiographique direct au foyer fin (0,3).

Resumé

A propos de 19 confrontations artériographiques pré-opératoires, anatomiques, et microangiographiques de tumeurs malignes du rein, les auteurs ont observé que l'artériographie ne montrait qu'une faible partie de la vascularisation tumorale, que dans les tumeurs apparemment avasculaires il existait toujours des vaisseaux néoformés.
Ils concluent donc à la nécessité d'améliorer la qualité de l'artériographie, d'utiliser de plus fortes quantités de produit de contraste en injection sélective et avec des substances pharmaco-dynamiques, enfin de recourir à l'agrandissement angiographique direct au foyer fin (0,3).

Die Nierenangiographie mit variabler Röntgenvergrößerung

H. Schreyer und K. Amplatz

Die Abklärung von krankhaften Prozessen der Gefäßperipherie der Niere wie auch der röntgenologische Tumornachweis im Bereiche dieses Organes macht die angiographische Darstellung kleiner Blutgefäße notwendig. Die Beurteilung derartiger kleiner Gefäße wird durch Kombination der Angiographie mit der direkten Röntgenvergrößerung verbessert. Bei der herkömmlichen Methode der direkten Röntgenvergrößerung dient der als Folge des großen Objekt-Film-Abstandes entstehende große „Objekt-Film-Raum" dazu, die Streustrahlung zu eliminieren. Aus diesem Grunde werden bei dieser Vergrößerungstechnik keine Raster verwendet. Liegt das zu vergrößernde Organ in einer Körperregion mit großem Querschnitt, muß als Folge davon der Raum zwischen Objekt und Film entsprechend groß dimensioniert sein, um die Streustrahlung zur Erzielung einer guten Bildqualität auf ein entsprechendes Ausmaß zu reduzieren. Dadurch werden die für die Vergrößerung verwendeten geometrischen Verhältnisse von der streustrahleneliminierenden Funktion des „Objekt-Film-Raumes" und damit vom Objekt-Film-Abstand abhängig. Das Vergrößerungssystem ist dadurch wenig flexibel. Die Erzeugung von relativ kleinen Vergrößerungen zwischen 1 : 1,5 und 1 : 1,8, wie sie bei der Verwendung eines 0,3 mm großen Brennfleckes zusammen mit einer hoch verstärkenden Folienkombination die beste Bildauflösung ergeben, wird schwierig. Ein weiterer Nachteil dieser Technik besteht darin, daß eine organgerechte Vergrößerung meist nicht möglich ist, d. h., in einem zweiten oder dritten Aufnahmeverfahren muß die röntgenologisch verdächtige Region zusätzlich herausvergrößert werden, was eine entsprechend häufige Wiederholung der Angiographie notwendig macht. Verwendet man jedoch neben dem für die Vergrößerung notwendigen größeren Objekt-Film-Abstand zur Streustrahleneliminierung zusätzlich einen Raster, werden die zur Vergrößerung verwendeten Abstandverhältnisse von der streustrahlenreduzierenden Funktion des Raumes zwischen Objekt und Film und damit von dem dafür notwendigen großen Objekt-Film-Abstand unabhängig. Dadurch wird die Vergrößerung variabel, d. h., bei Verwendung von entsprechenden Geräten können verschiedene Objektvergrößerungen erzeugt werden. Der Vorteil dieser Methode besteht darin, daß eine optimale dem Fokus und der Folien-Film-Kombination angepaßte Vergrößerung, die bei Verwendung eines 0,3 mm Fokus und einer hochverstärkenden Folien-Film-Kombination zwischen 1,5 und 2 liegt, leicht erzielt werden kann. Weiters ist eine organgerechte Vergrößerung, die bei der Niere von besonderer Bedeutung ist, möglich, d. h., die gesamte Niere kann primär mit einer Kontrastmittelinjektion vergrößert dargestellt werden, ohne daß in zusätzlichen Untersuchungsgängen einzelne Abschnitte herausvergrößert werden müssen.

An der Universitätsklinik für Radiologie in Graz werden Vergrößerungsangiographien der Nieren unter Verwendung des ATT3-Tisches und des Mimer3 durchgeführt. Der ATT3-Tisch (Accident Transport Table) ist ein für den Transport von Verletzten entwickeltes Gerät. Er eignet sich deshalb zur Vergrößerungsangiographie, da die Höhe seiner Tischplatte um 40 cm verstellbar ist. Die Verwendung des Mimer3 ist vorteilhaft, da sein Bildverstärker in Untertischposition gebracht werden kann. Durch die Mechanik des Gerätes ist der primäre Leuchtschirm des Bildverstärkers in Höhe der Filmebene einstellbar. Dadurch läßt sich die gewünschte Vergrößerung der Niere unter Durchleuchtungskontrolle auf dem Fernsehschirm durch entsprechendes Anheben der Tischplatte unter Sicht einstellen. Die bei der Vergrößerungsangiographie besonders wichtige Ausblendung auf das Organ wird durch diese technische Hilfe erleichtert, da die Begrenzung der Niere durch den nach einer Testinjektion von Kontrastmittel auftretenden nephrographischen Effekt deutlich ist, oder zumindest die Aufteilung der Nierenarterie im Bereiche des Hilus als Beziehungspunkt für die Bildeinstellung verwendet werden kann. Nach der Einblendung auf Objekt wird der Bildverstärker ausgeschwenkt und der Blattfilmwechsler in Aufnahmeposition geschoben. Bei der Verwendung dieser Geräte ergeben sich folgend3 Abstandsverhältnisse: Fokus-Film-Abstand: 70 cm – 100 cm. Bezogen auf die Niere als Objektebene läßt sich der Objekt-Film-Abstand jede beliebige Vergrößerung bis zu einem maximalen Wert von 1 : 2 erzeugt werden kann (Abb. 1). Als Raster wird der serienmäßig im Blattfilmwechsler eingebaute, auf 105 cm fokusierte 8 : 1 Raster verwendet. Folien: Siemens-Spezialfolien. Röntgen filme: Ilford-Red

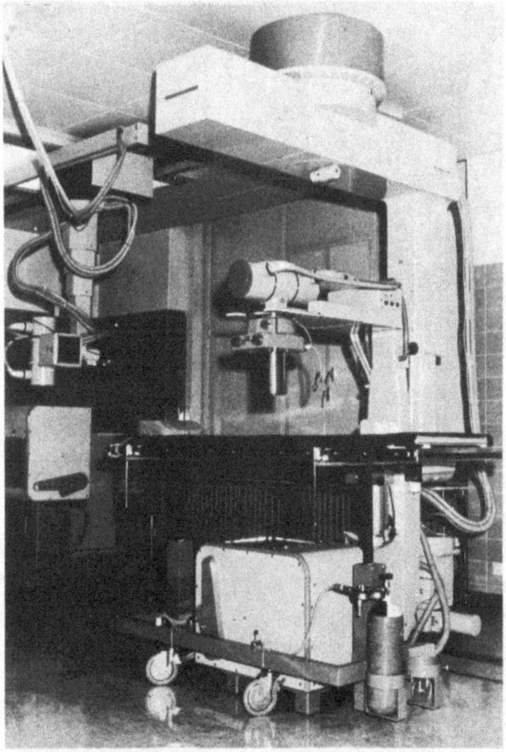

Abb. 1: Kombination des ATT3-Tisches und des Mimer3 zur Durchführung von Serienvergrößerungsangiographien der Niere. Die Tischplatte des ATT3-Tisches ist maximal angehoben. Die dadurch entstehende Aufnahmegeometrie ermöglicht Vergrößerungen von 1 : 2.

Seal, Kodak RPR. Maschinelle Filmentwicklung. Röntgengenerator: Siemens-Gigantos. Röntgenröhre: Biangulix, 0,3 mm Brennfleck mit 12 kW in 0,1 Sek. belastbar. Die Anwendung von Röntgenaufnahmeserien bis zu 2 Bildern pro sek. ist möglich.Bei adipösen Patienten wird die Bildfrequenz auf ein B9ld pro sek. reduziert, wodurch höhere mAs-Werte erreichbar sind. Wird die Aufnahmeserie mit einer auf einem Deckenstativ montierten Röhre durchgeführt, stehen, durch Verkleinerung des Fokus-Film-Abstandes auf 60 cm – 80 cm, für die Vergrößerungsangiographie günstigere Belichtungsdaten zur Verfügung. Die durch die Verkleinerung des Fokus-Film-Abstandes bedingte Defokusierung bewirkt bei dem verwendeten Raster noch keine Streifenbildung oder einen merkbaren Dosisabfall, wenn mit exakter Zentrierung und Einblendung auf das Objekt gearbeitet wird. Der Patient wird auf dem ATT-3-Tisch über dem Blattfilmwechsler geschoben, ohne daß eine Umlagerung notwendig ist. Mit den beschriebenen Geräten sind Vergrößerungsangiographien der Niere im täglichen Routinebetrieb durchfürhbar. Hierbei bringt die bessere Bildauflösung nicht nur Vorteile bei der Beurteilung kleiner Nierengefäße, sondern es kommen auch kleine Parenchymläsionen während des nephrographischen Effektes besser zur Darstellung. Hauptanwendungsgebiete der Vergrößerungsangiographie der Niere sind:

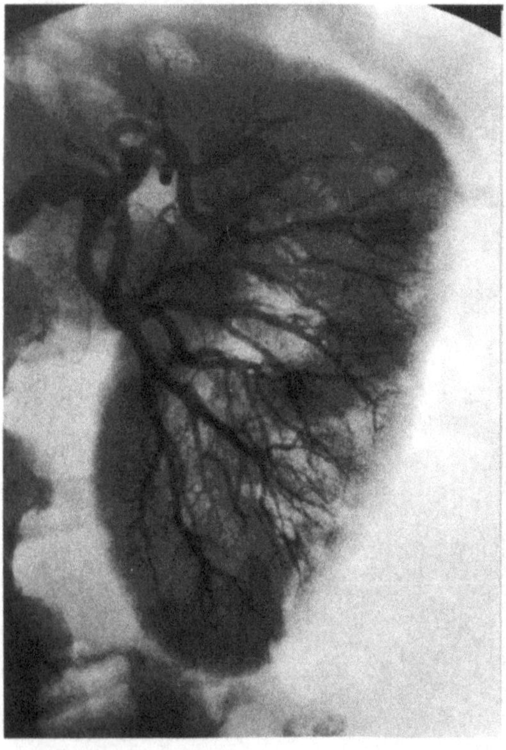

Abb. 2: Maligne Nephrosklerose der Niere bei Hypertonie infolge Nierenarterienstenose durch fibro-muskuläre Hyperplasie. Deutliche Kaliberschwankungen der kleinen Gefäße, sowie vereinzelte Gefäßabbrüche (Vergrößerung 1 : 2).

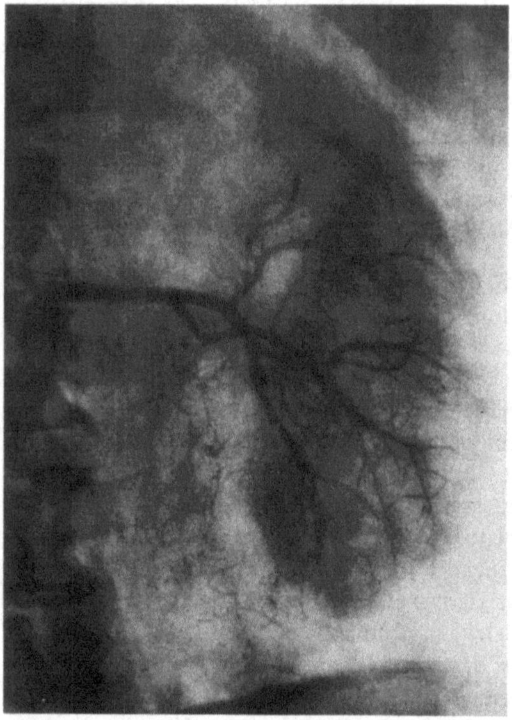

Abb. 3: Selektive Nierenarteriographie: Spreizung der intrarenalen Gefäße, sowie mäßige Rarifizierung derselben. Verdünnung des Parenchymmantels. Multiple unregelmäßig geschlängelte zarte Gefäße von unterschiedlichem Kaliber in der Region des Nierenbeckens bis zum unteren Nierenpol reichend (infiltrierend in die Umgebung einwachsendes Nierenbeckenkarzinom, Hydronephrose). (Vergrößerung 1 : 2).

1. Der Nachweis von primären und sekundären Erkrankungen der kleinen Nierengefäße (Abb. 2). 2. Die Diagnostik von entzündlich-destruierenden Nierenparenchymprozessen. 3. Der angiographische Nachweis von Abstoßungsreaktionen bei transplantierten Nieren. 4. Die Tumordiagnostik der Nieren (Abb. 3). Die verbesserte Detailerkennbarkeit auf den mit der beschriebenen Technik angefertigten Angiogrammen wird nicht nur durch die Objektvergrößerung, sondern auch durch die Verwendung des feinzeichnenden Fokus und die besonders wirksame Streustrahleneliminierung als Folge der Kombination eines Rasters mit einem größeren Objekt-Film-Abstand bewirkt, was auf Aufnahmen mit geringerer Vergrößerung von etwa 1 : 1,5 augenscheinlich wird. Die Vergrößerungsangiographie der Nieren sollte daher routinemäßig durchgeführt werden.

Möglichkeiten der Vergrößerungsangiographie am Körperstamm und den Extremitäten

E. Zeitler und D. Henninges

Voraussetzung für Vergrößerungsaufnahmen, die eine bessere Detailerkennbarkeit und einen Zuwachs an Information bringen können, ist die Verwendung eines Focus mit einer kleineren Kantenlänge als 0,20 mm. Wir haben Erfahrungen mit einer Mikrofokusröhre der Firma Siemens mit einem Focus von 0,1 bzw. 0,2 mm und einer Leistungsfähigkeit von 3 bzw. 5 kW bei 100 kV. Während für Einzelvergrößerungsaufnahmen eine ausreichende Belichtungszeit unabhängig von der Objektdicke möglich ist, sind für die Serienangiographie Belichtungszeiten von 0,16 sec und bei niedrigen kV bis 0,64 sec für eine ausreichende Belichtung gelegentlich zu lang. Bei großer Eigenbewegung des aufzunehmenden Objektes und der besonderen Objektdicke am Körperstamm ist die Aufnahmefrequenz von 1–2 Bildern pro Sekunde am geeignetsten.

Die technischen Möglichkeiten zur Vergrößerungs-Serienangiographie erfordern einen verkleinerten Fokus-Film-Abstand, damit eine genügende Dosis für die Bildgebung erzielt wird. Der Fokus-Filmabstand beträgt in den meisten Fällen 80, 90 oder 120 cm in Abhängigkeit von der gewünschten Vergrößerung. Für laterale Projektion bestehen die geringsten Schwierigkeiten bei der Vergrößerung des Objekt-Filmabstandes; bei frontalem Strahlengang ist entweder eine Erhöhung des Angiographietisches erforderlich, oder man lagert den Patienten lateral, und letztlich kann man auch einen Puck-Wechsler mit automatischer Höhenverstellung verwenden.

Vor dem Einsatz des Puck-Wechslers mit der Höhenverstellung war die Vergrößerungsangiographie von Oberbauchorganen nur als Einzelaufnahme möglich. Hierfür genügt es, eine Kassette in gegügendem Abstand unter dem Angiographietisch zu plazieren. Für die Serienangiographie mit Vergrößerungstechnik bestehen an Händen und Füßen gleich gute oder bessere Bedingungen als im Bereich der Hirnangiographie. Als Eigenbewegung kommt hier nur die Bewegung des Kontrastmittels im Gefäß zur Wirkung, und die Objektdicke ist für die Leistungsfähigkeit des Mikrofokus bei der Serienangiographie sehr günstig. Sicher sind Tumoren an Extremitäten selten, bei denen die Differentialdiagnose durch den Nachweis pathologischer Gefäße wichtig ist. Aber auch im Rahmen der Früherkennung und Differential-

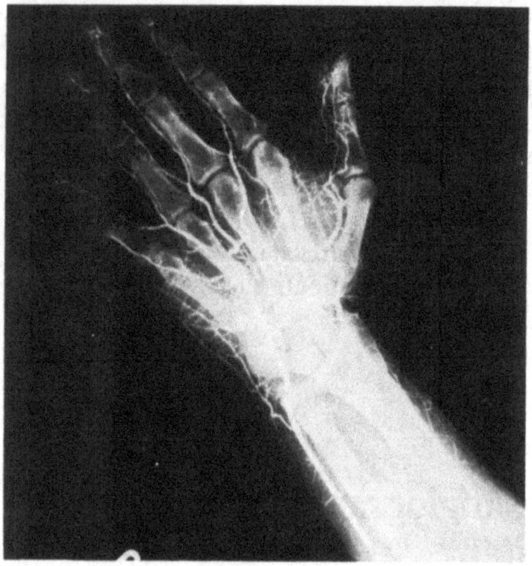

Abb. 1

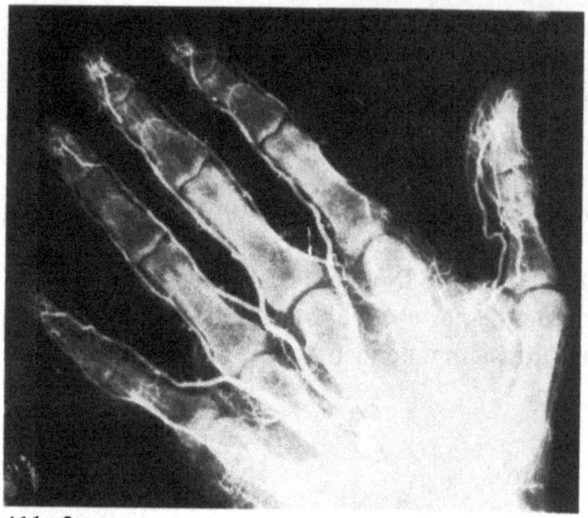

Abb. 2

diagnose der funktionellen und organischen Gefäßerkrankungen kann durch die Vergrößerungsangiographie eine differenziertere Analyse erfolgen, wie wir bisher in 75 Fällen gesehen haben.
Besonders bei dem Verdacht auf eine Thrombangiitis obliterans schafft die Vergrößerungsangiographie die Möglichkeit zur Frühdiagnose. Auch für die Diagnostik von Angiolopathien kann, wie die vergleichenden Aufnahmen von Fingerangiogrammen zeigen (Abb. 1 und 2), die direkte radiologische Vergrößerungsangiographie differenzierter einen Beitrag leisten, als die photographische Nachvergrößerung primär unvergrößerter Aufnahmen, obwohl der gleiche Mikrofokus hierfür verwendet wurde.
Die Bedeutung der Vergrößerungsangiographie mit Vergrößerungsfaktoren von 2 : 1 bis 4 : 1 besteht sicher nur in der Ergänzung zu Angiographien unter Standardbedingungen. Sie hat besondere Bedeutung beim Nachweis von Veränderungen an kleinen Gefäßen – also bei der Arteriosklerose und der Periarteriitis nodosa sowie bei tumorbedingten Veränderungen.
Unter diesem Gesichtspunkt ist besonders die Angiographie von Nieren, Pankreas und Magen eine Möglichkeit, die bisher möglichen Informationen bei der Tumordiagnostik zu verbessern.

Die Vergleiche von direkten radiologischen postmortalen Vergrößerungsangiogrammen mit photographischen Vergrößerungen zeigen deutlich Details, die ohne radiologische Vergrößerung nicht erkennbar waren.

Organ	Injektion	Fragestellung
Leber	Coeliaca	
Pankreas		Tumorgefässe
Magen		Tumorarrossion
Milz		Blutung
	Mesentericae	
Darm		
Niere	Renalis	Periarteriitis nodosa
Nebenniere	Phrenica ascendens	Arteriosklerose
Lunge	Bronchialis	
Nebenschilddrüse	Subclavia	
Schilddrüse		
Schädel	Carotis	
Gehirn	"	
	Vertebralis	
Spinalkanal	" intercostalis	
	Lumbalis	
Hände	Brachialis	Periphere Obliterationen
Füsse	Femoralis	+ Emboli

Abb. 3

Die Einsatzmöglichkeiten sind bei guten technischen Lösungen auch am Körperstamm und an den Extremitäten vielfältig (Abb. 3) und ihre Ergebnisse oft recht eindeutig. Wünschenswert ist die Entwicklung von Mikrofokusröhren mit noch höherer Belastbarkeit.

Mikroangiographische Untersuchungen über die zerebrale Ischämie und ihre klinischen Merkmale

M. Collard

Ins Deutsche übertragen von Dr. med. C. Scholten, Salzgitter-Ringelheim

Der tatsächliche Anteil der Arteriopathie an den psychischen Störungen des alten Menschen ist im Anfangsstadium ebenso schwierig festzustellen wie im Endstadium. Die quantitative Beurteilung der Kreislaufstörungen ist in vivo nur mit bestimmten Verfahren möglich, welche zwar diagnostische Aufschlüsse über die Arteriopathie geben, ohne aber deren Bedeutung für das Zustandsbild nachzuweisen. Psychische Störungen werden nicht selten einer herabgesetzten zerebralen Durchblutung zugeschrieben, obwohl sie in Wirklichkeit auf einer spezifischen Degeneration des Hirngewebes beruhen.

Die Darstellung des distalen arteriolären Gefäßnetzes mittels Arteriographie der Karotiden oder der Arteria vertebralis ist noch immer recht schwierig, selbst wenn die neuen angiographischen Verfahren mit direkter Vergrößerung verwendet werden. Dennoch ist die Untersuchung der Karotiden, der Vertebralarterien sowie des Zustandes der intrakraniellen Gefäße unerläßlich, um etwaige Beziehungen zwischen einer kortikalen Ischämie und Veränderungen an den großen Gefäßen nachzuweisen. Weiterhin vermag die Angiographie auch direkte Hinweise auf Kreislaufstörungen zu geben, je nach dem chronologischen Ablauf der einzelnen Phasen der Untersuchung.

Die intrakarotidiale Injektion bestimmter Radio-Isotopen (markierte Proteine, Xenon) vervollständigt die Untersuchung von Kreislaufstörungen in vivo; hierbei wird lediglich die Verringerung des Blutstromes nachgewiesen, ohne speziellen Hinweis, ob diese auf einer arteriellen Gefäßschädigung oder einer kortikalen Arteriolosklerose beruht.

Die vorliegende Arbeit bezieht sich auf mikroangiographische Untersuchungen an 54 Gehirnen von Patienten in verschiedenen Stadien der senilen Demenz; diese wurden aus 88 Fällen aufgrund technischer Kriterien ausgewählt. Die mikroangiographischen Befunde wurden mit den diagnostischen Ergebnissen der angiographischen und Isotopen-Untersuchungen in vivo verglichen.

Methodik

a. postmortal

Post mortem wird ein Katheter in die Karotiden und die Vertebralarterien eingeführt; unter moduliertem Druck wird sodann ins Gehirn eine Kontrastmittel-Suspension injiziert. Diese besteht aus einer Mischung von Bariumsulfat (Mikrotrast), Agar-Agar und 10%igem Formalin. Die Injektion erfolgt mit einer Vorrichtung, welche den Wechsel von systolischem und diastolischem Druck in vivo simuliert, um eventuelle Extravasate zu vermeiden. Im Laufe der Injektion werden standardisierte Röntgenaufnahmen gemacht, um die Vorgänge bei der fortschreitenden intrakraniellen Kontrastdarstellung genau zu verfolgen. Anschließend wird das Gehirn in parallele Schnitte von 3 mm Dicke zerlegt und mikroradiographische Aufnahmen auf einem Film mit hohem Auflösungsvermögen angefertigt (Micronmask Agfa-Gevaert).

Mittels der Mikrodensitometrie läßt sich die Vaskularisierung einer Hirnwindung durch Berechnung des Verhältnisses zwischen den strahlendurchlässigen Bezirken und dem kontrastgefüllten arteriolo-kapillären Netz bestimmen.

b. in vivo

Die Prüfung der Hirnfunktion wird mittels EEG, Rheographie, Angiographie und Isotopenuntersuchungen durchgeführt (bikompartimentale Methode); hierdurch wird die gleichzeitige Untersuchung der grauen und der weißen Substanz ermöglicht.
Für diese Untersuchungen wurden die Patienten in drei Gruppen eingeteilt:

1. Patienten ohne klinische oder sonstige Anzeichen einer zerebralen Gefäßerkrankung.
2. Patienten mit zerebralen Kreislaufstörungen und leichteren Verhaltensstörungen.
3. Patienten mit ausgeprägter Arteriosklerose und seniler Demenz.

Ergebnisse

Aus den mikroangiographischen Untersuchungen wurden diejenigen Fälle ausgewählt, welche eine gleichmäßige Auffüllung des arteriolo-kapillären Netzes ohne Artefaktbildung aufweisen (54 von 88).
Die mikroangiographische Symptomatologie der Arteriolosklerose entspricht derjenigen, welche in vivo an den Hauptarterien, den Karotiden und Vertebralarterien beobachtet wird. Die kortikalen Arteriolen sind gewunden, ihr Kaliber ist unregelmäßig mit abwechselnden Stenosen und poststenotischen Erweiterungen. Im weniger fortgeschrittenen Stadium finden sich neben axialen Arteriolen mit normalem Aussehen solche, die gewunden und stenosiert sind. Bei den schweren Formen der Erkrankung ist die kortikale Gefäßversorgung stark herabgesetzt. Außerdem stellen sich die drainierenden Venen vorzeitig dar, zu den arteriolosklerotischen Veränderungen kommt also eine vorzeitige venöse Ableitung hinzu. Zudem ermöglicht die Mikroangiographie eine einfache Unterscheidung zwischen corticaler Ischämie auf dem Boden einer Arteriolosklerose und einer Ischämie aufgrund eines Erweichungsherdes mit venösem Shunt, der auf den Vaskularisationsverhältnissen eines größeren corticalen Bezirks beruht.
In der ersten Gruppe (als normal anzusehende Fälle) finden sich arteriosklerotische Veränderungen im Bereich der großen Arterien, wobei die funktionellen Kreislaufparameter relativ normal sind. Die arteriolosklerotischen Veränderungen sind zart, ihre Auswirkung hängt vom Alter des Patienten ab; sie finden sich durchgehend von 67 Jahren ab und erreichen ihr Maximum in der Gruppe der 80 bis 90jährigen.
Mittels der Elektroenzephalographie und der Pneumenzephalographie kann eine zum Zeitpunkt der Untersuchung schon bestehende asymptomatische zerebrale kortikale Atrophie nachgewiesen werden.
In der zweiten Gruppe sind die arteriosklerotischen Veränderungen mit funktionellen Störungen verbunden, welche durch Diffusionsmessungen (Xenon-Methode) und in geringerem Maße auch durch Angiographie nachgewiesen werden können.
Die mikroangiographisch nachweisbaren arteriolosklerotischen Veränderungen sind eindeutig häufiger und betreffen in fast gleicher Weise den gesamten Cortexbereich. Die zerebrale Atrophie, wie sie durch fraktionierte und anatomisch kontrollierte Enzephalographie nachweisbar ist, tritt dagegen viel seltener auf.

In der dritten Gruppe sind im EEG stets Veränderungen nachweisbar; die Kreislaufuntersuchungen zeigen eine Beschleunigung der intrakraniellen Zirkulation mit vorzeitiger venöser Auffüllung. Während angiographisch nur unbedeutende Gefäßveränderungen bestehen, zeigt die Mikroangiographie erhebliche diffuse Veränderungen im Sinne einer kortikalen Arteriolosklerose.

Diskussion

Um die morphologischen Ergebnisse der zerebralen Angiographie zu vervollständigen, ist es erforderlich, die arterielle Kreislaufzeit und das

Sichtbarwerden der drainierenden Venen zu vergleichen; hierzu muß das Kontrastmittel unter konstanten Druckverhältnissen in die Karotiden eingespritzt werden.

Die Kreislaufzeit kann in diesen Beobachtungsserien genau verglichen werden; in speziellen Fällen läßt sich eine eventuelle Verschlechterung des zerebralen ischämischen Syndroms mittels dieser funktionellen Parameter, die als Ergänzung zu den morphologischen Aussagen dienen, feststellen.

Die arteriolären Veränderungen an der Cortex, wie sie die Mikroangiographie zeigt, sind bei Patienten mit Wandveränderungen der Karotiden oder Vertebralarterien sehr viel unscheinbarer. Umgekehrt zeigen die mikroangiographischen Bilder beträchtliche periphere arterioläre Veränderungen bei Patienten mit normalen Karotiden oder Vertebralarterien. Dieses Verhältnis ist sowohl bei den als normal anzusehenden Fällen der ersten Gruppe wie auch bei Fällen mit psychischen Veränderungen wechselnden Ausmaßes (Gruppe 2 und 3) konstant. Schließlich zeigen anatomische Kontrollen, daß bei 50% der untersuchten Gehirne (Gruppe 2 und 3) die degenerativen zerebralen Veränderungen mit einer kortikalen Arteriolosklerose verbunden sind.

Die reine senile Demenz auf der Grundlage einer elektiven Degeneration des Hirngewebes, unabhängig von Gefäßveränderungen, ist durch fortschreitende Gedächtnisstörungen und herabgesetzte Intelligenzleistung charakterisiert; sie führt in den schweren Fällen zu einem weitgehenden geistigen Abbau. Wenn die Veränderung eine Hauptarterie betrifft, so ist die Demenz durch fokale neurologische Zeichen kompliziert, welche auch diagnostische Hinweise geben; hingegen sind die neurologischen Störungen bei Patienten mit psychischen Veränderungen oft schwer nachzuweisen.

Im EEG ist eine allgemeine Niederspannung vorhanden, ohne daß sich feststellen läßt, ob der herabgesetzte Sauerstoffverbrauch auf zellulären oder vaskulären Vorgängen beruht.

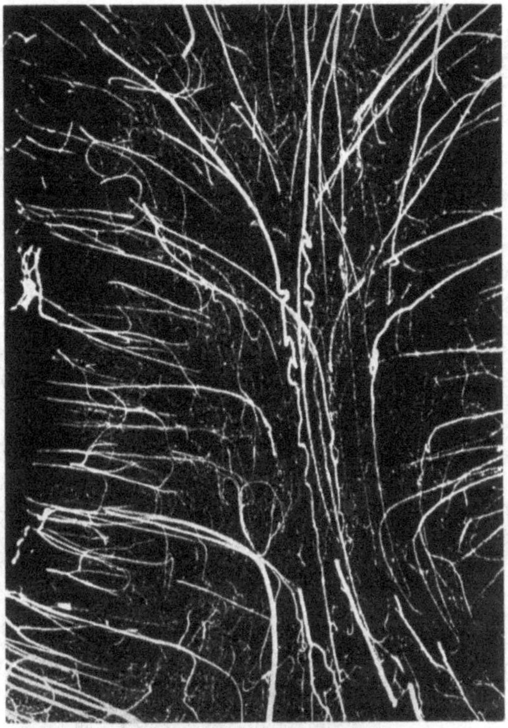

Fig. 1: Beginnende kortikale Arteriosklerose.

Bezirke mit Demyelinisation und Erweiterung der perivaskulären Räume sowie Verringerung der Neuronen sind vor allem an der parieto-temporalen-occipitalen Kreuzung lokalisiert, das heißt in dem Bezirk, wo eine terminale Vaskularisation besteht, ohne Möglichkeit einer Kollateralen-Bildung. Bei den Formen der Demenz mit kortikaler Arteriolosklerose ist der Verlauf der senilen Demenz beschleunigt, jedoch sind außer Sprachstörungen keine fokalen neurologischen Zeichen vorhanden.

Schlußfolgerungen

Die kombinierte klinische, angiographische und mikroangiographische Untersuchung ermöglicht beim alten Menschen die Abgrenzung von zwei verschiedenen Formen der zerebralen Ischämie mit psychischen Störungen.

Die arteriosklerotischen Veränderungen, wel-

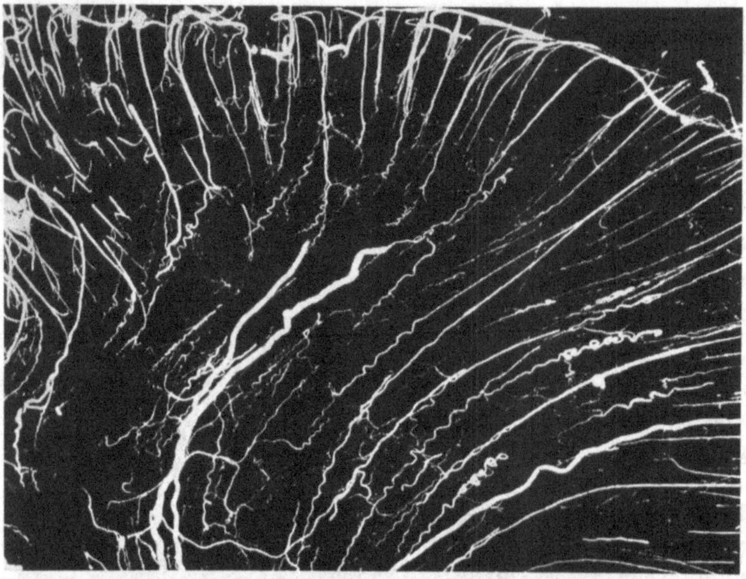

Fig. 2: Mäßig ausgeprägte kortikale Arteriolosklerose.

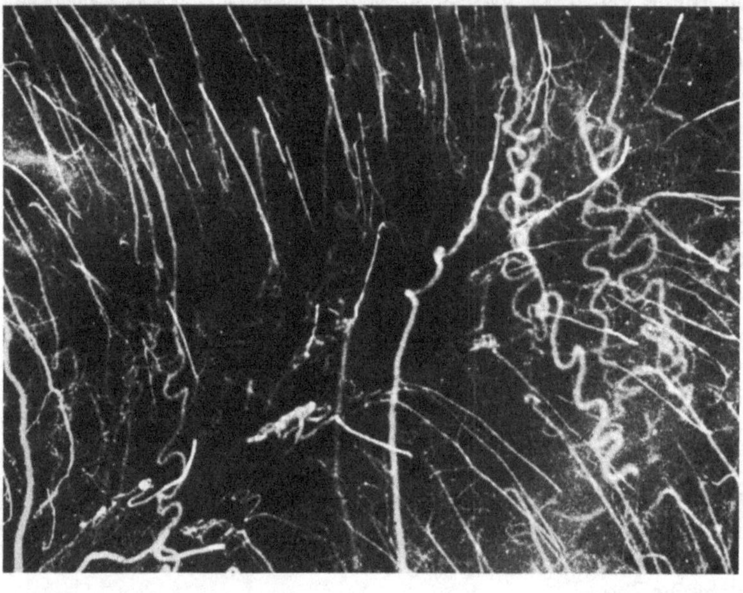

Fig. 3: Schwere kortikale Arteriolosklerose.

che die großen Arterien betreffen, führen zu einer systematisierten Ischämie an der parietotemporalen-occipitalen Kreuzung, wo die zerebrale Vaskularisation terminaler Art und ohne Kompensationsmöglichkeit durch Kollateralen ist. Der Druckunterschied zwischen normalem Karotiden-Gefäßnetz und dem pathologisch veränderten Gefäßnetz ist für die Lokalisation der ischämischen Zone verantwortlich. In diesem Falle bleibt das kortikale arterioläre Gefäßnetz unverändert, und die Symptome der Demenz sind schwach im Verhältnis zu den neurologischen Störungen. Diese Form der zerebralen Ischämie ist bei alten Menschen der Gruppe 1, die als normal anzusehen sind, nachweisbar.

Die Gefäßveränderungen können sich an den kortikalen Arteriolen lokalisieren, während die Hauptarterien intakt bleiben. Bei dieser Form sind die Verhaltensstörungen schwereren Grades, und der geistige Abbau ist offensichtlich. Es besteht eine signifikante Parallele zwischen dem Grad der Diffusion des Radioisotops, der Arteriolosklerose und dem Ausmaß der senilen Demenz. Keine Zeichen für zerebrale Atrophie finden sich im EEG oder bei anatomischer Kontrolle. Die Kreislaufstörungen sind ebensogut mittels der Serienangiographie wie mit Isotopenmethoden nachweisbar; der Hirnkreislauf ist beschleunigt, und die Fixierung der Isotopen ist im Bereich der grauen Substanz herabgesetzt.

Diese Beobachtungen ermöglichen, das Problem einer eventuellen Therapie der cerebralen Ischämie unter einem speziellen Gesichtswinkel zu betrachten. Es ist anzunehmen, daß der Angriffspunkt von Medikamenten, denen eine gefäßerweiternde Wirkung zugeschrieben wird, ein kortikaler ist; eine solche vasomotorische Wirkung kann nur bei intakten Arteriolen erwartet werden. In diesem Falle sind die Veränderungen an den Karotiden lokalisiert, in geringerem Ausmaß auch an den Vertebralarterien.

Patienten mit leichteren psychischen Störungen im Rahmen einer senilen Demenz und einem pathologischen Befund an den Karotiden, Vertebralarterien oder der sonstigen Arterienstämme weisen eine verhältnismäßige Intaktheit der kortikalen Arteriolen auf.

Jedenfalls zeigen die Untersuchungen von *Quadbeck* u. Mitarb., daß beim cerebralen ischämischen Syndrom in 15% der Fälle der Hirnkreislauf beeinträchtigt ist, bei weiteren 15% dagegen gesteigert. Daraus geht hervor, daß in 70% der Fälle der Hirnkreislauf innerhalb normaler Grenzen liegt. In diesen Fällen müssen also andere pathogenetische Faktoren in Betracht gezogen werden, vor allem Veränderungen im Glukosestoffwechsel des Gehirns.

In bestimmten Fällen können Medikamente, welche den Glukose-Stoffwechsel oder den Übertritt von Glukose in die Zellen fördern, von Einfluß sein. In anderen Fällen von cerebraler Ischämie vermag das Gehirn nicht mehr den erforderlichen Sauerstoff für den Glukosestoffwechsel aufzunehmen, das klinische Zustandsbild ist jedoch das gleiche. Bei diesen speziellen Formen der cerebralen Ischämie ist naturgemäß die Wirkung von Medikamenten, welche die corticalen Arteriolen erweitern, nur gering.

Die Indikation für eine Therapie der ischämischen Kreislaufstörungen beim alten Menschen kann daher wie folgt gestellt werden:

Eine internistische Therapie ist nur bei solchen Patienten erfolgreich, deren Eignung angiographisch festgestellt wurde und wo das Pneumencephalogramm eine irreversible cerebrale Atrophie ausschließen ließ.

Mittels der Angiographie kann also nicht nur eine kausale Diagnostik im Rahmen einer cerebralen Ischämie mit Demenzsyndrom erstellt werden, sondern es ist dadurch auch eine Auswahl solcher Patienten möglich, die für eine Therapie in Frage kommen, welche das meist irreversible Fortschreiten der Erkrankung aufzuhalten vermag.

Tierexperimentelle Untersuchungen zur Vaskularisation eines Transplantationstumors

L. V. Habighorst, H. H. Stelzig, N. Doetsch, H. J. Klaas und F. K. Kößling

Der angiographische Nachweis von Tumoren beruht auf der Darstellung einer eigenen Tumorvaskularisation und auf Beziehungen der Neoplasie zu ihrer Umgebung.

Die Entwicklung der Gefäßversorgung eines schnell wachsenden Tumors untersuchten wir am Myelosarkom T 58 (*Oberling* und *Guérin*) der Ratte. Dieser Tumor wird in fortlaufender Transplantation seit 1965 in unserem Institut gehalten. Bei insgesamt 120 Ratten eines einheitlichen Händlerstammes wurde eine Tumorzellsuspension entweder intramuskulär in den rechten Oberschenkel oder subkutan in die rechte Leiste implantiert.

Die subkutanen Tumoren entwickeln sich lange Zeit abgekapselt, nicht infiltrierend. In 10 Tagen erreichen sie Durchmesser von 1,5 bis 2,0 cm, in 20 Tagen etwa 3 bis 5 cm und führen nun zur Nekrose der darüberliegenden Haut. Metastasen treten in den regionalen Lymphknoten auf. Bei intramuskulärer Implantation wächst der Tumor rasch expansiv und destruierend in der Beinmuskulatur.

Zwischen dem 3. bis 25. Tag nach Tumorimplantation wurden unmittelbar nach Abtöten der Tiere unter konstantem Injektionsdruck Arteriographien von der Aorta thoracica und Venographien von der Vena cava inferior aus durchgeführt. Die Aufnahmen wurden unter Weichstrahlbedingungen mit 35 KV auf einen folienlosen Materialprüfungsfilm (Definix® Kodak) angefertigt.

Aus allen Entwicklungsstadien wurden außerdem Mikroangiogramme angefertigt (Micro 60, C. H. F. Müller, Filmmaterial Gevaert Scientic E 56 NUC, Exposition 5–10 min. bei 20 KV und 8 mA, FFA 25 cm).

Zur Makro- und Mikroangiographie verwendeten wir Micropaque® (*Nicholas*) als Kontrastmittel.

Nach intramuskulärer Tumorimplantation in einen Oberschenkel zeigt sich eine allmählich zunehmende Vermehrung der Arterien. Am 8. Tag (Abb. 1a) ist die arterielle Gefäßvermehrung noch diskret und nur im Vergleich zur Gegenseite erkennbar. Auffällig ist die Auffüllung von Venen im Arteriogramm schon zu diesem Zeitpunkt als Zeichen arteriovenöser Kurzschlußverbindungen. Das aus der klinischen Serienangiographie bekannte Zeichen eines arteriovenösen Shunts, die vorzeitige

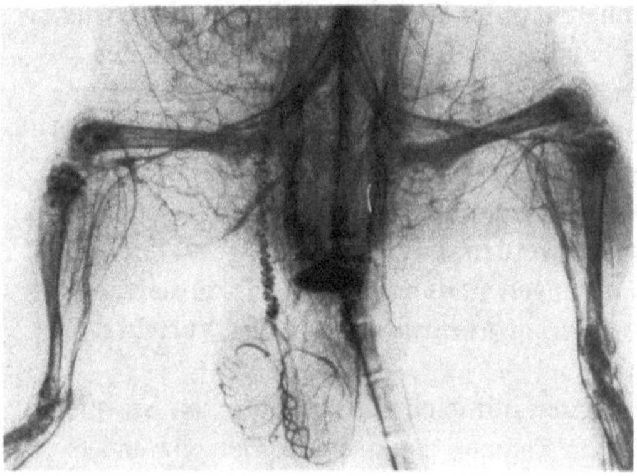

Abb. 1a: Intramuskulärer Tumor im rechten Oberschenkel Arteriogramm, 8. Tag.

Venenfüllung, ist im postmortalen Angiogramm nicht als zeitliches Füllungsereignis zu erfassen, da nur eine passive und statische Gefäßfüllung vorliegt. Arteriovenöse Shunts sind hier nur am Auftreten gefüllter intra- und posttumoraler Venen zu erkennen.

Zu früherem Zeitpunkt und deutlich stärker als die Arterien füllen sich die Venen des Tumorbereichs auf (Abb. 1b).

Der Tumor zeigt in diesen Entwicklungsstadien bis etwa zum 11. Tag einen diffusen Gefäßversorgungstyp, d. h. er wird von seinen Arterien und Venen diffus durchsetzt. Er wächst

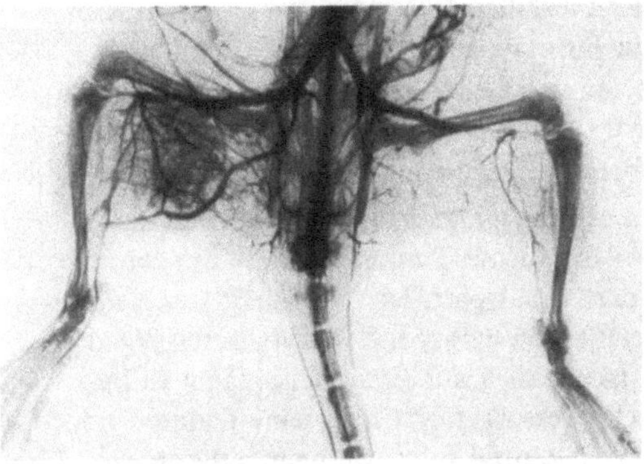

Abb. 1b: Intramuskulärer Tumor im rechten Oberschenkel. Venogramm, 5. Tag.

destruierend in der Muskulatur, aus der er seine Gefäßverzweigungen bezieht.
Im Mikroangiogramm (Abb. 2) zeigt sich der Unterschied zwischen den Gefäßen im Skelettmuskel, die sich regelmäßig am Verlauf der Muskelfasern orientieren, und dem bizarren, engmaschigen, knäulartigen Netz großkalibriger Gefäße des Tumors.

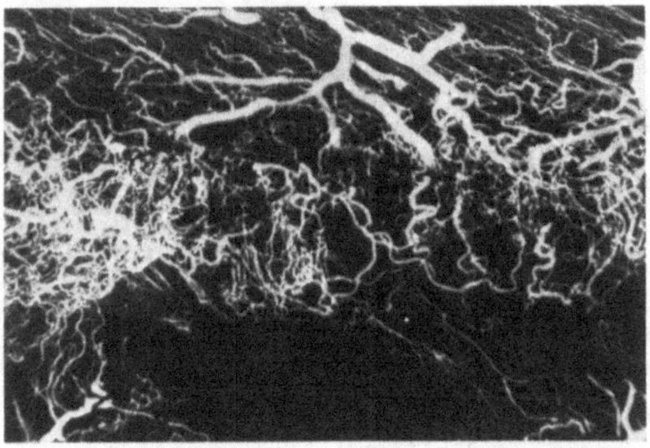

Abb. 2: Mikroangiogramm, intramuskulärer Tumor, 160fache Vergrößerung.

Bei subkutaner Tumorlokalisation in einer Leiste finden sich im Arteriogramm bis etwa zum 11. Tag spärliche und zarte arterielle Gefäße, die den Tumor umspinnen (Abb. 3a). Im Venogramm vom 11. Tag (Abb. 3b) stellen sich weite, den Tumor umgebende Venen dar, mit Abfluß überwiegend in eine erweiterte lumbale Vene sowie zu den Venen des Oberschenkels.

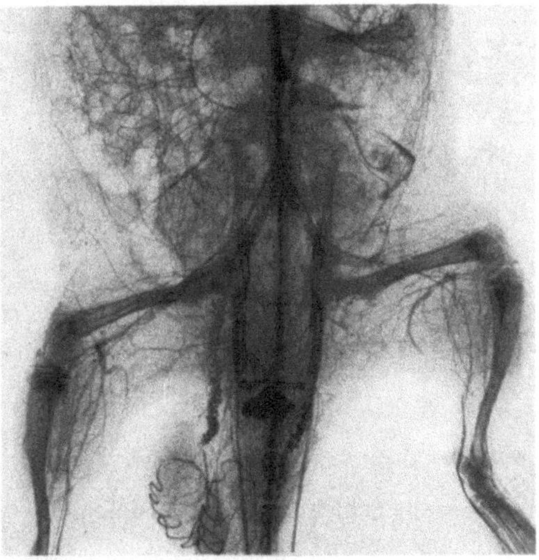

Abb. 3: Subkutaner Tumor in rechter Leiste.
a. Arteriogramm, 8. Tag.

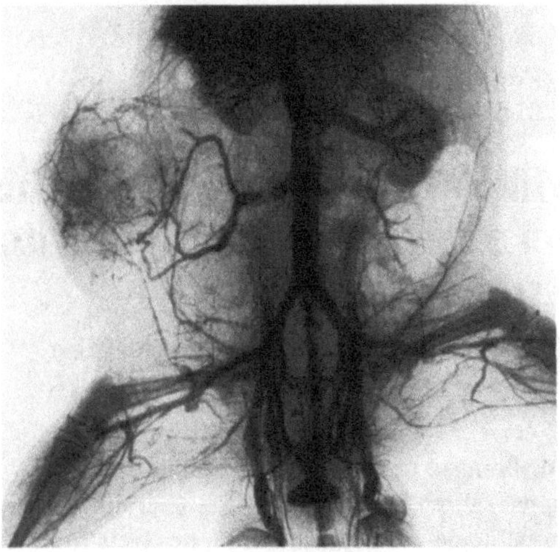

b. Venogramm, 11. Tag.

Bei fortgeschrittenen Tumorstadien, z. B. im Arteriogramm des 25. Tages (Abb. 4), zeigt sich eine charakteristische Schichtung: Außen die peritumorale Gefäßschicht, wobei zahlreiche Venen über arteriovenöse Kurzschlüsse aufgefüllt sind, nach innen gefolgt von einer Schicht kleiner Tumorgefäße, weiter innen eine Schicht von Kontrastmittel-Extravasaten und zentral eine gefäßfreie Nekrosezone. Eine

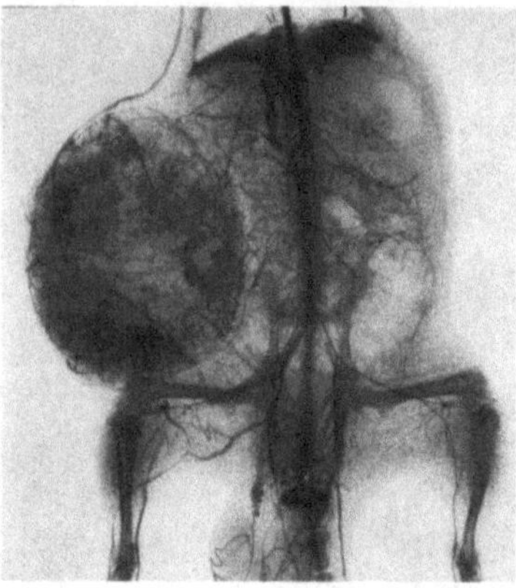

Abb. 4: Subkutaner Tumor, Arteriogramm, 25. Tag.

entsprechende Schichtung ist im histologischen Präparat zu erkennen.
Bei subkutanen Tumoren fand sich in allen Entwicklungsstufen dieser periphere Versorgungstyp. Der diffuse Versorgungstyp bei intramuskulären Tumoren zeigt sich jedoch nur bis etwa zum 11. Tag. Mit dem Auftreten von Nekrosen im intramuskulären Tumor tritt auch hier nach und nach ein peripherer Gefäßtyp auf.

Im Mikroangiogramm (Abb. 2) zeigt sich, daß das dichte Tumorgefäßnetz die zentrale Nekrose ausspart. Die neu gebildeten Tumorgefäße vom embryonalen Typ, deren Wand ausschließlich aus Endothelschläuchen besteht, versorgen nur noch eine dünne Tumorschale, zentral folgt wie beim subkutanen Tumor eine gefäßfreie Zone der Nekrose.

Zusammenfassend ergeben unsere angiographischen Untersuchungen am Myelosarkom T 58 der Ratte eine unterschiedliche zeitliche und topische Entwicklung der Arterien und Venen des Tumors in Abhängigkeit vom Ort der Tumorimplantation.

Mikroradiographische und histologische Untersuchungen bei experimenteller hypervitaminotischer Arterienverkalkung

H.-H. Stelzig, F. K. Kößling und R. Hülse

Bei eingehenden Untersuchungen der Arterienverkalkungen des Menschen konnten in den letzten Jahren neue Erkenntnisse über die Morphologie und Morphogenese der Gefäßkalkzinosen gewonnen werden. Diese Erkenntnisse waren insbesondere deshalb möglich, weil die Gefäße nicht nur histologisch, sondern auch ganz systematisch mikroradiographisch untersucht wurden. Nachdem ein Einblick in die Formen und den Ablauf der spontanen Mineralisation der Arterien des Menschen vorhanden war, lag es nahe, die Arterienverkalkung im Tierexperiment zu untersuchen. Dazu wurden zwei Gruppen ausgewachsener männlicher Bastard-Kaninchen in Einzeldosen von 1 mg insgesamt 3–15 mg Dihydrotachysterin bzw. in Einzeldosen von 1–3 mg insgesamt 8–27 mg Vitamin D_3 oral verabfolgt.
Von den Untersuchungen am Menschen ist bekannt, daß die Verkalkung der muskulären Arterien an der inneren elastischen Membran beginnt. Dabei kann die Membran flächenhaft mineralisiert werden. Gröbere körnige Kalkpartikel treten ausschließlich an der Mediaseite der Membrane elastica interna auf. Auch im Tierexperiment erfolgte die Mineralisation in allen untersuchten Gefäßprovinzen zuerst an den inneren elastischen Membranen. Frühe Mineralisationsstadien zeigen, daß die Elastika-Verkalkung in kleinen Flecken und Feldern beginnt, die die Tendenz haben, sich flächenhaft zu vereinigen. Die inneren elastischen

Membranen erscheinen wie mit Kalk bestäubt oder wie mit einem feinen Kalkmantel überzogen und lassen sich mikroradiographisch insbesondere an den Becken- und Beinarterien, aber auch an großen Eingeweideästen der Aorta vielfach in ganzer Ausdehnung darstellen. Die Membranen zeigen überall rhythmisch aufeinander folgende kräftige zirkuläre und dazwischen wesentlich feinere und dichtere axiale Falten. An den Becken und Beinarterien kommt es im Bereich der kräftigen zirkulären Falten zu ebenfalls zirkulär angeordneten körnigen Verkalkungen (Abb. 1). Solche in räumlicher Beziehung zu mineralisierten Anteilen

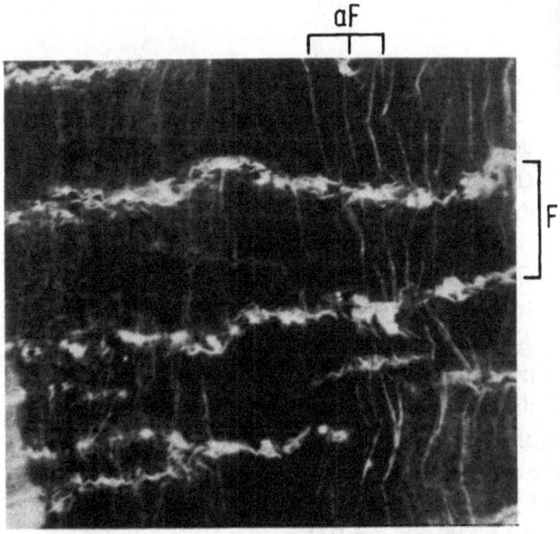

Abb. 1: Staubförmige Mineralisation der inneren elastischen Membran. Zahlreiche Kalkkörner in zirkulären Falten (F), dazwischen zarte axiale Falten (aF) der Elastica interna. Kaninchen 1 (Zust. n. 15 × 1 mg DHT), A. femoralis, Durchsicht-Mikroradiogramm, Gefäßachse vertikal, mikr. Vergr. 40 ×.

der inneren elastischen Membran systematisch angeordneten Kalkkörner sind auch in muskulären Arterien des Menschen häufig nachgewiesen worden.
In der Tunica media entsteht eine typische Mediaverkalkung, die röntgenmorphologisch der Mediaverkalkung des Menschen entspricht. Dabei bilden sich in schmalen zirkulär orientierten Arealen feine aus filiformen Elementen bestehende büschelförmige Verkalkungen. Diese Kalkeinlagerungen zeigen eine deutliche Tendenz zur Aggregation und führen in der Aorta zu schlanken in Ringsegmenten angeordneten Kalkschollen (Abb. 2).

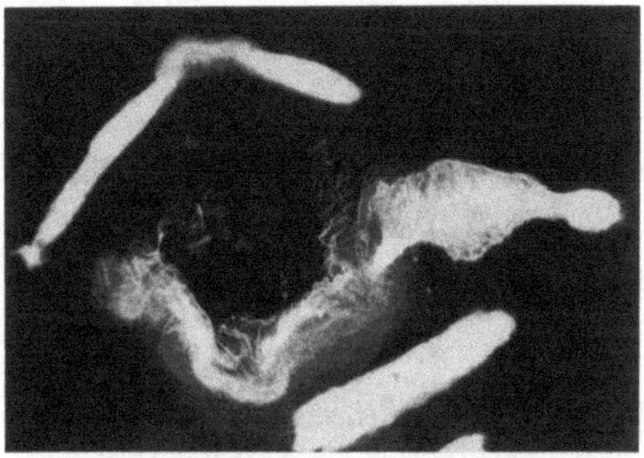

Abb. 2: Schmale zirkulär orientierte Mediakalkschollen um einen Gefäßabgang gruppiert. Mineralisierte Anteile der inneren elastischen Membran und beginnende Mediaverkalkung in der distalen Lippe des Gefäßabganges. Kaninchen 1 (Zust. n. 15 × 1 mg DHT), Aorta abdom., Durchsicht-Mikroradiogramm, Gefäßachse vertikal, mikr. Vergr. 40 ×.

Histologisch beginnt die Kalzifikation in der Aorta mit feinkörnigen Ablagerungen um lumennahe elastische Lamellen, seltener auch in der intermembranösen Grundsubstanz und hier häufig um myogene und kollagene Faserelemente (Abb. 3). Der Prozeß führt bei

Abb. 3: Verkalkung elastischer Lamellen (rechts) mit feinkörniger Mineralisation der intermembranösen Grundsubstanz (links). Kaninchen 2 (Zust. n. 5 × 1 mg DHT), Aorta abdom., Querschnitt, Kossa und Aldehyd-Fuchsin, mikr. Vergr. 400 ×.

stärkerer Ausprägung über Verkalkungen einzelner und häufig benachbarter elastischer Lamellen zu homogenen Kalzifizierungen von Gefäßwandsektoren, in denen Faserstrukturen bzw. interlamelläre Grundsubstanz nicht mehr differenzierbar sind.

Die Tierversuche erwiesen sich als geeignete Modelle zum Studium der formalen Genese der Arterienmineralisation. Dabei wurden Befunde erhoben, die der spontanen Mediaverkalkung des Menschen ähneln oder sogar mit ihr identisch sind.

Zusammenfassung der Ergebnisse des Themas „Mikroangiographie"

Moderator: F. E. Stieve

Zur Abhandlung des Themas „Mikroangiographie" war es notwendig, zunächst einmal zu klären, was der Radiologe unter diesem Begriff versteht, denn auch im Schrifttum sind hierunter ganz verschiedene Darstellungsformen zusammengefaßt. Dies kam auch in der Breite und Verschiedenheit der dargebotenen Referate und Vorträge zum Ausdruck.
Es ist wohl angebracht, diesen Begriff nur für die Darstellung von Gefäßstrukturen am anatomischen Präparat zu verwenden, und für die Abbildung von kleineren Details am Lebenden im Röntgenbild den von *Hacker* gebrauchten Ausdruck „Detailangiographie" oder je nach der verwendeten Technik „Vergrößerungsangiographie" bzw. „Angiographie mit Hochleistungsapparaturen" zu verwenden.
Vergleichende Untersuchungen an anatomischen Präparaten und histologischen Schnitten einerseits, sowie Angiogrammen am Lebenden andererseits – hier seien besonders die eindrucksvollen Demonstrationen der Gruppe *Pinet* aus Lyon erwähnt – haben bewiesen, daß besonders bei gefäßarmen Tumoren und entzündlichen Veränderungen Gefäße mit einem Durchmesser bis herunter zu 50 μ diagnosewichtig sind. Die derzeit praktizierten Darstellungstechniken gestatten auch unter Anwendung von Spezialverfahren jedoch nur, Gefäßkaliber mit einem Durchmesser bis zu 100 μ abzubilden.

Der Hinderungsgrund für eine Darstellung kleinerer Details am Lebenden liegt, wie aus dem Beitrag von *Bäuml* und *Widenmann* hervorging, nicht so sehr an der Leistung der Abbildungssysteme, sondern an den derzeitig verwendeten Kontrastmitteln, die bei diesen Gefäßkalibern nicht den erforderlichen Kontrast zu erzeugen in der Lage sind.
Als Darstellungstechniken haben sich gleichermaßen die Vergrößerungsaufnahmen als auch die Angiographie mit Hochleistungsapparaturen als wertvoll erwiesen. Es gehört ohne Zweifel zu den großen Verdiensten von Herrn *Ecoiffier,* hier durch die Verwendung leistungsfähiger Apparaturen und Röhren die Diskussion über die Grenzen der Abbildungsmöglichkeiten wieder in Gang gebracht zu haben. Die von ihm gezeigten Bilder waren für den Arzt eindrucksvoll und überzeugend. Als Anwendungsgebiete sind für die erstgenannten Methoden vor allem die Organe zu nennen, die keine oder nur geringe Bewegungen aufweisen. Dies ist vor allem der Gesamtbereich des Schädels, wobei wegen der objektbedingten Rauschstrukturen als Ergänzung die Subtraktionstechnik die Detailerkennbarkeit an den Gefäßen zusätzlich wesentlich verbessern kann.
Auch an anderen ausgewählten Organsystemen ist die Vergrößerungsangiographie als Ergänzungsmethode dann indiziert, wenn man sich

auf den üblichen Angiogrammen über Einzelheiten im Gefäßmuster und dessen Strukturen nicht im klaren ist. Bei der Hochleistungsangiographie sind besonders an Organen mit schnellen Bewegungen Verbesserungen für die Diagnostik zu erwarten. Dies betrifft im besonderen das Herz mit seinen Binnenräumen und Gefäßen.
Die Apparate- und Röhrentechnik erfordert danach einesteils Röhren mit kleinen Brennflecken, die trotzdem stark belastbar sein sollten, und auf der anderen Seite Röhren mit großen Leistungen bis zu 150 kW und mehr, bei denen zwangsläufig größere Brennflecke verwendet werden müssen. Als Spannungsoptimum wurden Werte zwischen 70 und 80 kV empfohlen.

Wie auch die Diskussion ergab, sind auf dem Detektorgebiet aussichtsreiche Entwicklungen im Gange. Sie betreffen gleichermaßen die Bildverstärker, bei denen eine Auflösung bis zu 5 P/mm angekündigt wird, als auch die Folienfilmsysteme, bei denen eine Verbesserung des Auflösungsvermögens und der Empfindlichkeit möglich erscheint. Als eine weitere Verbesserung der Erkennbarkeit wurde auch in der wissenschaftlichen Ausstellung die Anwendung spezieller Farbverfahren zur Variation des wahrnehmbaren Kontrastes und des Bildumfanges, wie sie jetzt im monochromatischen Film angeboten werden, diskutiert.

Selbst die Aussprache am Ende der Thematik ließ noch viele Fragen offen. Sie demonstrierte jedoch, daß auf allen Teilgebieten der Darstellung kleiner Details Entwicklungen im Gange sind, die eine Verbesserung der Diagnostik erwarten lassen. Die Abhandlung des Themas dürfte daher für Radiologen und die in der Entwicklung Tätigen gleichermaßen Anregungen mit auf den Weg gegeben haben.

IV. DIE DARSTELLUNG DER KORONARIEN IM RÖNTGENBILD

Anatomie der Koronararterien, ihre Anomalien und Darstellung im Röntgenbild

W. Rudolph* und J. Jehle

Die selektive Koronararteriographie erlaubt eine exakte Beurteilung der Anatomie menschlicher Koronararterien in vivo. Mit dieser Methodik lassen sich nicht nur die Hauptstämme wie rechte Koronararterie, Ramus descendens und Ramus circumflexus der linken Koronararterie, sondern auch Gefäße bis zu einem Durchmesser von 0,1 bis 0,2 mm sichtbar machen.

Auf Grund von 350 koronararteriographischen Untersuchungen, die nach der *Sones*- oder *Judkins*-Technik durchgeführt wurden, soll im Folgenden beschrieben werden, wie sich die Koronararterien röntgenologisch in den verschiedenen Projektionen darstellen und welche Anomalien auftreten können.
Die rechte Koronararterie verläuft nach ihrem Ursprung aus dem rechten Aortensinus im Sulcus atrioventricularis bogenförmig nach caudal in Richtung auf das Crux cordis. Im Bereich der Hinterwand des Herzens kann sie auf verschiedene Weise enden. Sie gibt in ihrem Verlauf mehrere Äste ab, die in Ursprung und Anzahl variieren (Abb. 1).

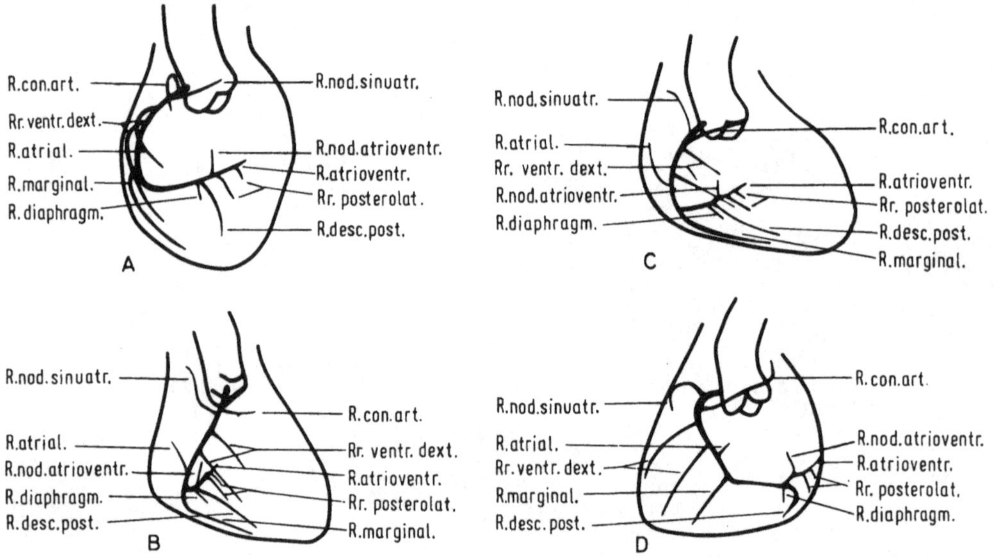

Abb. 1: Schematische Darstellung der rechten Koronararterie mit ihren Ästen in linksschräger (A), rechtsschräger (B), dorsoventraler (C) und linksseitlicher (D) Projektion.

* Mitglied des SFB 73.

In ca. 60% der untersuchten Patienten geht als erstes Gefäß ein Ramus coni arteriosi aus der rechten Koronararterie ab. Er ist ein relativ kleiner Ast, der die Ausflußbahn des rechten Ventrikels ungefähr in Höhe der Pulmonalklappenebene überquert und sich sehr gut in rechtsschräger Projektion beurteilen läßt. In ca. 40% entspringt die Konusarterie direkt aus der Aorta ca. 1 mm vom Ostium der rechten Koronararterie entfernt. Sie färbt sich dann bei der selektiven Koronararteriographie entweder nicht oder nur ganz schwach durch zurückströmendes Kontrastmittel an.

Als nächster Ast der rechten Koronararterie läßt sich in ca. 60% der Patienten ein Ramus nodi sinuatrialis nachweisen. Röntgenologisch ist er in rechtsschräger Projektion sicher zu identifizieren. Als ein nicht allzu dünnes Gefäß zieht er entgegengesetzt zur Richtung der Konusarterie unterhalb des rechten Herzohres zur Basis der Vena cava superior und zum Sinusknoten, läuft durch ihn hindurch und gibt Äste an beide Vorhöfe ab. In etwa 40% entspringt die Sinusknotenarterie vom Anfangsteil des Ramus circumflexus der linken Koronararterie. Sie zieht dann in der Nähe des linken Herzohres nach rechts cranial und verläuft dorsal der Aorta zur Basis der Vena cava superior um in gleicher Weise zu enden (Abb. 2).

Im anterolateralen Bereich des Sulcus atrioventricularis gibt die rechte Koronararterie einen oder mehrere Äste (Rami ventriculi dextri) ab, die sich über die Wand des rechten Ventrikels verteilen. Am häufigsten sind zwei Rechtsventrikeläste nachweisbar. Diese Gefäße variieren relativ stark in ihrer Länge. Als relativ konstanter größerer Ast der rechten Koronararterie folgt dann der Ramus marginalis, der entlang des Margo acutus zur Herzspitze zieht. Etwa auf gleicher Höhe entspringt meist ein atrialer Ast, der in entgegengesetzter Richtung zum Ramus marginalis verläuft. Die genannten Arterien stellen sich besonders gut in rechtsschräger Projektion dar. Zwischen dem Margo acutus

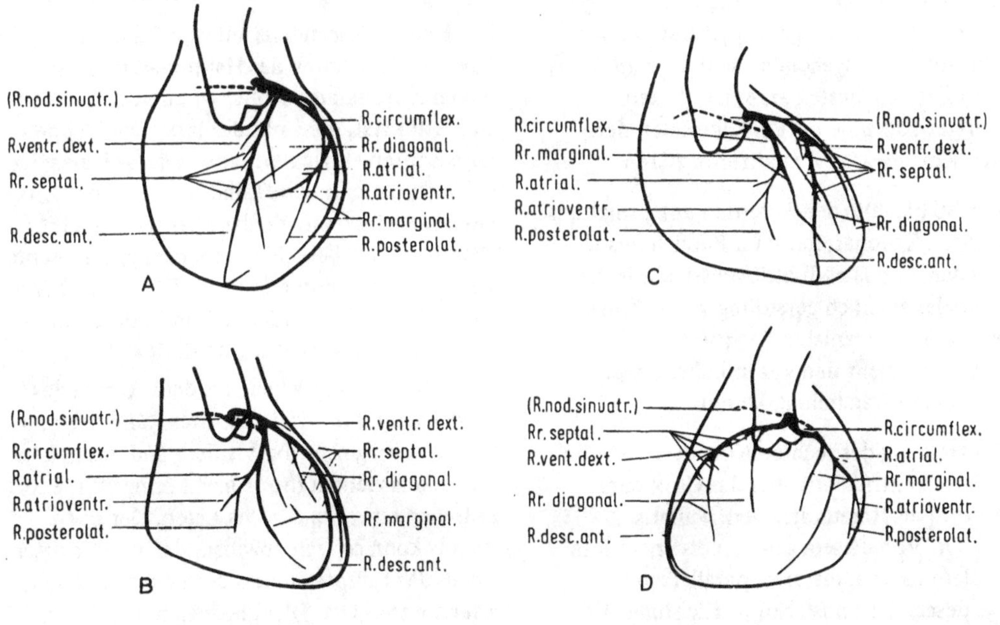

Abb. 2: Schematische Darstellung der linken Koronararterie mit ihren Ästen in linksschräger (A), rechtsschräger (B), dorsoventraler (C) und linksseitlicher (D) Projektion.

und dem Crux cordis kann die rechte Koronararterie noch kleine Äste (Rami diaphragmales) zur diaphragmalen Fläche des rechten Ventrikels abgeben.

Im Bereich des Sulcus interventricularis posterior formt die rechte Koronararterie häufig in Höhe des Crux cordis einen charakteristischen U-Bogen, der besonders gut in dorsoventraler und linksschräger Projektion sichtbar wird.

Der Ramus descendens posterior, der in der Regel als der eigentliche Endast der rechten Koronararterie zu betrachten ist, entspringt entweder direkt vom U-Bogen oder kurz davor und zieht im Sulcus interventricularis in Richtung auf die Herzspitze. Gelegentlich können zwei etwa parallele Äste mit nahbeieinander liegendem Ursprung den beschriebenen Verlauf nehmen. Es ist aber auch möglich, daß einer dieser Äste etwa in der Mitte zwischen Margo acutus und Crux cordis von der rechten Koronararterie abgeht und in schräger Richtung über die Hinterwand des rechten Ventrikels zum Sulcus interventricularis posterior gelangt. Der Ramus descendens posterior ist sehr gut in der dorsoventralen Projektion abzugrenzen. Dagegen ist er in rechtsschräger Projektion, in der sich die von ihm abgehenden sehr kleinen septalen Äste am besten erkennen lassen, schwieriger von anderen Ventrikelästen der rechten Koronararterie zu differenzieren.

In etwa 80 bis 90% der Patienten entspringt aus der rechten Koronararterie im Bereich des U-Bogens der Ramus nodi atrioventricularis. Er ist ein schmales ziemlich geradlinig verlaufendes Gefäß, das nach cranial in Richtung auf die Aortenwurzel zieht und gut in linksschräger Projektion zur Darstellung kommt.

Die Fortsetzung der rechten Koronararterie im Sulcus atrioventricularis über das Crux cordis hinaus wird als Ramus atrioventricularis bezeichnet. Von diesem gehen meist zwei Rami posterolaterales ab, die etwa parallel zum Ramus descendens posterior in Richtung auf die Herzspitze verlaufen und dementsprechend auch im gleichen Strahlengang gut zu beurteilen sind. Sie versorgen Teile der Hinterwand des linken Ventrikels.
Selten teilt sich die rechte Koronararterie vor dem Margo acutus in zwei Äste von etwa gleicher Größe. Der mehr cranial gelegene erreicht im Sulcus atrioventricularis die Hinterwand des Herzens und gibt den Ramus descendens posterior ab. Der caudale Ast zieht schräg über die Vorderwand des rechten Ventrikels und endet auf dessen diaphragmaler Seite.

Der Hauptstamm der linken Koronararterie stellt sich nach Abgang aus dem linken Aortensinus als relativ großes aber kurzes Gefäß dar, das nach links ventral und etwas caudal verläuft und in rechtsschräger Projektion gut zu erkennen ist. Bei der selektiven Arteriographie gelangt die Katheterspitze manchmal in direkten Kontakt mit der Teilungsstelle in Ramus descendens anterior und Ramus circumflexus, so daß eine unterschiedliche Kontrastmittelfüllung dieser beiden großen Äste resultieren kann. Zur Beurteilung der Bifurkation wählt man am besten die linkslaterale Projektion, in der beide Gefäße in entgegengesetzter Richtung entlang des Herzschattens verlaufen (Abb. 2).

Der Ramus descendens anterior bildet die direkte Fortsetzung des Hauptstammes der linken Koronararterie und ist zugleich ihr konstantester Ast, der links der Pulmonalklappe im Sulcus interventricularis anterior zur Herzspitze verläuft, diese umgreift und im vorderen Drittel des Sulcus interventricularis posterior endet. Dieser Verlauf läßt sich besonders gut in rechtsschräger Projektion erkennen. Das Gefäß kann aber auch in allen anderen Standardprojektionen sicher abgegrenzt werden.

In der Regel entspringen aus dem Ramus descendens anterior zwei oder drei Rami diagonales, die schräg über die Vorderwand des linken Ventrikels ziehen. Ihre Anzahl schwankt jedoch zwischen einem und sechs Ästen. Der obere Ramus kann so früh abgehen, daß er als drittes Gefäß des Hauptstammes der linken Koronararterie imponiert. Die diagonalen Äste lassen sich am besten in linksschräger Projektion identifizieren.

Aus dem Ramus descendens anterior gehen auch ein oder mehrere Äste zum rechten Ventrikel hervor, die angiographisch bei Koronargesunden jedoch häufig nicht sicher nachzuweisen sind.

Die Zahl der septalen Äste des Ramus descendens anterior ist sehr variabel, am häufigsten finden sich vier bis sechs derartige Gefäße. Im Allgemeinen werden die mehr cranial gelegenen Äste angiographisch besser als die caudalen sichtbar, da sie länger und dicker sind. In der rechtsschrägen Projektion können sie durch ihren typischen Abgang etwa im Winkel von 90°, ihren geradlinigen Verlauf und den Mangel an Bewegung während der Herzaktion von den Rami diagonales gut differenziert werden.

Der Ast der linken Koronararterie, der im linken Sulcus atrioventricularis in Richtung auf das Crux cordis zieht, wird als Ramus circumflexus bezeichnet. Er endet in der Regel bereits etwas distal des Margo obtusus. In rechtsschräger Projektion sieht man, daß er zuerst von der Richtung des Hauptstammes nach caudal abweicht.

Vom Anfangsteil des Ramus circumflexus entspringen meist ein oder mehrere Äste zum linken Vorhof und gegebenenfalls die Sinusknotenarterie, die entgegengesetzt zur Richtung der übrigen Gefäße des Circumflexsystemes verlaufen.

Weiter gibt der Ramus circumflexus mehrere Äste zur Seiten- und Hinterwand des linken Ventrikels ab, die als Rami marginales und Rami posterolaterales bezeichnet werden. Die Marginaläste, meist zwei bis drei an der Zahl, sind die größten und konstantesten Gefäße der Circumflexarterie und verlaufen im Bereich des Margo obtusus etwa parallel dem Ramus descendens. Die kleineren Rami posterolaterales, von denen sich in der Regel ein oder zwei Äste abgrenzen lassen, versorgen Teile der Hinterwand des linken Ventrikels und ziehen in Richtung auf die Herzspitze. Die Circumflexarterie kann entweder als Marginalast oder als Ramus posterolateralis auslaufen, sie kann aber auch mit einem kleinen Ramus atrioventricularis im Sulcus vor dem Crux cordis enden. Die genannten Gefäße sind eindeutig in rechtsschräger Projektion abzugrenzen.

Gelegentlich kann sich der Ramus circumflexus kurz nach seinem Ursprung in zwei parallele Äste von etwa gleicher Größe aufteilen, von denen der mehr cranial gelegene Äste zum linken Vorhof abgibt und Circumflexarterie des linken Vorhofes genannt wird. Vom mehr caudal gelegenen Gefäß gehen die Ventrikeläste ab.

Das Gebiet des Crux cordis ist die Region mit den häufigsten Variationen, insbesondere im Hinblick auf den Ursprung des Ramus descendens posterior.

Wenn dieser Ast von der rechten Koronararterie abgeht, was in ca. 80 bis 90% der Patienten zu beobachten ist, spricht man von einer Rechtsdominanz. Wird nicht nur, wie in der Regel, etwa die Häfte des diaphragmalen Anteiles des linken Ventrikels von der rechten Koronararterie versorgt, sondern die gesamte Hinterwand des linken Ventrikels, kann von einer stark dominierenden rechten Koronararterie gesprochen werden. Der Ramus circumflexus der linken Koronararterie endet bei diesen Patienten mit seinen Ästen im Bereich des Margo obtusus. Obwohl nach dieser Betrachtungsweise die rechte Koronararterie als die dominierende bezeichnet wird, ist die linke Koronararterie für die Blutversorgung des Herzens immer die bedeutendere.

Bei einer Linksdominanz, die sich bei ca. 10 bis 20% der Patienten fand, wird der Ramus descendens posterior von der linken Koronararterie gebildet. Diese Arterie versorgt dann den gesamten linken Ventrikel und gibt auch die av-Knotenarterie ab. Die rechte Koronararterie erreicht den Sulcus interventricularis posterior nicht. Meist ist der marginale Ast kräftiger ausgebildet als der Hauptstamm der rechten Koronararterie.

Neben den relativ häufigen Variationen der Koronargefäße hinsichtlich Anzahl, Abgang und Ausbreitungsgebiet der Äste von linker und rechter Koronararterie sind eine größere Anzahl seltener Anomalien beschrieben worden.

So kann das Koronarostium ein oder mehrere Zentimeter über dem Bulbus aortae liegen. Meist ist nur eine Koronararterie betroffen (Abb. 3a).
Zu den nicht ganz seltenen Anomalien zählt das Auftreten mehrerer Ostien, insbesondere der bereits beschriebene isolierte Abgang einer Konusarterie (Abb. 3b).
Gelegentlich entspringt der Ramus descendens anterior und der Ramus circumflexus der linken Koronararterie aus zwei vollständig getrennten Ostien des linken Aortensinus (Abb. 3c).

Ist nur ein Koronarostium nachzuweisen, so kann die linke Koronararterie als distale Fortsetzung der rechten gelten (Abb. 3d_1), oder die rechte Koronararterie kann als Ast aus dem Ramus descendens anterior der linken Koronararterie entspringen (Abb. 3d_2). Es können aber auch völlig atypisch verlaufende Äste das Versorgungsgebiet der fehlenden Koronararterie mitversorgen.
Neben dem Abgang einer Koronararterie aus dem posterioren Aortensinus wurde auch das Vorkommen einer akzessorischen Koronararterie aus dem linken Ventrikel beschrieben. Wenn beide Koronararterien mit getrennten Ostien aus einem Aortensinus entspringen, liegt ein transponierter Abgang vor (Abb. 3e).

Als weitere Anomalie ist der Koronararterienursprung aus der Pulmonalarterie zu erwähnen. Es können die linke Koronararterie, die rechte Koronararterie oder beide Koronararterien betroffen sein. Der Abgang der linken Koronararterie von der Arteria pulmonalis findet sich von den genannten drei Möglichkeiten am häufigsten (Abb. 3f).

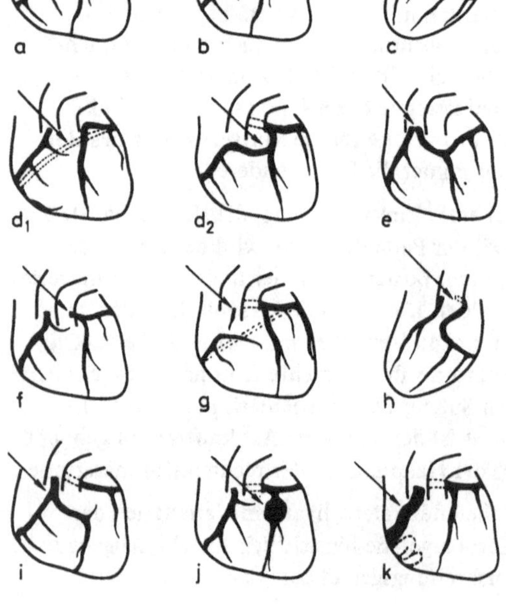

Abb. 3: Schematische Darstellung wichtiger Koronararterienanomalien in ventraler oder dorsaler (c, h) Ansicht.

a. Hoher Koronararterienabgang.

b. Isolierter Abgang des Ramus coni arteriosi vom rechten Aortensinus.

c. Getrennter Abgang des Ramus circumflexus und Ramus descendens anterior der linken Koronararterie vom linken Aortensinus.

d. Singuläre Koronararterie:
d_1 Distale Fortsetzung der rechten Koronararterie bildet linke Koronararterie.
d_2 Abgang der rechten Koronararterie aus dem Ramus descendens der linken Koronararterie.

e. Abgang beider Koronararterien aus einem Aortensinus.

f. Koronararterienabgang aus der Arteria pulmonalis.

g. Hypoplastische Koronararterie.

h. Abgang des Ramus circumflexus aus dem rechten Aortensinus bei normalem Ursprung des Ramus descendens anterior aus dem linken Aortensinus.

i. Abgang des Ramus descendens anterior von der rechten Koronararterie bei normalem Ursprurg des Ramus circumflexus aus dem linken Aortensinus.

j. Koronararterienaneurysma.

k. Arteriovenöse Koronarfistel.

Ist eine der beiden Koronararterien hypoplastisch, wird die Blutversorgung distal des Gefäßes von Ästen der anderen Koronararterie mitübernommen (Abb. 3g).
Weiterhin kann der Ramus circumflexus entweder isoliert aus dem rechten Aortensinus (Abb. 3h) oder vom Anfangsteil der rechten Koronararterie entspringen, während der Ramus descendens anterior regelrecht aus dem linken Aortensinus austritt. Es kann aber auch umgekehrt sein, daß der Ramus descendens anterior aus der rechten Koronararterie abgeht, und der Ramus circumflexus seinen Ursprung aus dem linken Aortensinus nimmt (Abb. 3i).
Die seltenen Koronaraneurysmen sind bei multiplen Auftreten meist an den Teilungsstellen der Koronararterien lokalisiert. Singuläre Aneurysmen liegen ostiumnah (Abb. 3j).

Die meist angeborenen arteriovenösen Koronarfisteln können zusammen mit anderen Herzfehlern vorliegen. Wahrscheinlich als Folge einer erheblichen Durchflußsteigerung findet sich eine aneurysmatische Erweiterung der betroffenen Arterie. Verbindungen wurden zwischen den Koronararterien einerseits und dem rechten oder linken Herzen einschließlich der Koronarvenen andererseits beschrieben (Abb. 3k).

Die genaue Kenntnis normaler Koronararterien und ihrer Variationen im Röntgenbild ist die Voraussetzung für die Abgrenzung angeborener Koronaranomalien und erworbener, meist arteriosklerotischer Koronargefäßveränderungen. Wenn man sich die Fortschritte der letzten Jahre auf dem Gebiet der Diagnostik und Therapie der koronaren Durchblutungsstörungen vor Augen hält, wird die zunehmende Bedeutung der röntgenologischen Beurteilung des Koronargefäßsystemes offenkundig.

Physiologie und Pathophysiologie des Koronarkreislaufs im Angiogramm

R. Felix und P. Thurn

Zur Physiologie

Zwei Parameter bestimmen den koronaren Fluß, wenn man einmal von der Viskosität absieht. Es handelt sich um Druck und Widerstand. Durchblutungsstörungen im Koronarkreislauf erfolgen nicht durch Erhöhungen oder Verminderungen des Druckgefälles sondern durch Vergrößerung oder Verkleinerung des Widerstandes bzw. des Gefäßquerschnitts. Hier interessieren daher in erster Linie die Einflüsse auf den Koronarwiderstand. Man unterscheidet im wesentlichen eine *myokardiale* und eine *vasale* Komponente desselben.
Die durch den Kontraktionsablauf des Herzmuskels als Summe von Förder- und Hemmwirkung entstehende Erhöhung des Gesamtströmungswiderstandes im Koronarsystem faßt *Bretschneider,* 1957 als *myokardiale* Komponente des Koronarwiderstandes zusammen. Der Einstrom in die Koronararterien findet vorwiegend in der Diastole statt und zeigt ein frühdiastolisches Maximum. In Systole wird der Einstrom in die mittleren und inneren Myokardschichten stark gedrosselt. Die koronaren Venen werden dagegen während der Kammersystole entleert. Die systolische Einstromhemmung ist für den re. Ventrikel insgesamt geringer, da der intramurale Druck nur 1/5 desjenigen im li. Ventrikel beträgt. Der treibende Aortendruck ist aber für beide Ventrikel der gleiche.
Auf Grund der dargestellten Bedingungen wird für den Koronareinstrom die sog. „*koronarwirksame Diastolendauer*“ entscheidend. Es

handelt sich dabei um die haemodynamische Diastole minus Erschlaffungsphase. Hohe Frequenzen führen zu einer relativen Verlängerung der Systolendauer. Dadurch entsteht eine verlängerte Behinderung des koronaren Einstroms. Weiterhin nimmt der koronare Einflußwiderstand mit Erhöhung des enddiastolischen Füllungsdrucks und Zunahme der Druckanstiegsgeschwindigkeit im linken Ventrikel zu.

Die *vasale* Komponente des Koronarwiderstandes wird vom Querschnitt und vom Tonus der arteriellen Gefäße, besonders der kleinen, bestimmt. Auf den Tonus bzw. den Querschnitt wirken besonders die Katecholamine bzw. β-Rezeptorstimulatoren und -blocker sowie Hypoxie und Nitroglycerin ein.

Nach *Ahlquist*, 1948 weist das sympathische Nervensystem zweierlei Rezeptoren auf – *α- und β-Rezeptoren.* Eine Stimulation der β-Rezeptoren führt allgemein zu einer Gefäßdilatation durch Erschlaffung der Gefäßmuskulatur und eine Stimulation der α-Rezeptoren führt allgemein zu einer Gefäßkonstriktion.

Nach Applikation von Noradrenalin, Adrenalin und Isoproterenol (spezifischer β-Stimulator) steigt die Koronardurchblutung an. *Adrenalin* und *Isoproterenol* bewirken dies sowohl durch eine Steigerung des O_2-Verbrauches infolge vermehrter Herzarbeit als auch durch eine Dilatation der Koronargefäße. *Rudolph* et al., 1968 fanden beim Menschen nach Adrenalin eine Zunahme der Koronardurchblutung bei direkter Dilatation der Koronargefäße, wobei der O_2-Mehrverbrauch mit dem O_2-Angebot korrelierte. *Noradrenalin* dagegen steigert den Koronarfluß nur durch den erhöhten O_2-Verbrauch. Es hat auf Grund seiner α-stimulierenden Aktivität eine pressorische Wirkung.

Angiographisch resultiert sowohl beim Noradrenalin als auch beim Isoproterenol eine extramurale Gefäßdilatation im Vergleich zur Ausgangssituation. Primäre Dilatation und sekundäre Dilatation als Folge einer Mehrarbeit des Herzmuskels sind angiographisch nicht voneinander zu unterscheiden. Beim Noradrenalin kann man gelegentlich die drucksteigende Wirkung an der Zunahme des Aortendurchmessers erkennen.

β-Blocker in hoher Dosierung vermindern die Koronarperfusion. *Wolfson* et al., 1966 fanden bei 5 mg Propranolol Senkungen der Koronarperfusion um 25 % mittels der Krypton-85-Methode bei 13 Patienten mit obstruktiven Koronarveränderungen. Andere Untersucher sprecher dagegen von 5–10 % Perfusionsminderung.

Der Einfluß einer *Hypoxie* ist allgemein bekannt. Die Koronardurchblutung steigt auf das 4–5fache an. Angiographisch kann man nach Atmung eines Sauerstoffmangelgemisches von 8 Vol. % O_2 über 10 min. eine maximale extramurale Koronardilatation beobachten. Es gibt zwei Erklärungen für die Wirkung des absinkenden Sauerstoffpartialdruckes auf die vasale Komponente des Koronarwiderstandes. Entweder werden Metaboliten frei (z. B. Adenosin), die direkt oder über Rezeptoren wirken, oder der verminderte Sauerstoffdruck erregt direkt O_2-mangelempfindliche Rezeptoren.

Nun noch zum Einfluß des *Glycerintrinitrates.* Koronarographisch konnten extramurale Koronardilatationen beim Menschen beobachtet werden (*Lickoff* et al., 1964; *Gensini* et. al., 1971). Letztgenannte Autoren finden 60 min. nach 2,6 mg Nitroglycerin oral und geschluckt eine Zunahme der extramuralen Koronardurchmesser im Mittel von 10 Untersuchungen um 14,1 %. Darunter hatten 9 Patienten normale Koronararterien und 1 Patient eine Koronarsklerose. Auch nach *Fam* et al., 1965 bewirkt Glycerintrinitrat eine Dilatation der großen Koronarien und erweitert gleichzeitig die Gefäße zu einem ischaemischen Muskelbezirk.

Bei perlingualer Applikation konnten *Gorlin*, 1959; *Bernsmeier*, 1961 und *Bing*, 1968 keine bzw. eine nicht signifikante koronare Durchblutungszunahme beobachten. Untersuchungen von *Carson* et al., 1969 haben dann auch gezeigt, daß die myokardiale Durchblutung bei koronarinsuffizienten Patienten kurz ansteigt, um dann wieder abzusinken. Die Durchblutung verläuft also biphasisch.

Zur Pathophysiologie

Zur Aufklärung der Pathophysiologie im Angiogramm bei Koronarverschluß haben wir Untersuchungen an mittlerweile über 150 Hunden durchgeführt. Während einer Thorakotomie wird eine Schlinge hoch um den Ramus interventricularis anterior gelegt. Der Thorax wird dann verschlossen und die Untersuchung kann später bei Spontanatmung stattfinden. Die Schlinge kann während des Versuches von außen her zugezogen werden, ohne daß ein weiterer und zusätzlicher Reiz auf das Tier trifft. Zusätzlich werden Wärmeleitsonden in das Myokard eingepflanzt, die es gestatten, die lokale myokardiale Durchblutung fortlaufend zu registrieren.

Abb. 1a zeigt ein normales Koronarogramm in Systole. Abb. 1b gibt dieselbe Herzphase etwa 30 min. nach *Okklusion* des Ramus interventricularis anterior wieder. Wir haben 50 Untersuchungen dieser Art durchgeführt und können generell folgendes feststellen: In 49 von 50 Untersuchungen werden die restlichen freien Koronararterien (Ramus circumflexus und re. Koronararterie) nicht weiter und nicht enger. Es tritt weder eine reflektorische Vasokonstriktion noch eine Vasodilatation auf. In der Literatur wird von beidem gesprochen.

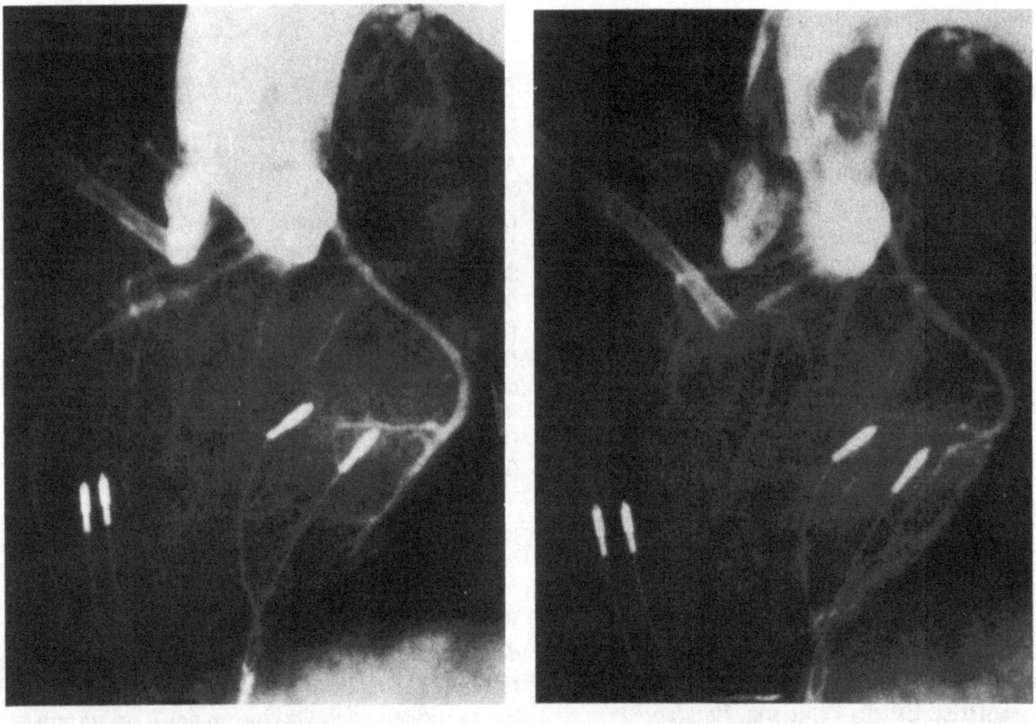

Abb. 1: Koronarogramm beim Hund.
a. Normalsituation vor Okklusion des Ramus interv. ant.
b. Zustand 30 min. nach Okklusion des Ram. interv. ant. Keine Dilatation und keine Vasokonstriktion der übrigen freien extramuralen Koronararterien. Geringer Rückgang des Aortendurchmessers wegen Okklusions-bedingter Verminderung des Systemdrucks.

Sofort nach Okklusion des Ramus interv. ant. sinkt die Perfusion im Verschlußbereich, d. h. im Versorgungsbereich des Ram. interv. ant., auf 45,4 ± 2,89% (n = 20) der Ausgangsgröße ab. In einem später untersuchten Kollektiv von 21 Tieren, die speziell nach dem angiographischen Kriterium einer *fehlenden retrograden Versorgung* nach Verschluß des Ram. interv. ant. ausgesucht wurden, ergab sich für den gleichen Parameter ein Wert von 48,46 ± 6,02% der Ausgangsdurchblutung. Eine Abhängigkeit der Restdurchblutung im Versorgungsbereich der Verschlußarterie von der Existenz interkoronarer Anastomosen läßt sich daher bei akuter Okklusion des Ram. interv. ant. nicht nachweisen. Im Mittel aller Untersuchungen tritt im normal vascularisierten Myokard (Versorgungsbereich des Ramus circumflexus der linken Koronararterie) keine Änderung der lokalen Myokardperfusion ein. Dies entspricht auch der fehlenden Änderung der extramuralen Koronardurchmesser im Angiogramm nach Verschluß des Ram. interv. ant. (Abb. 1b).

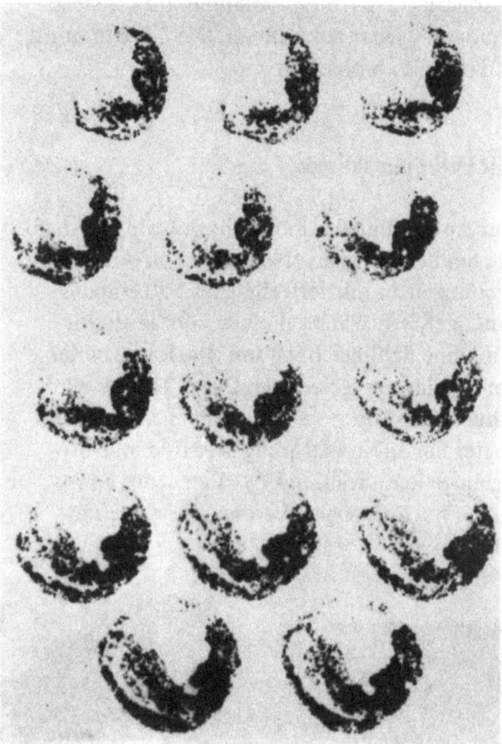

Abb. 2: Autoradiogramm der Myokardperfusion. Methode vgl. Text.

Das Herz ist von der Spitze (li. oben) bis zur Basis (re. unten) in Scheiben aufgeschnitten worden. Jede Scheibe wird einzeln autoradiographiert. Zustand nach Okklusion des Ram. interv. ant.

Durchblutungsausfall in der li. Ventrikelvorderwand (↑). Ein subepicardialer Durchblutungssaum bleibt beim Hund nahezu regelmäßig im Infarktbereich erhalten (↕). In 24 derartigen Untersuchungen tritt keine Durchblutungszunahme in der Infarktrandzone auf (keine sog. „Infarktrandzonenhyperämie“).

Gleichzeitig kann man nun Autoradiogramme der Myokardperfusion herstellen (*Flohr* und *Hoppe*, 1969). Diese Autoradiogramme werden in der Weise hergestellt, daß Jod-131-markierte Partikel in den linken Ventrikel injiziert werden. Sie verteilen sich in der gleichen Weise wie der Blutstrom und die Verteilung der Aktivität ist damit repräsentativ für die anteilige Durchblutung. Anschließend wird das Herz von der Basis bis zur Spitze in Scheiben aufgeschnitten. Jede Scheibe wird dann einzeln autoradiographiert.

Abb. 2 zeigt die Verteilung der Myokardperfusion im Autoradiogramm nach Verschluß des Ramus interv. ant. Perfusionsausfall in der linken Ventrikelvorderwand (↑). Wesentlich ist, daß in 24 Untersuchungen regelmäßig keine reaktive Perfusionszunahme in der Infakrtrandzone auftritt. Es tritt keine sog. *Randzonenhyperämie* ein. Ein kleiner subepikardialer Durchblutungssaum im Ischaemiebezirk bleibt beim Hund nahezu regelmäßig erhalten (Abb. 2; (↕)).

Es sollen noch kurz die *Folgen des Verschlusses des Ram. interv. ant. für die Funktion des Ventrikelmyokards* besprochen werden. Etwa 3–4 Herzaktionen nach Okklusion des Ram. interv. ant. tritt eine Kontraktionsinsuffizienz des Ventrikelmyokards ein. Im Laevokardiogramm kann man in dieser Situation großbogige Vorwölbungen der linksventriculären Vorderwand beobachten. Durch den in Systole ansteigenden intrakavitären Druck wird die Wand sogar nach außen vorgestülpt. Man nennt heute dieses Phänomen auch *Dyskinesie* der Wand. Hinter diesen dys- bzw. akinetischen Wandbezirken bleibt das Kontrastblut liegen und wird die Thrombosegefahr in diesen Abschnitten erkennbar. Das Blut, welches hinter diesen akinetischen bzw. dyskinetischen Wandbezirken dem Ventrikelzentrum am nächsten liegt, wird vom Schlagvolumen scheibenförmig mitgerissen, so daß angiographisch bis in den Ausflußtrakt hinein *schlierenförmige Schichtungsphänomene* resultieren.

Noch kurz zu dem Problem der *kollateralen Blutversorgung* im Angiogramm. Wird eine Koronararterie verschlossen, so hängt es vom Querschnitt der Kollateralen bzw. Anastomosen ab, ob es zu einer retrograden Versorgung der Verschlußarterie kommt. Reicht der Querschnitt für die retrograde Versorgung aus, so fließt das Blut in die Verschlußarterie retrograd über einen ungewöhnlich langen Weg ein und der Druckaufbrauch über die gesamte Strecke ist entsprechend hoch. Nach experimentellen Untersuchungen beträgt der Druck basisnahe an der Verschlußposition im okkludierten Gefäß je nach Anastomosenquerschnitt um 10 mm Hg (sog. „*back pressure*").

Daher tritt das angiographische Phänomen auf, daß der Durchmesser des retrograd versorgten Gefäßes immer ungewöhnlich klein ist, bzw. im Experiment kleiner erscheint als zuvor bei normaler antegrader Versorgung. Bei länger bestehendem Verschluß passen sich die Gefäßdurchmesser auch organisch an das verminderte Stromvolumen an.

Nun zum Schluß noch jenen für den Radiologen besonders wesentlichen Punkt – die *Kontrastmitteleigenwirkung* auf die Myokardperfusion. Wir verfügen über eigene Untersuchungen mit Urografin^{x} und Angiografin^{x}. Die lokale Myokarddurchblutung wurde mittels Wärmeleitsonden gemessen.
Bei der Übersichtstechnik folgt der Urografin-Injektion in den Aortenbulbus zunächst eine etwa 1 min dauernde Phase der myokardialen Perfusionsminderung. Dieser Perfusionsrückgang ist wahrscheinlich Folge der hohen Viskosität des Kontrastmittels (8,3 cP bei 37 Grad C).

In der 2. min. p. i. steigt die Perfusion wieder an, um etwa in der 3. min. p. i. ihr Maximum zu erreichen, welches über dem Ausgangsniveau liegt. Die Durchblutungssteigerung hält etwa für 20–30 min. an. Die mitgeteilten Ergebnisse gelten für 1,0–1,5 ml/kg Körpergewicht. Die extramuralen Koronardurchmesser zeigen bei diesen Durchblutungsänderungen keine eindeutig nachweisbare Zu- oder Abnahme.
Bei Verwendung von Angiografin, welches eine geringere Viskosität hat (5,1 cP bei 37 Grad C), sind die Reaktionen insgesamt geringer als beim Urografin. Eine Signifikanz ist hierfür jedoch auf Grund der starken Streuung der Einzelwerte nicht zu erbringen.
Nach einer Untersuchung von *Bussmann* et al., 1971 läuft bei *selektiver Injektion* in eine Koronararterie der Flußminderung eine Phase der Flußerhöhung voraus, die vermutlich allein Folge des aufgewandten Injektionsdruckes ist. Anschließend ist der Perfusionsverlauf der gleiche wie bei der Injektion in den Aortenbulbus.

Zusammenfassung

Es werden die Physiologie und die Pathophysiologie des Koronarkreislaufes aus der Sicht der Koronarographie erläutert.

Die vasale Komponente des Koronarwiderstandes kann im Angiogramm unmittelbar untersucht werden, die myokardiale dagegen nicht. Die verschiedenen Einflüsse auf die vasale und myokardiale Komponente werden im Einzelnen besprochen.
Im Rahmen der Pathophysiologie werden die Folgen der Koronarokklusion für die extramuralen Koronararterien, für die lokale Myo-

karddurchblutung und für die Ventrikelwandfunktion erwähnt. Die Verteilung der Myokardperfusion beim Myokardinfarkt wird autoradiographisch untersucht.

Am Schluß werden die Eigenwirkungen der Kontrastmittel auf die Myokardperfusion bei der Übersichts- und selektiven Koronarographie dargelegt.

Indikation und Technik der Koronarographie: Supravalvuläre Methode

A. Düx

Die Kontrastmitteldarstellung der Koronararterien ist die Voraussetzung für eine exakte Diagnostik vaskulär bedingter myocardialer Durchblutungsstörungen. Hierdurch können bereits zu Lebzeiten des Patienten Ursprungs- und Verlaufsanomalien der Koronararterien, Aneurysmen und AV-Fisteln sowie Gefäßstenosen und Verschlüsse im extramuralen Gefäßabschnitt lokalisiert und ihre funktionellen Auswirkungen auf die Koronarzirkulation bei Berücksichtigung des Kollateralkreislaufes und der Durchströmungszeit im Serienangiogramm beurteilt werden. Da eine derartige präzise Aussage über die Myocarddurchblutung durch keine anderen klinischen, elektrokardiographischen und labortechnischen Untersuchungsmethoden möglich ist und da die Koronarographie heute von methodischer und apparativer Seite bereits als Routineuntersuchung unter spezieller Fragestellung betrachtet werden kann, wird sie in Zukunft immer häufiger bei Patienten mit klinischen Zeichen einer myocardialen Durchblutungsstörung zur Anwendung kommen. Dies hängt einmal mit der allgemeinen Häufigkeitszunahme der Koronarsklerose und zum anderen mit der Entwicklung leistungsfähiger Operationsverfahren, z. B. dem aorto-koronaren Venenbypass zusammen. Aufgrund des koronarographischen Befundes kann bei einem koronarkranken Patienten entschieden werden, ob konservativ zu behandeln ist oder ob und welche chirurgische Maßnahme zur Verbesserung der Myocarddurchblutung anzuwenden ist.

Die gesamte klinisch-diagnostische Problematik läßt sich anhand von zwei Beispielen erörtern. Im ersten Falle (Abb. 1a u. b) war bei einem 33jährigen Patienten mit pektanginösen Beschwerden und normalem Ruhe-EKG ein unauffälliges Koronarogramm zu erzielen. Bei einem 49jährigen Patienten (Abb. 2) 7 Wochen nach Vorderwandinfarkt besteht ein erheblich verändertes Koronarogramm mit Verschluß des Ramus descendens anterior sinister, hochgradigen Stenosen an der kompensatorisch erweiterten rechten Koronararterie und einem bereits mäßig entwickelten Kollateralkreislauf. Während man dem Infarktpatienten (Abb. 2) zu einem aorto-koronaren Venenbypass raten würde, kann dem jüngeren Patienten (Abb. 1) die Angst vor einer koronaren Herzerkrankung trotz der Angina pectoris-ähnlichen Anfälle genommen werden.

Bei Übersichtskoronarogrammen in linker Seitenlage des Patienten (Abb. 1a u. b) lassen sich wegen der gleichzeitigen Kontrastfüllung beider Koronararterien und des Bulbus aortae durch die Einzelbildanalyse der Filmserie erhebliche Bewegungs-, Form- und Lageänderungen der extramuralen Koronararterien während des Herzzyklus aufzeigen.

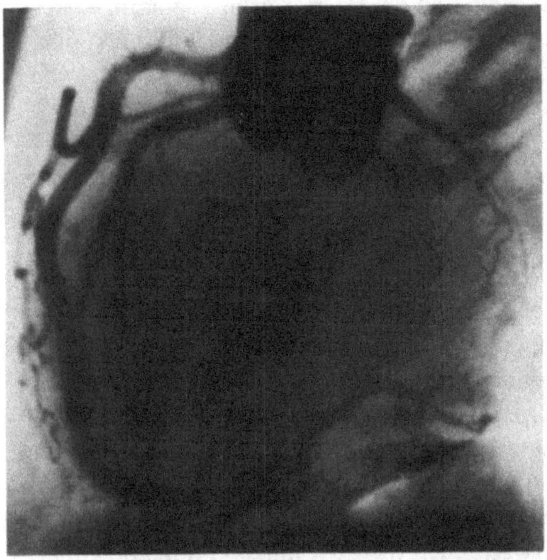

a. späte mechanische Systole.

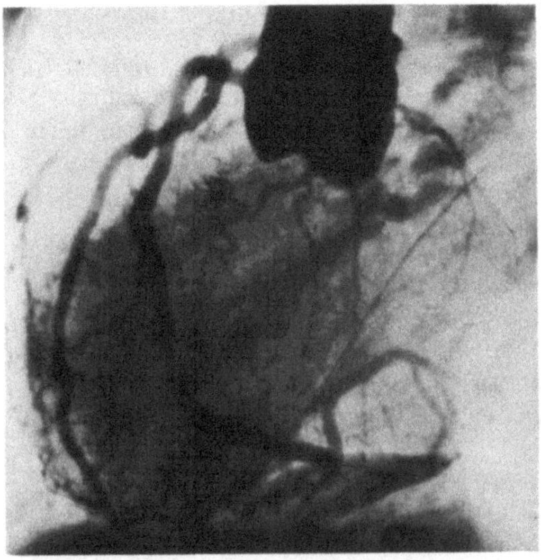

b. späte Ventrikeldiastole.

Abb. 1 a u. b: 33 Jahre ♂: Pektanginöse Beschwerden bei normalem Ruhe-EKG. Übersichtskoronarogramm links seitlich: Angeborener Rechtsversorgungstyp bei sonst normalem Gefäßbefund. Erhebliche Lageänderungen der extramuralen Koronararterien während des Herzzyklus.

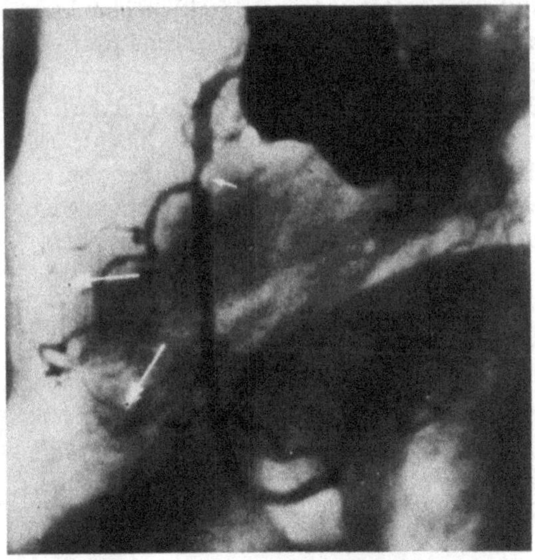

Abb. 2: 49 Jahre, ♂: Koronarogramm 7 Wochen nach klinisch gesichertem Vorderwandinfarkt (Infarkt-EKG). Ostiumnaher Verschluß des Ramus descendens anterior sinister mit verspäteter retrograder Füllung der distalen Gefäßabschnitte über mäßig entwickelten Kollateralkreislauf (⇆). Umschriebene hochgradige Stenose der adaptativ erweiterten rechten Koronararterie (←), über die die Kollateralzirkulation erfolgt. Zusätzliche Ostiumstenose der rechten Koronararterie.

Indikation

Eine Indikation zur Koronarographie besteht einmal unter *praeoperativen Aspekten* und zum anderen unter *klinisch-diagnostischen Aspekten*. Im einzelnen lassen sich folgende Hauptindikationen aufzählen:

1. Patienten mit dauerhaften pektanginösen Beschwerden und pathologischem Ruhe-EKG, insbesondere wenn ein Infarktverdacht besteht, zur Festlegung des Therapieplans, d. h. ob konservativ oder operativ zu behandeln ist.

2. Klinischer Verdacht auf eine arterio-venöse Koronarfistel bzw. Verdacht auf Koronararterienaneurysma.

3. Klärung der anatomischen Gefäßverhältnisse vor transventrikulärer Operation eines Klappenfehlers zum Ausschluß oder Nachweis einer atypisch verlaufenden oder entspringenden Koronararterie.

4. Pektanginöse Beschwerden und EKG-Veränderungen bei einem Patienten nach Thorax-

trauma zum Ausschluß oder Nachweis eines operablen Koronararterienverschlusses.

5. Beurteilung der Kollateralzirkulation und des Schweregrades der Koronarsklerose nach überstandenem Myokardinfarkt bei einem noch arbeitsfähigen Patienten zur Festsetzung des Therapieplanes und der zumutbaren Rehabilitationsmaßnahmen.

6. Manifeste oder unklare Zeichen einer Koronarerkrankung bei normotonen Patienten in gutachterlicher Fragestellung, insbesondere bei Patienten in beruflich verantwortungsvoller Position, z. B. Flugzeugführer, Busfahrer usw.

7. Ungeklärte Cardiomegalien mit diastolischer Druckerhöhung im linken Ventrikel zum Ausschluß oder Nachweis einer Koronararterienanomalie.

8. Objektivierung des Operationsresultates, besonders wenn eine neuere oder modifizierte Methode zur Verbesserung der Myokarddurchblutung angewandt wurde.

9. Überprüfung des Therapieplanes bzw. Feststellung des Behandlungsergebnisses nach medikamentöser Langzeitbehandlung mit koronarspezifischen Medikamenten, um auf diese Weise zu einer vereinheitlichten und wirkungsvollen Behandlung der durch Koronarsklerose bedingten Durchblutungsstörungen zu gelangen.

Die Beantwortung dieses Fragenkatalogs ist nur durch technisch einwandfreie Koronarogramme möglich. Letzteres ist immer dann gegeben, wenn eine optimale Kontrastierung der Koronararterien und eine scharfe Markierung der Gefäßränder gewährleistet wird. Diese diagnostische Forderung wirft jedoch mehrere apparativ technische und methodische Probleme auf, weil die Koronarographie am schlagenden Herzen durchgeführt wird. Während der Herzaktion machen die extramuralen Koronararterien die Bewegungs- und Formänderungen der Herzhöhlen und des Aortenbulbus mit, so daß vor allem zu Beginn der Ventrikeldiastole und der mechanischen Systole Bewegungsgeschwindigkeiten bis zu 400 mm/sek. auftreten können. Deshalb sind bei einem Koronarogramm extrem kurze Belichtungszeiten, d. h. 1/1000 sek. und kürzer anzustreben, um innerhalb der Filmserie möglichst viele Einzelaufnahmen mit scharfer Gefäßmarkierung zu erhalten. Fällt die Filmexposition in die Bewegungsspitze einer Koronararterie, dann lassen sich Konturunschärfen kaum vermeiden, wie durch Beispiele belegt werden konnte. Darüberhinaus bieten schnelle Serienbilder die Gewähr, daß störende passagere Überlagerungen einzelner Gefäßabschnitte infolge der ständigen Lageänderung der extramuralen Äste während des Herzzyklus aufgrund der Einzelbildanalyse zu keiner Fehlinterpretation zu führen brauchen.
Weiterhin sollten bei der Koronarographie des Erwachsenen trotz der kurzen Filmexposition 90 kV nicht überschritten werden, um eine Überstrahlung kleinerer kontrastgefüllter Arterien zu vermeiden und kontraststarke Koronarogramme zu erhalten. Mit Hilfe eines Hochleistungsgenerators und einer 150 kW-Röhre kann heute diesen Forderungen weitgehend Rechnung getragen werden.
Bei der Übersichtskoronarographie und auch bei der selektiven Koronarographie möchte ich der Großformatfilmserie den Vorzug geben, einmal wegen der besseren Detailerkennung und zum anderen, weil man unmittelbar nach der Untersuchung und für jeden glaubhaft demonstrabel die Diagnose stellen kann. Das gilt vor allem für den Routinebetrieb mit hoher Untersuchungsfrequenz, z. B. für die Röntgenabteilung in größeren Krankenanstalten, in denen bereits heute die apparativen und technischen Voraussetzungen zur Durchführung einer Koronarographie gegeben sein dürften.

Methodik

Wenn die apparativen und technischen Voraussetzungen gegeben sind, erhebt sich die Frage, welche koronarographische Methode angewandt werden sollte. Nach meiner Meinung sollte trotz der verschiedenen Auffassungen und praktischen Erfahrungen mit der einen oder anderen Untersuchungstechnik immer die Methode angewandt werden, die unter den gegebenen Umständen und bei der klinischen Fragestellung für den Patienten risikoarm ist, für den Untersucher leicht durchführbar ist und für die klinischen Belange eine einwandfreie Diagnostik gewährleistet.

Im Laufe der Zeit haben sich im wesentlichen zwei koronarographische Untersuchungsmethoden entwickelt, und zwar die sogenannte *Übersichtskoronarographie* bzw. die *supravalvuläre Methode* mit Kontrastmittelinjektion in den Bulbus aortae und gleichzeitiger Kontrastdarstellung beider Koronararterien und die *selektive Koronarographie* mit Kontrastdarstellung jeweils einer einzelnen Koronararterie nach vorheriger Sondierung derselben. Trotz der relativ einfach gewordenen Durchführbarkeit der selektiven Koronarographie, besonders wenn man die von Judkins empfohlene Technik mit dem von ihm entwickelten Spezialkatheter anwendet, und der allgemeinen Tendenz in Richtung auf die selektive Gefäßdarstellung sollen die Vor- und Nachteile der *Übersichtskoronarographie* dargelegt und an Beispielen demonstriert werden.

Durch die Verwendung des *Paulin*'schen *Doppelringkatheters* mit nach außen gerichteten Seitenlöchern im Bereich der Katheterspirale sind am schlagenden Herzen diagnostisch ausreichende Koronarogramme mit geringem Risiko für den Patienten und innerhalb sehr kurzer Zeit, d. h. innerhalb von wenigen Minuten zu erzielen. Im Gegensatz zu der selektiven Koronarographie wird nur einmal ein Spezialkatheter eingeführt und nur einmal Kontrastmittel injiziert. Bei richtiger Lage des Doppelringes im Aortenbulbus in Höhe der Koronarostien wird durch die ständige Berieselung der Koronarostien bzw. der Bulbusinnenwand während der protrahierten Kontrastmittelinjektion über 2–3 sek., d. h. über mehrere Herzzyklen, eine optimale Koronararteriendarstellung erreicht, wie anhand von Beispielen bewiesen werden konnte. Die extramuralen Koronararterienäste sind übersichtlich dargestellt. Infolge der regelmäßigen Applikation eines koronarerweiternden Mittels, z. B. Persantin, Intensain, Ildamen u. a. (*Pharmako-Koronarographie*) werden die Koronararterien außer an den pathologisch veränderten Wandabschnitten weitergestellt. Infolge der pharmakologischen Beanspruchung der Koronarreserve sind auf diese Weise stenosierende Gefäßprozesse leichter abgrenzbar.

Bei zu hoher Schlagfrequenz des Herzens, d. h. bei mehr als 90 Schlägen/Min., sollte bei der Übersichtskoronarographie zusätzlich eine *medikamentöse Frequenzverlangsamung*, z. B. durch einen Beta-Rezeptorenblocker, angestrebt werden.

Unter diesen Voraussetzungen sind bei *richtiger Katheterringlage* und leistungsfähiger Röntgenapparatur trotz der ständigen Form- und Lageänderungen der extramuralen Koronararterien diagnostisch einwandfrei verwertbare Koronarogramme, d. h. Koronarogramme mit gutem Kontrast und scharfer Gefäßkontur zu erhalten. Die *störende Überlagerung* der proximalen Abschnitte der linken Koronararterie im linken Seitenbild durch die kontrastgefüllte Aorta während der Kontrastmittelinjektion wird durch Serienaufnahmen unmittelbar nach Ende der Kontrastmittelinjektion wettgemacht. Ebenfalls können während der systolischen passageren Freispülung der Aorta mit nicht kontrastiertem Ventrikelblut während der Kontrastmittelinjektion die proximalen Gefäßabschnitte der linken Koronararterien beurteilt werden. Auf diese Weise lassen sich also stenosierende Gefäßveränderungen im proximalen Bereich der linken Koronararterie und am Koronarostium im Übersichtskoronarogramm beurteilen.

Diagnostisch unzureichende Koronarogramme können immer dann resultieren, wenn

1. der Katheterring nicht in unmittelbarer Nähe der Koronararterienabgänge zu liegen kommt und

2. wenn ein deutliches Mißverhältnis zwischen Katheterringdurchmesser und Aortendurchmesser besteht.

Eine ungleichmäßige Kontrastfüllung der Koronararterien tritt dann auf, wenn sich die Katheterspirale aus irgendeinem Grunde aufgerollt hat oder bei Instabilität des Doppelringes an der horizontalen Umbiegungsstelle schräg zum Aortendurchmesser gestellt hat. Weiterhin tritt eine unzureichende Kontrastmittelfüllung der Koronararterien bei zu hoher oder zu tiefer Lage der Katheterspirale hinsichtlich der Koronararterienabgänge auf. Bei zu tiefer Lage kann der Katheterring nämlich infolge des normalen diastolischen Tiefertretens in den linken Ventrikelausflußtrakt eintauchen bzw. zu einer Schlußunfähigkeit der Aortenklappe führen, so daß es zu einer störenden Kontrastmittelfüllung des linken Ventrikelkavums kommt. Hierdurch können größere Koronararterienabschnitte überlagert, bzw. nicht beurteilbar werden. Durch Probeinjektion einer kleineren Kontrastmittelmenge in In- und Exspiration vor der abschließenden Kontrastmittelinjektion muß die zu hohe oder die zu tiefe Katheterringlage vermieden werden.
Ein weiterer Unsicherheitsfaktor besteht in dem *Mißverhältnis* zwischen Katheterringdurchmesser und Aorteninnendurchmesser. Die Ursache liegt oft darin, daß vor der Koronarographie der effektive Aortendurchmesser nicht sicher abgeschätzt werden kann. Bei zu großem Ring und zu kleinem Aortendurchmesser kommt es zwangsläufig zu einer Schrägstellung und Verformung des Ringes in der Aorta und zu einer inhomogenen Kontrastmittelfüllung der Koronararterien.
Bei zu kleinem Ring und zu weiter Aorta resultiert einmal eine instabile Ringlage wegen des fehlenden Widerlagers der Katheterspirale an der Aorteninnenwand, wie es z. B. bei der poststenotischen Dilatation bei einem Aortenfehler oder der allgemein sklerotisch bedingten Aortendilatation der Fall sein kann, wie durch Beispiele belegt werden konnte. Zum anderen kann der Katheterring in eine der drei Aortenklappentaschen eintauchen, so daß eine einseitige Kontrastmittelverteilung in vorwiegend einer Koronararterie eintritt. Hierdurch kann allerdings ein ausgezeichnetes semi-selektives Koronarogramm erzielt werden, wie durch Beispiele belegt werden konnte.

Durch eine Verbesserung des Kathetermaterials – bisher wurde von uns zur Durchführung eines Übersichtskoronarogramms ein selbst gefertigter Katheter aus grauem Kifa-Kathetermaterial genommen – könnte nach meiner Meinung eine bessere Stabilisierung des Doppelringes, besonders an der horizontalen Umbiegungsstelle, und eine jeweilige bessere Anpassung an den zum Teil unterschiedlichen Aorteninnendurchmesser entweder durch Öffnen oder Engstellung der Katheterspirale erreicht werden.

Da der für die Koronarographie verwandte Ringkatheter ohne Schwierigkeit unter fortlaufender EKG-Registrierung auch bis in den linken Ventrikel vorgeschoben werden kann, besteht im Anschluß an die Übersichtskoronarographie bei jedem Patienten die Möglichkeit der unmittelbaren *Druckmessung* in Aorta und linkem Ventrikel und wenn nötig der *selektiven Laevokardiographie.*

Für die Übersichtskoronarographie benötigt man in der Regel 60 ml Kontrastmittel. Das zur praeoperativen Beurteilung der Wandfunktion des linken Ventrikels notwendige Laevokardiogramm kann deshalb ohne Risikosteigerung für den Patienten mit weiteren 30 ml Kontrastmittel angefertigt werden. Auf die Erstellung eines zweiten Übersichtskoronarogramms in einer anderen Aufnahmeposition, wie dies bei der selektiven Koronarographie regelmäßig durchgeführt wird, haben wir aus Gründen der Kontrastmittelüberdosierung bisher verzichtet. Ein wesentlicher Vorteil ist hierdurch nicht zu erwarten, vorausgesetzt, daß von vornherein mit präziser Technik gearbeitet wird.

Zusammenfassung

Die Koronarographie ist heute als Spezialuntersuchung zur präzisen Diagnostik myokardialer Durchblutungsstörungen allgemein anerkannt. Wir sind seit einigen Jahren aus dem Pionierstadium herausgetreten, so daß die Koronarographie als Routineuntersuchungsmethode unter spezieller Fragestellung betrachtet werden kann. Es gibt heute sowohl unter klinisch-diagnostischen Aspekten als auch ganz besonders unter praeoperativen Gesichtspunkten klar formulierbare Indikationen für die Koronarographie. Da durch die Übersichtskoronarographie diagnostisch einwandfrei verwertbare Koronarogramme zu erzielen sind, bieten sich trotz des allgemeinen Trends in Richtung auf die selektive Gefäßdarstellung folgende Vorteile:

1. Schnelle Durchführbarkeit, was besonders in hoch frequentierten Röntgenabteilungen größerer Krankenanstalten von ausschlaggebender Bedeutung sein kann,

2. Risikoarmut für den Patienten, wenn die allgemein notwendigen Vorsichtsmaßnahmen berücksichtigt werden. Wenn auch das Übersichtskoronarogramm hinsichtlich der feinsten Detailerkennung der kleineren Gefäße hinter der des selektiven Koronarogramms einzuordnen ist, so möchte ich bei Berücksichtigung der Tatsache, daß der aorto-koronare Venenbypass heute die Methode der Wahl bei der operativen Verbesserung der Myokarddurchblutung darstellt, glauben, daß das Übersichtskoronarogramm in vollem Maße auch den praeoperativen Ansprüchen genügt.

Koronarographie, Kontrastmittel und Injektionstechnik

N. Schad

Die bekannteste *haemodynamische Wirkung* einer Kontrastmittelinjektion in die Gefäße oder das Herz ist ein Blutdruckabfall (Tab. 1).

Die peripheren Gefäße erweitern sich und die periphere Durchblutung steigt an. Das Blutvolumen nimmt zu, da die hypertonische Kontrastmittellösung Wasser aus den roten Blutkörperchen und dem Gewebe in den intravasculären Raum zieht. Die Herzfrequenz fällt ab, kann aber auch unbeeinflußt bleiben oder ansteigen. Eine Reflexbradykardie wird vagal ausgelöst entweder über Dehnungsrezeptoren in der Lunge, dem Carotissinus, der Aorta oder den Koronarien.

Bei Injektion in die rechte Herzseite steigen die rechtsseitigen Druckwerte bis zum linken Vorhof und dem enddiastolischen Druck des linken Ventrikels an, während der systolische Ventrikeldruck und der Systemblutdruck abfallen. Der Widerstand im pulmonalen Kreislauf steigt, der des großen Kreislaufs fällt.

Tab. 1:

HEMODYNAMIC EFFECTS OF INJECTIONS OF CONTRAST MEDIUM (I)

Blood Pressure ↓	+ *Dilatation of Peripheral Vessels*
Peripheral Resistance ↓	
Blood Flow ↑ peripheral – aortic – carotid – coronary	

HEMODYNAMIC EFFECTS OF INJECTIONS OF CONTRAST MEDIUM (II)

Blood Volume ↑	Hypertonic Solutions Draw H_2O
Heart Rate ↓ or no or ↑	Vagal Response to Stretch or baroreceptors: lung – carotid sinus – aorta – coronaries
Pressure ↑	LV: End-diastolic – LA – PA – RV – RA – Venous

Welches sind nun die Wirkungen *einer selektiven Kontrastmittelinjektion in die Koronarien?*

Auch bei der Koronarographie kommt es oft zu einer vorübergehenden bradykarden Reaktion (Tab. 2). Wie in den peripheren Gefäßen nimmt der Gefäßwiderstand ab und die Durchblutung zu. Das Koronarblutvolumen ist vermehrt.

Tab. 2:

EFFECTS OF CORONARY INJECTIONS
OF CONTRAST MEDIUM

Bradycardia

Coronary – Blood Flow ↑ Resistance ↓
– Blood Volume ↑

Myocardial Contractility ↓ Systolic Pressure ↓
LV-End-diastolic Pr. ↑

Cellular Metabolic + Morphological Changes

ECG-Changes: Depolarization + Repolarization

Zudem nimmt aber die Myokardkontraktilität ab. Das Kontrastmittel wirkt depressorisch, der systolische Druck fällt, der end-diastolische Druck steigt an. Es werden zelluläre metabolische und morphologische Veränderungen beobachtet und regelmäßig treten elektrokardiographische Veränderungen in der De- und Repolarisationsphase auf.

Welches sind die Ursachen dieser Wirkungen? Mehrere auslösende Mechanismen kommen in Betracht, die in den physikalischen und chemischen Eigenschaften des Kontrastmittels und der Bildung eines Bolus während der Injektion liegen. Diese Mechanismen sind experimentell nicht immer zu trennen.

Der *Kontrastmittelbolus* verdrängt zunächst den nutritiven Koronarflow. Injiziert man Kontrastmittel in ein kleines Gefäß, so kann man den Blutflow auf 20–25% vermindern, der Rest ist Kontrastmittel. Der Bolus kann demnach einen vorübergehenden *ischaemischen Effekt* auslösen. Je länger die Injektion dauert, d. h. je länger der Bolus ist, um so ausgeprägter müßte diese Wirkung sein und um so länger müßte sie andauern. Ein Teil des Kontrastmittels verläßt dann das Kapillarbett und kommt mit der *Zelle* in Berührung, kann also *direkt toxisch* wirken.

Carson und *Lazarra* injizierten eine Mischung von ^{125}J markiertem Albumin und ^{130}J markiertem Hypaque in die Koronararterie des Hundes und maßen die Aktivitäten im Koronarvenenblut. Die frühe Konzentration des Hypaque im Koronarvenenblut ist niedriger als die des Albumins, weil das Kontrastmittel in das Gewebe abgewandert ist. Die späte Hypaquekonzentration ist dagegen höher, da das Hypaque aus dem Gewebe wieder zurückfließt.

Das Kontrastmittel kommt also mit der Zelle in Berührung und verursacht *metabolische und morphologische Veränderungen,* wie wir aus den Untersuchungen von *Oppenheimer* wissen (Tab. 3). Nach Kontrastmittelinkektion in die Hundekoronarie steigt im Koronarvenenblut der Lactat- und Pyruvatspiegel an. Dies deutet

Tab. 3:

EFFECTS OF CORONARY INJECTIONS
OF CONTRAST MEDIUM (I)

Cellular Metabolic + Morphological Changes
Lactat ↑ Pyruvat ↑ Free fatty acid uptake ↑
Mitochondria damage (Enzyme inhibition?)

Bradycardia Stretch receptors – chemoreceptors

Coronary – Blood Flow ↑ after initial, short
– Resistance ↓ decrease
– Blood Volume ↑ (biphase change)

EFFECTS OF CORONARY INJECTIONS
OF CONTRAST MEDIUM (II)

Myocardial Contractility ↓ Early blood pressure ↓
dp/dt ↓
LVEDP ↑
LV-volumes ↑
Cardiac work ↑ ↓

Electrocardiographic Changes
QRS – vector shift toward side of injection
T – vector shift away from side of injection

darauf hin, daß anärob vermehrt Milchsäure gebildet wird und dadurch die Laktatextraktion vermindert ist. Elektronenmikroskopische Untersuchungen zeigten dabei, daß die Mitochondrien in ihrer Form verändert sind, sich aber erholen.

Die *Bradykardiereaktion* ist dagegen nach *Carson* und *Lazarra* reflektorisch neural über Dehnungsrezeptoren in den Koronarkapillaren und kleinen Venen ausgelöst. Bei vermehrter Dehnung nimmt die Vagusaktivität auf den Sinusknoten zu. Mit Atropin oder bilateraler Vagotomie kann sie verhindert werden, so daß die Autoren eine direkte Kontrastmittelwirkung oder Anoxie des Sinusknotens durch die Injektion ausschließen.

Die Bradykardie wird durch Koronarinjektion verschiedener hypertoner Lösungen, aber nicht durch 0,9% Kochsalzlösung, ausgelöst. Sie ist stärker ausgeprägt bei großen Molekülen, die weniger permeabel sind. Deshalb läßt sich annehmen, daß Wasser aus dem Gewebe in das Kapillargefäßbett einströmt und dieses ausdehnt, worauf der Bradykardiereflex einsetzt. *Lehan* u. M. sahen nach Koronarinjektionen von Diatrizoat im Koronarvenenblut eine 35–50% Abnahme des Haematokrits, Haemoglobins und Proteins, die auf das Einströmen von Wasser aus dem Gewebe zurückgeführt wird. Nach Kontrastmittelpassage kam es zum Wiederanstieg dieser Werte über den Ausgangswert, so daß eine Rückkehr von Wasser aus dem Gefäßbett ins Myokard angenommen wurde.

Der signifikanten Zunahme der *Koronardurchblutung* geht häufig eine vorübergehende Phase der Flowabnahme voraus, die ein Minimum in weniger als 20 sec erreicht. Dies beobachteten auch *Felix* u. M. bei Wärmeleituntersuchungen an Hunden und Injektion in den Aortenbulbus. Nach einer kurzfristigen Verminderung der Durchblutung von 30–60 sec, setzte eine Vermehrung ein, die etwa 30 min. dauerte.

Die initiale Flowabnahme wird auf Gefäßspasmus, hohe Kontrastmittelviskosität mit Änderung der Blutviskosität und auf eine zeitweilige Aggregation der roten Blutkörperchen mit vorübergehender mechanischer Blockierung des Gefäßbettes zurückgeführt. Dann folgt die Phase der Flowvermehrung und Widerstandserniedrigung. Mit den größten verwandten Kontrastmittelmengen stellte sich im Versuch der Flow nach 4 min. auf den Ausgangswert wieder ein.

Die Abnahme der *Myokardkontraktilität* wurde durch direkte Messung am linken Ventrikel des Hundes nachgewiesen. Sowohl nach selektiver Koronarinjektion verschiedener Kontrastmittel, wie nach Injektion in die Aorta ascendens. Die herabgesetzte Kontraktilität äußert sich in einem Anstieg des enddiastolischen Druckes und in einem Abfall des systolischen Druckes. *Judkins* u. M., und wir verwandten diesen Parameter zum Vergleich verschiedener Kontrastmittel bei Koronarinjektionen am Hund.

Abb. 1–4 zeigen die massivste Senkung des systolischen Druckes, die wir bei Injektion von 6,5 ml Renographin 76% in die linke Hundekoronarie erhielten. Die Veränderungen setzen ein mit dem 4. Schlag nach Injektionsende, erreichen ihr Maximum nach 7 Schlägen und klingen wieder ab bis nach 11 sec.
Nach *Gensini* u. M. ist der Anstieg des enddiastolischen Druckes bei Coronarographie statistisch signifikant und stärker ausgeprägt bei Patienten mit Koronarerkrankung, vor allem wenn der linke Ventrikel vergrößert ist, sich schlecht kontrahiert oder mittelgroße bis große Aneurysmen vorhanden sind.

Bei Injektion in den linken Vorhof oder die Aorta des Menschen fällt nach *Bouchard* u. M. das dp/dt Maximum des linken Ventrikels ab, während der enddiastolische Druck ansteigt. Beide Veränderungen sind etwas ausgeprägter bei der Aorten- als bei der Vorhofinjektion. Dies wird auf die Nähe des Koronarbettes zur Aorta zurückgeführt.

Carleton maß die linksventrikulären Dimensionen während der ersten 5 Schläge der Injektion in den linken Ventrikel und fand keine Dimensionsänderungen während der ersten zwei

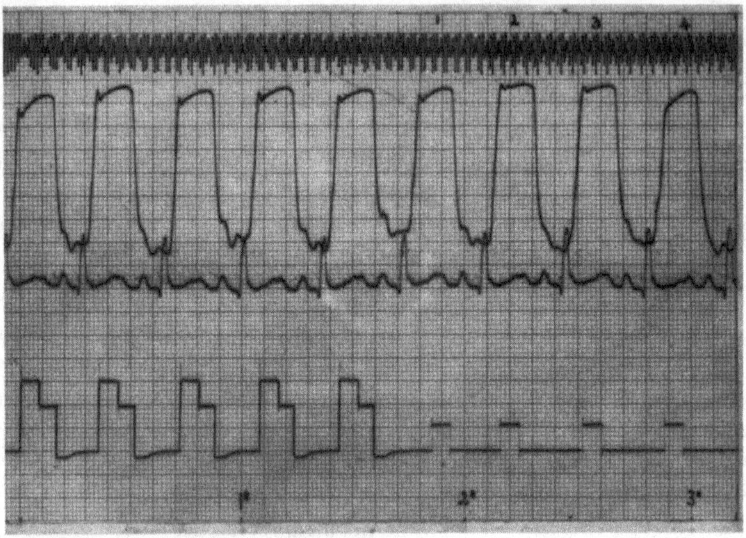

Abb. 1

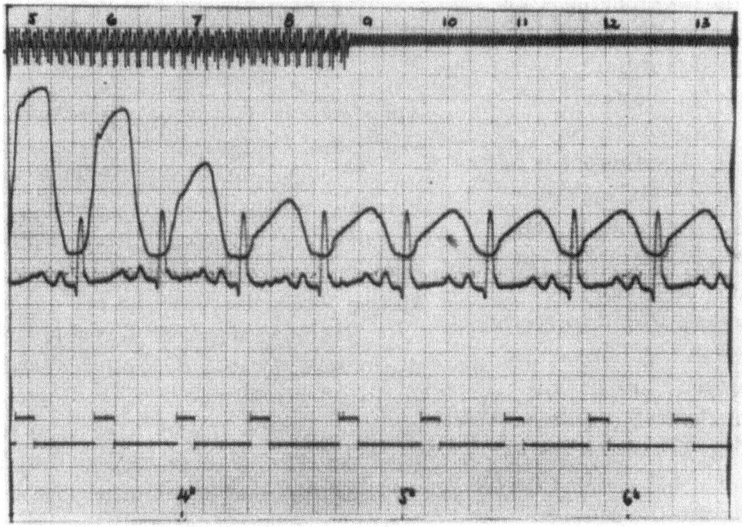

Abb. 2

Zyklen nach Darstellung des linken Ventrikels, d. h. das injizierte Volumen selbst hatte keinen Einfluß. Vom 3. bis 5. Schlag an nahmen aber die enddiastolischen und endsystolischen Dimensionen progressiv zu, der negative inotrope Effekt setzte ein.
Auch die Leistung des linken Ventrikels, berechnet aus der Druck-Volumenschleife, kann herabgesetzt sein, wie *Bjoerk* zeigte. Die Veränderungen konnten 5–8 sec nach Kontrastmittelinjektion in den linken Ventrikel, die Aorta oder linken Vorhof des Menschen nachgewiesen werden.
Demnach ist der *Blutdruckabfall* bei Injektionen in das Herz oder die Aorta zunächst Folge der herabgesetzten Myokardkontraktilität, später auch der peripheren Gefäßerweiterung. Im Tierversuch wird ein Blutdruckabfall auch beobachtet, wenn durch bilaterale Vagotomie die neuralen Einflüsse auf die Peripherie ausgeschaltet sind und wenn die Bradykardie durch einen Schrittmacher verhindert wird, woraus

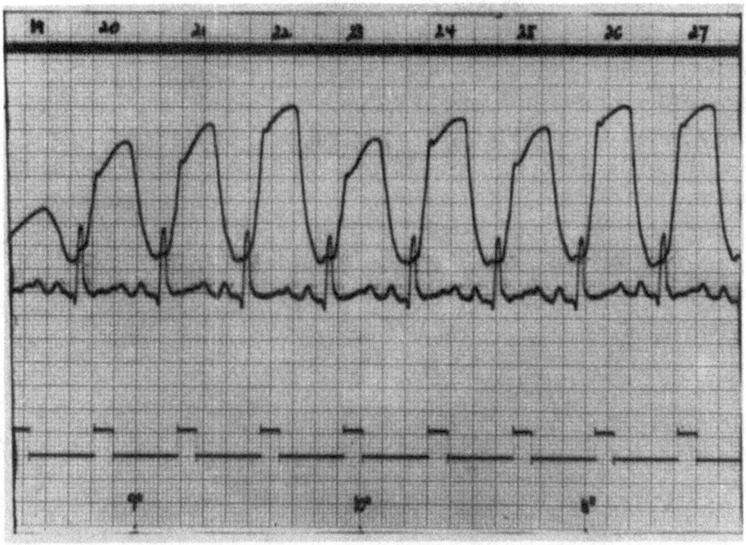

Abb. 3

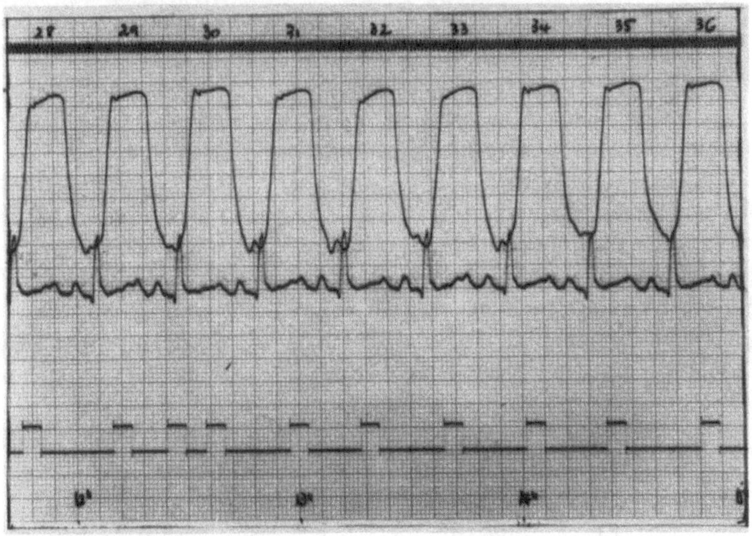

Abb. 4

Abb. 1–4: Abfall des systolischen Druckes nach 5 intermittierenden Injektionen von je 1,3 ml Renographin, 76 in die linke Hundekoronarie.

sich ursächlich die direkte depressorische Wirkung des Kontrastmittels auf die Myokardkontraktion ergibt. Bei starkem Blutdruckabfall kann sogar die Koronarperfusion vermindert werden.

Die *Elektrokardiographischen Veränderungen* bestehen in einer Abwanderung des QRS-Vektors zur Seite der Injektion und des T-Vektors von der Seite der Injektion weg. Die Veränderungen dauern 10–20 sec an. Während der Injektion oder anschließend kann es zu ventrikulären Extrasystolen kommen bis zum Bild des Kammerflimmerns.

Neben der Viskosität des Kontrastmittels könnte auch sein pH von Bedeutung sein. In der chemischen Zusammensetzung spielt neben dem Anion das Kation, vor allem der *Natriumgehalt* eine wichtige Rolle. Wir wissen heute – nachdem eine Kontrastmittelfirma unvermittelt den Natriumgehalt von 190 meq/L auf 40 meq/L verminderte und darauf vermehrt Kammerflimmern beobachtet wurde – daß ein bestimmter Natriumgehalt nötig ist. Im allgemeinen sind die Methylglucaminsalze der Kontrastmittel weniger toxisch als die Natriumsalze. *Gensini* und *Di Giorgi* fanden bei Hundekoronarographie, daß die reinen Methylglucaminsalze des Diatrizoat weniger Repolarisationsstörungen im EKG hervorriefen als die entsprechenden reinen Natriumsalze. Die Toxizität der reinen Natriumsalze nahm von 50 bis 80% schrittweise zu. Mischungen beider Salze lagen in ihrem Effekt dazwischen. Ein ischaemischer Bluteffekt wurde angenommen, da Injektion physiologischer Kochsalzlösung und 5% Glucose, aber nicht von Blut, die gleiche Wirkung hatte.

Simon u. M. untersuchten an Hunden das Auftreten von Kammerflimmern nach Koronarinkektion von NMG Diatrizoat verschiedener Natriumkonzentrationen zwischen 40 und 190 meq/L. Mit steigender Natriumkonzentration traten weniger Extrasystolen und weniger Kammerflimmern auf.

Das Natriumion erhöht entweder die Kapillarpermeabilität für das Anion oder vermehrt die Leitfähigkeit infolge der stärkeren Jonisation als das Methylglucaminsalz. Unterschiede in der Toxizität bei gleicher Jonisation wären dann dem Anion zuzuschreiben. Albumin und Dextrangaben erniedrigen die Leistungsfähigkeit und Toxizität. Zuviel Natrium ist ebenso schädlich, wie zu wenig; wo das Optimum liegt, wissen wir heute noch nicht.

Was kann man nun gegen diese Wirkungen tun, wie kann man sie einschränken?

Es lag nahe, dem Kontrastmittel Calcium zuzugeben, ein natürlicher kardialer Stimulator, das wahrscheinlich die Brücke bildet zwischen Erregung und Kontraktion. Die Zugabe von Calcium-Jonen zum Kontrastmittel hat im allgemeinen eine gewisse Schutzwirkung, die größer ist, wenn Calcium zum Natriumsalz des Metrizoats als zum Methylglucaminsalz verabreicht wird. *Salvesen* u. M. zeigten am isolierten Herzen, daß eine optimale Calciumzugabe sogar die Amplitude der Herzkontraktion erhöhen konnte. Der depressorischen Wirkung, die vor allem von der Toxizität und dem relativ hohen Natriumgehalt abhängt, weniger vom Anion selbst, konnte durch Calciumgabe entgegengewirkt werden.

Das Isopaque coronar enthält pro ml 0,35 mg Calcium, das 1,1% der 77% Lösung ausmacht, während der Natriumanteil 10% ist. Bei den Katzenversuchen von *Lund Nilsen* u. M. und den Hundeversuchen *Judkins* ergab sich, daß die depressorische Wirkung auf den linken Ventrikel gemessen an den Druckwerten gerin-

Tab. 4:

FALL IN MAXIMUM SYSTOLIC PRESSURE

	5 × 1.3 ml Intermittent (n = 17)	6.5 ml Continuous (n = 17)	Intermittent Minus Continuous
Mean	3.1 mm Hg	9.9 mm Hg	6.73 mm Hg
Standard Deviation	23.6	9.7	10.81
Range	0–53.8 mm Hg	0–31.5 mm Hg	–
T Value			2.5669
Significance			.025‹p‹0.01

ger ist als mit anderen kein Calcium enthaltenden Kontrastmitteln. Dies ist von Bedeutung, da Koronarpatienten häufig eine verminderte Kontraktilität aufweisen, so daß eine weitere Steigerung des enddiastolischen Druckes unerwünscht ist. Eine weitere Vorsichtsmaßnahme wäre es den Kontrastmittelbolus nicht zu lange zu machen, d. h. nur kurz zu injizieren, um die Kontaktzeit zwischen Kontrastmittel und Myokard zu verkürzen. Den Einfluß der Zeit zeigt die folgende Untersuchung.
Wir injizierten die gleiche Kontrastmittelmenge von 6,5 ml beim gleichen und einmal kontinuierlich beginnend in Diastole und 5 mal intermittierend, d. h. 1,3 ml diastolisch in die linke Koronarie. Die Tabelle 4 zeigt den Effekt auf den systolischen Ventrikeldruck, verglichen sind 17 solche intermittierenden mit 17 kontinuierlichen Injektionen. Die kontinuierliche Injektion von 6,5 ml verursacht beim gleichen Hund eine signifikant geringere Abnahme des maximalen systolischen Druckes als die fünf aufeinanderfolgenden intermittierenden Injektionen à 1,3 ml, wahrscheinlich weil sich die kontinuierliche Injektion nur auf 2–3 Herzschläge erstreckt, statt auf fünf und der Bolus also kürzer ist. Die kontinuierliche Injektion erzeugt aber eine höhere Konzentration. Die höhere Konzentration über eine kürzere Zeit wurde also besser ertragen als die niedrigere Konzentration über eine längere Zeit. Für die Information ist es aber in der Regel nicht nötig, länger als über drei Herzschläge hinweg zu injizieren.

Sieht man einen positiven Befund auf dem Monitor, ist man leicht geneigt, weiter zu injizieren, um den Befund länger und im Detail betrachten zu können. Dies kann bei ausgedehnten Koronarveränderungen gefährlich werden. Das Gleiche gilt in diesem Fall für häufiges Wiederholen der Injektion in kurzen Zeitabständen. Die zeitliche Beschränkung der Injektion wird auch um so dringender, je mehr wir in das Feld der Mikroangiographie vordringen. Um kleine Gefäße kontrastreich darzustellen, benötigen wir wegen der geringen Schichtdicke und der Übertragungseigenschaften eine hohe Kontrastmittelkonzentration. Diese sollte jedoch wegen der Nähe des sensiblen Kapillarbettes nicht zu lange andauern, sondern rasch durch nachfolgendes Blut ausgewaschen werden. Auch sollte man keine höheren Konzentrationen als nötig verwenden, da die vaskuläre Reaktion in der Regel mit der Konzentration zunimmt, d. h. man sollte nicht mehr als nötig injizieren.
Die Injektion müßte volumenmäßig und zeitlich definiert sein. Dies ist aber präzis nur mit einem Kontrastmittelinjektor möglich, der in bestimmten Fällen indiziert ist und der es ermöglichen muß, mit niedrigen konstanten Injektionsflows zu injizieren und der Luftfreiheit garantiert.

Der Fortschritt in der Herstellung von weniger toxischen Kontrastmitteln sollte deshalb durch Fortschritte in der Injektionstechnik ergänzt werden, damit die Angiographie die Funktion der hochspezialisierten parenchymatösen Organe unserer Patienten weniger beeinträchtigt.

Koronarographie mit 70 mm-Aufnahmen vom Bildverstärker

J. Kaude

Bei der Angiographie der Koronargefäße müssen schnell bewegliche, feine Strukturen von relativ geringer Kontrastdichte scharf dargestellt werden. Diese Aufgabe erfordert eine kurze Belichtungszeit, die Anwendung eines Brennfleckes von kleiner Kantenlänge und ein Abbildungssystem mit kontrastreicher Bildwiedergabe ohne Unschärfe.
Da die Bewegungsgeschwindigkeit der Koronararterien 100 mm/sec und oft mehr beträgt, würde auch bei einer Belichtungszeit von nur 10 msec die Bewegungsunschärfe mindestens 1 mm im Bilde betragen, was im Hinblick auf das kleine Gefäßkaliber der Koronararterien sehr beachtlich ist.
Bei Bildverstärkeraufnahmen mit einem Brennfleck von 0,6 mm Kantenlänge beträgt die Belichtungszeit etwa nur 1/3 der Belichtungszeit, die für Großformataufnahmen mit einem 1,0 mm Brennfleck notwendig ist. Somit fällt die Bewegungsunschärfe bei Bildverstärkeraufnahmen weniger ins Gewicht.
Bei Verwendung eines Brennfleckes von 0,3 mm Kantenlänge mit 12 kW bedeutet das eine Verlängerung der Belichtungszeit für Bildverstärkeraufnahmen um etwa 50%, wenn man eine geometrische Vergrößerung um etwa 2mal anwendet und dabei den Streustrahlenraster entfernt (Abb. 3). Die Belichtungszeit ist jedoch immer noch wesentlich kürzer als für Großformataufnahmen.
Seit 1969 haben wir an der Universität Lund Bildverstärkeraufnahmen im Serienbetrieb (6 Bilder in der Sekunde) bei der Koronarographie verwandt. Wir arbeiten mit Bildverstärkern in 2 Ebenen, wobei wir in beiden Ebenen die 70 mm-Kamera mit einer 35 mm Filmkamera ersetzen können.
Nach transfemoraler, selektiver Katheterisierung der Koronararterie folgt die erste Aufnahmeserie in seitlicher (horizontaler) Strahlenrichtung. Danach werden 2 Aufnahmeserien angefertigt, wobei der Patient in etwa 45° nach links gedreht ist, die eine in horizontaler und die andere in vertikaler Strahlenrichtung. Die Untersuchung ist somit insgesamt in drei verschiedenen Strahlenrichtungen durchgeführt, wobei die Lage des Patienten nur einmal geändert werden mußte. Die Einstellung und der gesamte Untersuchungsgang wird unter Durchleuchtungskontrolle und genauer Einblendung durchgeführt. Die Aufnahmeserien werden jedoch nicht simultan vorgenommen, um eine Verschlechterung der Bildqualität durch Streustrahlen zu vermeiden. Bei Verwendung eines Brennfleckes von 0,6 mm Kantenlänge werden Aufnahmen mit 320 mA und 80 bis 100 kV mit Belichtungsautomatik erzielt (Abb. 1). Die Belichtungszeit ist etwa 3 bis 8 msec.

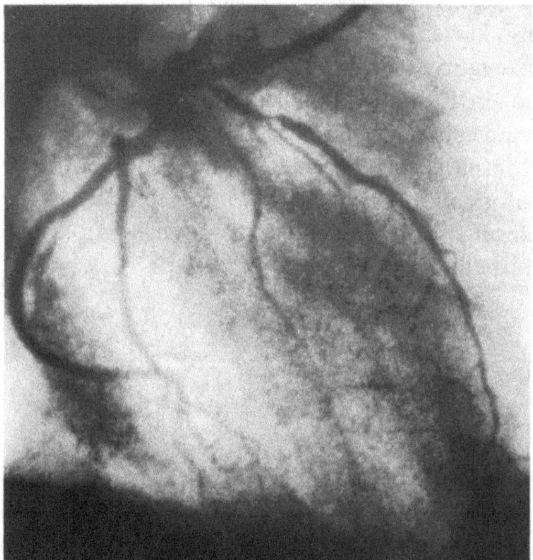

Abb. 1: Selektive Koronarographie der linken Koronararterie über 25 cm Bildverstärker.
Stenosen im proximalen Anteil des Ramus descendens anterior. 90 kV, 320 mA, etwa 8 msec.

Für die Koronarographie haben wir keine elektronenoptische Vergrößerung bei dem uns bisher zur Verfügung gestandenen 25/15 cm Bildverstärker angewandt, weil dann die Belichtungszeit etwa dreimal länger und damit fast so lang wäre wie bei Großformat-Serienaufnahmen. Wir haben jedoch mit einem in der Erprobung befindlichen 27/19 cm Bildverstärker der Siemens AG, mit Caesium-jodid-Eingangsschirm die elektronenoptische Vergrößerung, also das 19 cm Feld, angewandt, die eine 1,4fache Vergrößerung ergibt und etwa die doppelte Belichtungszeit erfordert. Mit diesem Bildverstärker können wir je nach Herzgröße die Technik der geometrischen oder elektronenoptischen Vergrößerung wahlweise anwenden, immer das ganze Herz darstellen und haben damit eine weitere Verbesserung der Bildqualität erzielt (Abb. 2).

Mit der Bildverstärker-Aufnahmetechnik im Serienbetrieb lassen sich die Vorteile eines Röhrenfokus von kleiner Kantenlänge (0,6 oder 0,3 mm) und einer kurzen Belichtungszeit neuerdings mit Einsatz der Caesium-jodid-Bildverstärker mit einem guten Auflösungsvermögen (30–40 Linienpaare/cm) vereinigen. Dadurch ist diese Methode zur morphologischen Studie der Koronargefäße der Großformat-Aufnahmetechnik vorzuziehen.

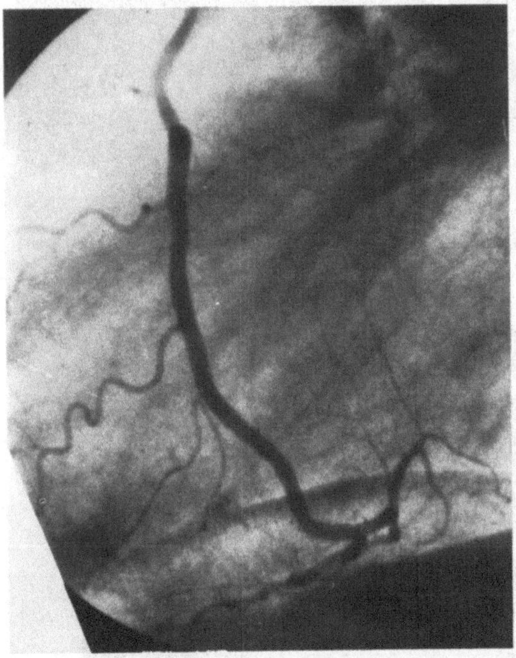

Abb. 2: Selektive Koronarographie der rechten Koronararterie über Bildverstärker mit Caesium-jodid-Eingangsschirm (19 cm Feld). Normaler Befund.

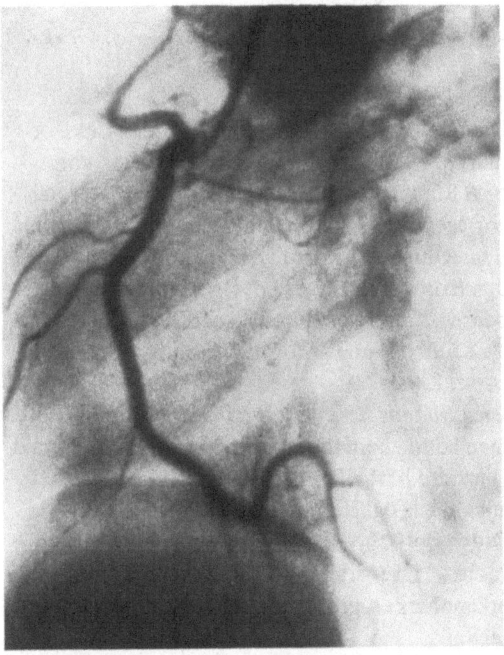

Abb. 3: Selektive Koronarographie der rechten Koronararterie, 19 cm Feld des Caesium-jodid-Bildverstärkers. Mit Anwendung eines Brennflecks von 0,3 mm Kantenlänge und damit einer längeren Belichtungszeit (in diesem Falle etwa 25 msec) kann auf manchen Aufnahmen die Bewegungsunschärfe störend werden.

Analyse koronarangiographischer Befunde mit unterschiedlichen Aufnahmesystemen

D. Henninges und E. Zeitler

Bei der Koronarangiographie kommen verschiedene Aufnahmesysteme zur Anwendung (Abb. 1):

Aufnahmesystem:		Format:	Frequenz:
		under-framing	
Cine	35 mm	in-framing	48-80 / sec
		over-framing	
	(zooming)		
Mittelformat	70 mm	BV-Kamera	4-6 / sec
	100 mm	BV-Kamera	
Grossformat	35 mm	schwarz-weiss	4-6 / sec
		Medichromefilm	

Abb. 1

Die *Großformataufnahme* mit Filmen des Formats 35 X 35 cm, die in einer Frequenz von 4–6 Filmen/sec gewechselt werden, bietet hervorragende Möglichkeiten der *morphologischen* Beurteilung der Koronarsklerose. Dies ist für den Koronarchirurgen im Operationssaal vor oder während des Eingriffs besonders wertvoll als Kontroll- und Informationsmöglichkeit (Abb. 2 + 3).

Die *Cinepuls-Kinematographie* mit 35 mm-Filmen kann ebenfalls eine exakte morphologische Diagnose herbeiführen. Gleichzeitig gibt sie auch die Möglichkeit einer *Funktionsanalyse.* Durch optische Bildvergrößerung wie bei der In- bzw. Over-framing-Technik ist die Detailerkennbarkeit größer als bei der Underframingtechnik.

Eine noch bessere Detailanalyse ist nach unseren Erfahrungen im Kinofilm mit dem Bildverstärker *Sirecon H 2* möglich.

Die *Seriographie im Mittelformat mit der BV-Kamera* – wir haben Erfahrungen mit der 70 mm-Kamera der Firma Philips – hat in Abhängigkeit von der Qualität des Bildverstärkers sowie des Filmmaterials ebenfalls eine weitere Verbesserung gebracht. Sie ermöglicht kontrastreiche Coronarogramme zu erstellen, deren Informationswert hinsichtlich morphologischer Details über dem des Kinofilms, aber unter dem der Großformataufnahme liegt (Kaude).

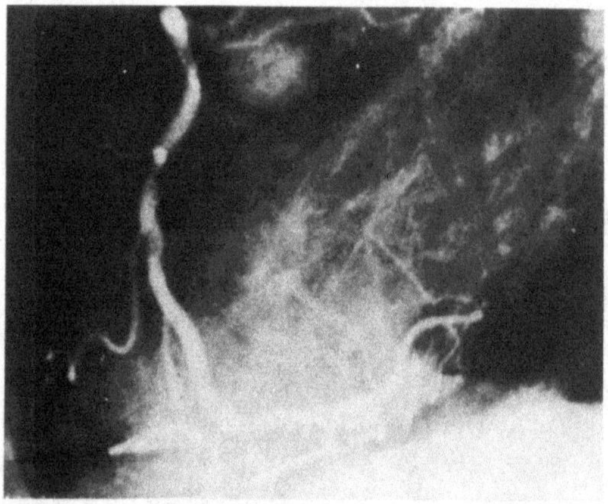

Abb. 2

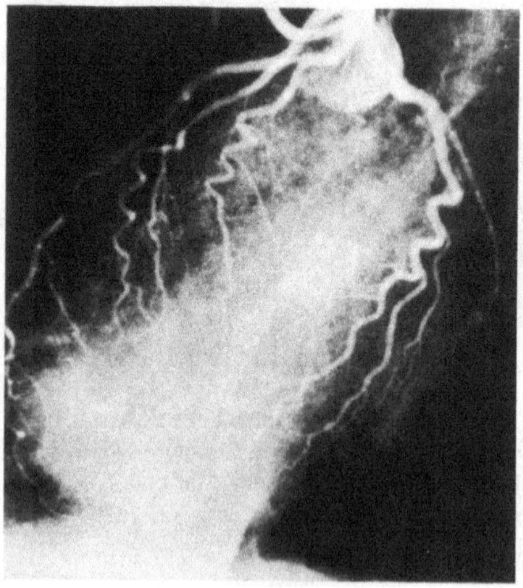

Abb. 3

Unter 150 selektiven Coronarographien, bei denen stets *gleichzeitig* Großformataufnahmen und Kinematogramme angefertigt wurden,

mußten wir *in 5 Fällen eine Befunddivergenz* feststellen.
Dabei erfolgte die Dokumentation der Großformataufnahmen jeweils bei lateraler und linker vorderer Schrägprojektion, die der Kinematogramme in linker und rechter vorderer Schrägprojektion.
Entgegen dem Vorschlag von *Judkins* wurde also bei beiden Aufnahmesystemen je 1 Projektion weggelassen, *dennoch* war das Koronarsystem stets insgesamt in 3 Ebenen dokumentiert!
Trotz unterschiedlicher Bewertung in den beiden Verfahren war in der Synthese aller Befunddokumentationen immer eine exakte Diagnose möglich. Lediglich in 1 Fall führte die auswärtige Überbewertung des kinematographischen Befundes in 1 Ebene im Zusammenhang mit der klinischen Symptomatik zu einer unnötigen Operation, die eine Befundverschlechterung brachte.

Die 5 Befunddivergenzen lauteten im einzelnen

Fall 1: Die *Großformataufnahme* zeigte fälschlicherweise einen *Verschluß* des R. desc. ant., das Kinematogramm demonstrierte dagegen lediglich eine hochgradige *Stenose.*

Fall 2: Die *Großformatangiographie* dokumentierte eine vermeintliche *Stenose,* während die Kinematographie in Wirklichkeit nur eine *Muskelbrücke* stets während der systolischen Phase deutlich erkennen ließ.

Fall 3: Im *Kinematogramm* war ein auf den Großaufnahmen in einer anderen Projektion (lat.) deutlich zu erkennender Verschluß nicht zu identifizieren, da ein kräftiges Kollateralgefäß vom 1. Septumast als unmittelbare Fortsetzung fehlinterpretiert worden war.

Fall 4: Das *Kinematogramm* ließ in einer Projektion eine Stenose am Ursprung des R. desc. ant. vermuten, was jedoch die Großaufnahmen und die Kinematographie in anderer Position nicht bestätigten.

Fall 5: Im *Kinematogramm* war ein Normalbefund registriert worden, die Großformataufnahmen demonstrierten jedoch richtigerweise eine *Stenose* am R. circumflexus.

Zusammenfassend wären also mit der Großformatangiographie allein in 2 von 150 Fällen Fehldiagnosen gestellt worden, die Kinematographie allein hätte in 1 Fall von 150 zu einer Fehlinterpretation geführt. In 2 von 150 Fällen wurde der Beweis erbracht, daß nur eine Befunddokumentation in mehreren, d. h. 3 Ebenen garantiert, daß nichts übersehen wird.

Unsere Analyse soll demnach zeigen:

1. Eine optimale Befundinterpretation ist erst durch die *Kombination* von Kinematographie und Großformatangiographie möglich. – Die Großformataufnahme mit *Medichromefilm* kann für die Erkennung extracardialer Kollateralen für den Chirurgen von Vorteil sein.

2. Auf die Kinematographie kann in *keinem* Fall verzichtet werden. Dagegen ist bei Verwendung der modernen Bildverstärker die Qualität von Kinofilm und Mittelformatangiographie so gut, daß unter besonderen Umständen auf die Großformatkoronarogramme verzichtet werden kann.

3. Es ist erforderlich, Koronarographien *in 3* – mindestens 2 Projektionen anzufertigen. Im Hinblick auf Verringerung von Untersuchungsrisiko, Strahlenbelastung und Kosten genügt es, wenn jede Kranzarterie zwar in 3 Ebenen – in jeder jedoch nur 1 × dokumentiert wird.

Großbildkoronarangiographie in der Diagnostik der Koronarsklerose

E. Aldor und H. Heeger

Der rasche Fortschritt in der Möglichkeit chirurgischer Intervention bei der koronaren Herzkrankheit hat in den letzten Jahren zu einer immer weiteren Perfektionierung der für den Chirurgen unerläßlichen angiographischen Diagnostik geführt. Dabei hat sich die Großbildkoronarographie besonders bewährt, da auf diese Weise dem Chirurgen eine anschauliche Dokumentation in den Operationssaal mitgegeben werden kann. Überdies gibt das großformatige, stehende Bild dem Befunder bessere Möglichkeiten anatomische Details abzuklären. Um mit einem Blattfilmwechsler angefertigte großformatige Koronarogramme zu erhalten, ist jedoch eine Technik der selektiven Koronarsondierung nötig, bei der eine konstante Lage des Koronarographiekatheters gewährleistet wird. Im Gegensatz zu der *Soon*'schen Methodik ist dies mit speziell geformten Kathetern, wie sie von *Judkins, Amplatz, Bourassa* u. a. angegeben wurden, bei transfemoral-retrograder Katheterisierung möglich. Welche Katheterform im einzelnen Anwendung findet, ergibt sich aus der Anatomie der jeweiligen Aorta bzw. des Abganges der Kranzgefäße. Eine weitere Voraussetzung ist die Möglichkeit, den Patienten in verschiedene Durchleuchtungsrichtungen bringen zu können, ohne wesentliche Manipulationen durchführen zu müssen, da nur auf diese Weise die Erhaltung der richtigen Katheterlage gewährleistet erscheint. Wir verwenden zu diesem Zweck eine Röntgen-Drehmulde, mit deren Hilfe der Patient passiv, also ohne sich zu bewegen in jede gewünschte Lage gedreht werden kann. Da durch Zwischenschalten der Drehmulde der Patienten-Filmabstand in der a-p Ebene zu groß würde, verwenden wir für unsere Großbildangiogramme die seitliche AOT-Ebene, da wir hier den Patienten direkt an den Blattfilmwechsler heranbringen können. Dabei hat sich uns routinemäßig für die Darstellung der linken Kranzarterie eine Rotation des Patienten im Uhrzeigersinn um 60° am besten bewährt, was für die seitliche Ebene einer Aufnahmerichtung in etwas zu gering gedrehtem I. schrägen Durchmesser entspricht. Die rechte Kranzarterie versuchen wir im fast seitlichen Strahlengang abzubilden, doch sind wir hier oft gezwungen, leichte Verdrehungen des Patienten, wie sie bei der Sondierung des rechten Ostiums nötig sind, beizubehalten, da die Sondierung des rechten Koronarostiums technisch meist schwieriger ist als links und der Katheter manchmal schwer in einer stabilen Lage gehalten werden kann.

An Hand von zwei Abbildungen darf ich die Leistungsfähigkeit der Methode demonstrieren.

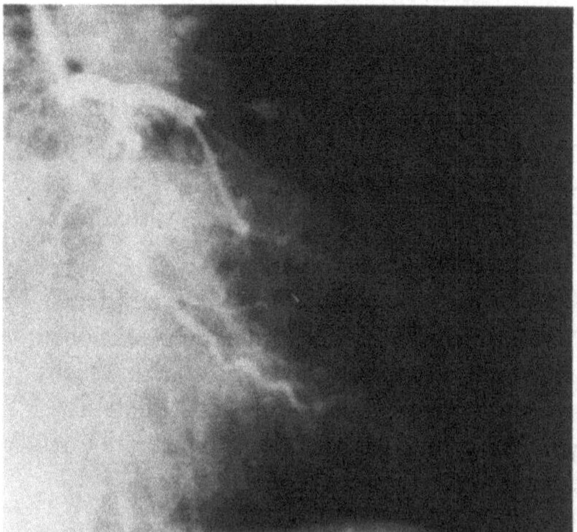

Abb. 1: Ein Großbildangiogramm bei selektiver Darstellung der linken Kranzarterie. Es besteht eine hochgradige Stenosierung im Bereich des ramus desc. ant.

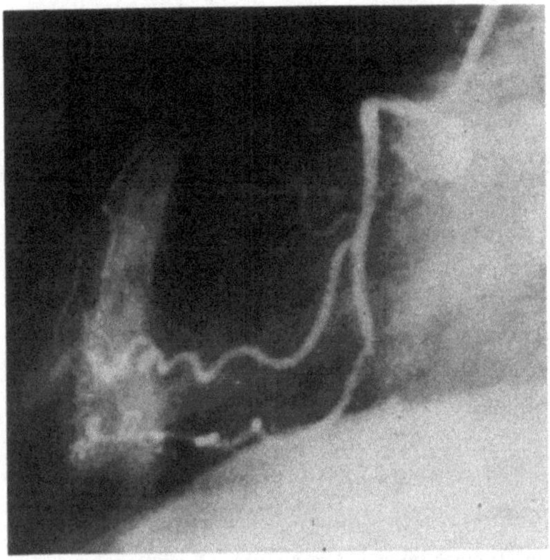

Abb. 2: Die rechte Koronararterie ist selektiv dargestellt. Man sieht einen Verschluß des Hauptstamms, wobei es über den Kantenast und andere marginale Äste zu einer Kollateralverbindung zum ramus desc. ant. der linken Kranzarterie kommt, die ebenfalls verschlossen war.

Um jedes Mißverständnis auszuschließen, möchte ich jedoch betonen, daß bei jeder Koronarangiographie selbstverständlich auch eine Cineangiographie, wenn möglich in mehreren verschiedenen Durchleuchtungsrichtungen durchgeführt werden muß.
Nur unter Zuhilfenahme des bewegten Bildes des Cineangiogramms ist eine funktionelle Beurteilung der koronaren Strömung möglich. Die wesentlich kürzere Belichtungszeit des Einzelbildes im Cineangiogramm, die bei etwa 1 msec. liegt, bietet überdies die Möglichkeit, eventuelle diagnostische Unklarheiten im Großbildkoronarogramm, die manchmal durch Bewegungsunschärfen entstehen, da hier mit Belichtungszeiten von etwa 50 msec. gearbeitet werden muß, eindeutig abzuklären.
Unserem Bestreben um die Abklärung des einzelnen Falles genügt aber auch diese Forderung noch nicht. Wir führen heute bei jeder Koronarangiographie eine Flow-Messung mit Xenon^{133} und eine Myocardszintigraphie mit makroaggregierten Jod Albumin Partikeln durch. Wir glauben, daß so auch eine weitere funktionelle Beurteilung besonders im Hinblick auf die Funktionsfähigkeit eventuell bestehender Kollateralbahnen möglich ist.
Das Großbildkoronarogramm ist aber unserer Meinung nach ein wichtiger Teil der koronarographischen Untersuchung.

Der Mechanismus der selektiven Koronarkatheterisierung mit dem Amplatz-Katheter

H. Schreyer, U. Schwarz und W. Klein

Wie bei jeder Methode der transfemoralen selektiven Koronararteriographie muß auch bei den von *Amplatz* und Mitarb. (1967) entwickelten Kathetern für die linke wie auch für die rechte Koronararterie ein besonders geformter Katheter verwendet werden. Das Ende des für die linke Koronararterie verwendeten Katheters ist hakenförmig, die Spitze hat in einem Bereich von 2 cm eine Verjüngung des Kalibers auf Fr. 5. Das Kaliber des übrigen Katheters beträgt Fr. 8. Der verjüngte Teil weist eine zusätzliche Krümmung auf, um ein obstruierendes Vordringen des Katheters in distale Koronarabschnitte zu verhindern (Abb. 1a). Für die linke Koronararterie wird der Polyurethankatheter mit eingewebtem Drahtnetz, entsprechend den unterschiedlichen Größenverhältnissen der Aorta, in 3 verschiedenen Größen hergestellt. Die Auswahl einer den Größenverhältnissen des Bulbus aortae angepaßten Kathetergröße ist für das Gelingen der selektiven Aufsuchen der linken Koronararterie notwendig. Bei den meisten

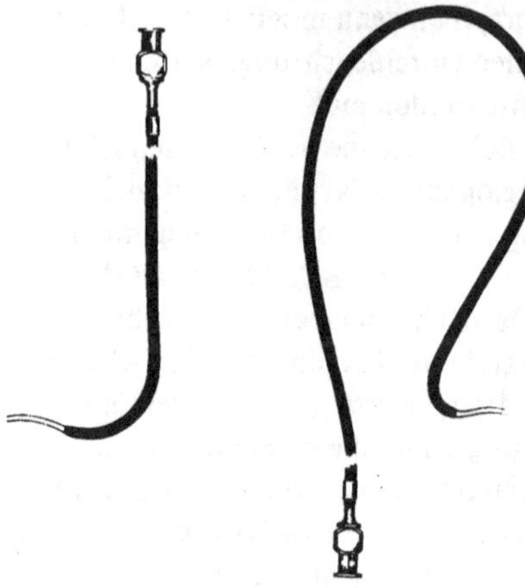

Abb. 1 a (links): Katheter für die linke Koronararterie nach *K. Amplatz.* Abb. 1 b (rechts): Katheter für die rechte Koronararterie nach *K. Amplatz.*

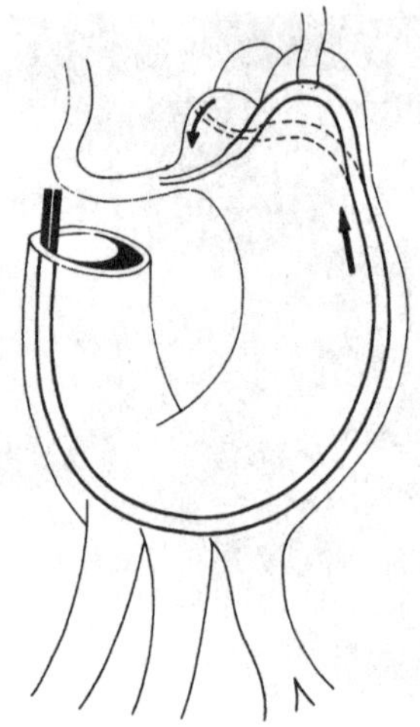

Abb. 2: Mechanismus der selektiven Katheterisierung der linken Koronararterie. Die Spitze des Katheters richtet sich durch Anpressen der Kurve im Bereich des distalen Endes des Katheters gegen die Aortenklappen entlang der Bulbuswand auf und dringt in das Koronarostium ein.

Patienten gelingt dies mit dem mittleren Katheter. Bei Einführen des Katheters in den Bulbus aortae dreht sich der Katheter derartig, daß seine Spitze in den linken Sinus weist. Preßt man nun die Kurve des Katheters gering gegen die Aortenklappen, so richtet sich die Katheterspitze auf. Sie steht hierbei senkrecht zur Wand des Bulbus aortae und dringt in entsprechender *Höhe in das Koronar*ostium ein (Abb. 2). Ist die richtige Lage des Katheters durch eine Kontrastmitteltestinjektion verifiziert, wird der Katheter etwas zurückgezogen, wodurch er sich an der Gegenwand der Aorta und an der Wand des Koronarostiums abstützt (Abb. 3 a). Zu große und zu kleine Katheter zeigen im Bulbus ein charakteristisches Verhalten. Sind diese Zeichen zu erkennen, muß der Katheter gegen einen solchen passender Größe ausgetauscht werden.

Das Verhalten eines zu großen Katheters: Bei der Einführung des Katheters in den Bulbus aortae biegt sich während des Anpressens der Kurve des Katheters gegen die Aortenklappen die kaliberschwächere Spitze an der Gegenwand des Bulbus aortae nach kaudal um und bildet dadurch einen nach unten offenen spitzen Winkel. Hat sich der Katheter durch weiteren Druck gegen die Aortenklappen vollständig aufgerichtet, so reicht er über das Koronarostium hinaus und kann in dieses nicht eindringen. Der Katheter nimmt dadurch eine charakteristische J-Form an (Abb. 3b).

Das Verhalten des zu kleinen Katheters: Der zu kleine Katheter neigt dazu, durch die Aortenklappen in den Ventrikel vorzudringen. Wenn sich seine Spitze aufrichtet, erreicht er das Ostium nicht, d. h., trotz richtiger Lage der Katheterspitze gelingt es nicht, die Spitze in das Ostium einzuführen (Abb. 3c). Kontrastmitteltestinjektionen zeigen meist eine semiselektive Füllung der Koronararterie. Ein weiteres Zeichen besteht darin, daß die Spitze zwar in das Koronarostium vordringt, jedoch hier nicht zu fixieren ist und durch den Blutstrom während der Systole aus dem Ostium herausgeschleudert wird.

Der rechte Katheter, dessen kleinste Größe für die Katheterisierung der Koronararterie meist die geeignete ist, unterscheidet sich in der Form seiner distalen Kurven nicht vom linken Katheter. Damit jedoch die Katheterspitze im Bulbus aortae nach ventral weist, hat der Schaft des

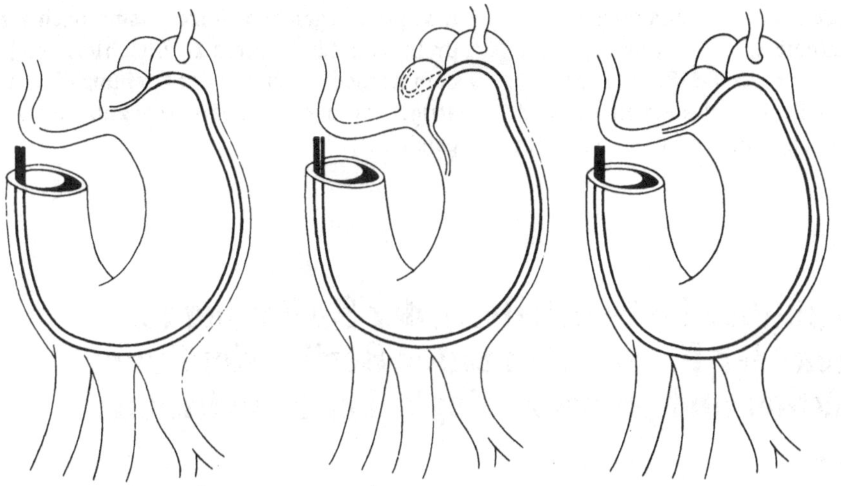

a b c

Abb. 3a–c: a. Durch leichtes Rückziehen des Katheters ist dieser durch Abstützung an der dem linken Koronarostium gegenüberliegenden Wand der Aorta fixiert.
b. Verhalten eines zu großen Katheters im Bulbus: Die Spitze des Katheters biegt sich anfänglich nach kaudal um. Später ist der Katheter J-förmig konfiguriert. Die Spitze liegt über dem linken Koronarostium.
c. Zu kleiner Katheter. Die Spitze reicht nicht bis zum linken Koronarostium.

Katheters eine dem Aortenbogen angepaßte Krümmung (Abb. 1b). Im Gegensatz zur linken Koronararterie, die durch Anpressen des Katheters gegen die Aortenklappen und das dadurch bedingte Aufrichten der Katheterspitze selektiv aufgesucht wird, dringt der rechte Katheter in das Koronarostium direkt ein (Abb. 4). Eine

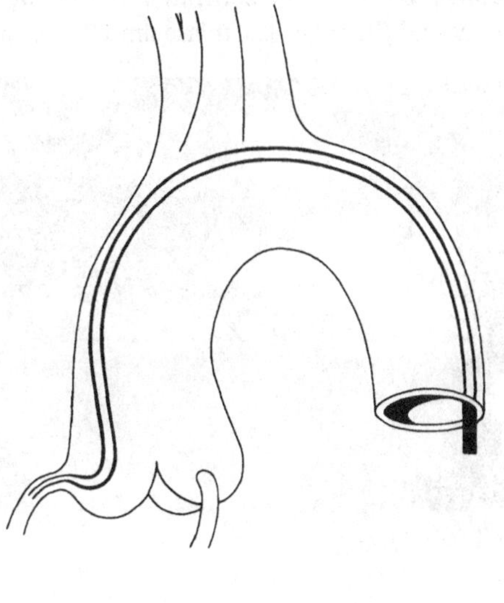

Abb. 4: Der rechte Koronararterienkatheter in situ. Die Katheterspitze dringt rechts direkt in das Ostium ein, ohne daß der Katheter gegen die Aortenklappen angepreßt werden muß.

besondere Manipulation zur Fixierung des Katheters im rechten Ostium ist nicht notwendig. Zu beachten ist, daß die Reaktion der Katheterspitze auf die Manipulation des Untersuchers infolge der Krümmung des Aortenbogens sich entgegengesetzt verhält als bei der abdominellen Aortographie. Weist die Katheterspitze, nachdem sie in die Aorta ascendens oder den Bulbus aortae vorgeschoben wurde nicht nach ventral, sondern auf die linke oder rechte Seite des Patienten, so muß sie durch entsprechende Drehung des Katheters in die richtige Position, also nach ventral gebracht werden, damit das rechte Koronarostium selektiv aufgesucht werden kann. Um nun die Katheterspitze von der rechten Seite des Patienten nach ventral zu drehen, muß man den Schaft des

Katheters gegen den Uhrzeigersinn drehen, damit sich die Katheterspitze im Uhrzeigersinn nach ventral bewegt. Weist die Katheterspitze hingegen auf die linke Seite des Patienten, wird der Schaft im Uhrzeigersinn gedreht, damit sich die Spitze gegen den Uhrzeigersinn nach ventral dreht. Um die Rotation zu erleichtern, soll mit dem Katheter während der Drehung eine ruckartige Vor- und Rückwärtsbewegung durchgeführt werden.

Kinematographische Beurteilung der Strömung im Gefäßsystem der Koronarien unter Berücksichtigung der Herzaktion und pharmakologischer Einwirkungen

H. Zimmermann

Mit Hilfe der Röntgenkinematographie lassen sich Strömungsvorgänge im Gefäßbereich gut beobachten und bei gleichzeitiger Einblendung von Meßgrößen wie Ekg, Druckkurven in das Kinobild können diese in Beziehung zu Kreislauf und Herzaktion analysiert werden.

Von besonderem Interesse ist der coronare Strömungsablauf, der vom peripheren Kreislauf erheblich abweicht. *Gregg, Wiggers, Cotton* u. a. haben im Tierversuch nachgewiesen, daß während der Systole eine weitgehende Blockierung der Koronarströmung eintritt, nach Flowmetermessungen von *Gregg* und *Anrep* konnten im Bereich der linken Koronararterie sogar rückläufige Strömungsbewegungen registriert werden. Wenn bei selektiver Koronarangiographie am Hundeherzen der Kontrastmittelstrom in die linke Koronararterie konstant gehalten wird und dem Blutstrom aus der Aorta in das Gefäß so angepaßt wird, daß die Kontrastdichte nicht dominiert, so läßt sich kinematographisch eine rhythmische Zu- und Abnahme der Kontrastdichte im Gefäß erkennen, die in Abhängigkeit zur Herzaktion steht. Die Zunahme der Kontrastdichte während der Systole läßt sich mit der Drosselung des Bluteinstromes aus der Aorta erklären, während die mit Übergang in die Diastole zu beobachtende Aufhellung auf einen erneuten Einstrom kontrastfreien Blutes aus der Aorta hinweist.

In dieser Phase lassen sich auch deutliche Strömungseffekte entlang der Gefäßwand erkennen, die sich aus der noch unvermischten Blut- und Kontrastsäule ergeben.
Die von *Gregg* und Mitarb. mittels Flowmeter registrierte systolische Rückstrombewegung konnte erst dadurch sichtbar gemacht werden, daß der intrakoronaren Kontrastinjektion eine kleine Luftblase beigeben wurde, die sich als kleine Aufhellung innerhalb des kontrastdichten Gefäßes abhob und so die feinen Schwankungen innerhalb des Gefäßschattens anzeigte.

So läßt sich mit Ablauf der aortalen Druckkurve der gleichmäßige Abstrom während der Diastole erkennen (Abb. 1) eine zunehmende Verlangsamung und Stase der Luftblase am Übergang

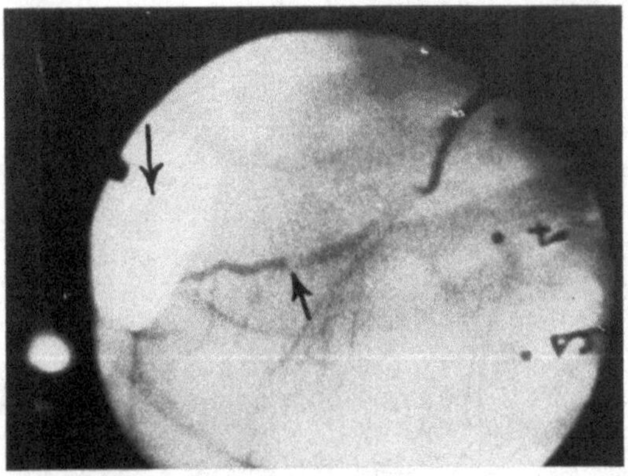

Abb. 1

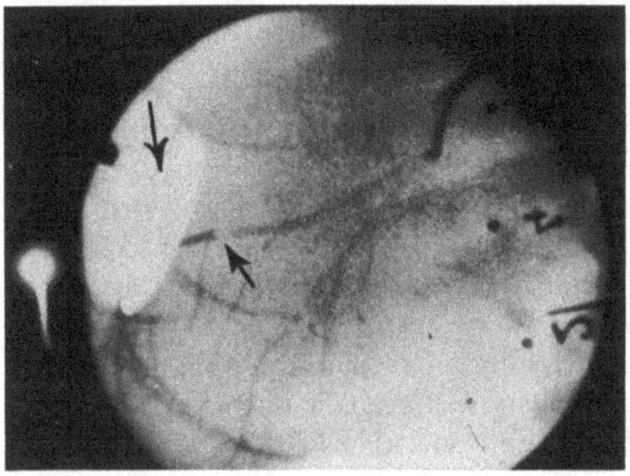

Abb. 2

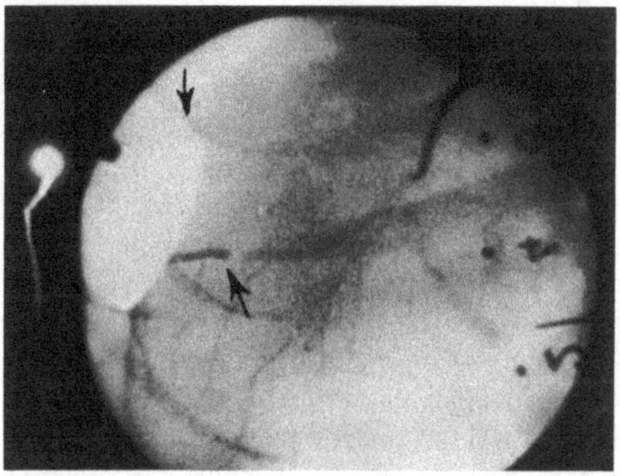

Abb. 3

zur Systole (Abb. 2) und schließlich zum Zeitpunkt der maximalen Anspannung eine kleine Rückstoßbewegung (Abb. 3), die sich besonders gut an der Lageverschiebung zu den kleinen Gefäßabgängen abgrenzen läßt.
Da bei der selektiven Koronarangiographie der Sinus venosus kontrastdicht zur Darstellung kommt, ergibt sich die Möglichkeit auch den venösen Rückstrom kinematographisch zu beobachten und die Kreislaufzeit von Beginn der Kontrastinjektion bis zum Zeitpunkt der Anfärbung des Sinus venosus zu messen. Dabei läßt sich vor allem die Wirkung gefäßerweiternder und -verengender Pharmaka in ihrer verkürzenden bzw. verlängernden Umlaufzeit gegenüber stellen. Schließlich ergibt sich auch die Möglichkeit, die Wirkung verschiedener Kontrastmittel auf die Kontraktilität des Herzmuskels und Veränderungen des miteingeblendeten Elektrocardiogrammes registrieren zu können.

Verlaufsbeobachtung nach simultaner direkter und indirekter Revaskularisation des Herzens

C. A. Pierach

Zusammenfassung

Zwischen 1968 und 1972 wurden von unserer Arbeitsgruppe an 524 Patienten revaskularisierende Eingriffe am Herzen vorgenommen. Eine Kombination von direkter (aorto-koronarer Venen-Bypass) und indirekter (Implantation einer oder beider Aa. mammariae internae) Revaskularisation wurde 119 mal durchgeführt, wobei die Operationsmortalität 4% betrug. Nachuntersuchungen an 40 Patienten mittels Angiographie und/oder Autopsie zeigten, daß 24 von 53 implantierten Aa. mammarıe ınternae sichtbare Kollateralen zum Koronargefäßsystem gebildet hatten. Sechs implantierte Aa. mammariae ınternae waren verschlossen Funfzehn der 42 eingesetzten Venen-Bypass-Grafts waren verschlossen. Sektionen an sechs Patienten zeigten, daß fünf Venen-Bypass-Grafts wenıgstens teilweise durchgängig waren Bei 14 von

15 Patienten mit verschlossenen Venen-Bypass-Grafts war wenigstens eine der implantierten Aa. mammariae internae durchgängig, allerdings nur in acht Fällen mit sichtbaren Kollateralen. Bei 17 Patienten waren sowohl die Venen-Bypass-Grafts als auch die implantierten Aa. mammariae internae offen, wobei letztere in zehn Fällen Kollateralen aufwiesen. Angina pectoris war in allen Untergruppen vermindert, doch fand sich die deutlichste Besserung bei jenen Patienten, die sowohl offene Venen-Bypass-Grafts als auch offene Implantate hatten. Der nicht seltene Verschluß der Venen-Bypass-Grafts und die relativ häufige Kollateralbildung von implantierten Aa. mammariae internae aus, lassen eine Kombination dieser beiden Revaskularisationsverfahren sinnvoll erscheinen.

Beide der häufig angewandten chirurgischen Behandlungsverfahren der koronaren Herzkrankheit haben ihre Nachteile: Die Implantation einer oder beider Aa. mammariae internae kann zwar Angina pectoris lindern, doch benötigt die Ausbildung der dazu erforderlichen Kollateralen relativ viel Zeit, in welcher der Patient einem eher höheren Risiko ausgesetzt ist. Der aorto-koronare Venen-Bypass kann zwar die Durchblutung des Herzens sofort verbessern, doch mehren sich die Berichte über nachteilige Veränderungen der Venen-Bypass-Grafts. Ein weiterer Unterschied dieser beiden Revaskularisationsverfahren ist in ihrer Anwendbarkeit zu sehen: Bypass-Grafts sind nur dann sinnvoll, wenn sie eine relativ proximal gelegene Koronarstenose umgehen und wenn das periphere Koronarsystem einen guten Abfluß gewährleistet; demgegenüber eignen sich implantierte extrakardiale Arterien (z. B. *Vineberg*sche Operation) zur Revaskularisation ischämischen Myokards bei diffuser Koronarsklerose.

Im folgenden soll unsere Erfahrung mit dieser kombinierten chirurgischen Revaskularisation des Herzens dargestellt werden.

Patienten

Zwischen Mai 1968 und April 1972 wurden an 524 Patienten revaskularisierende Eingriffe am Herzen vorgenommen. Die Mehrzahl der Patienten, nämlich 364, erhielten Venen-Bypass-Grafts (128 je einen, 221 je zwei und 15 je drei Grafts). An 41 Patienten wurde eine Gasendarterektomie vorgenommen. Bei 119 Patienten wurden direkte und indirekte Revaskularisation kombiniert. Während oder unmittelbar nach dem Eingriff verstarben fünf (= 4%) der letztgenannten Patientengruppe. Koronarangiographie und Ventrikulographie bestimmten das chirurgische Vorgehen. Bei den 119 Patienten wurden während der kombinierten Revaskularisation 144 Bypass-Grafts eingesetzt und zusätzlich bei 100 Patienten eine und bei 19 Patienten beide Aa. mammariae internae implantiert. Ein Patient wurde ein zweites Mal operiert, als sein erster Venen-Bypass thrombosiert war.

Acht Patienten, die verstorben waren und 32 Patienten, an denen eine Nachuntersuchung etwa ein Jahr nach dem Eingriff (2–25 Monate) durchgeführt worden war, bilden die Grundlage dieser Arbeit. Das Durchschnittsalter der Patienten zum Zeitpunkt der Operation betrug 50 Jahre (34–65 Jahre); es handelt sich um 37 Männer und drei Frauen. Bei allen Patienten war vor und nach der Operation eine selektive Koronarographie durchgeführt worden. In den meisten Fällen wurde die Technik nach *Sones* und *Shirey* benutzt. Die Angiogramme wurden unabhängig vom klinischen Befund ausgewertet und die Schwere der Koronarsklerose nach einem Gradsystem unterteilt (Tab. 1). Die implantierten Aa. mammariae internae und die der V. saphena entstammenden Bypass-Grafts wurden angiographisch nachuntersucht, wobei nach Möglichkeit eine selektive Angiographie durchgeführt wurde, unter Vermeidung eines Verschlusses der Gefäßöffnung mittels Katheter.

Acht Patienten erhielten vor und nach der Operation orale Antikoagulantien, weitere sechs Patienten waren vor und 12 Patienten nur nach

Tab. 1: Koronarskleroseausmaß an prä- und postoperativen Angiogrammen

Kranzgefäß	Durchschnittlicher Grad*	
	präoperativ	ein Jahr nach der Operation
A. coronaria dextra	3,75 (41)	4,4 (28)
R. descendens anterior	3,34 (41)	3,79 (29)
R. circumflexus	3,04 (41)	3,29 (28)

* 1: gelegentliche Stenose (bis 10% Einengung); 2: mäßiggradige Stenose (10 bis 50% Einengung); 3: schwere Stenose (50 bis 90% Stenose); 4: fast vollständiger Verschluß; 5: vollständiger Verschluß.
( ) Anzahl untersuchter Gefäße.

der Operation antikoaguliert. Die Vorgeschichte ergab bei 25 Patienten einen Myokardinfarkt vor der Operation, bei acht Patienten sogar zwei Infarkte. Ein Patient überlebte seinen zweiten Infarkt neun Monate nach der Operation, während er mit Antikoagulantien behandelt wurde; sein Venen-Bypass war zwar stenosiert, doch angiographisch durchgängig, während sein A. mammaria interna-Implantat verschlossen war. Autoptisch fanden sich drei weitere Myokardinfarkte, die in engem zeitlichen Zusammenhang mit der Operation aufgetreten waren. Ein Patient erlag fünf Monate nach der Operation einem autoptisch nachgewiesenen Infarkt.

Ergebnisse

Eine Einteilung der Patienten je nach Zustand der revaskularisierenden Gefäße führt zu den Tab. 2 bis 4. Die Todesfälle sind zusätzlich in Tab. 5 zusammengefaßt.

Verschlossener Venen-Bypass und offenes A. mammaria interna-Implantat:

Diese Gruppe (Tab. 2) von 15 Patienten hatte ein Durchschnittsalter von 50 Jahren und unter-

Tab. 2: Verschlossener Venen-Bypass und offenes A. mammaria interna-Implantat

	Patient (Alter)	Venen-Bypass zu	Implantat Zahl	Implantat Kolateralen	Angina pectoris vor Operation	Angina pectoris nach Operation	Antikoagulantien vor Operation	Antikoagulantien nach Operation
1	(51)	R	1	ja	2	0	ja	ja
2	(65)	LAD	2	ja	3	2	nein	nein
5	(55)	R & LAD (Y)	1	ja	3	2	nein	ja
7	(54)	R	2	1–ja	3	1	ja	nein
8	(45)	R	1	ja	3	2	nein	nein
12	(51)	R	2	1 offen	0	2	ja	nein
13	(36)	LAD	1	nein	2	1	nein	nein
15	(49)	R	2	ja	4	1	nein	nein
21	(46)	R & LAD (Y)	1	nein	3	0	nein	ja
22	(43)	R	1	ja	0	0	nein	ja
23	(45)	LAD	1	nein	4	0	nein	ja
25	(57)	R	2	ja	3	0	nein	ja
31	(46)	R	1	nein	3	0	ja	nein
32	(46)	LAD	1	nein	4	4	nein	nein
40	(58)	R	1	nein	3	0	nein	nein

Legende: R: A. coronaria dextra; LAD: R. descendens anterior; CMX: R. circumflexus; Y: Venen-Bypass-Graft von einem Ausgangspunkt an der Aorta zu zwei Gefäßen im Koronarsystem; die Angina pectoris wurde in einer 0 bis 4-Skala eingeteilt (in Anlehnung an die Klassifizierung der New York Heart Association): 0: keine Angina pectoris, jedoch fanden sich bei einzelnen Patienten präoperativ Beschwerden wie Kurzluftigkeit, rasche Ermüdbarkeit und unspezifische Symptome; 1: leicht; 2: mäßig; 3: schwer; 4: Angina decubitus. Antikoagulantien beziehen sich auf den langfristigen Gebrauch von Dicumarolpräparaten.

schied sich hierin nicht von den anderen Patienten. Vier Bypass-Grafts zum R. descendens anterior (= R. interventricularis anterior) und zwei Y-förmige Grafts waren verschlossen. Neun implantierte Aa. mammariae internae zeigten angiographisch eindeutige Kollateralen zum Koronargefäßsystem. Zwei Patienten dieser Gruppe wiesen keine Besserung ihres Beschwerdebildes auf. Sechs der 15 Patienten erhielten orale Antikoagulantien nach dem Eingriff; vier dieser 6 Patienten hatten zwar erkennbare Kollateralen von den Implantaten aus, doch waren ihre Bypass-Grafts verschlossen.

Offener Venen-Bypass und offenes A. mammaria interna-Implantat:
Das Durchschnittsalter dieser Gruppe (Tab. 3) von 17 Patienten lag mit 58 Jahren etwas höher.

Tab. 3: Offener Venen-Bypass und offenes A. mammaria interna-Implantat

	Patient (Alter)	Venen-Bypass zu	Implantat Zahl	Implantat Kollateralen	Angina pectoris vor Operation	Angina pectoris nach Operation	Antikoagulantien vor Operation	Antikoagulantien nach Operation
3	(52)	R	1	ja	4	1	nein	ja
4	(66)	R	1	ja	4	0	nein	nein
6	(52)	R	1	nein	2	1	nein	nein
10	(47)	R	1	nein	0	0	ja	ja
12	(47)	R	2	1–ja	2	0	nein	ja
16	(51)	LAD	1	nein	2	0	ja	ja
19	(47)	R	1	ja	3	0	nein	ja
20	(55)	LAD	1	nein	1	0	ja	ja
24	(38)	LAD	1	ja	4	0	nein	nein
26	(67)	CMX	1	ja	2	1	nein	nein
27	(62)	R	2	nein	2	0	nein	nein
28	(52)	R	2	1–ja	4	1	nein	nein
29	(50)	LAD	1	nein	4	0	nein	ja
30	(46)	R	1	ja	4	0	ja	ja
32	(46)	R	1	nein	4	4	nein	nein
38	(46)	R	2	ja	3	0	nein	nein
39	(65)	R	2	ja	4	0	ja	ja

Legende: s. Tab. 2.

Fünf Bypass-Grafts zu Ästen der A. coronaria sinistra und 12 Bypass-Grafts zur rechten Koronararterie waren offen. Zehn A. mammaria interna-Implantate hatten sichtbare Kollateralen zum Kranzgefäßsystem gebildet. Elf Patienten waren postoperativ völlig beschwerdefrei, ein Patient gab keine Besserung an. Zehn Patienten erhielten postoperativ Antikoagulantien, doch findet sich nur eine schwach-positive Korrelation zur Ausbildung von Kollateralen vom Implantat.

Offener Venen-Bypass und verschlossenes A. mammaria interna-Implantat:
Die fünf Patienten dieser Gruppe (Tab. 4) lagen altersmäßig zwischen den vorgenannten Gruppen. Bei diesen Patienten war ein Bypass zur A. coronaria dextra angelegt worden und gleichzeitig eine A. mammaria interna in die Wand des linken Ventrikels implantiert worden. Alle Patienten erhielten postoperativ Antikoagulantien. Diese Gruppe zeigte als Kollektiv die geringste postoperative Besserung.

Tab. 4: Offener Venen-Bypass und verschlossenes A. mammaria interna-Implantat

Patient	(Alter)	Venen-Bypass zu	Angina pectoris vor Operation	Angina pectoris nach Operation	Antikoagulantien vor Operation	Antikoagulantien nach Operation
8	(35)	R	2	2	nein	ja
14	(60)	R	3	3	ja	ja
17	(58)	R	0	0	ja	ja
18	(65)	R	1	0	nein	ja

Legende: s. Tab. 2.

Frühe und späte Todesfälle:
Vier Patienten verstarben in engem zeitlichen Zusammenhang mit der Operation (Tab. 5). Vier weitere Patienten starben 2, 5, 11 und 33 Monate nach dem Eingriff. Da drei Patienten zwischen Operation und Tod angiographiert worden waren, sind diese Patienten auch in obigen Tabellen an entsprechender Stelle aufgeführt. Die beiden Patienten, welche am längsten überlebten, hatten Antikoagulantien erhalten, die anderen Patienten nicht. Autoptisch fand sich bei allen Patienten eine mehr oder minder deutlich ausgeprägte Herzvergrößerung, wobei das schwerste Herz 700 g wog. Drei von sechs Venen-Bypass-Grafts waren weit offen, doch handelte es sich um drei Frühtodesfälle. Bei einem Patienten, der zwei Monate nach der Operation verstorben war, lag ein Verschluß beider Venen-Bypass-Grafts und der implantierten A. mammaria interna vor. Bei zwei Patienten wiesen die Venen-Bypass-Grafts eine ausgeprägte subintimale fibröse Hyperplasie auf. Bei zwei der fünf Autopsien zeigten die implantierten Aa. mammariae internae mikroskopisch Gefäßneubildungen, die wir als Kollateralen auffassen.

Diskussion

Trotz weiter Verbreitung von direkter und indirekter Revaskularisation scheint eine Kombination dieser beiden Verfahren selten angewandt zu werden. Favaloro wies als erster auf die Bedeutung dieser Kombination hin; die Operationsletalität lag bei seinen Patienten in etwa gleichem Bereich wie für die direkte und indirekte Revaskularisation allein. Eine Umfrage bei kardiovaskulären Zentren in USA ergab eine Operationsmortalität von 2,8% für 455 kombinierte Revaskularisationen des Jahres 1970. In unserem Krankengut machte die Patientengruppe, bei welcher ein kombinierter Eingriff vorgenommen wurde, 22,6% aller revaskularisierenden Operationen aus.

Die Implantation einer extrakardialen Arterie in ischämisches Myokard verschlechtert den Zustand des Herzens wenigstens so lange, bis Kollateralen ausgebildet sind. Dieser Prozeß braucht etwa sechs Wochen. Ist der Anschluß aber einmal hergestellt, so scheinen Spätkomplikationen seitens des Implantates kaum zu befürchten. Demgegenüber vermag ein Venen-Bypass-Graft die Blutversorgung des Myokards sofort zu verbessern, doch eignen sich nur Kranzgefäße mit relativ proximaler Stenose und gutem peripheren Gefäßkaliber für die Anlegung eines solchen Grafts. Zudem ist die Zahl der Grafts, die pro Patient angelegt werden kann, begrenzt; Y-förmige Grafts, die man auch mit der Form eines Kleiderbügels vergleichen kann, haben sich bei uns nicht bewährt. Spätverschlüsse von Venen-Bypass-Grafts werden in 32–50% der Patienten beobachtet, wobei niedrige Flußmengen im Bypass (< 40 ml/min) und geringe Durchmesser der Koronararterie an der Anschlußstelle besonders ungünstig wirken.

Tab. 5: Frühe und späte Todesfälle

Patient (Alter)	Venen-Bypass	Implantat Zahl	Angina pectoris vor Operation	Angina pectoris nach Operation	Antikoagulantien vor Operation	Antikoagulantien nach Operation	Zustand der revaskularisierenden Gefäße angiographisch Venen-Bypass	angiographisch Implantat	autoptisch Venen-Bypass	autoptisch Implantat
32 (46)	R & LAD	2	4	4	nein	nein	R–offen LAD–verschlossen	offen	R–verschlossen LAD–verschlossen	offen
33 (57)	R	1	2		nein	nein			offen	verschlossen
34 (64)	R	1	2		ja	nein				
35 (37)	R	1	4		ja	nein			offen	offen
36 (48)	R	2	4		nein	nein			offen	offen
37 (46)	R	2	3	4	nein	nein			verengt	offen mit Kollateralen
38 (46)	R	2	3	0	ja	ja	offen	offen mit Kollateralen		
39 (65)	R	2	4	0	nein	ja	verengt	offen mit Kollateralen	ausgeprägte subintimale fibröse Hyperplasie	offen mit Kollateralen

Legende: s. Tab. 2.

Anschluß Tab. 5:

Todesursache	postoperative Überlebenszeit	Herzgewicht g	Sektion
verstarb während Angiographie	2 Monate	510	frischer Myokardinfarkt
Arrhythmie	13 Tage	600	Phäochromozytom
akute intestinale Blutung	23 Tage		
Kammerflimmern	5 Tage	560	frischer Myokardinfarkt
Schock	1 Tag	380	
Herzversagen	5 Monate	700	frischer Myokardinfarkt
kollabiert; Tod bei Ankunft im Krankenhaus	33 Monate		
Kammerflimmern	11 Monate	630	ausgeprägte Myokardfibrose; kein Anhalt für frischen Myokardinfarkt

In diesen Fällen scheint uns die Implantation einer oder beider Aa. mammariae internae indiziert. Es sei auch bedacht, daß sich arteriosklerotische Veränderungen recht oft in peripheren Abschnitten des Herzkranzgefäßsystems finden, was nicht immer aus den Koronarogrammen hervorgeht.
Die postoperative Anwendung oraler Antikoagulantien folgte keiner strengen Regel; unsere Ergebnisse lassen keinen Schluß bezüglich ihres Nutzens für die revaskularisierenden Gefäße zu.

Zwar ist der günstige Einfluß revaskularisierender Eingriffe auf das Beschwerdebild der Patienten auch in unseren Untersuchungen ersichtlich, doch wäre eine objektivere Erfassung der Leistungsbreite des Herzens oder der Myokarddurchblutung wünschenswert. Eine um so größere Rolle spielt die Angiographie, die eine wesentliche Untersuchung in der Verlaufsbeobachtung der Patienten darstellt. Die von uns bevorzugte Technik nach *Sones* und *Shirey* läßt sich auch wiederholt am gleichen Gefäß anwenden, wobei wir die alte Arteriotomie wiederbenutzen.
Die Operationsmortalität im hier referierten Krankengut betrug 4% und scheint uns im Vergleich zur „natürlichen“ Mortalität von 3% jährlich bei Patienten mit Angina pectoris annehmbar. Die geringe Häufigkeit postoperativer Myokardinfarkte kontrastiert mit der hohen präoperativen Infarktfrequenz, doch erlauben unsere Untersuchungen nicht den Schluß, daß die Revaskularisation tatsächlich Infarkte verhindert und somit das Leben verlängern kann. Das rasche Fortschreiten einer einmal begonnenen Koronarsklerose ist aus einem Vergleich unserer prä- und postoperativen Koronarogramme ersichtlich und bestätigt die Erfahrungen anderer Untersucher (siehe Tab. 1). Das Überwiegen von Venen-Bypass-Grafts zur rechten Kranzarterie erklärt sich wenigstens teilweise dadurch, daß dieses Gefäß besonders häufig arteriosklerotisch verändert ist (siehe Tab. 1). Wenngleich sich bei allen unseren Gruppen im Kollektiv eine Besserung der pectanginösen Beschwerden fand, so ist dieses doch am deutlichsten bei jenen Patienten, die sowohl einen offenen Venen-Bypass als auch eine offene implantierte A. mammaria interna hatten (Tab. 3). Selbst bei jenen Patienten, bei denen sich bei der Nachuntersuchung ein Verschluß des Venen-Bypass fand, möchten wir einen günstigen Effekt der kombinierten Revaskularisation annehmen, denn es erscheint uns durchaus denkbar, daß der Bypass solange funktionierte, bis Kollateralen von der implantierten A. mammaria interna aus gebildet waren.

Schlußfolgerungen

Die Revaskularisation des Myokards durch Anlegen eines Venen-Bypass-Grafts kann durch gleichzeitige Implantation einer oder beider Aa. mammariae internae bereichert werden, falls sich eine diffuse Koronarsklerose findet. Eine Kardiomegalie stellt eine relative Kontraindikation dar. Der Angiographie der revaskularisierenden Gefäße kommt eine wesentliche Rolle im Rahmen der Nachuntersuchungen zu. So konnte gezeigt werden, daß bei 14 von 40 Patienten, an denen simultan eine kombinierte Revaskularisation vorgenommen worden war, beide zusätzlichen Quellen der Blutzufuhr wirksam zu sein schienen.

Die hier referierten Operationen wurden ausgeführt von Drs. N. K. Jensen, W. R. Schmidt, J. J. Garamella, M. F. Lynch, A. M. Bilgutay und W. D. Kelly, deren überaus kollegiale Zusammenarbeit ich gerne dankbar anerkenne. Für die Hilfe bei der Auswertung und Zusammenstellung der Unterlagen danke ich Frau Joy Thoma und Melanie King.

Selective coronary Arteriography by the Percutaneous Femoral Artery approach according to Bourassa

A. Essinger

Semi-selective coronary arteriography as described by *Paulin* was first introduced in our department in 1963, and over a thousand patients have been examined with this method, and this without any casualty over a peiod of seven years. Since the introduction of aorto-coronary venous by-pass, by *Favaloro* and *Effler*, there has been a need for better demonstration of collateral peripheral coronary circulation and this brought many cardio-vascular centers, and specially their radiological team to developp selective coronary angiography through the femoral route. In the last five years, many reports have demonstrated the feasibility of transfemoral approach for the selective study of the coronary tree, and this in very large series of patients. This led us change our method of investigation and introduce in June 1970 the selective technique described by the french Canadians *Bourassa* and *Lespérance*.

The method uses manually prepared white radiopaque polythelene catheters with two different shapes in order to enter successively the right and left coronary orifice, and this by immersing the catheter in boiling water after having tapered the tip over a distance of approximately 1 cm (fig. 1). The introduction of the catheters in the femoral artery is made according to the well-known *Seldinger* technique, using either a standard stainless steel guide-wire or a teflon-coated one. The cannulation of the coronary arteries is remarkably simple, and usually few manipulations, if any, are required to enter the coronary ostia, this under pressure monitorization and permanent EKG control. The left coronary artery is cannulated in the antero-posterior projection, while the right one is entered either in a left anterior oblique or in a true lateral one, using for these projections a *Nordenström* C-arm.

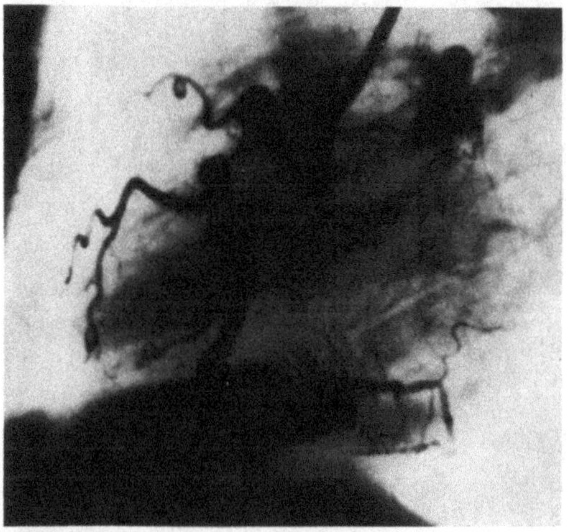

Fig. 1: ♂ 52 years.
"Impending infarct". Severe stenosis of the right coronary artery (lateral view).

Three different projections of the right and left coronary arteries are obtained: the great stability of the catheters allows us to run the examination first on 35 mm cine, and secondly on large sized films, thus allowing to appreciate as well the dynamic as well as lesions on very fine vessels. A left ventriculography done on cine only, with an occluded tip catheter, always completes the examination often made on an ambulatory basis, under local anesthesia, without heparinization of the patient, and without any kind of premedication. The examination can be usually completed in thirty minutes, but some patients required only 20 minutes while others needed 90 minutes, this depending on the anatomy of the coronary arteries as well as of the arteriosclerotic changes of the thoracic and abdominal aorta. Urografin 76% has been used in most our patients; a manual injection of 4 to 8 cc with a 10 cc seringue usually permits an excellent opacification of the right and left coronary vessels. For the left ventriculogra-

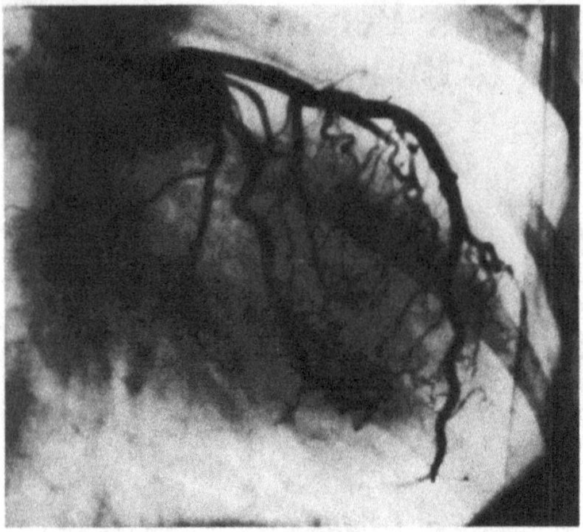

Fig. 2: ♀ 60 years.
Slight stenosis of the anterior descending (right anterior oblique view).

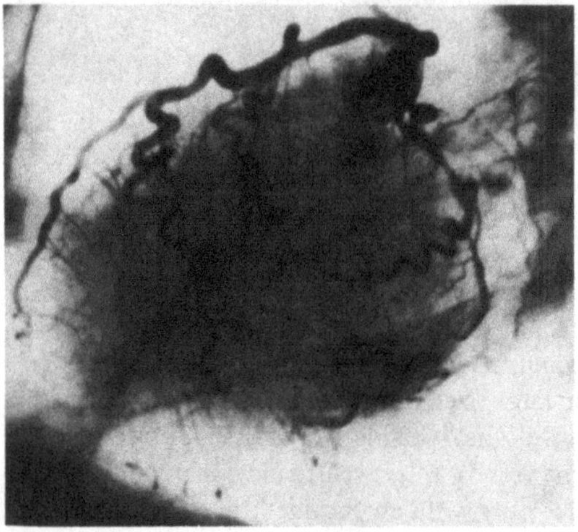

Fig. 3: ♂ 55 years.
Multiple lesions of the circumflex, of the postero-lateral bronches, and collateral circulation to the right coronary artery (lateral view).

phy, we have been using 25–30 cc Urografin 76% with an automatic injector; since we have started volume measurement in the left anterior oblique projection, the amount of contrast used has been slightly increased.
From June 1970 to December 1972, 510 patients have been examined with the Bourassa technique; there were 94 females (18,7%) amongst them. The oldest patient examined with this method was 76 years old, while the youngest one was 23. In 20 patients, different catheters than those described by *Bourassa* had to be used either for the right or the left coronary artery. In 7 elderly patients with an average age of 65, where the femoral approach was not possible due to severe arteriosclerotic changes in the iliac arteries, the Sones technique was used, with poor results due to tortuosity of the brachio-cephalic trunk and to arteriosclerotic plaques at the site of the cut-down, which resulted that three patients developped a thrombosis of the brachial artery, which have been cured surgically a few hours after the end of the examination.

As complications, we have had one episode of ventricular fibrillation, with rapid and uneventful defibrillation. A dissection of a right coronary artery has occured in one instance, with no electrocardiographic changes, due to the fact that the patient had a 90% stenosis of the middle third of that coronary, which was operated on an emergency basis, with excellent results. A young woman developped a thrombosis at the site of puncture, which had to be cured surgically. One casualty has to be reported in a man, who had three cardiac arrest in the 24 hours before the examination, which was done on an emergency basis. These figures can be compared to those of *Bourassa,* who reports in a study of 1000 consecutive cases 0,4% vascular complications, 1,0% cardiac complications (ventricular fibrillation, infarct and coronary dissection) and 0,2% casualty.

In order to assess patency of aorto-coronary vein grafts, the original shape of the *Bourassa* catheters had to be slightly modified, particularly for studying the grafts for the left side, which are usually implanted anteriorly on the aorta. 57 grafts could thus be studied in a period varying from twelve to eighteen months post-operatively. When the graft was occluded, the sight of implantation could usually be

detected by the catheter, and a slight irregularity of the aortic wall could be demonstrated angiographically.
As a vascular radiologist, we gave our preference to the femoral approach as compared to the brachial one, this route being used daily for the selective catheterisation of abdominal and cephalic arteries. The femoral artery has a much larger calibre than the brachial artery, and therefore less frequent thrombotic complications are encountered at the site of entry of the catheter. Furthermore, the cannulation of the coronary arteries is much easier by the femoral approach than from the brachial artery the *Sones* technique requires a lot of training to be fully succesfull, and even than, a lot of manipulations and a long fluoroscopy time are required to enter both coronary ostia.
Our preference was given to the *Bourassa* technique, the complications rate being very low, and the catheters manipulation being very easy. The *Judkin's* catheters have been used here and there, but there rigidity causes intimal lesions, and their irregular wall favours the formation of thrombi. Furthermore, the shape of the right coronary catheter requires a number of manipulations to enter the right coronary artery, which can be avoided by using a proper shaped one as the *Bourassa* for instance. Percutaneous femoral approach obviates the need for dissection of an brachial artery, with all the disadvantages of such an approach, such as numbness of the arm and hand, diminution or absence or radial pulse at the end of the examination. Furthermore, it allows easy projections of the coronary tree, in all the oblique views as well as the true lateral one, as the patient may easily put both his hands behind his head during the course of the examination.
Nevertheless, if the *Bourassa* technique is a very safe and handy method for studying the coronary arteries, one should not limit itself to one single method, but should be able, if necessary for the demonstration of the coronary arteries, to be able to use other ways of approach, such as *Sones* for instance.

Postoperative Koronarographie

M. Wiljasalo und O. Korhola

Im Krankenhaus Meilahti der Universität Helsinki wurden in den Jahren 1969 bis 1972 230 Koronarangiographien durchgeführt. Dabei war zunächst die Methode nach *Paulin* und in neuerer Zeit vermehrt die Technik nach *Judkins* verwandt worden. 40 dieser Koronarangiographien waren postoperativ durchgeführt worden. Wir haben den *Judkins*-Katheter modifiziert, indem wir die Spitze steiler gebogen haben. Die A.mammaria interna läßt sich selektiv mit diesem Kathetertyp oder mit einem *Paulin*-Katheter semiselektiv darstellen.

Zur Überprüfung der postoperativen Nahtverhältnisse haben wir diese Kathetertechnik zunächst an 10 Hunden unmittelbar postoperativ durchgeführt. Die Ergebnisse waren sehr gut, es kam zu keinen Komplikationen.
Die postoperative Koronarographie läßt sich mit der Technik nach *Paulin* semiselektiv oder mit der Technik nach *Judkins* selektiv durchführen. Die Darstellung des Mammaria-interna-Transplantates ist rein aortographisch oder selektiv möglich.

Nach Koronararterien-Chirurgie ist bei 40 Patienten eine postoperative Koronarangiographie durchgeführt worden. Sowohl selektive als auch semiselektive Techniken wurden angewandt: Bei Zustand nach aorto-koronarem Bypass, nach Arteria-mammaria-Bypass und nach Gasendarterektomie.

Die besseren Ergebnisse ließen sich mit der selektiven Technik erzielen. Die semiselektive Technik hat sich bei uns nur dann bewährt, wenn der Verdacht auf einen Verschluß des Bypasses besteht.

In 8 % der von uns untersuchten Fälle war der Bypass postoperativ verschlossen. Komplikationen haben wir während der postoperativen Koronarangiographie nicht beobachtet.

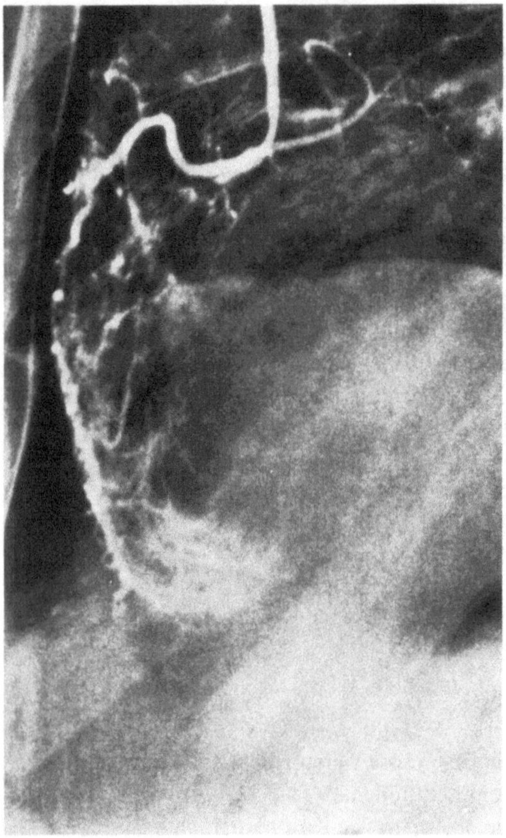

Abb. 1: Rechte selektive Katheterisierung, Hauptäste verschlossen.

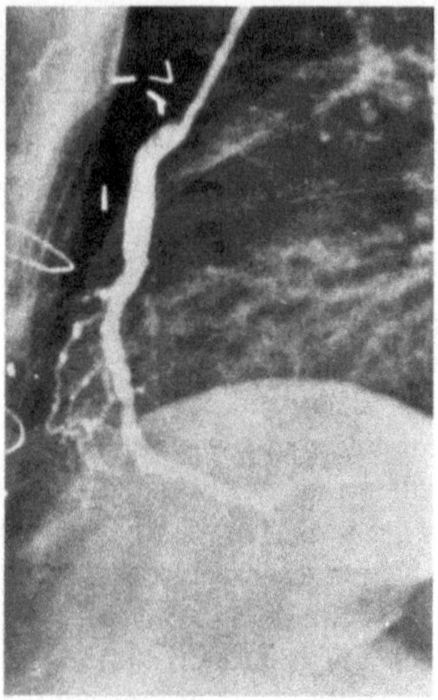

Abb. 2: Selektive postoperative Darstellung des Bypasses (hier war auch eine Gasendarteriektomie durchgeführt worden), Darstellung der rechten Koronararterie.

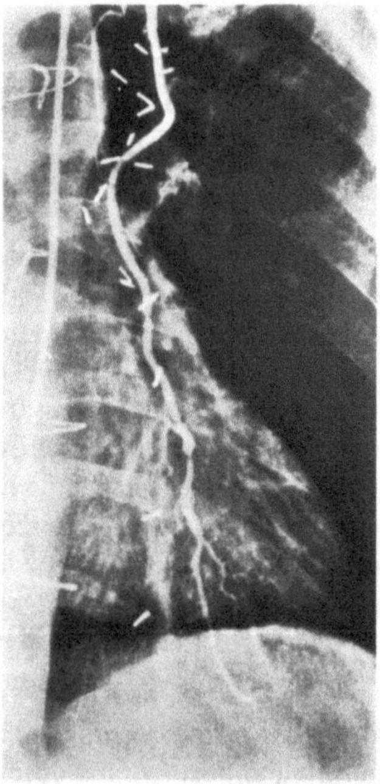

⟶

Abb. 3: Derselbe Patient: Katheterisierung der Arteria mammaria interna, Darstellung der Arteria anterior descendens, die in der Peripherie durch einen Mammaria-interna-Bypass dargestellt ist.

V. DIE RÄUMLICHE ZUORDNUNG DES GEFÄSS-SYSTEMS IM ANGIOGRAPHISCHEN BILD

Stereofernsehen mit Stereokinematographie, eine praxisgerechte Lösung mit modernen Röntgenanlagen

K. Dümmling und W. Maaß

Das Konzept der im folgenden beschriebenen Einrichtung für Stereokino und Stereofernsehen geht zurück auf die Arbeiten von *Lindblom, Webster, Sones* mit Kok und eine Zusammenarbeit mit *Stauffer* in Philadelphia. Eine Stereoanlage nach diesem Konzept ist bereits seit 1970 in Betrieb (Prof. van de Velde, Prof. Kunnen, Academisch Ziekenhuis, Gent, Belgien). Sie ist als Zwei-Ebenen-Einrichtung für die Cardangiographie aufgebaut.

Beim Cineradiographicum in Antwerpen wurde 1970 zum ersten Mal darüber berichtet. Hier soll der inzwischen verbesserte Stand dieser Einrichtung beschrieben werden.

Die Abb. 1–3 geben einen Überblick über die Stereoeinrichtung. Abb. 1 zeigt links die beiden übereinander angeordneten Röntgenröhren, die bei Stereobetrieb abwechselnd auf den seitlichen Bildverstärker strahlen. Unter dem Tisch befindet sich ein gleiches Stereopaar von Röntgenröhren für die sagittale Strahlenrichtung. Hinter der Strahlenschutzwand mit Bleiglasfenstern sind die beiden Röntgengeneratoren in einer Montagewand angeordnet (Abb. 2).

Mit dieser Anlage ist wahlweise Mono- oder Stereodurchleuchtung und Mono- oder Stereokinobetrieb möglich. Für den Monobetrieb können sowohl die rechte wie die linke Röntgenröhre der jeweiligen Ebene angewählt werden. Für den Kinobetrieb ergeben sich insgesamt 15 Auswahlmöglichkeiten mit zwei Röntgenröhren in zwei Ebenen. Es wurden jedoch nicht 15 Tasten für diese

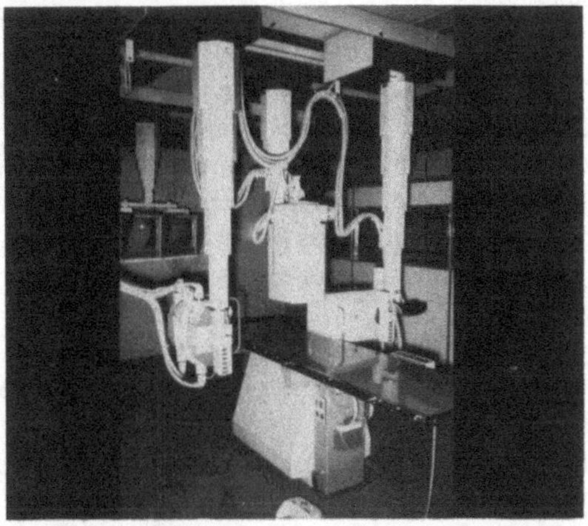

Abb. 1

Abb. 2

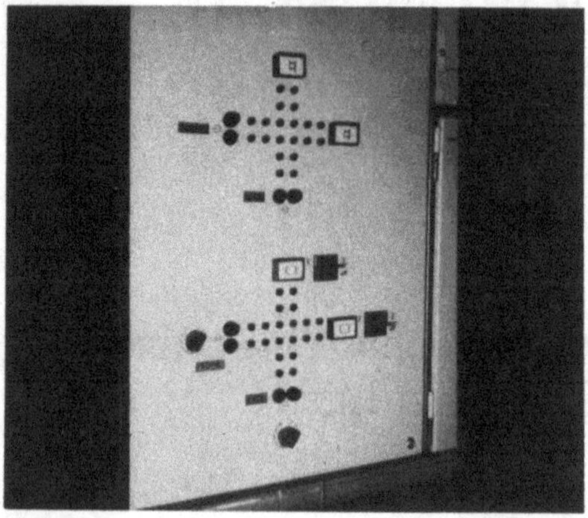
Abb. 3

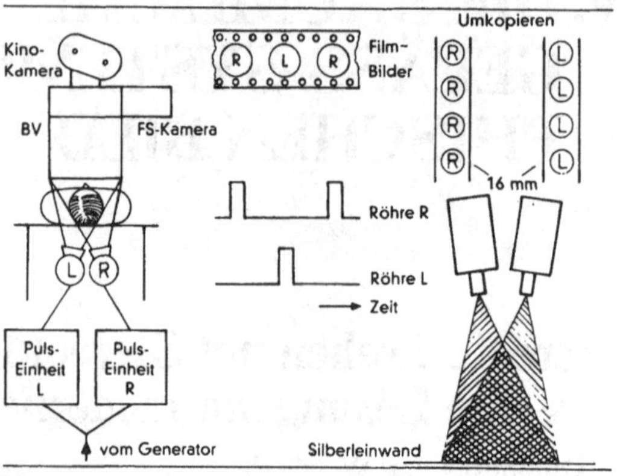

Röntgenstereoanlage
mit Fernsehen und Kinokamera
Abb. 4

vielen Möglichkeiten vorgesehen, sondern in einem Bedienfeld jeder Röhre eine Taste zugeorndet (Abb. 3). Da der Durchleuchtungsbetrieb vielfach mit einer anderen Röhrenanwahl als der Kinobetrieb erfolgt, enthält das Bedienfeld die Tasten getrennt für beide Betriebsarten, oben für Kinobetrieb, unten für Fernsehdurchleuchtung. Werden z. B. im Durchleuchtungsbedienfeld die beiden sagittalen Röhrentasten (ganz unten) gedrückt und im Kinobedienfeld alle Röhrentasten, so erfolgt die Kathetereinführung bei Stereodurchleuchtung in der p.a-Richtung und die Injektion wird in beiden Ebenen mit synchron laufenden Kinokameras in Stereo aufgenommen.
Nach diesem allgemeinen Überblick wird kurz auf die prinzipielle Arbeitsweise beim Stereo-Kino- und -Durchleuchtungsbetrieb eingegangen. Es werden einige wichtige Probleme behandelt, wie die Halbbildtrennung bei der Bildverstärker-Fernsehanlage und bei der Betrachtung, das Problem der ausreichenden Bildfrequenz für eine flimmerfreie Betrachtung, die Stereomitbeobachtung während der Stereo-Kinoaufnahme und die Bandspeicherung des Stereofernsehsignals. Abb. 4 zeigt die prinzipielle Arbeitsweise für eine Ebene bei Stereokino. Beide Röntgenröhren sind an denselben Hochspannungsgenerator angeschlossen. Es handelt sich um die für den Kinobetrieb üblichen gittergesteuerten Röhren, die abwechselnd von den zugehörigen Pulseinheiten eingeschaltet werden. Auf den Bildverstärker treffen abwechselnd, wie in der Mitte des Bildes angedeutet, kurze Strahlenimpulse der rechten und linken Röntgenröhre.

Bei der Aufnahme einer Kinoszene steuert die Kinokamera abwechselnd die rechte und die linke Pulseinheit. Auf dem 35-mm-Originalfilm wechseln Rechts- und Links-Bilder einander ab. Die Filmauswertung erfolgt nach dem Umkopieren auf zwei 16-mm-Filme nach dem sogenannten Zweibandverfahren. Das heißt, der Rechts- und der Links-Film werden durch zwei gekoppelte und synchron laufende Projektoren auf dieselbe Leinwand projiziert. Die Bildtrennung erfolgt dabei nach dem Polarisationsverfahren.

Abb. 5 zeigt die Arbeitsweise bei der Stereo-Fernsehdurchleuchtung. Hier erfolgt die alternierende Ansteuerung der Pulseinheiten im Abtastrhythmus der Fernsehanlage. Die Fernsehbilder stellen abwechselnd Rechts- und Links-Bilder dar. Sie werden über einen elektronischen Umschalter zwei nebeneinander angeordneten Sichtgeräten zugeführt. Der Betrachter trägt eine Prismenbrille zur Konvergenzunterstützung. Polarisationsfilter auf den Sichtgeräteschirmen und ein polarisierender Belag auf den Prismen sorgen dafür, daß jedes Auge nur das zugehörige Halbbild sieht, wie durch die gekreuzten Lichtbündel

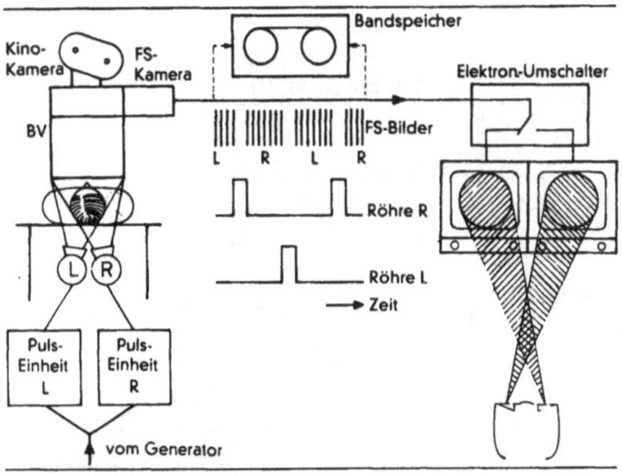

Röntgenstereoanlage
mit Fernsehen und Kinokamera

Abb. 5

angedeutet. Auf diese Weise sieht der Betrachter ein stereoskopisches Bild ohne ein störendes rechtes und linkes Nebenbild.

Im Bild ist weiterhin angedeutet, daß das Fernsehsignal wie üblich auf Bandspeicher aufgenommen werden kann. Handelt es sich dabei um die Registrierung einer Stereoszene, so erfolgt die Wiedergabe über den elektronischen Umschalter auf den beiden Sichtgeräten. Für die Stereobetrachtung ist es dabei wesentlich, daß die richtige Zuordnung der Halbbilder zu den Sichtgeräten gegeben ist. Hierzu wird jedem Rechtsbild des Fernsehsignals bei der Aufnahme ein Kennimpuls zugemischt. Bei der Wiedergabe steuert dieser Impuls den elektronischen Umschalter.

Die Ausführung der Primenbrille zeigt Abb. 6. Die Prismen nehmen nur den oberen Teil der

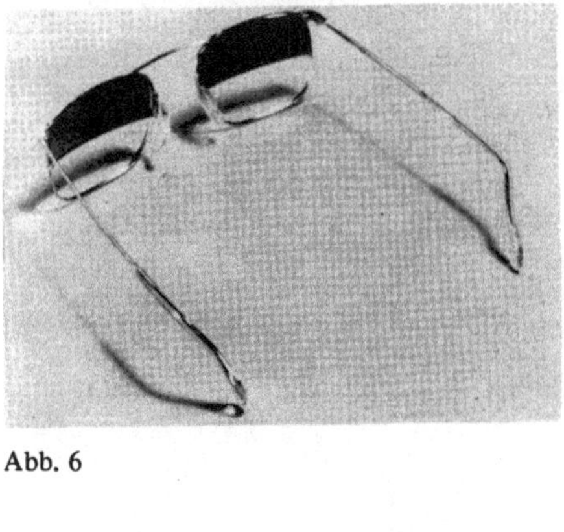

Abb. 6

Brille ein, so daß der Betrachter beim Blick nach unten, z. B. zum Einführen des Katheters, nicht durch eine zusätzliche Konvergenz seiner Sehrichtung gestört ist.

Die Prismenbrille ersetzt die zuerst verwendete Brille mit Umlaufblenden zur Trennung der Stereohalbbilder bei der sequentiellen Darbietung auf einem Sichtgerät.

Die Darbietung der Stereohalbbilder auf getrennten Sichtgeräten erlaubt neben der Stereobetrachtung mit der Prismenbrille natürlich auch die getrennte Betrachtung der rechten und linken Halbbilder. Dies hat sich für das Einrichten des Patienten und die Einstellung der Strahlenblenden gut bewährt.

Bei der üblichen Fernsehabtastung mit 50 Halbbildern pro Sekunde zeigt jedes Sichtgerät nur 25 rechte bzw. linke Halbbilder pro Sekunde. Infolge dieser niedrigen Bildfrequenz ergibt sich ein störendes Flimmern. Bei der Verschmelzung der Halbbilder zu einem stereoskopischen Bild ist die Flimmerempfindung zwar geringer, sie hat sich in der Praxis jedoch als Behinderung herausgestellt, vor allem bei den für die Herzkatheterisierung manchmal langen Durchleuchtungszeiten. Zur Abhilfe wurden an dieser Einrichtung die Fernsehanlagen auf eine höhere Bildfrequenz umgestellt. Statt 50 Halbbilder pro Sekunde werden 100 abgetastet. Jedes Sichtgerät zeigt damit 50 rechte bzw. linke Stereohalbbilder pro Sekunde, womit das Problem des Flimmerns gelöst ist. Damit die Verdopplung der erforderlichen Frequenzbandbreite gelingt, mußte eine weitere Änderung der Fernsehabtastung vorgenommen werden. Diese ist in Abb. 7 schematisch angedeutet. Von der Abtastung des runden Bildfeldes durch ein Raster mit einem Höhen- zu Breitenverhältnis von 3 : 4 und 50 Halbbildern pro Sekunde, mit jeweils 625/2 Zeilen, wurde übergegangen auf eine quadratische Abtastung mit 525/2 Zeilen pro Halbbild. Der Abtaststrahl braucht somit nur einen kürzeren Weg zurückzulegen als bisher. Seine Geschwindigkeit wird deshalb nicht doppelt so hoch wie bisher, sondern nur 1,4fach vergrößert. Im Bild sind die wichtigsten Konsequenzen dieser Änderung der Fernsehabtastung angegeben. Die Änderung der Zeilenzahl

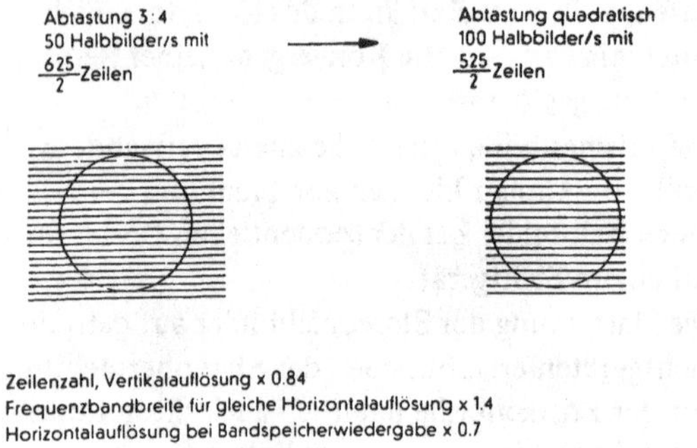

Konsequenzen beim Übergang von 50-Hz- auf 100-Hz-Fernsehen

Abb. 7

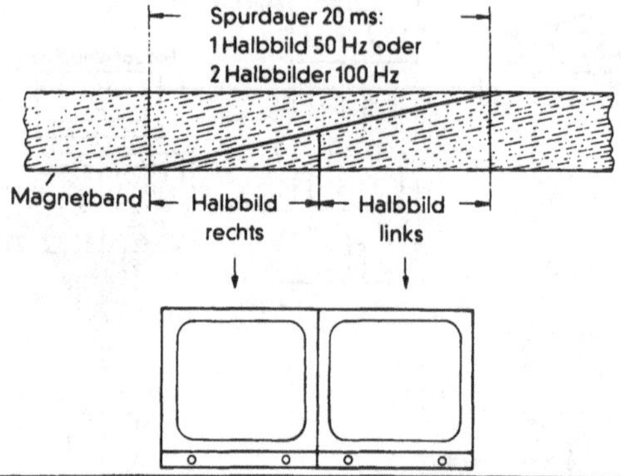

Bandspeicherung bei 100-Hz-Fernsehen

Abb. 8

bedingt eine Abnahme der Vertikalauflösung auf das 0,84fache. Die erhöhte Abtastgeschwindigkeit des Elektronenstrahls erfordert bei gleicher Horizontalauflösung eine Erhöhung der Frequenzbandbreite auf das 1,4fache.

Infolge einer ausreichenden Bandbreitenreserve der verwendeten Fernsehanlagen ist dieser Bandbreitenerhöhung bereits Rechnung getragen, so daß sich bei der Fernsehdurchleuchtung die gleiche Horizontalauflösung ergibt wie bisher bei der Abtastung mit 50 Halbbildern pro Sekunde.

Bei der Bandspeicherwiedergabe liegen die Verhältnisse jedoch anders. Hier ist keine Reserve an elektrischer Bandbreite gegeben, so daß die Horizontalauflösung auf das 0,7fache absinkt. Insgesamt stellt diese Abtastart einen Kompromiß dar, der sich inzwischen im praktischen Betrieb bewährt hat.

Für die Bandspeicherung des 100 Hz-Fernsehsignals ergeben sich keine besonderen Anforderungen an den Bandspeicher. Die Aufzeichnung erfolgt genau wie beim üblichen Fernsehsignal. Die Dauer jeder der schräg auf das Magnetband aufgezeichneten Spuren, von denen eine in Abb. 8 hervorgehoben ist, beträgt wie sonst 20 ms. Darin sind nun jedoch zwei Fernsehhalbbilder enthalten, bei Stereobetrieb ein rechtes und linkes Halbbild. Lediglich bei der Wiedergabe ist für die schon erwähnte Zuordnung der Halbbilder zu den beiden Sichtgeräten zu sorgen. Bei der Standbildwiedergabe wird immer wieder dieselbe Spur abgetastet. Da eine Spur zwei Halbbilder enthält, ist sogar das wiedergegebene Standbild ein Stereobild.

Der Übergang von 50- auf 100 Hz-Fernsehen hat eine weitere wichtige Konsequenz für die Fernsehmitbeobachtung während der Stereokinematographie. Der Stereokinobetrieb erfolgt an dieser Anlage vorzugsweise mit 100 Bildern pro Sekunde, und zwar netzsynchron.

Somit laufen die Kino- und Fernsehkameras frequenz- und phasengleich und die Fernsehmitbeobachtung bei der Stereokinematographie erfolgt ebenfalls stereoskopisch. Auf diese Weise erhält

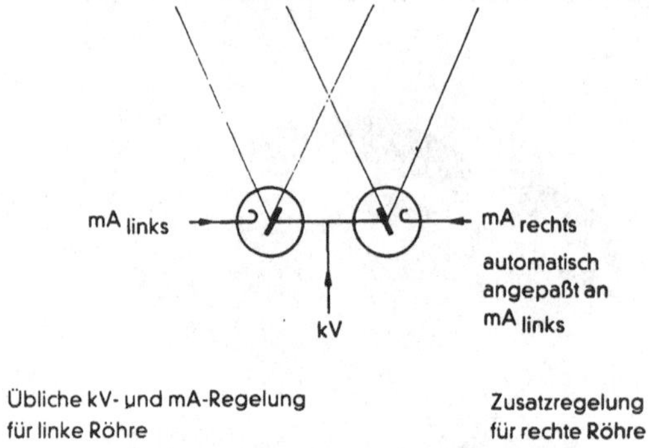

Belichtungsangleich für Stereohalbbilder

Abb. 9

man ein besonders gut beurteilbares Bild vom Verlauf des Kontrastmittels bei der Injektion.

Beim Stereokinobetrieb mit nur 50 Bildern pro Sekunde ist ebenfalls eine stereoskopische Fernsehmitbeobachtung gegeben, jedoch mit einem leichten Flimmern des Bildes.

Ein weiteres Problem ist die Erzielung der gleichen Helligkeit (Abb. 9) für beide Stereohalbbilder. Für eine Röntgenröhre, z. B. die linke, werden Hochspannung und Röhrenstrom durch die übliche Regelung für Durchleuchtung und Kinobetrieb eingestellt. Bei der rechten Röntgenröhre sorgt eine Zusatzregelung für eine automatische Anpassung der mA-Werte an die Werte der linken Röhre.

Schließlich soll noch eine Maßnahme beschrieben werden, mit der eine saubere Trennung der Stereohalbbilder möglich ist. Diese Trennung ist das Kernproblem bei jeder Stereoanlage, bei der die Rechts- und Linksbilder in rascher Folge erzeugt und über den Röntgenbildverstärker und die Fernsehkamera sequentiell übertragen werden. Schon ein geringer Nachleuchteffekt des Röntgenbildverstärkers und ein geringes Restsignal infolge der Trägheit der Fernsehaufnahmeröhre führen zu störenden Resten des einen Stereohalbbildes im anderen.

Auch bei der Verwendung eines Plumbicons als Fernsehaufnahmeröhre verbleiben Rest- oder Nebenbilder, die das Zustandekommen eines räumlichen Bildeindruckes erschweren.

Abb. 10 zeigt schematisch den Übergang von der normalen Betriebsart des Plumbicons zu einer Betriebsart mit Kompensation der Störbilder.

Links oben ist ein Stereopaar, bestehend aus zwei aufeinanderfolgenden Bildverstärker-Ausgangsbildern, skizziert. Bei der Abtastung der Speicherplatte des Plumbicons durch den Elektronenstrahl entsteht ein Fernsehbildsignal mit den angedeuteten Störbildanteilen.

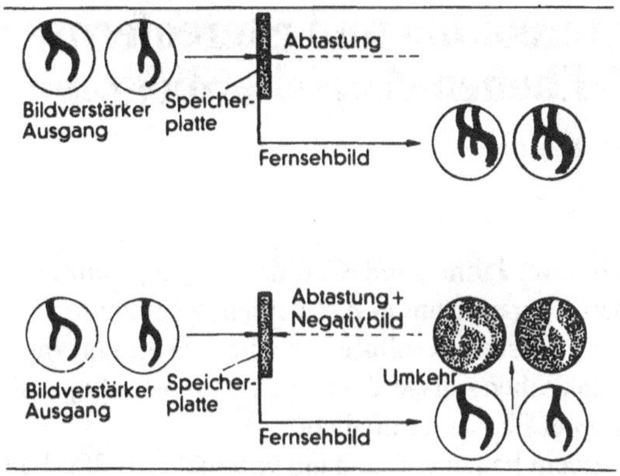

Kompensation der Störbilder

Abb. 10

Der untere Teil des Bildes zeigt die Kompensation der Störbilder. Hierzu wird der Elektronenstrahl nicht nur zur Abtastung benutzt, sondern auch zum Aufschreiben eines Negativbildes auf die Speicherplatte. Das Negativbild wird gerade so star aufgeschrieben, daß es entgegengesetzt gleich ist zu dem Störbild, das infolge der Trägheit des Plum bicons entsteht. Mit dieser Maßnahme ist es gelungen, ein störbildfreies Stereofernsehbild zu erhalten.

Die Stereotechnik ist, ebenso wie der übliche Monobetrieb, mit dem entsprechenden Komfort einer automatischen Belichtungsregelung, einer stereoskopischen Fernsehmitbeobachtung während der Kinematographie und der Bandspeicherung des Stereosignals durchführbar.

Die flimmerfreie und störbildfreie Stereofernsehdurchleuchtung kann als besonderer Fortschritt angesehen werden. Mit der Existenz dieser einen Biplan-Stereo-Anlage ist zwar noch kein allgemeine Durchbruch der Stereotechnik gegeben. Die Erfahrungen an dieser Anlage haben jedoch gezeigt, daß die Stereo-Kinematographie und das Stereofernsehen aus dem Experimentierstadium herausgewachsen sind.

Stereokino und Stereofernsehdurchleuchtung in der 2-Ebenen-Angiokardiographie

M. Kunnen

Vor zwei Jahren, anläßlich des 5. Symposium cineradiographicum in Antwerpen, zeigten wir unsere ersten Resultate mit einer neuen kineangiographischen Anlage, die eine Stereokineradiographie in zwei Ebenen ermöglichte.

Seitdem haben wir, anhand von mehr als 300 Fällen – sowohl angeborener als erworbener Herzfehler – den großen Nutzen dieser Untersuchungstechnik beweisen und ihre Methodik weiter verbessern können. Insbesondere konnte hier seit anderthalb Monaten noch ein wesentlicher Fortschritt durch den Einsatz von den neuentwickelten 35 mm Hochgeschwindigkeitskameras Arritechno gemacht werden. Diese Kameras gewährleisten nicht nur eine Bildfrequenz von 100, sondern sogar von 150 Bilder/ pro Sek., was somit eine weitere Verlangsamung der Stereokinoangiokardiographie ermöglicht.

Ein weiterer Vorteil ist durch den netzsynchronen Kinokameralauf gegeben; auch bei 100 Bildern pro Sekunde, wird ein stereoskopisches Fernsehbild mitbetrachtet und auf Magnetband mittels eines Sirecord X-Bandspeichers aufgezeichnet; beim Einsatz zweier Bandspeicher liegt die stereoskopisch-angiokardiographische Information sowohl der P-A- als auch der seitlichen Ebene unmittelbar vor; auch verlangsamte Wiedergabe und selbst Stereo-Standbildbetrachtung ohne Flimmern ist ohne weiteres möglich.

Diese Röntgenanlage (Abb. 1) umfaßt folgende wesentliche Elemente:

Zwei Sirecon-Duplex Bildverstärker der neuen Generation, die ein noch wesentlich schärferes Bild liefern und zudem weniger Bildremanenz aufweisen, und zwar im Vergleich zu der früheren, wenn auch schon dunkelgetasteten Ausführung.

Jedem Bildverstärker sind zwei gittergesteuerte Röntgenröhren Biangulix bei Brennfleckengröße 0,6 × 0,6 mm mit einer Belastbarkeit von je 30 kW zugeordnet.

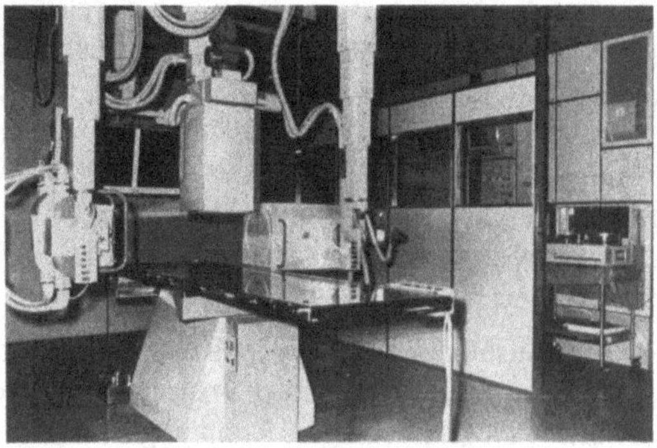

Abb. 1: Anlage für Stereokino und Stereofernsehdurchleuchtung in der 2-Ebenenangiokardiographie.

Man bemerkt die lateral aufgehängten Röhren; die P-A-Röhren sind hinter der Strahlenschutzwand des Angiotisches versteckt.

Der Fokus-Bildverstärker-Abstand beträgt stets 100 cm und der Winkel zwischen den beiden, von den stereokopisch zusammenhängenden Röhren gebildeten Zentralstrahlen, 10°.

Nach unserer Erfahrung ist dieser Stereowinkel von 10° optimal: der Stereoeffekt ist noch nicht zu stark und der Stereotiefenbereich reicht aus für die Untersuchung des Herzens und der großen Gefäße die Bilder können noch sehr gut stereoskopisch verschmolzen werden.

Jeder Bildverstärker ist mit einer 35 mm Röntgenkinokamera „Arritechno“ und mit einer Plumbikon-Videokamera verbunden.

Man bemerkt die zwei gekoppelten, mit Polarisationsfiltern versehenen 100 Hz-Fernsehmonitoren für die stereoskopische Fernsehbetrachtung. Ein Bedienungskasten kontrolliert sämtliche Kombinationen: Mono-, Stereo-, P-A-Aufnahme, Seitenaufnahme und 2-Ebenenbetrieb, und zwar für Kino und für Durchleuchtung.

Zur Filmaufnahmetechnik kurz Folgendes:

Die Kameras für den P-A-Film und den Profilfilm zeichnen gleichzeitig stereoskopische Bilder auf.

Die Kameras laufen, wie jetzt schon üblich, im 2-Ebenenbetrieb synchron, mit einer Phasenverschiebung von 180°. Man bemerkt die Alternierung der Röntgenimpulse (Abb. 2).

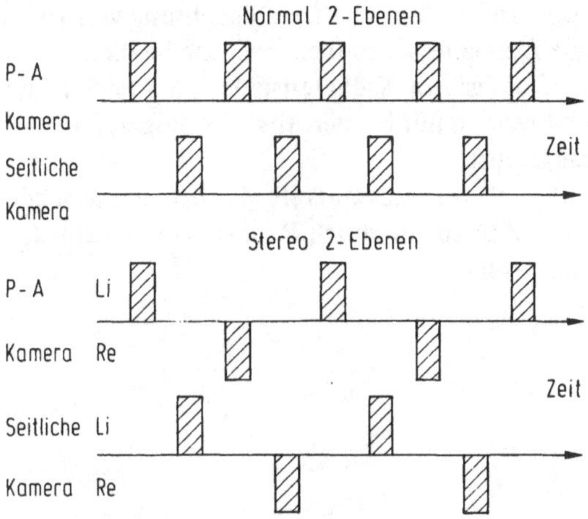

Abb. 2: Alternierung der Röntgenimpulse in Normal-2-Ebenen-Kino-Betrieb und in Stereo-2-Ebenen-Kino-Betrieb.

Bei unserer Stereo-2-Ebenen-Anlage, werden in beiden Ebenen, die Röntgenimpulse darüberhinaus, über die rechte und die linke Röhre verteilt. Auf diese Weise erhält man einen P-A und einen Profil-35 mm-Negativfilm, mit aufeinanderfolgenden Rechts-Links-Bildern.

Dieser Originalfilm wird dann, anhand einer Universalfilmkopiermaschine, laut einer von uns entwickelten Methode, auf zwei 16 mm-Filme kopiert; auf einem ersten Film die Bilder für das linke und auf einem zweiten Film die Bilder für das rechte Auge.

Beim Kopiervorgang wird jedes Bild verdoppelt, sodaß eine ausgesprochene Verlangsamung bei der Projektion ohne störendes Flimmern erzielt wird. Hierzu sind insgesamt vier Kopierdurchgänge erforderlich (Abb. 3). Bei jedem Durchgang wird der 35 mm-Originalfilm mit einer 35 mm-Maskenfilmschleife in Kontakt gebracht.

Der Maskenfilm enthält abwechselnd vollständig geschwärzte und ganz helle Bilder. Um Staubablagerung und Verschmutzung der hellen Bilder der Maske zu vermeiden, wurden die Bildteile völlig ausgestanzt.

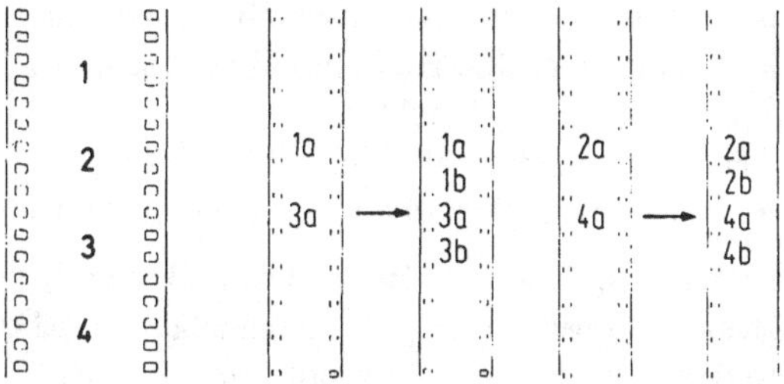

Abb. 3: Die vier Kopierdurchgänge für die Verteilung und Verdoppelung der 35 mm-Stereokinobilder auf zwei 16 mm-Filme.

Beim Kopieren wird also jedes zweite Bild des Originalfilmes abgedeckt. Beim ersten Kopierdurchgang werden alle ungeraden Bilder, z. B. die für das linke Auge bestimmte, kopiert, unter gleichzeitiger Abdeckung aller geraden Bilder.

Also bekommen wir die Bilder 1 a, 3 a, usw. . . . auf dem 16 mm-Film. Beim zweiten Kopierdurchgang werden dieselben ungeraden Bilder noch einmal auf demselben positiven 16 mm-Film aufgezeichnet; zuerst ist jedoch der Kopierfilm um ein Bild in der Kopiermaschine verschoben worden.

Wir erhalten also die Bilder 1b, 3b, usw. . . .
Der 16 mm-Kopierfilm weist nun eine kontinuierliche Serie ungerader verdoppelter Bilder auf.

Die geraden Bilder werden auf die gleiche Weise kopiert, d. h. unter Abdeckung der ungeraden Bilder: also bekommen wir zuerst 2a, 4a und dann 2b, 4b, usw. . . .

Die Projektion erfolgt anhand zweier elektro-mechanisch gekoppelter Spezialprojektoren von Bell & Howell, Typ 173. Das von den Projektoren ausgehende Licht wird polarisiert und die Betrachtung erfolt mit Stereo-Polarisationbrillen.

Zum Schluss möchte ich noch kurz das Stereofernsehen behandeln.

Wie schon erwähnt, wird bei 100 Hz-Röntgenkino ein stereoskopisches Fernsehbild mitbetrachtet und simultan auf Magnetband gespeichert. Mittels zweier Bandspeicher kann die Angiokardiographie in 2 Ebenen, unmittelbar nach Belieben verlangsamt und sogar in Standbild, stereoskopisch erfaßt werden.

Mittels einer polarisierten Prismenbrille werden die flimmerfreien 100 Hz-Fernsehbilder sehr gut stereoskopisch verschmolzen.
Aber auch die Stereofernsehdurchleuchtung ist ohne weiteres möglich und von großem Nutzen.

Hierbei werden, wie die Herren Dümmling und Maass im vorigen Vortrag im Detail erläutert haben, pro Sekunde 100 Röntgenimpulse von je 1 ms, abwechselnd durch die linke und die rechte Röntgenröhre aufgebracht und die somit entstehenden Videosignale den gekoppelten 100 Hz-Fernsehmonitoren zugeführt. Wir verwenden seit ungefähr 5 Monaten diese neue Ausführung.

Das Betrachten des stereoskopischen Fernsehbildes mittels Prismenbrille ist absolut nicht ermüdend.

Durch die dreidimensionale Lokalisierung des Katheters, können wir nun für den Katheterismus völlig auf die seitliche Durchleuchtung verzichten; alle Elemente der seitlichen Ebene bleiben also während des ganzen Katheterismus in der Parkstellung und werden nur bei der Angiokardiographie herangeführt.
Der Katheterismus verläuft also bedeutend schneller und ist zudem durch Raumgewinn erheblich angenehmer.

Diagnostischer Wert einer neuen einfachen Stereoeinrichtung für die Angiographie

D. Beduhn, H. Gajewski, U. Goering und W. Wenz

Trotz vieler Anläufe ist es bisher nicht geglückt, Röntgenstereoaufnahmen in nennenswertem Umfange in die klinische Diagnostik einzuführen. Der erforderliche technische Aufwand, sieht man einmal von der Aufnahme ruhender Objekte ab, ist meistens zu groß.
Für die Entstehung eines räumlichen Eindruckes bietet aber gerade das Gefäßbild seinem Aufbau nach dem Betrachter optimale Voraussetzungen. Stereoangiographien können im Bauchraum einen besseren Einblick in die komplizierte Gefäßarchitektur geben. Bei der räumlichen Zuordnung von Gefäßen zweiter und dritter Ordnung und damit bei der Beurteilung pathologischer Organveränderungen, sind genauere diagnostische Aufschlüsse als bei der Angiographie in 2 Ebenen zu erwarten.

Bereits 1961 versuchte *Hettler* ein stereoskopisches Verfahren in die abdominale Angiographie einzuführen. Grundprinzip seiner Methode war die Verwendung einer gebräuchlichen Serienapparatur mit der wechselweisen Abdeckung der einander gegenüberstehenden, simultan geschalteten Röhren.

Wir haben mit einer technisch einfachen Stereoeinrichtung Versuche unternommen, um den diagnostischen Wert von Stereoaufnahmen in der viszeralen Angiographie zu prüfen. Es gibt verschiedene Verfahren, nach denen die für räumliche Wahrnehmung erforderliche Bildparallaxe der beiden Stereoaufnahmen erzeugt werden kann. Voraussetzung für das räumliche Sehen ist, daß die strahlengeometrischen Bedingungen, die zur Erzielung einer ausreichenden Tiefenwahrnehmung bei der Betrachtung der Stereoaufnahmen notwendig sind, eingehalten werden (Abb. 1 a).
Für unsere Stereoeinrichtung ist nur eine Röntgenröhre erforderlich. Der Patient wird dabei zwischen zwei Aufnahmen in der Längsachse um einen definierten Winkel gedreht. Natürlich kann das Röntgenstrahler-Bildaufzeichnungssystem auch um den ruhenden Patienten geschwenkt werden (Abb. 1b).

Für die Lagerung und Drehung des Patienten verwenden wir eine motorisch angetriebene Drehmulde (Abb. 2). Auf der Kopfseite der Mulde

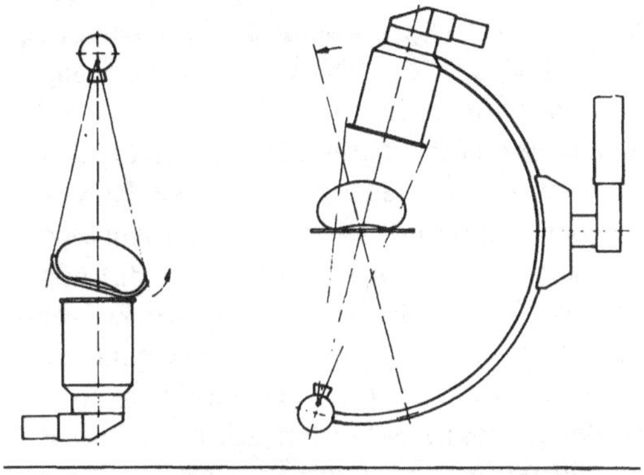

Abb. 1: Röntgenstereoverfahren mit einem Röntgenstrahler und Drehung des Objekts oder des Aufnahmesystems.

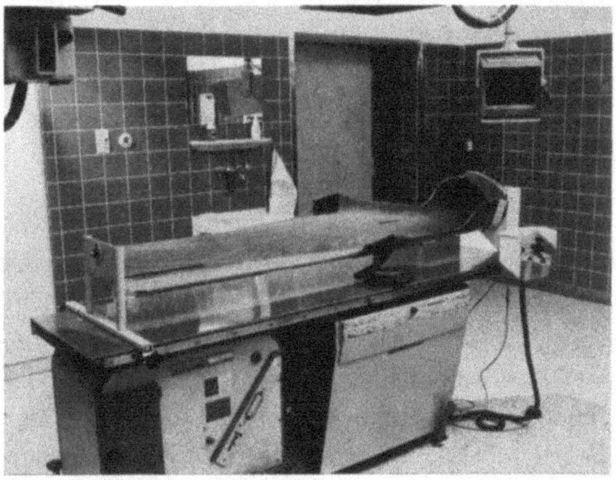

Abb. 2: Drehmulde für die Stereoangiographie auf dem Angiographietisch.

können Drehgeschwindigkeit und Drehwinkel durch verstellbare Endkontakte vor Beginn der Untersuchung bestimmt werden, so daß ungewollte extreme Schräglagen des Patienten vermieden werden können. Die Versuche haben gezeigt, daß ein Drehwinkel von 60 Grad, d. h. eine Drehung von 30 Grad nach jeder Seite, dem Patienten ohne weiteres zugemutet werden kann.

Die Drehmulde wird mit dem fixierten Patienten während des Kontrastmitteldurchflusses mit konstanter Geschwindigkeit von 10 bis 12 Grad in der Sekunde von einer Endstellung in die entgegengesetzte Endstellung gedreht. Mit einer Frequenz von 2 Bildern pro sec. werden dabei Aufnahmeserien belichtet und die Untersuchung kann entweder mit einer 70 mm-Serienkamera *Sirecon* 25/15 H und Untertisch-Röntgenstrahler durchgeführt werden, oder man verwendet den AOT-Blattfilmwechsler und die Obertischröhre, wie bei der gewöhnlichen Routineangiographie.
Die Belichtungszeiten sind der Drehgeschwindigkeit so angepaßt, daß sich die Bewegungsunschärfe infolge der Drehung des Patienten noch nicht nachteilig auf die Bildgüte auswirkt. Sie liegen mit dem 1 mm-Brennfleck zwischen 20 und 30 ms.

Je zwei aufeinanderfolgende Bilder der Aufnahmeserie ergeben jeweils ein Stereobildpaar, weil sie aus zwei um 5 bis 6 Grad voneinander abweichende Projektionsrichtungen belichtet werden. Durch die Drehung des Patienten während der Angiographie erhält man mit unserer Methode eine Serie von Stereoaufnahmen mit verschiedenen Einblickseinrichtungen in das Objekt. Natürlich können die Bilder der Serie auch als Einzelaufnahmen betrachtet werden. Wegen der wechselnden Projektionsrichtung von Aufnahme zu Aufnahme erhält man dabei zusätzliche Informationen über die räumliche Zuordnung der einzelnen Gefäße, die sich durch Aufhebung von Überlagerungen ergeben können.
Um trotz der p.a.-Strahlenrichtung bei den Aufnahmen über den Bildverstärker das Gefäßsystem bei der Stereobetrachtung vor der Wirbelsäule zu sehen, muß der Patient während der Serienaufnahme von seiner linken in die rechte Schräglage gedreht werden.
Stellenweise kann der räumliche Eindruck beeinträchtigt werden, wenn sich Teile des Objekts, wie z. B. Darmschlingen, ihre Form von einer Aufnahme zur nächsten wandeln, Organe verlagern oder sich der angiographische Füllungszustand wesentlich ändert. Apnoe während der Aufnahmeserie ist unbedingte Voraussetzung für einwandfrei beurteilbare Angiogramme. Die gleiche Problematik der Verlagerung von Organen und Darmschlingen während der Serienangiographie begegnet uns natürlich bei der Subtraktion der viszeralen Angio-

graphie. Die rasche Änderung des Gefäßbildes im Intervall von einer halben Sekunde ist durch eine langsame, kontinuierliche Injektion mit der Druckspritze zu vermeiden.
An Beispielen läßt sich der diagnostische Wert der Serienangiographie demonstrieren (Abb. 3). Zweifellos bedarf es einer Umstellung, um den räumlichen Effekt solcher Aufnahmen zu erfassen. Bei der normalen Coeliacographie im a.p.-Strahlengang läßt sich nicht differenzieren, wie die großen Gefäße aus dem Truncus coeliacus mit ihrem Gefäßnetz in der Tiefe verlaufen und welche Gefäße in gleicher Ebene liegen. Plastisch wird das ganze Bild erst bei stereoskopischer Betrachtung. Jetzt bekommt man einen räumlichen Eindruck und kann die Gefäßverläufe auch in der sagittalen Ebene wahrnehmen. Das Beispiel der Coeliacographie zeigt bei der stereoskopischen Betrachtung wie die Arterien zunächst nach vorne ziehen, um dann bogenförmig wieder nach dorsal umzuschlagen. Dieser Tiefeneindruck eröffnet eine ganz neue Dimension. Häufig dauert es eine Weile, bis man dieses neue „Raumgefühl" empfindet. Auch der Verlauf der Mes. superior mit seinen Ästen kann bei der stereoskopischen Betrachtung des Angiogramms räumlich wahrgenommen werden. Besonders eindrucksvoll ist der Verlauf der A. colica media. Im Stereobild zieht dieses Gefäß, das als zweiter Ast rechts aus der Mesenterica superior entspringt, zunächst direkt nach vorne, zeichnet im rechten Unterbauch einen Bogen, um dann nach hinten links zu ziehen. Auch die anderen Mesenterialäste lassen sich im Stereoangiogramm wesentlich räumlicher erfassen. Diesen räumlichen Eindruck hat man bei der Angiographie im a. p. Strahlengang bisher nie empfinden können. Vielmehr hat man sich bei der konventionellen Betrachtung der Angiogramme daran gewöhnt, das Gefäßnetz nur in einer Ebene zu sehen. Mit der stereoskopischen Betrachtung ist die Beziehung der einzelnen Organe zueinander im Bauchraum wesentlich einfacher zu erfassen. Im Spätbild der Mesentericographie ist deutlich zu erkennen, daß die Darmschlingen im rechten Mittelbauch vor dem kontrastgefüllten Nierenbecken liegen.

Auch an der Niere liefert die Stereoangiographie weitere Informationen. Im Stereoangiogramm kann der Verlauf der einzelnen intrarenalen Gefäße in der Niere richtig erkannt und räumlich zugeordnet werden. Am Beispiel einer Nierencyste läßt sich sehr schön demonstrieren, wie die kleinen Gefäßäste um die Cyste von ventral und dorsal herumziehen. Dieser Eindruck ist uns bisher im Nierenangiogramm immer verwehrt worden.

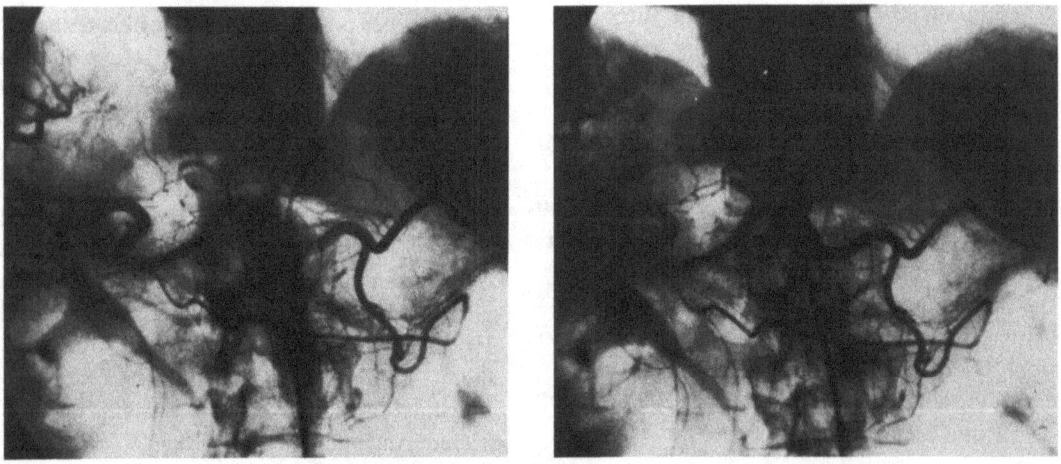

Abb. 3: Stereobildpaar einer Coeliacographie. Das Bild rechts ist in einer um 5–6° gedrehten Projektionsrichtung gegenüber dem linken Bild aufgenommen.

Hauptindikationsgebiet der Stereoangiographie im Bauchraum bleibt trotzdem das Pankreas, da es bis heute noch keine überzeugende Untersuchungsmethode für dieses so problematische Organ gibt.

Gerade die Differenzierung zwischen Tumor und entzündlicher Pankreaserkrankung bereitet immer wieder größte Schwierigkeiten. Das Stereoangiogramm vermittelt einen hervorragenden räumlichen Einblick in die Gefäßarchitektur des Pankreas, das von mehreren größeren Arterien versorgt wird. Auf der einen Seite ist die räumliche Zuordnung zu den Nachbarorganen mühelos möglich und auf der anderen Seite können pathologische Veränderungen wie Gefäßstenosen oder -verschlüsse, aber auch Kaliberschwankungen und Wandunregelmäßigkeiten an den kleineren Gefäßen wie der A. pancreatica dorsalis oder A. pancreatica magna plastisch dargestellt werden. Durch die Tiefenwirkung der Stereoskopie ist es möglich, die schwierige angiographische Pankreasdiagnostik zu erleichtern.

Zusammenfassung

Mit einer technisch einfachen Stereoeinrichtung wird der diagnostische Wert von Stereoaufnahmen der viszeralen Angiographie geprüft. Zur Erzeugung der für die räumliche Wahrnehmung erforderlichen Bildparallaxe des Stereobildpaares wird bei feststehender Röntgenröhre eine Drehung des Patienten angewandt. Bei kontinuierlicher Drehung des Patienten mit bestimmter Geschwindigkeit in einem passend gewählten Winkelbereich kann entweder mit einer 70 mm-Serienkamera und Untertischröntgenstrahler oder mit dem AOT-Blattfilmwechsler und der Obertischröhre ohne wesentlichen technischen Aufwand automatisch eine Folge solcher Stereobildpaare von hohem diagnostischen Wert aufgenommen werden. Erst die stereoskopische Betrachtung gestattet eine räumliche Darstellung des viszeralenGefäßsystems mit ihren Organen. Der räumliche Einblick in die Gefäßarchitektur kann die schwierige angiographische Diagnostik, die besonders bei der Pankreasbeurteilung auf große Schwierigkeiten stößt, erleichtern. Die durch die Stereoangiogramme erzeugte Tiefenwirkung kann bei der Beurteilung der Angiogramme eine große Hilfe bedeuten.

Der Informationswert der abdominellen Angiographie in 2 Ebenen

P. Gerhardt, H. J. Schneider und J. Schröder

Die viscerale Angiographie hat durch die gezielte Darstellung auch kleinster Gefäßäste und durch die Anwendung von Pharmaka einen Stand ereicht, der zur Zeit nur durch die Erweiterung der technischen Möglichkeiten wesentlich verbessert werden kann.
Ein entscheidender Fortschritt wurde durch die gleichzeitige Darstellung der Gefäße in 2 Ebenen erzielt.
Es hat sich jedoch gezeigt, daß die synchrone oder alternierende Belichtung der Filme beider Ebenen bei großen Feldern mit einer die Bildqualität erheblich verringernden Streustrahlendosis einhergeht. Während bei der alternierenden Belichtung der Film einer Ebene belichtet wird, wird der Film der zweiten Ebene in die Aufnahmeposition und ein zweiter aus der Aufnahmeposition in die Auffangkasette befördert. Obwohl die Filme in dieser Phase nicht an die Folien angepresst sind, erfolgt eine Belichtung des Films durch die entstehende Streustrahlung.
Wir haben mit einem Alderson-Phantom die den

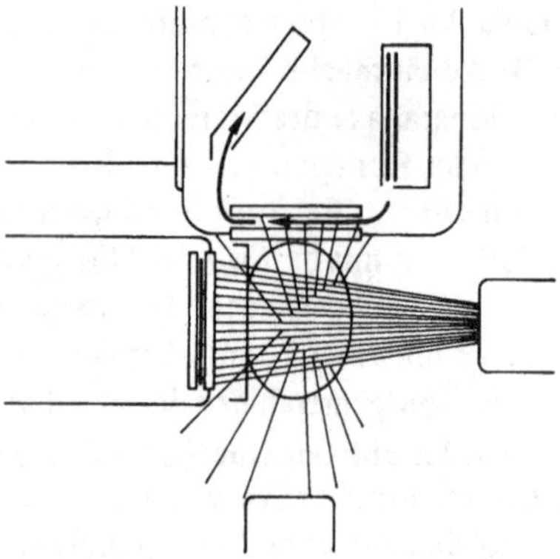

Abb. 1: Schematische Darstellung der 2-Ebenen-Angiographie. Die bei der Belichtung in sagittaler Ebene entstehende Streustrahlung trifft bei synchroner Belichtung den in der Aufnahmekasette liegenden Film der seitlichen Ebene oder bei alternierender Belichtung diesen Film während des Transports.

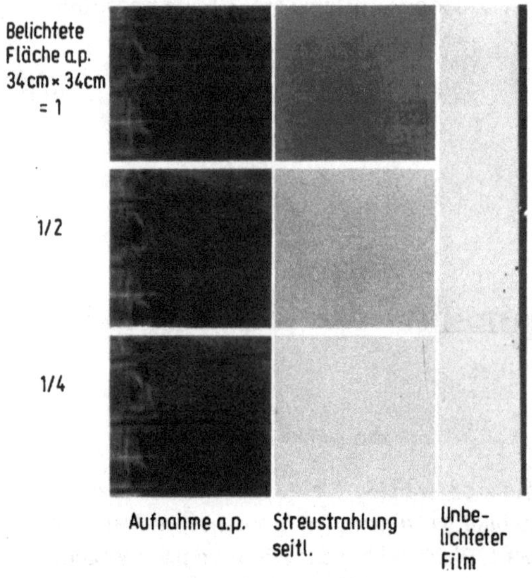

Abb. 2: Schwärzungsvergleiche mit einem Alderson-Phantom. Der a.p-Film wird durch die Nutzstrahlung, der daneben gezeigte Film nur durch die Streustrahlung im seitlichen AOT geschwärzt. Die Schwärzung durch Streustrahlung beträgt bei einer Größe des sagittalen Feldes von 34 × 34 cm 2,1, bei einer Feldgröße von 17 × 17 cm 1,3 und bei einer Feldgröße von 9 × 9 cm 0,4.

nicht direkt belichteten Film treffende Streustrahlung photometrisch gemessen.
Die Messungen ergaben bei einer belichteten Fläche von 34 × 34 cm eine maximale Schwärzung durch Streustrahlung von 2,1 gegenüber 2,3 im mittleren Abschnitt des zur Aufnahme belichteten Films. Wird das Feld auf die Hälfte verkleinert, beträgt die Schwärzung des durch Streustrahlung belichteten Films noch 1,3 und bei Reduzierung der Feldgröße auf ein Viertel 0,4.

Die zusätzliche Schwärzung der Filme durch die Streustrahlung bedeutet bei großen Feldern eine solche Qualitätsminderung der Aufnahmen, daß auch die alternierende Belichtung in der Praxis nicht zu empfehlen ist. Ein weiterer Nachteil ist die instabile elektrische Synchronisierung der beiden Ebenen mit daraus sich ergebenden Folgerungen.

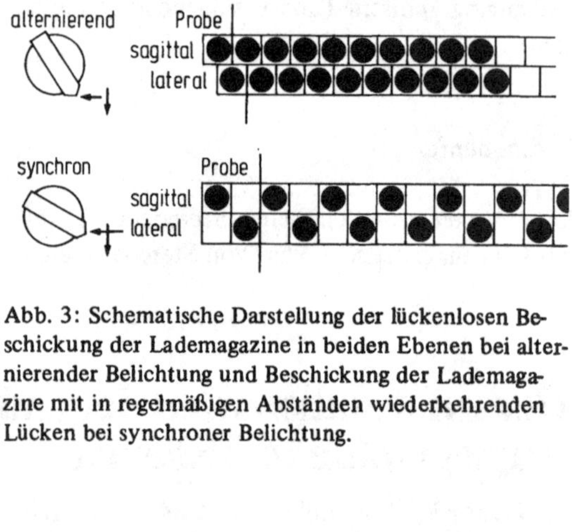

Abb. 3: Schematische Darstellung der lückenlosen Beschickung der Lademagazine in beiden Ebenen bei alternierender Belichtung und Beschickung der Lademagazine mit in regelmäßigen Abständen wiederkehrenden Lücken bei synchroner Belichtung.

Sehr gute Bildqualitäten werden jedoch dann erreicht, wenn nur jedes zweite Fach in den Lademagazinen belegt wird, und zwar z. B. 1, 3, 5 im sagittalen *AOT* und 2, 4, 6 im seitlichen *AOT*.
Bei der Belichtung einer Ebene ist die Aufnahmekassette der anderen Ebene leer, so daß jegliche Schwärzung eines Films durch Streustrahlung entfällt. Voraussetzung für dieses Aufnahmeprogramm ist jedoch die Verdoppelung der gewünschten Aufnahmefrequenz, da jedes zweite Fach der Lademagazine nicht beschickt wurde.

Die Vorteile der 2-Ebenen-Angiographie soll an einigen Beispielen demonstriert werden.
Zunächst erlaubt die unseres Erachtens notwendige Übersichtsaortographie eine exakte Bestimmung der Gefäßabgänge.
Der große Vorteil der seitlichen Übersichtsaortographie geht aus folgenden Beispielen hervor.

Auf dem Bild im sagittalen Strahlengang ist der Abgang der Arteria coeliaca nicht zu erkennen (Abb. 4).
Auf der seitlichen Aufnahme (Abb. 5) sind die im spitzen Winkel nach caudal verlaufenden Arteriae coeliaca und mesenterica superior dargestellt. Diese Aufnahme erleichtert die Wahl des Katheters für die selektive Arteriographie wesentlich. Bei extrem steilem Abgang kann die Aufnahme schon vor etwaigen Sondierungsversuchen klären, daß der transaxilläre Weg für die selektive Darstellung der visceralen Gefäße notwendig ist.

Man erkennt neben der schweren Arteriosklerose einzelner Gefäße mit partieller Stenose und poststenotischer Erweiterung der Arteria hepatica communis auf dem Seitenbild eine geringe Verschmälerung des Lumens der Arteria coeliaca von dorsal und eine Impression der Vorderwand der Aorta als Hinweis auf einen raumfordernden Prozeß.

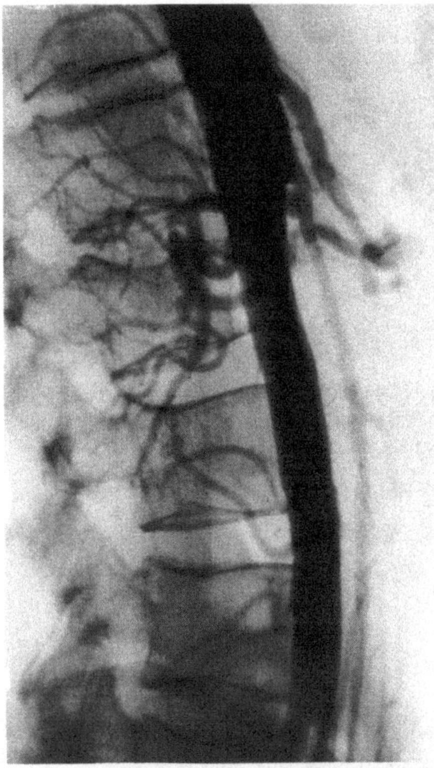

Abb. 5: Die zur Abb. 4 gehörige Seitenaufnahme zeigt deutlich eine tumorbedingte Impression von Aorta und Arteria coeliaca, die auf der a.p.-Aufnahme nicht zu erkennen ist.

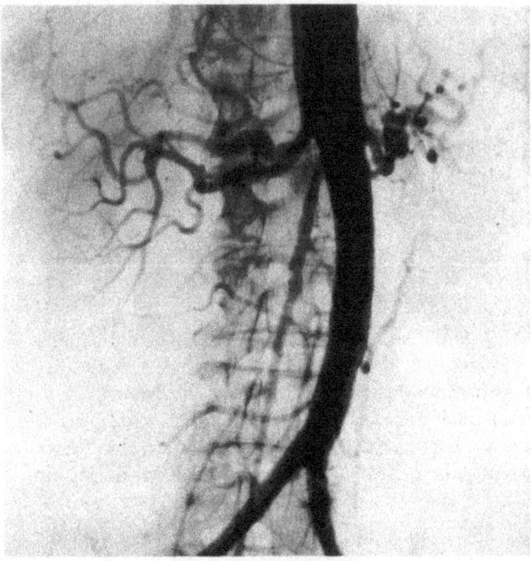

Abb. 4: Übersichtsaortographie im sagittalen Strahlengang mit Arteriosklerose einzelner Gefäße. Auf der a.p.-Aufnahme ist kein Beweis für das Vorliegen eines Tumors zu erkennen (Patientin Sch.).

Die selektive Arteriographie ergibt den Beweis für das Vorliegen eines Pankreas-Neoplasmas mit Ummauerung und Einengung der Arteria lienalis (Abb. 6). Auf dem dazu gehörigen Seitenbild (Abb. 7) ist die oben beschriebene Ausdehnung der Impression der Arteria coelica von dorsal zu erkennen, die weiteren Aufschluß über die Ausdehnung über den inoperablen Tumor gibt, der die Vena lienalis verschlossen hat.
Ein anderes Beispiel eines inoperablen Pankreastumors mit hochgradiger Einengung der Arteria hepatica communis und der Arteria lienalis sehen

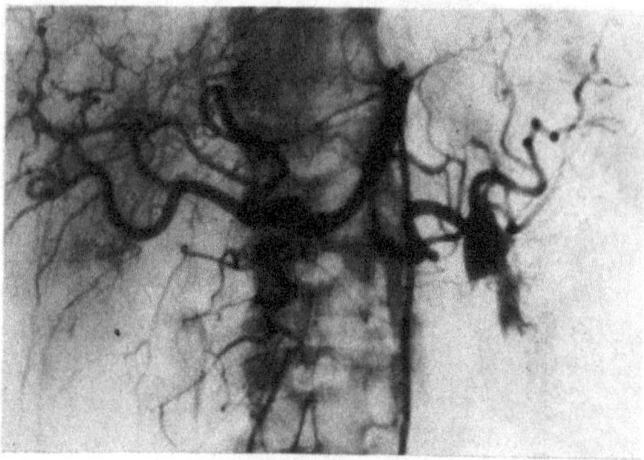

Abb. 6: Zu Abb. 4 gehörige selektive Coeliacographie im sagittalen Strahlengang mit Ummauerung der Arteria lienalis bei Pankreas-Carcinom.

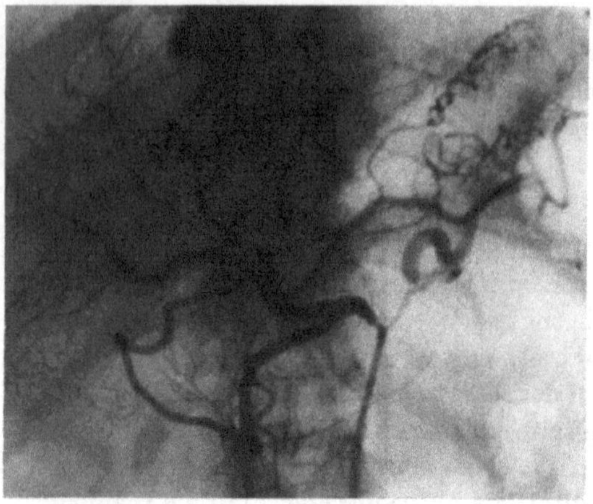

Abb. 8: Selektive Coeliacographie (Patientin W.) mit Ummauerung der Arteria hepatica communis und der Arteria lienalis.

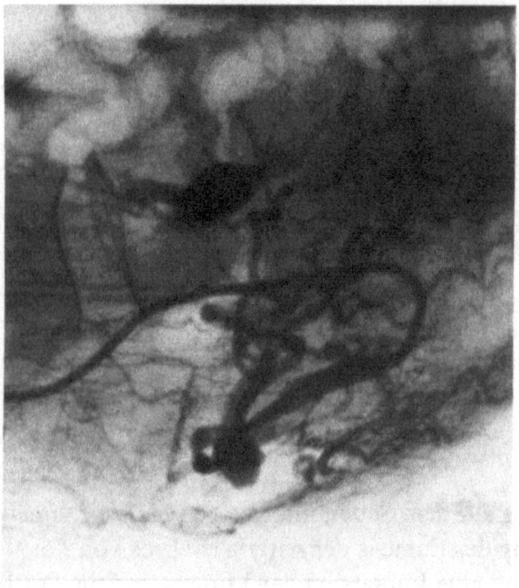

Abb. 7: Selektive Arteriographie zu Abb. 5 im seitlichen Strahlengang mit Einengung der Arteria coeliaca und damit zusätzlicher Aussage über die Ausdehnung des Tumors.

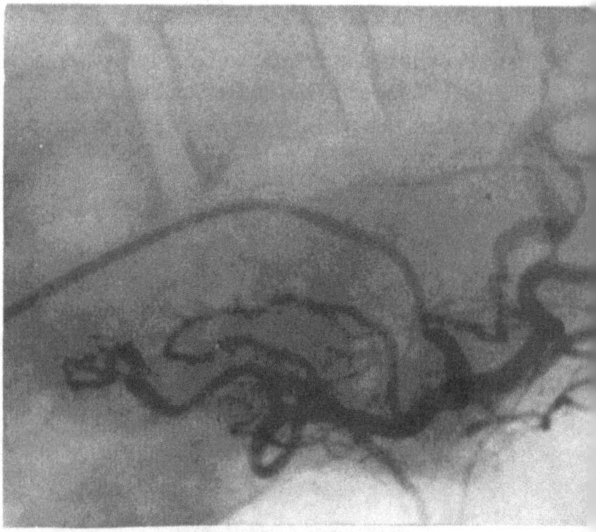

Abb. 9: Seitliche Aufnahme zu Abb. 8. Die ummauerte Gefäßstrecke der Arteria lienalis kann lediglich auf dieser Aufnahme beurteilt werden. Man sieht einen von ventral nach dorsal verlaufenden Gefäßabschnitt, der typische Tumorzeichen erkennen läßt und der auf der a.p.-Aufnahme nicht in gleicher Deutlichkeit dargestellt ist.

wir in der Abb. 8. Die Strecke der Stenose der Arteria lienalis und die dadurch nachzuweisende Ausdehnung des Tumors wird jedoch erst auf dem Seitenbild (Abb. 9) sichtbar. Die topographische Zuordnung eines raumfordernden Prozesses durch die seitliche Angiographie wird oft erheblich erleichtert, wie auch aus dem nächsten Beispiel hervorgeht.

Die Infusionsurographie bei diesem 50jährigen Patienten ergab eine Caudalverlagerung und Achsenkippung der rechten Niere (Abb. 10).

Aufgrund der Szintigraphie (Abb. 11) wurde die Diagnose eines raumfordernden Prozesses im rechten Leberlappen gestellt.

Die Angiographie der Arteria coeliaca zeigt eine Verlagerung der Arteria hepatica communis nach links und der Arteria hepatica propria und hepatica dextra nach cranial (Abb. 12).

Auf der seitlichen Aufnahme sieht man eine Einengung des Anfangsteiles der Arteria coeliaca und eine maximale Verlagerung der Leberarterien nach ventral bei deutlicher Streckung der intrahepatischen Äste (Abb. 13).

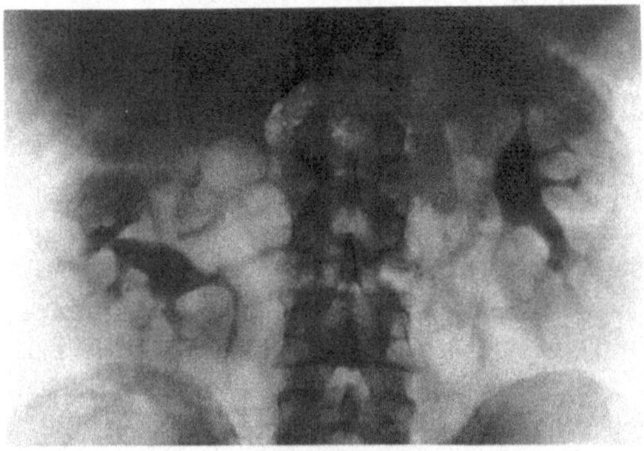

Abb. 10: Infusionsurogramm mit Verlagerung der rechten Niere nach caudal bei Verdacht auf raumfordernden Prozeß im rechten Oberbauch (Patient F.).

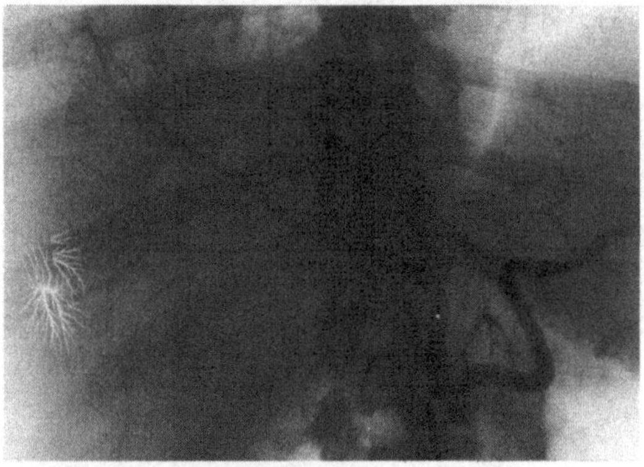

Abb. 12: Coeliacographie zu Abb. 10 und 11 mit Verlagerung der Arteria hepatica nach links und relativ geringer Kontrastierung der Lebergefäße, die gestreckt verlaufen.

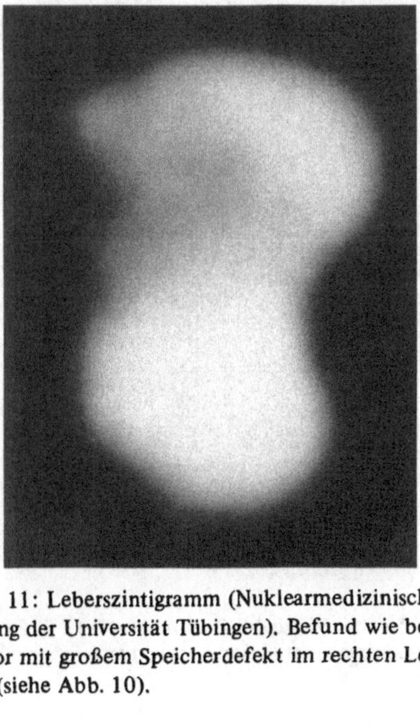

Abb. 11: Leberszintigramm (Nuklearmedizinische Abteilung der Universität Tübingen). Befund wie bei Lebertumor mit großem Speicherdefekt im rechten Leberlappen (siehe Abb. 10).

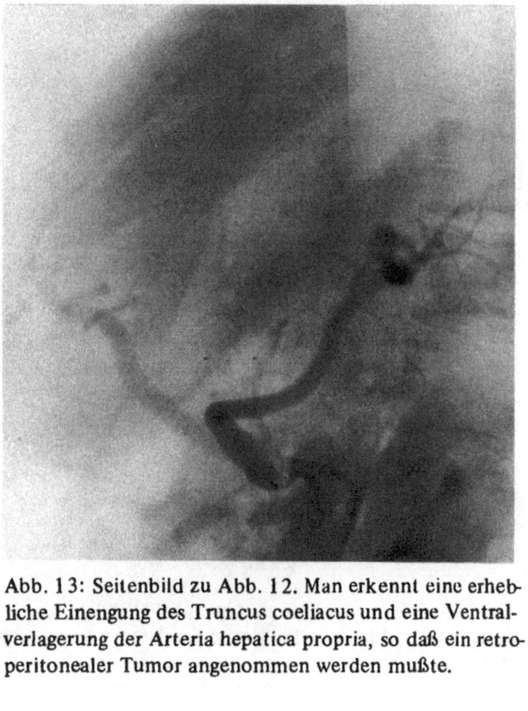

Abb. 13: Seitenbild zu Abb. 12. Man erkennt eine erhebliche Einengung des Truncus coeliacus und eine Ventralverlagerung der Arteria hepatica propria, so daß ein retroperitonealer Tumor angenommen werden mußte.

Dieser Befund war durch einen retroperitonealen Tumor (Neurinosarkom) hervorgerufen, der durch die Kompression der Arteria coeliaca und der Arteria hepatica communis zu einer verminderten Durchblutung der Leber und zur Verschmälerung des rechten Leberlappens geführt hat.

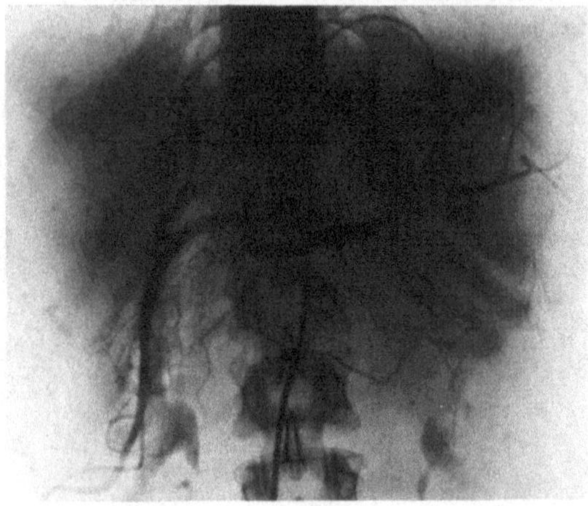

Abb. 14: Selektive Coeliacographie mit atypisch verlaufender Arteria gastroduodenalis und Arteria gastroepiploica dextra (Patientin We.).

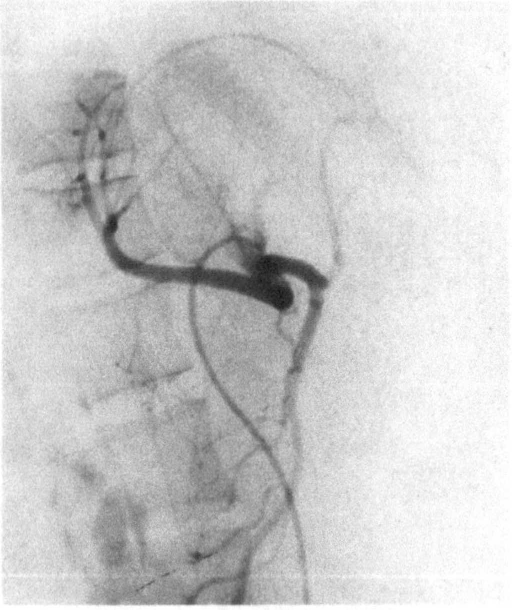

Abb. 15: Seitenaufnahme zu Abb. 14. Erhebliche Verlagerung der Milz nach dorsal und cranial und Impression der Arteria lienalis von ventral und cranial.

Bei der nächsten Patientin war 4 Wochen vor der Angiographie ein rasch größer werdender Tumor im gesamten linken Abdomen bemerkt worden.

Die Coeliacographie im sagittalen Strahlengang ergibt eine Verlagerung der Arteria gastroduodenalis und der Arteria gastroepiploica dextra nach rechts, einen gestreckten Verlauf der Arteria lienalis und ein nach cranial bogig ausgespanntes Gefäß, das aus der Arteria lienalis entspringt (Abb. 14).
Auf der Seitenaufnahme (Abb. 15) erkennt man, daß die Milz weit nach dorsal und cranial, die Arteria lienalis nach caudal verlagert ist.
Der aus der Arteria lienalis abgehende Gefäßast verläuft von dorsal nach ventral unterhalb des linken Zwerchfells.
Die venöse Phase des Angiogramms zeigt im a.p.-Bild eine deutliche Verlagerung der nach caudal gut abgrenzbaren Milz (Abb. 16) und auf der Seitenaufnahme die Impression der Vena lienalis von cranial und ventral (Abb. 17). Aufgrund dieser und weiterer radiologischer Untersuchungen,

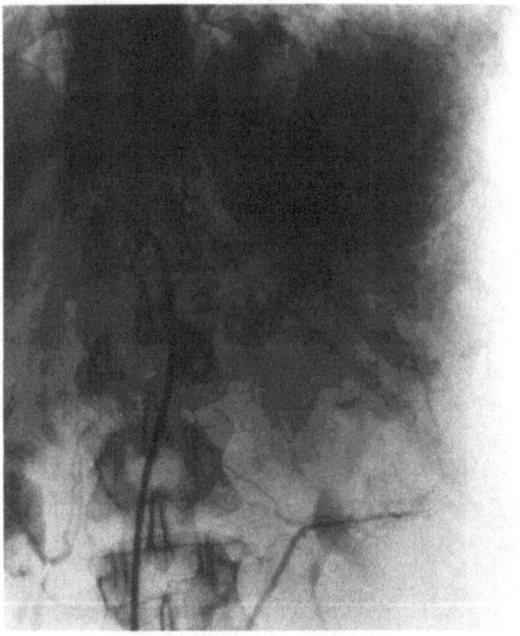

Abb. 16: Venöse Phase der Coeliacographie mit Parenchymanfärbung der Milz, siehe Abb. 14.

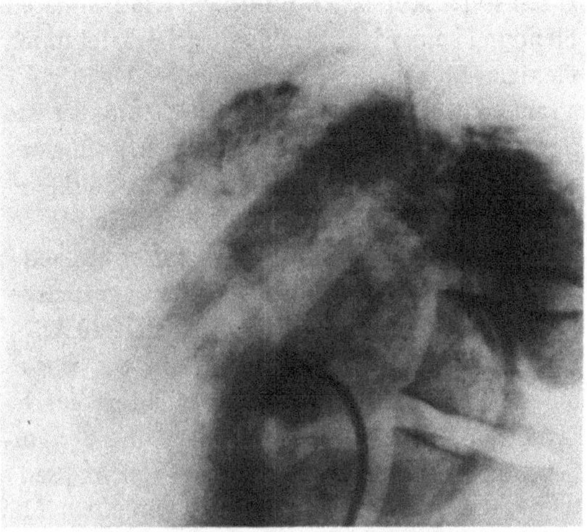

Abb. 17: Seitenaufnahme zu Abb. 16. Die Milz ist durch einen raumfordernden Prozeß nach cranial und dorsal verlagert. Die Vena lienalis ist durch den Tumor imprimiert.

vor allem der Darstellung der Arteria mesenterica superior, wurde die operativ gesicherte Diagnose eines malignen Tumors des Mesenterium gestellt.

Diese wenigen Beispiele mögen demonstrieren, daß der Informationswert der visceralen 2-Ebenen-Angiographie sehr groß sein kann. Unsere Erfahrungen lassen sich dahingehend zusammenfassen:

1. Mit Hilfe der seitlichen Aortographie ist die Orientierung über die Gefäßabgänge und die Wahl des zu verwendenden Katheters erleichtert. Evtl. ergibt sich aus dem Bild die Notwendigkeit, den transaxillären Weg zu wählen, wenn eine weitergehende Gefäßselektion erfolgen soll.

2. Die an die zweite Ebene gekoppelte Durchleuchtungseinrichtung ermöglicht eine sichere Katheterführung, vermeidet damit zusätzliche Komplikationen z. B. durch eine etwaige Intimaverletzung und verkürzt die Untersuchungszeit.

3. Die Ausdehnung eines raumfordernden Prozesses ist besser zu beurteilen.

4. Der vom Tumor befallene oder ummauerte Gefäßabschnitt ist in 2 Ebenen exakt zu bestimmen.

5. Einengungen oder Arrosionen der vorderen und hinteren Gefäßwand sind nachweisbar.

6. Die Differentialdiagnose zwischen Arteriosklerose und Gefäßstenose wird erleichtert.

Zusammenfassung

Es wird anhand mehrerer Beispiele der Informationswert der visceralen abdominellen Angiographie in 2 Ebenen demonstriert. Es werden einige Punkte hervorgehoben, die die 2. Ebene als besonders wertvoll kennzeichnen. Das Untersuchungsverfahren führt, wenn die technischen Voraussetzungen gegeben sind, zu einer wesentlichen Erleichterung des Arbeitsganges und damit zu einer geringeren Belastung des Patienten.

Technik und Ergebnisse der Stereoangiographie bei der Tumorsuche im Abdomen

P. J. Prager, M. Georgi, J. Pingel und H. Munzinger

Für die räumliche Beurteilung pathologischer Veränderungen im Bereich der Abdominalorgane bietet die Stereoangiographie gegenüber Bildserien in zwei Ebenen wesentliche Vorteile. Ein stereoskopisches Bildpaar gibt, durch die in ihm vorhandenen parallaktischen Verschiebung, außer seinem morphologischen Inhalt, noch ein meßbares Bild wieder. Hiermit hat man die Möglichkeit, bei entsprechender Technik, einer objektivierbaren topographischen Lokalisation sämtlicher Veränderungen, eine Möglichkeit, die für Radiotherapeuten wie Chirurgen von großem Interesse ist. Da es sich bei der Angiographie um die Erfassung eines schnell ablaufenden Prozesses handelt, erfordert die Anfertigung von stereoskopischen Aufnahmen die Erfüllung bestimmter technischer Voraussetzungen: Das Zeitintervall zwischen stereoangeordneten Aufnahmen darf nicht über 0,5 sec. liegen, da sonst vergleichbare Stereobilder nicht erfaßt werden können. Das heißt, eine schnelle Aufnahmefrequenz und ein schneller Filmwechsel müssen gewährleistet sein. Ausgehend von einer allgemeingebräuchlichen Serienangiographieanlage lassen sich diese Bedingungen einfach und ohne größere finanzielle Belastung erfüllen. Wir selbst haben mit folgender Anordnung sehr gute Erfahrungen sammeln können (Abb. 1): Die Röhren werden parallel

Abb. 1: Serienangiographieanlage in Stereoanordnung.

in Stereoposition gebracht, wobei der Fokus-Fokusabstand 18 cm, der Fokus-Filmabstand 110 cm betragen. Das Verhältnis der beiden Größen zueinander beträgt also 1 zu 6 und gibt einen sehr guten stereoskopischen Eindruck. Die Formateinblendung beider Nutzstrahlenkegel erfolgt durch Plexiglas-Bleischeiben. Die Lamellen des Streustrahlenrasters müssen dabei in Richtung der Brennflecke der Röhren ausgerichtet sein. Durch eine einfache Flip-Flop-Schaltung werden nun die Röhren auf Stereobetrieb geschaltet. Hierbei wird, filmgesteuert vom AOT-Wechsler aus, ein alternierender Röhrenbetrieb auf zwei getrennte Generatoren eingestellt. Die so geschaltete Anlage ist für die Routineuntersuchung betriebsbereit, die Angiographie wird wie üblich durchgeführt. Wenn eine genaue Ausmessung der vorliegenden Veränderungen erfolgen soll, müssen vorher lediglich Stereoaufnahmen von einem Maßstabmodell mit Grundplatte und Aufnahmen vom Patienten mit Markierung der Bauchdecken, z. B. mit einem Drahtgitter, aufgenommen werden. Bei der abdominellen Stereoangiographie wird die Filmfrequenz durch das hohe notwendige MaS-Produkt auf zwei Bilder pro Sekunde begrenzt. Die Betrachtung der Aufnahmen kann durch freies stereoskopisches Sehen oder unter Zuhilfenahme optischer Hilfsmittel wie Spiegelstereoskope oder Stereobinokel erfolgen. Mit einem Röntgenstereokomparator kann eine stereometrische Auswertung auf elektronischer Basis vorgenommen werden.

Die Stereoangiographie im Abdominalbereich gebrauchen wir, außer wenn eine genaue Tumorlokalisation und Ausdehnungsbestimmung gewünscht wird, vornehmlich bei der Tumorsuche im Versorgungsgebiet des Truncus coeliacus und seiner Äste, weniger häufig bei der Tumordiagnostik im Bereich der Nieren. Am Beispiel eines Stereoangiogramms einer Coeliacographie erkennt man deutliche Verdrängungserscheinungen im Verlauf der atypisch aus der Arteria mesenterica-superior entspringenden Arteria hepatica-dextra. Es handelt sich hier um eine sehr große Lebermetastase bei einer wegen Collum-Ca. operierten Patientin. Die eingezeichnete Markierung entspricht jeweils dem vorher aufgenommenen Maßstabmodell. Der stereometrisch ermittelte Sagittalschnitt läßt eine erhebliche Tiefenausdehnung dieses Tumors erkennen.

Eine unter gleichen Bedingungen aufgenommene linksseitige selective Nierenangiographie zeigt eine etwa 9 X 10 cm große gut vascularisierte Raumforderung am oberen Nierenpol. Es handelt sich hierbei um ein Hypernephrom. Stereoskopisch betrachtet läßt sich dieser Tumor deutlich im ventralen Nierenabschnitt lokalisieren.

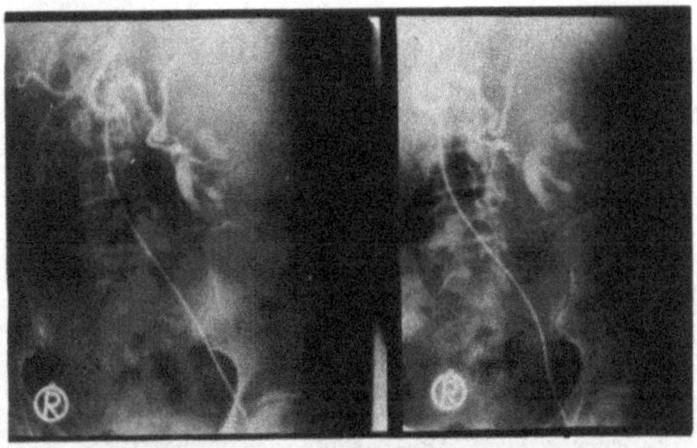

Abb. 2: Darstellung eines Milztumors durch eine Stereocoeliacographie.

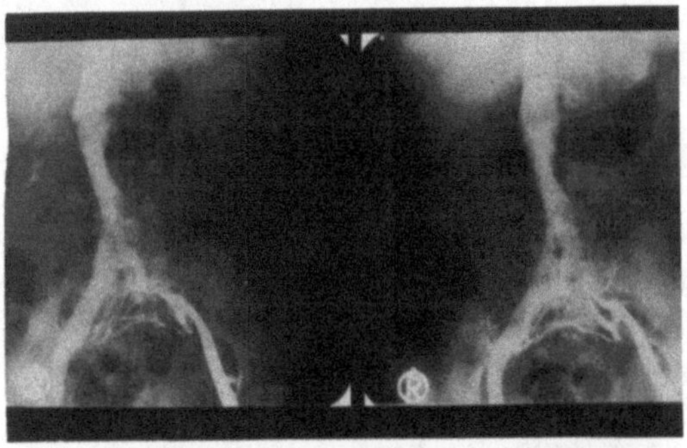

Abb. 3: Stereoskopisches Bild einer Cavographie mit durch Lymphknotenpakete verursachten Veränderungen.

Eine andere Stereocoeliacographie (Abb. 2) gibt mit sehr gutem räumlichen Eindruck das Bild eines gefäßlosen Milztumors mit Caudaldislokation der linken Niere.

Eine unter Stereobedingungen aufgenommene Cavographie (Abb. 3) zeigt eine Verdrängung der Vena cava nach rechts mit bogenförmigen Pelottierungen linksseitig durch Lymphknotenpakete sowie einen Abbruch der Vena iliaca linksseitig mit kräftigem Kollateralkreislauf über Sacral- und Lumbalvenen. Bei stereoskopischer Betrachtung imponiert zusätzlich eine Verdrängung der Vena cava nach ventral, eine Tatsache, die bei Durchführung der Strahlenbehandlung Berücksichtigung fand.

Zusammenfassung

Gegenüber Serienangiographien in zwei Ebenen bietet die Stereoangiographie in vielen Fällen einen zusätzlichen Informationsgewinn durch die Möglichkeit einer genauen Ausmessung und topographischen Lokalisation. Ausgehend aus einer gewöhnlichen Serienangiographieanlage läßt sich leicht und ohne größeren finanziellen Aufwand die Möglichkeit der Stereoangiographie herstellen. Eine solche Anlage wird beschrieben, einige Beispiele von Stereoangiographien werden demonstriert.

Die Bedeutung der Schräg- und Seitenprojektionen bei der Beurteilung von arteriosklerotischen Veränderungen in Bauchaorta und Iliakalarterien

R. Köhler

Viele Gefäßchirurgen haben darauf hingewiesen, daß bei Operationen wegen Obliteration oder Stenose in der kaudalen Aorta oder den unteren Extremitäten die wirkliche Veränderungen meistens bedeutend umfassender sind, als das Angiogramm erwiesen hat. Der Engländer *Dyde* hat in Lancet 1968 das dorsale Übergewicht der Veränderungen hervorgehoben.
Die gleiche Beobachtung hatte der finnische Chirurgieprofessor Tala schon vor mehreren Jahren bei gefäßchirurgischen Operationen gemacht und mir mitgeteilt. Diese Wahrnehmung sowie ein großes Interesse für eine Klärung der Pathologie der viszeralen Hauptstämme im Zusammenhang mit arteriosklerotischer Insuffizienz in den unteren Extremitäten war die Ursache dessen, daß wir schon 1966 routinemäßig eine Angiogrammserie seitlich der Aorta abdominalis in Anschluß an Unterextremitätsangiographien aufzunehmen begannen. Bei pathologischem Befund in den Beckenarterien wurde des weiteren eine Bildserie in Schrägprojektion von der unteren Aorta bis zur Inguinalregion aufgenommen.
Derartige Seitenangiogramme aus den Jahren 1966–70 habe ich geprüft und bei 100 Fällen Größe und Lokalisation der Arterioskleroseveränderungen registriert, soweit sie die Aortawand zum mindesten ventral oder dorsal affiziert hatten. Auf entsprechende Weise habe ich in 100 Fällen die Frequenz der Arterioskleroseveränderungen bei Beckenschrägangiographien mit der Frequenz der Veränderungen in entsprechenden a.p.-Angiogrammen verglichen.
In der Aorta waren bei 100 Fällen die dorsalen Veränderungen größer als die ventralen bei 57 Fällen, sie waren gleich groß in 41 Fällen und nur in zwei Fällen ventral größer. Im Iliakalgebiet waren die entsprechenden Zahlen 38, 39 und 3. Folgende Abb. (1) zeigt bei a) einen Fall mit gleich großen Veränderungen dorsal und ventral sowie bei b) und c) Fälle mit deutlich kräftigeren Veränderungen dorsal.

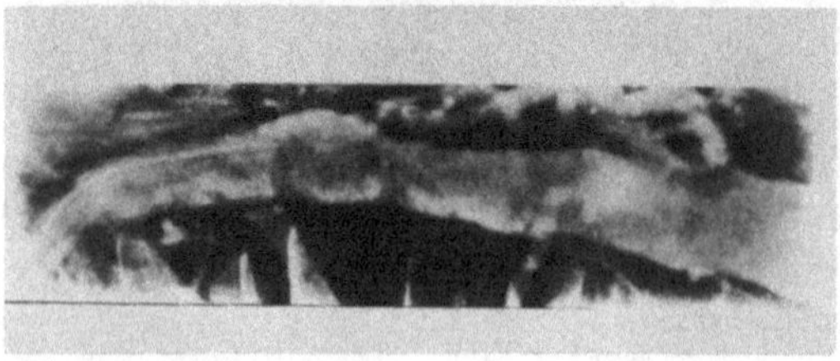

Abb. 1 a

Abb. 1 b

Abb. 1 c

Die Bedeutung multipler angiographischer Projektionen wird erläutert durch die Bilder, die ich jetzt zeigen werde. Ein Aortenaneurysma kann in zwei Projektionen bedeutend vollständiger als nur in der a.p.-Richtung beurteilt werden. In der nächsten Abb. (2) erscheint das ventrale Aortenaneurysma kaum auf dem a. p.-Angiogramm, dagegen aber ausgezeichnet in Seitenansicht. Das Iliaca communis-Aneurysma lag vorzugsweise ventral und medial.

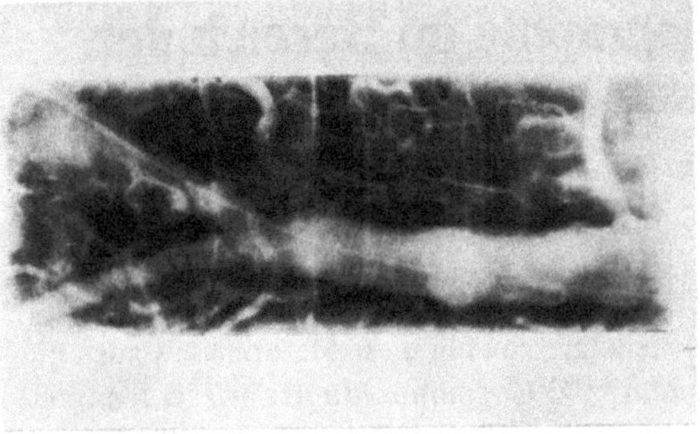

Abb. 2a

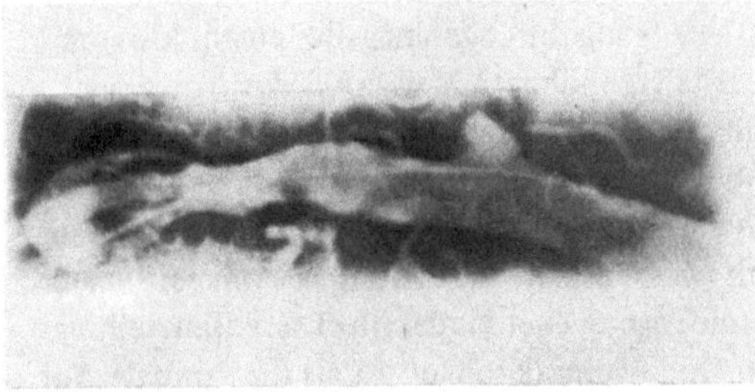

Abb. 2b

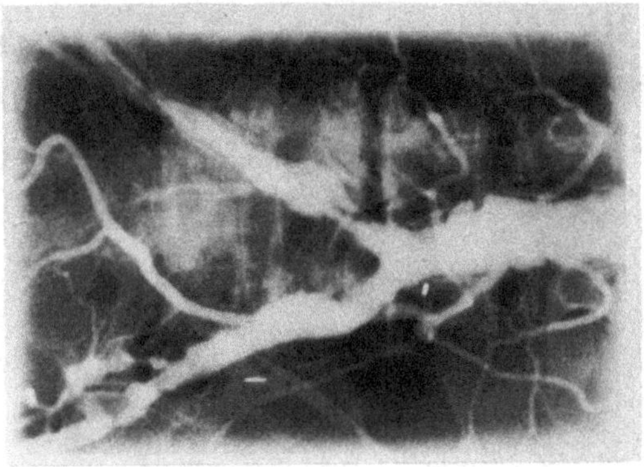

Abb. 3a

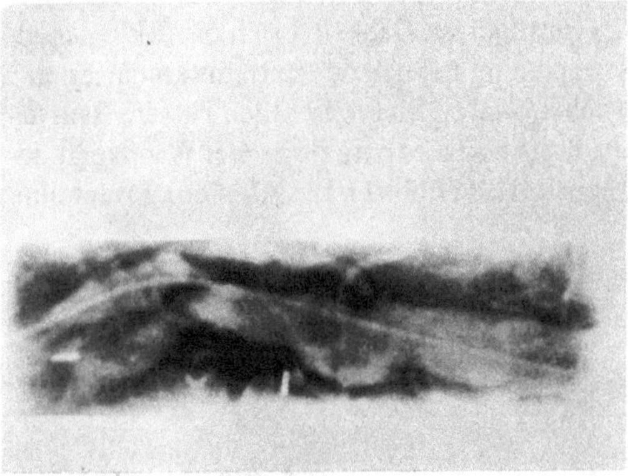

Abb. 3b

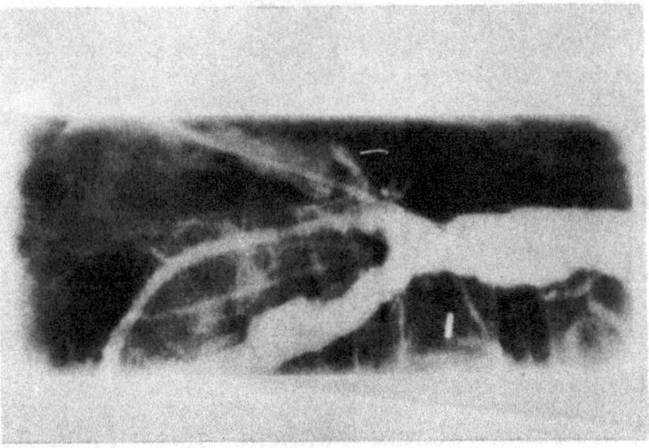

Abb. 3c

Die folgende Abb. (3) veranschaulicht den Wert einer Kombination von a. p.- und Schrägprojektion bei iliakalen Angiographien. Die großen Plaques auf der linken Seite sehen auf dem a. p.-Bild besser aus, dagegen sind die rechtseitigen auf dem Schrägbild besser bestimmt. Es ist wichtig nicht stereotyp an nur zwei Ebenen bei Angiographien festzuhalten, wie das nächste Bild zeigt. In bezug auf die Beurteilung der Aorta sind die a. p.- und Seitenprojektion am wertvollsten. Die proximale rechte Arteria iliaca dagegen zeichnet sich am besten in rechter Schrägprojektion ab, wo die Gefäßverengung ungefähr in der Bildebene liegt. Das gleiche Prinzip wenden wir ja z. B. bei Colonuntersuchungen an.

Zusammenfassend möchte ich noch einmal das dorsale Übergewicht arteriosklerotischer Veränderungen in der unteren Aorta und den Iliakalarterien hervorheben. Bei Angiographien dieser Gefäße oder noch mehr peripher müssen wir, um eine hinreichende diagnostische Exaktheit zu erlangen, für eine durch die örtlichen Umstände bedingte multidirektionelle Technik eintreten, die sich auf optimale Projektionen im Verhältnis zu dem untersuchten Verlauf des Gefäßes gründet. Unvollständigkeiten in dieser Hinsicht sind wahrscheinlich die Hauptursache der Diskrepanz zwischen Operations- und Röntgenbefunden bei gefäßchirurgischen Eingriffen in der unteren Aorta und distal davon.

Die Wertigkeit der 2-Ebenenangiographie im Bereich der Bauchaorta und der Beckenarterien

D. Mack, H. J. Scherer, B. Kramann und P. Maurer

Die Art eines Rekonstruktionsverfahrens ist für den Gefäßchirurgen immer von den pathologischen Veränderungen an der Gefäßwand abhängig. In vielen Fällen kann die Angiographie bereits eine Entscheidung fällen, ob zur Beseitigung einer Stenose oder eines Verschlusses die halboffene Ringdesobliteration nach Vollmar oder der Bypass günstiger ist. Dabei hat sich die 2 Ebenenangiographie im Bereich der Extremitätenarterien bewährt, weil sie eine wesentlich bessere Beurteilung des Ausmaßes pathologischer Wandveränderungen zuläßt (Abb. 1). Die Abbildung zeigt eine

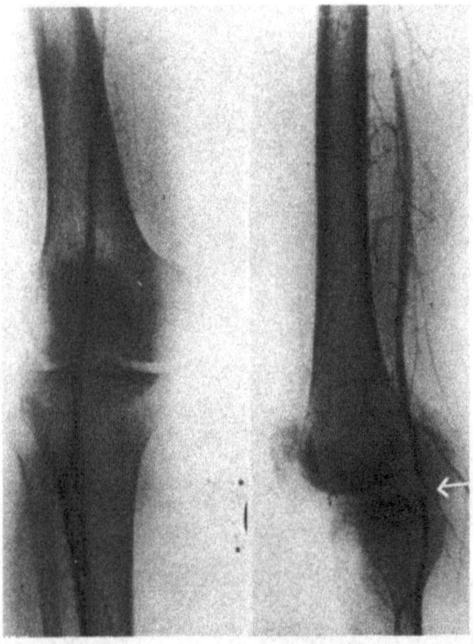

Abb. 1

mäßige Intimasklerose sämtlicher dargestellter Arterien im anterioposterioren Strahlengang, während in der seitlichen Ebene ein fast vollständiger Verschluß der arteria poplitea zu sehen ist. Dieser erheblich bessere Aussagewert hat uns veranlaßt zu untersuchen, ob mit der 2 Ebenenangiographie im Bereich der Aorta abdominalis und der Beckenarterien ähnliche Ergebnisse zu erzielen sind.

An der Aorta abdominalis haben wir immer die Katheterangiographie, über deren Technik Herr Scherer berichtet hat, angewandt. In der Beckenetage sowohl diese Methode, als auch die *Seldinger*-Angiographie von der arteria femoralis communis aus. Es wurde jeweils eine Serienangiographie im anterio-, posterioren und im seitlichen Strahlengang durchgeführt. Bei einem klinisch bereits erkennbaren Verschluß der Aorta oder einer Beckenarterie hat nach unseren Untersuchungen die 2 Ebenenangiographie keine bessere Aussagekraft und ist deshalb auch nicht erforderlich (Abb. 2). Die Abbildung läßt im seitlichen Strahlengang eher eine schlechtere Beurteilung der Gefäßveränderungen zu als die lumbale Aortographie.

Wenn bei der klinischen Untersuchung eines Patienten ein Strömungsgeräusch über der Aorta oder den Beckenarterien zu hören war, haben wir seit Beginn unserer Untersuchungen die Angiographie in 2 Ebenen durchgeführt.

Die Angiogramme in der seitlichen Ebene ergaben auch hier keine bessere Beurteilungsmöglichkeit arteriosklerotisch bedingter Stenosen im Bereich derAorta abdominalis oder der Beckenarterien. Mit ein Grund dafür dürfte in dem dicken Weichteilpolster zu suchen sein, das den Gefäßen in der seitlichen Ebene vorgelagert ist. Es kommt dadurch zu einer flaueren Kontrastmitteldarstellung, was die Beurteilung der Gefäßwandveränderungen erschwert.

Für die Wahl eines Rekonstruktionsverfahrens ist die 2 Ebenenangiographie jedoch sehr wertvoll (Abb. 3). Während auf der Abbildung im anterioposterioren Strahlengang ein nahezu gradliniger Verlauf der rechten Beckenarterie zu sehen ist, zeigt das Angiogramm in der seitlichen Ebene eine starke Schlängelung *beider* Beckenarterien. Patienten, die derartige Befunde im Angiogramm aufweisen, operieren wir nicht mehr mit der retrograden Ringdesobliteration, weil in diesen Fällen die Gefahr der Perforation sehr groß ist. Wir er-

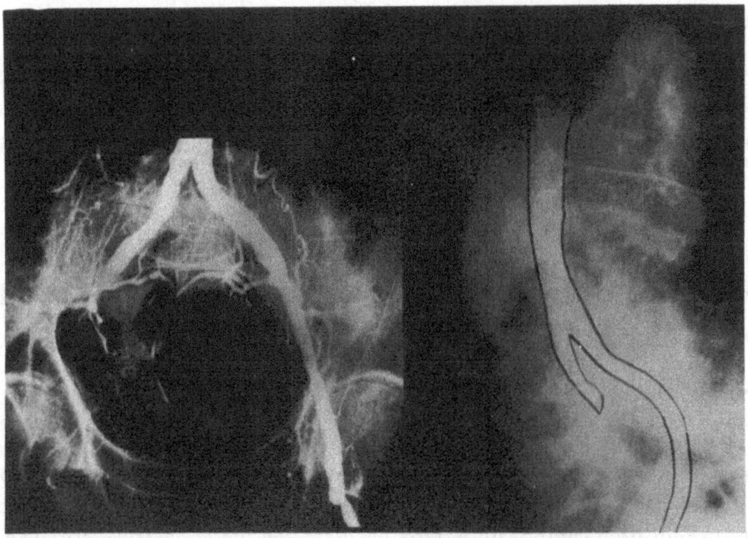

Abb. 2

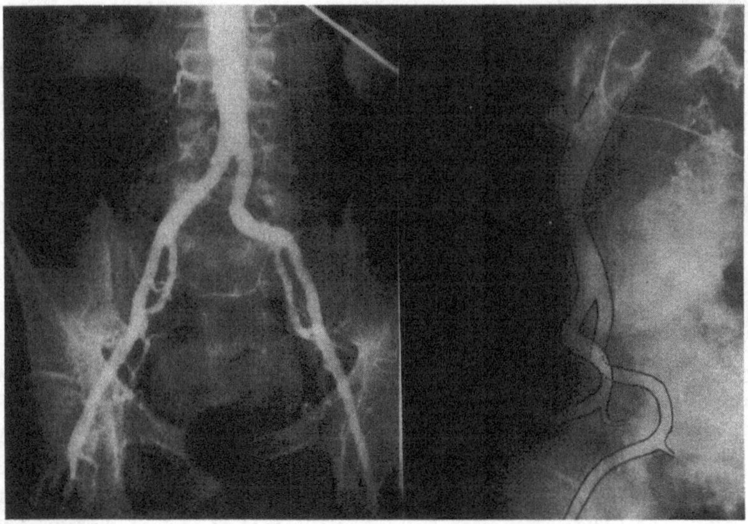

Abb. 3

setzen dann die Beckenarterien durch einen aortofemoralen Dacron Bifurcations By-pass, den wir bei älteren Patienten extraperitoneal anlegen.

Wenn sich im seitlichen Strahlengang kein Kinking zeigt, bevorzugen wir bei Patienten jenseits des 65. Lebensjahres wegen der geringeren Belastung die retrograde Ausschälungsplastik mit dem Ringstripper.

Bei Verschlüssen oder Stenosen der Äste der Aorta abdominalis ist die Angiographie in 2 Ebenen ebenfalls sehr wertvoll, weil sich Abgangsstenosen in der seitlichen Ebene besser beurteilen lassen. Besonders das echte Malabsorptionssyndrom stellt hierfür eine Indikation dar.

Bei unseren Versuchen, in deren Verlauf wir 31 Katheterangiographien der Aorta und 40 Katheter-

angiographien der Beckenarterien von der Arteria femoralis aus durchgeführt haben sind wir zu folgendem Ergebnis gekommen:
Sklerotische Wandveränderungen und Verschlüsse der Aorta abdominalis und der Beckenarterien sind für den Gefäßchirurgen mit der 2 Ebenenangiographie nicht leichter zu beurteilen. Für die Wahl des Rekonstruktionsverfahrens der Aorta abdominalis ist sie von höherem Aussagewert als die einfache lumbale Aortographie.

Die translumbale 2-Ebenenangiographie der Bauchaorta nach einem neuen Katheterverfahren

H. J. Scherer, P. Mutzenbach und B. Kramann

Es bleibt unvermeidbar, daß wir als Gefäßchirurgen von Zeit zu Zeit eine durch Punktion geschädigte, meist sklerotisch veränderte Arterie nach Angiographie versorgen müssen (Abb. 1). Gleichzeitig muß hervorgehoben werden, daß die Katheterangiographie heute zur wertvollen, ja unersetzbaren Routinediagnostik geworden ist. Nach großen Sammelstatistiken ergibt sich dabei je nach dargestellter Gefäßregion und angewandter Technik eine Komplikationsrate zwischen 0 bis rund 13 %. Die Ursachen für diese Komplikationen sind sehr vielfältig und hinreichend bekannt. Wir wissen auch, daß bei der direkten Aortographie die geringste Komplikationsquote besteht. Zweifellos läßt die Gefäßdarstellung in 2 Ebenen für die Operationsindikation eine bessere Beurteilung der morphologischen Befunde zu. Jedoch ist die apparative Voraussetzung für diese 2-Ebenen-Angiographie in Serienaufnahmen nur selten gegeben. Um dennoch Gefäßkontrastbilder in 2 Ebenen darstellen zu können und dabei die Komplikationsrate so niedrig wie möglich zu halten, haben wir versucht, unter Beibehaltung der Kathetermethode die Punktionen von Arterien mit kleineren Durchmessern zu umgehen.

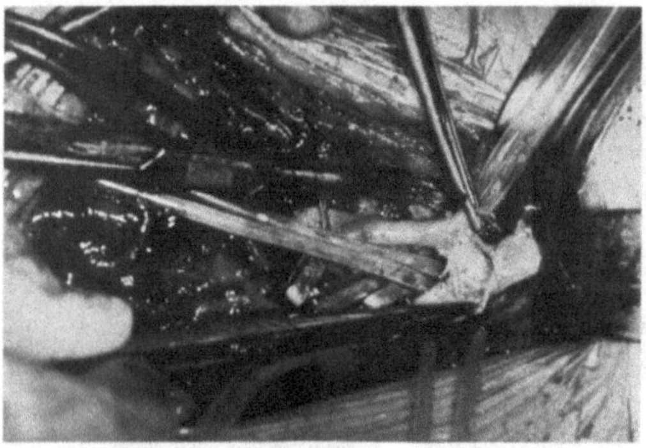

Abb. 1: Operationssitus einer nach *Seldinger*-Katheterisation geschädigten, sklerotisch veränderten Femoralarterie links.

Unser technisches Vorgehen dabei: wir verwenden für die direkte Serien-Aorto-Arteriographie den *Angiorapid*. Es erfolt die Direktpunktion der Aorta in der vorgesehenen Höhe von lumbal her in üblicher Weise bei Bauchlage des vollnarkotisierten Patienten. Die jetzt verwendete Punktionskanüle weist nach Entfernung des Troikars und des scharfen Nadelanteiles eine lichte Weite von 2 und einen äußeren Durchmesser von 2,5 mm auf, ist also dicker als die gewöhnlich verwendeten Punktionsnadeln. Einführen eines gelben Katheters nach *Oedmann–Ledin,* der an der Spitze offen ist und weitere 5 seitliche Löcher aufweist (Abb. 2). Sobald die gebogene Katheterspitze die vorgesehene Gefäßprovinz erreicht hat, wird die starre Hülse über den Katheter entfernt. Aber auch ohne die äußere Punktionskanüle als Leitschiene kann die Lage des Katheters noch korrigiert werden. Die Injektion des Kontrastmittels erfolgt maschinell mit der *Contrac*-Spritze bei einem flow von 11 bis 12 ml/sec. Serienaufnahmen im ap.-Strahlengang können jetzt geschossen

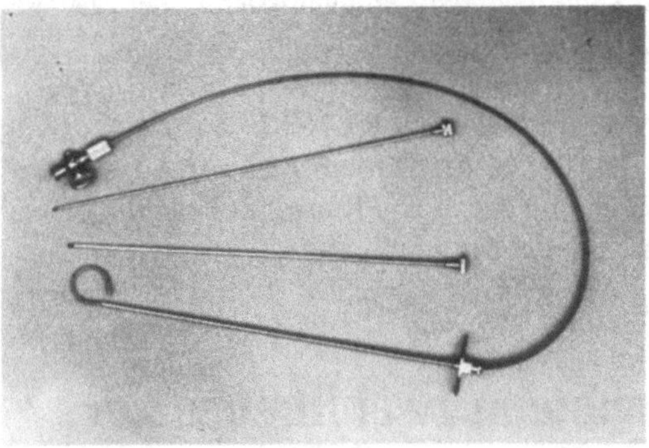

Abb. 2: 3-teilige Aorten-Punktionskanüle mit dazu passendem Katheter nach *Oedmann–Ledin.*

werden. Für die Angiographie im seitlichen oder evtl. schrägen Strahlengang ist – wie auch bei der *Seldinger*-Katheterisierung – die Umlagerung des Patienten erforderlich. Diese Manipulation kann aber nach Entfernung der starren Kanüle jetzt völlig gefahrlos vorgenommen werden. Beispielsweise wird über eine translumbal vorgenommene Aortenpunktion mit dieser Kathetermethode die Darstellung des Aortenbogens ebenso ermöglicht. – Es ist ohne weiteres denkbar, daß nach diesem Verfahren auch die selektive Darstellung einzelner Gefäßbezirke unter Verwendung eines mit einem entsprechenden Führungsdraht bestückten Katheters möglich ist.

(a)

(b)

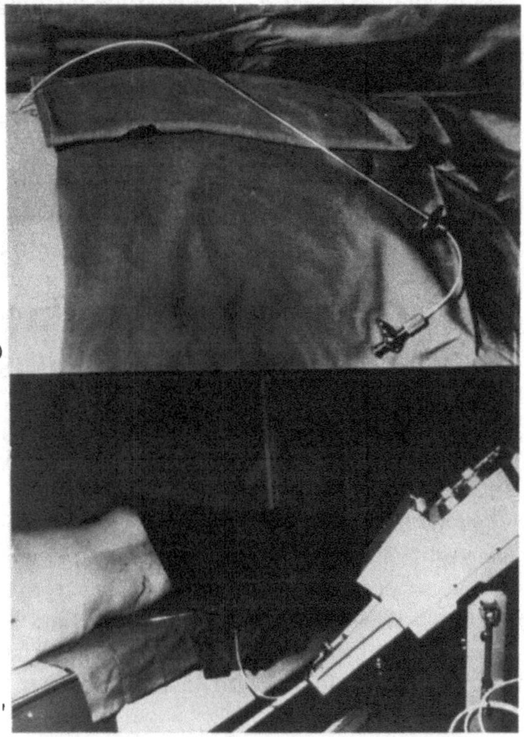

Abb. 3a: Patient in Bauchlage im Zustand nach Direktpunktion der Aorta, translumbal eingeführtem Katheter und Entfernung der äußeren Punktionskanüle.

Abb. 3b: Patient nach Umlagerung auf die linke Seite bei intra-aortal liegendem Katheter zur Erstellung der seitlichen Serienangiogramme. – *Contrac*-Spritze.

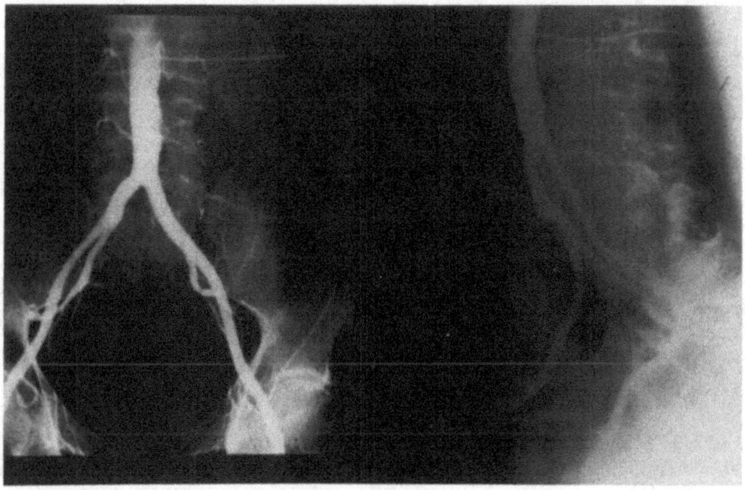

Abb. 4: Beispiel einer translumbalen Katheter-Arterio-Aortographie in 2 Ebenen: die im a.p.-Strahlengang nur mäßig veränderten Beckenarterien zeigen bei seitlicher Aufnahme deutliches „kinking" und Stenosen.

Wir sehen nach bisherigen, zahlenmäßig allerdings noch geringen Erfahrungen folgende Vorteile dieses Verfahrens:

1. Einfache und sichere Technik
2. Direktpunktion des größtlumigen arteriellen Gefäßes
3. Wegfall eines möglichen Arteriospasmus
4. Keine Traumatisierung mittlerer oder kleinerer Arterien
5. Möglichkeit der gefahrlosen Umlagerung des Patienten und damit der Mehrebenen-Angiographie
6. Die Gefahr der Thrombenanlagerung am Katheter und dadurch auftretender Komplikationen erscheint in der großlumigen Aorta geringer.

Die Bedeutung der Ventrikulographie in zwei Ebenen zur Beurteilung des Kontraktionsverhaltens des linken Ventrikels bei koronarer Herzkrankheit

H. J. Becker, G. Kober, M. Kaltenbach, P. Spitz und G. Hornung

Über die Notwendigkeit die selektive Koronarangiographie mit einer Ventrikulographie zu kombinieren bestehen keine Meinungsverschiedenheiten, da Auswirkungen der Koronarsklerose auf das Myokard nur hierdurch genügend beurteilt werden können. Am häufigsten wird die linke Kammer in der rechtsvorderen Schrägprojektion gefilmt. Bei Auswertung von 460 selektiven Koronarangiogrammen mit Ventrikulographie hat sich gezeigt, daß in dieser einen Ebene vorwiegend das Kontraktionsverhalten der Vorderwand und der diaphragmalen Hinterwand beurteilbar ist. Über

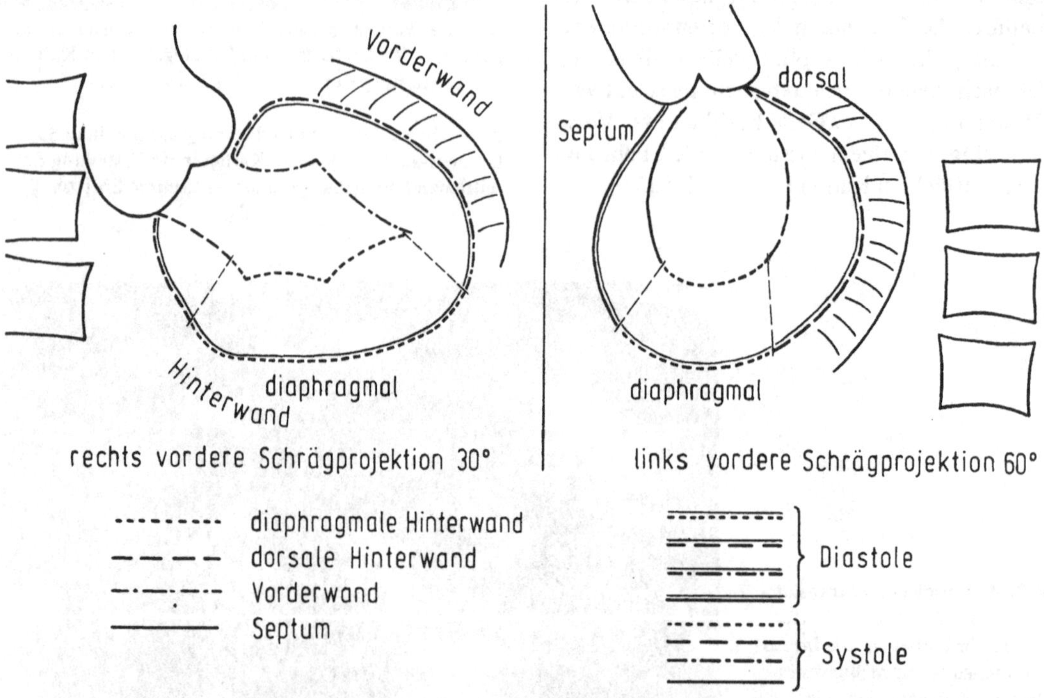

Abb. 1: Schematische Darstellung des Angiogramms der linken Kammer in zwei Ebenen, jeweils in Endsystole und Enddiastole. Das Angiogramm zeigt ein normales Kontraktionsverhalten aller vier Wände des linken Ventrikels.

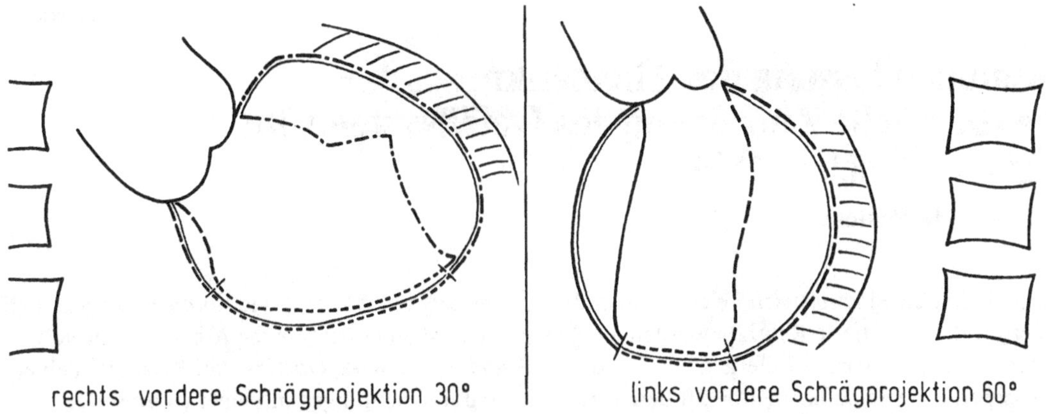

Abb. 2: Linksventrikuläres Angiogramm nach diaphragmalem Hinterwandinfarkt, der an der weitgehend aufgehobenen Kontraktion der betroffenen Wand gut zu erkennen ist.

die Funktion der septalen und dorsalen Wand kann dagegen nur eine Aussage gemacht werden, wenn außer der Füllung der linken Kammer in rechtsvorderer Schrägprojektion (mit Drehung des Patienten um 30–50°) auch eine in linksvorderer Schrägprojektion (mit Drehung des Patienten um 40–60°) erfolgt (siehe Abb. 1). Erst die Auswertung beider Ebenen gestattet zum Beispiel bei einem Hinterwandinfarkt die sichere Aussage ob nur die dorsale oder diaphragmale Hinterwand (siehe Abb. 2 und 3) betroffen ist oder ob ein Kontraktionsausfall der gesamten Hinterwand vorliegt. Der Nachweis einer guten Kontraktionsfähigkeit der dorsalen Hinterwand ermöglicht erst die Indikationsstellung zur Implantation der Arteria thoracica interna in dieses Gebiet, wenn dies nach dem Koronarogramm und klinischen Befund für erforderlich gehalten wird. Außerdem entscheidet unter anderem bei einem Vorderwandaneurysma das Ausmaß der Mitbeteiligung des Septums über die Operabilität.

Die gleichzeitige Erfassung der Druckwerte in der linken Kammer und der Druckanstiegsgeschwindigkeit ergänzen den angiographischen Befund, sie sind jedoch keineswegs immer gleichsinnig verändert wie das Ventrikulogramm. Das Risiko der Ventrikulographie ist auch bei Verwendung des Sones-Katheters, der Seitenlöcher und ein Endloch besitzt, gering. Bei rund 1000 Kontrastmittelinjektionen in die linke Kammer wurden von uns bislang keine ernsten Komplikationen beobachtet. Ein Film mit Beispielen wurde demonstriert.

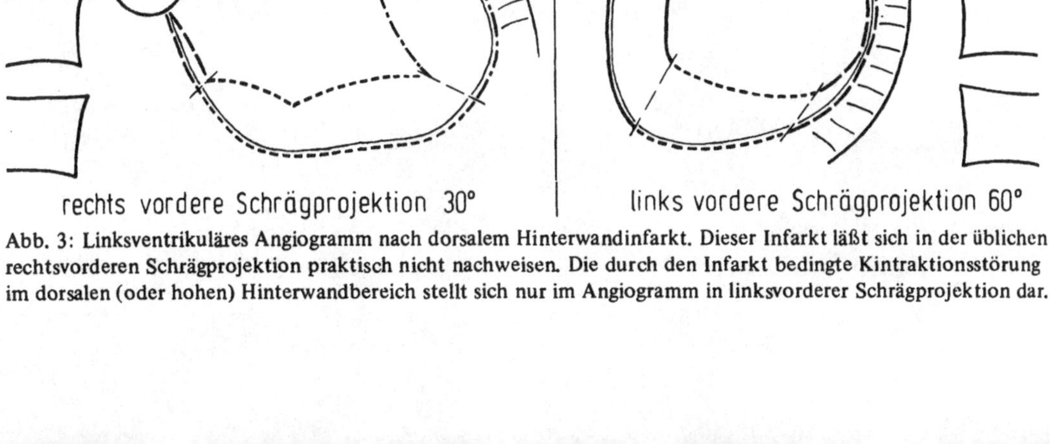

Abb. 3: Linksventrikuläres Angiogramm nach dorsalem Hinterwandinfarkt. Dieser Infarkt läßt sich in der üblichen rechtsvorderen Schrägprojektion praktisch nicht nachweisen. Die durch den Infarkt bedingte Kintraktionsstörung im dorsalen (oder hohen) Hinterwandbereich stellt sich nur im Angiogramm in linksvorderer Schrägprojektion dar.

Zusammenfassung des Themenkreises V – Die räumliche Zuordnung des Gefäßsystems im angiographischen Bild

Moderator: H. Pokieser

Durch eindrucksvoll kasuistisch belegte und bildmäßig gut dokumentierte Referate wurden die Bedeutung und diagnostische Relevanz von angiographischen Röntgenaufnahmen in 2-Ebenen aufgezeigt. Für die Darstellung im Bereiche von Gehirn und Herz routinemäßig üblich bzw. obligat, haben im besonderen die Referate von *Gerhardt* und Mitarbeitern (Tübingen), *Köhler* (Helsinki) sowie *Mack* und Mitarbeitern (München) die Wichtigkeit und Aussagekraft der zweiten Ebene für viscerale Angiographien und die untere Aorta sowie die Beckengefäße anschaulich dargelegt.

Hinsichtlich stereoskopischer und stereographischer Verfahren wurden von den Referenten *Dümmling* und *Maass* (Erlangen) die technischen Voraussetzungen sowie von *Kunnen* (Belgien) die klinische Anwendung von Stereofernsehen und -kinematographie erörtert und demonstriert. Die dem Auditorium gebotene Vorführung von Kontrastdarstellungen der Herzhöhlen und selektiven Coronarographien unterstrich in überaus eindrucksvoller Weise den praktischen klinischen Wert dieser technisch und finanziell sehr aufwendigen Einrichtungen. Von besonderem Interesse erscheint auch die Information der Referenten über die routinemäßig angewendete Stereofernsehdurchleuchtung bei der Durchführung kardioangiographischer Untersuchungen und selektiver Gefäßdarstellungen. Im Vergleich zu dem von *Dümmling* und *Maass* sowie *Kunnen* vorgestelltem Stereosystem berichtete die Arbeitsgruppe von *Beduhn, Gajewski, Goering* und *Wenz* (Heidelberg) über ihre Erfahrungen mit einer technisch sehr einfachen Einrichtung zur Anfertigung stereoskopischer Röntgenaufnahmen von Visceralangiogrammen. Die Bilder werden unter Verwendung nur einer feststehenden Röntgenröhre durch phasenweise Verlagerung des Patienten in einer Drehmulde hergestellt und vermitteln einen guten räumlichen Eindruck über abnorme Gefäßverläufe im Abdominalbereich.

In der anschließenden ausführlichen und sehr angeregten Diskussion werden die Fragen der praktischen Anwendung stereoskopischer Verfahren sowie verschiedene optische und mechanische Auswertungsmöglichkeiten erörtert.

Zusammenfassend kann festgestellt werden, daß die praktische Bedeutung stereoskopischer und stereographischer Verfahren sowie auch die Wertigkeit der 2-Ebenen-Angiographie zweifelsfrei feststeht. Technisch optimale Lösungen erfordern heute allerdings einen für viele Spitalserhalter noch zu hohen Kostenaufwand, sodaß die altbekannten, technisch und finanziell weniger aufwendigeren 2 Ebenen- und Stereoeinrichtungen nach wie vor ihre Bedeutung für den praktischen Betrieb haben.

VI. ERFASSUNG DYNAMISCHER VORGÄNGE MIT HILFE DER ANGIOGRAPHIE UND VERWANDTER VERFAHREN

Viszerale Pharmakoangiographie

M. Cen und W. Frik

Seit 40 Jahren wurde immer wieder versucht, den Einfluß vasoaktiver Pharmaka bei der Angiographie diagnostisch zu nutzen. Zuerst konnten mit Gefäßdilatatoren gewisse Erfolge bei der Angiographie der Extremitäten erzielt werden. Bei der viszeralen Angiographie haben sich vasodilatatorisch wirkende Pharmaka für die indirekte Darstellung der abführenden Venen bewährt. Zur Beurteilung des venösen Pfortaderkreislaufes bei Zustand nach Splenektomie ist die indirekte Portographie mittels Mesentericographie für die Erfassung der bestehenden Dynamik des Pfortoaderabflusses die einzig mögliche Methode. Wegen der schwachen Kontrastmittelanfärbung ist jedoch die Aussagekraft der konventionellen Mesentericographie in der venösen Phase begrenzt. Nach Applikation von Bradykinin in die A. mesenterica superior nimmt der periphere Widerstand ab und die Durchblutung zu und die entsprechenden Venen füllen sich praller. Voraussetzung für die bessere Darstellung der Venen ist jedoch die Erhöhung der Kontrastmittelmenge und des Kontrastmittelinjektionsflusses.

Durch die organspezifischen, kurzzeitig hyperämisierenden Pharmaka läßt sich auch die Kapillarphase verbessern, so daß auch deren Aussagekraft erhöht und die genaue Abgrenzung des entsprechenden Organs möglich wird. Gewisse Erfolge wurden bereits bei der Darstellung des Pankreas erzielt. Z. B. durch das Sekretin wird das Aufnahmevermögen des Kapillarbettes im Pankreas vergrößert. Wenn dieses erhöhte Aufnahmevolumen für das Kontrastmittel voll ausgenutzt werden soll, muß man natürlich sowohl die Kontrastmittelmenge pro Zeiteinheit als auch das gesamte Kontrastmittelvolumen gegenüber der konventionellen Angiographie erhöhen. Bei gleichbleibender Kontrastmittelmenge und Durchfluß pro Zeiteinheit ist die Pharmakoangiographie mit einem vasodilatatorischen und hyperämisierenden Pharmakon wegen des stark verdünnten Kontrastmittelbolus enttäuschend und dieser Fehler kann die Pharmakoangiographie ungerechtfertigt in Mißdredit bringen.

Der diagnostische Wert der Pankreasanfärbung ist sehr umstritten und ich möchte hier darauf nicht eingehen. Gestatten Sie mir aber anhand von zwei Beispielen zu verdeutlichen, daß das Problem nicht in der Darstellung des Pankreas liegt, sondern vielmehr in der Interpretation der Anfärbung. Hier handelt es sich um ein relativ großes Pankreas. Nach den Labor- und klinischen Befunden dürfte dieser Patient keine Pankreaserkrankung haben. Auf diesem Bild sehen Sie eine inhomogene Darstellung des Pankreas mit welligen Konturen, auch bei diesem Patienten waren die Diastasewerte nicht erhöht und klinisch bestand kein Anhalt für eine Pankreaserkrankung.

Bei der Diagnostik zahlreicher entzündlicher, degenerativer und insbesondere maligner Erkrankungen bietet sich demnach an erster Stelle die Beurteilung der Gefäßstruktur an. Für die Bewertung dieser sog. Angioarchitektonik genügt meist die konventionelle, selektive Organangiographie, in manchen Fällen reicht sie jedoch zum Nachweis kleinerer, umschriebener Veränderungen nicht aus. Neben der superselektiven Angiographie wurde deshalb versucht, die unterschiedliche Reaktion des Gefäßsystems auf vasopressorische Substanzen zu nutzen. Auf diesem Bild (Abb. 1)

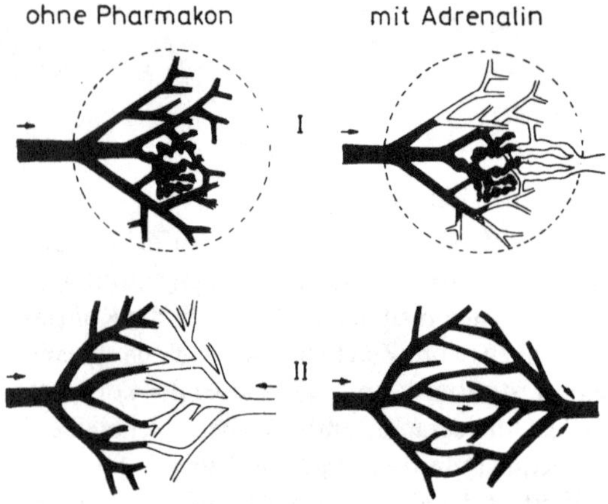

Abb. 1

sehen Sie mehrere Angiographien schematisch dargestellt. Die linke Reihe zeigt die Angiographien ohne Pharmakon. In der rechten Reihe stehen die entsprechenden Angiographien nach der intraarteriellen Adrenalinapplikation. Das erste Beispiel stellt einen gefäßreichen Tumor mit arteriovenösen Kurzschlüssen dar. Durch die Adrenalininjektion wird die gesunde Peripherie blockiert, das Kontrastmittel in die Tumorgefäße abgeleitet und eine isolierte, nicht überlagerte Darstellung der Tumorgefäße erzielt; denn die Tumorgefäße vom embryonalen Typ reagieren auf Adrenalin nicht. Bei der Pharmakoangiographie mittels Adrenalin kann man also in der Regel den Tumor exakt abgrenzen, seine anatomische Zuordnung präoperativ genau beurteilen und über die Gefäßversorgung des Tumors bessere Aussagen machen . Außerdem führt die Adrenalininjektion durch Blockierung der gesunden Peripherie zu einem relativ größeren Kontrastmittelangebot an den Tumorkreislauf, der das Kontrastmittel über seine arteriovenösen Anastomosen wenig verdünnt in die Tumorvenen abgibt. Die ausbleibende Beimischung mit venösem Blut aus dem gesunden Parenchym verhilft zusätzlich zu einer kontrastreichen Darstellung der abführenden Tumorvenen. Die selektive Nierenangiographie mit Adrenalin ist deshalb auch für die indirekte Nephrophlebographie bei gefäßreichen Tumoren zur Abklärung einer Tumorinvasion der Venen zu empfehlen. Auf diesem Angiogramm ist die Vena renalis trotz der selektiven Nierenangiographie nicht abgrenzbar. Bei der Wiederholung der selektiven Nierenangiographie mit Adrenalin erkennt man eine gute Kontrastmittelanfärbung der Vena renalis, wodurch eine Thrombose der Vena renalis ausgeschlossen werden konnte. In Fällen mit wenigen oder fehlenden arteriovenösen Kurzschlüssen ist jedoch die Cavographie nach intraaortaler Adrenalininjektion der selektiven Pharmakoangiographie vorzuziehen. Die durch Adrenalininjektion bedingte Konstriktion der kleinen Nierenarterien führt zu einer Druckminderung in den Nierenvenen. Hierdurch wird der retrograde Einstrom des Kontrastmittels von der unteren Hohlvene in die Nierenvenen erleichtert. Die retrograde Füllung der Nierenvenen bei der Cavographie nach intraaortaler Adrenalininjektion beschränkt sich allerdings meistens auf den Hauptstamm. Seine Darstellung ist jedoch in der Mehrzahl der Fälle für die Einleitung der entsprechenden Therapie ausreichend. Auf dieser Cavographie nach intraaortaler Adrenalininjektion sehen Sie beide Vv. renales gut angefärbt. In diesem Fall stellt sich die rechte Nierenvene gut dar. Dagegen kann man links eine Nierenvenenthrombose erkennen, die in die Vena cava inferior hineinragt.

Das schematisch dargestellte zweite Beispiel (Abb. 1) stellt ein Organ dar, daß von zwei Arterien versorgt wird, wie das Pankreas. Wenn man nur eine von beiden Arterien katheterisiert und Kontrastmittel injiziert, erzielt man gewöhnlich eine Darstellung nur einer Hälfte des Organes. Bei einer so unvollständigen Darstellung der Pankreasarterien in der konventionellen selektiven Angiographie ist eine bessere Darstellung der Pankreasarterien mittels Adrenalin möglich; denn das Adrenalin erzeugt eine starke Tonuserhöhung der Arterienwand und der Injektionsdruck wird durch die dann starrwandigen Arterien bis in die Peripherie fortgeleitet. Die Gefäße, die sich bei der ersten Angiographie ohne Pharmakon nicht dargestellt haben, werden auch von der Adrenalininjektion nicht erreicht. Sie stehen deshalb während der Druckinjektion des Kontrastmittels nicht unter Adrenalinwirkung und lassen sich über die interarteriellen Anastomosen retrograd darstellen (Abb. 1 und 2).

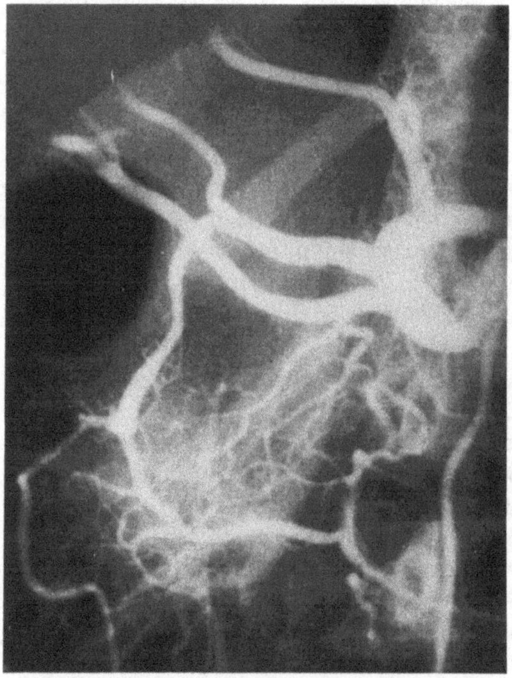

Abb. 2

Sowohl die bessere Darstellung der Anastomosen als auch der Tumorgefäße ist mittels Adrenalin auch dadurch bedingt, daß die Verweildauer der Kontrastmittelsäule in der entsprechenden Versorgungsarterie verlängert wird. Die Verlangsamung des Blutstromes führt zu einem relativ wenig verdünnten Kontrastmittel bolus, ohne die Kontrastmittelmenge pro Zeiteinheit zu vergrößern. Die relative Erhöhung des Kontrastmittelangebotes in den interessierenden Arterienästen erlaubt sogar sowohl die Reduzierung der applizierten Kontrastmittelmenge als auch des Injektionsdruckes, wodurch das Risiko der Untersuchung für den Patienten herabgesetzt wird. In dieser Hinsicht ist die superselektive Angiographie mit der Pharmakoangiographie bedingt zu vergleichen. Durch die superselektive Angiographie ist das entsprechende Kontrastmittelangebot an die darzustellenden Arterien mit kleiner Kontrastmittelmenge wohl gewährleistet. Ob das Risiko der Untersuchung für den Patienten bei der superselektiven Angiographie auch so gering gehalten wird, wie bei der Pharmakoangiographie mit Adrenalin, möchte ich bezweifeln.

Wir stimmen dennoch überein mit den Kollegen, die bei dem fraglichen Befund im Pankreasbereich die superselektive Angiographie der Pharmacoangiographie vorziehen. Bei der Klärung eines fraglichen Angiographiebefundes ist eine wirklich gelungene superselektive Angiographie hinsichtlich ihrer Aussagekraft in der Differentialdiagnose der Pharmakoangiographie meistens überlegen. Wenn aber der konventionellen selektiven Angiographie kein Hinweis über die Lokalisation des pathologischen Organprozesses zu entnehmen ist oder die gefäßanatomischen Verhältnisse des Pankreas unklar oder für die superselektive Angiographie ungeeignet erscheinen (Abb. 2), möchte ich der Pharmakoangiographie mit Adrenalin in der Untersuchungsreihe einen Platz vor der superselektiven Angiographie einräumen. Vor allem verursacht die Pharmakoangiographie keine zusätzliche Belastung für den Patienten durch erneute Kathetermanipulationen und die Untersuchungsdauer wird höchstens 5 min, also unbedeutend, verlängert. Man gewinnt außerdem dabei eine Angiographie in einer zweiten Ebene, da wir Pharmakoangiographien im 2. schrägen Durchmesser anfertigen. Nach der Klärung der gefäßanatomischen Verhältnisse durch die Pharmakoangiographie kann man dann die superselektive Angiographie, sofern es möglich und notwendig ist, immer noch vornehmen.

Zu den pharmakodynamischen Wirkungen des intraarteriell applizierten Adrenalins gehört auch die mehr oder weniger starke Retention des Kontrastmittels in der entsprechenden Arterie bei gleichzeitiger proximaler Verlängerung der Kontrastmittelsäule. Diesen Effekt kann man ausnützen, um solche Arterien darzustellen, deren superselektive Katheterisierung manchmal schwierig sein kann, z. B. die A. phrenica inferior (Abb. 3),

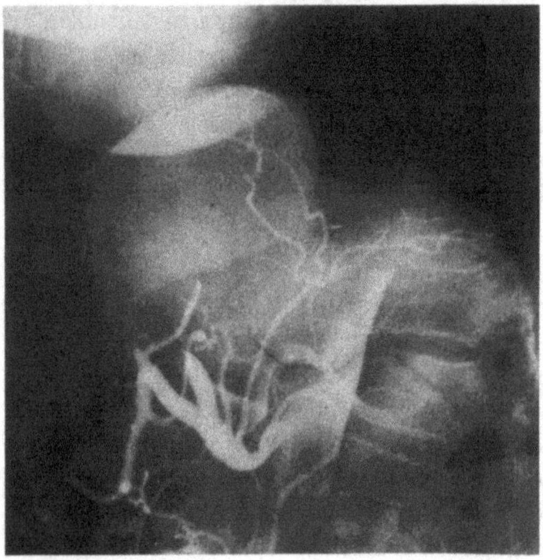

Abb. 3

die A. suprarenalis inferior oder auch z. B. die A. pancreatica dorsalis. Die proximale Verlängerung der Kontrastmittelsäule durch die Blockierung der Peripherie mittels Adrenalin kann man natürlich auch bei der sog. Rückflußarteriographie (Gegenstromangiographie) nutzen. Der sonst erforderliche höhere Injektionsdruck bei einer Rückflußarteriographie ohne Adrenalin kann nach Applikation von Adrenalin reduziert werden.

Die Arteriographie wurde in der letzten Zeit auch als Methode der Wahl in der Diagnose akuter Magen-Darmblutungen anerkannt. Auch beim Nachweis einer Blutungsquelle kann man gegebenenfalls die Aussagedraft der Arteriographie durch eine Pharmakoangiographie mit Adrenalin erhöhen, worauf wir auf der letzten Tagung in Baden-Baden eingingen. Wichtig ist auch die blutstillende Wirkung der gefäßverengenden Medikamente, die nach der selektiven Angiographie als ebenfalls selektive arterielle Infusion angeschlossen werden, um die Blutung unter Kontrolle zu bringen. Die lokalisierte Gefäßverengung mit reduziertem Blutdurchfluss und die verkürzte Blutkoagulationszeit (Wright), welche die Möglichkeit einer Thrombosierung und damit des Verschlusses eines blutenden Gefäßes verbessern, ist die theoretische Überlegung dieser Methode. Sie wurde von Baum und Mitarb., Rösch und Mitarb. und Slezak und Mitarb. tierexperimentell untermauert und in der Humanmedizin mit Erfolg verwendet. Wir haben bis jetzt nur einmal den Vorrang vor den Chirurgen gehabt und durften diese Methode bei einer akuten gastrointestinalen Blutung mit Erfolg verwenden. Es handelte sich um einen jungen Patienten, bei dem vier Wochen nach einem schweren Verkehrsunfall mit operativer Versorgung einer Leberruptur, eine akute gastrointestinale Blutung auftrat. Es bestand der Verdacht auf ein Stress-Ulcus. Die sofort durchgeführte Coeliacographie ließ die Blutungsquelle im Bereich des Duodenums mit einem großen Extravasat unschwer erkennen. Wir haben anschließend durch den liegenden Katheter im Truncus coeliacus 10 μg Suprarenin/min über 10 min infudiert. Auf eine Kontrollangiographie wurde wegen der gefäßerweiternden Wirkung des Kontrastmittels verzichtet, da uns die unmittelbar danach durchgeführte Operation über die Wirkung unserer Infusion Auskunft geben konnte. Bei der Operation bestand keine Blutung mehr und wir hatten den Eindruck, daß die Sistierung der Blutung während der Operation dem Chirurgen sehr angenehm war.

Cine-Densitometrie

F. Heuck, H. K. Deininger und K. Vanselow

In der Radiologie sind verschiedenartige Untersuchungsverfahren zur Beurteilung der Kreislauffunktionen eingesetzt worden. Als Indikatoren sind entweder Kontrastsubstanzen oder radioaktiv-markierte Stoffe verwendet worden, Im Prinzip sind diese Methoden den bekannten Verfahren der Farbstoffverdünnungsuntersuchungen sehr ähnlich. Die Isotopenverfahren haben die breiteste Anwendung zur Kreislaufanalyse gefunden. Heute beschränkt sich diese Methode nicht allein auf eine Funktionsmessung mit Szintillationszählern. Der Einsatz der Gammakamera in Verbindung mit Datenverarbeitungsanlagen erschließt neue Möglichkeiten. Bei gutem zeitlichem Auflösungsvermögen des Durchflusses radioaktiver Substanzen ist die räumliche Bildauflösung jedoch sehr viel schlechter als die eines Röntgenfilmes.
Die Angiographie mit hoher Bildfrequenz erlaubt eine Analyse der Kreislauffunktionen im großem Kreislauf und den Parallelkreisläufen der Organe. Bisher wurde vorwiegend der arterielle Schenkel der Strombahn untersucht, während der Kapillarkreislauf – also die Gewebsdurchblutung und ihre Störungen – sowie der venöse Abschnitt der Strombahn weniger beachtet worden sind. Sehr rasche Bewegungsabläufe können nur dann analysiert werden, wenn die Aufnahmefrequenz entsprechend hoch gewählt wird. Für das Studium der arteriellen Strömungsphänomene sind Bildfrequenzen von 80–200 Bildern pro Sekunde erforderlich, so daß nur die Röntgenkinematographie die notwendigen Voraussetzungen zur Kreislaufanalyse schaffen kann. Die im Röntgenbild, im Kinofilm oder im Bildbandspeicher enthaltene Information kann mit Hilfe der Photometrie oder Densitometrie analysiert werden. Bei Einsatz der Röntgenkinematographie wird von „Cine-Densitometrie", unter Zugrundelegung der Bildverstärkerfernsehtechnik von „Video-Densitometrie" gesprochen. Beide Methoden sind bisher zur Kreislaufanalyse herangezogen worden, so daß die kritische Betrachtung der Angio-Cine-Densitometrie unter Berücksichtigung des verwandten, jedoch andersartigen Verfahrens vorgenommen werden soll.

1. Kritische Betrachtungen zur Angiodensitometrie

Eine *Wertung der Verfahren* zur densitometrischen Analyse des Kreislaufes muß in erster Linie das Auflösungsvermögen sowie das Signalstörverhältnis berücksichtigen. Von diesen beiden Faktoren hängt in starkem Maße die Aussagefähigkeit der Methode und damit der Wert des Meßergebnisses ab. Prinzipiell werden alle densitometrischen Meßverfahren durch Vorgänge ermöglicht, denen verschiedene physikalische Effekte wie Umwandlung von Strahlungsenergie in elektrische Energie und elektrischer Energie in Lichtenergie (Bildwandler) oder in Schwärzungen einer Filmschicht zugrunde liegen. Diese physikalischen Effekte führen eine Meßwertwandlung durch. So werden Lichtsignale in ein elektrisches Signal und elektrische Signale in ein mechanisches Signal, wie sie z. B. im *EKG*-Gerät als Schreiber vorliegen, transformiert. Die Leistungsfähigkeit einer solchen Meßwandlerkette wird beschränkt durch das Auflösungsvermögen und das Signalrauschverhältnis.

a. *Das Auflösungsvermögen*

Die durch die Meßapparatur bedingte Grenze des Auflösungsvermögens wird durch die kleinste Einheit, die eben noch analysiert werden kann, bestimmt. Wir unterscheiden ein zeitliches Auflösungsvermögen, das von der Aufnahmebildfrequenz abhängt und ein räumliches Auflösungsvermögen, das charakterisiert ist durch die Anzahl einzelner Symbole, z. B. Striche, die pro Millimeter noch aufgelöst werden können. In unserem Beispiel der Kreislauf-Densitometrie ist ferner die Kontrastmittelkonzentration im Gefäßlumen oder im Gewebe für das Auflösungsvermögen bedeutsam.

b. *Das Signalrauschverhältnis*

Unter diesem Begriff ist das Verhältnis eines Signales zu den verschiedenen Störfaktoren zu verstehen. Es ist das quantitative Maß für die Auflösung der Signale aus dem Rausch- und Störpegel. Für die Densitometrie ist von Interesse die räumliche und zeitliche Auflösung aus dem Rausch- und Störpegel. Der räumliche Faktor wird durch die Körnigkeit des Bildes bestimmt. Zeitliche Schwankungen haben einen Einfluß auf das Signal-Rauschverhältnis. Ferner sind die Größe der Intensitätsschwankungen und Dichteunterschiede im Meßareal, Schwankungen des Bildstandes und der Bildfolge nicht ohne Einfluß.

Wenn wir unter den genannten Gesichtspunkten die Cine-Densitometrie und die Video-Densitometrie gegenüberstellen, so liegt die durch die Meßapparatur bedingte Grenze des Auflösungsvermögens bei der Video-Densitometrie in den 50 Halbbildern oder Zwischenbildern pro Sekunde, die nur mit großem apparativen Aufwand überschritten werden könnte. Bei der Cine-Densitometrie können Aufnahmefrequenzen bis zu 200 Bildern und mehr pro Sekunde erreicht werden. Die Grenze des Verfahrens liegt nicht bei der Filmempfindlichkeit, sondern wird durch das Röntgenquantenrauschen bestimmt. Je mehr Bilder pro Sekunde gefordert werden, um so weniger Röntgenquanten stehen zur Verfügung, so daß sich die Körnigkeit im Bild erhöht. Das zeitliche Auflösungsvermögen ist für Geschwindigkeitsmessungen bedeutsam. Die Möglichkeit einer 8fach höheren Bildfolge der Cine-Densitometrie gegenüber der Video-Densitometrie kann sehr wichtig sein, da sich z. B. ein angenommener Fehler von 40 % in der Video-Densitometrie bei 200 Bildern pro Sekunde durch die Cine-Densitometrie auf 5 % reduzieren ließe.

Hinsichtlich des Signal-Rauschverhältnisses ist für *beide Verfahren* das Quantenrauschen der Röntgenstrahlung bedeutsam. Das Filmkorn spielt demgegenüber keine große Rolle. In der Cine-Densitometrie können noch Unterschiede der Entwicklung des Filmes einen Einfluß haben. Für die Video-Densitometrie ist die unterschiedliche Empfindlichkeit der Fläche der Fernsehaufnahmeröhre ein wichtiger Faktor. Ferner sind das Rauschen des Magnetbandes, das Abheben vom Aufnahme- oder Wiedergabekopf, Schwankungen der Intensität durch äußere Einflüsse wie Magnetfelder u. a. Faktoren zu beachten. Für beide Verfahren können Intensitätsschwankungen störend wirken, die in Schwankungen der Spannungsversorgung begründet sind. Neben dem Einfluß der Spannungsversorgung muß bei der Video-Densitometrie die Alterung der Elektronik und damit Änderungen der Verstärkung, der Kennlinie des logarithmischen Verstärkers und der Fernsehaufnahmeröhre beachtet werden. Ferner sind die Moiréschen Figuren zu berücksichtigen. In der Cine-Densitometrie kommen Helligkeitsschwankungen der Projektionslampe durch Störungen in der Spannungsversorgung und durch Alterung des Drahtes der Glühbirne in Betracht. Alle densitometrischen Meßmethoden müssen sich also mit zahlreichen Störfaktoren auseinandersetzen. Zur Beseitigung dieser Störungen können drei Wege beschritten werden:

1. Die Störung kann am Entstehungsort selbst beseitigt werden.
2. Die Störung läßt sich rechnerisch eliminieren.
3. Die Störung wird im Meßvorgang beseitigt.

Bei der Röntgen-Cine-Densitometrie ist die Eliminierung der Störung im Meßvorgang selbst technisch am leichtesten zu realisieren. Hierzu bietet sich die Quotienten-Densitometrie an, über deren Prinzip und theoretische Grundlagen bereits mehrfach und zuletzt vor diesem Kreis auf der Arbeits- und Fortbildungstagung 1970 berichtet worden ist (Heuck 1970). Die Quotienten-Densitometrie ist prinzipiell vergleichbar mit einer Balkenwaage, bei der unabhängig von äußeren Einflüssen der Wägevorgang durchgeführt werden kann, da störende Einflüsse auf beide Waagschalen gleichmäßig einwirken. Betont sei, daß dieses Prinzip gleichermaßen auf die Video-Densitometrie anwendbar ist.

2. Methodik der Cine-Densitometrie

Im eigenen Arbeitskreis wurde zur Cine-Densitometrie das Quotientenmeßverfahren in der Weise eingesetzt, daß Fotowiderstände Verwendung fanden, die paarweise angeordnet werden, so daß die jeweils zwischen 2 Punkten bestehenden Helligkeitsdifferenzen in einen Photostrom unterschiedlicher Spannung umgewandelt werden (Vanselow, Heuck u. Piepgras 1968, Heuck und Vanselow 1971). Als wesentliches Bauelement ist eine Brückenschaltung zu nennen, die einerseits 2 konstante Widerstände, andererseits die beiden variablen Photowiderstände für die Messung enthält. Es kommt nur dann zu einer Spannungsänderung, wenn sich auch die Photowiderstände in unterschiedlichem Ausmaße ändern. Bei einer gleichsinnigen Änderung der paarweise angeordneten Meßzellen um denselben Betrag tritt eine Spannungsschwankung nicht auf. Hierdurch werden alle nicht durch die in das Gefäßlumen injizierte Kontrastsubstanz hervorgerufenen Helligkeitsänderungen eliminiert, so daß ausschließlich das anflutende Kontrastblut sowie die Kontrastkonzentration erfaßt werden. Alle Verfahren, die nicht nach diesem Prinzip arbeiten, können die Mehrzahl der genannten Störfaktoren nicht mit der gleichen Präzision ausscheiden.

Vor der Gewinnung von Meßergebnissen müssen eine Reihe von Fragen geklärt werden. So sind die Informationen, die einem in das Gefäßlumen eingegebenen Kontrastmittelbolus innewohnen, ferner die eingegebene Kontrastmittelmenge, die Kontrastkonzentration, die Injektionsdauer, die zur Verfügung stehende Meßstrecke und die Bildaufnahmefrequenz von Bedeutung. Ein besonderes Gewicht kommt der Relation von Meßstrecke/Bildfrequenz der Röntgenkinematographie und der Strömungsgeschwindigkeit des Blutes zu. Ohne auf die Strömungsphysiologie im einzelnen einzugehen und die Passagemessungen mit Indikatoren im Blut im besonderen zu besprechen, sei betont, daß die mittlere Verweildauer eines Indikators im Gefäßsystem Rückschlüsse auf die Strömungsgeschwindigkeit des Blutes ermöglicht. Theoretisch läßt sich die erforderliche Aufnahmefrequenz des Röntgenkinofilmes bei einer bestimmten Strömungsgeschwindigkeit errechnen, wenn eine

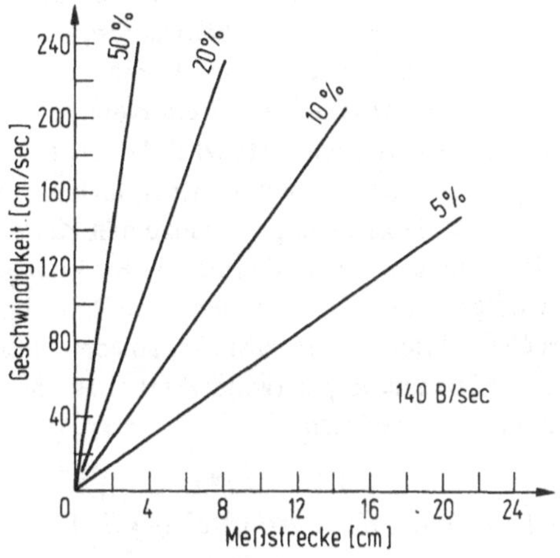

Abb. 1 a: Meßgenauigkeit bei vorgegebener Bildaufnahmefrequenz in Abhängigkeit von der Geschwindigkeit und der Meßstrecke.

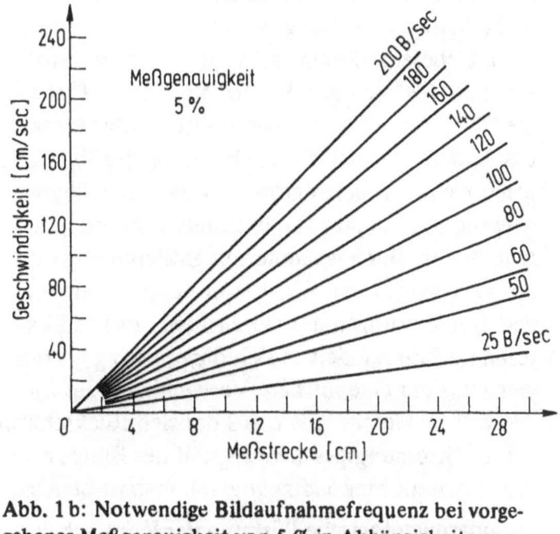

Abb. 1 b: Notwendige Bildaufnahmefrequenz bei vorgegebener Meßgenauigkeit von 5 % in Abhängigkeit von der Geschwindigkeit und der Meßstrecke.

gewisse Fehlerbreite unterstellt wird (Abb. 1). Bei einer kurzen Meßstrecke sollten mehrere Injektionen kleiner Kontrastmittelmengen erfolgen. In Vorversuchen konnte ermittelt werden, daß nach Injektion einer geringen Kontrastmittelmenge von 0,2–0,5 ml eine wesentliche Beeinflussung der Strömungssituation nicht eintritt. Da bei einem solchen Vorgehen nur ein kleiner Teil der Kennlinie des Filmes, also der Schwärzungskurve, ausgesteuert wird, können lineare Verhältnisse angenommen werden, wodurch die Weiterverarbeitung des Meßwertes sehr erleichtert wird. Die mehrfache Injektion einer kleinen Kontrastmitteldosis erlaubt ferner die Erfassung der einzelnen Phasen der Pulswellen, aus denen die mittlere Strömungsgeschwindigkeit bestimmt werden kann. Bei Kenntnis des Gefäßdurchmessers läßt sich aus den Meßwerten der Strömungsgeschwindigkeit auch das Stromvolumen errechnen.

a. *Zur Technik der Kontrastmittelinjektion*

Der Einfluß des Injektionsmodus.

Ein Einfluß der phasischen Stromstärke der A. renalis durch eine *stoßweise Injektion von Kontrastsubstanz* muß nur dann berücksichtigt werden, wenn eine *größere Menge* in kurzer Zeit eingegeben wird. Die Applikation einer *kleinen Kontrastmitteldosis* dürfte, abgesehen von der pharmakologischen Wirkung der Lösung, ohne Einfluß auf die Nierenströmung sein. Bei laminarer Strömung bewegt sich der Axialstrom rascher fort als die Randströmung. Röntgenkontrastsubstanzen und andere, dem Blutstrom beigemengte Indikatoren kleiner Teilchengröße bewegen sich überwiegend mit der langsamen Randströmung, während die im Blut suspendierten größeren Partikel mit dem schnelleren Axialstrom fortbewegt werden. Bei Messungen des Durchflusses mit Indikatoren im Blut handelt es sich daher streng genommen stets um eine mittlere Verweildauer des Indikators im Gefäßsystem, aus der sich Rückschlüsse auf die Strömungsgeschwindigkeit des Blutes ergeben, wenn die Meßbedingungen konstant bleiben.

Die pharmakologische Wirkung der Kontrastsubstanz.

Die Angio-Cine-Densitometrie ist geeignet, pharmakologische Einflüsse auf die Strombahn zu untersuchen. Ein solches Pharmakon stellt das für die Untersuchung benutzte Röntgenkontrastmittel dar. Es konnte gezeigt werden, daß zur Analyse des Organkreislaufes der Niere *eine* arterio-venöse Kontrastmittelpassage ausreicht. Außerdem ist bekannt, daß die Kontrastmittelwirkung am Gefäßsystem erst nach wenigen Sekunden auftritt (Thurau 1964), also zu einem Zeitpunkt, an dem die kinematographische Aufzeichnung der Kontrastmittelpassage bereits beendet ist. Die erste Kontrastmittelanwendung ist folglich durch eine Gefäßreaktion und durch die Rezirkulation des Indikators unbeeinflußt. Durch Vergleich der Strömungszeiten einer ersten und einer nachfolgenden Kontrastmittelinjektion kann die Gefäßreaktion der verwendeten Substanz überprüft werden. Die zeitliche Differenz zwischen den beiden Injektionen ist in Abb. 2 in Korrelation zum Alter aufgetragen. Es fällt auf, daß in jüngeren Jahren eine deutliche Verlängerung der Durchflußzeit resultiert. Dieser Befund läßt auf eine Vasokonstriktion im Bereich der renalen Endstrombahn schließen (Deininger 1972), die durch die erste Applikation der Kontrastsubstanz ausgelöst wurde.

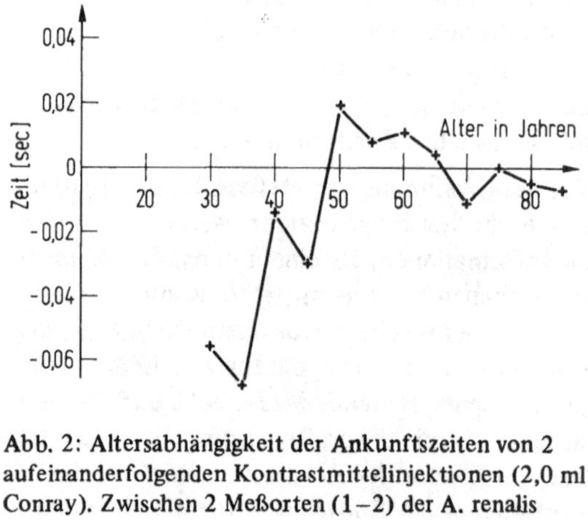

Abb. 2: Altersabhängigkeit der Ankunftszeiten von 2 aufeinanderfolgenden Kontrastmittelinjektionen (2,0 ml Conray). Zwischen 2 Meßorten (1–2) der A. renalis verlängert sich nach der Erstinjektion die Strömungszeit bis zum 5. Lebensjahrzehnt, so daß die Differenz der Flußzeit negativ wird. Im höheren Lebensalter ist eine Reaktion der Nierenarterien nach Kontrastmittelapplikationen nicht mehr nachweisbar.

In fortgeschrittenem Lebensalter tritt diese nicht mehr auf, was für eine altersbedingte Minderung der Gefäßkontraktilität als Folge der Rigidität der Gefäßwand spricht. Die pharmakologische Kontrastmittelwirkung ist außerdem für die verschiedenen trijodierten Kontrastsubstanzen unterschiedlich und bei den Jothalamaten am geringsten.

b. *Zur Auswertung der Densitometerkurven*

An vorher markierten Meßorten werden nach Eingabe der Kontrastsubstanz Densitometerkurven gewonnen, deren weitere Analyse durch einfache Messungen oder mit Hilfe eines Computers vorgenommen werden kann. Auf die Methodik der metrischen Auswertung soll hier nicht im einzelnen eingegangen werden (Heuck und Vanselow 1971). Kurvenanalysen mit Hilfe eines Rechners sind in Zusammenarbeit mit Epple und Decker am Institut für Biomedizinische Technik durchgeführt worden. Die Datenverarbeitungsanlage erlaubt neben der Vereinfachung der Angio-Densitometrie auch die Erkennung und weitgehende Eliminierung von Störungen und ermöglicht die Auswertung einer großen Anzahl von Fällen bei Variationen mehrerer Parameter. Es können relativ einfache statistische Zusammenhänge zwischen einzelnen Meßergebnissen und Krankheitsbefunden erkannt werden. Wenn diese Zusammenhänge bekannt sind, so lassen sich automatische Meß- und Auswerteanlagen für die klinische Anwendung erstellen. Ein wichtiges Hilfsmittel ist dabei das Dialogsystem. Es erlaubt ungeschulten Kräften, komplizierte Meßsysteme ohne die Gefahr zu bedienen, daß Bedienungsfehler oder Verwechslungen zu falschen und nicht erkennbaren Ergebnissen führen.
Für die *klinische Anwendung* densitometrischer Verfahren ist der Geräteaufwand und damit der finanzielle Aufwand einer Methode nicht unbedeutend. Bei einem solchen Vergleich dürfte die Video-Densitometrie bedeutend schlechter abschneiden. Ferner muß die hohe Störanfälligkeit komplizierter elektronischer Systeme berücksichtigt werden. Schließlich sollte erwähnt werden, daß die Archivierung von Röntgenkinofilmen mit der in ihnen gespeicherten Information die Möglichkeit eröffnet, zu einem späteren Zeitpunkt die vorhandene Information zu Vergleichszwecken erneut zu gewinnen, um Befundänderungen objektivieren zu können. Die Angiokinematographie hat gegenüber allen anderen Verfahren zur Analyse eines Organkreislaufes den Vorteil, daß die zur Messung herangezogenen Zonen anatomischen Strukturen zugeordnet werden können, die sich auch bei einer Kontrolle exakt wiederfinden und lokalisieren lassen.

3. **Vorläufige Ergebnisse**

Die Anwendung der Angio-Cine-Densitometrie soll an Hand einiger Beispiele des Nierenkreislaufes dargelegt werden. Der Informationswert der Cine-Densitometrie des Organkreislaufes der Niere ist in Tab. 1 zusammengestellt. Im eigenen Arbeitskreis wurde ein Teil dieser Parameter aufgrund der Untersuchungen von 139 Nierengesunden bestimmt und Normwerte dafür aufgestellt. Hierzu waren über 4400 Einzelmessungen notwendig. Die Mittelwerte bzw. der Streubereich dieser Bestimmungen sind für die einzelnen Gefäßabschnitte der Niere angegeben. Bei Erkrankungen der Niere kommt es zu Abweichungen einzelner oder mehrerer dieser Parameter, die somit eine weitergehende Differenzierung des jeweiligen Krankheitsbildes und wahrscheinlich auch dessen Schweregrad ermöglichen. Vergleichende Untersuchungen zu verschiedenen Nierenleiden müssen jedoch noch in größerer Zahl vorgenommen werden, um statistisch verbindliche Aussagen machen zu können. Der Nachweis eines pathologischen Befundes soll am Beispiel eines hypernephroiden Nierencarcinoms demonstriert werden (Abb. 3). Der Befund ist charakteristisch für weitere 8 Hypernephrome, bei denen der renale Kreislauf cine-densitometrisch analysiert wurde. Grundsätzliche Abweichungen des totalen Nierendurchflusses waren nicht zu beobachten und die Strömungsgeschwindigkeit in der A. renalis war ebenfalls innerhalb des Norm-

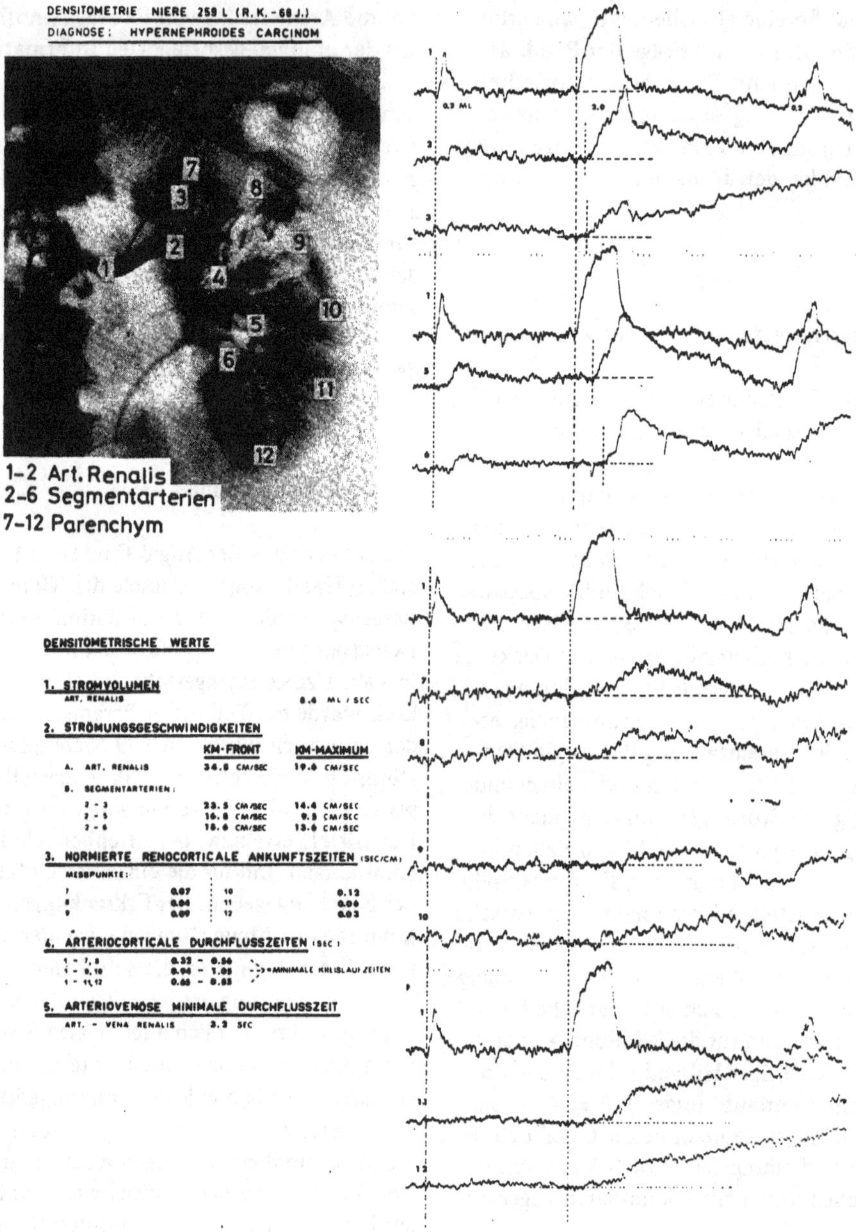

Abb. 3: Angiodensitometrische Meßkurven und -orte einer Niere mit hypernephroidem Carcinom. Deutliche Unterschiede der Strömungsgeschwindigkeiten, normierten renocorticalen Ankunftszeiten und arterio-corticalen Durchflußzeiten im Tumorbereich.

bereiches. Auffällig sind jedoch die stark erhöhten Flußgeschwindigkeiten in den Segmentarterien, die den Tumor versorgen. Daraus ergibt sich eine relative Minderdurchblutung des intakten Nierenparenchyms zugunsten des Tumorgewebes. Andererseits ist im Tumorbereich eine deutliche Verkürzung der renocorticalen Ankunftszeit zu beobachten, ohne daß es nachfolgend zu einem adaequaten Anstieg der Kontrastdichte, also einer Parenchymphase kommt. Auffällig sind vielmehr eine geringe Anhebung des Kurvenniveaus und verstärkte Schwankungen der densitometrischen Meßkurve im Vergleich mit dem Nullpegel. Dieser Befund läßt darauf schließen, daß das dem Tumor zuströmende Kontrastblut intravasal bleibt, im Tumorbereich zwar lange verharrt (Pseudoparenchymeffekt von Hypernephromen), jedoch innerhalb der intravasalen Räume häufig verlagert wird (Pendelblut in Tumorseen und tumorbedingten arteriovenösen Shunts).

Es konnte gezeigt werden, daß die Angio-Cine-Densitometrie der Nierenstrombahn nach Injektion kleinster Kontrastmittelmengen ohne jeden störenden Einfluß auf die Strömungssituation Messungen der Strömungsgeschwindigkeit des Blutes in den einzelnen Abschnitten dieses Organkreislaufes erlaubt. Bei Kenntnis des Gefäßdurchmessers der A. renalis und ihrer Segmentarterien kann das Blutstromvolumen errechnet werden. Im arteriellen Schenkel der Strombahn können Unterschiede der Segmentdurchblutung der Niere ermittelt werden. Krankhafte Veränderungen lassen sich nachweisen und Seitendifferenzen der gesunden zur kranken Niere objektivieren. Das Verfahren erlaubt also eine Analyse der Nierendurchblutung nach topographischen Gesichtspunkten und die Konstruktion von Strömungskarten wie dies von unserem Arbeitskreis für die Hirnstrombahn bereits durchgeführt würde (*Heuck* u. *Piepgras* 1969, *Heuck, Piepgras* und *Vanselow* 1970). Der besondere Vorteil der Angio-Cine-Densitometrie einer Organstrombahn liegt in ihrer Anwendbarkeit am wachen Menschen unter weitgehend physiologischen Bedingungen.

Weitere Untersuchungen werden zeigen, ob die getrennte Analyse von Nierenrinde und Nierenmark möglich ist. Aussichtsreich erscheint es ferner, die Beeinflussung der Nierenstrombahn durch verschiedene Pharmaka am lebenden Menschen zu untersuchen und die erhobenen Befunde mit den Untersuchungsergebnissen anderer Methoden zu vergleichen oder zu kombinieren. Über die Gewebsdensitometrie, also die Analyse der kapillären Strombahn in einem Organ wurde am Beispiel des Hirngewebes an anderer Stelle berichtet (*Piepgras, Heuck* und *März* 1969). Für die Nierenstrombahn stehen solche Untersuchungen noch aus.
Es ergibt sich ferner die Möglichkeit, die Ausscheidungsfunktion dieses Organes nach topographischen Gesichtspunkten zu untersuchen. Da das räumliche Auflösungsvermögen annähernd unbegrenzt ist, und die Grenze der zeitlichen Auflösung der Angio-Cine-Densitometrie die bisher bekannten Verfahren ebenfalls erreicht, erscheint eine Weiterentwicklung der Methode und ihr breiter Einsatz in der klinischen Forschung und Routine sinnvoll.

Tab. 1: Möglichkeiten einer renalen Kreislaufanalyse mit der Angiocinedensitometrie

1. Renales Stromvolumen (ml/sec)

A. renalis	11,0 ± 7,5	KM–Front
	10,6 ± 7,7	KM–Maximum

2. Durchfluss in Segmentarterien (ml/sec)

3. Strömungsgeschwindigkeiten (cm/sec)

A. renalis	28,2 ± 15,0	KM–Front
	25,4 ± 15,3	KM–Maximum
Segmentarterien		
	17,3 ± 10,3	KM–Front
	14,0 ± 8,6	KM–Maximum

4. Renale Durchflusszeiten (sec) anatomisch definierter Messwege

A. Arteriovenöse Durchflusszeit	4,5 ± 2,6
B. Renocorticale Kreislaufzeit	0,3 - 1,2
C. Normierte corticale Ankunftszeit	0,074 ± 0,033 sec/c
D. Zwischenzeiten intrarenaler Kreislaufabschnitte	
E. Renale Transit- bzw. renopyelale Passagezeit und corticopyelale Ankunftszeit	
F. Impulszeiten (Länge des Kontrastbolus)	

Zusammenfassung

Die Zielsetzung und die Methodik der Röntgen-Cine-Densitometrie mit Hilfe des „Quotientenmeßverfahrens" werden besprochen. Ausführlich wird auf die Fehlermöglichkeiten und ihre Eliminierung eingegangen. In kritischer Gegenüberstellung von Röntgen-Cine-Densitometrie und Video-Densitometrie werden die Vor- und Nachteile der beiden Meßverfahren unter besonderer Berücksichtigung des Auflösungsvermögens sowie der Problematik des Signalrauschverhältnisses dargelegt. Die Möglichkeiten der Cine-Densitometrie des Nierenkreislaufes werden an einigen Beispielen demonstriert. Ergebnisse der densitometrischen Analyse des arteriellen Schenkels der Nierenstrombahn bei Gesunden werden den Befunden bei Nierenerkrankungen am Beispiel des Nierentumors gegenübergestellt. Der Informationswert der quantitativen renalen Kreislaufanalyse wird besprochen. Abschließend wird der Einsatz der Angio-Cine-Densitometrie der Nierenstrombahn in der klinischen Routinediagnostik erörtert.

Videodensitometrie*

P. Heintzen, J. Bürsch, R. Simon und A. Wessel

1. Technische Grundlagen der Methode und neuester Entwicklungsstand

Die Videodensitometrie nimmt unter den Verfahren zur statischen oder dynamischen Röntgendensitometrie insofern eine Sonderstellung ein, als das primär mit Hilfe der Röntgentechnik entworfene Bild *zeilenförmig abgetastet* und in ein elektrisches *Analogsignal* umgesetzt wird. Die Amplitude dieses sogenannten Videosignals ist damit zu jedem Zeitpunkt ein Maß für die entsprechende Bildhelligkeit. Durch elektrische Synchronzeichen (Vertikal- und Horizontal-Impulse) lassen sich Bildabtastung und Wiedergabe derart steuern, daß die Videosignalamplituden bestimmten Ortskoordinaten des Bildes eindeutig zugeordnet werden können. Die Auswertung der *Videosignale* zur Messung der Röntgenstrahlenschwächung durch absorbierende Medien, d. h. zur Röntgendensitometrie, wurde erstmals von *Sturm, Sanders* und *Wood* vorgeschlagen.

Das zu diesem Zwecke entwickelte Registrierinstrument – das *Videodensitometer* – besteht aus 2 Einheiten, dem Fenstergenerator und Videointegrator. Der Fenstergenerator erlaubt aus der gesamten Bildinformation *die* Ausschnitte herauszublenden, deren Helligkeit im Bilde analysiert werden soll. Diese Bildteile werden gleichzeitig am Fernsehmonitor durch eine größere Helligkeit gekennzeichnet. Nur *die* Videosignale, die dem gewählten Bildausschnitt entsprechen, werden einem schnellen, elektrischen Integrator zugeleitet, aufsummiert und mit Hilfe einer Tast- und Halteschaltung am Ende jedes Halbbildes dem nachgeschalteten Meß- und Anzeigeinstrument zugeführt. Ein solches Standardvideodensitometer erlaubt die Messung der arithmetisch gemittelten Leuchtdichte innerhalb rechteckiger Meßfenster beliebiger Größe. Mehrere derartige Videodensitometer können gleichzeitig zur Densitometrie verschiedener Bildteile verwendet werden.

Da nach dem *Lambert-Beer*'schen Schwächungsgesetz – das nach ausgedehnten Untersuchungen in definierten Bereichen auch auf die Röntgenstrahlenabsorption durch Kontrastmittel angewendet werden kann – nicht die

* Mit Unterstützung der STIFTUNG VOLKSWAGENWERK.

Leuchtdichte selbst, sondern deren Logarithmus der Konzentration und Schichtdicke des Kontrastmittels proportional ist, muß zur quantitativen Kontrastmittel*mengen*messung das Videosignal logarithmiert werden, bevor über ausgedehnteren Arealen mit inhomogener Kontrastmittelverteilung die Summation oder Integration der Videosignale innerhalb des Meßfernsters erfolgt. Das Standardvideodensitometer ist deshalb für quantitative Messungen durch einen logarithmierenden Verstärker zu ergänzen, dessen linearer Arbeitsbereich etwa 2 Dekaden betragen sollte.

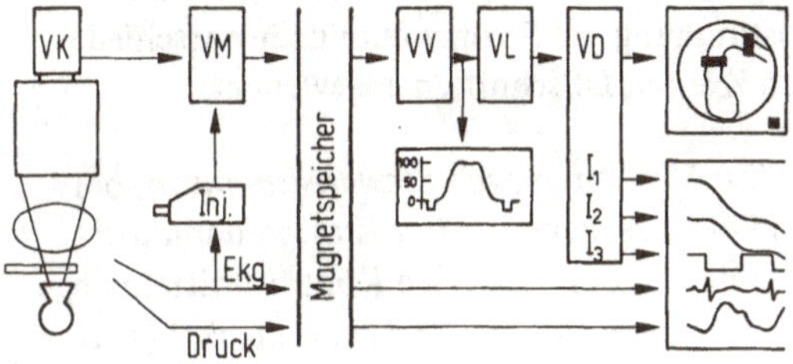

Abb. 1

Wie anderenorts beschrieben, können die primär rechteckigen Meßareale mit Hilfe geeigneter Konturenspeicher auch beliebig geformt und damit unregelmäßigen Herz, Gefäß- und Organflächen angepaßt werden. Neuerdings wurde in unserer Arbeitsgruppe eine *Mehrebenen-Speichermatrix* entwickelt, die unter Einsatz der *Farbfernsehtechnik* die Messung der Bildhelligkeit in mehreren rechteckigen oder beliebig geformten und sich überschneidenden Arealen erlaubt, die durch unterschiedliche Farbgebung gekennzeichnet sind (s. Abb. 2). Eine derartige, optimierte videodensitometrische Meßtechnik kann mit netz- bzw. fernsehsynchroner Strahlenpulsung in einer – oder alternierend in zwei Ebenen – durchgeführt werden. Auch die Möglichkeit einer gleichzeitigen videometrischen *Dimensionsmessung* sei hier nur kurz hingewiesen.

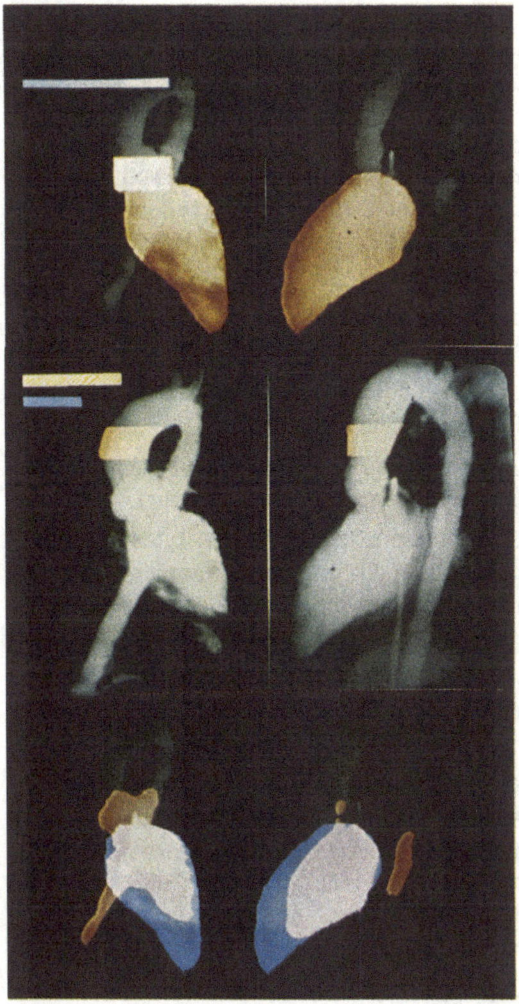

Abb. 2

2. Vergleich mit anderen densitometrischen Verfahren

Die selektive Photometrie am Bildverstärkerausgangsleuchtschirm mit Hilfe der Fernsehtechnik hat gegenüber anderen röntgendensitometrischen Verfahren u. a. folgende Besonderheiten:

a. Das örtliche und zeitliche Auflösungsvermögen entspricht dem Frequenzgang des Fernsehkanals, d. h. bei etwa 5 MHz Bandbreite lassen sich in der Regel bei der gebräuchlichen

Fernsehnorm 50 Halbbilder/sec. mit 312,5 Zeilen und etwa gleicher Bildpunktzahl pro Zeile übertragen. Das zeitliche und örtliche Auflösungsvermögen ist also gegenüber der Kinedensitometrie eingeschränkt, aber für fast alle röntgendensitometrischen Belange voll ausreichend. Grundsätzlich kann das zeitliche Auflösungsvermögen (z. B. auf 100 Halbbilder/sec.) erhöht werden.

b. Zu den besonderen Vorzügen der Videodensitometrie gehört:

1. der weite Bereich der linearen Übertragungsfunktion der Fernsehkette,

2. die elektronische Wählbarkeit beliebig formbar, sich überlappender Meßbereiche,

3. die sequentielle Abtastung des Bildareals und damit die Möglichkeit zur *Mengen*densitometrie nach Logarithmierung der Videosignale,

4. die Speicherung der Bildinformation auf Magnetband, d. h. ohne Verwendung eines weiteren, erst zu entwickelnden Informationsträgers mit nicht linearer Kennlinie (Röntgenfilm),

5. ermöglicht die Tatsache, daß die gesamte Bildinformation als elektrisches Signal vorliegt, die direkte, strenge Synchronisierung mit anderen elektrischen Analogsignalen wie dem intrakardialen Druck und EKG mit verschiedenen Methoden, und

6. gelingt die gleichzeitige, videodensitometrische und videometrische *Kombination von Dichte und Dimensionsmessung*. Schließlich kann mit Hilfe der „Projektionskamera" auch die hochfrequente, kinematographische Bildinformation in den Fernsehkanal übertragen werden, so daß die bisher entwickelten Fernseh-Computersysteme auch zur kine-videodensitometrischen Analyse eingesetzt werden können.

3. Anwendungsmöglichkeiten der Videodensitometrie zur Kreislaufanalyse

Die *Video*densitometrie ist bisher von verschiedenen Arbeitsgruppen hauptsächlich zur Untersuchung dynamischer Dichteschwankungen über verschiedenen Organen unter physiologischen und pathologischen Bedingungen herangezogen worden. Sie hat sich insbesondere in der Kombination mit der Indikatorverdünnungstechnik zur Analyse der *Herz- und Kreislauffunktion* bewährt. Dabei wird ein Röntgenstrahlen absorbierendes Kontrastmittel nicht nur zur morphologischen Darstellung der Herz- und Gefäßabschnitte verwendet, es werden vielmehr die örtlichen und zeitlichen Schwankungen der Konzentration und Schichtdicke des Indikators „Kontrastmittel" in geeigneter Weise gemessen und registriert.
Folgende Meßprinzipien wurden bisher zur Bestimmung der Stromvolumina in verschiedenen Kreislaufabschnitten angewendet:

1. Das Verfahren nach *Stewart-Hamilton*, bei dem entsprechend der Farbstoffverdünnungstechnik aus der injizierten Kontrastmittelmenge und der im arteriellen Kreislaufschenkel (z. B. über der Aorta) gemessenen Konzentrations- bzw. Mengen-Zeitkurve das Herzzeitvolumen bestimmt werden kann. Dabei ermöglicht die Röntgendensitometrie die Messung mit Hilfe eines den Körper durchdringenden Meßstrahles, d. h., *ohne* daß zur Indikatormessung *Sonden* in den betreffenden Kreislaufabschnitt eingeführt werden müssen.

2. Mit Hilfe *zweier* videodensitometrischer *Meßfenster* in definiertem Abstand kann bei Kenntnis des Querschnittes des zwischen den Meßfenstern gelegenen Gefäßabschnittes aus der *Differenz der mittleren Zirkulationszeiten* an beiden Meßorten die Stromstärke in dem betreffenden Gefäß bestimmt werden. Bei gleicher Übertragungscharakteristik beider Videodensitometer ist die Kurvenkalibrierung sowie die Kenntnis der Menge des Injektates nicht erforderlich. Bei diesem Verfahren darf zur zuverlässigen Bestimmung der Gefäßdimension eine bestimmte Kontrastmittelkonzentration im Gefäß nicht unterschritten werden. Andererseits können die erforderlichen Kontrastmittelkonzentrationen durch Viskositäts-

erhöhungen den physiologischen Durchfluß erheblich beeinflussen. Auch erfordert das Verfahren ausreichend lange Meßstrecken zwischen beiden Fenstern, da die Meßfehler erheblich ansteigen, wenn die Differenz der mittleren Zirkulationszeit 0,2 sec. unterschreitet. Durch diese Faktoren wird daher die Anwendbarkeit dieses Meßprinzips begrenzt.

3. Die Bestimmung des Herzzeitvolumens ist auch mit flächenförmigen Meßfenstern über der linken Herzkammer und Aorta möglich, ohne daß die über einem Aortenvolumen gemessene Mengenzeitkurve kalibriert werden müßte. Das Gesamtinjektat kann über dem Ventrikel bei ein- oder zweimaliger diastolischer Injektion als relativer Ausschlag erfaßt werden und unter Berücksichtigung der Empfindlichkeit und Lichtstreuung im Bereich beider Meßfenster zur Auswertung der Mengenzeitkurven nach *Stewart-Hamilton* benutzt werden.

4. Die Kontrastmittel*mengen*densitometrie über einer Herzkammer ermöglicht durch Registrierung von Auswasch- und Rückwaschkurven die Bestimmung der *Residualfraktion* sowie der *Regurgitationsfraktion* für beide Herzkammern bei intakten bzw. insuffizienten arteriellen Klappen. Diesem Verfahren zur Diagnostik und Quantifizierung von arteriellen Klappeninsuffizienzen mit Hilfe der Videodensitometrie dürfte in der klinischen Kardiologie eine besondere Bedeutung zukommen.

5. Die Zwei-Fenster-Mengenmeßtechnik über einer Herzkammer und einem nachgeschalteten Gefäßsegment, dessen Volumen geometrisch bestimmt werden kann, erlaubt die Berechnung der endsystolischen und enddiastolischen Kammervolumina, sowie der Differenz beider Werte, des Schlagvolumens.

6. Die Bestimmung der *Stromstärkeverteilung* an Gefäßaufzweigungen ist durch eine weitere Zwei-Fenstermeßtechnik über geometrisch definierten Gefäßvolumina möglich.

4. Möglichkeiten der Strömungsmessung in Teilkreisläufen am Beispiel der Nierendurchblutung

Ausgedehnte Untersuchungen der Nierendurchblutung mit Hilfe der unter Punkt 2 beschriebenen Bestimmung der Differenz der mittleren Zirkulationszeiten hatten – in Übereinstimmung mit anderen Untersuchern – zu unvertretbar großen Fehlern geführt. Mit der neuen Methode der Blutverteilungsmessung gelang es erstmals die Stromstärkerelation in beiden Nierenarterien mit befriedigender Genauigkeit zu bestimmen. Bei gleichzeitiger elektromagnetischer Flußmessung an beiden Nierenarterien ergab sich eine gute Korrelation zwischen densitometrisch und elektromagnetisch bestimmter Durchblutungsrelation beider Nieren bei normaler und experimentell einseitig gedrosselter Nierendurchblutung (vgl. Abb. 3).

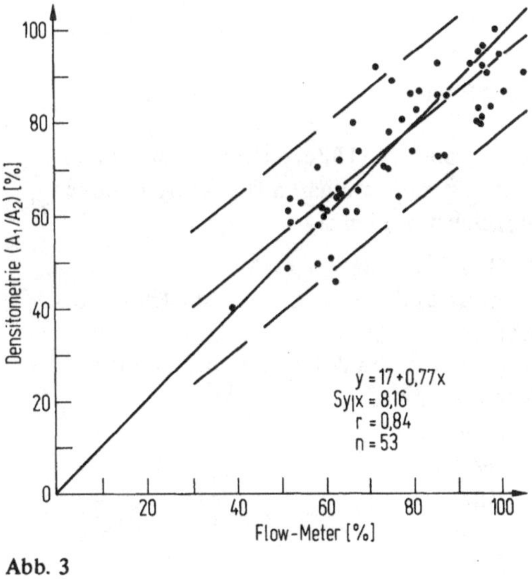

Abb. 3

Bisher liegen mit keinem anderen röntgendensitometrischen Verfahren bzw. Meßprinzip Messungen der Nierendurchblutung vor, deren Brauchbarkeit und Meßgenauigkeit durch kritischen Vergleich mit einer wissenschaftlichen fundierten Vergleichsmethode gesichert wären.

Somit erlaubt die hier beschriebene Technik der quantitativen Videodensitometrie auf verschiedenen Wegen die Erfassung fundamentaler Kreislaufgrößen durch eine zusätzliche, spezifisch röntgendensitometrischer Auswertung der angiokardiographischen Bildinformation.

Zusammenfassung

Die methodischen Grundlagen, deren neuester Entwicklungsstand und die Besonderheiten der Röntgen-Videodensitometrie werden dargestellt. Die verschiedenen Meßprinzipien zur Bestimmung von Stromvolumina im großen und kleinen Kreislauf sowie in Teilkreisläufen werden beschrieben.
Experimentelle Vergleichsuntersuchungen der Nierendurchblutungsrelation mit der elektromagnetischen Durchflußmessung und Videodensitometrie ergaben eine gute Korrelation der Meßwerte.
Die beschriebene Technik der quantitativen Videodensitometrie ermöglicht die Messung fundamentaler Kreislaufgrößen durch eine zusätzliche, spezifisch röntgendensitometrische Auswertung der angiokardiographischen Bildinformation.

Gammakamera bzw. Sequenzszintigraphie

K. zum Winkel

Einleitung

Szintigraphische Untersuchungen der Hämodynamik mit stationären Detektoren können ausgeführt werden an

1. Herz und Lunge
2. Aorta und großen Arterien im Thorax und Abdomen
3. großen Venen des oberen und unteren Körperstammes
4. Hirn
5. Nieren
6. Milz
7. Leber
8. Extremitäten.

In Form der Perfusion ausgeführt sind dabei abzugrenzen

1. eine arterielle Phase
2. eine parenchymatöse bzw. kapilläre Phase.

Nur selten läßt sich eine venöse Phase nachweisen. Mit der Szintigraphie der Hämodynamik ergeben sich grundsätzlich Möglichkeiten

1. zum Nachweis einer Ischämie, resp. einer Minderdurchblutung, besonders beim Durchströmungsvergleich in symmetrischen Regionen wie der Nieren oder der Hirnhemisphären,
2. zur Differenzierung von bereits diagnostizierten – vaskularisierten oder gefäßarmen – Tumoren,
3. zum Nachweis von gefäßreichen Tumoren.

Als Radiopharmaka kommen in Betracht:

1. intravasal verbleibende Substanzen wie Indium 113m-Transferrin oder radioaktiv markiertes Serumalbumin,
2. Substanzen mit relativ geringer extravasaler Diffusion wie Technetium 99m-Pertechnetat,
3. in den Arteriolen bzw. Kapillaren verbleibende Makroaggregate,
4. mit hoher Spezifität von einem Ausscheidungsorgan wie Niere oder Leber extrahierte Substanzen, z. B. mit Radiojod markierte Hippursäure oder Bromsulphthalein.

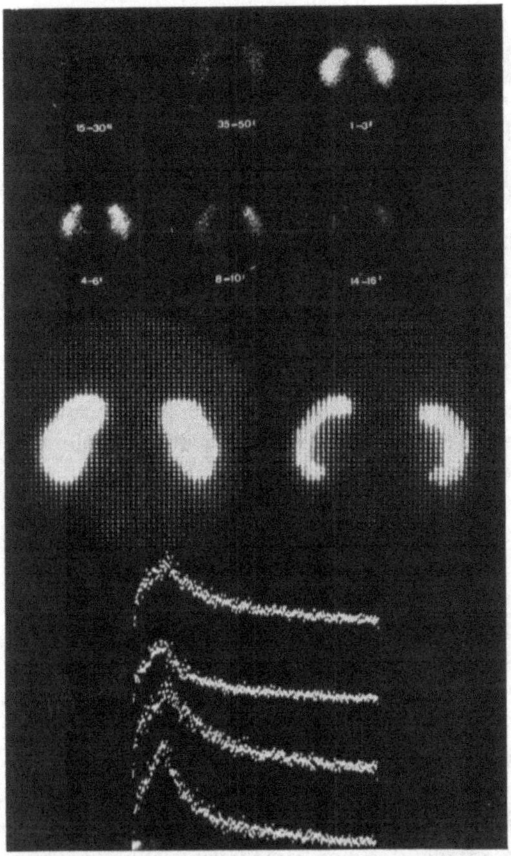

Abb. 1: Sequenzszintigraphie nach 500 μCi ^{131}J-o-Jodhippursäure i. v. beim Nierengesunden: Regelrechte Anflutung in beiden Nieren, unauffällige Verteilung, regelrechter intrarenaler Transport und zeitgerechte Entleerung. Regions of interest: Beide Nieren und die Nierenrinde bds. Integrale Funktionskurven (von oben nach unten Nierenrinde rechts, Nierenrinde links, rechte Niere, linke Niere): Das Radioaktivitätsmaximum wird über der Nierenrinde frühzeitiger erreicht als über dem Gesamtorgan.

Mit der Gammakamera nach Anger läßt sich die Radioaktivitätsverteilung in einem kreisförmigen Sichtbereich von 27 cm Durchmesser simultan erfassen. Abhängig von der nachzuweisenden Radioaktivität können Expositionszeiten bis 1 sec und weniger zur Anwendung kommen. Polaroidaufnahmen vom Oszilloskop ermöglichen Sequenz- bzw. Serienszintigraphien.

Technik

Angeschlossen an eine Nuclear Chicago Szintillationskamera verwenden wir eine Intertechnique-Einheit mit 4096 Kanalkernspeicher, Speicheroszilloskop und digitalem Ampexband. Die elektronische Datenverarbeitung gestattet nach Abschluß der Untersuchung die Anfertigung von Szintiphotos unter veränderten Bedingungen und die simultane Aufzeichnung der integralen Funktionskurven von 4 „regions of interest", die mittels eines „light pen" auszuwählen sind. Die Kurven repräsentieren die Radiopharmakokinetik der "regions of interest".

Wir injizieren 500μCi ^{131}J-o-Jodhippursäure i. v. und fertigen Szintiphotos beider Nierenregionen von 15–30 und 35–50 sec sowie von 1–3, 4–6, 8–10, 14–16 und 24–26 min an. Zur Perfusion werden mehrere mCi^{99m}TcO_4 i. v. verabfolgt und Szintiphotos der Nierenregionen im Abstand von 5 bzw. 10 sec angefertigt. Die elektronische Datenverarbeitung benötigt mit Rückspielen des digitalen Bandes, Festlegung der regions und Aufzeichnung der Kurven durchschnittlich 8, maximal 15 min.

Ergebnisse

Die hier vorgestellten Resultate beschränken sich auf die szintigraphische Untersuchung der renalen Hämodynamik. Die Serienszintigraphie am nierengesunden Hund (zum Winkel et al., 1968) ergibt nach der intraaortalen Injektion von tubulär sezernierten bzw. rein glomerulär filtrierten Radiopharmaka eine gleichmäßige Anflutung und Verteilung der Radioaktivität, eine Verkleinerung des Parenchymareals von 20–40 sec entsprechend dem Substanztransport im Nierenmark, eine erneute Vergrößerung von 40–60 sec wegen des Transports durch das distale Tubuluslumen und anschließend eine zunehmende Konzentration im peripelvinen Bereich sowie eine deutliche Entleerung.
Unter gleichen Versuchsbedingungen zeigen sich bei akuter einseitiger Minderdurchblutung

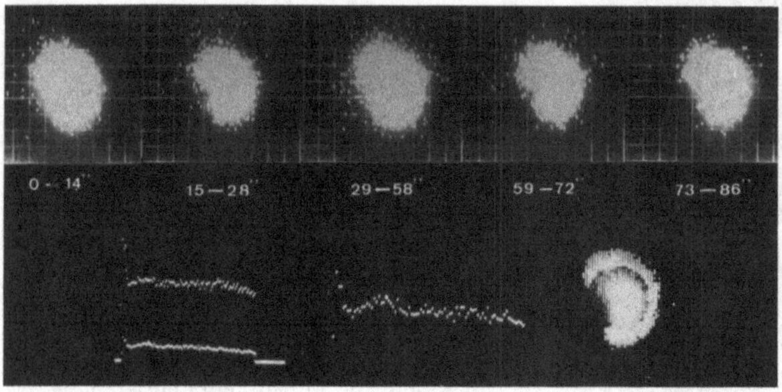

Abb. 2: Serienszintigraphie, integrale Funktionskurven über Gesamtniere und Nierenrinde (links unten sowie Mitte) und "regions of interest" nach Radiohippursäure intraarteriell: Verkleinerung des Nierenparenchyms von 15–28 und ab 59 sec. Die Serienszintigramme wurden vom Oszilloskop entsprechend der Nierenrindenfunktionskurven gewonnen.

mit einem mittleren Druck in der Nierenarterie von 40 mmHg verminderte Anflutung, verspätete Konzentration und wegen des reduzierten Harnzeitvolumens verlängertes Verweilen des Radiopharmakons im Nierenbecken. Wird der Druck auf 30 mmHg verringert, fehlt die renale Anreicherung eines glomerulär filtrierten Radiopharmakons vollständig; doch wird die tubulär sezernierte Radiohippursäure noch in geringem Umfang renal abgelagert.

Beim Menschen sind nach intraarterieller Injektion von Hippursäure ähnliche Größenveränderungen der renalen Radioaktivitätsverteilung entsprechend dem Substanztransport im Nephron festzustellen. Die Passagezeit von der Nierenarterie bzw. Nierenrinde bis zur Nierenvene beträgt 6 sec. Der Transport des Radiopharmakons im Nephron läuft verzögert ab bei einer Harnwegstauung.

Nierenarterienstenosen führen im Sequenzszintigramm in 67% zur herabgesetzten Anflutung, in 54% zur reduzierten Konzentration, in 35% zum verkleinerten Parenchym und in 28% zur verspäteten Evakuierung aus dem Nierenbecken (Feine und zum Winkel). Lageabhängige Durchblutungsstörungen lassen sich bei der Nephroptose gut erkennen durch die Untersuchung im Liegen und im Sitzen. Auch segmentale Durchblutungsminderungen sind einfach nachzuweisen. Doppelseitige Arterienstenosen bewirken in beiden Nieren verzögerte Anflutungen. Einige Patienten hatten keine Abweichungen im Sequenzszintigramm, doch offenbarte die Datenverarbeitung die herabgesetzte Konzentration der durchblutungsgeminderten Niere. Schließlich muß jedoch erwähnt werden, daß die Symptome der herabgesetzten Anflutung, der verzögerten maximalen Konzentration und der verspäteten Entleerung auch bei entzündlichen Erkrankungen wie der Pyelonephritis anzutreffen sind.

Niereninfarkte kennzeichnen sich durch herabgesetzte bis aufgehobene Hippursäurekonzentration in peripheren Parenchymbezirken. Die vollständig aufgehobene Radioaktivitätsablagerung im gesamten Organ deutet – z. B. bei der Nierentransplantation – auf eine Thrombose der Arteria renalis; bei der Nierenvenenthrombose findet sich eine herabgesetzte Hippursäureablagerung.

Tierexperimentelle und klinische Erfahrungen haben uns gezeigt, daß bei der Abstoßungsreaktion eines Transplantates über die verspätete Anflutung, den verzögerten intrarenalen Transport und die verspätete Evakuierung hinaus ein Abfall der Radioaktivität innerhalb 20 sec festzustellen war, der als verminderte tubuläre Extraktion für Radiohippursäure gedeutet werden muß.

Die initiale Anflutung in den Nieren bringt Hinweise zur Differenzierung raumfordernder Prozesse, die sich als Bezirke mit aufgehobener Radioaktivitätskonzentration manifestieren. Bei gut vaskularisierten Tumoren findet sich innerhalb von 30 bis spätestens 40 sec nach der intravenösen Injektion von Radiohippursäure eine vermehrte Radioaktivitätsablagerung in einer Region, die anschließend stets ausgespart bleibt. Diesen zuerst von Rosenthall beschriebenen Umkehreffekt haben Schenck und Mitarbeiter mit einer Ausnahme bei 10 Patienten mit gefäßreichen Nierentumoren beobachtet, doch war linksseitig die Abgrenzung bei gleichzeitiger Splenomegalie schwierig. Die Perfusion nach Pertechnetat i. v. läßt die Hypervaskularisierung noch besser abgrenzen. Intratumorale Nekrosen lassen jede Radioaktivitätsablagerung vermissen, auch fehlt hier die sonst übliche initiale Radioaktivitätszacke auf den integralen Funktionskurven.

In Nierenzysten fehlt die initiale Radioaktivitätsanflutung sowohl nach der i. v. Injektion von Hippursäure wie von Pertechnetat.

Der Vergleich von Serienszintigraphie und Angiographie bei 65 Patienten ergab eine Überlegenheit der Szintigraphie in der Diagnostik von Nierenbeckentumoren (4 Patienten, kein Befund angiographisch gesichert) und Pyelonephritis (9 Patienten, nur 4 angiographisch erkannt). Die Angiographie war überlegen in der Erkennung der Nierenarterienstenose und in der Differenzierung von Hypernephromen und Zysten. Gleiche diagnostische Resultate zeigten beide Methoden bei der Hydronephrose und der Schrumpfniere.

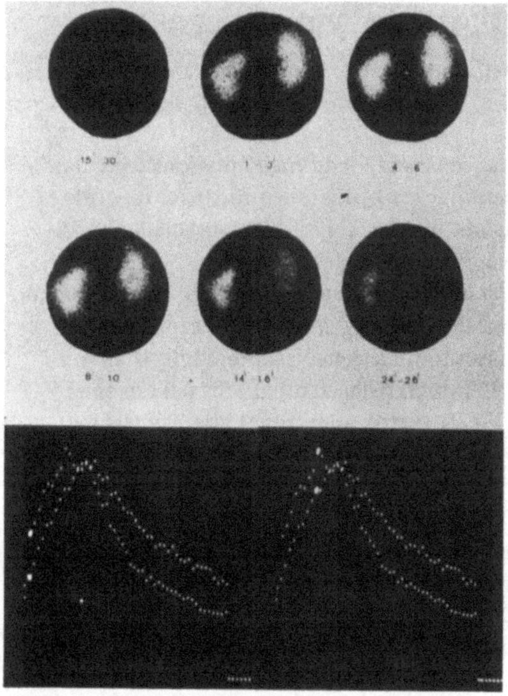

Abb. 3: Verminderte Anflutung, verspätetes Maximum und verzögerte Entleerung in der Sequenzszintigraphie und in den integralen Funktionskurven beider Nieren (übereinander projiziert) bei einem Patienten mit linksseitiger Pyelonephritis; im Angiogramm kein Hinweis für Nierenarterienstenose.

Zusammenfassung

In Kombination mit der elektronischen Datenverarbeitung bildet die Serienszintigraphie mit der Gammakamera eine wichtige Methode zur Erfassung dynamischer Vorgänge. Die Angiographie wird nicht ersetzt, sondern in wertvoller Weise ergänzt durch die Registrierung der Anflutung und Konzentration, der intrarenalen Transportvorgänge und der Evakuierung der oberen Harnwege. Renale Ausscheidung und Perfusion lassen sich im Gesamtorgan wie in wählbaren Teilbezirken untersuchen. Indikationen zum Studium der renalen Hämodynamik bilden der Verdacht auf Arterienstenose, Niereninfarkt, Arterienthrombose, Abstoßungsreaktion bei Nierentransplantation, Pyelonephritis und raumfordernde Prozesse wie Tumoren, speziell des Pyelons und solitäre wie multiple Zysten.

Digitales Autofluoroscope

P. Reindl

Das von *Bender* und *Blau* entwickelte digitale Autofluoroscope wurde primär für die Aufnahme dynamischer Funktionsabläufe konzipiert.
Der Unterschied zum Prinzip der Anger-Kamera besteht in erster Linie im Detektor, der statt eines großflächigen Natriumjodidkristalles 294 Einzelkristalle enthält. Sie sind in einer 14 × 21 Matrix angeordnet, die Abmessung eines Kristalls beträgt 0,9 cm im Quadrat bei einer Dicke von 3,8 cm.
Die Umwandlung, Weiterleitung und Zuordnung der auftreffenden Gamma-Quanten geschieht mittels Lichtleitern und 35 Photomultipliern. Die Anordnung der einzelnen Systeme in der xy-Koordinate bewirkt, daß das im jeweiligen Kristall auftreffende Ereignis der korrespondierenden Position in einem 294-Kanal-Kernspeicher exakt zugeordnet wird. Ein zweiter Kernspeicher dient zur Korrektur der Kristallinhomogenität bei der Wiedergabe. Die in beiden „memories" gespeicherten Informationen werden digital auf einem Magnetband festgehalten.
Dadurch kann die Wiedergabe digital über einen Prozeßrechner, Ausdrucker oder über Iso-Impuls-Zonen erfolgen, sowie analog über einen helligkeitsgesteuerten Bildschirm und als Polaroid- oder 35-mm-Film.
Die Wiedergabe eines dynamischen Funktionsablaufes als Kurve über einem interessierenden Bezirk geschieht als sog. „region of interest" mittels eines Dreifachschreibers, nachdem vorher die gewünschten Compartments mit einer Lichtdiode markiert wurden. Damit wird im Rahmen der Methode eine weitgehend störende Backgroundaktivität vermieden.
Die Schwerpunkte unserer dynamischen Untersuchungen mit dem Autofluoroscope bei einer Zahl etwa von 5000 Fällen lag bislang auf dem Gebiet der Neuroradiologie, der Nierenfunktionsdiagnostik, Leber- und Lungenfunktion.
Die statischen Untersuchungen umfaßten in erster Linie die Hirnszintigraphie sowie quantitative Verteilungsmessungen bei Knochenszintigrammen mit Strontium 85 und Strontium 87^{m}.
Erlauben Sie mir, Ihnen anhand einiger Fall-Beispiele unsere Methodik bei den einzelnen Untersuchungen zu demonstrieren, wobei es uns vor allem darauf ankam, die Korrelation und den Vergleich zur radiologischen Diagnostik herzustellen.
Für die Hirnszintigraphie erfolgt die Injektion des 99 m Tc O_4 routinemäßig vorwiegend in pa-Projektion vor der Kamera, um auf diese Weise eventuelle Gefäßprozesse im Hals bzw. pathologische Durchströmungsereignisse im Hemisphärenbereich zu erfassen, vor allem auch hinsichtlich einer gezielten Angiographie. Die Injektion erfolgt als Bolus nach der *Oldendorf*-Methode, also am mit Blutdruckmanschette über dem systolischen Blutdruck gestauten Arm. Die Dosis beträgt 15 m Ci in maximal 2 ccm, die Akkumulationszeit pro Bild 1 Sekunde.
Entsprechend der angiographischen Darstellung der Halsgefäße vom Aortenbogen aus werden sequenzszintigraphische Bilder der Hals- und Hirndurchblutung angefertigt. Gleichzeitig werden Kurven über dem Halsbereich und den Hemisphären geschrieben, wobei wir aufgrund einer genügend großen Anzahl klinischer Normalfälle diesen Kurven im Seitvergleich eine semi-quantitative Aussage hinsichtlich Durchströmungszeit und -größe beimessen können.
Jedoch ergeben sich aufgrund der Anatomie im Halsbereich durch den geringen Abstand von A. carotis communis und A. vertebralis, in der pa.-Projektion zwangsläufig bei der Erfassung vasculärer Erkrankungen Schwierigkeiten. Hier könnte jedoch durch die getrennte Aufzeichnung der Durchströmung in ap- und pa-Projektion mit 2 Nukleiden, z. B. Indium 113^{m} und Tc 99^{m}, eine Verbesserung der Diagnostik möglich sein.

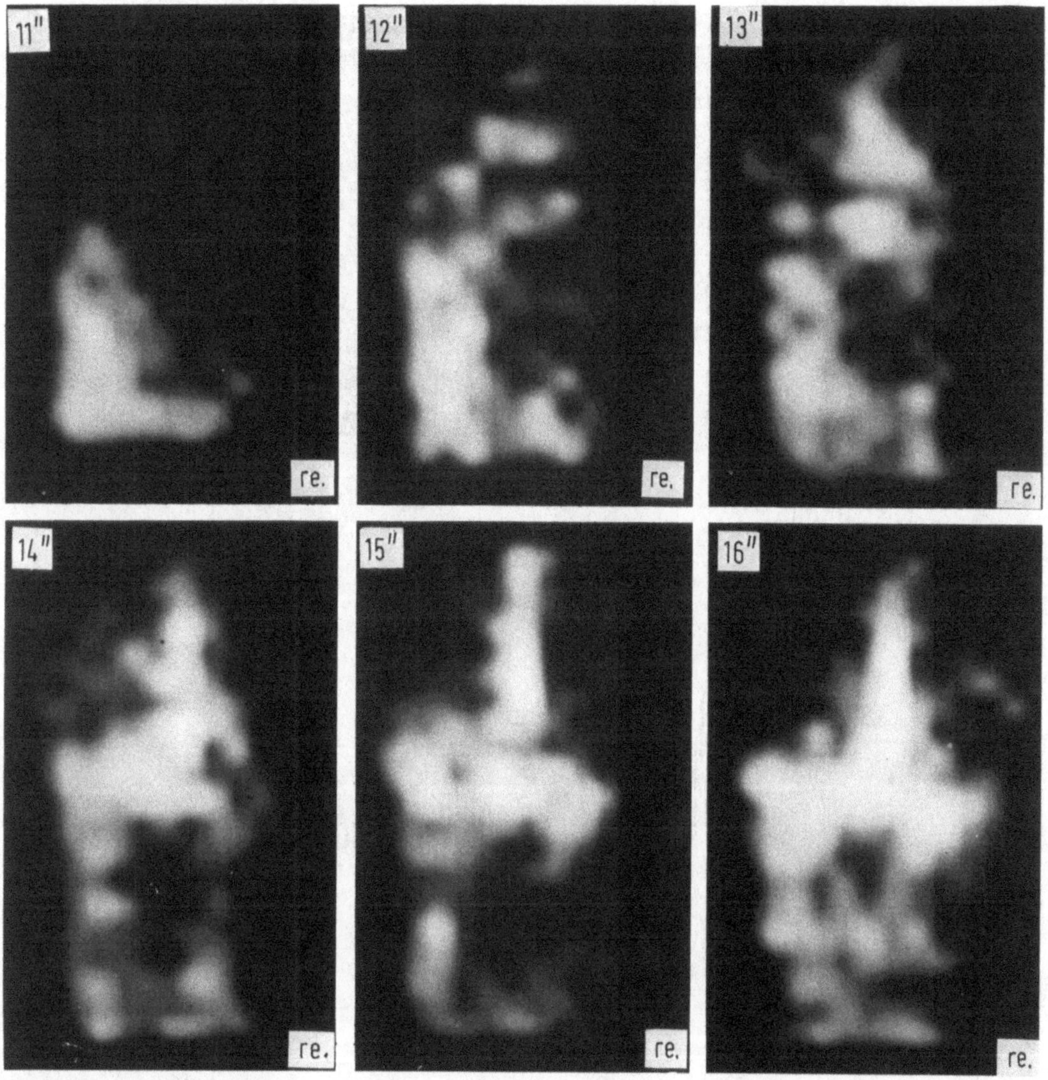

Abb. 1: zeigt die Kamerasequenz im Hals-Hirnbereich pa-Projektion (Zeitabstand 1 Sek.) bei einem 38jähr. Patienten mit linksseitiger Hemiparese.
Dabei zeigt sich eine deutliche Seitdifferenzierung im Halsbereich mit verminderter Aktivitätspassage rechts, sowie verzögerter intracerebraler Aktivitätsaufbau rechts.

Wir betrachten deshalb diese Methode bei dieser Fragestellung derzeit noch als „screening", wobei wir jedoch auch der Meinung sind, wie u. a. *Rösler* und Mitarbeiter schon beschrieben haben, daß aufgrund der Erfassung der Strömungsdynamik Differenzierungen in der Artdiagnose eines cerebralen Prozesses möglich sind (Abb. 1–3).
Die Funktionsuntersuchungen im Bereich der Leber mit Jod 131 markierten Substanzen – wie Bromsulphan und Bengalrosa – betreffen die Fragestellung der Parenchymfunktion hinsichtlich der Extraktions- und Exkretionsleistung insgesamt, sowie Störungen im Bereich der abführenden Gallenwege. Als Compartments werden dabei die Leber sowie Gallenblasenbereich und Intestinum verglichen.
Das Hauptgewicht unserer Untersuchungen liegt

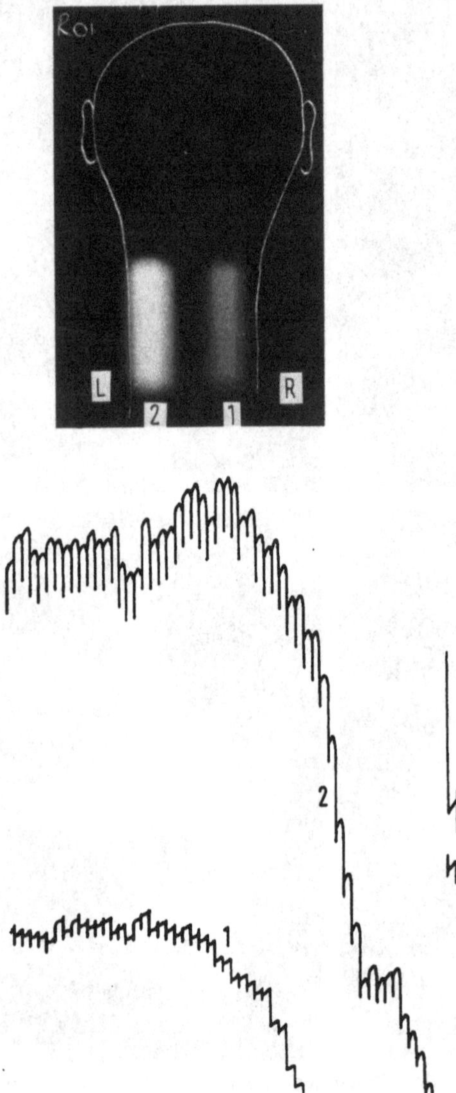

Abb. 2: zeigt die selektiven Kurven über dem Halsbereich (linkes Kurvenpaar) mit deutl. quant. Differenz, sowie vermindertem Durchfluß rechts intracerebral.

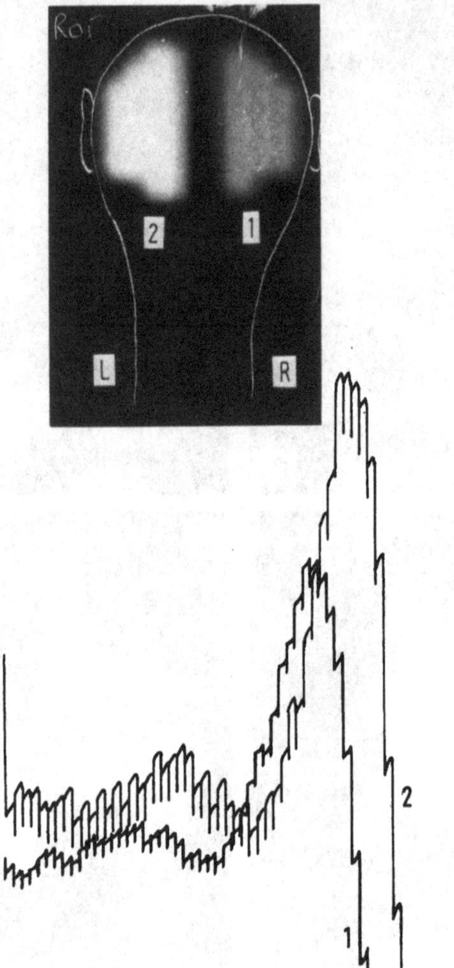

Abb. 3: zeigt das Angiogramm mit Stenose bei a-carotis interna rechts.

derzeit auf dem Gebiet der Nierenfunktionsdiagnostik. Sie umfaßt auf dem nuklearmedizinischen Sektor außer der Clearance die statische Szintigraphie, die Hippuran-Nephrographie mit Sequenz sowie die Durchblutung.
Zur Erfassung der Durchströmung verwenden wir derzeit vorwiegend 99 m Tc O in einer Dosis von 10 mCi, ebenfalls als Bolus-Injektion. Als Compartments dienen Nierenareal, Aorta, A. renalis sowie ggf. die Leber. Das Akkumulationsintervall beträgt 1 Sekunde pro Bild.

Gerade aus der Durchströmungssequenz bzw. Kurve ergeben sich bei renalen Gefäßprozessen sowie für die Differenzierung raumfordernder Prozesse neue diagnostische Möglichkeiten.

Zum Winkel, wie u. a. Pfannenstiel und Mitarbeiter haben bereits auf diese Möglichkeiten hingewiesen.

In der Nephrographie ergeben sich durch die Möglichkeit der selektiven Untersuchung einzelner Compartments in der Beurteilung neue Differenzierungen.

Wir überblicken derzeit eine Zahl von 182 Fällen, bei denen das Angiogramm zum Vergleich zur Verfügung stand.
Dabei zeigte sich bei raumfordernden Prozessen eine Übereinstimmung in 92%, bei Parenchymerkrankungen 81%, wobei hier eine Differenz bei entzündlichen Befunden bestand, die angiographisch noch nicht sicher nachweisbar waren.

Bei den Gefäßerkrankungen bzw. -anomalien betrug die Übereinstimmung 87%, hier bestanden divergente Befunde bei 4 angiographisch nachgewiesenen Stenosen, die jedoch von seiten der nuklearmedizinischen Diagnostik funktionell noch nicht relevant erschienen.
Aufgrund der vergleichenden Ergebnisse von Angiogramm und nuklearmed. Untersuchungen glauben wir, daß, abgesehen von Hippuransequenz und selektivem Kameranephrogramm, bei gezielter Fragestellung auch die Erfassung der Durchströmung über den Wert eines Screenings hinausgeht und ihren festen Platz in der Reihe der einzelnen radiologischen Untersuchungen hat.

Nierendurchblutungsmessung mit radioaktiven Isotopen zum Zeitpunkt der selektiven Nierenangiographie*

P. E. Peters, J. O. Eichling, R. J. Stanley, C. S. Coble und M. M. Ter-Pogossian

Nach der physiologischen Literatur nimmt die Nierenrinde ca. 70% des Gesamtvolumens einer Niere ein und erhält 80–90% der Durchblutung (*Ullrich, Deetjen* et al.). Trotz dieses Gefäßreichtums ist eine befriedigende röntgenologische Beurteilung der Nierenperipherie auch mit selektiver Kontrastmittelinjektion gegenwärtig noch nicht möglich. Mit Hilfe von radioaktiven Isotopen kann man jedoch zum Zeitpunkt der Nierenangiographie die Durchblutung der Nierenperipherie bestimmen und erhält somit funktionelle Daten, die die morphologische Information der Röntgenuntersuchung sinnvoll ergänzen. Die Methode wurde 1963 von *Thorburn* und Mitarb. erstmals im Tierversuch angewandt. Noch im gleichen Jahr wurden Nierendurchblutungsmessungen am Menschen durchgeführt (*Kemp* et al.). Das technische Vorgehen ist einfach: Vor der selektiven Kontrastmittelinjektion injiziert man eine kleine Menge eines gut diffusiblen radioaktiven Indikators in die Nierenarterie. Das Auswaschen der Aktivität wird mit Hilfe eines von dorsal gegen die Nieren gerichteten Szitillationsdetektors

* Mit Unterstützung der NIH (HE 1385110 und RR 00396) und der Deutschen Forschungsgemeinschaft.

registriert. Wir haben zu diesem Zweck eine stabile Sperrholzplatte entworfen, die auf den Angiographietisch aufgelegt wird (Abb. 1).

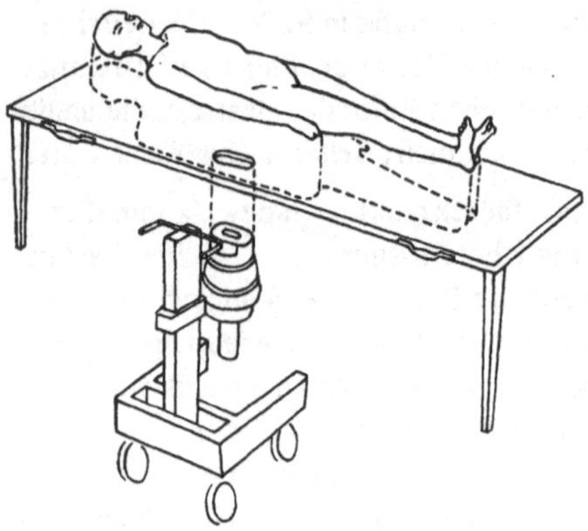

Abb. 1: Lagerungsplatte.
Die zu untersuchende Niere wird unter Durchleuchtung über die Markierungsvorrichtung gebracht. Anschließend wird die Lagerungsplatte seitlich verschoben, so daß die Meßsonde von dorsal her in Position gebracht werden kann.

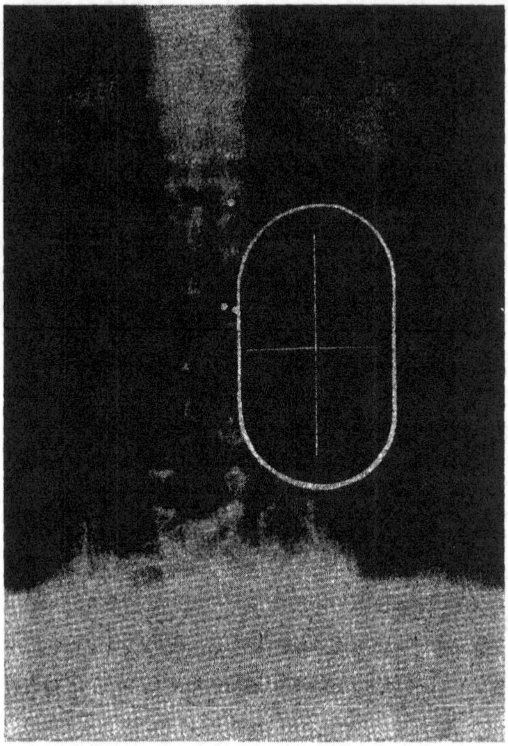

Abb. 2: Röntgenaufnahme des Abdomens zur Demonstration der Markierungsvorrichtung.

Unter Durchleuchtung wird die zu untersuchende Niere exakt in das „Fadenkreuz" der Markierungsvorrichtung gebracht (Abb. 2). Dadurch ist gewährleistet, daß die Niere im Gesichtsfeld der Meßsonde liegt. Der Kollimator ist so ausgelegt, daß möglichst wenig von den großen Gefäßen und von den Nachbarorganen mit erfaßt werden.

Ein Indikator für Organdurchblutungsmessungen nach dem modifizierten *Kety-Schmidt*-Prinzip muß folgende Bedingungen erfüllen:

1. Er muß frei diffusibel sein, d. h. es muß sich ein sofortiges Gleichgewicht der Konzentration des Indikators im Blut und im Gewebe einstellen.

2. Der Abtransport des Indikators darf nur auf dem Blutwege erfolgen.

3. Der Indikator darf nicht rezirkulieren.

Diese Voraussetzungen werden mehr oder weniger vollständig von den inerten Gasen erfüllt, von denen ^{133}Xenon und ^{85}Krypton die weiteste Verbreitung gefunden haben.
Wir möchten hier mit dem radioaktiven ^{15}O markierten Wasser einen Indikator vorstellen, der von uns erstmals zur Messung der Nierendurchblutung des Menschen eingesetzt wurde.
Der radioaktive Sauerstoff wird gewonnen durch Bombardierung von Stickstoff mit 7 MeV Deuteronen in einem Zyklotron. In Form von $C^{15}O_2$ wird er durch heparinisiertes Patientenblut geleitet, wo es unter Einwirkung der Carboanhydrase zur Bildung radioaktiven Wassers kommt.
Radioaktives Wasser bietet gegenüber den inerten Gasen eine Reihe von Vorteilen, die hier nur stichwortartig aufgeführt werden können:

1. Hohe Löslichkeit in Gewebe und Blut.

2. Der Gewebeblutverteilungskoeffizient ist proportional zum Wassergehalt des Blutes und dem des zu untersuchenden Gewebes und damit leicht zu bestimmen und auch im pathologischen Fall weitgehend konstant. Demgegenüber ist der Gewebeblutverteilungskoeffizient für die inerten Gase schwierig zu ermitteln und sehr stark abhängig vom Lipidgehalt des zu untersuchenden Organes.

3. Energiereiche 511 keV-Strahlung.

4. Sehr kurze Halbwertszeit (122,5 sec), daraus resultierend: geringe Strahlenbelastung.

5. Hohe spezifische Aktivität (bis zu 80 mCi/ml).

Die kurze Halbwertszeit limitiert allerdings auch den Einsatz dieses Indikators. Trotz der hohen spezifischen Aktivitäten die erzielt werden können, ist die Anwendung nur in Instituten möglich, in deren unmittelbarer Nähe ein Zyklotron steht. Nachteilig ist außerdem, daß radioaktives Wasser nach der Injektion in das Organ rezirkuliert, wobei jedoch dank des enorm großen Verteilungsraumes (Körperwasser) die rezirkulierende Menge bei der Niere nur ca. 1–2% beträgt. Diese geringe Aktivität beeinflußt die Ergebnisse nur wenig, zumal bei der Kurvenanalyse die Rezirkulation berücksichtigt werden kann.

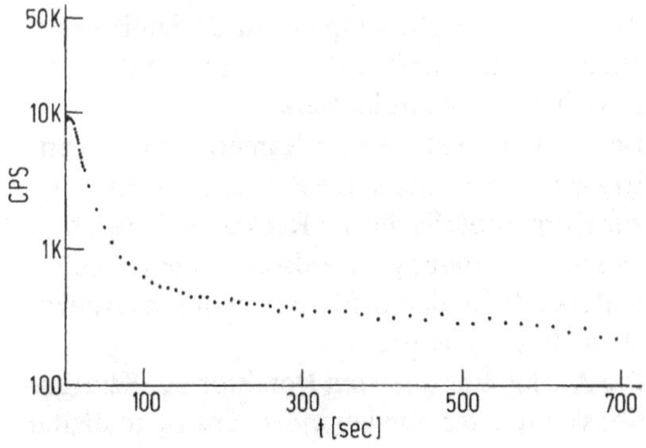

Abb. 3: $H_2{}^{15}O$-Auswaschkurve eines potentiellen Nierenspenders. Normalbefund. Semilogarithmische Darstellung. Originalausdruck des Laborcomputers.

Die registrierten Auswaschkurven (Abb. 3) werden je nach Fragestellung analysiert. Die Compartment-Analyse (manuell oder mit Hilfe des Computers) ergibt bei der Untersuchung mit radioaktivem Wasser 2 oder 3 Compartments und erlaubt eine Aussage über die intrarenale Blutstromverteilung. (Einzelheiten dazu siehe *Thorburn* et al. und *Ladefoged*.) Die stochastische Methode nach *Zierler* dient zur Berechnung der mittleren Nierendurchblutung in ml/min/100 g. Die „initial-slope"-Methode (*Hollenberg* et al.) führt ebenfalls zur Bestimmung der mittleren Nierendurchblutung, wobei jedoch die hohe Rindendurchblutung den Mittelwert etwas beeinflußt. Es handelt sich hierbei um eine graphische Methode, der der Fehler der Subjektivität anhaftet, die aber andererseits den Vorteil hat, daß man sie rasch ohne Hilfsmittel überall durchführen kann.

Mit der letztgenannten Methode berechneten wir eine mittlere Nierendurchblutung von 372 ml/min/100 g bei 4 Normalpersonen, die als potentielle Nierenspender untersucht wurden. Dieser Wert liegt etwas höher als der von *Hollenberg* et al. mit ^{133}Xenon erhobene Normalwert von 338 ml/min/100 g. 10 hypertensive Patienten konnten nach dem Röntgenbefund und der Nierendurchblutungsmessung den von *Hollenberg* et al. beschriebenen 3 Kategorien der essentiellen Hypertonie zugeordnet werden: 3 Patienten mit unkomplizierter essentieller Hypertonie (mittlerer Blutdruck 123 mmHg) wiesen eine mittlere Nierendurchblutung von 339 ml/min/100 g auf. Bei 4 Patienten waren röntgenologisch diskrete Veränderungen kleiner intrarenaler Gefäße erkennbar, bei ihnen war die mittlere Nierendurchblutung bereits auf 221 ml/min/100 g eingeschränkt (mittlerer Blutdruck 130 mmHg). 3 weitere Patienten zeigten deutliche intrarenale Gefäßveränderungen i. S. einer schweren Hypertonie. Die entsprechenden Werte der Nierendurchblutung betrugen nur noch 119 ml/min/100 g (mittlerer Blutdruck 149 mmHg).

Bei gleichzeitiger Bestimmung der Reninwerte im Nierenvenenblut läßt sich die Reninsekretionsrate seitengetrennt bestimmen und daraus sehr exakt die Operationsindikation bei renovaskulär bedingtem Hochdruck stellen. Eine weitere Domäne der Nierendurchblutungsmessung sind die Fälle mit akutem oligurischen Nierenversagen, bei denen der Methode möglicherweise sogar eine prognostische Bedeutung zukommt (*Hollenberg* et al. 1968).

Zusammenfassung

Die Nierendurchblutungsmessung mit radioaktiven Isotopen ist eine funktionelle Ergänzung des morphologischen Befundes der Röntgenuntersuchung, die ohne zusätzliche Belastung für den Patienten zum Zeitpunkt der Angiographie durchgeführt werden kann. Radioaktives Wasser $H_2{}^{15}O$ als Indikator ist den inerten Gasen in verschiedener Hinsicht überlegen, es bleibt jedoch seiner kurzen Halbwertszeit wegen den wenigen Instituten mit eigenem Zyklotron vorbehalten.

Die Wertigkeit des Isotopennephrogrammes bei Nierenarterienstenosen unter Anwendung eines data store-play-back-Systems*

H. Umek, H. Czembirek, H. Frischauf, H. Imhof und H. Pokieser

Die hämodynamisch wirksame Nierenarterienstenose führt über eine Minderdurchblutung der Niere zur Freisetzung von Renin (*Sarre* 1961, *Weidmann* 1967). Der Folgezustand – die renal bedingte Hypertonie – stellt eine schwerwiegende Bedrohung für den Patienten dar. Bei frühzeitigem Erkennen der Gefäßveränderung erlauben gefäßchirurgische Eingriffe Abhilfe.

Seit den positiven Erfahrungen von *Tauxe* 1961, *Doig* 1963, *Taplin* 1963, *Winter* 1964, wird das Isotopennephrogramm mit seinen methodischen Modifikationen immer häufiger als Routineuntersuchung zur Abklärung herangezogen (*zum Winkel* 1964, *Hör* 1966, *Rösler* 1968, *Pabst* 1970). Die vorliegende Studie vergleicht isotopennephrographische Befunde mit dem angiographischen Korrelat und versucht eine Bewertung der nuklearmedizinischen Methode unter Verwendung eines data store-play back-Systems.

* Mit Unterstützung des Jubiläumsfonds der Österreichischen Nationalbank und der Ludwig Boltzmann Gesellschaft.

Patientengut

Bei 21 Patienten mit Nierenarterienstenose wurden Isotopennephrogramme und renale Angiogramme erhoben.

Methodik

Zur Isotopennephrographie wurde den Patienten J-131-Hippursäure (2,0 μCi pro kg Körpergewicht) intravenös injiziert.
Der Detektor einer *Anger*-Kamera (Pho-Gamma III) wurde dem sitzenden Patienten senkrecht zur Körperoberfläche am Rücken aufgesetzt. Durch Verwendung eines divergierenden Kollimators erfaßte der Meßkopf sowohl die Nieren- als auch die Blasenregion.
Die Analog-Impulse vom Detektor der Szintillationskamera führten wir einem analog to digital Converter (*ADC*) zu. Die digitalisierten Impulse wurden einer 256 X 256 Matrix zugeordnet und über einen recorder controller nach Impuls-Phasenmodulation in Form von „Words“ mit

einem video-tape recorder (*IVC*) im binär decimal code auf Magnetband aufgezeichnet.

Die Untersuchungsdauer betrug 15 Minuten. Die Auswertung erfolgte im play back nach Transformierung der digitalen Banddaten in analoge über einen digital to analog converter (*DAC*). Im analogen Teil der Anlage bestand die Möglichkeit mittels Comperator-Schaltungen zwei Meßregionen („regions of interest") beliebiger Form und Größe einzublenden. Die Adjustierung beider „regions of interest" erfolgte an Hand digitaler Szintiphotos.
Über ratemeter und Zweifachschreiber wurden die integralen Meßwerte beider Nierenregionen kurvenmäßig erfaßt.
Die Nierenangiographie wurde als lumbale Übersichtsaortographie mit „tip occlusion" durchgeführt. Unklare Gefäßbefunde ergänzten wir fallweise durch selektive Nierenarteriographie.

Klassifizierungsschema

Die Bewertung der Isotopennephrogramme wurde nach qualitativen Gesichtspunkten vorgenommen.
Im Isotopennephrogramm lassen sich grundsätzlich 3 Phasen unterscheiden:

Phase I (sogenannte Initialphase, Durchblutungsphase), entspricht dem Transport des radioaktiven Indikators durch renovaskuläre, pararenale und extravaskuläre Kompartimente.

Phase II (sogenannte Sekretionsphase), erfaßt die renale Funktionsphase und entspricht annähernd dem effektiven renalen Plasmafluß.

Phase III (sogenannte Exkretionsphase), kommt durch die Ausscheidung der Testsubstanz in die ableitenden Harnwege zustande.

In Anlehnung an *Hör* (1966) erfolgte die vergleichende Auswertung der isotopennephrographischen und angiographischen Befunde nach dem Schweregrad der Gefäßveränderungen im Angiogramm:

Gruppe I keine Hypertonie
Angiogramm: kleine arteriosklerotische Plaques an der Abgangsstelle der Nierenarterie
Isotopennephrogramm: unauffällig

Gruppe II Hypertonie
Angiogramm: Stenose mit Einengung des Gefäßquerschnittes auf weniger als die Hälfte, peripheres Gefäßbild unauffällig
Isotopennephrogramm: Veränderungen der Phase I und/oder Phase II

Gruppe III Hypertonie
Angiogramm: Stenose mit Einengung des Gefäßquerschnittes auf die Hälfte, eventuell Rarefizierung des peripheren Gefäßbildes
Isotopennephrogramm: Veränderungen der Phase I, II und III

Gruppe IV Hypertonie
Angiogramm: Stenose mit Einengung des Gefäßquerschnittes auf mehr als die Hälfte, Rarefizierung des peripheren Gefäßbildes, eventuell Organverkleinerung
Isotopennephrogramm: Akkumulation-, Isosthenurie- oder Nephrektomie-Typ

Gruppe V Hypertonie
Angiogramm: Segmentarterienstenose
Isotopennephrogramm: bei regionaler Auswertung Veränderungen der Phase I und Phase II

Ergebnisse

In der Gruppe I (mit 4 Patienten zwischen 59 und 63 Jahren) fanden sich als Zufallsbefund einer Aortographie arteriosklerotische Plaques am Abgang der Nierenarterien. Das Isotopennephrogramm war unauffällig.
Gruppe II umfaßt 2 Patienten. Im Isotopennephrogramm zeigte ein Patient eine Höhenreduktion der Durchblutungsphase. Der zweite Patient ließ einen abgeflachten Anstieg der Sekretionsphase mit einem im Vergleich zur Gegenseite verzögert auftretenden Aktivitätsmaximum gleicher Höhe erkennen.
6 Patienten mit einer Einengung der Nierenartrie auf die Hälfte wurden der Gruppe III zuge-

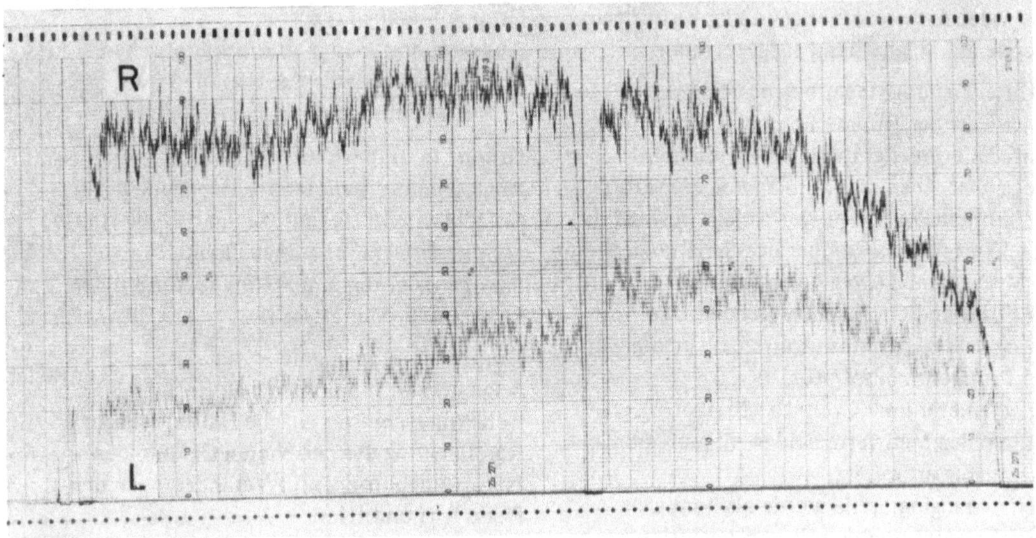

Abb. 1: Isotopennephrogramm: rechte Niere: verzögertes Aktivitätsmaximum; linke Niere: Höhenreduktion der Initialphase, verzögertes und erniedrigtes Aktivitätsmaximum (Nierenarterienstenose links und Tubulosekretionsschaden rechts).

ordnet. Dreimal zeigte das Angiogramm eine zusätzliche kollaterale Blutversorgung der Niere über erweiterte Harnleitergefäße gepaart in zwei Fällen mit einer Rarefizierung der Gefäßperipherie bei erhaltener Organgröße.
Im Isotopennephrogramm fand sich in vier Fällen eine Höhenreduktion der Durchblutungsphase. Der Anstieg der Sekretionsphase war abgeflacht, das Aktivitätsmaximum erniedrigt, die Gipfelzeit im Vergleich zur Gegenseite verlängert und an der oberen Normgrenze. Bei einer Patientin (Abb. 1) war zusätzlich das Isotopennephrogramm der kontralateralen Niere pathologisch verändert. Dies ist als Ausdruck einer bereits faßbaren Tubulosekretionsstörung der ursprünglich gesunden Niere im Gefolge eines *Goldblatt*-Mechanismus aufzufassen.
In der Gruppe IV sind sechs Patienten zusammengefaßt. Der Gefäßbaum der stenosierten Nierenarterie war in vier Fällen rarefiziert und die Niere in ihrer Gesamtheit verkleinert. Einer dieser Fälle ließ bereits Gefäßveränderungen an der kontralateralen Niere erkennen. Ein weiterer Fall zeigte eine weitgehende Schrumpfung der (Abb. 2a) zunächst gesunden linken Niere

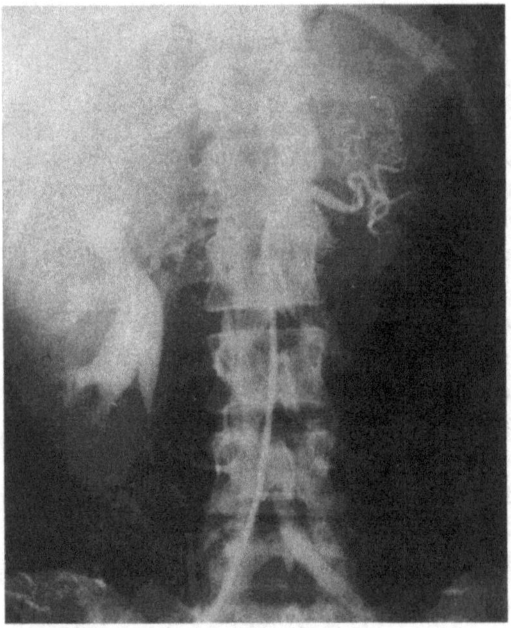

Abb. 2a: lumbale Übersichtsaortographie: verkleinerte linke Niere mit rarefiziertem Gefäßbaum bei unauffälliger Nierenarterie.

als Hochdruckfolge mit Afunktion im Urogramm. Die rechte Nierenarterie (Abb. 2b) war stenosiert, das Organ wurde zusätzlich über reichliche Kollateralen aus Harnleitergefäßen und Lumbalarterien versorgt und war kompensatorisch vergrößert.

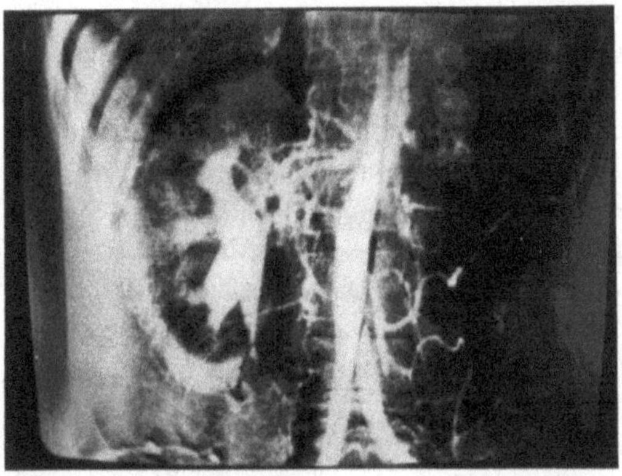

Abb. 2b: hochgradige Nierenarterienstenose (rechts) mit kollateraler Blutversorgung des kompensatorisch hypertrophierten Organes.

Die zugehörigen Isotopennephrogramme ließen bei vier Patienten eine Höhenreduzierung der Durchblutungsphase erkennen. In Abhängigkeit vom Schweregrad der Stenose bot die Niere dieser Seite fünfmal das Bild eines Isosthenurie-Typs, einmal einen Nephrektomie-Typ.

In beiden Fällen (Gruppe V) mit Stenosierung einer Segmentarterie (Abb. 3a) waren im Isotopennephrogramm zunächst nur die Zeichen eines verlängerten intrarenalen Transportes des Radioindikators gegeben. Erst die in Kenntnis des Angiogrammes durchgeführte regionale Auswertung der Funktionskurven ergab die für eine Nierenarterienstenose (Abb. 3b) typischen Veränderungen der Phase I und II.

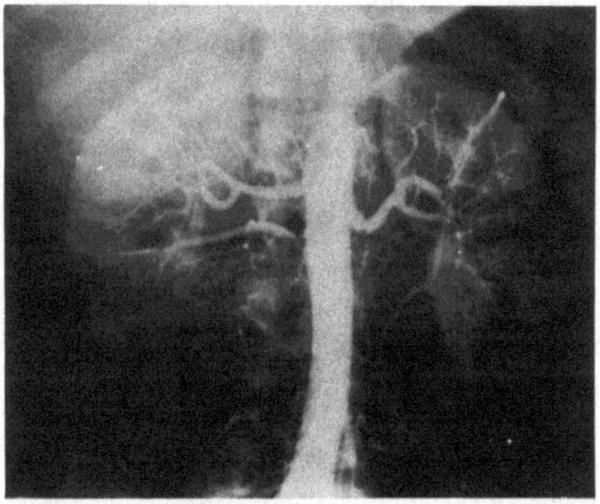

Abb. 3a: lumbale Übersichtsaortographie: hochgradige Stenose der caudalen Segmentarterie rechts.

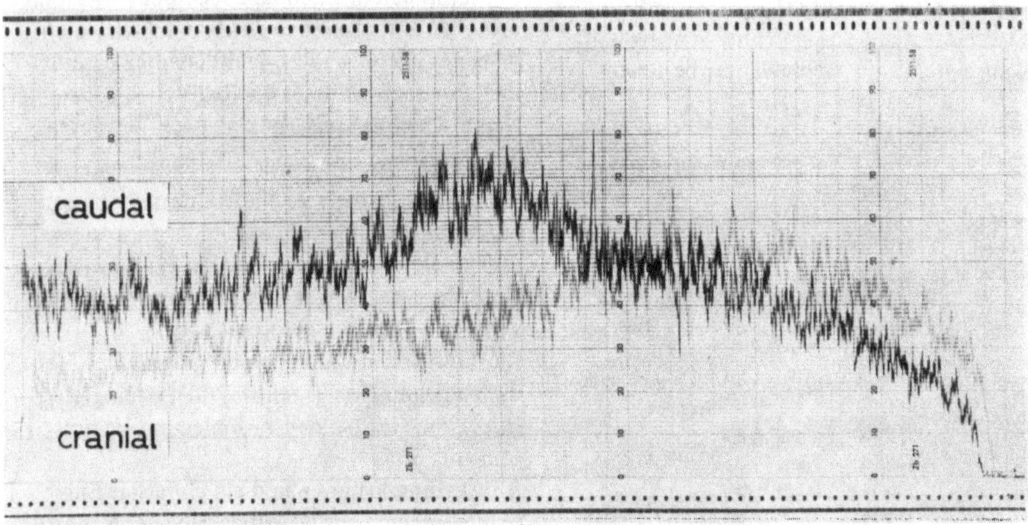

Abb. 3b: regionales Isotopennephrogramm rechts: unauffälliger Kurvenverlauf über der cranialen Region. Höhenreduktion der Initialphase, deutlich verzögertes Aktivitätsmaximum mit abgeflachtem Anstieg über der caudalen Region.

Diskussion

Auf Grund des vorliegenden Patientengutes fühlen wir uns zu folgenden Aussagen berechtigt: Das Konzept, eine *Anger*-Kamera mit divergierendem Kollimator und data store play back-System zu verwenden, erwies sich als nützlich. Schwierigkeiten der Lokalisation von Nieren und Harnblase, wie sie bei Anwendung von Einzeldetektoren bestehen, entfallen.
Die binär decimale Codierung der Meßdaten verhindert einen Informationsverlust durch falsche Empfindlichkeitseinstellung der Apparatur, der rein analogen Aufzeichnungssystemen anhaftet.
Die Speicherung der Untersuchungsdaten auf Magnetband erlaubt jederzeit eine neuerliche Auswertung mit abgeänderten „regions of interest". Wie wir zeigen konnten, deckten erst die gezielt erhobenen regionalen Isotopennephrogramme in zwei Fällen mit Segmentarterienstenosen die typischen Veränderungen auf.
Die Treffsicherheit der von uns angegebenen Methode zum Nachweis einer Nierenarterienstenose beträgt in unserem Krankengut 86%. Wie ein Vergleich mit anderen Autoren (Tab. 1) zeigt, sinkt die Treffsicherheit des isotopennephrographischen Nachweises bei Vorliegen segmentaler Stenosen auf 40%.
Wesentlich erscheint uns, daß eine Schädigung der kontralateralen Niere bei länger bestehendem Hochdruckleiden auf Grund des Isotopennephrogrammes früher als im Angiogramm zu erkennen war.
Die Veränderungen im Isotopennephrogramm bei Nierenarterienstenose sind typisch, doch keineswegs spezifisch und bestärken unsere Ansicht, daß sich das Isotopennephrogramm zwar als Vorfelduntersuchung bewährt, eine Interpretation des causalen Zusammenhanges jedoch nur auf Grund des Angiogrammes möglich ist. Weder ein normales noch ein pathologisches Isotopennephrogramm wird letztlich bei juveniler Hypertonie eine ausreichende Entscheidungsbasis für das weitere therapeutische Vorgehen darstellen. Dies kann nur die Synopsis aller zur Verfügung stehender diagnostischer Methoden in der Reihenfolge: Urogramm, Isotopennephrogramm, Nierenangiographie, seitengetrennte Reninbestimmung und intra- oder präoperative Messung eines Druckgradienten.

Tab. 1:

Autor		Fälle	Treffsicherheit in %
Tauxe et al.	(1961)	27	97
Hunt et al.	(1962)	15	100
Stewart et al.	(1962)	19	100 bei einseitiger Stenose
			67 bei beidseitiger Stenose
			40 bei segmentaler Stenose
Quinn	(1963)	27	89
Winter	(1963)	56	85
Scholz	(1964)	10	90
Hör et al.	(1966)	13	85
zum Winkel	(1971)	38	67
eigene Fälle	(1972)	21	86

Zusammenfassung

Nach intravenöser Injektion eines nierenpflichtigen radioaktiven Indikators (J-131-Hippuran) werden vom Detektor einer *Anger*-Szintillationskamera kommende Meßimpulse in codierter Form mit einem video-tape recorder aufgenommen. Die anschließende elektronische Einblendung der Nierenareale erlaubt über Ratemeter und Zweifachschreiber die Registrierung der Nephrogrammkurven im play-back-Verfahren.
Mit diesem System wurden 21 Fälle angiographisch diagnostizierter Nierenarterienstenosen untersucht.
4 Fälle ohne Hypertonie zeigten ein normales Nephrogramm, wie es für hämodynamisch nicht wirksame Stenosen gefordert wird.
Die Treffsicherheit der nephrographischen Verdachtsdiagnose einer renovaskulär bedingten Hypertonie lag bei den 17 Fällen mit Hypertonie bei 86%.
Auswertungskriterien und ein einfaches Einteilungsschema zur Klassifizierung der Nephrogramme in Korrelation zum angiographischen Befund werden erörtert.

Dynamisch-morphologische Studien bei der gekippten Niere

P. Reindl und J. Neumann

Der Einfluß der Nephroptosis auf das Nephrogramm bei Aufzeichnung in sitzender oder stehender Position war in zahlreichen Arbeiten Gegenstand näherer Untersuchungen.
Ich darf hier nur auf Veröffentlichungen von *Taplin, z. Winkel* und *Büll* hinweisen.
Es zeigt sich dabei vor allem eine Störung der Exkretion und weniger der Sekretionsleistung.

Ein weiterer Faktor im Rahmen der Veränderungen im Nephrogramm, wie auch dem Pyelogramm, dürfte die Kippung einer Niere ohne wesentliche Ptosis sein.
Ein Phänomen, dem u. E. bislang möglicherweise nicht die entsprechende Bedeutung beigemessen wurde.
Bei einem Untersuchungsgut von 1500 Patienten, bei denen Infusionspyelogramm und nuklearmedizinische Funktionsdiagnostik durchgeführt wurden, fanden sich in 66 Fällen Zeichen der Kippung einer Niere.
Es soll jedoch im Rahmen dieses Vortrages zur Objektivierung der typischen Veränderungen nur auf die Einflüsse der gekippten, nicht ptotischen Niere eingegangen werden, die bei Untersuchung im Liegen nephrographisch (*RNG*) und pyelographisch normal waren.

Diese Anomalie zeigte sich in 32 von 66 Fällen aus dem angegebenen Untersuchungsgut.

Die Veränderungen waren, abgesehen von prozentualen Schwankungen, bei der quantitativen Auswertung in allen Fällen die gleichen. Ich darf mich aus diesen Gründen auf die Demonstration eines Falles beschränken.
Zuerst die einzelnen Untersuchungen in liegender Position.
Dabei zeigte sich im Infusionspyelogramm das Nierenhohlsystem und den Ureterabgang betreffend ein unauffälliges Bild.
Das selektive Kameranephrogramm (Autofluoroscope) lag, bewertet nach Phase 1, Aktivitätsdifferenz im Maximum, zeitl. Erreichung des Kulminationspunktes sowie Wertung der Exkretionszeit, völlig im Normbereich, wobei wir für T 1/2 E als obere Grenze 7 Minuten annehmen (Abb. 1).

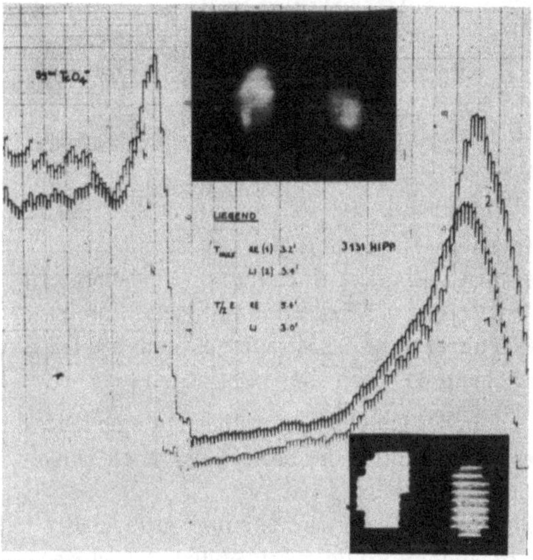

Abb. 1

Die Durchströmung mit 99 m Tc O_4 ergab ebenfalls keine quantitative Differenz in der vergleichenden Untersuchung.
Das Szintigramm im Liegen zeigte in Lage, Form und Größe unauffällige Nieren.
Derselbe Fall nun in sitzender bzw. in stehender Position.
Hier kam es im Infusionspyelogramm infolge der Lageveränderung zu einer Projektion der cranialen Kelchgruppe auf den oberen Nierenbeckenbereich. Zudem resultierte aus der Kippung ein höherer Ureterabgang.
Das selektive Kameranephrogramm (Abb. 2) ist über der linken Niere weiterhin unauffällig, jedoch zeigt sich rechts eine deutliche Differenz in Phase 1, sowie in der Aktivitätsdifferenz im

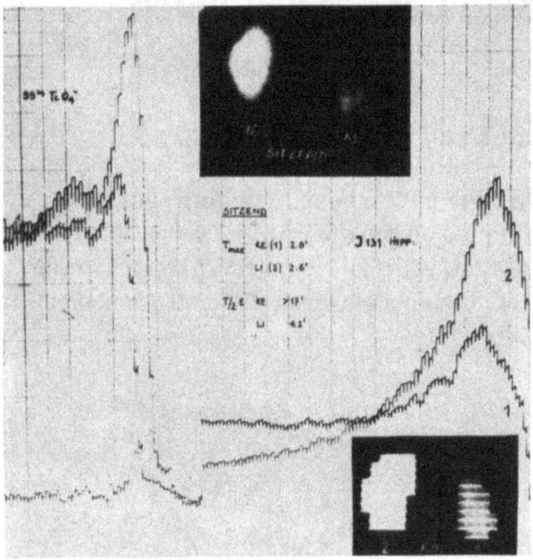

Abb. 2

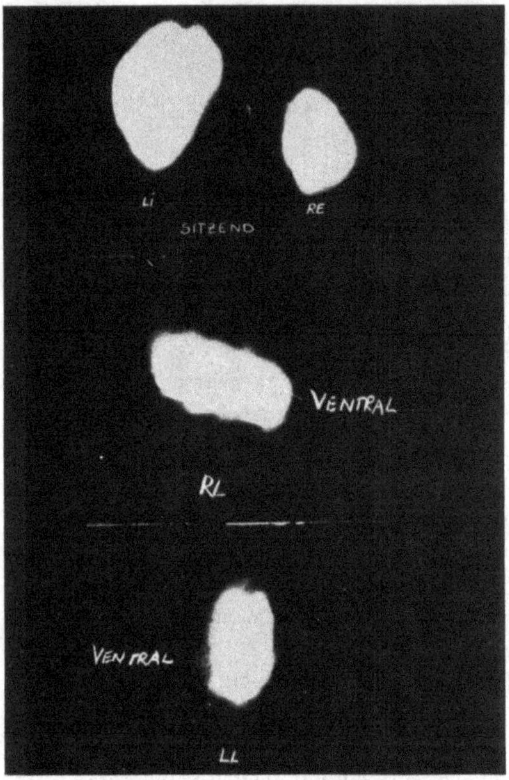

Abb. 3

Maximum. Die Sekretionsphase ist nur unwesentlich verbreitert, doch besteht eine deutliche Verzögerung der Exkretion mit Retention im Nierenbecken bis 20 Minuten pi, wobei T 1/2 E bei einem Wert von über 17 Minuten liegt.

Auch in der Durchströmung besteht eine Differenz zu ungunsten der betroffenen Niere (linkes Kurvenpaar).

Das Nephrogramm wird bei uns routinemäßig in sitzender Position durchgeführt. Ausschlaggebend für die Wiederholung im Liegen war die Diskrepanz im Szintigramm zwischen liegender und sitzender Position.

Hierbei kam es bei gekippter Niere im Sitzen nur zu einem rundlichen Aktivitätsbild des betreffenden Organs, sozusagen das Projektionsbild eines gekippten Elypsoids.

Das entsprechende seitliche Szintigramm der Niere zeigte ein deutliches Abgleiten des unteren Nierenpols nach ventral, wobei wir ein Abweichen von mehr als 35° von der Vertikalen als signifikant betrachten (Abb. 3).

Als ursächliches Moment für die typischen Veränderungen der Funktionskurven sind neben einer Exkretionsstörung vor allem auch eine Beeinflussung der Durchblutung anzusehen.

Eine Beeinflussung durch meßgeometrische Faktoren könnte jedoch bis zu einem gewissen Grad eine Rolle spielen.

Zusammenfassend kann man sagen, daß der gekippten, nicht ptotischen Niere, auch bei der geringen Zahl von 32 Fällen, aus der Konstanz der Kriterien eine klinische Bedeutung beizumessen ist. Vor allem hinsichtlich der therapeutischen Konsequenz, da auf lange Sicht durch die Lageveränderung und die dadurch bedingte Exkretionsstörung manifeste Schädigungen zu erwarten sind.

Die regionale Perfusion der Lungen mit semiquantitativer Computerauswertung*

H. Imhof, K. H. Kärcher, W. Schlick und H. Umek

Die Lungenszintigraphie mit Jod-131- oder Tc-99m-Makroaggregaten (*MAA*) ist eine bereits anerkannte Methode zur Beurteilung der Lungenperfusion.
Zusätzlich ist es nun möglich, unter Einsatz einer Angerszintillationskamera, eines 4096-Kanalspeichers und eines computerkompatiblen Magnetbandes rasch ablaufende regionale Durchblutungsänderungen zu erfassen und mit Hilfe eines Computerprogramms semiquantitativ zu beurteilen.

Methodik

Wir verwenden als radioaktive Indikatoren i. v. injiziertes Tc-99m-Albumin, das mit dem Blutstrom wandert und nicht abgeatmet wird, und Tc-99m-MAA, die zu einer partiellen Lungenmikroembolisation führen. Injektion und Untersuchung erfolgt in Rückenlage. Die auf dem Detektor der Szintillationskamera auftreffenden Gammastrahlen werden in elektrische Impulse umgewandelt und entsprechend ihrer Lokalisation im 4096-Kanalspeicher aufsummiert. In Zeitintervallen von 1,2 Sek. werden die so aufsummierten Zählraten digital auf ein Computerkompatibles Magnetband übertragen und im off-line Verfahren ausgewertet (1. und 2. Abbildung).
Das Auswertungsprogramm ermöglicht die Wiedergabe von Einzel- oder Summenszintigrammen, wobei der Aktivitätsbereich in 7 Grauwertstufen mit jeweils 2 Sigmaabständen unterteilt wird. Eine zusätzliche Bildverbesserung kann durch digitale Filterung mit bis zu 7 Wienerfiltern erreicht werden. Dies ist aber so zeitaufwendig, daß eine routinemäßige Anwendung nicht in Frage kommt. Ferner ist es möglich, bis zu 10 regionale Zeitaktivitätskurven gleichzeitig auszudrucken. Diese Kurven werden in der Zeitrichtung mit Hilfe einer Gauß-Funktion geglättet. Überdies können regionale Differenz- und Quotientenkurven in ihrem zeitlichen Verlauf dargestellt werden. Mit Hilfe eines Spezialprogramms erhalten wir für jede Region die Anstiegszeit bis zum Erreichen des Aktivitätsmaximums (= Einstromzeit), wobei der 0-Punkt extrapoliert wird, und die Zeit des Aktivitätsabfalles bis zur Hälfte des Aktivitätsmaximums (= Abstromzeit), so wie die jeweils bis zu diesen beiden Zeitpunkten gemessene Gesamtaktivität, die für die Berechnung der pro Zeiteinheit ein- bzw. abströmenden Aktivität erforderlich ist.

Ergebnisse

Unsere Normalwerte stammen bis jetzt von 7 Patienten, bei denen kein Anhaltspunkt für eine Störung der pulmonalen oder cardialen Funktion bestand. Bei 2 Patienten mit Lungenmetastasen zeigt sich ein relativ rascher Blutein- und Abstrom, wobei als Ursache sekundärblastomatös bedingte AV-shunts anzunehmen sind (Tab. 1). Ein deutlich verzögerter Abstrom aus dem rechten Herzen und ein verspäteter Ein- und Abstrom in die Lungen bzw. aus den Lungenarealen trat bei 7 Patienten mit nachgewiesenem Mitralvitium und Linksherzversagen auf. Übereinstimmend mit bisherigen Untersuchungen zeigen sich diese Veränderungen bei leichteren Fällen nur in den caudalen, in schweren auch in den cranialen Bereichen. Eine quantitative Aussage über eine einfache Korrelation zum Vorhofsdruck läßt sich infolge der zu geringen Fallzahl noch nicht machen.
Der Vergleich unserer nuklearmedizinischen

* Mit Unterstützung des Jubiläumsfonds der Österreichischen Nationalbank.

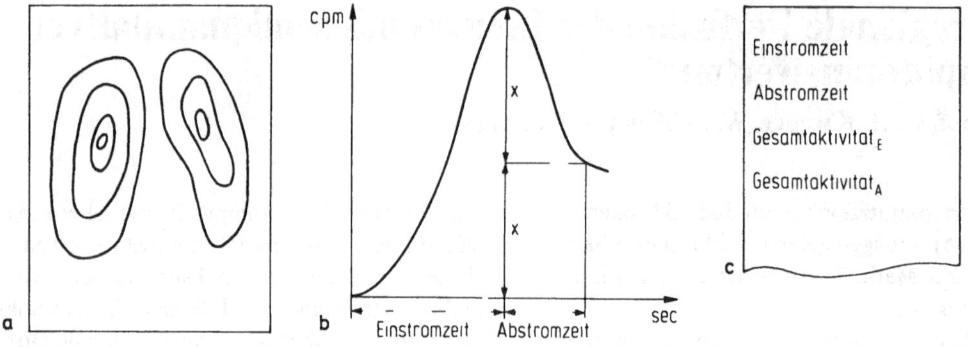
cpm
x
x
Einstromzeit
Abstromzeit
sec
Einstromzeit
Abstromzeit
Gesamtaktivität E
Gesamtaktivität A
a
b
c

Abb. 1

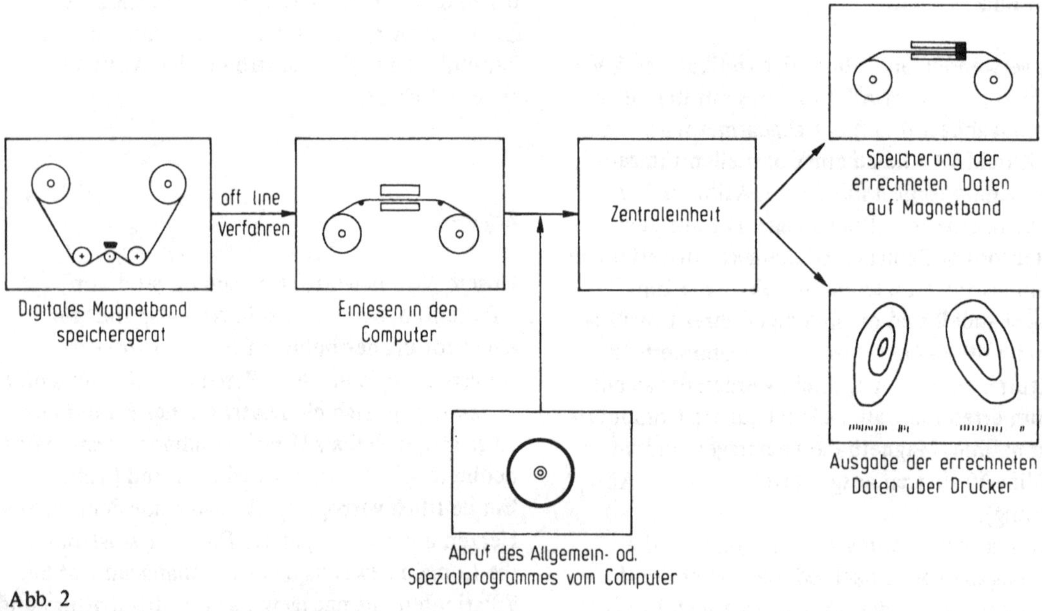
off line
Verfahren
Digitales Magnetband speichergerät
Einlesen in den Computer
Zentraleinheit
Speicherung der errechneten Daten auf Magnetband
Ausgabe der errechneten Daten über Drucker
Abruf des Allgemein- od. Spezialprogrammes vom Computer

Abb. 2

Tab. 1:

	Einstrom in die rechte Lunge		Einstrom in die linke Lunge	
	Normalwerte	$Fall_{III}$	Normalwerte	$Fall_{III}$
oben	6,0–9,0″	5,4″	5,6– 9,0″	6,0″
Mitte	6,0–9,0″	5,4″	5,4– 9,0″	6,0″
unten	6,0–9,0″	5,4″	7,2–10,2″	6,0″
	Abstrom aus der rechten Lunge		Abstrom aus der linken Lunge	
	Normalwerte	$Fall_{III}$	Normalwerte	$Fall_{III}$
oben	4,8–7,2″	3,6″	5,4–7,2″	3,6″
Mitte	4,8–6,0″	3,6″	4,8–7,2″	3,6″
unten	4,8–7,2″	5,4″	5,4–7,2″	5,4″

Ergebnis: verkürzter Einstrom in die rechte Lunge
verkürzter Abstrom aus beiden Lungenober- und mittelgeschossen.

Ergebnisse mit den klinischen Daten und mit der Lungenfunktionsprüfung zeigt, daß durch diese Methode eine brauchbare zusätzliche Funktionsaussage erzielt werden kann.

Weitere Untersuchungen betreffen die Perfusionsänderungen, die während und nach Strahlentherapie von Lungentumoren auftreten. Es wurden 8 Patienten bis zu 7 Monaten nach erfolgter Strahlentherapie kontrolliert. Insgesamt wurden 26 Kontrollen durchgeführt.
2 Patienten konnten jeweils 4 mal nachuntersucht werden. Es zeigte sich (Abb. 3) eine deutliche Verlängerung der Einstromzeit und soweit beurteilbar, auch der Abstromzeit, wobei die relative Gesamtaktivität über dem bestrahlten Areal eher zunimmt. Dies ist wohl im Sinne einer Strahlenfibrose zu deuten.
Im ersten Monat ist dieser Anstieg der integrierten Aktivität während der Einstromzeit besonders deutlich, wie sich aus dem Quotienten der korrespondierenden Lungenareale erkennen läßt (Abb. 3).

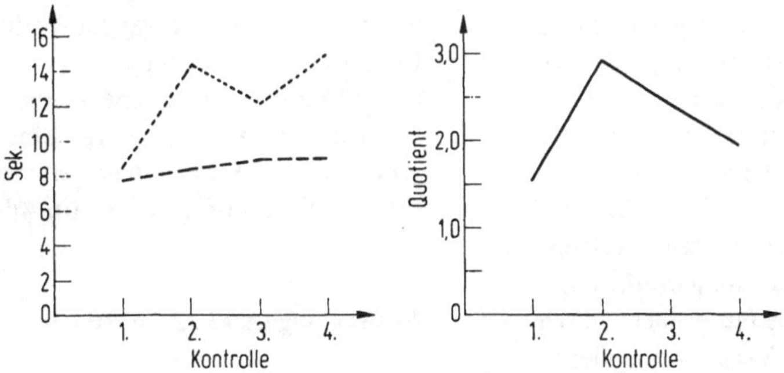

Abb. 3

Zusammenfassung

Es wird über eine nuklearmedizinische Methode zur Messung der regionalen Lungenperfusion mit Computerauswertung berichtet. Die Veränderungen bei Patienten mit sekundärer-pulmonaler Hypertension, mit primären und sekundären Lungentumoren und Patienten während und nach Strahlentherapie eines Tumors werden diskutiert.

Der pharmakoangiographische Adrenalineffekt in der Angioszintigraphie des Pankreas*

H. Czembirek, H. Imhof, H. Pokieser und H. Umek

Die Qualität der Darstellung des Pankreasparenchyms durch Angiographie oder Szintigraphie ist weiten Schwankungen unterworfen. Selbst fehlende Organanfärbung im Arteriogramm erlaubt keine diagnostischen Rückschlüsse, sofern andere Symptome fehlen. Auch die Pharmakoangiographie mit Sekretin hat nicht die erwartete Verbesserung der Parenchymdarstellung gebracht. Die Pankreasszintigraphie ist trotz verschiedener Modifikationen mit einem hohen Prozentsatz inkompletter Pankreasdarstellungen belastet.
Versuche Jod ^{131}-Makroaggregate durch einen in der Arteria coeliaca liegenden Katheter zu injizieren, haben zu keiner befriedigenden Darstellung des Pankreas geführt. Aktivitätsanreicherungen über Milz, Magen und Leber standen einer Abgrenzung des Pankreas entgegen.
Bessere Ergebnisse werden nach selektiver Angioszintigraphie (*ASG*) und nach Hormonstimulierung mit 75 Se-Selenmethionin mitgeteilt. Durch superselektive Applikation von 75 Se-Methionin in die Arteria gastroduodenalis, Arteria pancreatica dorsalis und Arteria lienalis hat *Reuter* bei 4 Fällen eine intensive Teildarstellung des Pankreas erzielt.
Da superselektive Sondierungen der Pankreasgefäße meist schwierig und oft unmöglich sind, die bisher geübten Methoden keine verläßliche Pankreasparenchymdarstellung erbringen, haben wir versucht die gefäßverengende Wirkung des Adrenalin zur Verbesserung des Angioszintigrammes der Bauchspeicheldrüse heranzuziehen.

* Mit Unterstützung des Jubiläumsfonds der Österreichischen Nationalbank.

Methode und Material

Die Injektion von Adrenalin in den Truncus coeliacus bewirkt eine starke Kontraktion der Arteria hepatica communis und der Arteria lienalis, eine geringere Verengung der Arteria gastrica sinistra und der duodenalen Gefäße, während die Pankreasarterien schwächer reagieren. Dadurch kann es bei nachfolgender Kontrastmittelinjektion zu einer besseren Durchströmung der Pankreasgefäße kommen. Diesen Effekt nutzten wir an 20 Patienten zur Angioszintigraphie des Pankreas.
5 Minuten nach selektiver Zoeliakographie wurden 10 ug Adrenalin (Suprarenin-Höchst) injiziert. Um die Adrenalinwirkung zu überprüfen, folgte 20 Sekunden nach der Injektion des Suprarenins eine Bildserie, daran anschließend die langsame manuelle Injektion von 3–5 mCi 99m Tc-Mikrosphären (durchschnittliche Teilchengröße 45 Mikron) durch den liegenden Zoeliakakatheter. Die Szintigramme wurden nach Entfernung des Katheters und Blutstillung innerhalb der folgenden 30 Minuten mit einer Gammakamera (Pho Gamma III, Nuclear Chikago) angefertigt. Eine Kontrollgruppe von 20 Patienten erhielt 99m Tc-Mikrosphären ohne Vorinjektion von Adrenalin.

Auswertung und Ergebnisse

Die Zoeliakogramme von 20 Patienten vor und nach Adrenalininjektion wurden zunächst hinsichtlich des Darstellungsumfanges und des Adrenalineffektes beurteilt und dann mit den auf Polaroidbildern festgehaltenen Angioszintigrammen verglichen. Die Auswertung erfolgte für Leber, Milz, Magen und Pankreas, wobei Pankreaskopf, Pankreaskörper und Pankreas-

schwanz getrennt beurteilt wurden. Die Qualität der Angiogramme und Szintigramme wurde mit schlecht, gut und sehr gut bewertet.
(Tab. 1) Gute bis sehr gute Angioszintigramme aller drei Pankreasabschnitte fanden wir in 6 Fällen (Abb. 1). Nur in 3 Fällen traf diese Qualifikation auch auf die Angiogramme zu.

Tab. 1: Kombinierte und isolierte Darstellung der Pankreasregionen durch PSG's und Angiogramme (berücksichtigt sind nur Untersuchungen mit guter oder sehr guter Qualifikation)

Dargestellte Organbereiche	PSG	Angiogramme (ohne und mit Adrenalin)
Caput + Corpus + Cauda	6	3
Caput + Corpus	3	5
Caput	5	1
Corpus	–	1
Cauda	–	2

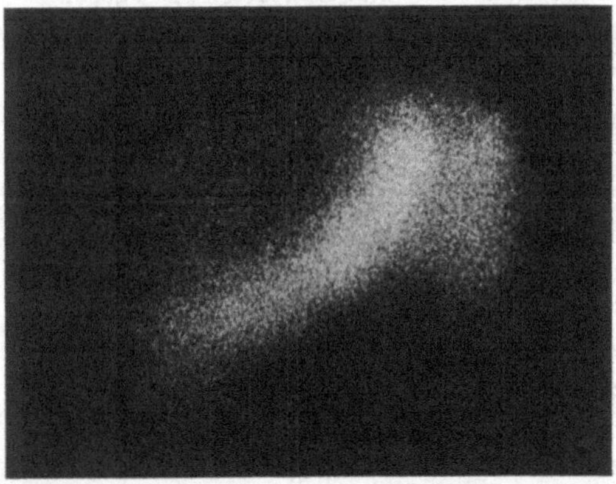

Abb. 1

Eine kombinierte Darstellung von Kopf- und Körperbereich zeigte sich 3 mal, die der Angiogramme allerdings 5 mal.

Der Pankreaskopf war 5 mal isoliert gut oder sehr gut zu erkennen, während nur 1 Angiogramm ausschließlich gute Pankreaskopfdarstellung zeigte.
Körper und Schwanz der Bauchspeicheldrüse waren niemals szintigraphisch isoliert zu sehen, wohl aber 1 bzw. 2 mal am Angiogramm dargestellt.
(Tab. 2) Der Kopfbereich der Bauchspeicheldrüse war insgesamt 14 mal gut bis sehr gut abzugrenzen, wobei 9 mal auch eine der beiden angiographischen Serien in diese Qualitätsgruppe fallen.

Tab. 2: Qualität der Angiogramme und Perfusionsszintigramme (N = 20)

	Angiogramme gut oder sehr gut	PSG gut oder sehr gut
Caput Pancr.	9	14
Corpus Pancr.	7	9
Cauda Pancr.	3	6

Der Körperbereich war in 9 Fällen szintigraphisch gut bis sehr gut markiert, 7 mal angiographisch gut und 2 mal schlecht dargestellt.

Die Cauda pancreatis war 6 mal gut oder sehr gut zu differenzieren, obwohl nur 3 gute Angiogramme dieser Region vorlagen.
Eine deutliche Aktivität über dem Magen fand sich in 10 Fällen, wobei 6 mal der Pankreasschwanz und 1 mal der Pankreaskörper überlagert und dadurch nicht abgrenzbar war (Abb. 2).

Durch Milzaktivität war bei 6 Fällen die Differenzierung des Caudaabschnittes erschwert, 2 mal ließ sich trotzdem der Pankreasschwanz gut abgrenzen (Abb. 3).
In der Leber fand sich nur bei 4 Fällen ausge-

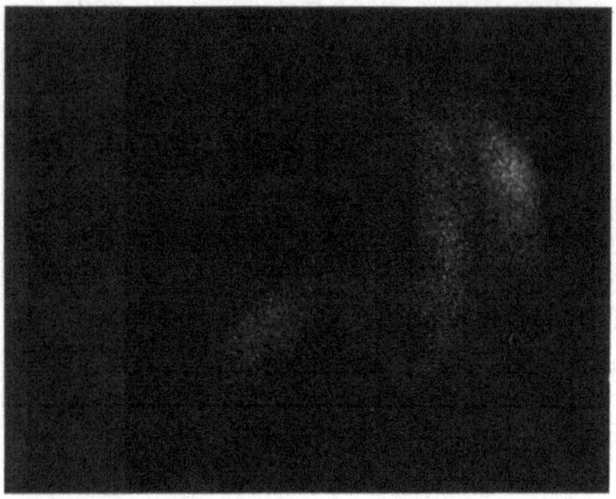
Abb. 2

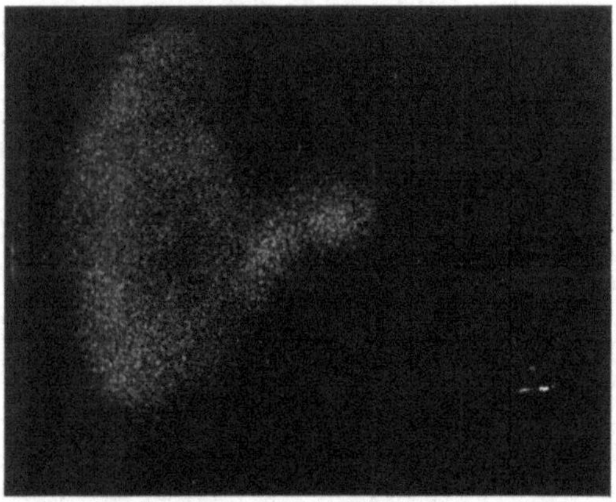
Abb. 3

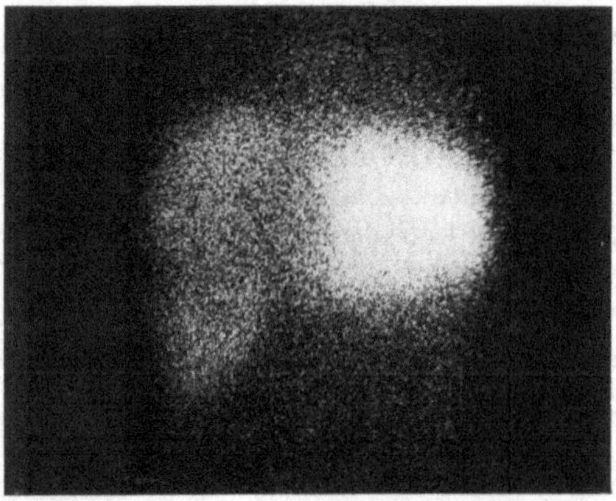
Abb. 4

prägte Aktivitätsanreicherung, wobei 2 mal durch Hepatomegalie eine Organabgrenzung des Pankreas nicht möglich war, 2 mal jedoch die Bauchspeicheldrüse von einer normal großen Leber gut abgesetzt war.
Demgegenüber zeigte die Kontrollgruppe mit 20 Angioszintigrammen ohne Adrenalin 7 mal eine Pankreaskopfdarstellung, während der Körperabschnitt 8 mal gut oder sehr gut markiert waren. Die Caudaregion blieb stets durch Magen und Milzaktivität überlagert und nicht beurteilbar. Aktivitätseinlagerungen in Milz, Leber und Magen fand sich 16,8 und 11 mal (Abb. 4).

Diskussion und Schlußfolgerung

Stellt man *ASG*'s mit Adrenalin der Serie ohne Adrenalin gegenüber, so findet die geänderte Hämodynamik auch im *ASG* ihren Niederschlag. Die Frequenz guter Pankreaskopfdarstellungen im *ASG* war nach Adrenalin doppelt so hoch wie in der Kontrollgruppe. Während die Markierung der Pankreaskörperregion in beiden Serien gleichoft aufschien, zeigte sich 6 mal intensive Nuklideinlagerung im Pankreasschwanz gegenüber keiner einzigen in der Kontrollserie.
Nach Adrenalingabe blieb die Aktivitätseinlagerung in die Leber bei 16 von 20 Fällen schwach oder fehlend, für Milz (12 von 20) und Magen (10 von 20) war die Reduktion des Partikeleinstromes weniger ausgeprägt. Die Analyse schlechter *ASG*'s zeigt Beziehungen zur Qualität der Angiogramme. Fehlender Markierung des Pankreaskopfes in 6 Fällen, stehen 6 mangelhafte Gefäßfüllungen gegenüber, bei 12 schlechten Szintigrammen des Pankreaskörpers bzw. 14 des -schwanzes, lagen nur 2 bzw. 1 gutes Angiogramm vor. Auffallend war die Beobachtung, daß 6 guten *ASG*'s aller drei Pankreasabschnitte nur 3 gut zu klassifizierende Angiogramme entsprachen.
Demnach erbringt die Angioszintigraphie des Pankreas unter Adrenalinwirkung wohl eine

deutlich höhere Frequenz von Parenchymdarstellungen gegenüber dem Angioszintigramm ohne gefäßverengendes Pharmakon; trotzdem schränkt die fehlende Abgrenzungsmöglichkeit von Pankreasteilbereichen bei intaktem Parenchym in einem bis zwei Drittel der Fälle die Brauchbarkeit dieser Methode ein. Da zudem gute oder ausbleibende Partikelfixation sowohl in gesunden als auch in pathologisch veränderten Organen (3 mal) nachzuweisen war, erfährt diese Methode im diagnostischen Einsatz eine weitere Einschränkung.

Angiographische Untersuchungen bei abdominellen Strömungsgeräuschen

U. Klein und H. G. Heinze

Klinisch verifizierte abdominale Strömungsgeräusche erfordern eine arteriographische Abklärung, um gefäßpathologische Prozesse zu erkennen und zu lokalisieren. Die Arteriographie bietet hierbei die Grundlage für jeden gefäßchirurgischen Eingriff.

Die Abb. 1 a zeigt das Phonogramm eines durch eine arteriovenöse Fistel nach Nephrektomie (Abb. 1 b) hervorgerufenen typischen abdominalen Strömungsgeräusches.
Unter dem Zeichen dieses klinischen Leitsymptoms sollen einige Ursachen, die zu solchen Geräuschen führen können, besprochen werden.

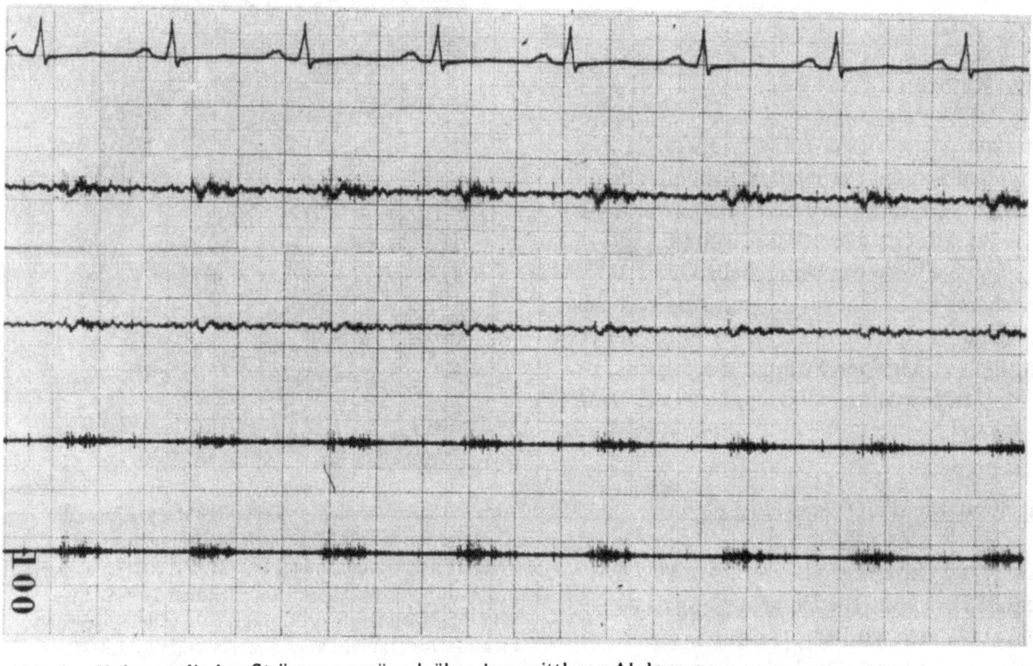

Abb. 1 a: Holosystolisches Strömungsgeräusch über dem mittleren Abdomen.

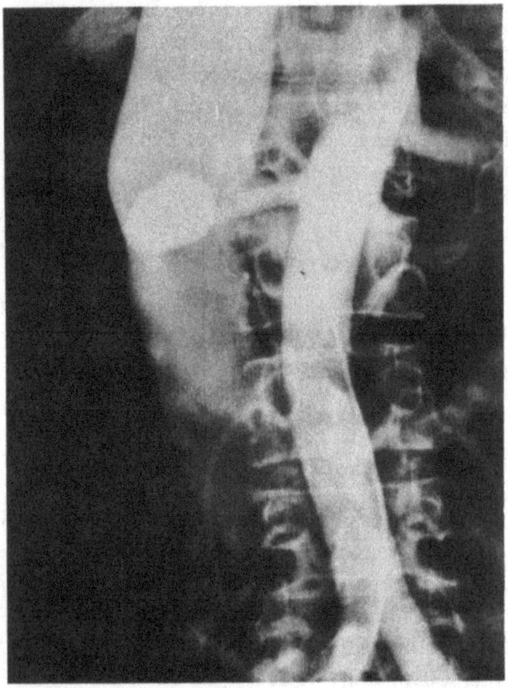

Abb. 1 b: Arterio-venöse aneurysmatische Fistel nach Nephrektomie. Dilatation der Vena cava caudalis (retrograde Strömung des Kontrastblutes).

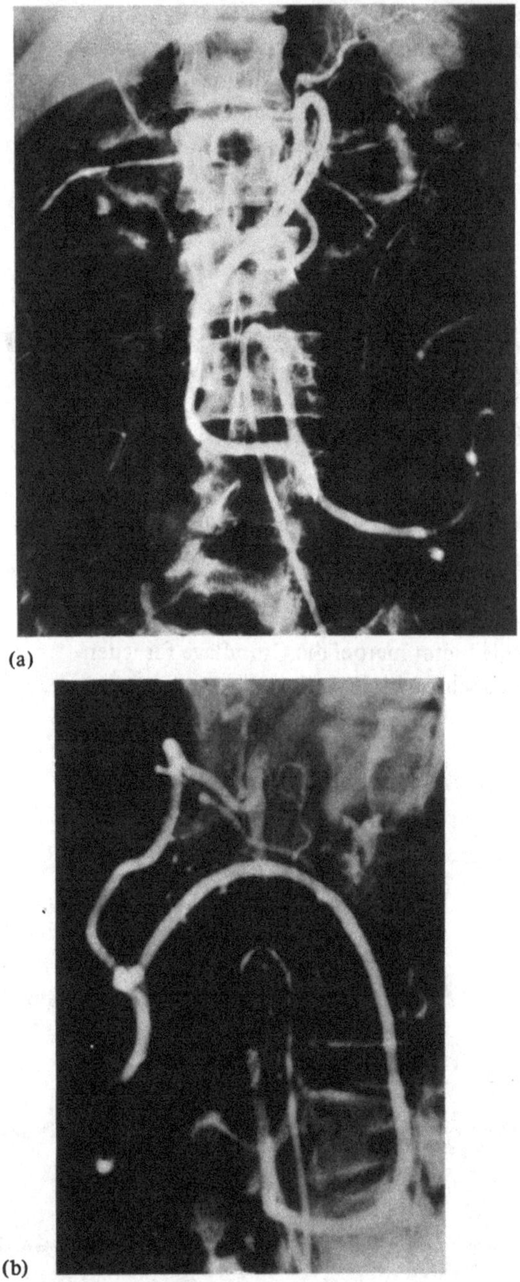

(a)

(b)

Abb. 2: Anlagebedingter Verschluß des Ostiums der A. mesenterica cranialis. Selektive Darstellung der A. mesenterica caudalis in a. p. – (a) und seitlicher (b) Projektion wegen lautem, fauchendem Strömungsgeräusch li. abdominal. Retrograde Auffüllung der A. mesenterica cranialis über eine Riolan'sche Anastomose.

Gefäßstenosen

Unter den Stenosen der großen Äste der Aorta abdominalis ist die Nierenarterienstenose die häufigste. Allerdings ist ein Strömungsgeräusch nur in 30 %–50 % dieser Fälle hörbar. Angiographisch stellt die poststenotische Dilatation ein sicheres Kriterium zur Abgrenzung gegenüber funktionellen Spasmen dar. Sie ist Folge der poststenotisch veränderten Strömungsmechanik, d. h. der hinter der Stenose entstandenen Turbulenz.

Umgehungskreisläufe

Hinter einem Strombahnhindernis sinkt der arterielle Druck ab. Die Vergrößerung des Druckgradienten wird an praeformierten Brükkengefäßen wirksam. Die Folge davon ist ein vermehrtes Strömungsvolumen, eine Dilatation und eine Längenzunahme dieser Kollateralgefäße. Je nach Lokalisation des Strombahnhindernisses kann eine Umkehr der Strömungsrichtung in den Kollateralen erfolgen und ein Entzugsphänomen (Steal-Effekt) im Bereich der Quellarterie entstehen. Ätiologisch stehen die erworbenen Gefäßverschlüsse im Vordergrund. Demgegenüber sind die angeborenen Gefäßveränderungen mit Umgehungskreislauf selten. So konnten wir kürzlich über einen angeborenen Verschluß der A. mesentarica cranialis bei einer 19jährigen Patientin berichten, bei der das craniale Mesentericastromgebiet retrograd über eine Riolan'sche Anastomose aufgefüllt wurde (Abb. 2). Anlaß zur Angiographie war auch hier ein abdominales Strömungsgeräusch, das als Zufallsbefund im Rahmen einer Herzuntersuchung wegen einer Pulmonalstenose entdeckt wurde. Die Kenntnis dieser lebenswichtigen Anastomose ist aber für spätere eventuell notwendig werdende abdominale Operationen wichtig.

Aneurysmen

Die häufigste Ursache für Aneurysmen der Organarterien ist die Arteriosklerose. Ferner kommt eine mykotische, eine traumatische sowie eine konnatale Entstehungsursache in Betracht.
Milzarterienaneurysmen sollen in ca. 5 % aller Coeliacographien vorhanden sein. Verkalkungen sind selten, so daß eine Diagnosestellung ohne Angiographie kaum möglich ist. Ihre Diagnostik kann jedoch wichtig werden, da eine unklare Oberbauchsymptomatik auch einmal durch ein rupturierendes Milzarterienaneurysma verursacht sein kann.

Arterio-venöse Fisteln

Arterio-venöse Fisteln verursachen in der Regel ein charakteristisches, kontinuierliches Gefäßgeräusch. Im Abdomen stellen solche Fisteln allerdings eine Rarität dar. Sie entstehen in der Hauptsache nach operativen Eingriffen aufgrund von Sammelligaturen der Arterie und Vene. Unbehandelt führen große A-V-Fisteln wegen der erheblichen Volumenbelastung des kleinen und großen Kreislaufs letztlich zum Tod durch Herzversagen. Die rechtzeitige Erkennung und Behandlung dieses Zustandsbildes entscheidet daher über das Schicksal des Patienten.
Aus den genannten Fakten läßt sich ableiten, daß bei jedem abdominalen Strömungsgeräusch die Angiographie indiziert ist, um Ursachen sowie pathophysiologische und morphologische Verhältnisse abzuklären.

Die Dissektion als angiographische Komplikation

J. Balau, F. Kleinschmidt, D. A. Loose und H. J. Maurer

Intramurale Kontrastmittelinjektionen mit nachfolgender Dissektion der Gefäßwandschichten sind neben Thromboembolien und Nachblutungen gefürchtete Komplikationen angiologischer Untersuchungen.
Während in kasuistischen Beiträgen immer wieder auf die z. T. tödlichen Gefahren iatrogener dissecierender Aneurysmen nach Angiographien hingewiesen wird, werden in der täglichen Praxis des öfteren Dissektionen beobachtet, die komplikations- und symptomlos verlaufen.

Es scheint uns daher gerechtfertigt, zur Frage der Häufigkeit und des Risikos von dissezieren-

den Gefäßverletzungen anhand des eigenen Krankengutes Stellung zu nehmen.
Unsere Beobachtungen stützen sich auf 1350 Arteriographien des Bauchraumes und der Extremitäten, die in den letzten 4 Jahren in der Röntgenabteilung der Chirurgischen Universitätsklinik Düsseldorf durchgeführt wurden. Davon wurden 1160 Untersuchungen in der typischen, indirekten, transfemoralen Technik nach *Seldinger* vorgenommen. Bei den restlichen 190 Angiographien, bei denen ein transfemoraler Zugang nicht möglich war, wurde das Kontrastmittel durch hohe translumbale Aortenpunktion appliziert.
Im allgemeinen wurde das Kontrastmittel mit Kontrac-Injektion bei einer Flußrate von 20 ml/ Sec. injiziert. Bei ca. 300 Patienten erfolgte die Injektion mit der *Gidlund*-Spritze mit 4–6 atü. Die Untersuchungen wurden meistens in tiefer Intubationsnarkose durchgeführt.
Die Altersverteilung der Patienten reichte von 2–78 Jahren und lag im Mittel bei einem Lebensalter von 56 Jahren. Bei den meisten Patienten – etwa 60% – wurde die Angiographie zur Abklärung arterieller Durchblutungsstörungen durchgeführt, während bei den restlichen 40% die Frage nach abdominellen, hauptsächlich urologischen Tumoren gestellt war.
Bei 40 Angiographien, das heißt bei 3% der Untersuchungen, konnten Dissektionen mit unterschiedlicher Ausdehnung und Lokalisation nachgewiesen werden. Neben vereinzelten kleinen, strichförmigen intramuralen Kontrastmitteldepots ohne wesentliche Abscherung der Gefäßwandschichten wurden meist ausgedehnte, 7–15 cm lange Dissektionen im Bereich der abdominellen Aorta und der iliacalen Gefäße beobachtet. Bis auf einen 36jährigen Mann, bei dem ein kleines, intramurales Depot gesetzt worden war, traten Dissektionen erst bei den Patienten jenseits des 50. Lebensjahres auf, wobei der größte Teil mit 26 dissezierenden Aneurysmen jenseits des 6. Dezeniums gefunden wurde.
Nach diesen Erfahrungen kommt es zu Dissektionen im allgemeinen nur bei vorgeschädigtem, arteriosklerotisch verändertem Gefäßsystem, bei dem es durch ausgedehnte Kalkplaquebildung und atheromatöse Ulcerationen leicht möglich ist, die Gefäßwand zu unterspülen oder mit dem Katheter zu unterfahren.
In Übereinstimmung mit anderen Untersuchern konnten wir bei direkten translumbalen Aortographien eine wesentlich höhere Dissektionsrate von 7% nachweisen, im Gegensatz zu den indirekten, transfemoralen Angiographien, wo die Dissektionsfrequenz bei 2% lag.
Bis auf einen Fall verliefen die beobachteten Dissektionen ohne wesentliche Symptome oder Komplikationen. Lediglich bei 12 ausgedehnten Dissektionen kam es während der Narkose zu kurzfristigen hypotonen Blutdruckkrisen. Bei allen Patienten mit Dissektionen wurde im Anschluß an die Untersuchung eine sofortige Aufnahme in der Intensivstation eingeleitet, um für eventuelle Spätkomplikationen gewappnet zu sein. Keiner der Patienten klagte nach Aufwachen aus der Narkose über nennenswerte Beschwerden. Auch im weiteren Verlauf der stationären Behandlung zeigten sich keine Besonderheiten.
Den einzigen Zwischenfall erlebten wir bei einem 63jährigen Patienten. Bei ihm zeigte zwar das indirekte transfemorale Angiogramm keine Dissektion, es kam jedoch nach Ziehen des Katheters zu einem Verschluß der punktierten linken Arteria femoralis. Unter dem Verdacht einer Katheterembolie wurde der Verschluß operativ angegangen. Dabei zeigte sich jedoch, daß die Arteria femoralis durch eine 12 cm lange, aufgerollte Intimaabscherung, die beim Ziehen des Katheters entstanden sein mußte, verschlossen war.
7 Patienten wurden nach der dissektionsauslösenden Angiographie nochmals im Abstand von 2–3 Tagen oder mehreren Wochen arteriographiert, z. T., weil die erste Untersuchung kein klares Ergebnis gebracht hatte, z. T., weil weiterhin Durchblutungsstörungen bestanden. Bei diesen 7 Nachuntersuchungen fanden sich keine Zeichen einer noch bestehenden Dissektion. Die Gefäßverletzungen hatten sich spontan zurückgebildet.

Obwohl nach diesen Erfahrungen dissezierende Gefäßverletzungen nach Angiographien relativ ungefährlich sind, soll auf eine wichtige Besonderheit und Nebenwirkung der Dissektion hingewiesen werden. Bei 9 der untersuchten Dissektionen konnten in den distal der Verletzung gelegenen Gefäßabschnitten – meist in den Iliacalgefäßen – ausgedehnte Verschlüsse ohne Kollateralkreislauf nachgewiesen werden. Da vor der Untersuchung bei diesen Patienten die vom Verschluß betroffenen Gefäße gut fühlbar waren, mußte es sich um einen durch die Gefäßverletzung bedingten Verschluß handeln. In der Literatur sind derartige Pseudo-Verschlüsse bekannt. Sie sind meist durch die abgescherte, sich ins Gefäßlumen vorwölbende ausgesackte Intima verursacht. Unseres Erachtens dürften für diese Verschlüsse zum Teil auch durch die Gefäßläsion ausgelöste Spasmen verantwortlich sein; denn bei 3 Patienten mit Pseudoverschlüssen konnte in einer sofort angeschlossenen zweiten Angiographie bei fortbestehender Dissektion eine Lösung des Verschlusses nachgewiesen werden. Bei den übrigen 6 Pseudoverschlüssen wurde eine zweite Angiographie nach einigen Tagen durchgeführt, wobei mit der Spontanremission der Dissektion der Verschluß sich ebenfalls zurückgebildet hatte.

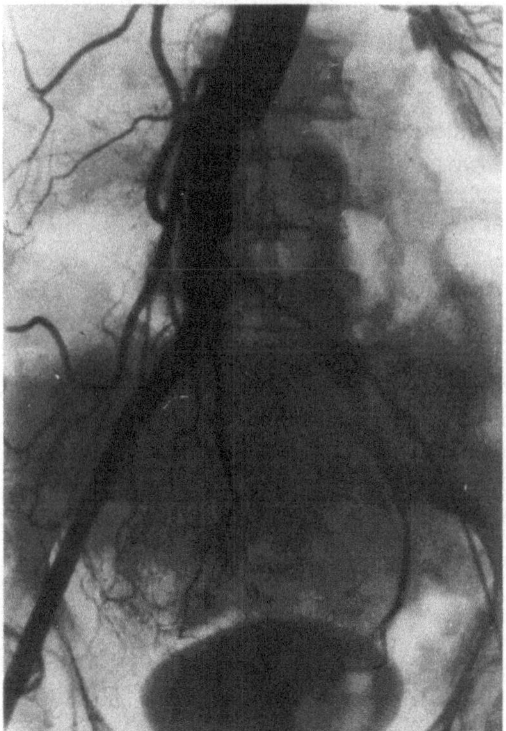

Abb. 1 a: Bei arteriosklerotisch stark verändertem Gefäßsystem ausgedehnte bifurkationsnahe Dissektion der abdominellen Aorta mit durch Spasmus oder Intimavorwölbung bedingtem Verschluß der linken A. iliaca communis bei transfermoraler Aorto-Arteriographie.

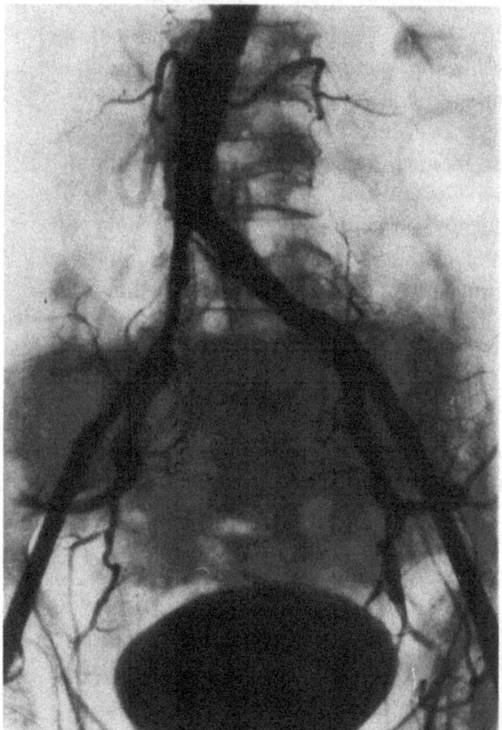

Abb. 1 b: Bei sofortiger Kontroll-Arteriographie nach Zurückziehen des Katheters vollständige Lösung des Verschlusses mit durchgängigen Iliacalgefäßen bds. ohne sicheren Nachweis einer noch bestehenden Dissektion.

Vergleicht man unsere Ergebnisse mit anderen Sammelstatistiken, fällt die große Diskrepanz über Häufigkeitsangaben von angiographisch bedingten Dissektionen auf. Bei den translumbalen direkten Aortographien werden in verschiedenen Arbeiten Häufigkeitswerte von 1–10%, bei den retrograden transfemorale um 1‰–10% angegeben. Der Unterschied dieser Werte dürfte wohl in der Verschiedenheit der untersuchten Patientenkollektive liegen. Betrachtet man bei unseren Angiographien allein das Patientenkollektiv, bei dem nicht obstruktive Gefäßprozesse im Vordergrund standen, sondern die Angiographien zur Tumordiagnostik durchgeführt wurden, so zeigt sich, daß bei diesem die Dissektionshäufigkeit nur 1% betrug, während bei Patienten mit Gefäßerkrankungen die Dissektionen in etwa 4% der Fälle auftraten.

Die günstige Prognose, die wir bei Dissektionen nachweisen konnten, soll jedoch nicht darüber hinwegtäuschen, daß schwere tödliche Folgeerkrankungen z. B. Rupturen und Nachblutungen, möglich sind, wie im Schrifttum hinreichend bekannt ist. Unseres Erachtens liegt die Hauptgefahr jedoch in der Vortäuschung von falschen angiographischen Befunden mit durch Intimavorwölbung oder Spasmen bedingten Pseudoverschlüssen, die zu nicht gerechtfertigten gefäßchirurgischen Schritten veranlassen können.
Voraussetzung zur Vermeidung von Dissektionen ist das exakte Einführen des Katheters unter Durchleuchtungskontrolle, sowie die genaue Überprüfung der intravasalen Lage des Katheters durch Nachweis einer pulsierenden Blutung am äußeren Katheterende und durch Probekontrastmittelinjektion unter Durchleuchtungskontrolle. Es ist jedoch zu bemerken, daß sich bei erheblich arteriosklerotisch-veränderten Gefäßen bei der transfemoralen Angiographie der Katheter oft ohne jeglichen Widerstand in weiten Abschnitten intramural verschieben läßt. Im Durchleuchtungsbild wird dann eine anatomische Lage des Katheters vorgetäuscht.

Weiterhin kann es auch bei regelrechter, durch Probeinjektion nachgewiesener intravalaser Lage des Katheters zu einer Dissektion kommen, und zwar, wenn der Katheter unter einem sklerotischen Plaque liegt und dieses bei hohem maschinellen Injektionsdruck unterspült wird. Ebenso kann der Katheter durch den Rückstoß bei der Injektion unter einer arteriosklerotischen Läsion verlagert werden und so zu einer Dissektion führen.
Abschließend ist besonders unter forensischen Gesichtspunkten zu betonen:
1. Dissektionen sind auch bei exakter Durchführung der Angiographie nicht immer zu vermeiden.
2. In Anbetracht der guten Prognose unter konservativer Behandlung sollte bis auf wenige Fälle von chirurgischen Eingriffen Abstand genommen werden. Es sollte jedoch jeder Patient mit einer Dissektion unter Bedingungen einer modernen Intensivstation einige Zeit beobachtet werden.

Zeichnerische Auswertung von angiographischen Kinofilmen als Methode der Strömungsanalyse

B. Mayr, R. Bartl und U. Klein

Die zeichnerische Auswertung radiologischer Kinofilme hat sich als Methode zur Analyse von Organbewegungen bewährt (*Grosse-Wilde*). Insbesondere kann sie bei angiographischen Kinofilmen zur Erfassung von Strömungsgeschwindigkeiten verwendet werden. Wir haben uns speziell mit der Hämodynamik der Nierenarterie befaßt.

Im Rahmen einer Nierenangiographie wurde über einen selektiven Katheter ein Kontrastmittelbolus von 1 ml mittels einer EKG-gesteuerten Injektionsspritze (Contrac 3 E) injiziert. Wegen des beinahe rechteckigen Injektionsimpulses und des damit verbundenen raschen Druckanstieges ist der Kontrastmittelbolus scharf abgrenzbar. Mit einer Arri-Filmkamera wurden 50 Bilder/sec angefertigt. Die Auswertung der Filme erfolgte am Arri-Viewer, wobei die Fortbewegung der Bolusspitze von Bild zu Bild gezeichnet wurde. Die Meßpunkte wurden jeweils an die Spitze der Kontrastmittelsäule gelegt.

Abb. 1 a zeigt eine *elektromagnetisch* gemessene Flowkurve der Arteria renalis einschließlich des Druckablaufes in der Aorta abdominalis. Die Form dieser Durchblutungskurve (ml/min) ist identisch mit der Blutstromgeschwindigkeitskurve (cm/sec), da der Durchmesser der Arteria renalis während einer Herzaktion annähernd konstant bleibt (*Wetterer, Bartl*).

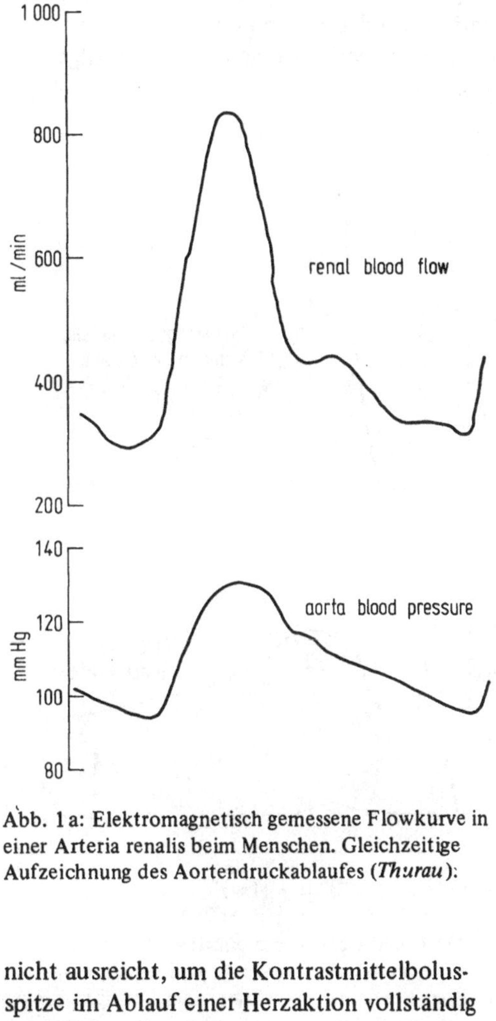

Abb. 1 a: Elektromagnetisch gemessene Flowkurve in einer Arteria renalis beim Menschen. Gleichzeitige Aufzeichnung des Aortendruckablaufes (*Thurau*):

Die Strömungsgeschwindigkeiten, die innerhalb einer Herzaktion – wie sie Abb. 1 a zeigt – während einer bestimmten kurzen Zeitspanne auftreten, unterscheiden sich erheblich. Um diesen Ablauf tatsächlich erfassen zu können, messen wir mit der oben beschriebenen Methode die einzelnen Geschwindigkeiten der Kontrastmittelbolusspitze in jedem Kurventeilstück. Die Strömungsgeschwindigkeiten in den Nierenarterien sind allerdings so groß (bis über 100 cm/sec), daß die Länge der Nierenarterien nicht ausreicht, um die Kontrastmittelbolusspitze im Ablauf einer Herzaktion vollständig zu verfolgen (im Gegensatz zur Femoralarterie, die eine ausreichende Länge aufweist (*Heuck*)). Deswegen ist es notwendig, mit Hilfe der *EKG*-Steuerung der Injektionsmaschine mehrere Kontrastmittelboli in den verschiedenen Herzphasen zu injizieren. Die dabei gemessenen Geschwindigkeiten wurden in einem Koordinatensystem in Beziehung zu ihren *EKG*-Phasen aufgetragen. Die Verbindung dieser Punkte ergab dann die in Abb. 1b gezeichnete Strömungsgeschwindigkeitskurve innerhalb einer Herzphase in einer Nierenhauptarterie, aus der planimetrisch die mittlere Strömungsgeschwindigkeit errechnet wurde. Die Form dieser kinematographisch ermittelten Kurve ist annähernd identisch mit der physiologischen Flowkurve einer Nierenarterie, wie sie in Abb. 1a aufgezeichnet ist.

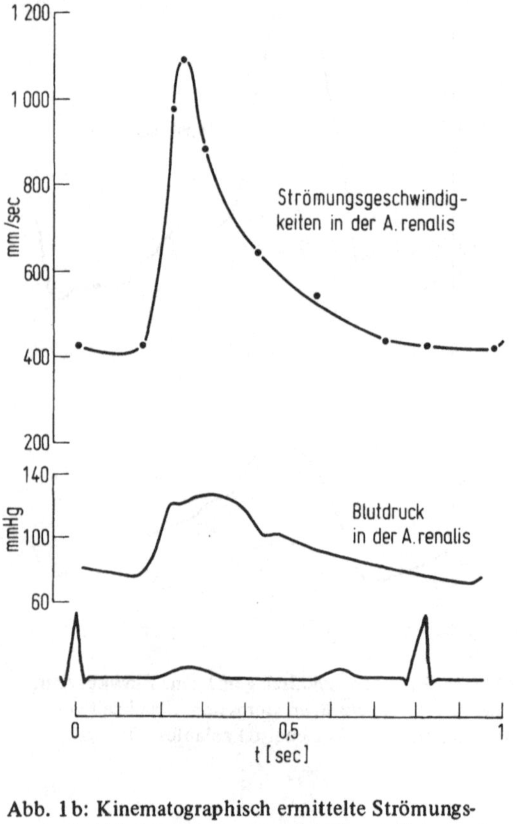

Abb. 1b: Kinematographisch ermittelte Strömungsgeschwindigkeitskurve in einer Arteria renalis in Abhängigkeit von der Herzaktion. Gleichzeitige Druckaufzeichnung in der Arteria renalis.

Mit Hilfe dieser Methode kann somit ermittelt werden:

1. Der Ablauf der Blutströmungsgeschwindigkeit während einer Herzaktion. Diese Messung kann nicht nur in der Nierenhauptarterie, sondern auch in accessorischen und in intrarenalen kleineren Arterien bis zu einem Durchmesser von 1 mm (Abb. 2) erfolgen.

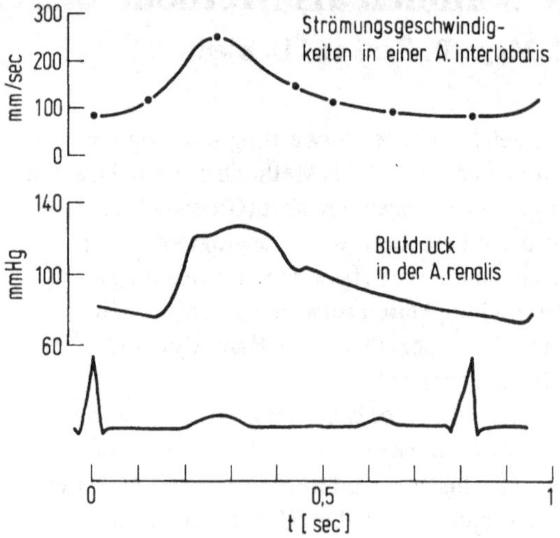

Abb. 2: Kinematographisch ermittelte Strömungsgeschwindigkeitskurve in einer Arteria interlobaris (Durchmesser 1 mm) in Abhängigkeit von der Herzaktion. Gleichzeitige Druckaufzeichnung in der Arteria renalis.

2. Die Durchblutung der Niere als Produkt aus mittlerer Strömungsgeschwindigkeit und Arterienquerschnitt.

Von insgesamt 58 untersuchten Patienten mit normalen und pathologisch veränderten Nieren betrug die Durchblutung bei 25 normalen Nieren durchschnittlich 580 ml/min, bei 12 gefäßreichen Nierenkarzinomen durchschnittlich 830 ml/min und bei 9 Schrumpfnieren durchschnittlich 290 ml/min. Die Durchblutungswerte bei normalen Nieren entsprechen den in der Literatur angegebenen Werten.

Zusammenfassung

Die Methode der zeichnerischen Auswertung angiographischer Kinofilme ermöglicht eine Strömungsanalyse in den Nierenhauptarterien sowie in kleineren Gefäßen bis zu einem Durchmesser von 1 mm. Damit gelingt es, die Organdurchblutung aus mittlerer Strömungsgeschwindigkeit und Gefäßquerschnitt zu ermitteln.

Erfassung dynamischer Vorgänge kombinierter thermographischer und angiographischer Untersuchungen der unteren Extremität

M. Johne und R. Sörensen

Die Thermographie stellt die bildliche Wiedergabe von Oberflächentemperaturen dar. Sie ist eine kontaktlose Temperaturmessung, die auf der Tatsache beruht, daß jeder Körper, dessen Temperatur über der des absoluten Nullpunktes liegt, einen Teil seiner Wärmeenergie in Form von Infrarotstrahlung abgibt. Mit Hilfe eines Indium-Antimonid-Detektors, dessen Leitfähigkeit sich proportional der auftreffenden Infrarotstrahlung ändert, wird die unsichtbare Infrarotstrahlung in ein elektrisches Signal umgesetzt und sichtbar auf einem Leuchtschirm wiedergegeben. Die Dokumentation der Messung erfolgt durch Fotografie des Leuchtschirmbildes.

Untersuchungsgang

Die Patienten wurden bei einer konstant gehaltenen Raumtemperatur von 21°C bei entkleideter unterer Extremität für etwa 10 Minuten auf einen Tisch gelagert. Dann wurden die Thermogramme der Fußsohlen in Rückenlage, daran anschließend die der Unterschenkel im Sitzen und danach die der gesamten unteren Extremität von ventral, dorsal und seitlich im Stehen angefertigt.
Da es sich um ein nicht selektiertes Krankengut handelte, ergaben die Arteriographien nur in einer verschwindend kleinen Anzahl streng einseitige Befunde. In der überwiegenden Mehrzahl der Fälle bestanden in wechselnder Anzahl Stenosen und Verschlüsse sowie generalisierte Gefäßprozesse an einer oder an beiden Extremitäten nebeneinander.

Eigene Beobachtungen

Insgesamt wurden 39 Patienten klinisch, angiographisch und thermographisch untersucht. In 13 Fällen ließ sich angiographisch ein pathologischer Befund vorwiegend rechts, in 15 Fällen vorwiegend links und in 11 Fällen beidseits lokalisieren.
Es sollten die Möglichkeiten und Grenzen der Thermographie als *vororientierende* Untersuchung vor einer Beinarteriographie anhand folgender Fragestellungen überprüft werden:

1. Läßt sich ein angiographischer Befund (Stenose oder Verschluß) anhand einer *umschriebenen* oder *generalisierten* Temperaturerniedrigung über der betroffenen Extremität nachweisen?

2. Besteht eine Korrelation zwischen *klinischen* und *thermographischen* Befunden?

Ergebnisse (Tab. 1)

Eine sehr gute Korrelation zwischen angiographischem und thermographischem Befund zeigte sich in 13 Fällen, eine teilweise Übereinstimmung in weiteren 9 Fällen. Als sehr gute

Tab. 1: Kombinierte thermographisch-angiographische Untersuchungen

	Gesamtzahl der untersuchten Patienten	39
	Angiographischer Befund vorwiegend rechts	13
	Angiographischer Befund vorwiegend links	15
	Angiographischer Befund beidseits	11
I	Klinischer Befund – Thermographischer Befund	
	sehr gute oder gute Übereinstimmung	in 24 von 39 Fällen
	geringe oder keine Übereinstimmung	in 15 von 39 Fällen
II	Angiographischer – Thermographischer Befund	
	sehr gute Übereinstimmung in	13 Fällen
	teilweise Übereinstimmung in	9 Fällen
	regelrechter Befund in	4 Fällen
	scheinbar paradoxer Befund in	6 Fällen
	paradoxer Befund in	7 Fällen

Übereinstimmung wurde angesehen, wenn sich neben einer lokal erniedrigten Oberflächentemperatur am Unter- oder Oberschenkel auch eine relative oder absolute Temperaturerniedrigung in der Peripherie, d. h. über der Fußsohle entsprechend der angiographisch stärker betroffenen Seite nachweisen ließ. Als teilweise Übereinstimmung wurde angesehen, wenn sich die angiographisch festgestellte Einschränkung der Durchblutung als lokale oder periphere Temperaturerniedrigung nachweisen ließ.
In 17 Fällen zeigte sich im Thermogramm keine Erniedrigung der Oberflächentemperaturen. Im Zusammenhang mit dem klinischen Befund konnte geklärt werden, daß in 6 Fällen eine ausgeprägte Varicosis, Hautulzerationen oder Phlebitiden zu einer Überlagerung des thermographischen Befundes geführt hatten, so daß der Nachweis einer Temperaturerniedrigung nicht möglich war.

In 4 Fällen ergab sich ein Befund, der als „unauffällig“ klassifiziert wurde. Er entsprach im Temperaturverlauf an der gesamten unteren Extremität und über der Fußsohle den Befunden, die wir thermographisch bei 20 gesunden jugendlichen Vergleichspersonen gewinnen konnten.

In 7 Fällen ließ sich ein *„paradoxer“* Befund erheben: Angiographisch wurde eine Stenose oder ein Verschluß festgestellt, thermographisch ergaben sich über den Fußsohlen relativ und absolut erhöhte Temperaturen.

Unter alleiniger Berücksichtigung der klinischen Befunde (Varicosis, Ulzerationen, Fußpulse, Einschränkung der Gehstrecke) ergab sich eine Übereinstimmung mit dem thermographischen Befund in 24 der 39 untersuchten Fälle. Das heißt, hier zeigten sich Temperaturerhöhungen und Temperaturerniedrigungen entsprechend dem klinischen Befund. In 15 Fällen ließ sich ein entsprechender klinischer Befund thermographisch nicht feststellen.
Die Vielfalt und die damit auch verbundene Vieldeutigkeit der Thermogramme soll an 2 Fällen demonstriert werden.
In den hier gezeigten Farbthermogrammen entsprechen die wärmeren Regionen den Farben am rechten Skalenende, also rot und gelb. Die Farben am linken Skalenende, hellblau und dunkelblau, symbolisieren kältere Regionen. Den einzelnen Farbsprüngen entsprechen Temperatursprünge von jeweils 1 oder 2°C. Eine Umrechnung der relativen Temperaturdifferenzen in absolute Temperaturdifferenzen ist mit Hilfe des gleichzeitig mit dargestellten Referenzstrahlers möglich.

Fall I

Klinischer Befund: Zustand nach Varizenoperation beidseits, abgeheiltes Ulcus am rechten Unterschenkel.
Angiographischer Befund: Generalisierter degenerativer Gefäßprozeß mit Verschluß der linken Femoralis superficialis, peripheres Anschlußsegment Tibialis posterior.

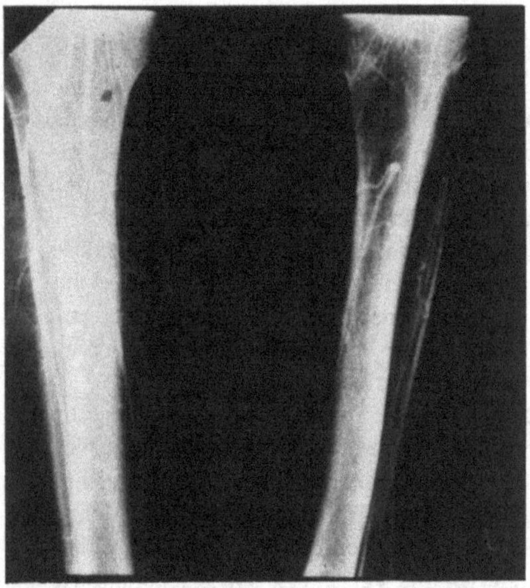

Abb. 1

Thermographischer Befund: Keine erniedrigten Temperaturen im Bereich des linken Unterschenkels, vielmehr sind die Temperaturen über dem Fußrücken und den Zehen rechts erniedrigt.

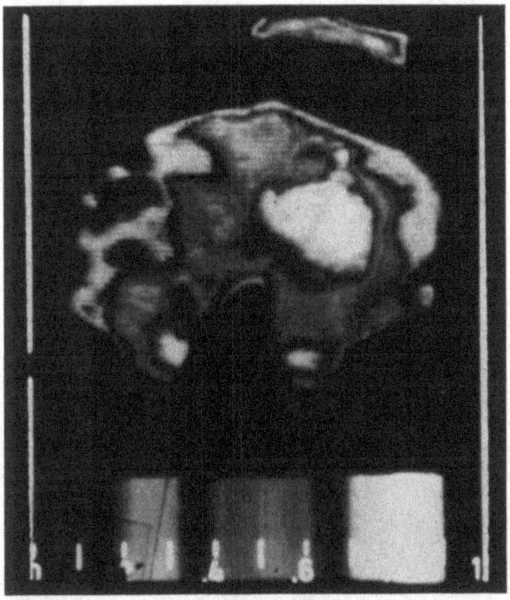

Abb. 2

Die rechtsseitig im Bereich des Oberschenkels stark ausgeprägte Varicosis kommt im dorsalen Übersichtsbild als rechtsseitige Temperaturerhöhung in diesem Bereich zur Darstellung.

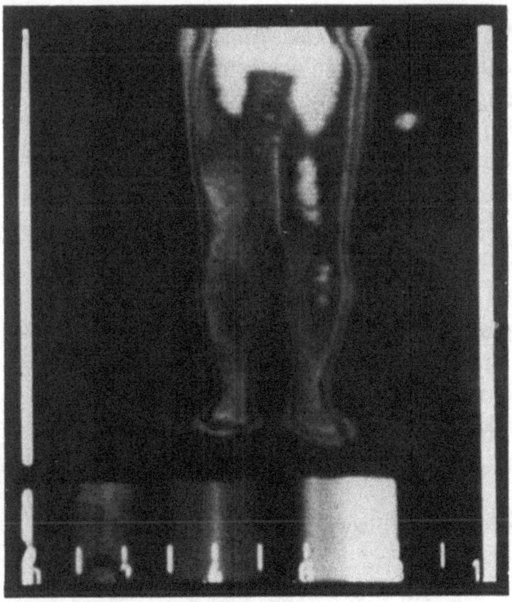

Abb. 3

Bei unauffälligem angiographischen rechtsseitigen Befund zeigen sich im Zusammenhang mit dem abgeheilten Ulcus am rechten Unterschenkel verringerte Temperaturen über der rechten Fußspitze.
Die auch am linken Bein vorhandene Varicosis läßt den thermographischen Nachweis von linksseitig verminderten Temperaturen entsprechend dem angiographischen Befund nicht zu. Aufgrund der Rekanalisierung kann eine ausreichende Versorgung des distalen linken Unterschenkels angenommen werden. Die thermographischen Befunde zeigen jedoch über der Fußsohle eine deutliche Temperaturerhöhung als Zeichen einer eingeschränkten Durchblutung.

Fall II

Klinischer Befund: Ruheschmerz im Bereich der linken Wade. Livide Verfärbung des linken Fußes. Diabetische Gangrän der 1.–3. Zehe links.
Arteriographischer Befund: Nierenarterienstenose rechts, erhebliche arterio-sklerotische Veränderungen in der abdominalen Aorta sowie in den Iliacae communes und externae.

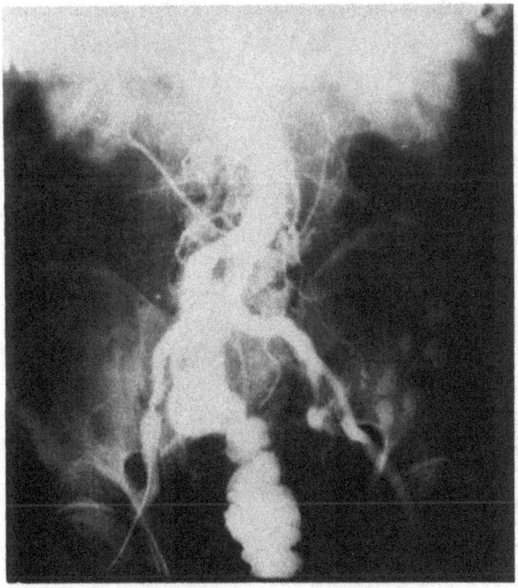

Abb. 4

Stenose der Femoralis communis rechts, Stenose der Tibialis anterior rechts.

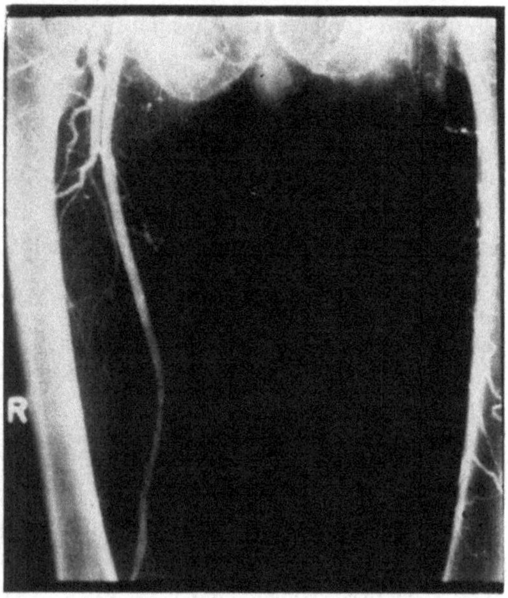

Abb. 5

Verschluß der Femoralis superficialis links an ihrer Teilungsstelle mit der A. femoralis profunda. Die distalen Gefäße sind bis in die Peripherie hin beidseits dargestellt.

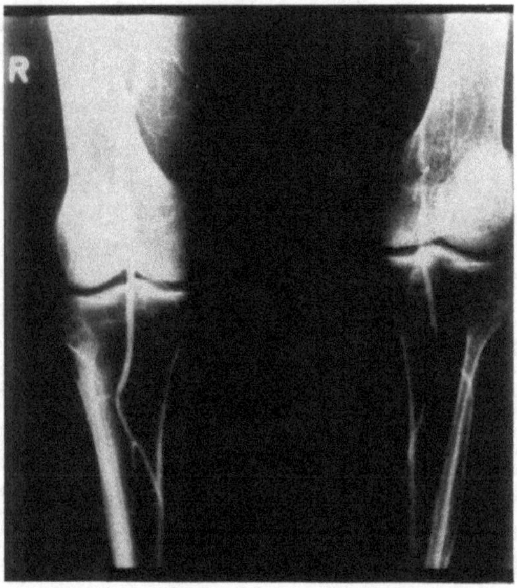

Abb. 6

Thermographischer Befund: Entsprechend dem angiographischen Befund läßt sich hier thermographisch die deutliche Durchblutungsminderung der linken unteren Extremität nachweisen.

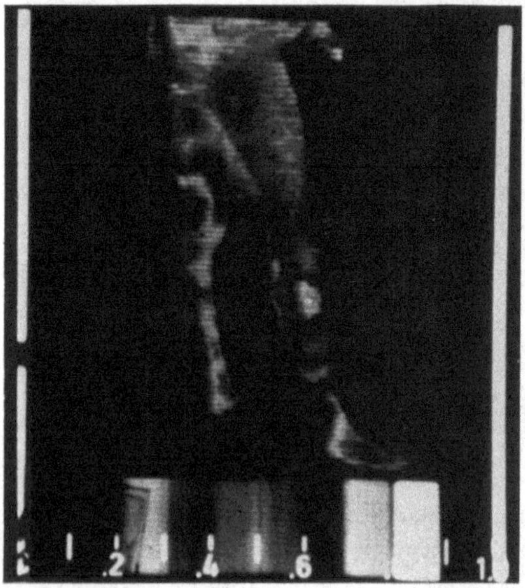

Abb. 7

Während in dem gleichzeitig angefertigten Infrarotfoto die Gangrän der 2. und 3. Zehe links dargestellt ist, zeigt das Thermogramm den diffusen Befall *aller* Zehen links sowie zusätzlich die deutliche Temperaturerniedrigung über der Großzehe rechts.
Daneben besteht eine nahezu symmetrische Temperaturerhöhung über beiden Fußsohlen.

Die anhand der Thermographie zu treffende Aussage lautet: Neben der bereits bestehenden Gangrän der 3 ersten Zehen links ist ein Fortschreiten des Befundes auf die Zehen 4 und 5 links sowie 1 rechts zu erwarten.

Schlußfolgerungen

Trotz der geringen Anzahl der untersuchten Fälle erscheinen folgende Aussagen möglich:

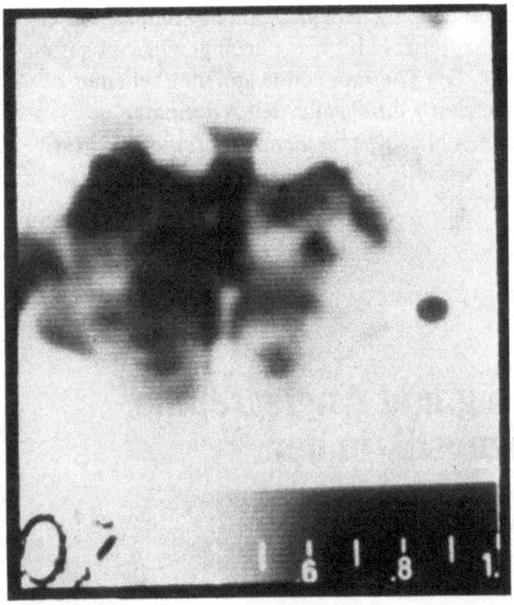

Abb. 8

1. Das thermographische Bild liefert eine *Vielzahl* von Informationen (Fall I), wobei oft oberflächennahe venöse und entzündliche Prozesse den Befund entscheidend beeinflussen. Bei angiographisch nahezu symmetrischen pathologischen Prozessen zeigt die Thermographie oft bei Übereinstimmung mit dem klinischen Befund eine eindeutige Seitenbevorzugung. Bei angiographisch überwiegend einseitig lokalisierten pathologischen Prozessen läßt sich manchmal anhand der Thermographie eine zusätzliche Information über die Gegenseite gewinnen (Fall II).

2. Eine genaue topographische Lokalisation des Verschlusses oder eine sichere graduelle Korrelation zur Schwere des stenosierenden Prozesses ist nicht immer möglich. Entzündliche oder atrophische Prozesse, die weit in der Peripherie gelegen sind und zu denen anhand der Angiographie eine Aussage nur schwierig möglich ist, werden bei einer thermographischen Untersuchung der unteren Extremität sehr genau erfaßt und lassen sich klar einordnen.

3. Die erniedrigten Temperaturen über dem abgeheilten Ulcus am rechten Unterschenkel (Fall I) gestatten anhand der Thermographie den Nachweis eines atrophischen Prozesses und erlauben den Ausschluß einer entzündlichen Reaktion.

4. Die unserer Meinung nach interessanteste Beobachtung stellen 7 als „paradox" klassifizierte Befunde dar: Angiographisch zeigte sich ein stenosierender Gefäßprozeß, thermographisch ergaben sich relative und absolute Erhöhungen der Oberflächentemperaturen über den Fußsohlen. Dieser Befund zeigte sich vorwiegend bei inkompletten Gefäßverschlüssen oder Verschlüssen, bei denen eine Rekanalisation angiographisch nachgewiesen wurde. Er ließ sich nicht bei massiven akuten kompletten Verschlüssen nachweisen. Unter der Annahme, daß der angiographische Befund die Durchblutung der tiefen Gewebsschichten widerspiegelt und der thermographische Befund die Durchblutung des subkutanen Gewebes, erscheint die Annahme gerechtfertigt, daß Muskel- und Hautdurchblutung sich gegenläufig verhalten. Ob dieser Mechanismus im Sinne eines „Umgehungskreislaufes" interpretiert werden kann oder ob er auf eine Vasodilatation infolge einer Sympathikuswirkung zurückgeführt werden muß, muß anhand von zusätzlichen Untersuchungen entschieden werden. Ebenso ist es nicht möglich, anhand der wenigen Fälle prognostische Rückschlüsse aus dem Fehlen oder Vorliegen eines solchen Mechanismus zu ziehen.

Zusammenfassung

Bei 39 Patienten wurden eine Arteriographie sowie eine Thermographie nach einem Standardprogramm durchgeführt. Neben einer Vielfalt von Informationen, wie sie sonst nur durch gleichzeitige angiographische, phlebographische und klinische Untersuchungen erhalten werden, liefert das Thermogramm der unteren Extremität auch die Vieldeutigkeit eines solchen Befundes. Dabei überlagern sich oft oberflächennahe temperaturerhöhend wirkende Vorgänge und tiefergelegene temperaturerniedrigend wirkende Prozesse. Interessanterweise wurden bei angiographisch nachgewiesener eingeschränkter Durchblutung der tiefen Gewebsschichten thermographisch erhöhte Hauttemperaturen festgestellt. Die ersten Ergebnisse zeigen, daß die Vereinfachung „angiographisch Stenose – thermographisch kalt" nicht uneingeschränkt gelten kann. Die Thermographie eröffnet bei einer gleichzeitig durchgeführten Arteriographie daher vielleicht eine mehr funktionelle Betrachtungsweise.

Die Korrelation von Druckmessung und Angiographie als Beitrag zur funktionellen Diagnostik in der Röntgenologie

A. Grüntzig, J. Wellauer und W. Wirth

In der Diagnostik arterieller Gefäßkrankheiten ist die Angiographie inzwischen unentbehrlich geworden.
Die Darstellung der Gefäßmorphologie mit Kontrastmittel erlaubt jedoch keine Schlüsse auf die funktionelle Wirksamkeit der dargestellten Stenosen und Kollateralgefäße.
Die Ergänzung der Angiographie durch simultane prä- und poststenotische Druckmessung eröffnet nun für den Röntgenologen die Möglichkeit, dem einweisenden Arzt neben dem Gefäßbild auch einen Hinweis auf das aktuelle, entlang der Stenosen auftretende Druckgefälle zu liefern.
Die Druckmessung wird am liegenden Patienten direkt vor der Kontrastmittelinjektion ausgeführt und ist der Blutdruckmessung nach *Riva-Rocci* ähnlich.
Die parallel geschaltenen Druckmanschetten werden am Arm und Knöchel des betroffenen Beines angelegt (Abb. 1). Das Stethoskop wird durch Ultraschall-Transducer (Arteriosonde, Hoffmann-La Roche AG; Doppler-Ultraschall-Gerät, Modell 802, Parks Electronics Lab., Beaverton, Or.) oder Oszillographen (Zweikanal-Simultan-Pulsorette, Fa. Rose KG, Trier) ersetzt.

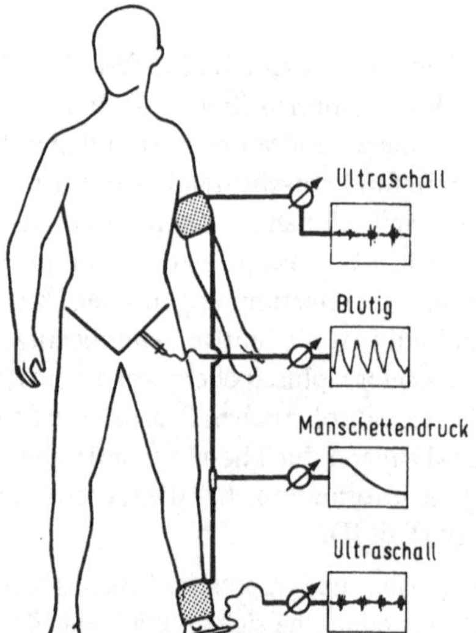

Abb. 1: Die Druckmessung am Arm (Arteriosonde) und Knöchel (Doppler-Ultraschall-Gerät) erfolgt durch simultanes Ablassen des suprasystolischen Druckes in den parallel geschalteten Manschetten. Wenn am Arm und Knöchel die ersten pulssynchronen Signale auftreten, so lassen sich die systolischen Drucke über den gleichzeitig mitregistrierten Manschettendruck ablesen. Der systolische und diastolische Druck in der A. femoralis wird blutig gemessen.

Neben dieser indirekten Blutdruckmessung wird über die bereits liegende Seldinger Nadel in der a. femoralis comm. oder über einen Katheter in der Aorta der Druck blutig registriert (*LVDT* Pressure Transducer, Biotronex Lab., Silver Spring, Md.). Die einzelnen Meßwerte werden über einen Mehrfach-EKG-Schreiber (Minograf, Elema-Schönander, Stockholm) zusammengefaßt.

Die indirekte Blutdruckmessung am Arm und Knöchel erfolgt, indem die Luft aus den anfangs suprasystolisch aufgeblasenen Manschetten abgelassen wird und beim ersten Auftreten pulssynchroner Strömungssignale der Druck am Manometer abgelesen oder – wie in Abb. 2 – über den Manschettendruck (Druckwandler EMT 34, Elema-Schönander, Stockholm) errechnet wird.

Die Übereinstimmung der Resultate dieser indirekten Blutdruckmessung an Arm und Knöchel mit der direkten blutigen Messung des Druckes in diesen Gefäßen wird als gut bezeichnet. Das trifft auch für die poststenotisch niedrigen Drucke in den Knöchelarterien zu. Allerdings kann man in diesen Arterien mit den genannten Methoden nur den systolischen Druck bestimmen.

Dieser ist jedoch von den bekannten Druck- und Durchflußgrößen für unsere Zwecke der geeignete, da er auf hämodynamisch bedeutsame Stenosen unter Ruhebedingungen als erster reagiert.

Von Gefäßgesunden weiß man, daß der systolische Druck in den größeren Arterien peripherwärts eher zunimmt, d. h. daß der systolische Druck in den Knöchelarterien höher oder zumindest gleich dem Druck in der a. femoralis oder a. brachialis ist. Das bestätigte sich auch bei unseren Messungen. So ergab sich z. B. bei Pat. W. A. (Abb. 2, 3) in der a. femoralis ein um 35 mm Hg höherer Druck als in der a. brachialis.

Wird also zwischen Arm und Leiste oder zwischen Leiste und Knöchel ein Druckabfall registriert, so sind Stenosen oder Verschlüsse zwischen diesen Meßpunkten anzunehmen. Ihre Lokalisation und Morphologie wird durch die anschließende Angiographie dargestellt. Im Falle des oben erwähnten Patienten wurde ein

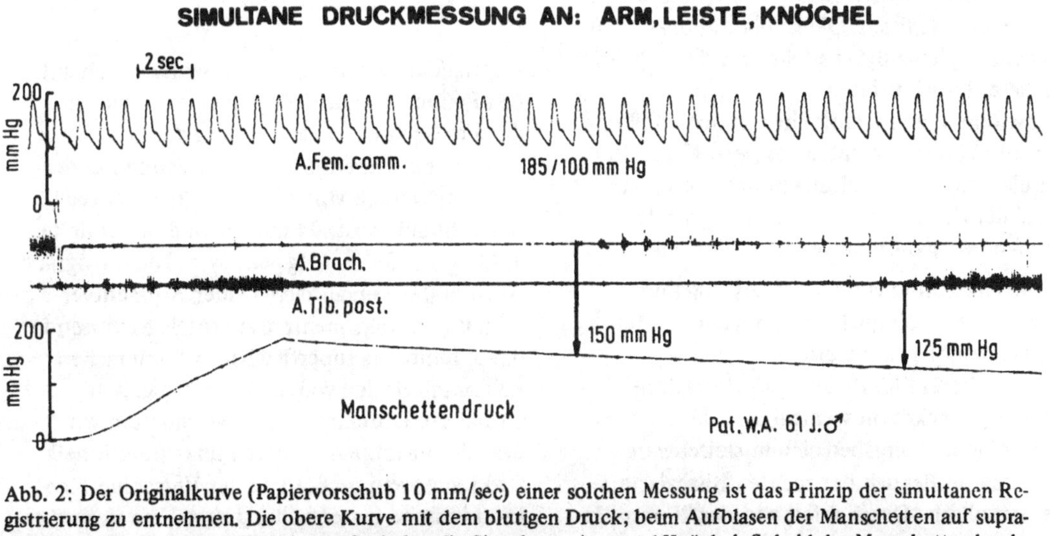

Abb. 2: Der Originalkurve (Papiervorschub 10 mm/sec) einer solchen Messung ist das Prinzip der simultanen Registrierung zu entnehmen. Die obere Kurve mit dem blutigen Druck; beim Aufblasen der Manschetten auf suprasystolische Werte (untere Kurve) verschwinden die Signale am Arm und Knöchel. Sobald der Manschettendruck auf 150 mmHg abfällt, treten pulssynchrone Signale über der a. brachialis, bei 125 mmHg über der a. tibialis post. auf. Die Druckmessung ergibt also folgende Drucke: Arm 150 mmHg, Knöchel 125 mmHg (beides systolisch) und Leiste 185/100 mmHg. Der systolische Druckabfall von 60 mmHg ist durch die Implantation eines Saphena-Bypass nach Aneurysmaresektion verursacht, dessen Nahtstellen röntgenologisch einwandfrei zur Darstellung kamen (Abb. 3).

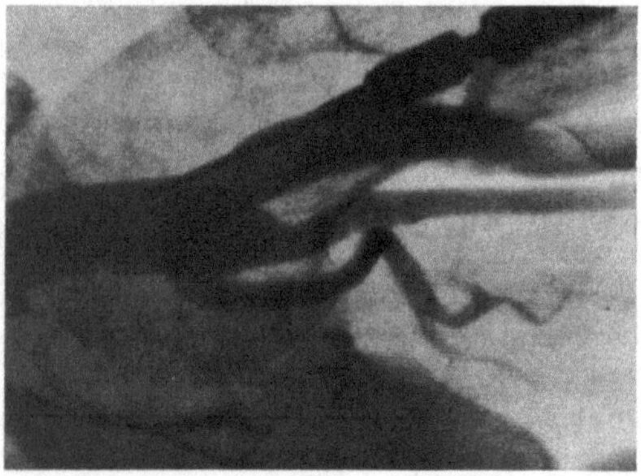

Abb. 3: Bei diesem 61j. Patient wurde ein Aneurysma der linken distalen a. femoralis superfic. und a. poplitea reseziert* und durch einen Saphena-Bypass vom Beginn der a. femoralis superfic. bis zur Unterschenkel-Trifurkation ersetzt. Proximale (Abb.) und distale Insertionsstellen mit geringen Kontrastmittelaufhellungen jedoch ohne eindeutige Stenosen. In Saphena-Mitte Venenklappenkontur; das Angiogramm wurde am 10. postoperativen Tag angefertigt.

* PD Dr. U. Brunner, Chirurgische Klinik B der Universität Zürich.

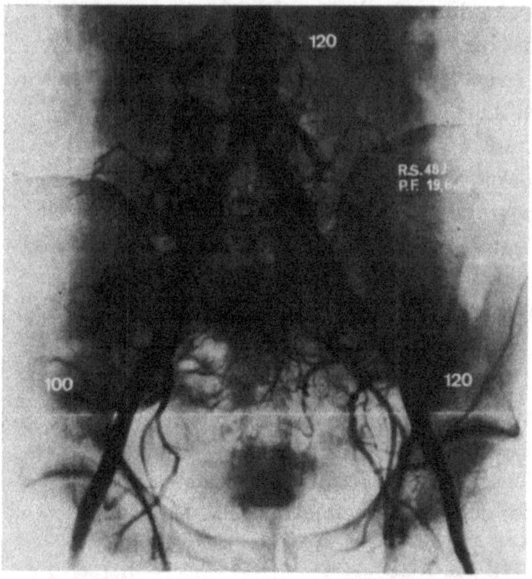

Abb. 4: Aortogramm mit leistenförmigen arteriosklerotischen Plaques direkt nach Abgang der rechten a. iliaca und leichten Stenosierungen vor der Aufteilung in die iliaca externa und interna, bei arteriosklerotischen Wandveränderungen auch links. Der systolische Druck in der Aorta 120 mmHg, rechte a. femoralis 100 mmHg, linke a. femoralis 120 mmHg. Darstellung eines beginnenden Kollateralkreislaufes rechts.

Druckabfall zwischen Leiste und Knöchel von 60 mm Hg gemessen. Die Implantationsstellen und der Saphena-Bypass führten offensichtlich zu dieser Druckdifferenz.
Da zwischen dem systolischen Druckabfall und der Durchblutungsreserve des betroffenen Beines eine direkte Beziehung besteht, kann an Hand der Druckwerte der Schweregrad der Durchblutungsstörung geschätzt werden.

Die Kombination von Druckmessung und Angiographie soll noch an drei weiteren Beispielen demonstriert werden:
Abb. 4: Dieser 48j. Patient gab eine schmerzfreie Wegstrecke von weniger als 200 m an. Angiographisch ergaben sich mittelschwere Stenosen im Bereich der rechten Illiacalarterie. Der systolische Druckabfall von nur 20 mm Hg zwischen Aorta und a. femoralis wies jedoch daraufhin, daß die funktionelle Wirksamkeit dieser Stenosen nicht sehr ausgeprägt sein konnte. Das stand im Gegensatz zu der relativ kurzen Gehstrecke. Weitere angiologische Untersuchungen deckten den Widerspruch auf. Der Patient litt zusätzlich an einer Ischialgie, die die Claudicatio verschlimmerte.
Abb. 5: Bei diesem 66j. Patient wurden in der Aorta ein Druck von 125 mm Hg, in der rechten a. tibialis post. 94 mm Hg und in der linken a. tib. post. 88 mm Hg gemessen. Die retrograde Aortographie ergab rechts einen Segmentverschluß und links mehrere subtotale Stenosen in der a. femoralis superficialis. Die Unterschenkelstammarterien waren durchgängig. Auf Grund der Druckmessungen vermuteten wir, daß die subtotalen Stenosen links funktionell wirksamer sein mußten als der Verschluß rechts. Die klinische Untersuchung bestätigte unseren Befund: nach 334 m (Laufband 3,2 km/h, 12,5 % Steigung) traten in der linken Wade Claudicationsschmerzen auf, rechts dagegen nicht. Entsprechend wurde im Reflexogramm des *ASR* nur links eine Verlängerung der Rela-

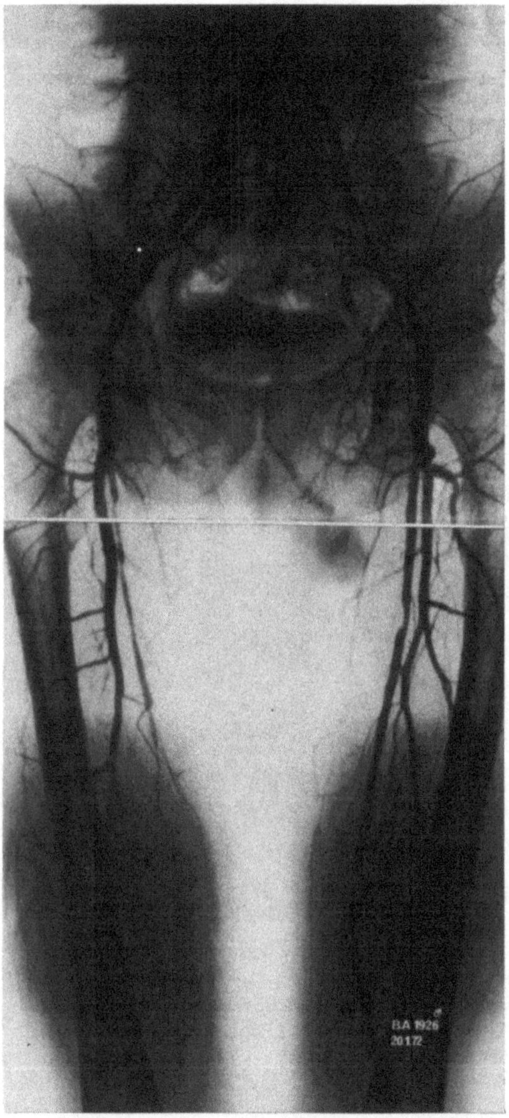

Abb. 5: Aortogramm mit Stenosierungen und einem Totalverschluß in der rechten a. femoralis superfic. mit kräftigen Kollateralen über die a. femoris profunda. Links mehrere subtotale Stenosierungen in der a. femoralis superfic., beginnende Kollateralisation über die a. femoris prof. Der systolische Druck in der Aorta 125 mmHg, a. tib. post. rechts 94 mmHg, links 88 mmHg. Die a. poplitea und die Unterschenkelstammgefäße frei durchgängig. Trotz des Totalverschlusses rechts ein höherer Druck in der Peripherie. Die Claudicationsbeschwerden links wurden erst seit einigen Wochen vom Pat. bemerkt. Zuvor litt er an Claudicationsbeschwerden rechts, die bis zum Ereignis links, nach ca. 700 m auftraten.

xationsphase (*TRT*) und zwar um 45% beobachtet.

Abb. 6: Dieser 66j. wurde vor vier Jahren endarterektomiert. Trotz des röntgenologischen Aspektes teils stenosierender, teils aneurysmatischer Wandveränderungen konnte kein systolischer Druckabfall festgestellt werden. Die funktionelle Leistungsfähigkeit mußte somit recht gut sein.

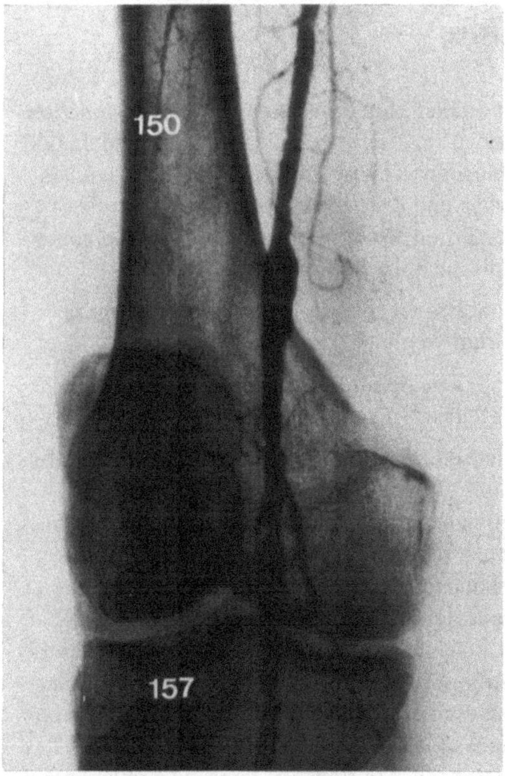

Abb. 6: Status nach Endarterektomie der a. femoralis superfic. und poplitea vor vier Jahren. Anhaltender Operationserfolg ohne Druckabfall in der Peripherie. Röntgenologisch stenosierende und aneurysmatische arteriosklerotische Wandveränderungen. (Patient M. W., 65 Jahre, Ausschnitt aus der Femoralisangiographie, die übrigen Gefäßabschnitte weitgehend unauffällig.)

Wie diese Beispiele gezeigt haben, ergeben sich aus der Kombination von Gefäßbild und Druck wertvolle Hinweise auf die Hämodynamik der dargestellten Strombahnhindernisse.

Dadurch wird die durch funktionelle Angaben ergänzte Angiographie zu einer noch besseren Entscheidungshilfe und Therapiekontrolle für den Angiologen und Gefäßchirurgen.

Den Herren PD Dr. *A. Bollinger*, Dr. *F. Buholzer* und Prof. Dr. *W. Rutishauser* von der Poliklinik des Departementes für Innere Medizin der Universität Zürich sei für Ihre stets freundliche Beratung und praktische Unterstützung unserer Arbeit sehr herzlich gedankt.

Phleboskopische Strömungskontrolle

R. Nißl

Es sei hier kurz über unsere Erfahrung berichtet, die wir im Laufe von 20 Jahren bei rund 15 000 phleboskopischen Untersuchungen gesammelt haben und die sich als Strömungskontrolle bewährten. Was soll uns eine phlebographische Untersuchung für Ergebnisse bringen?

1. Sollen die morphologischen Verhältnisse geklärt werden?

2. Sollen die Strömungsverhältnisse und die Abflußzeiten aufgezeigt werden?

Hier soll nun Punkt 2 – die Strömungsverhältnisse – kurz besprochen werden.
Wir haben sämtliche phlebographischen Methoden durchprobiert und sind zu dem Ergebnis gekommen, daß eine richtige Strömungskontrolle nur durch die phleboskopische Untersuchung möglich ist. Ausschlaggebend ist für die venöse Zirkulation die Beschaffenheit der Klappen des tiefen Venensystems und die Funktion der Wadenmuskelpumpe, sowie der Zustand des oberflächlichen Venensystems. Alle phlebographischen Untersuchungen funktionieren recht gut beim normalen tiefen Venensystem. Anders wird aber die Sache beim postthrombotischen Zustandsbild. Hier ist das Bildmaterial bei blindgeschossenen Aufnahmen zum größten Teil recht unbefriedigend und die Aussagen über die Strömungsverhältnisse werden problematisch. Diese Nachteile haben uns zur Phleboskopie mit gezielten Aufnahmen gebracht. Es soll hier nicht mehr auf die Durchführungsdetails eingegangen werden, da diese zur Genüge bekannt sind. Die Methode ist einfach und gibt uns Aufschlüsse sowohl über die Klappenfunktion und die Strömungsverhältnisse, als auch über die Funktion der Wadenmuskelpumpe (Abb. 1). Bei der Klappeninsuffizienz sinkt die

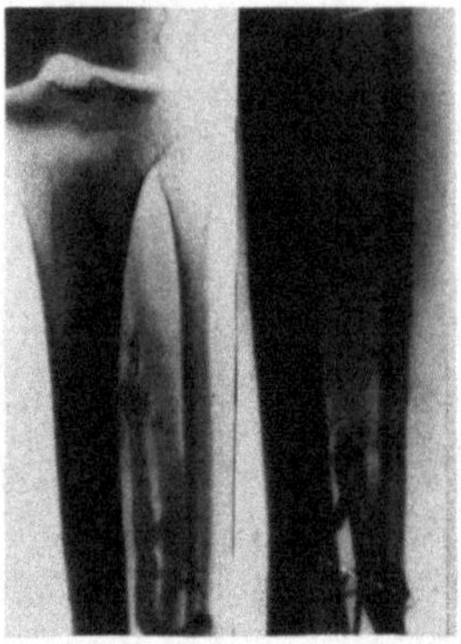

Abb. 1: Phleboskopische Überprüfung der Klappen.
Bild links: Druck auf den Knöchel. Das Kontrastmittel steigt in den tiefen Unterschenkelvenen.
Bild rechts: Wegnahme des Drucks. Das Kontrastmittel sinkt nach distal hin ab; die Klappen sind insuffizient.

durch Massage hinaufgepumpte Kontrastmittelsäule wieder nach distal ab. Bei der suffizienten Klappe bleibt das Kontrastmittel in den Klappen hängen, und man bekommt das typische Bild der Klappengrenze. Wenn man zusätzlich den Patienten kurz pressen läßt, stellen sich die tiefen Klappen besonders gut dar und es kann ihre Schlußfähigkeit beurteilt werden, ohne daß eine spezielle Pressphlebographie ausgeführt werden muß. Weiter können die Strömungsverhältnisse beurteilt werden, welches der beiden

Venensysteme, das oberflächliche oder das tiefe Venensystem den Hauptabfluß des venösen Blutes übernimmt (Abb. 2). Beim postthrom-

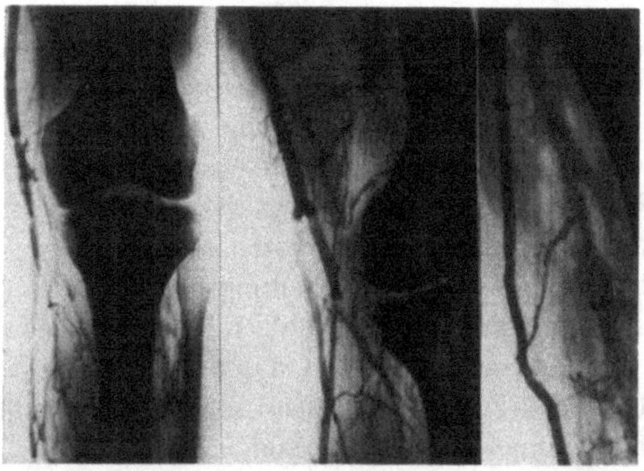

Abb. 2: Funktionsbild beim postthrombotischen Syndrom. Postthrombotischer Schaden des tiefen Venensystems vom Stadium 3. Das tiefe Venensystem nur schwach angefärbt. Hauptabfluß durch oberflächen Kollateralkreislauf I. Ordnung – Vena saphena magna. Diese stark angefärbt.

botischen Syndrom kann gerade dies den Ausschlag geben, ob am oberflächlichen Venensystem Veränderungen operativ angegangen werden dürfen oder nicht. Bei der Beurteilung der Abflußzeit begnügen wir uns meist im groben mit folgender Einteilung, wobei als normale Abflußzeit ca 25 bis 30 Sekunden gelten.

1. Zu rascher Abfluß; dies beobachtet man bei ausgedehnten, sehr frischen Thrombosen des tiefen Venensystems im frühesten Stadium.

2. Normale Abflußzeit, bei normalem tiefen Venensystem.

3. Leicht verzögerte Abflußzeit, z. B. bei Klappeninsuffizienz, wie sie bei übergewichtigen Patienten meist zu sehen ist.

4. Stark verzögerte Abflußzeit, durch Hängenbleiben des Kontrastmittels in den tiefen Beinpartien beim postthrombotischen Syndrom.

Ferner erlaubt uns die Phlebographie eine Beurteilung der Strömungsverhältnisse der Wadenvenen sowie die Feststellung ihrer Suffizienz oder Insuffizienz. Weiter sieht man bei der Phlebographie auch die Strömungsverhältnisse in den Venae perforantes. Auch ist es mit der phleboskopischen Untersuchung möglich, bei Kontrolluntersuchungen nach operativen Eingriffen am Venensystem, wie z. B. bei der Operation nach Palma eine Beurteilung des Operationserfolges zu geben (Abb. 3).

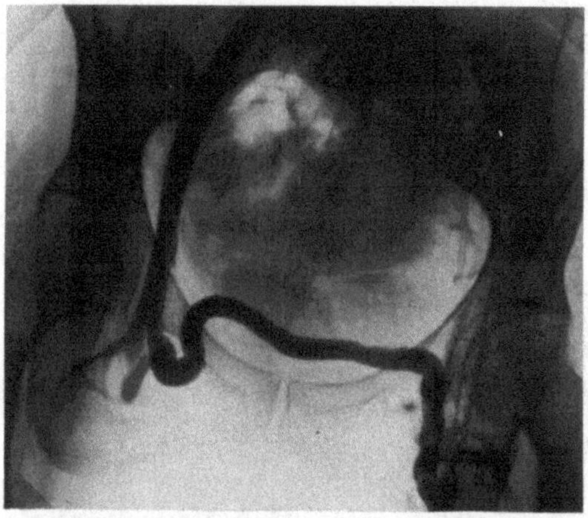

Abb. 3: Abflußkontrolle nach Palma-Operation, bei abgelaufener Thrombose der Beckenvenen links. Hauptabfluß durch Anastomose auf die rechte Seite.

Die Phleboskopie scheint uns aus dem Gebrachten daher derzeit die beste Methode röntgenologisch die Strömung zu überwachen.

Radiokardiographie mit Gamma-Kamera und Datenverarbeitungsgerät

E. Tähti, T. Heiskanen und J. Peräsalo

Die Untersuchungen wurden mit einer Gamma-Kamera und daran angeschlossenem Vielkanalanalysator sowie magnetischer Bandspeicherung durchgeführt. Als radioaktiver Indikator wurde 113 m Indium verwendet, dessen Halbwertzeit 100 Minuten beträgt. 10 mCi wurden als Bolus in eine Kubitalvene injiziert. Normalerweise haben wir die Messungen so durchgeführt, daß sich die Gamma-Kamera über dem Patienten befand. Alle Informationen werden auf Magnetband gespeist, dessen Kapazität vier Bilder pro Sekunde beträgt. Auf dem Oszilloskop des Analysators kann später der Kreislauf des Isotops über das Herz in den kleinen Kreislauf und zurück in die linke Herzhälfte beobachtet werden (Abb. 1).

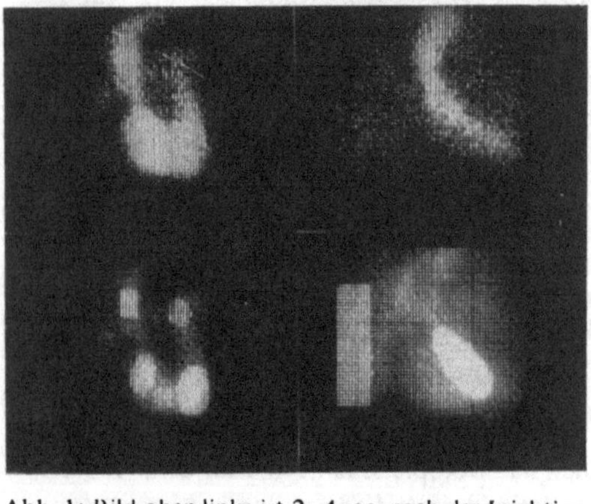

Abb. 1: Bild oben links ist 2–4 sec. nach der Injektion aufgenommen und Bild oben rechts 8–10 sec. Die unteren Bilder zeigen die abgegrenzten interessanten Areale.

Der Vielkanalanalysator hat 4000 Bildelemente. Auf der Bildröhre des Oszilloskops können mit einem Leuchtstift vier interessante Areale abgegrenzt werden, von denen die Zeitaktivitätskurven des Isotops ermittelt werden. Diese Zeitaktivitätskurven können numerisch ausgewertet werden und die Ergebnisse einer größeren Datenverarbeitungsmaschine zugeführt werden. In diesem Fall handelt es sich um einen Univac 1108 Computer, der sich vier Kilometer entfernt in einem Datenverarbeitungszentrum befindet. Die Datenverarbeitungsmaschine ist so programmiert, daß in einigen Sekunden die Volumina der Herzhöhlen, das Verhältnis von Pulmonal- zu Systemkreislauf sowie das Gesamtblutvolumen gemessen werden können.

Abb. 2 zeigt die Radiogrammkurven eines normalen Patienten. Hier die Mittelwerte für Herzhöhlenvolumina von sieben normalen Patienten:

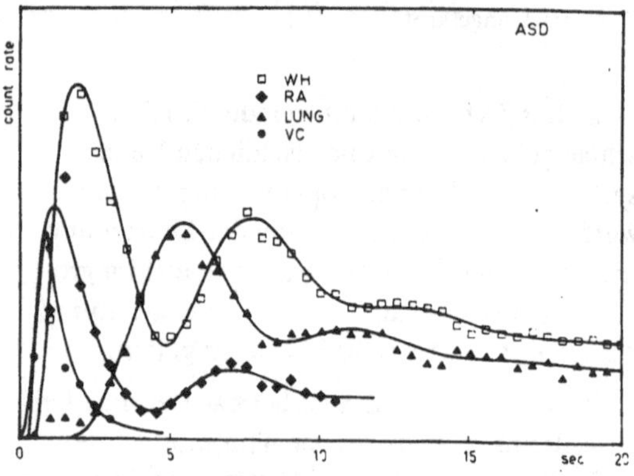

Abb. 2: Die Radiokardiographiekurven eines normalen Patienten.

Herzhöhlen- und Pulmonalblutvolumen bei 7 normalen Patienten.

	Mittelwert	S. D.
Rechter Vorhof	85 ml	28
Rechte Kammer	112 ml	28
Lungen	368 ml	35
Linkes Herz	254 ml	58

Auf dem nächsten Bild die Radiokardiographiekurven eines Patienten mit Vorhofseptumdefekt (Abb. 3).

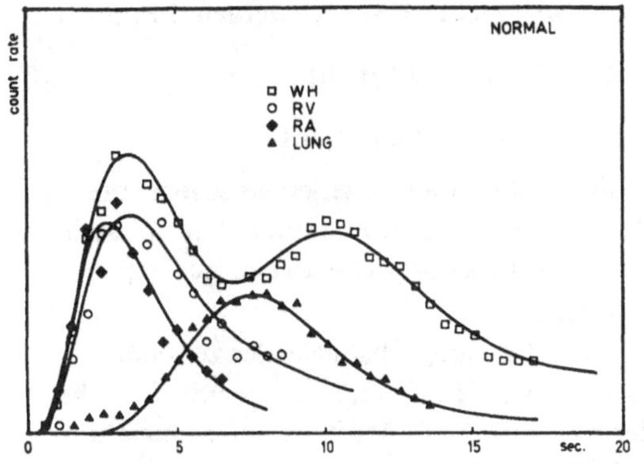

Abb. 3: Die Radiokardiographiekurven eines Patienten mit Vorhofseptumdefekt.

Herz- und Pulmonalblutvolumen bei 2 Patienten mit Links-rechts-Shunt (*ASD*).

	RV	RK	Lungen	LV und LK
Pat. 8	125	198	615	280
Pat. 9	113	125	334	180

Wir haben den Eindruck gewonnen, daß die Radiokardiographie bei kardiovasculären Erkrankungen als präliminäres Auslese-Verfahren von Bedeutung ist. Zusätzlich zur visuellen Information können die erwähnten Volumina quantitativ bestimmt werden. In dieser Hinsicht hat die Methode ihren Wert bei der Auswahl der Patienten für größere angiokardiographische Untersuchungen.

Kombinierte angiographische und szintigraphische Untersuchung zur Erfassung der zerebralen Hämodynamik

E. Ogris, F. Olbert und H. Denck

Zur Messung von cerebralen Durchblutungsveränderungen können verschiedenste Meßgrößen herangezogen werden. Die gebräuchlichsten davon sind die Angabe der Durchblutung pro Volumseinheit Gewebe, die Angabe von Zirkulationszeiten im weitesten Sinn sowie Größen des Sauerstoffmetabolismus. Untersuchungen der regionalen Hirndurchblutung werden praktisch immer mit sogenannten frei diffusiblen Tracern ausgeführt. Unsere Untersuchung befaßt sich mit den Aussagen, die in dieser Fragestellung durch Verwendung nicht diffusibler Tracer verbunden mit externer Messung gemacht werden können.

Methodik

Als Methode diente die Funktionsszintigraphie nach intravenöser oder wahlweise intraarterieller Injektion von ^{99m}Tc-Pertechnetat.

Die intraarterielle Injektion erfolgte vom Aortenbogen aus im Anschluß an die angiographische Untersuchung der großen extracraniellen Gefäße. Die Untersuchungen wurden mit Hilfe einer Szintillationskamera in Verbindung mit einem 4096-Kanalkernspeicher und einem sogenannten Data-Storage-Play-Back-System ausgeführt. Die gleichzeitig über verschiedenen, frei wählbaren Regions of Interest (*ROI*) erhaltenen Zeit-Aktivitätskurven wurden im sogenannten Time-Multiplex-Verfahren in den Vielkanalkernspeicher mit einer, der Geschwindigkeit des registrierten dynamischen Vorganges entsprechend gewählten Zeitkonstante eingespeichert, wo sie ausgewertet und von dessen Oszilloskopschirm sie photographiert wurden.
Bei unseren Untersuchungen wurden als ROIs die beiden Hemisphären in Frontalprojektion ausgewählt, um ihre jeweilige Durchblutung miteinander vergleichen zu können.
40 Patienten wurden auf diese Weise kombiniert

angiographisch sowie mittels der Funktionsszintigraphie untersucht. Um Aufschluß über die Verdünnung des als Bolus injizierten radioaktiven Tracers durch das vorangeschaltete zentrale Blutvolumen zu erhalten und dessen Einfluß auf das Untersuchungsergebnis abschätzen zu können, wurde die Perfusionsangioszintigraphie mit ^{99m}Tc-Pertechnetat bei vier Patienten nicht nur intravenös, sondern auch vom Aortenbogen aus intraarteriell durchgeführt. Dabei wurde als repräsentative Kreislaufzeit des extracraniellen Gefäßabschnittes die Erscheinungszeit (*Ta*) des Tracers vom Aortenbogen bis zu dessen Eintreffen im Syphon der A. carot. int. bestimmt und mit der serienangiographisch ermittelten Zeit verglichen. Auch wurden die einzelnen Phasen der Perfusionsangioszintigraphie mit den korrespondierenden Bildphasen der angiographischen Untersuchung verglichen.

Ergebnisse und Diskussion

Bei Verwendung eines sogenannten nicht diffusiblen Tracers ist die Kurvenform der über einer bestimmten ROI registrierten Zeit-Aktivitätskurve abhängig

1. vom Injektionsmodus, d. h. vom Injektionsvolumen und der Geschwindigkeit der Injektion,
2. von der Entfernung der Injektionsstelle zur untersuchten Region und der durch das dazwischenliegende Kreislaufsystem bedingten Umformung des injizierten Bolus,
3. von der Rezirkulationszeit des verwendeten Tracers, sowie
4. von der Verformung der Zeit-Aktivitätskurve durch die Art der Registrierung, d. h. bei Verwendung von radioaktiven Stoffen als Indikator von der gemessenen Impulsrate und der Zeitkonstante des registrierenden Ratemeters.

Die bei Verwendung von diffusiblen Tracern gebräuchliche Berechnung der Durchblutung pro Volumeneinheit Gewebe durch die mathematische Formel der initialen Höhe gebrochen durch die Fläche unter der Zeit-Aktivitätskurve kann dabei nicht verwendet werden. Lediglich

$$(F = \lambda \frac{H}{A} \text{ ml/9/min})$$

unter der Voraussetzung, daß

1. die Injektion intraarteriell als sogenannte Deltafunktion (Impulsfunktion, d. h. so rasch wie möglich, idealerweise als einziger Impuls) und
2. noch dazu möglichst nahe der zu untersuchenden ROI erfolgt, kann die initiale Höhe der Kurve ein Maß für die als Bolus injizierte Gesamtaktivität sein.

Unter diesen Voraussetzungen kann eine wichtige, für den jeweiligen untersuchten Pool charakteristische Kreislaufgröße, die sogenannte *mittlere Transitzeit* bestimmt werden. Sie wird aus der Formel

$$\bar{t} = \frac{\int_0^\infty C(t)\,dt}{H}$$

berechnet, wobei H die initiale größte Höhe der Kurve und das Integral die Fläche unter der Zeit-Aktivitätskurve bedeutet. Die sogenannte mittlere Transitzeit ist ein Maß für die mittlere Zeit der Passage eines Indikator- oder Tracerpartikels vom zuführenden arteriellen Gefäß zum abführenden venösen Gefäß des untersuchten Pools. Mathematisch ausgedrückt stellt sie die Summe aller, beim Durchströmen des untersuchten Pools auftretenden einzelnen Transitzeiten dar, gebrochen durch die Häufigkeit mit der sie vorkommen. Zum Unterschied von den Indikatorverdünnungsmethoden mit Farbstoffen, wo die Konzentrationsveränderung pro Zeiteinheit für einen bestimmten Indikator in dem aus dem Pool austretenden Gefäß gemessen werden muß, liegen die Vorteile bei der Verwendung von radioaktiven Stoffen als Indikatoren darin, daß durch *externe Messung* die Menge des pro Zeiteinheit im Pool verbleibenden Tracers gemessen wird.

Es resultiert daher die Beziehung

$$\bar{t} = \frac{\int_0^\infty Q(t)\,dt}{Q_{max}}$$

wobei Q_{max} die Höhe der extern registrierten Kurve über dem gemessenen Pool und das Integral die Fläche der extern registrierten Zeit-Aktivitätskurve nach Bolusinjektion des Tracers darstellt. Q(t) bedeutet die pro Zeiteinheit im Pool verbleibende Tracermenge.
Bei intraarterieller Injektion des Tracers, wo ein rascher Austritt der Aktivität aus dem untersuchten Pool in die Zirkulation erfolgt, spielt die Rezirkulation keine große Rolle, wie unsere Zeit-Aktivitätskurven nach Injektion vom Aortenbogen aus zeigen. Die Berechnung des Integrals unter der Kurve bereitet daher keine großen Schwierigkeiten. Doch selbst unter diesen optimalen Bedingungen kann nur die mittlere Pool-Transitzeit und keine Druchblutungsgröße entsprechend der grundsätzlichen Beziehung $\bar{t} = \frac{V}{F}$
errechnet werden, da das zur Berechnung von F, der Durchblutung, notwendige virtuelle Verteilungsvolumen V des Tracers zur Zeit des Equilibriums bei nicht diffusiblen Tracern nicht bestimmt werden kann. Insofern erscheint die Verwendung nicht diffusibler Tracer also den frei diffusiblen Tracern völlig unterlegen zu sein. Die Vorteile einer Untersuchung mit nicht diffusiblen Tracern sind jedoch folgende:

1. ist sie einfach, weil sie intravenös erfolgen kann,

2. kann sie beliebig oft wiederholt werden,

3. erlaubt sie die Beurteilung der Durchblutung beider Gehirnhälften in ihrer Relation zueinander in einem einzigen Arbeitsgang,

4. erlaubt sie Rückschlüsse auf die Beeinflussung der Durchblutung einer betreffenden Hemisphäre durch kollaterale Zirkulation, wie speziell eines Cross flow von der kontralateralen Seite.

Nachteile die dabei in Kauf genommen werden müssen, sind andererseits:

1. daß auch extracranielles Gewebe in die Messung mit einbezogen wird und

2. ein durch das vorgeschaltete Kreislaufsystem (bei intravenöser Injektion hauptsächlich durch das cardiopulmonale Blutvolumen) verdünnter Bolus die zu untersuchende Region erreicht.

Es ist daher notwendig, bei intravenöser Injektion die äußeren Bedingungen durch Verwendung derselben Aktivität, desselben Injektionsvolumens derselben Punktionsstelle sowie gleich rascher Injektion möglichst konstant zu gestalten, um vergleichbare Werte zu erhalten. Unter diesen Bedingungen sind auch aus den bei intravenöser Injektion erhaltenen Zeit-Aktivitätskurven Parameter bestimmbar, die *klinisch relevante Zirkulationsmeßgrößen* darstellen. Nach unseren Erfahrungen sind diese Meßgrößen sogar bei der Untersuchung der Durchblutung einzelner Organregionen charakteristische Werte und sind somit für die klinische Auswertung durchaus brauchbar.

Bei diesen Zirkulationsparametern handelt es sich um Begriffe, die bereits von den Indikatorverdünnungsmethoden her bekannt sind. Es handelt sich im einzelnen um die sogenannte Erscheinungszeit „Ta", die sogenannte Anstiegszeit „Ts", die sogenannte Passagezeit „Tp" und die sogenannte modale Transitzeit „Tr", die die Zeit zwischen den Wendepunkten der Zeit-Aktivitätskurve darstellt (Abb. 1). Die bei Verwendung der intravenösen Injektionstechnik erhaltenen Werte sind in folgender Tabelle zusammengefaßt (Tabelle 1).

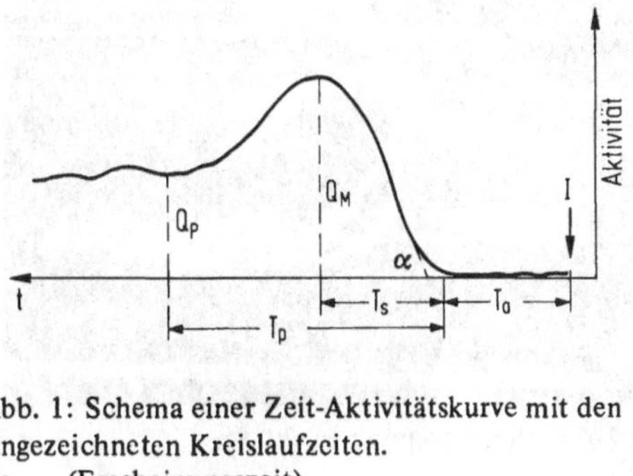

Abb. 1: Schema einer Zeit-Aktivitätskurve mit den eingezeichneten Kreislaufzeiten.
Ta (Erscheinungszeit)
Ts (Anstiegszeit)
Tp (Passagezeit)
Qm (höchste Aktivität)
Qp (Aktivität zur Zeit des ersten Minimums).

Tab. 1:

	Normal	Verschlüsse	Stenosen
Ta	10,5 ± 1,4 sec	12,3 ± 4,4 sec	10,5 ± 2,1 sec
Ts	8,8 ± 1,2 sec	11,0 ± 4,6 sec	10,5 ± 2,1 sec
Tp	32,1 ± 3,5 sec	38,1 ± 8,8 sec	34,5 ± 12,0 sec
Tr	7,8 ± 0,9 sec	12,1 ± 4,1 sec	10,2 ± 3,1 sec
	n = 29	n = 4	n = 7

Die Analyse der über beiden Hemisphären als ROI registrierten Zeit-Aktivitätskurven, die bei vier Patienten sowohl nach intravenöser Injektion als auch nach intraarterieller Injektion vom Aortenbogen aus aufgezeichnet wurden, zeigt die deutliche Verformung des injizierten Bolus durch den vorangeschalteten Kreislaufabschnitt und dessen Blutvolumen (Abb. 2). Durch den

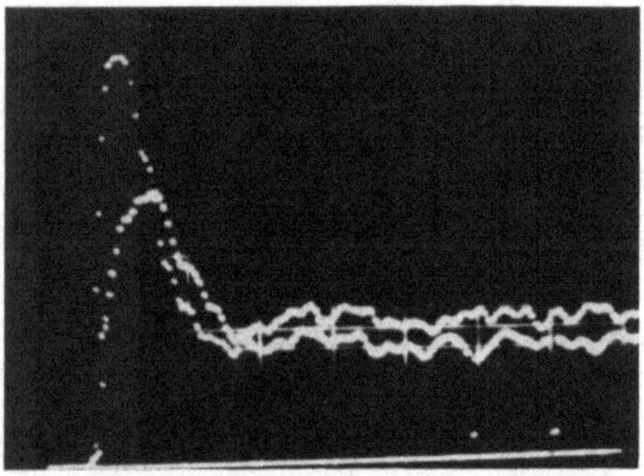

Abb. 2a: nach Injektion vom Aortenbogen aus.

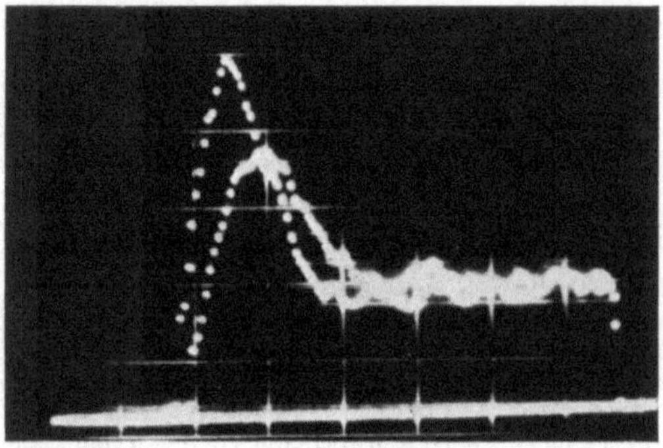

Abb. 2b: nach intravenöser Injektion.

Abb. 2: Zeit-Aktivitätskurve über beiden Hemisphären bei einem Patienten mit Verschluß der A. carot. int. links (niedrige Kurve)

Verdünnungseffekt kommt es dabei zu einer Verringerung der größten Höhe und zu einer Verbreiterung der Zeit-Aktivitätskurve. Ein Vergleich der beiden die Hemisphären durchströmenden Integralaktivitäten zeigt jedoch, daß sowohl nach intravenöser als auch nach intraarterieller Injektion vom Aortenbogen aus dasselbe Verhältnis zueinander besteht.

Zwischen den einzelnen Bildfolgen der Angiographie und der Perfusionsangioszintigraphie konnte eine ausgezeichnete Übereinstimmung gefunden werden. Grobe Veränderungen an den großen extracraniellen Gefäßen sowie im Bereich der A. cerebri media, wie Stenosen, Kinking und Kollateralkreisläufe, können mit großer Sicherheit mittels der Funktionsszintigraphie erkannt werden, wie dies an zwei ausgewählten Fällen demonstriert werden soll (Abb. 3, 4). Von wesentlicher Bedeutung für eine vergleichende Beurteilung der Ergebnisse von Angiographie und Perfusionsangioszintigraphie ist die Tatsache, daß mit der erstgenannten Untersuchungsmethode die morphologischen Details einer cerebrovasculären Erkrankung, mit der letztgenannten jedoch die daraus resultierenden Veränderungen der regionalen Hirndurchblutung erfaßt werden können. Dies kommt sowohl in den einzelnen Bildphasen der serienszintigraphischen Untersuchung wie auch in den Veränderungen der gleichzeitig über den Hemisphären registrierten Zeit-Aktivitätskurven zum Ausdruck.

Die für den extracraniellen Kreislauf repräsentative Kreislaufzeit, gemessen vom Aortenbogen bis zum Siphon der jeweiligen A. carotis interna zeigte, daß eine gute Übereinstimmung zwischen beiden Methoden besteht. Die mit der Serienangiographie gemessenen Kreislaufzeiten waren jedoch wegen der unterschiedlichen Viskosität der verwendeten Indikatoren im Durchschnitt länger (Abb. 5). Die registrierte Zeitaktivitätskurve weist deutliche Schwankungen durch die einzelnen Pulswellen auf. Die bereits von vielen Autoren geforderte herzphasengesteuerte Untersuchung des Aortenbogens und seiner Gefäße findet durch die mit

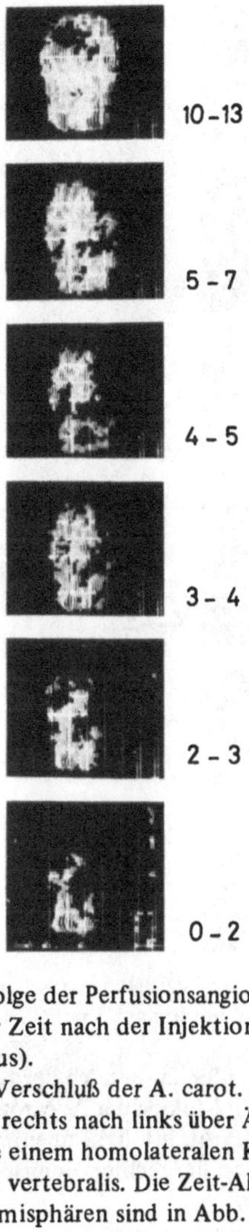

Abb. 3a: Bildfolge der Perfusionsangioszintigraphie mit Angabe der Zeit nach der Injektion (Injektion vom Aortenbogen aus).
Es besteht ein Verschluß der A. carot. int. links mit Cross flow von rechts nach links über Äste der A. cerebri front. sowie einem homolateralen Kollateralkreislauf über die A. vertebralis. Die Zeit-Aktivitätskurven über beiden Hemisphären sind in Abb. 2 dargestellt.
Deutliche Minderperfusion der linken Hemisphäre mit verzögertem venösen Abstrom im Bild 10–13 sec. p. i.

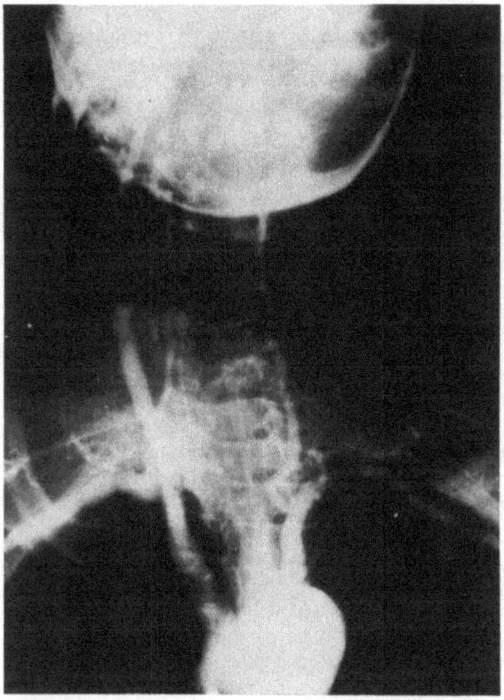

Abb. 3b

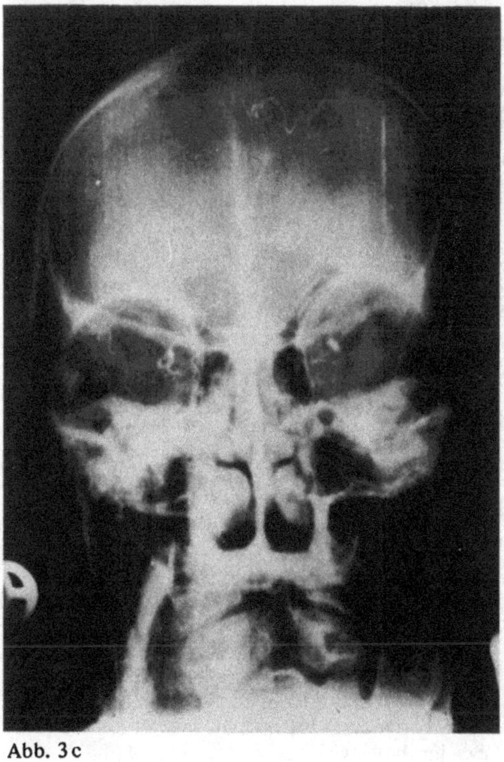

Abb. 3c

Abb. 3b: Aortenbogenangiographie, die Gefäßsituation zeigend.

Abb. 3c: Demonstration des Cross flow über A. cerebri front. links nach selektiver Angiographie der A. carot. int. rechts.

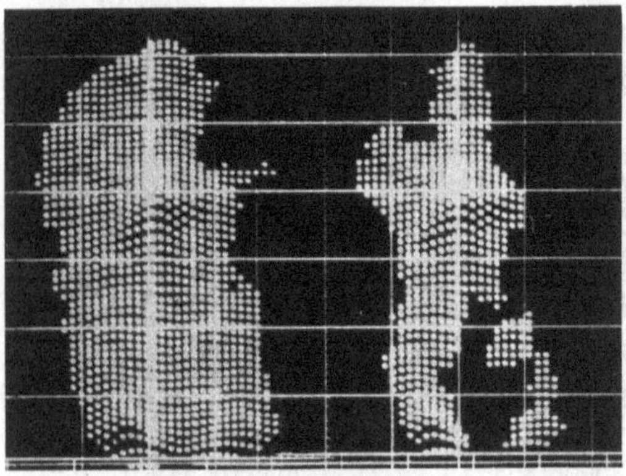

Abb. 3d: Digitales Kernspeicherbild entsprechend der Früharteriellen Phase des Angiogramms mit Verschluß der A. carot. int. links und A. cerebri media links, cross flow von rechts nach links. Gute Darstellung der A. carot. int. rechts und der A. vertebralis links.

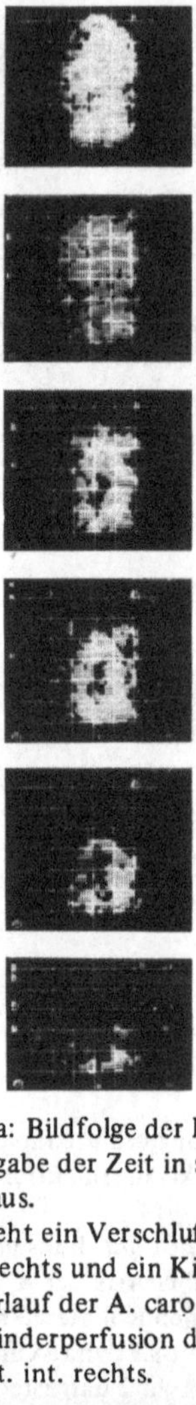

Abb. 4a: Bildfolge der Perfusionsangioszintigraphie mit Angabe der Zeit in sec nach Injektion vom Aortenbogen aus.
Es besteht ein Verschluß im Bereich der A. cerebri media rechts und ein Kinking der A. carot. int. rechts. Der Verlauf der A. carot. int. links unauffällig. Deutliche Minderperfusion der rechten Hemisphäre und der A. carot. int. rechts.

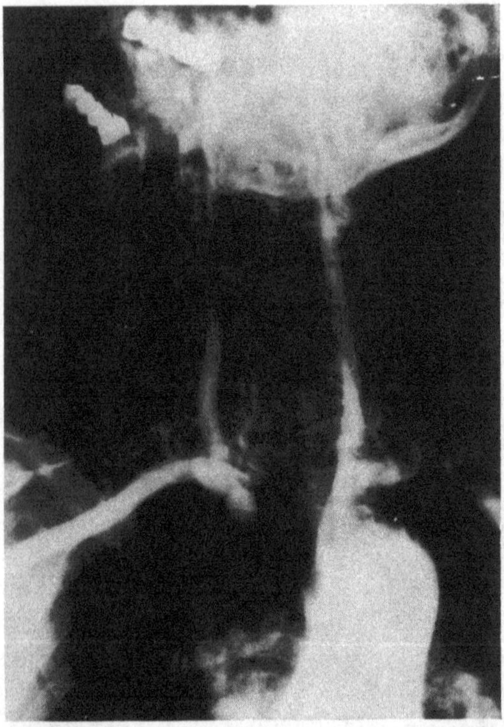

Abb. 4b: Aortenbogenangiographie mit den großen Gefäßen im Halsbereich.

Abb. 4c: Minderperfusion der A. carot. int. rechts durch Kinking im Subtraktionsbild.

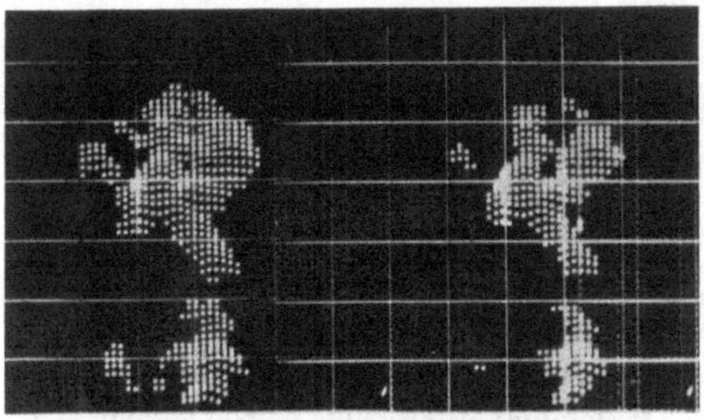

Abb. 4d: Digitales Kernspeicherbild der Früharteriellen Phase des Angiogramms entsprechend mit Verschluß einzelner Äste der A. cerebri media rechts und Minderperfusion der A. carot. int. rechts infolge Kinking. Unregelmäßige Darstellung der A. carot. int. links infolge arteriosklerotischer Wandveränderungen.

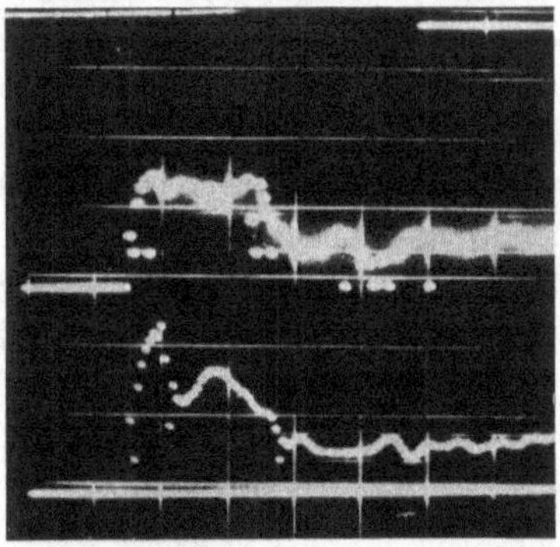

Abb. 4e: Zeit-Aktivitätskurve über dem Siphon der A. carot. int. (obere Kurve rechts, untere Kurve links) die Minderperfusion in diesem Bereich zeigend. Einzelne Kurvengipfel durch die hintereinander eintreffenden Pulswellen bedingt.

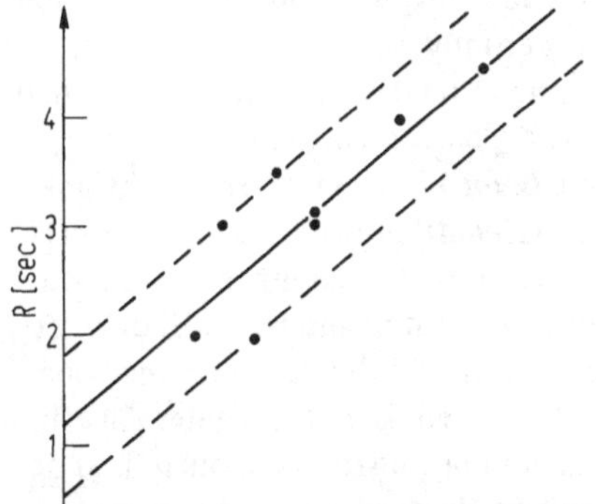

Abb. 5: Aortenbogen-Siphon-Zeiten gemessen mittels Serienangiographie (R) und Perfusionsangioszintigraphie (N) einander gegenübergestellt.
(y = 0,92 x - 0,54, r = 0,861).

radioaktiven Substanzen erhaltenen Zeit-Aktivitätskurven ihre Bestätigung und sollte daher wenn möglich bei der Angiographie bzw. bei der Perfusionsangioszintigraphie angewendet werden.

Zusammenfassung

(1) Es besteht eine sehr gute Übereinstimmung zwischen den Bildfolgen der Serienangiographie und der Perfusionsangiographie, wobei mit der einen Methode die morphologischen Details cerebrovasculärer Erkrankungen, mit der anderen deren funktionelle Auswirkungen auf die regionale Hirndurchblutung sichtbar gemacht werden können. Die Perfusionsangioszintigraphie ist daher eine einfache, rasche und aussagekräftige Suchmethode zur Erfassung cerebrovasculärer Gefäßveränderungen besonders was die A. cerebri media und den extracraniellen Gefäßabschnitt der A. carotis interna betrifft.

(2) Die relative Durchblutung der beiden Hemisphären zueinander weist sowohl nach intravenöser als auch nach intraarterieller Injektion vom Aortenbogen aus dasselbe Verhältnis auf.

(3) Die angiographisch ermittelten extracraniellen Kreislaufzeiten (Aortenbogen-Siphon-Zeit) sind im Durchschnitt etwas länger als die mittels radioaktiver Methoden gefundenen Zeiten. Der Unterschied dürfte darauf zurückzuführen sein, daß Indikatoren mit differenter Viskosität injiziert werden, zumal bei der Angiographie ein Röntgenkontrastmittel, bei der Perfusionsangioszintigraphie ein radioaktiver Tracer in wäßriger Lösung injiziert wird. Es besteht jedoch eine gute Korrelation der mittels beider Methoden gefundenen Kreislaufzeiten.

(5) Zur Indikationsstellung für einen gefäßchirurgischen Eingriff sollten zur weitestmöglichen praeoperativen Abklärung beide Methoden herangezogen werden. Dies gilt auch für postoperative Kontrollen.

Zusammenfassung des Themenkreises VI – Erfassung dynamischer Vorgänge mit der Hilfe der Angiographie und verwandter Methoden

Moderator: A. Breit

Aussagemöglichkeit und Leistungsfähigkeit angiographischer und nuklearmedizinischer Verfahren zur Erfassung der Kreislaufdynamik sind nur dann richtig zu verstehen, wenn man sich über die physiologischen Grundlagen der Kreislaufregulation im klaren ist. Es wurden deshalb einleitend die Möglichkeiten experimenteller physiologischer (*Thurau*, München) und pathophysiologischer Verfahren (*Sherwood*, London), mit denen die Durchblutung der Niere und deren Änderung aufgezeigt werden können, diskutiert.
Thurau demonstrierte dabei an den Möglichkeiten experimentell-physiologischen Arbeitens die Durchblutungsgrößen im Rindengebiet sowie im äußeren und inneren Nierenmark. Dabei beschränken sich die Kenntnisse auf die Durchblutung im Gebiet der Arterien und Arteriolen bis zu den Glomeruli, während eingehendere Beobachtungen über die Verhältnisse im Gebiet der medullären Zone fehlen.

Sherwood stellte bei Untersuchungen an Hunden die Durchblutung im normalen Kreislauf der bei verschiedenen Hypertonieformen sowie chronischen Erkrankungen des Gefäßsystems an der Niere gegenüber. Von ihm wurde besonders der Wert des intravenösen Pyelogramms hervorgehoben, dem er bei guter Technik ebenfalls weitreichende Aussagen über den Blutkreislauf zuerkennt.
Die viscerale Pharmakoangiographie bringt nach *Cen* und *Frick* nicht nur bei der Untersuchung der Nieren aufschlußreiche Ergebnisse, wobei allerdings diese Methode nicht so sehr zur Erfassung der Dynamik benutzt wird, sondern dazu bestimmt ist, Gefäßbezirke isoliert darzustellen. Bei der Untersuchung des Pankreas führt die Angiographie in Verbindung mit der Angioszintigraphie (*Pokieser* und Mitarbeiter) zu wertvollen Erkenntnissen.

Densitometrische Verfahren wie die Videodensitometrie (*Heintzen*) und die Cinedensitometrie (*Heuck* und Mitarbeiter) scheinen einen weiteren Fortschritt im Vergleich zur üblichen Angiographie zum Studium von Durchblutungsfragen und der damit verbundenen dynamischen Vorgänge zu bringen. Die Konzentration des Indikators an den verschiedenen Orten des Organs und deren zeitlicher Ablauf kann damit bestimmt werden. Die bereits vorliegenden Normalwerte für die arterielle Strombahn stimmen gut mit den auf andere Weise ermittelten Größen überein. Physiologische Alterungsvorgänge sowie krankhafte Veränderungen lassen sich davon trennen. Ihre Einführung in die Klinik erfordert auf jeden Fall wegen der Vielzahl der zu erfassenden Größen eine Verarbeitung in elektronischen Datenverarbeitungsanlagen.
Praxisreif erscheint bisher vor allem die Auswertung der Kinofilme mit zeichnerischen Methoden. Die Strömungsverhältnisse im Angiogramm erlauben bei den derzeit zur Verfügung stehenden Aufzeichnungssystemen immerhin die Messung der Durchblutung in den Arterien bis herunter zu einem Durchmesser von etwa 1 mm. Von den nuklearmedizinischen Methoden sind gleichermaßen die Sequenzszintigraphie (*zum Winkel*) und die Funktionsszintigraphie (*Reindl*) geeignet. Der Transport im untersuchten Organ kann mittels geeigneter Radiopharmaka damit qualitativ im Bildablauf als auch quantitativ durch selektive Funktionskurven erfaßt werden. Die Störung der Kinetik, vor allem auch in begrenzten Regionen, und der Vergleich mit der kontralateralen Seite bei paarigen Organen kann wichtige Erkenntnisse schon vor der eigentlichen Kontrastmitteluntersuchung aufzeigen.
Über beide Verfahren liegen in der Klinik bereits Erfahrungen vor, die beweisen, daß sie

derzeit für die Diagnostik wertvolle Aussagen erlauben. Sie können darüber hinaus mit relativ geringen Eingriffen am Patienten und einer geringen Strahlenbelastung gewonnen werden.

Für die Klinik wichtige Ergebnisse brachten Arbeiten von *Peters* und Mitarbeiter bezüglich der Nierendurchblutung mit radioaktiven Isotopen zum Zeitpunkt der selektiven Nierenangiographie. Morphologisch-dynamische Studien mit Isotopen bei Nierenstenosen (*Umek* und Mitarbeiter) und bei gekippten Nieren (*Reindl* und *Neumann*) ergeben wichtige Einblicke in die Durchströmung der Niere bei verschiedenen Lagen und Körperhaltungen. Als Screening-Untersuchung scheint die Radiocardiographie mit Kamera und Datenverarbeitung eine Rolle zu spielen (*Tähti*).

Vergleiche über die Wertigkeit der einzelnen angeführten Verfahren auf breiterer Basis sind bisher noch selten durchgeführt worden. Ein Vergleich der Angiographie mit der Thermographie und der Angiographie in Korrelation zu Druckmessungen zeigen, daß sich zwar die einzelnen Methoden ergänzen und damit eine detailliertere Aussage erlauben, in vielen Fällen jedoch nicht eindeutig korrelieren lassen. In der leider sehr kurzen Diskussion kam zum Ausdruck, daß es dringend notwendig ist, an den einzelnen Organen die Wertigkeit der diskutierten Untersuchungsmethoden untereinander zu vergleichen, um die Indikation für jede einzelne Methode abgrenzen zu können. Alle Referenten und Diskussionsredner waren sich dabei einig, daß dieses in der Praxis noch nicht genügend beachtete Gebiet einer intensiven Erforschung bedarf, um auf breiter Basis für die Diagnostik eingesetzt werden zu können.

Zusammenfassend wurde festgestellt: Dynamische Vorgänge sind im typischen Angiogramm nur begrenzt erfaßbar, durch die verschiedenen Verfahren der Densitometrie und der Nuklearmedizin sind wesentliche Aussagen möglich, allerdings fehlen noch genügend Vergleiche, die die Aussagemöglichkeiten der einzelnen Methode bewerten und deren Indikation abgrenzen können. Absolute Bestimmungen der Blutverteilungen zum Beispiel in der Niere sind derzeit nur im physiologischen Experiment durchführbar.

VII. FILM UND FERNSEHEN

Problematik der Film- und Fernsehproduktion

H. J. Gnamm

Jeder von Ihnen kann jetzt oder in naher Zukunft die Absicht haben, ein wissenschaftliches Thema filmisch zu dokumentieren und muß sich dabei mit den Problemen der Film- und Fernsehproduktion auseinandersetzen. Ihnen dabei viel Ärger zu ersparen, Sie vor finanziellen Schäden zu bewahren, ist Sinn meines Vortrages.
Die Aufnahmen für derartige Filme können auf Filmmaterial oder durch elektronische Bildaufzeichnung erfolgen. Welche Art gewählt wird, hängt von der Möglichkeit der Aufnahme, vom geplanten Einsatz und den dabei zur Verfügung stehenden Kommunikationsmitteln – und letztlich vor allem vom vorhandenen Geld ab.

Ein Wissenschaftler, der eine neue Idee filmisch dokumentieren will, vergißt in seiner natürlichen Begeisterung zu oft, daß eine solche Filmproduktion in erster Linie Geld kostet.

Meiner Erfahrung nach enthält aber nahezu kein Forschungsetat für diesen Zweck Geld und so weit ich weiß, ist es sogar schwierig für die Herstellung eines Lehrfilmes zur Demonstration bei wissenschaftlichen Vorlesungen, Etatmittel zu bekommen.
Dies trotz der Erkenntnis, daß die Wissenschaft vor der dringenden Aufgabe steht, immer mehr Wissen an immer mehr Menschen zu vermitteln.

Bis aber die einzelnen Universitäten über eigene Filmzentren verfügen, mit welchen sie in der Lage sind, solche Filme selbst zu produzieren, dürften noch einige Jahre ins Land ziehen. So wird es noch lange Zeit bei dem heutigen Zustand bleiben, daß der einzelne Wissenschaftler gezwungen ist, seine Filme selbst zu konzipieren, selbst herzustellen oder – was vernünftiger ist – herstellen zu lassen.
Entschließt er sich jedoch für den Alleingang, so nimmt ein solches Vorhaben oft einen recht abenteuerlichen Verlauf.
Ein Beispiel für viele darf ich aus meiner Tätigkeit der letzten Zeit herausgreifen.
Ein Arzt entschloß sich, einen Dokumentationsfilm über eine neue medizinische Erkenntnis herzustellen. Er fand sogar eine Industriefirma, die ihn dabei finanziell unterstützen wollte.

Er beauftragte den Fotografen seines Institutes, die notwendigen Filmaufnahmen durchzuführen. Es bestand sogar eine Art Drehbuch. Die Aufnahmetechnik des Fotografen war noch nicht einmal schlecht, aber es fehlte eben beiden, dem Arzt und dem Fotografen die notwendige Erfahrung und die Kenntnis der technischen Zusammenhänge einer Filmproduktion.

Die Herstellungskosten, die sich beide errechneten, waren in Unkenntnis der gesamttechnischen Notwendigkeiten einer Filmproduktion zu nieder angesetzt und schon nach kurzer Zeit weit überschritten. Die Dreharbeiten zogen sich über Monate hin, und es wurde dabei eine Unmenge von Filmmaterial verbraucht. Und was das Schlimmste war: es wurden dabei verschiedene Materialien und verschiedene Formate benutzt.
Als dann schließlich das Industrieunternehmen darauf drängte, doch eine Filmproduktionsfirma zu Hilfe zu nehmen, war der entstandene finanzielle Schaden nicht mehr gut zu machen.

Unsere Kunden aus Wissenschaft und Technik teilen sich im Großen und Ganzen in zwei

Gruppen auf. Sie unterscheiden sich dadurch, daß die eine Gruppe den Versuch, einen Film mit eigenem Personal und eigenen oft recht mangelhaften filmtechnischen Hilfsmitteln zu produzieren, nach trüben Erfahrungen aufgegeben hat und sich vertrauensvoll an die Filmindustrie wendet. Die andere Gruppe hat dieses Stadium noch nicht erreicht und kommt nur zur Endfertigung, meist hilfesuchend zu uns. Sie ist immer noch in filmischem Amateurdenken verhaftet.

Wenn man solche Kunden zu überzeugen versucht, ihre nächsten Filmproduktionen doch gleich in Zusammenarbeit mit uns oder doch zumindest unter Beratung eines Filmfachmannes durchzuführen, so spürt man häufig in ihrer Ablehnung die Überlegung, daß der Filmfachmann ja doch nicht die medizinischen Probleme oder Aufgabenstellung verstehe und somit auch nicht in der Lage sei, derartige Filme zu produzieren oder gar als Regisseur in Tätigkeit zu treten.

Ich produziere seit über 16 Jahren nahezu ausschließlich Filme für Wissenschaft und Technik. Ich bin dabei nicht nur als Produktionsleiter, sondern fast immer auch als Regisseur tätig. Natürlich kann ich nicht Mediziner, Radartechniker, Maschineningenieur, Chemiker, Kunststoffexperte, Datenverarbeiter, Brückenbauer, Sonartechniker, Elektroniker oder Atomphysiker in einer Person sein.

Aber ich kann mir Mühe geben, mich in diese Fachgebiete mit Hilfe meines wissenschaftlichen Auftraggebers soweit zu vertiefen, daß ich die in den geplanten Filmen behandelten Themen wenigstens ungefähr begreifen kann und für meinen Auftraggeber ein brauchbarer Partner bin.

Damit bin ich bei einem Punkt angelangt, der für eine fruchtbare und für beide Seiten erfolgreiche Zusammenarbeit von Bedeutung ist.

Suchen Sie den richtigen Partner für Ihr Filmvorhaben.

Lernen Sie Ihn zunächst kennen – ihn und seine Mitarbeiter. Fragen Sie notfalls Kollegen, die bereits Filme produzieren ließen. Gehen Sie nicht zu den billigsten Firmen. Eine Filmproduktion muß auch für den wissenschaftlichen Film die Anwendung moderner filmtechnischer Geräte, den Einsatz guter Mitarbeiter auf den Gebieten der Kameraführung, des Bildschnittes, der Gestaltung, der Tontechnik gewährleisten können.

Haben Sie Ihre Wahl getroffen, so beginnt die eigentliche Zusammenarbeit mit Produktionsbesprechungen, in welchen Sie sich die Zeit nehmen und die Geduld haben müssen, dem Filmteam zu erläutern, was für einen Film es produzieren soll.

Es muß erkennen können:

1. Das Thema des Filmes und seine besondere Aussage bzw. was der Film erreichen soll.
2. Wen soll der Film ansprechen, wer ist das zukünftige Publikum.
3. Welche Einsatzmöglichkeiten stehen zur Vorführung später zur Verfügung.

Zunächst sollte versucht werden, ein Drehbuch oder auch nur ein Treatment für das geplante Filmvorhaben zu erstellen, um so Aufnahmematerial einzusparen, die Dreharbeiten vorher genau planen zu können und sie auf ein Minimum an Zeit zu beschränken. Nur so können die Produktionskosten genau kalkuliert und limitiert werden.

Der verantwortliche Produktionsleiter oder Produzent und der für die Filmproduktion vorgesehene Regisseur, haben während der Drehbucharbeiten dem Buchautor und dem auftraggebenden Wissenschaftler beratend zur Verfügung zu stehen.

Der Regisseur hat vor allem bei der Festlegung der Bildgestaltung des Filmes mitzuwirken und zu verhindern, daß ins Drehbuch Dinge aufgenommen werden, die nachher bildlich nicht darzustellen sind.

Der Produktionsleiter muß die Bearbeitung des Drehbuches dahingehend kontrollieren, daß die von wissenschaftlicher Seite geforderten Darstellungen im Rahmen der zur Verfügung stehenden finanziellen Mittel bleiben und soll

eventuell Vorschläge unterbreiten, wie man den gewünschten bildlichen Effekt auch mit billigeren Mitteln erreichen kann, ohne dabei die gewünschte Lehraussage oder wissenschaftliche Aussage zu beeinträchtigen.
Der Einwand, daß bei wissenschaftlichen Filmen keine Schauspieler zu führen und daher ein Regisseur überflüssig sei – oder ehrlicher gesagt: eingespart werden könne – ist meist nicht richtig.
Auch bei solchen Aufnahmen ist es seine Aufgabe, durch die Anwendung dramaturgischer Regeln bzw. Mittel, die Bildgestaltung so zu beeinflussen, daß ein Film entsteht, der seinen wissenschaftlichen Inhalt publikumswirksam darbietet.
Sie haben alle längst durch Film und Fernsehen zwischen gut und schlecht gemachten Filmen zu unterscheiden gelernt. Man kann nur in seltenen Fällen Aufnahmen rein wissenschaftlichen Inhaltes einfach hintereinanderkleben und mit einem Kommentar versehen zur Vorführung bringen. Es kommt heute bei den Ansprüchen des Publikums auf die Verpackung an. Ich bin der Meinung, daß man auch einen wissenschaftlichen Stoff im Film interessant darbieten sollte.
Spätestens nach Erstellung des Drehbuches ist die Produktion in der Lage, Ihnen ein verbindliches Kostenangebot zu unterbreiten. Alle zu einem früheren Zeitpunkt angeforderten Kostenangebote können nur als Richtpreis abgegeben bzw. gewertet werden.
Begnügen Sie sich nicht mit einem globalen Kostenangebot, in welchem lediglich pauschal ein Herstellungspreis für die geplante Filmherstellung genannt wird.
Verlangen Sie in einem schriftlichen Angebot eine genaue Aufzählung *der* Leistungen der Filmproduktion, die in dem vereinbarten Betrag enthalten sind.
Spätere Streitigkeiten und Ärger über eventuell auftauchende Nachforderungen sind damit von vornherein ausgeschlossen.
Jede seriöse Filmproduktion wird ohnehin ihr Angebot mit klar umrissenen Leistungen in dieser Form vorlegen.

Der nächste Schritt ist nun die gemeinsame Planung der Dreharbeiten.
Diese ist für einen wissenschaftlichen Film, in welchem z. B. bestimmte Krankheitsbilder, operative Eingriffe, Untersuchungen oder Behandlungen dargestellt und klinische Einrichtungen benutzt werden sollen, sehr viel schwieriger als für Filme, deren darzustellende Objekte oder Personen jederzeit zur Verfügung stehen.
Die Produktionsfirma ist zwar durch die Abgabe ihres Preises gebunden, aber sie hat selbstverständlich dabei auch ihre zu erbringenden Leistungen in einer bestimmten höhe limitiert.

Sie wird mit allen Mitteln versuchen, die Dreharbeiten rationell durchzuführen, und Sie müssen sie in diesem Bestreben durch die zeitgerechte Bereitstellung aller von Ihrer Seite zu erbringenden Leistungen unterstützen, denn es geht dabei auch um Ihr Geld.
Um alle anderen produktionstechnischen Fragen der Organisation und Terminierung brauchen Sie sich nicht zu kümmern. Dies ist Sache der Filmproduktion.
In nahezu allen Fällen meiner Praxis, entstand während dieser Vorarbeiten ein gutes Verhältnis zwischen Auftraggeber und Auftragnehmer, vor allem zwischen Wissenschaftler und Regisseur, was den nun einsetzenden Dreharbeiten zugute kommt. Sie ist entscheidend für das Gelingen des Filmes. Überlassen Sie dabei die bildliche Gestaltung dem Regisseur, aber übernehmen Sie selbst die Kontrolle der fachlich bzw. wissenschaftlich richtigen Darstellung.
Das gleiche gilt für die anschließenden Schnittarbeiten.
Filmherstellung ist im wahrsten Sinne des Wortes Teamwork, in welchem jeder Beteiligte mit seinem Fachwissen zum Gelingen des Filmes beizutragen hat.
Ob Wissenschaftler, Drehbuchautor, Regisseur, Kameramann, Produzent, Tonmeister, jeder einzelne ist für sein Fachgebiet verantwortlich.

Daß es innerhalb eines solchen Teams einer coordinierenden Funktion bedarf, fordert die

angestrebte Wirtschaftlichkeit eines solchen Vorhabens.
Diese Funktion liegt in den Händen des Produzenten oder des beauftragten Produktionsleiters.

Sind die wirtschaftlichen Mittel eines Auftraggebers jedoch so beschränkt, daß eine Auftragserteilung an eine Filmproduktion nicht möglich ist, so versichern Sie sich wenigstens der beratenden Mitarbeit eines Filmfachmannes. Dieser muß allerdings in der Lage sein, Ihnen beim Transponieren Ihres Fachwissens ins Optische zu helfen, den richtigen filmtechnischen Weg zu weisen und Sie vor finanziellem Schaden zu bewahren.
Ich habe in meinen Ausführungen versucht, Ihnen für zukünftige Filmvorhaben einen sicheren Weg zu weisen, den andere vor Ihnen bereits mit Erfolg beschritten haben. Meine Absicht war zu helfen, nicht zu kritisieren. Ich hoffe, daß mir dies gelungen ist.

VIII. FILMVORFÜHRUNGEN UND DISKUSSION

L'Artériographie Coronaire (film 16 mm - couleur - son optique)

M. Amiel, J. Delaye, J. Normand et F. Pinet

Ce film présente successivement:

– les techniques d'examen (injection globale pour l'ostium coronarien et sélective pour l'athérome tronculaire avec radiocinéma),

– l'anatomie radiologique,

– la séméïologie radiologique des différentes lésions athéromateuses ou non,

– les indications à titre diagnostic et thérapeutique, de l'exploration,

– les résultats de la chirurgie de revascularisation du myocarde.

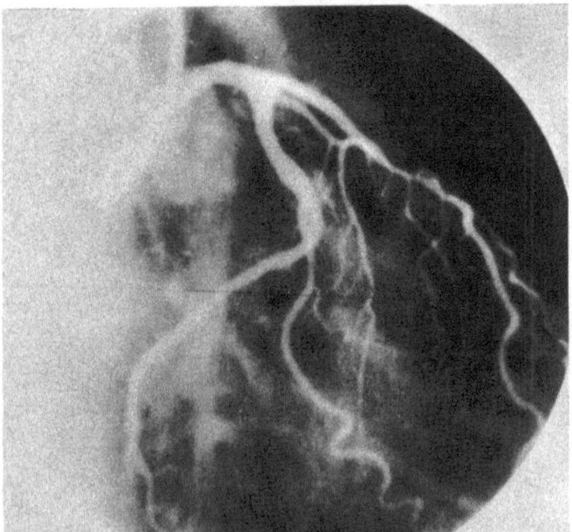

Fig. 1: Athérome coronarien avec sténose serrée de l'I.V.A. (coronaire gauche en oblique antérieure droite – Document 70 mm.

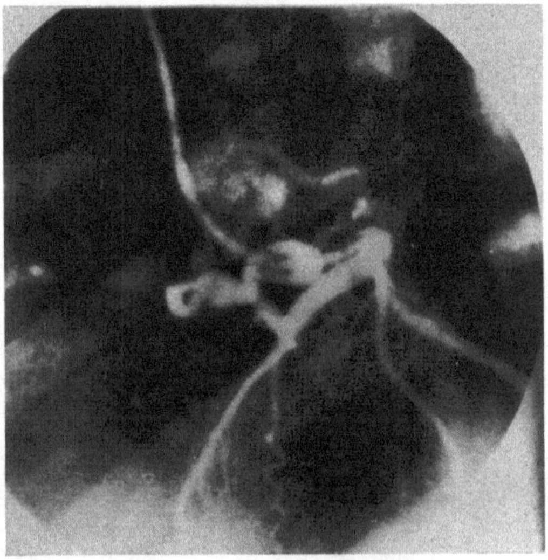

Fig. 2: Fistule coronaro-pulmonaire venant de l'artère coronaire gauche (oblique antérieure gauche – document 70 mm).

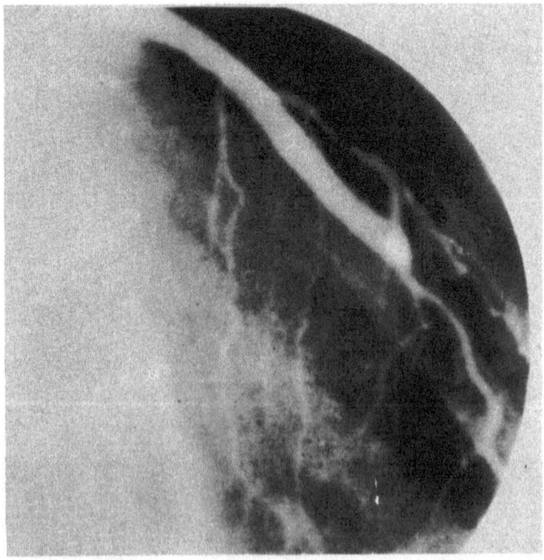

Fig. 3: Pontage veineux aorto-coronarien sur l'I.V.A. (oblique antérieure droite – Document 70 mm).

Intermittierender Ikterus bei biliopankreatischem Umgehungskreislauf der Papilla Vateri (Film 16 mm)

H.-P. Hebestreit

Die Ursache für einen intermittierenden Ikterus bei inkompletter Stenose der Papilla Vateri ist nach *Adolf* meist ein Papillenkarzinom. In 30% der Fälle werden anikterische Intervalle von 3–12 Monaten beobachtet. Die Ursache für das Intermittieren kann sowohl ein Gewebszerfall des Tumors als auch eine katarrhalische Entzündung sein. 98% aller Papillenstenosen sind nach *Niedner* entzündlich bedingt.
Klinisch werden vielfach Oberbauchschmerzen, Gallenkoliken, Leberzirrhose und Pankreatitis gleichzeitig beobachtet.
Bei Papillenstenose wurde von *Caroli, Hess* und *Niedner* ein biliopankreatischer Reflux beschrieben. Da der Druck im Pankreasgang höher ist als im Gallengang, ist ein Galleflluß in den Pankreasgang nur bei Druckerhöhung im Ductus Choledochus oder bei Erniedrigung des Pankreassekretionsdruckes möglich (*Harms* und *Kern*). Das ist auch bei einer Eigensekretion des Ductus pankreaticus minor (*Santorini*) möglich (*Opie*). In 90% der Fälle ist der Ductus pankreaticus major (*Wirsungiani*) und in 10% der Ductus pankreaticus minor (*Santorini*) der Hauptausführungsgang (*Swart*).

Kasuistik

Ein 66jähriger Patient wurde im Juni 1971 ikterisch und mit hohem Fieber aufgenommen. 2 Jahre zuvor war dieselbe Erkrankung schon einmal aufgetreten, begleitet von heftigen Oberbauchschmerzen. – Nach operativer Entfernung einer Schrumpfgallenblase wegen des passageren Verschlußikterus wurde bei einer routinemäßigen Kontrastuntersuchung des Ductus choledochus durch ein T-Drain ein haselnußgroßer Aussparungsbezirk präpapillär festgestellt. Der Ductus choledochus war stark aufgestaut. Das Kontrastmittel floß retrograd in den Pankreasgang und schien durch den Ductus pankreaticus minor in das Duodenum zu gelangen. Daher wurde zur weiteren Abklärung eine Kinematographie vorgenommen.

1. Diapositiv: T-Drain-Füllung, Röntgenaufnahme während Durchleuchtung: Der Ductus Choledochus ist stark aufgestaut, Aussparungsbezirk präpapillär. Darstellung des Ductus pankreaticus major und minor. Kontrastmittel im Duodenum.

2. Diapositiv: Ausschnittsvergrößerung aus dem Film: Gegenüber dem vorhergehenden Diapositiv ist hier zusätzlich der gesamte Pankreasgang bis zum Pankreasschwanz dargestellt. Teilweise Überlagerung durch sehr langes und verschlungenes T-Drain.

3. 16 mm Film: Der Film wurde mit einer Cine-Puls-Anlage und halbautomatischer Belichtung aufgenommen. Geschwindigkeit 24 Bilder/Sekunde. Es handelt sich um die verkleinerte Kopie eines 35 mm-Röntgenfilms, der mit einer Entwicklungsmaschine für Routine-Formate entwickelt wurde.
Es folgen 4 kurze Szenen, in denen jeweils eine Injektion durch das T-Drain in den Ductus choledochus erfolgt. Infolge eines Papillenverschlusses fließt das Kontrastmittel retrograd in den Ductus pancreatikus major, von dort in den Ductus pankreaticus minor und durch die Papilla duodeni minor in das Duodenum. Es handelt sich um einen Umgehungskreislauf der Vaterschen Papille (Papilla duodeni major).

Bei erhöhtem Injektionsdruck stellt sich außerdem der gesamte Pankreasgang dar. Ein geringer Kontrastmittelanteil fließt bei starkem Druck auch durch die Vatersche Papille.
Bei der Relaparatomie konnte weder ein Konkrement noch ein Papillentumor nachgewiesen werden. Es fanden sich nur Zeichen einer Entzündung. Eine Papillotomie wurde nicht vor-

genommen. Es erfolgte eine Choledocho-duodenostomie.
Wir sind der Ansicht, daß der Umgehungskreislauf die Ursache für das Intermittieren eines Ikterus u. a. sein kann und, daß wir erstmalig den kinematographischen Nachweis eines biliopankreatischen Umgehungskreislaufs erbracht haben.
Niedner beobachtete unter Durchleuchtung bei 6 Patienten mit Ostiumstenosen der Papilla Vateri eine Stromumkehr, ohne dieses jedoch durch Bildmaterial sicher belegen zu können.

Die trans-ossale Phlebographie der Wirbelsäule und des Spinalkanals

– Morphologie und Klinik –

H. J. Clemens und H. Vogelsang

Die Vertebralvenensysteme spielen bei den verschiedensten Erkrankungen des Brust-, Bauch- und Beckenraumes, der Halsregion und des Schädels eine Rolle, da sie als Kollateral-Kreislauf-System zwischen der Vena cava superior und der Vena cava inferior eingeschaltet sind. Das venöse Blut kann in diesem System auf jedes „Segment" verteilt werden. Eine Blutstromumkehr ist möglich.

Die beste Darstellungsmethode der Venensysteme der Wirbelsäule ist die trans-ossale Phlebographie. Diese Methode setzt sich zunehmend durch, nachdem nunmehr ausreichende anatomische Grundlagen vorhanden sind und technische Probleme bei der Phlebographie gelöst werden konnten.

Im ersten Teil des Films sind die anatomischen Details der Vertebralvenensysteme sowie die mögliche Blutstromrichtung in diesen Gefäßen mit Hilfe von Trickzeichnungen dargestellt. Diese Sequenz wird durch die Abbildung eines Original-Ausguß-Modelles abgeschlossen.

Der zweite Teil zeigt die Technik der trans-ossalen Phlebographie in Verbindung mit der Bildverstärker-Röntgen-Kinematographie sowie der Tomographie und die dadurch gewonnenen Aufnahmefolgen.
Im dritten, klinischen Teil werden Erkrankungen der Wirbelsäule und des Spinalkanals abgehandelt (paravertebrale und epidurale raumfordernde Prozesse, extradurale und kombinierte spinale Angiome, traumatische Veränderungen, Bandscheibenvorfälle und intradurale Tumoren etc.). Durch die ambulant durchführbare trans-ossale Phlebographie gelingt es, die bei den genannten Erkrankungen auftretenden pathologischen Prozesse im Bereich der Venenplexus, wie Verlagerungen, Einengungen und Unterbrechungen sichtbar zu machen. Damit ist Lokalisation und Ausdehnung bestimmbar. Diese Methode stellt ein wichtiges diagnostisches Hilfsmittel dar.
Technische Angaben:
Farbfilm 16 mm
Länge: 250 m
Spieldauer: 22 min.
Geschwindigkeit: 24 Bilder/sek.
Lichtton
Filmverleih: *Sandoz AG*, Nürnberg oder Basel

Zusammenfassung der Themenkreise VII und VIII – Film und Fernsehen und Filmvorführungen

Moderator: B. Söding

Den Referenten zum Thema Film und Fernsehen war die Aufgabe gestellt worden, Arzt und Filmproduzenten auf dem Anwendungsgebiet Medizin zusammenzuführen. Die ständige Zunahme des Lernstoffes während des Studiums, die Einführung neuer Methoden, die auf Fortbildungsveranstaltungen diskutiert werden müssen und die Notwendigkeit auch den Ärzten, die sich einer Weiterbildung zum Facharzt unterziehen, einen theoretisch fundierten Wissensstoff vermitteln zu müssen, erfordert die Einführung audiovisueller Methoden auch in der Medizin.

B. Söding begründete in der Einleitung, daß auf Spezialgebieten wie der Medizin der Filmproduzent meist keine Vorstellung hat, was den Mediziner tatsächlich interessiert bzw. was er eigentlich im Film zeigen möchte. Auf der anderen Seite hätten die Mediziner zu geringe Vorstellungen, welche Überlegungen erforderlich seien, um die Voraussetzung für einen guten Film, der für Unterricht und Fortbildung geeignet ist, zu schaffen. Meist würden die Fachleute aus der Film- und Fernsehindustrie erst zu einem Zeitpunkt zu solchen Vorhaben hinzugezogen, an dem schon ein Teil der zur Verfügung stehenden Mittel verbraucht sei oder es seien von vornherein nicht genügend Mittel vorhanden, um ein solches Unterfangen erfolgreich durchführen zu können. Der Informationswert schlechter Filme stände auf jeden Fall in keinem Verhältnis zu aufgewendeter Zeit und verbrauchten Geldmitteln.
Für einen guten vorführreifen Film sei es auf jeden Fall erforderlich, nicht nur eine Idee zu haben, sondern auch ein Drehbuch, in dem vor der eigentlichen Verfilmung alle wesentlichen Einzelheiten festzulegen sind, und eine ausreichende Ausrüstung, gleichgültig ob es sich um die Herstellung typischer konventioneller Filme handelt oder um Aufzeichnungen auf elektronischem Wege. Letztere gewinnt besonders zur Darstellung aktueller Vorgänge in Zukunft besondere Bedeutung.
In den nachfolgenden Referaten wurden zunächst Einzelheiten der Tontechnik besprochen, die immer dann Schwierigkeiten bereitet, wenn es sich um Aufnahmen handelt, bei denen die Tonführung nicht von vornherein festliegt (*K. Mandl*). Der Aufwand, der heutzutage auf diesem Gebiet getrieben wird, ist durch die Verschiedenartigkeit der zur Verfügung stehenden Medien meist mit verhältnismäßig umfangreichen technischen Maßnahmen verbunden.
H. Gnamm und *K. Götz* als auf dem Medizinsektor erfahrene Kameramänner berichteten anschließend über die Problematik der Film- und Fernsehproduktion. Sie liegt für den Hersteller einesteils in den nicht sehr präzisen Vorstellungen des Mediziners begründet, was er eigentlich darzustellen wünscht, auf der anderen Seite jedoch darin, daß die Vorgänge in der Medizin meist nicht wiederholbar sind. Eine Einmaligkeit der relativ kurzen Szene macht deshalb in vielen Fällen den Einsatz zusätzlicher elektronischer Mittel erforderlich. Sie fordert jedoch auf jeden Fall eine genaue Planung und Einweisung auch des auf medizinischem Gebiet erfahrenen Regisseurs und Kameramannes.
Lehrh. von Arnold und Richter betonte, daß ein guter Film nur mit professioneller Ausrüstung herzustellen ist. Kameras, wie sie im allgemeinen von Amateuren benutzt werden, reichen für die Herstellung geeigneter Filme in der Regel nicht aus. Besonders bei Darstellungen von operativen Eingriffen hat sich die Verwendung von Kameraausrüstungen bewährt, die durch fernsehtechnische Mittel eine Mitbeobachtung auf dem Fernsehschirm erlauben.

T. Nischwitz zeigte mit einem Film die heutigen Möglichkeiten des Trickfilms. Er ist besonders bei Verwendung audiovisueller Mittel geeignet, um aus der Vielfalt des Darzustellenden das herauszuholen, was für den Lernprozeß wichtig

ist. Die Tricktechnik beschränkt sich dabei nicht nur auf einfache Zeichentricks, sondern erlaubt die Ein- und Überblendung von gleichen Szenen. Solche Darstellungen sind jedoch nur in dafür speziell ausgerüsteten Tricklabors herzustellen. Sie werden heutzutage z. B. auch bereits für die Angiographie genutzt.
K. Köferl und *K. Eichstätt* demonstrierten, daß ähnliche Voraussetzungen für die Herstellung von Fernsehaufzeichnungen erforderlich sind. Hier bestehen auch für die Medizin in gut ausgerüsteten Fernsehstudios hervorragende Möglichkeiten. Durch die Fernsehtechnik können für ein breiteres Publikum Vorgänge sichtbar gemacht werden, die früher nur einzelne hätten beobachten können. Die Übertragung und Speicherung von Handlungen – auch in Farbe – hat heute schon einen Stand erreicht, der den Einsatz für Unterricht und Fortbildung lohnt. Die Verwendung geeigneter Speicherverfahren, wie Band und Plattenspeicher, erlauben dabei auch nachträglich noch eine Weiterverarbeitung aufgenommener Szenen auch in Zeitdehnung und Zeitlupe. Zusätzlich gestatten es die elektronischen Verfahren, jederzeit noch zusätzliche Informationen wie Zeitdaten, Bildunterschriften und ähnliches nachträglich in das Fernsehbild einzublenden bzw. simultan zu übertragen.

Das am nächsten Tage gezeigte Filmprogramm demonstrierte an einigen zwar aus sehr unterschiedlichen Arbeitsgebieten stammenden Filmen die Leistungsfähigkeit der Laufbilddarstellung. Die Lyoner Gruppe unter Amiel, Delahaye und Pipet zeigte einen ausgezeichneten Film über die Coronarangiographie, H. P. Hebestreit einen Film über den intermittierenden Ikterus bei biliopankreatischem Umgehungskreislauf der Papilla Vateri. *Clemens* und *Vogelsang* zeigten ihren Film über die trans-ossale Phlebographie der Wirbelsäule und des Spinalkanals. Hier werden zunächst die anatomischen Grundlagen des Venensystems sowie die möglichen Abflußrichtungen an Ausgußmodellen und Trickzeichnungen gezeigt, anschließend die Darstellung im Röntgenbild erklärt, sowie schließlich an Hand von pathologischen Befunden die Brauchbarkeit der Methode nachgewiesen. Schließlich zeigte *K. Decker* in einer für ihn charakteristischen Darstellungsweise einen technisch qualifizierten Film über die Physiologie und Pathophysiologie des Schluckaktes.
Die anschließende Diskussion demonstrierte vor allem, daß die Probleme beider Seiten auf ganz verschiedenen Ebenen zu suchen sind. Sie führte jedoch die am Film interessierten Kongressisten zusammen und gab beiden Seiten viele Anregungen.

Mitarbeiterverzeichnis

R. Adams, MD., Dept. of Radiology, Cardiovascular Laboratories Loma Linda University, Loma Linda, California 92354, USA

Dr. *K. Alexander,* Institut für Klinische Radiologie der Medizinischen Hochschule Hannover, D-3000 Hannover-Buchholz, Podbielskistraße 380

Dr. *E. Aldor,* Hanuschkrankenhaus, A-1140 Wien, H.-Collins-Straße 30

Dr. *M. Amiel,* Hôpital Cardiovasculaire, Rue du Doyen Lépine, F-69 Lyon 8e, Frankreich

Dr. *K. Amplatz,* Department of Radiology, University Hospital Minneapolis, Minnesota 55455, USA

Prof. Dr. *H. Anacker,* Institut für Röntgenologie und physikalische Therapie am Klinikum rechts der Isar, D-8000 München 80, Ismaninger Straße 22

Arnold & Richter KG, 8000 München 13, Türkenstraße 89

Dr. rer. nat. *A. Bäuml,* Bundesgesundheitsamt, Abteilung für Strahlenhygiene, Laboratorium für Dosimetrie und Strahlenphysik, D-8042 Neuherberg bei München, Ingolstädter Landstraße 1

Dr. med. *J. Balaun,* Facharzt für Radiologie, D-4048 Grevenbroich, Graf-Kessel-Str. 30

Dr. *R. Bartl,* Pathologisches Institut der Universität München, D-8000 München 15, Thalkirchnerstraße 36

Priv.-Doz. Dr. *G. Baumann,* Gefäßchirurgische Abteilung der Chirurgischen Universitätsklinik München, D-8000 München 15, Thalkirchnerstraße 48

Prof. Dr. *S. Bayindir,* Röntgenabteilung der Chirurgischen Universitätsklinik und Poliklinik Gießen, D-6300 Gießen, Klinikstraße 37

Dr. *H. J. Becker,* Zentrum Innere Medizin, Kardiologische Abteilung der Chirurgischen Klinik der Universität Frankfurt, D-6000 Frankfurt/Main Süd, Ludwig-Rehn-Straße 14

Dr. *J. C. Becker,* Service de Radiologie, Centre Hôpitalier et Universitaire de Besançon, F- Besançon, 2 Place Saint Jaques

Dr. *D. Beduhn,* Radiologische Klinik im Schwerpunktskrankenhaus, 633 Wetzlar

Dr. *L. Beltz,* Radiologische Klinik der Universität Bonn, D-53 Bonn 1, Venusberg

Dr. *S. Benetatos,* Department of Thoracic and Cardiovascular Surgery, The Red Cross General Hospital Ambelokipi, Athen 607, Griechenland

Dr. *D. W. Berenbeck,* Radiologisches Institut und Poliklinik der Universität zu Köln, D-5000 Köln 41, Joseph-Stelzmann-Straße 9

Robert N. Berk, MD., Dept. of Radiology, University Hospital, 225 West Dickinson Street, San Diego/California 92118, USA

Prof. Dr. *H. Bleifeld,* Abteilung Innere Medizin I der Rheinisch-Westfälischen Technischen Hochschule, D-5100 Aachen, Goethestraße 27/29

Prof. Dr. *E. Boijsen,* Röntgendiag Avd., Allmänna sjukhuset, Lunds Universitet, Malmö/Schweden

Prof. Dr. *A. Breit,* Strahlenabteilung des Städtischen Krankenhauses Passau, D-8390 Passau, Bischof-Pilgrim-Straße 1

Dr. *J. Bürsch,* Abt. für Kinder-Kardiologie und Bio-Medizinische Technik, Universitäts-Kinderklinik Kiel, 23 Kiel, Fröbelstr. 15

Priv.-Doz. Dr. *M. Cen,* Abteilung Radiologie der Medizinischen Fakultät der Technischen Universität Aachen, D-5100 Aachen, Goethestraße 27–29

Prof. Dr. *H. J. Clemens,* 1 Berlin 62, Hewahlstraße 10

Dr. *A. Clermont,* Hospital cardio-vasculaire et pneumologique, 59 Boulevard Pinel, F-69 Lyon 3', Frankreich

C. S. Coble, MD., Washington University, School of Medicine, Mallinckrodt Institute of Radiology, 510 S. Kingshighway Blvd., St. Louis, Mo. 63110, USA

Dr. *M. Collard,* Röntgendiagnostische Abteilung, Montignies-Le-Tilleul, Belgien

Dr. *H. Czembirek;* Röntgenabteilung der I. Medizinischen Univ.-Klinik Wien, A-1097 Wien, Spitalgasse 23

Prof. Dr. *K. Decker,* Neuroradiologische Abteilung der Nervenklinik der Universität München, D-8000 München 2, Nußbaumstraße 7

Dr. *H. K. Deininger,* Abteilung Neuroradiologie an der Universitäts-Nervenklinik, D-6650 Homburg/Saar

Dr. *J. Delaye,* Hôpital Cardiovasculaire, Rue du Doyen Lépine, F-69 Lyon 8e, Frankreich

Primarius Dozent Dr. *H. Denck,* I. Chirurgische Abteilung des Krankenhauses der Stadt Wien-Lainz, A-1130 Wien/Österreich

Prof. Dr. *L. Diethelm,* Institut für klinische Strahlenkunde der Universität Mainz, D-6500 Mainz, Langenbeckstraße 1

Dr. *N. Doetsch,* Krankenhaus Lahnstein, Innere Abteilung

Dipl.-Ing. *K. Dümmling,* Siemens AG, Bereich Röntgen, D-8520 Erlangen, Henkestraße 127

Prof. Dr. *A. Düx,* Röntgenabteilung des Maria-Hilf-Krankenhauses, D-4050 Mönchengladbach

Prof. Dr. *J. Écoiffier,* Hôpital Broussais, 96 rue Didot, F-75 Paris XIVe, Frankreich

Prof. Dr. *S. Effert,* Abteilung Innere Medizin I der Rheinisch-Westfälischen Technischen Hochschule, D-5100 Aachen, Goethestraße 27–29

J. O. Eichling, MD., Washington University, School of Medicine, Mallinckrodt Institute of Radiology, 510 S. Kingshighway Blvd., St. Louis, Mo. 63110, USA

K. Eichstätt, Ampex Corporation, 401 Broadway, Redwood City, California 94063

Priv.-Doz. Dr. *A. Eissinger,* Institut universitaire de Radiologie, Hospital, cantonal, CH-1011 Lausanne/Schweiz

Prof. Dr. *H. H. Ellegast,* Diagnostisches Röntgeninstitut an den Landeskrankenanstalten Salzburg, A-5020 Salzburg, Müllner Hauptstraße 48

Prof. Dr. *R. G. Favaloro,* Cordoba 3933, Buenos Aires, Argentinien

Priv.-Doz. Dr. *R. Felix,* Radiologische Klinik der Universität Bonn, D-5300 Bonn 1, Venusberg

Dr. *H. Flohr,* Radiologische Klinik der Universität Bonn, D-53 Bonn 1, Venusberg

Dr.-Ing. *K. Franke,* Siemens AG, Bereich Röntgen, D-8520 Erlangen, Henkestr. 127

Dr. *J. Freyschmidt,* Radiologische Universitätsklinik, D-3400 Göttingen, Goßlerstraße 10

Prof. Dr. *W. Frik,* Abteilung Radiologie der Medizinischen Fakultät der Technischen Universität Aachen, D-5100 Aachen, Goethestraße 27–29

Prof. Dr. *G. Friedmann,* Radiologisches Institut und Poliklinik der Universität zu Köln, D-5000 Köln 41, Joseph-Stelzmann-Straße 7

Doz. Dr. *H. Frischauf,* I. Medizinische Universitäts-Klinik, A-1090 Wien, Spitalgasse 23

Prof. Dr. *W. A. Fuchs,* Röntgendiagnostische Abteilung, Zentrales Röntgeninstitut der Universität Bern, CH-3008 Bern, Inselspital

Dr. phil. *H. Gajewski,* Siemens AG, Bereich Röntgen, D-8520 Erlangen, Henkestraße 127

M. P. Gander, MD., Dept. of Radiology, Cardiovascular Laboratories, Loma-Linda University, Loma-Linda, California 92354, USA

Prof. Dr. *A. Gebauer*, Röntgenabteilung der Med. Universitäts-Kliniken, D-6000 Frankfurt/M., Ludwig-Rehn-Straße 14

Priv.-Doz. Dr. *M. Georgi*, Universitäts-Strahlenklinik Heidelberg, Czernykrankenhaus, D-6900 Heidelberg, Voßstraße 3

Priv.-Doz. Dr. *P. Gerhardt*, Medizinisches Strahleninstitut der Universität Tübingen, Röntgenabteilung der Chirurgischen Klinik, D-7400 Tübingen, Calwer Straße 71

Med.-Dir. Prof. Dr. *R. Giessler*, Chirurgische Abteilung Aggertalklinik für Gefäßerkrankungen, D-525 Engelskirchen

H. Gnamm, Filmproduzent, D-8000 München 21, Villacher Straße 3

Ing. *U. Goering*, Siemens AG, Bereich Röntgen, D-8520 Erlangen, Henkestraße 127

K. Götz, Söding TV GmbH + Co., Bild + Ton International, D-8000 München 60, Planegger Straße 5

Dr. *J. Göthlin*, Centralröntgen, Universitetshospital, S-221 85 Lund, Schweden

G. Grames, MD., Dept. of Radiology, Cardiovascular Laboratories Loma Linda University, Loma Linda, California 92354, USA

Dr. *A. Grünzig*, Röntgendiagnostisches Zentralinstitut am Kantonsspital Zürich, CH-8006 Zürich, Rämistraße 100

Dr. *L. V. Habighorst*, Städt. Krankenhaus Kemperhof Koblenz, Radiologische Abteilung und Strahlenklinik

Doz. Dr. *H. Hacker*, Röntgenabteilung der Neurochirurgischen Klinik der Universität Frankfurt/Main, D-6000 Frankfurt/Main, Schleusenweg

Dr. *H. Hackstock*, Unfallkrankenhaus, A-4020 Linz, Blumenauerplatz 1

Dr. *W. Hanrath*, Abteilung Innere Medizin I der Rheinisch-Westfälischen Technischen Hochschule, D-5100 Aachen, Goethestraße 27/29

Dr. *P. H. Hebestreit*, Röntgeninstitut und Strahlenklinik der Städtischen Krankenanstalten Mannheim, D-6800 Mannheim, Postfach 23

Dr. *N. Heger*, Röntgenabteilung der Chirurgischen Universitätsklinik und Poliklinik Gießen, D-6300 Gießen, Klinikstraße 37

Doz. Dr. med. *H. Heeger*, Hanuschkrankenhaus, A-1140 Wien, H.-Collins-Straße 30

Doz. Dr. *H. G. Heinze*, Klinik und Poliklinik für Radiologie der Universität München, D-8000 München 2, Ziemssenstraße 1

Prof. Dr. *P. Heintzen*, Kardiologische Abteilung der Univ.-Kinderklinik Kiel, D-2300 Kiel, Fröbelstraße 15

Dr. *H. Heiskanen*, Meilahti Krankenhaus der Universität Helsinki, Röntgendiagnostische Abteilung, Helsinki 29, Haartmaninkatu 4, Finnland

Dr. *R. E. Hekster*, Academisch Ziekenhuis, Afdeling Radiologie, Leiden/Holland

Dr. *E. Henniges*, Röntgenabteilung der Aggertalklinik für Gefäßkrankheiten, D-5250 Engelskirchen

Prof. Dr. *F. Heuck*, Zentrales Röntgeninstitut des Katharinenhospitals, D-7000 Stuttgart N, Kriegsbergstraße 60

Dr. *H. H. Hilger*, Radiologisches Institut und Poliklinik der Universität zu Köln, D-5000 Köln 41, Joseph-Stelzmann-Straße 9

Dr. *G. Hornung*, Zentrum Innere Medizin, Kardiologische Abteilung der Chirurgischen Klinik, Röntgendiagnostische Abteilung der Chirurgischen Klinik der Universität Frankfurt/Main, D-6000 Frankfurt/Main Süd, Ludwig-Rehn-Straße 14

Dr. *R. Hülse*, Institut für Klinische Strahlenkunde der Universität Mainz, D-6500 Mainz, Langebeckstraße 1

Dr. *H. Imhof*, Röntgenabteilung der I. Medizinischen Universitäts-Klinik Wien, A-1097 Wien, Spitalgasse 23

Dr. *L. Inglese*, Istituto per lo studio e la cura delle malatte cardiovascolari e rheumatiche, I-60100 Ancona, Italien

Dozent Dr. *B. Jakobsson,* Röntgenavdelningen, Bannsjukhuset, Göteborg, Schweden

C. Jansen, MD., Dept. of Radiology, Cardiovascular Laboratories Loma Linda University, Loma Linda, California 92354, USA

Dr. *J. Jehle,* Kardiologische Abteilung der II. Medizinischen Klinik der Universität München, D-8 München 2, Ziemssenstr. 2

Dr. *U. Jobst,* Institut für Klinische Radiologie der Medizinischen Hochschule Hannover, D-3 Hannover-Buchholz, Podbielskistr. 380

Dr. *M. Johne,* Radiologische Klinik, Klinikum Steglitz der Freien Universität Berlin, D-1000 Berlin 45, Hindenburgdamm 30

Prof. Dr. *M. P. Judkins,* Dept. of Radiology, Cardiovascular Laboratories Loma Linda University, Loma Linda, California 92354, USA

Prof. Dr. *K. H. Kärcher,* Strahlentherapeutische Klinik der Universität Wien, A-1095 Wien, Alserstraße 4

Prof. Dr. *F. Kaindl,* Kardiologische Universitätsklinik Wien, A-1090 Wien, Garnisonsgasse 13

Dr. med. *M. Kaltenbach,* Zentrum Innere Medizin, Kardiologische Abteilung der Chirurgischen Universitätsklinik der Universität Frankfurt, D-6000 Frankfurt/Main Süd, Ludwig-Rehn-Straße 14

Dr. med. *V. Kammerer,* Abteilung Neuroradiologie an der Universitäts-Nervenklinik, D-6650 Homburg/Saar

Prof. Dr. *J. Kaude,* Department of Radiology University of Florida, Gainsville/Florida 32601, USA

Dr. *Z. Kéri,* Radiological Clinic of Med. Univ. Budapest, Budapest VIII, Ullöi ut 78

Dr. *H. J. Klaas,* Städt. Krankenhaus Kemperhof Koblenz, Chirurgische Klinik

Dr. *U. Klein,* Klinik und Poliklinik für Radiologie der Universität München, D-8000 München 2, Ziemssenstraße 1

Dr. *F. Kleinschmidt,* Chirurgische Klinik der Universität Düsseldorf, D-4000 Düsseldorf, Moorenstraße 5

Dr. *G. Kober,* Zentrum Innere Medizin, Kardiologische Abteilung der Chirurgischen Klinik der Universität Frankfurt, D-6000 Frankfurt/Main Süd, Ludwig-Rehn-Straße 14

H. Köferl, Ampex Europa GmbH, D-6000 Frankfurt/Main 70, Walter-Kolb-Straße 9/11

Doz. Dr. *R. Köhler,* Meilahti Krankenhaus der Universität Helsinki, Röntgendiagnostische Abteilung, 02700 Grankulla, Elinstigen 4, Finnland

Dr. *F. K. Kößling,* Pathologisches Institut der Städtischen Krankenanstalten Bremen

Priv.-Doz. Dr. *J. Kollath,* Röntgenabteilung der Chirurgischen Universitätsklinik, D-6000 Frankfurt/Main Süd, Ludwig-Rehn-Straße 14

Dr. *O. Korhola,* Meilahti-Krankenhaus der Universität Helsinki, Röntgenabteilung, Haarmaninkatu 4, Helsinki 29, Finnland

Doz. Dr. *E. Kotscher,* Röntgenabteilung Kardiologische Universitätsklinik Wien, A-1090 Wien, Garnisonsgasse 13

Dr. *J. R. Krahen,* Service of Radiologie, Centre Hospitalier et Universitaire de Besançon, F- Besançon, 2 Place Saint Jaque

Dr. *B. Kramann,* Institut für Röntgendiagnostik am Klinikum rechts der Isar der Techn. Universität München

Dr. *E. Krause,* Chirurgische Universitätsklinik der Universität Frankfurt, D-6000 Frankfurt/Main Süd, Ludwig-Rehn-Straße 14

Doz. Dr. *R. Krieg,* Röntgenabteilung des Bundeswehrkrankenhauses Hamm, D-4700 Hamm/Westfalen, Am Pilzholz 29

Dr. *B. Kunkel,* Neuroradiologische Abteilung der Nervenklinik der Universität München, D-8000 München 15, Nußbaumstraße 7

Dr. *M. Kunnen,* Akademisch Ziekenhuis, Universität Gent, Röntgendiagnostik-Department, B-9720 De Pinte, 37 Acacialaan

Dr. *E. Lehtinen*, Central Hospital, SF-33520 Tampere 5, Finnland

Prof. Dr. *J. Lissner*, Klinik und Poliklinik für Radiologie der Universität München, D-8000 München 2, Ziemssenstraße 1

Dr. *D. A. Loose*, Chirurgische Klinik der Universität Düsseldorf, D-4000 Düsseldorf 1, Moorenstraße 5

Prof. Dr. *K. E. Loose*, Chirurgische und Angiologische Abt. der Städt. Krankenanstalten, D-2210 Itzehoe/Holstein, Am Langen Peter

Dr. *W. Luyendijk*, Academisch Ziekenhuis, Afdeling Radiologie, Neurosurgery, Leiden/Holland

Dr. *D. Mack*, Chirurgische Klinik und Poliklinik rechts der Isar der Technischen Universität München, D-8000 München 80, Ismaningerstraße 22

Ing. (grad.) *W. Maass*, Siemens AG, Bereich Röntgen, D-8520 Erlangen, Henkestraße 127

K.-H. Mandl, Deutsches Olympia-Zentrum, D-8000 München 2, Augustenstraße 14a

M. Mansoor, Röntgendiagnostische Abteilung der Universitätsklinik Lund, Lund/Schweden

K. Martonffy, Radiologische Klinik der Med. Universität Budapest, Budapest VIII, Ullöi ut 78, Ungarn

Dr. *B. Matricali*, Academisch Ziekenhuis, Afdeling Neuroradiologie and Neurosurgery

Prof. Dr. *H. J. Maurer*, Röntgenavdelning Sentralsykehuset I Tromsø N-9012 Tromsø, Norwegen

Priv.-Doz. Dr. *P. Maurer*, Chirurgische Klinik und Poliklinik rechts der Isar der Technischen Universität München, D-8000 München 80, Ismaningerstraße 22

cand. med. *B. Mayr*, Klinik und Poliklinik für Radiologie der Universität München, D-8000 München 21, Agnes-Bernauer-Straße 109

Dr. *S. Megyaszai*, Radiological Clinic of Univ. Budapest, Budapest VIII, Ullöi ut 78, Ungarn

Dr. med. *W. Merx*, Abteilung Innere Medizin I der Rheinisch-Westfälischen Technischen Hochschule, D-5100 Aachen, Goethestraße 27/29

Dr. *H. Munzinger*, Universitäts-Strahlenklinik Heidelberg, Czernykrankenhaus, D-6900 Heidelberg, Voßstraße 3

Dr. *P. Mutzenbach*, Strahlenabteilung am Klinikum rechts der Isar der Technischen Universität München, D-8000 München 80, Ismaningerstraße 22

Dr. *I. Neumann*, Strahlenabteilung des Städtischen Krankenhauses Passau, D-8390 Passau, Bischof-Pilgrim-Straße 1

Th. *Nischwitz, Bavaria Atelier Gesellschaft mbH*, D-8000 München-Geiselgasteig, Bavaria-Film-Platz 7

Dr. *R. Nissl*, Röntgeninstitut, A-6020 Innsbruck, Neuhauserstraße 2

Dr. *J. Normand*, Hôpital Cardiovasculaire, Rue du Doyen Lépine, F 69 Lyon 8e, Frankreich

Dr. *R. Oberson*, Hospital cantonal Universitaire Institut de Radiologie Médicale, CH-1011 Lausanne/Schweiz

Prof. Dr. *H. Oeser*, Radiologische Klinik im Klinikum Steglitz der Freien Universität Berlin, D-1000 Berlin 45, Hindenburgdamm 30

Dr. *E. Ogris*, Röntgenabteilung des Krankenhauses Wien-Lainz, A-1130 Wien, Wolkensbergerstraße 1

Dr. *F. Olbert*, Konsiliararzt der Röntgenabteilung des Krankenhauses Wien-Lainz, A-1130 Wien, Wolkensbergerstraße 1

Doz. Dr. *T. Olin*, Lunds Universitet, S-22005 Lund/Schweden

Prof. Dr. *Olle Olsson*, Universitetklinikernas Röntgendiagnostik Avd., S-22005 Lund/Schweden

Dr. *R. Otto*, Hospital cantonal Universitaire Institut de Radiologie Médicale, CH-1011 Lausanne/Schweiz

Prof. Dr. *W. H. A. M. Penn,* Sint Radboud Ziekenhuis, Institut voor Radiologie, Nijmegen/Holland, Geert Grooteplein Zuid 18

Dr. *J. Peräsalo,* Meilahti Krankenhaus der Universität Helsinki, Röntgendiagnostische Abteilung, Helsinki 29, Haartmaninkatu 4, Finnland

Priv.-Doz. Dr. *P. E. Peters, MD.,* Deutsche Klinik für Diagnostik, 62 Wiesbaden, Ankammallee 33

Dr.-Ing. *M. Pfeiler,* Siemens AG, Bereich Röntgen, D-8520 Erlangen, Henkestraße 127

Priv.-Doz. Dr. *H. Piepgras,* Abteilung Neuroradiologie an der Universitäts-Nervenklinik, D-6650 Homburg/Saar

Dr. *C. A. Pierach,* Northwestern Hospital, Chicago Avenue at 27th street, Minneapolis, Minnesota 55407, USA

Prof. Dr. *A. Pinet,* Hôpital Cardiovasculaire, Rue du Doyen Lépine, F-69 Lyon 8e, Frankreich

Dr. *F. Pinet,* Hôpital Cardiovasculaire, Rue du Doyen Lépine, F-69 Lyon 8e, Frankreich

Dr. *J. Pingel,* Universitäts-Strahlenklinik Heidelberg, Czernykrankenhaus, D-6900 Heidelberg, Voßstraße 3

Dr. *M. Podzich,* Abteilung Neuroradiologie an der Universitäts-Nervenklinik, D-6650 Homburg/Saar

M. M. Ter-Pogossian, Washington University, School of Medicine, Mallinckrodt Institute of Radiology, 510 S. Kingshighway Blvd., St. Louis, Mo. 63110, USA

Dr. *A. Pokert,* Röntgenabteilung der Chirurgischen Univ.-Klinik Heidelberg, D-6900 Heidelberg

Oberarzt Dr. *H. Pokieser,* Röntgenabteilung der I. Medizinischen Univ.-Klinik Wien, A-1097 Wien, Spitalgasse 23

Dr. *L. Polemis,* Dept. of thoracie and Cardiovascular Surgery, The Red Cross General Hospital, Ambelokipi; Athen 607, Griechenland

Dr. *P. J. Prager,* Univ.-Strahlenklinik Heidelberg, D-6900 Heidelberg, Voßstraße 3

Dr. *E. Prombonas* (Adresse wie Polemis)

Prof. Dr. *G. E. Poulias,* Department of Thoracic and Cardiovascular Surgery, The Red Cross General Hospital Ambelokipi, Athen 607, Griechenland

Dr. *M. J. Raphael,* Ray Dept. Hammersmith Hammersmith Hospital, London W 12, Grait Britain

Dr. *P. Reindel,* Strahlenabteilung des Städtischen Krankenhauses Passau, D-8390 Passau, Bischof-Pilgrim-Straße 1

Dr. *J. P. Ricatte,* Service de Radiologie, Centre Hospitalier et Universitaire de Besançon, F-Besançon, 2 Place Saint Jaque

Dr. *Hans Richter,* Angiologische Klinik, D-6100 Darmstadt-Eberstadt, Heidelberger Landstraße 379

Dr. *K. Rittmeyer,* Radiologische Universitätsklinik, D-3400 Göttingen, Goßlerstraße 10

Prof. Dr. rer. nat. *R. Röhler,* Institut für medizinische Optik der Universität München, D-8000 München 13, Barbarastraße 16/4.

Dr. *F. J. Roth,* Röntgenabteilung der Chirurgischen Univ.-Klinik Heidelberg, D-6900 Heidelberg

Prof. Dr. *W. Rudolph,* Kardiologische Abteilung der II. Medizinischen Universitätsklinik, D-8000 München 2, Ziemssenstraße 1

Prof. Dr. *N. Schad,* The Edward Mallinckrodt Institute of Radiology, Washington University, 510 S. Kingshighway Blvd., St. Louis, Mo. 63110, USA

Priv.-Doz. Dr. *H. J. Scherer,* Chirurgische Klinik und Poliklinik rechts der Isar der Technischen Universität München, D-8000 München 80, Ismaningerstraße 22

Dr. med. *H. F. Schirmer,* Röntgenabteilung der Chirurgischen Universitätsklinik und Poliklinik Gießen, D-6300 Gießen, Klinikstr. 37

Dr. med. *W. Schlick*, Röntgenabteilung der I. Medizinischen Univ.-Klinik Wien, A-1095 Wien, Alserstraße 4

Dr. med. *K. Schmücker*, Radiologisches Institut und Poliklinik der Universität zu Köln, D-5000 Köln 41, Joseph-Stelzmann-Straße 7

Dr. *H. J. Schneider*, Medizinisches Strahleninstitut der Universität Tübingen, Röntgenabteilung der Chirurg. Klinik, D-7400 Tübingen, Calwerstraße 71

Doz. Dr. *H. Schreyer*, Zentralröntgeninstitut der Universität Graz, Landeskrankenhaus, A-8036 Graz

Dr. *J. Schröder*, Medizinisches Strahleninstitut der Universität Tübingen, Röntgenabteilung der Chirurg. Klinik, D-7400 Tübingen, Calwerstraße 71

Prof. Dr. *R. Schuster*, Röntgenabteilung der Medizinischen Klinik und Poliklinik der Universität Göttingen, D-3400 Göttingen, Humboldtallee 1

Dr. *G. Schwarz*, Zentralröntgeninstitut der Universität Graz, Landeskrankenhaus, A-8036 Graz

Th. Sherwood, MD., Hammersmith Hospital, Duncane Road, London W 12, Great Britain

Dr. *H. Sieberns*, Röntgenabteilung der Städtischen Krankenanstalten Itzehoe, D-2210 Itzehoe, Am langen Peter

Dr. *H. C. Siemensen*, Radiologische Universitätsklinik und Strahleninstitut, Universitäts-Krankenhaus Eppendorf, D-2000 Hamburg 20, Martinistraße 52

Dr. *R. Simon*, Abt. f. Kinder-Kardiologie und Bio-medizinische Technik, Universitäts-Kinderlkinik 23 Kiel, Fröbelstr. 15

Dr. *B. Skoutas*, Dept. of Thoracic. and Cardiovascular Surgery, The Red Cross General Hospital Ambelokipi, Athen 607, Griechenland

Bernhard Söding, Söding TV GmbH + Co, Bild + Ton International, 8 München 60, Planegger Straße 5

Dr. *P. Spitz*, Röntgendiagnostische Abteilung der Chirurgischen Klinik der Universität Frankfurt, D-6000 Frankfurt/Main Süd, Ludwig-Rehn-Straße 14

Dr. *E. Spritzendorfer*, Unfallkrankenhaus Linz, A-4020 Linz, Blumenanerplatz 1

Dr. *R. Sörensen*, Radiologische Klinik, Klinikum Steglitz der Freien Universität Berlin, D-1000 Berlin 45, Hindenburgdamm 30

Dr. *L. Szlávy*, Radiological Clinic of Med. Univ. Budapest, Budapest VIII, Ullöi ut 78, Ungarn

MD., *R. J. Stanley*, Washington University School of Medicine, Mallinckrodt Institute of Radiology, 510 S. Kingshighway Blvd., St. Louis, Mo. 63110, USA

Dr. med. *R. Steckenmesser*, Röntgenabteilung der Chirurgischen Universitätsklinik und Poliklinik Gießen, D-6300 Gießen, Klinikstraße 37

Prof. Dr. *H. H. Stelzig*, Stadtkrankenhaus Rüsselsheim/Main, Radiolog. Abteilung

Prof. Dr. *F. E. Stieve*, Bundesgesundheitsamt, Abteilung für Strahlenhygiene, D-1000 Berlin 33, Thielallee 88/92

Dr. *S. Syribeis*, Dept. of Thoracic and Cardiovascular Surgery, The Red Cross General Hospital, Ambelokipi, Athen 607, Griechenland

Prof. Dr. *E. Tähti*, Meilahti-Krankenhaus der Universität Helsinki, Röntgendiagn. Dpt., Helsinki 29, Haartmaninkatu 4, Finnland

Dr. *V. Tran-Minh*, Hôpital Cardiovasculaire, Rûe du Dayen Lépine, F-69 Lyon 8e, Frankreich

Dr. *E. Vallidi*, Athen 138/Griechenland, Herodotou 7

Prof. Dr. *E. Van de Velde*, Laboratorium voor Röntgendiagnose der Rijksuniversiteit Gent, B-9000 Gent, De Pintelaan 115, Belgien

Prof. Dr. *H. G. Vogelsang*, Strahleninstitut des Universitäts-Klinikums Steglitz, D-1000 Berlin 45, Hindenburgdamm 30

Prof. Dr. *E. Vogler*, Zentral-Röntgeninstitut der Universität Graz, A-8010 Graz, Auenbruggerplatz 1, Landeskrankenhaus

Prof. Dr. *P. Vuorinen*, Dpt. of Radiology, University of Oulu, SF-90 100 Oulu/Finnland

Priv.-Doz. Dr. *H. Wagner*, Institut für Klinische Radiologie der Medizinischen Hochschule Hannover, D-3000 Hannover-Buchholz, Podbielskistraße 380

Dr. *P. Weber*, Universitäts-Strahlenklinik Heidelberg, Czernykrankenhaus, D-6900 Heidelberg, Voßstraße 3

Prof. Dr. *F. Weill*, Service de Radiologie, Centre Hospitalier et Universitaire de Besançon, F- Besançon, 2 Place Saint Jaque

Prof. Dr. *J. Wellauer*, Röntgendiagnostisches Zentralinstitut am Kantonsspital Zürich, CH-8006 Zürich, Rämistraße 100

Dr. *H. H. Wendenburg*, Universitäts-Strahlenklinik Heidelberg, Czernykrankenhaus, D-6900 Heidelberg, Voßstraße 3

Prof. Dr. *W. Wenz*, Direktor des Institutes für Röntgendiagnostik der Universität, 78 Freiburg, Hugstetterstr. 55

Dr. *A. Wessel*, Abt. f. Kinder-Kardiologie und Bio-Medizinische Technik Universitäts-Kinderklinik 23 Kiel, Fröbelstr. 15

Prof. Dr. *H. van de Weyer*, Radiologische Abteilung und Strahlenklinik des Mutterhauses der Borromäerinnen, D-5500 Trier, Krahnenstraße 8–12

Dr. *M. H. Wholey*, Clinical Associate Professor of Radiology, University of Pittsburgh, School of Medicine Dept. of Radiology, Shadyside Hospital, Pittsburgh, Pennsylvania 15232, USA

Dr. *L. Wicke*, Röntgenabteilung des Krankenhauses Wien-Lainz, A-1130 Wien, Wolkensbergerstraße 1

L. Widenmann, MTA., Institut für Strahlenschutz der Gesellschaft für Strahlen- und Umweltforschung mbH, D-8042 Neuherberg, Ingolstädter Landstraße 1

Priv.-Doz. Dr. *H. Wieners*, Krankenhaus Holweide, D-5 KÖln 80, Neufelder Str. 32

Doz. Dr. *M. Wiljasalo*, Meilahti-Krankenhaus der Universität Helsinki, Röntgenabteilung, Haartmaninkatu 4, Helsinki 29, Finnland

Prof. Dr. *K. zum Winkel*, Universitäts-Strahleninstitut und -klinik im Städt. Krankenhaus Westend, D-1000 Berlin 19, Spandauer Damm 130

Priv.-Doz. Dr. *W. Wirth*, Röntgendiagnostisches Zentralinstitut der Universität Zürich, CH-8006 Zürich, Rämistraße 100

Dr. *A. Wittenberg*, Institut für Klinische Radiologie der Medizinischen Hochschule Hannover, D-3000 Hannover-Buchholz, Podbielskistraße 380

Ing. *H. Woelke*, C. H. F. Müller GmbH, 2000 Hamburg 1, Alexanderstraße 1

Prof. Dr. *E. Zeitler*, Röntgenabteilung der Aggertalklinik für Gefäßkrankheiten, D-5250 Engelskirchen

Priv.-Doz. Dr. *H. Zimmermann*, Strahlenabteilung des Kreiskrankenhauses München-Pasing, D-8000 München 60, Steinerweg 5

Prof. Dr. *Z. B. Zseböck*, Radiological Clinic of Med. Univ. Budapest, Budapest VIII, Ullöi ut 78, Ungarn

W DE G

Walter de Gruyter
Berlin · New York

J. Cervos-Navarro
(Editor)

The Pathology of Cerebral Microcirculation

Editorial board: F. Matakas, N. Grcevic, A. G. Waltz

1974. 517 pages. With 224 figures, 22 tables and
991 references. Cloth DM 140,– ISBN 3 11 004472 2

International Symposium Berlin, September 1973

The lectures concern the results from recent studies in cerebral circulation, especially in the microvasculature. The lecture material covers the entire gamut of circulatory derangements, from hemodynamic disturbances to morphological manifestations.

From the contents:
Development and Structure of Microvasculature of the CNS – Hemodynamics and Regulation of Cerebral Circulation – Pathology of Cerebral Microvasculature – Anoxia, Ischenia and Related Conditions – Human Pathology and Clinical Approach – List of Contributors – Subject Index.

Price is subject to change

Walter de Gruyter
Berlin · New York

Julian Mincu

Diabetic Macro- and Microangiopathy

Translated from the Rumanian

1975. Approx. 384 pages. With 200 illustrations.
Cloth approx. DM 96,– ISBN 3 11 004533 8

Contents:
Introduction – Angiopathy in Diabetics – Ocular Microangiopathy in Diabetis Mellitus – Renal Diabetic Angiopathy – Diabetic Macroangiopathy – Cutaneous and Muscular Angiopathy in Diabetis Mellitus – Diabetic Neuropathy.

Alois J. Beuren

Die angiokardiographische Darstellung kongenitaler Herzfehler

Ein Atlas
Mit Geleitwort von Helen W. Taussig und Gerhard Joppich

Quart. XVI, 312 Seiten. Mit 285 Abbildungen in 459 Einzeldarstellungen. 1966. Gebunden DM 175,– ISBN 3 11 000807 6

Nicht nur für den Kardiologen und Thoraxchirurgen, sondern auch für den praktischen Arzt, Pädiater, Internisten und Radiologen wird das Buch zu einem unentbehrlichen Standardwerk, welches nicht zuletzt durch das Literaturverzeichnis und ausführliche Sachverzeichnis eine Vollständigkeit erhält, die in dieser Form einmalig ist.

Preisänderungen vorbehalten

FSC
www.fsc.org
MIX
Papier | Fördert
gute Waldnutzung
FSC® C083411

Kolibri 360 GmbH
Ferdinand-Jühlke-Straße 7
99095 Erfurt, Deutschland
produktsicherheit@kolibri360.de